CONTEMPORARY

Advertising

The Irwin Series in Marketing

Gilbert A. Churchill, Jr., Consulting Editor
University of Wisconsin, Madison

CONTEMPORARY

Advertising

FIFTH EDITION

William F. Arens

◆

Courtland L. Bovée

With the editorial collaboration of Jack J. Whidden

IRWIN

Burr Ridge, Illinois
Boston, Massachusetts
Sydney, Australia

Cover Photo: *Sharon Hoogstraten*
Cover Calligraphy: *Linda Blackwell*

Senior sponsoring editor: *Stephen M. Patterson*
Developmental editor: *Eleanore Snow*
Marketing manager: *Jim Lewis*
Project editor: *Jane Lightell*
Production manager: *Ann Cassady*
Designer: *Michael Warrell*
Art coordinator: *Mark Malloy*
Photo research coordinator: *Patricia A. Seefelt*
Photo researcher: *Michael J. Hruby*
Compositor: *Better Graphics, Inc.*
Typeface: *10/12 ITC Garamond Light*
Printer: *Von Hoffmann Press, Inc.*

Library of Congress Cataloging-in-Publication Data

Arens, William F.
    Contemporary advertising / William F. Arens, Courtland L. Bovée ;
with the editorial collaboration of Jack J. Whidden.—5th ed.
        p.   cm. — (The Irwin series in marketing)
    Bovée's name appears first on previous editions.
    Includes bibliographical references and indexes.
    ISBN 0-256-13412-X
    1. Advertising.   I. Bovée, Courtland L.   II. Title.   III. Series.
HF5821.B62   1994
659.1—dc20   93–5995

Printed in the United States of America
1 2 3 4 5 6 7 8 9 0 VH 0 9 8 7 6 5 4 3

To Sid Bernstein
1907-1993

Known around the world as Mr. Advertising, Sid Bernstein worked at Crain Communications, Inc., for 71 years where he rose from teenage copy boy to editor of *Advertising Age* to company president and finally to chairman of the executive committee—a post he held until his recent passing at 86.

For the past 21 years, his weekly Con-SID-erations column probed, promoted, and provoked the advertising industry to which he was so deeply and personally committed. Both champion and critic, he believed that business, and particularly advertising, serves itself well when it serves the ultimate consumer well. On his election to the Advertising Hall of Fame in 1989, *Ad Age* said of him: "He has taught us to be true to the values that embody responsibility and progress, and he also challenges advertising to help mankind sustain its ideals."

Viewing it as crucially important to the industry's future, Mr. Bernstein was a fervent advocate of advertising education—not just advertising creativity, but the whole subject of marketing communications and promotion.

We were all lucky to have known him and to have been the recipients of his sometimes gruff advice, his often gentle encouragement, and his always caring conscience.

Thanks, Sid.

Foreword

By John E. O'Toole
*President, American Association
of Advertising Agencies*

A few decades ago advertising education and the textbooks accompanying it were regarded with a certain amount of scorn by those working in the field. They were regarded as "not in the real world," a criticism well warranted for the most part, and I say that not solely because of the wretched grades I received in the few advertising courses I tried as an undergraduate.

A walk through an advertising agency today, or through the marketing department of a manufacturing company, will demonstrate how dramatically all this has changed. Accounts, departments, and offices are headed by men and women trained initially in schools of business, journalism, or communication— and trained by faculties comprising both academic skills and "real world" experience.

The Fifth Edition of *Contemporary Advertising* is an equally dramatic example of this new relationship. Written by a successful advertising man and a respected educator, it not only represents a context vividly familiar to the practitioner but a treasury of insights, information, pertinent examples, and memory refreshers of surprising value. Its division of subjects knitted together with cross references, its sidebars and portfolios, all reflect the diversity that is advertising without lapsing into undue complexity.

But what most endears *Contemporary Advertising* to those of us laboring in the vineyard is its recognition of change. Early textbooks gave the impression that the craft of advertising was cast in bronze, as fixed in its course as the paths of the stars. This resulted in textual anachronisms that misled students and amused professionals. Bill Arens and Courtland Bovée understood from the beginning that change and unpredictability were endemic; they chronicled that change from edition to edition and, on occasion, predicted it. Their growing concentration on advertising as a multinational and global force is an example.

Advertising today is going through changes so vast and profound that many of us, while confidently proclaiming our theories, are not totally certain where it will all come out. It is prudent of the authors not to emulate us. But it is perceptive of them to cover some of the stronger currents of change and help the student toward a clearer view of the "real world." I'm referring specifically to the discussions of ethical problems involved in advertising to children and minority groups, to recent patterns in Supreme Court decisions concerning the First Amendment protection of advertising, and to the increasing importance of integrated marketing communications.

For all of these reasons, the Fifth Edition of *Contemporary Advertising* is not only an excellent introduction to a craft as endlessly fascinating as the audiences it addresses, but a clear and true reflection of the "real world."

Preface

British novelist Norman Douglas affirmed the global significance of advertising when he remarked, "You can tell the ideals of a nation by its advertisements." While advertising may have been viewed as a particularly American institution in the first half of the 20th century, that is certainly no longer the case. Everyone living and working in the modern world today is influenced by advertising. So the study of advertising is important, not only for students of business or journalism—who may be contemplating a career in the field—but also for students of sociology, political science, economics, history, language, art, or the sciences—any of whom may one day become advertisers themselves, and all of whom will continue to be consumers of advertising.

There are several broad reasons why students profit from studying advertising. It can help them to:

- Appreciate the important global effect of marketing communications on business, industry, and national economies.
- Comprehend how advertising supports the profession of journalism and relates to the whole field of communications.
- Perceive the real social and cultural role of advertising and, conversely, the impact of a society's values on advertising.
- Understand the strategic function of advertising within the broader context of business and marketing.
- Evaluate and appreciate the artistic creativity and technical expertise required in advertising.
- Discover what people in advertising and related disciplines do, how they do it, and the wide career opportunities these fields offer.

In addition, the study of advertising gives students many specific tools they can use in any subsequent profession. For example, it will help them learn to:

- Plan and think strategically.
- Gather both primary and secondary research data.
- Compute and evaluate the benefits of alternative courses of action.
- Cooperate with a team in developing creative solutions to a problem.
- Analyze competitive proposals.
- Understand why people behave the way they do.
- Express themselves and their ideas with clarity and simplicity.
- Persuade others to accept their point of view.
- Appreciate and differentiate quality in creative endeavors.
- Use data to speak with knowledge, confidence, and conviction.

TO THE STUDENT: FEATURES ORIENTED TOWARD THE 21ST CENTURY

In previous editions of *Contemporary Advertising,* our mission was to present advertising as it is actually practiced—to put flesh on the bones of academic theory. As we approach the 21st century, our purpose remains the same. Advertising should be taught as it really is—as a business, as a marketing tool, as a creative process, and as a dynamic, hybrid discipline employing elements of the various arts and sciences. We also believe advertising should be taught in a manner and style relevant to today's student.

For these reasons, we developed *Contemporary Advertising* around a number of exclusive student-oriented features.

Award-Winning Graphic Design

Contemporary Advertising has always been distinguished by its exceptional packaging and award-winning graphic design. For a book that purports to educate students about advertising design and art direction, that's important; and it contributes to learning by making the text material inviting and accessible to the widest range of students. In the Fifth Edition, the elegance of this design is further enhanced with beautiful new part and chapter openers and a redesign of all the technical illustrations for greater clarity and simplicity. The text material is made reader-friendly with part and chapter overviews and chapter learning objectives.

Chapter-Opening Vignettes

To capture and hold student interest, each chapter begins—not with a case—but with a story. Written in a warm, narrative style, each vignette depicts an actual situation that illustrates a basic concept in the study of advertising. Wherever possible, this opening example is then woven throughout the chapter to demonstrate how textbook concepts actually come to life in real-world situations. For example, the history of the world's most successful packaged good—Coca-Cola—is used throughout Chapter 1 to define the functions of advertising, to trace the development and growth of modern advertising, and to explain the economic functions of advertising. The recent successful launch of Claritin (already number one in the Canadian over-the-counter antihistamine market) is used to illustrate the depth and complexity of marketing and advertising research; and the whole subject of marketing and advertising planning is wrapped around the story of how Saturn was successfully introduced and advertised in the United States.

Extensive Illustration Program

The best way to teach is to set a good example. So each of the 18 chapters is beautifully illustrated in full color with currently running, award-winning ads, commercials, and campaigns that demonstrate the best in the business. In fact, *Contemporary Advertising* is the most heavily illustrated textbook on the market, and all the major media are represented—print, electronic, outdoor—in a balanced manner. All the examples and illustrations used in this text are carefully selected not only for their quality but also for their relevance to students.

Furthermore, we have included a mix of local, national, and international ads from business-to-business, consumer, and noncommercial campaigns. In-depth captions tell the stories behind many of the ads and explain how the ads demonstrate the concept discussed in the text.

The text is also heavily illustrated with diagrams, charts, graphs, and tables that encapsulate useful information on advertising concepts or about the advertising industry, media, and production.

Full-Color Portfolios

In addition to the individual print ads and actual frames from TV commercials, the book contains several multipage portfolios of outstanding creative work. These include: the Art Director's Portfolio, the Copywriter's Portfolio, Portfolio of Corporate Advertising, Portfolio of Outstanding Magazine Advertising, and many others.

Creative Departments

The Creative Department is a special section that appears in two chapters of the book and describes how an interesting ad was created from beginning to end. A print ad for Lipton International Soup Classics is featured in the first. And the second Creative Department features the creation of the very popular and current series of TV commercials for Taster's Choice coffee.

Advertising Laboratories

Active participation enhances learning, so Advertising Laboratories are incorporated into every chapter. These unique sidebars to the world of advertising introduce students to topics of current interest or controversy and then involve them in the subject by posing questions that stimulate critical thinking. Some of the many topics presented in Ad Labs include subliminal advertising, marketing warfare, bottom-up marketing, and the psychological impact of color.

Ethical Dilemmas in Advertising

Today's students will be 21st century practitioners. As such, they will face new and challenging ethical issues, and they will need to exercise greater sensitivity than their 20th century counterparts. Therefore, throughout the book, we have interspersed a series of nine current ethical dilemmas in advertising—to focus attention on the most critical social issues facing advertisers today. These include advertising to children, the targeting of ethnic minorities, negative political advertising, and others.

Practical Checklists

Advertising is a broad subject encompassing many disciplines, and one of the dilemmas faced by both advertising students and practitioners is how to handle and organize large amounts of information and then creatively convert this data into effective advertising. For this reason, students truly appreciate the numerous, handy checklists that appear regularly throughout the text. The checklists are useful for stimulating memory, organizing thinking, and reinforcing important concepts. Some of these include: Checklist of Product Marketing Facts for Copywriters; Checklist of What Works Best in TV; Checklist of Design Principles; and Checklist of Ways to Set Advertising Budgets, to mention just a few. In the years that follow, students who become practitioners will find these checklists an invaluable, practical resource for developing marketing and advertising plans, writing and designing effective ads and commercials, selecting and scheduling media, evaluating advertising work, and making advertising decisions. Thus, the checklists greatly enhance the long-term value of the book.

Local Advertising Coverage

Throughout the book, *Contemporary Advertising* addresses the needs of both small and large advertisers with its many examples, case histories, Ad Labs, checklists, and advertisements. Moreover, this is one of the few texts to devote adequate attention to the needs of the small retail advertiser by discussing how local advertisers can use integrated marketing communications.

TO THE PROFESSOR: CHANGES IN THIS EDITION

Our continuing goal has been to involve students personally as much as possible in the practical experiences of advertising while simultaneously giving them a solid understanding of advertising's role in both marketing management and the human communications process. In the pursuit of this objective, we have instituted a significant number of modifications and improvements in the Fifth Edition of *Contemporary Advertising*.

Up-to-Date and Concise

First, throughout the book, we updated all statistics and tables and also augmented the documentation of academic and professional source material, thereby giving *Contemporary Advertising* the most current and extensive compendium of academic and trade references in the field. We cited important recent research on topics ranging from the effects of advertising and sales promotion on brand-building to integrated marketing communications and international advertising law. And we introduced interesting new building-block models to facilitate student comprehension of the often-complex processes involved in human communication, consumer behavior, marketing research, and integrated marketing communications.

Second, the book is shorter. In response to student requests, we carefully edited, pruned, and tightened the text discussion to be more active, direct, and concise, thereby cutting some 100 pages from the book's total length.

Fresh, Contemporary, Relevant Examples

Many new, real-world examples were added. These were selected not only for their currency but also for their relevance to students. Likewise, many of the chapter-opening stories are new. Some of these include the advertising success stories of companies like Levi Strauss, Nike, Apple Computer, and Saturn. All the Ad Labs, checklists, and full-color portfolios were updated, expanded, or replaced with more recent examples.

Global Orientation Integrated Throughout

In light of the increasing globalization of business, we placed greater emphasis on international advertising by integrating this information throughout the book. International data is extensively revised and updated to reflect the increased importance of advertising in the new economic and marketing realities of Europe. Throughout the text, a new global icon is used to flag readers wherever international examples or data are used.

In recent years, the technology of advertising has changed dramatically. For example, in just the last five years, the computer revolutionized the way advertising is planned, designed, produced, and scheduled. The Fifth Edition of *Contemporary Advertising* continues to deal with this revolution in detail in several chapters.

Focus on Integrated Marketing Communications

A result of this technological explosion—and consequent market fragmentation—has been a growing interest on the part of major advertisers and agencies in the integration of all their marketing communications (IMC) programs. In response to this we added a new section: Part V, Integrated Marketing Communications. This final part of the book introduces, defines, and discusses the subject of IMC in detail and includes three chapters on the subject—including a new one on IMC, direct marketing, and sales promotion.

North American Perspective

Finally—thanks in large part to the contributions of the professional community—the North American perspective of the book, introduced in the Fourth edition, was augmented and expanded. This is important for two reasons.

First, *Contemporary Advertising* is widely used in Canada. Likewise, many of the academic and trade references for the text emanate from Canadian journals and trade publications. Therefore, we treated the subject of domestic advertising as it is practiced in *both* the United States and Canada. In so doing, we also included a wide variety of high-quality Canadian examples throughout the book—in both English and French—with which Canadian students and professors will be familiar. And wherever differences exist between Canadian and U.S. advertising, we attempted to point this out.

Second, it's important for U.S. students to understand the importance of our closest neighbor and largest trading partner, especially in light of the North American Free Trade Agreement now under consideration. (U.S. students are often not as knowledgeable about Canada as Canadian students are about the United States.)

Additional Pedagogical Aids

Each chapter concludes with a summary followed by questions for review and discussion. Both of these pedagogical aids are designed to help students review chapter contents and assimilate what they have learned. Throughout the text, key ideas and terms are highlighted with boldface type and are defined when introduced. The definitions of all these terms are collected at the end of the book in a thorough and extensive glossary.

Because of the inclusion of separate chapters on marketing and advertising research, integrated marketing communications, direct marketing and sales promotion, public relations and corporate advertising, and local and noncommercial advertising, this book will remain the most comprehensive and up-to-date text on the market.

While all chapters were edited and updated, other specific highlights of this revision include:

Chapter 1: The Dimensions of Advertising. This chapter was carefully edited, tightened, and shortened. At the same time, the growth and status of international advertising was appended to the section on the history of advertising.

Chapter 2: The Social, Ethical, and Regulatory Aspects of Advertising. This chapter offers a more balanced presentation of what's right and wrong about advertising. The discussion of commercial speech was updated with recent court rulings. Major differences between American and Canadian laws are highlighted, and a section on advertising laws in international markets was added.

Chapter 3: The Advertising Business. This chapter features a new opening story: how one of the top American ethnic-specialty agencies, Muse, Cordero, Chen, worked with Nike to target a new market segment, urban youth. The story is woven throughout the chapter to demonstrate what agency people do and how they work. New material was introduced on the hottest new agency discipline—account planning. And a whole new section was added on managing international advertising.

Chapter 4: The Importance of Marketing and Consumer Behavior to Advertising. In the discussion on the influence of culture and subculture, new information is presented relative to foreign cultures. Similarly, the influence of international legal and social environments on consumer purchasing behavior is also discussed.

Chapter 5: Market Segmentation and the Marketing Mix: Matching Products to Markets. A new story—the invention of blue jeans and the growth of the Levi Strauss company—highlights this chapter. The story also serves as a foil for demonstrating how market segmentation works. We enhanced this chapter with new material on products, services, and branding; and the subject of direct marketing is now discussed as an element of the promotion mix.

Chapter 6: Marketing and Advertising Research: Inputs to the Planning Process. The successful introduction of Claritin by Schering Canada to the over-the-counter antihistamine market is recounted in the chapter-opening story and used to demonstrate the basic steps in the research process. The chapter presents new sources of research information, shows new examples of how research affects advertising creativity, and discusses the problems of collecting primary and secondary data in foreign markets.

Chapter 7: Marketing and Advertising Planning. A new chapter-opening story—the successful introduction of the Saturn automobile—serves as a foil for the principles and concepts discussed throughout this chapter. The Saturn story, highlighted with many illustrations and specific examples, also demonstrates the importance of integrated marketing communications.

Chapter 8: Creative Copywriting. The beginning of this chapter has been extensively revised—along with a new story on 4day Tire Stores—to bring the discussion of creative strategy and copywriting more in line with the book's earlier discussion of the human communications process and consumer behavior. We expanded the sections on how advertisers develop the copy platform and the big idea in advertising. To assist in understanding the objectives of good copy, the copywriter's pyramid, introduced in the Fourth Edition, is illustrated alongside an ad to show how each step of the pyramid relates to a section of the ad. Also introduced in this chapter is information on writing copy for international markets. The chapter is accented with a completely new illustration program—of both domestic and international ads—that students will find relevant and timely.

Chapter 9: Creative Art Direction. Material on television creativity—previously in Chapter 11—was moved to the section in this chapter dealing with the role of art in radio and television commercials. A completely new illustration program is included, and the art director's portfolio contains current, student-relevant ads to enliven the text matter.

Chapter 10: Creative Production: Print Media. The material on typesetting was updated with greater detail on how to specify type, and new examples demonstrate the possibilities offered by typography. The chapter was carefully edited throughout to ensure students gain the most practical information possible on how to produce quality print media materials. Some new terms were introduced, and the section on how to think like a printer to save money on print runs was edited for greater clarity.

Chapter 11: Creative Production: Electronic Media. A new section on the value of good talent (actors and presenters) to radio and television commercials is introduced following the chapter-opening story of Motel 6. The Creative Department on the very popular campaign for Taster's Choice coffee shows the most recent commercial in this campaign and serves as a climax to the chapter and the whole creative unit by showing how these commercials were developed and shot, from concept through production.

Chapter 12: Media Planning and Selection. The chapter was carefully revised to reflect the changing role of media planners from space or time specialists to advertising generalists, knowledgeable about all forms of marketing communications. We made the writing style more lively to quickly engage students in chapter topics. The chapter expands the coverage of value-added media options, and the discussion of media objectives and strategy was strengthened with the introduction of concepts parallel to other strategic discussions in the book—for example, the 4Ms of the Media Mix. The availability and economics of foreign media are new to this chapter. And examples were added to enrich the material and engage student interest.

Chapter 13: Print Media. The award-winning, business-to-business campaign for Continental Bank provides a fresh opening for this chapter, which was completely reorganized for a more logical presentation. The worldwide nature of print media is discussed, and the chapter was carefully edited for currency and clarity. For purposes of brevity, the discussion of the advantages and drawbacks of print media was moved to a checklist.

Chapter 14: Electronic Media. The discussion of broadcast and cable TV was integrated to eliminate redundancy and unnecessary length. New material on infomercials was added, and information on expanding TV technology was updated. A new checklist is introduced to enumerate the pros and cons of electronic media.

Chapter 15: Direct Mail, Outdoor, Transit, and Supplementary Media. The previous lengthy discussion of the pros and cons of direct mail was abbreviated and moved to a checklist. The section on outdoor media starts with a new, local advertising story that students will enjoy. And the chapter material was expanded to cover the supplementary media.

Chapter 16: IMC: Direct Marketing and Sales Promotion. This completely new chapter defines integrated marketing communications as both a concept and a process, explains the current evolution in marketing thinking that creates so much interest in IMC programs, and cites the latest research on this topic. We use the unbridled success of Apple Computer as the chapter-opening story to demonstrate one of the best implementations of IMC to date. Since direct marketing and sales promotion play such important roles in IMC, those topics are also covered in-depth in this chapter. This discussion includes the basics of these disciplines, the strategies and tactics employed, and the controversy surrounding advertising versus promotion expenditures.

Chapter 17: IMC: Public Relations and Corporate Advertising. This chapter was refocused to illustrate the role of these disciplines in integrated marketing communications programs. The differing perspective of advertising and PR practitioners was expanded. A completely new illustration program adds currency and relevance to the chapter.

Chapter 18: Integrated Marketing Communications for Local and Noncommercial Advertisers. The discussion of integrated marketing communications concludes with a discussion of how local and noncommercial advertisers, who typically lack the funding of large national advertisers, can employ IMC to achieve their marketing objectives.

SUPPLEMENTARY MATERIALS

While the text itself is a complete introduction to the field of advertising, it is accompanied by a number of valuable supplemental materials designed to assist the instructor.

Instructor's Manual

Written with the assistance of Bonnie Dowd of Palomar College, the Instructor's Manual offers a wealth of new suggestions for classroom lectures and discussions. It includes a lecture outline for each chapter and answers to all discussion questions, as well as suggested workshops, projects, and debates.

Video Supplements

To illustrate how the principles discussed in the text are actually applied in business, the book is supplemented by two special video programs and a Video Instructor's Guide. The authors produced one video exclusively for *Contemporary Advertising* for instructor use in the classroom. It includes a wide variety of both domestic and international commercials specially referenced with voice-over introductions to specific chapters. This video is not only text-specific in subject matter, it also includes many of the commercials discussed in the text—such as the Nike campaign from Chapter 3, the Claritin campaign from Chapter 6, the Saturn campaign from Chapter 7, and the Taster's Choice and Gotcha campaigns from Chapter 11—to mention just a few.

The second video was produced by the Advertising Educational Foundation, to whom we express our deep gratitude and appreciation, and includes a behind-the-scenes look at the advertising process at work. Included on the video are: the development of a TV commercial designed to introduce a new Johnson & Johnson product, ACUVUE Disposable Contact Lenses; the production of a print ad for JELL-O gelatin; and a summer TV ad for Coca-Cola. These are all excellent adjuncts to the chapters on creativity and production.

Offered at no charge to adopters of *Contemporary Advertising,* these video supplements are designed to help the instructor teach real-world decision making and demonstrate some of the best current examples of television advertising from around the world.

Color Transparencies

Also available to instructors is a high-quality selection of overhead transparencies. These include more than 50 additional ads not found in the text and a selection of many of the important models and graphs presented in the text—all produced in full color.

Testing Systems

An extensive bank of objective test questions carefully designed to provide a fair, structured program of evaluation is available in several formats:

Irwin Computerized Test Generator System—a convenient and flexible question retrieval device for mainframe systems, providing an extensive bank of questions to use as is or with additional questions of your own.

COMPUTEST—a microcomputer testing system that provides convenient and flexible retrieval from an extensive bank of questions to use as is or with additional questions of your own.

COMPUGRADE—a microcomputer gradebook that stores and prints all grades by name or ID number. Capable of weighting and averaging grades.

Teletest—a toll-free phone-in service to request customized exams prepared for classroom use.

USES FOR THIS TEXT

Contemporary Advertising was written for the undergraduate student in liberal arts, journalism, and business schools. However, because of its practical, hands-on approach, depth of coverage, and marketing management emphasis, it is also widely used in independent schools, university extension courses, and courses on advertising management. The wealth of award-winning advertisements also makes it a resource guide to the best work in the field for students in art and graphic design courses and for professionals in the field.

Many of the stories, materials, and techniques included in this text come from our own personal experiences as a full-time marketing and advertising executive and as a college professor. Others come from the experiences of friends and colleagues in the business. We hope this book will be a valuable resource guide, not only in the study of advertising but later on in the practice of it as well. In all cases, we hope readers will experience the feel and the humanness of the advertising world—whether they intend to become professionals in the business, to work with practitioners, or simply to become more sophisticated consumers.

Acknowledgments

We are deeply indebted to many individuals in advertising and related fields for their personal encouragement and professional assistance. These include, but are certainly not limited to: Ella Strubel, Wally Petersen, Joe Silberman, and Mark Hart at Leo Burnett; Dennis Chase and Dave Kelley at *Advertising Age;* Tom Exster at *American Demographics;* Joyce Harrington at the American Association of Advertising Agencies; Rena Spangler at the Advertising Educational Foundation; Bob Pritikin at the Mansion, San Francisco; Vonda LePage, FCB/Leber Katz; Kevin Tedesco and Fred Posner at N.W. Ayer; David Kreinick, Creative Media, Inc.; Peter Farago at Farago Advertising; Hank Seiden, the Seiden Group; Joy McBride at McCann Erickson, San Francisco; Jigisha Patel at Chiat/Day, Los Angeles; Adelaide Horton, Chiat/Day, New York; Maryanne O'Brien, Patricia Davidson, Nadine Howe at Fallon McElligott; Cindi Rowe, BBDO/West; Ann Jenneman Smith at Procter & Gamble; Thomas Hripko, the Richards Group, Dallas; Larry Jones and Nicholetta Poloynis at Foote, Cone & Belding, Los Angeles; Russ Hanlin, Sunkist Growers; P. J. Santoro at Levi Strauss & Co.; Pamela Scott at Hal Riney & Partners; Mike Salisbury, Salisbury Communications; Gerry Rubin at Rubin Postaer; Jo Muse, Mavis Cordero, Berni Neal, Jimmy Smith, and Phil Byrd at Muse, Cordero, Chen; Scott Bedbury at Nike; Larry Light of the Coalition for Brand Equity; Joe Sedelmaier and Marsie Wallach, Sedelmaier Film Productions; Raphaële at Raphaële Digital Transparencies; and Paula Veale at the Ad Council.

For their warm, open, and gracious contributions of time, counsel, and materials, we extend our appreciation, *avec tous nos remerciements,* to all our Canadian friends, especially Joe Mullie at the Association des Agences de Publicité du Québec; Chuck McDonald and Robert West at Schering Canada; François Duffar, Daniel Rabinowicz, Pierre Délagrave, Nicole Lapierre, Normand Chiasson, Ian Saville, Jocelyn Laverdure, and Manon Caza at Cossette Communication-Marketing; Marcel Barthe, Optimum; François Descarie, Impact Research; Yves Gougoux, Caroline Jarvis, and Sylvie Thauvette at BCP Stratégie Créativité; Jacques LeFebvre, MacLaren LINTAS, Montreal; André Morrow, Marketel; André Beauchesne at Bos; Maryse Parent of Parent & Richard Communications; Patrick Pierra at *InfoPress;* J. Richard Genin at the Television Bureau of Canada; Paul Lavoie at Taxi; Jane Williams at Young & Rubicam, Montreal; *et particulièrement,* Marcel Gilbert and Patrice Lafleur at the Quebec government office in Los Angeles; Jean Pelletier and the Publicité-Club de Montréal; Normand Grenier at Communications Grenier; and Elisabeth Cohen at the Biodome in Montreal.

We also appreciate the timely assistance of Duncan Milner, Jennifer Wilson, and Hugh Duthie at Chiat/Day (Toronto); Allison Findley, Ogilvy & Mather, Toronto; and Nancy Birnbaum, Kathleen Vollebregt, Rick Davis, Daryl Sykes, Kevin Spreckmeester, and Susan Murray at Young & Rubicam/Toronto; Peter Stringham and Larry Tolpin of BBDO/Baker Lovick; Geoff Roche at Geoffrey Roche & Associates; Bill Durnan, MacLaren LINTAS, Toronto; and Laura Medcalf at *Marketing* magazine.

For great support and assistance, we are indebted to the Canadian Consulate General in Los Angeles, especially Pamela Johnson and Rosalind Wolfe; and for helping us navigate the Canadian legal waters, we appreciate the generous contributions of Eric Gross of Gowling and Henderson, Toronto; Bryan Fraser of Hooey-Remus, Toronto; and Robert Legault of Legault & Joly, Montreal.

Special thanks also to several good, longtime friends whose contributions, continuous support and wise counsel we appreciate far more than they could ever know: Al Ries at Trout & Ries; Susan Irwin at McCann-Erickson; John O'Toole at the American Association of Advertising Agencies; Brad Lynch at the Ad Council; Victoria Horstmann at Bloom/FCA; Jan Sneed at Ketchum Advertising; Sid Stein at Rutgers University; Rance Crain at *Advertising Age;* Larry Londre at University of Southern California; Ken Longman at Longman-Moran Analytics; Randy Grimm at National Decision Systems; Gary Corolis at MacLaren LINTAS/ Toronto; Cecil Scaglione at Scaglione Communications; Robert Baxter at McGill University; and, for patient and loyal support, Stanley L. Urlaub.

In addition, we are appreciative of the moral support, encouragement, generous assistance and friendship of Larry Mattera, Tom Michael, Roger Tilton, Alayne Harris, Kelly Seagraves, Professor E. L. Deckinger, Suzie Toutant, Jim Moran, Rob Settle, Pam Alreck, Joe Hoyt, Bruce Henderson, Rick Rivers, Bill Kimmelman, Jann Pasler, Atsuo Mihara, Mary Beth McCabe, Barnard and Sylvia Thompson, Don and Ann Ritchey, Carlos and Yolanda Cortez, Susan Harding, Jim and LeAnna Zevely, Fred and Brenda Bern, Bill and Olivia Werner, Alan and Rita Moller, and—for giving so much to so many for so long—Stanley D. Woodworth and Sid Bernstein, gone from our midst but never forgotten.

We appreciate the love and patience of our far-flung families, the Arenses, Bovées, and Whiddens, and especially Olivia, for her unwavering support.

Likewise, great appreciation to Dan Weinberg, Amanda Gomez, Rebecca Smith, and Bonnie Dowd for timely editorial help and for being there when we needed them most.

In the effort to make this the most timely and current book on the market, the huge Irwin A-team, which invariably found a way to do the impossible, was led by Steve Patterson, Eleanore Snow, Michael Warrell, Mike Hruby, Jane Lightell, Merrily Mazza, Irene H. Sotiroff, Ann Cassady, Mark Malloy, Pat Seefelt, John Black, Bill Setten, and Jerry Saykes, all of whom had to put up with us on an almost daily basis. We appreciate your tolerance of our individual and collective idiosyncrasies and foibles, and we thank you for a job incredibly well done.

We also wish to recognize and thank the American Association for Education in Journalism and Mass Communication and the American Academy of Advertising, two organizations whose publications and meetings provide a valuable forum for the exchange of ideas and for professional growth.

We are deeply grateful to the many instructors, professors, practitioners, and academic reviewers whose ideas, critical insights, and suggestions were invaluable in the preparation of this edition. These include, but are certainly not limited to, the following individuals: Hugh G. Daubek, Purdue University, Calumet; Leslie Cole, Vice President, Burrell Advertising, Inc.; Joby John, Bentley College; Susan A. Schneider, Endicott College; Ivan L. Preston, University of Wisconsin, Madison; Ronald D. Taylor, Mississippi State University; Peter B. Turk, University of Akron; Sharon Brock, Ohio University; James W. Taylor, Shay Sayre, and J. Nicholas De Bonis, California State University, Fullerton; Karen Porter, University of Montana; Kak Yoon and Kevin Hall, Florida International University; Marilyn Kern-Foxworth, Texas A&M University; Michael F. Weigold, University of Florida, Gainesville; D. Joel Whalen, DePaul University; G. Gelderloos, Grand Rapids Junior College; and Jim Hutton, University of St. Thomas.

To all of you, thank you. You make it happen.

The Authors

Contents in Brief

Contents

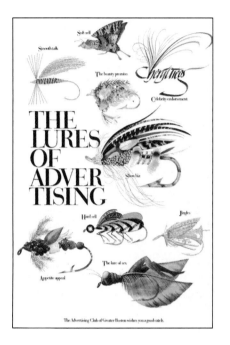

P A R T II

Developing Marketing and Advertising Strategies 100

P A R T **III**

Creating Advertisements and Commercials   232

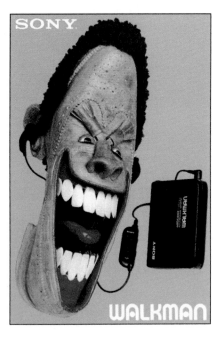

McDonald's vous sert une pizza fraîche et cuite au four en moins de cinq minutes. Ça, c'est du sport!

P A R T ▼

Integrated Marketing Communications 486

CONTEMPORARY

Advertising

P · A · R · T

I

Advertising Perspectives

There are many ways to look at advertising—as a business, as a creative process, as a social phenomenon, and as a fundamental ingredient of a free enterprise system. The first part of this text defines advertising, outlines its functions and scope, examines how it affects the economy, discusses its social and legal ramifications, and looks at who the major participants are in the advertising business, as it is practiced in the United States and Canada.

Chapter 1, "The Dimensions of Advertising," gives an overview of the

profession. It defines advertising and discusses its various functions and classifications. The chapter focuses on how technology has affected the evolution of advertising and discusses advertising's impact on the free enterprise system around the world.

Chapter 2, "The Social, Ethical, and Regulatory Aspects of Advertising," discusses some of the common criticisms of advertising and debates the ethical and social responsibilities of companies that advertise. It describes the role government, industry, and consumer groups play in regulating advertising. Finally, it

compares important laws governing the practice of advertising in the United States and Canada with those in foreign countries.

Chapter 3, "The Advertising Business: Agencies and Clients," shows how people and groups organize themselves—as advertisers and agencies—to create and produce advertising. The chapter describes the role of advertising agencies and the way clients structure their advertising departments. Finally, the chapter discusses critical factors that affect the client-agency relationship.

The Dimensions of Advertising

Objective: To define advertising and introduce the profession. You will learn the basic terminology used in advertising; the many ways advertising is classified; the evolution of advertising technology and strategic thinking; the functions and effects of advertising; and advertising's overall impact on the economy. These basic elements set the framework for the more detailed study to follow.

After studying this chapter, you will be able to:

- Define advertising and differentiate it from public relations.

- Understand and describe the different classifications of advertising.

- Discuss key milestones in the evolution of modern advertising.

- Explain the significance of marketing warfare to produce advertising.

- Enumerate some of the most important functions of advertising.

- Debate the effect of advertising on the value and price of products.

- Explore the impact of advertising on competition and consumer choice.

H e didn't realize it at the time, but Dr. John S. Pemberton, an inconspicuous pharmacist in Atlanta, Georgia, invented what would become the most successful consumer product in history. In fact, it would revolutionize the beverage industry and write a whole new chapter in the history of marketing and advertising.

As legend goes, Dr. Pemberton developed his concoction in 1886 while working over a three-legged pot in his backyard. From the juices of certain plants and nuts, he produced a sweet-tasting brown syrup. When he accidentally mixed it with soda fountain water, the syrup created a remarkable, sparkling taste. On May 8, 1886, Jacobs' Pharmacy in downtown Atlanta started selling Pemberton's elixir for 5 cents a glass. It was an immediate success. On May 29, a newspaper ad in the *Atlanta Journal* invited Atlantans to try "the new and popular soda fountain drink." The ad also proclaimed that Coca-Cola, as Pemberton called it, was "delicious and refreshing," a theme that continues to this day in all Coke's advertising, domestic and worldwide. As one contemporary ad agency put it, Coke's advertising was the campaign that conquered the world (see Exhibit 1–1).

Through the years, the Coca-Cola Company has used a variety of advertising slogans and headlines, including:

The great national temperance beverage.

Thirst knows no season.

The pause that refreshes.

Enjoy Coca-Cola.

For a complete list of Coca-Cola's slogans, campaigns, and themes spanning more than 100 years, see Ad Lab 1–A. ◆

ADVERTISING DEFINED

What is advertising? According to McCann Erickson, the advertising agency that has developed Coca-Cola's national campaigns for many years, advertising is "Truth well told." This philosophy, echoed by Coke's management in its annual report 25 years ago, continues today:

EXHIBIT • 1–1

This self-promotion ad for The Richards Group advertising agency in Dallas points out that Coca-Cola succeeded in "conquering the world" by choosing the right weapon—advertising.

ONLY ONE LAUNCHED A CAMPAIGN THAT CONQUERED THE WORLD.

[Coke's advertising] should be a pleasurable experience, refreshing to watch and pleasant to listen to. It should reflect quality by being quality. And it should make you say, "I wish I'd been there. I wish I had been drinking Coke with these people."[1]

That's what advertising is to Coca-Cola. But can the same be said for other goods and services?

Albert Lasker, the father of modern advertising, said advertising is "salesmanship in print." But he offered that definition long before radio and television, at a time when the nature and scope of advertising were quite limited.

Today, we may define advertising as a communication process, a marketing process, an economic and social process, a public relations process, or an information and persuasion process. However, in this book, we use the following definition:

Advertising is the nonpersonal communication of information, usually paid for and usually persuasive in nature, about products (goods and services) or ideas by identified sponsors through various media.

Let's take this definition apart and analyze its components. Advertising is directed to groups of people rather than individuals and is therefore *nonper-*

AD LAB 1–A   It Had to Be Good to Get Where It Is!

1886 Drink Coca-Cola.	1933 Don't wear a tired, thirsty face.
1904 Delicious and refreshing.	1935 Coca-Cola . . . the pause that brings friends together.
1904 Coca-Cola . . . satisfies.	
1905 Coca-Cola revives and sustains.	1937 America's favorite moment.
1905 Wherever you go . . . you'll find Coca-Cola.	1938 The best friend thirst ever had.
1906 The drink of quality.	1938 Thirst asks nothing more.
1906 The great national temperance beverage.	1939 Coca-Cola goes along.
1907 Coca-Cola is full of vim, vigor and go—is a snappy drink.	1939 Coca-Cola has the taste thirst goes for.
	1939 Whoever you are, whatever you do, wherever you may be, when you think of refreshment, think of ice-cold Coca-Cola.
1908 Get the genuine.	
1909 Whenever you see an arrow, think of Coca-Cola.	
1911 Enjoy a glass of liquid laughter.	1940 Within easy reach of your thirst.
1917 Three million a day.	1940 America's year-round answer to thirst.
1920 Coca-Cola . . . good things from 9 climes poured into a single glass.	1941 Work refreshed.
	1941 Coca-Cola belongs . . .
1922 Thirst knows no season.	1942 The only thing like Coca-Cola is Coca-Cola itself.
1923 Enjoy thirst.	1942 Coca-Cola has that extra something.
1925 It has the charm of purity.	1942 The best is always the better buy.
1925 With a drink so good . . . 'tis folly to be thirsty.	1942 It's the real thing.
1925 Six million a day.	1943 Universal symbol of the American way of life . . . Coca-Cola.
1926 Coca-Cola is the shortest distance between thirst and refreshment.	
	1943 With a taste all its own.
1927 It had to be good to get where it is.	1945 The happy symbol of a friendly way of life.
1927 Around the corner from anywhere.	1945 Why grow thirsty?
1027 At the little red sign.	1946 The world's friendliest club . . . admission 5¢
1928 Coca-Cola . . . a pure drink of natural flavors.	1946 Yes.
1929 The best served drink in the world.	1947 Coca-Cola . . . continuous quality.
1929 The pause that refreshes.	1947 Continuous quality is quality you trust.
1932 Ice-cold sunshine.	1947 The quality of Coca-Cola is a friendly quality you can always trust.
1932 Thirst come, thirst served.	
1933 Bounce back to normal.	

sonal. These groups might be teenagers who enjoy rock concerts or adults who attend investment seminars.

Direct-mail advertising often attempts to personalize the message by inserting the receiver's name in the letter. But direct mail is still nonpersonal; a computer inserts the name.

Most advertising is *paid for* by sponsors. General Motors, Kmart, Coca-Cola, and Sonja's local fitness salon pay money to the newspaper or to the radio or TV station to carry the ad we read, hear, and see. But some sponsors don't have to pay for their ads. The American Red Cross, United Way, and American Cancer Society are three of many organizations whose public service messages are customarily carried at no charge.

Most advertising is intended to be *persuasive*—to win converts to a good, service, or idea. A company usually sponsors advertising to convince people its product will benefit them. Some ads, though, such as legal announcements, are intended merely to inform, not to persuade.

In addition to promoting tangible **goods** such as suits, soap, and soft drinks, advertising also helps publicize the intangible **services** of bankers, beauticians, and bike repair shops. And increasingly, advertising is used to sell a wide

1948	Where there's Coke there's hospitality.		1968	Tells your thirst to go fly a kite.
1949	Coca-Cola . . . along the highway to anywhere.		1968	Wave after wave—drink after drink.
1950	Thirst, too, seeks quality.		1968	For twice the convenience, bring home two cartons of Coke.
1951	For home and hospitality.		1968	It's twice time.
1951	You taste its quality.		1970	It's the real thing.
1952	What you want is a Coke.		1971	I'd like to buy the world a Coke.
1952	Coke follows thirst everywhere.		1972	Coke . . . goes with the good times.
1953	Drive safely . . . Drive refreshed.		1975	Look up America, see what we've got.
1953	Midsummer magic.		1976	Coke adds life . . .
1955	Bright and bracing as sunshine.		1980	Have a Coke and a smile.
1956	Coca-Cola . . . makes good things taste better.		1982	Coke is it.
1956	The friendliest drink on earth.		1985	We've got a taste for you (new Coke).
1956	Gives a bright little lift.			America's real choice (Coca-Cola Classic).
1956	Coca-Cola puts you at your sparkling best.		1986	Catch the Wave (new Coke).
1957	Sign of good taste.			Red, white and you (Coca-Cola Classic).
1958	The cold, crisp taste of Coke.		1988	Can't beat the feeling (Coca-Cola Classic).
1959	Cheerful life of Coke.		1989	Can't beat the real thing (Coca-Cola Classic).
1959	Relax refreshed with ice-cold Coca-Cola.		1991	Can't beat the real thing (Coca-Cola Classic).
1959	Be really refreshed.		1992	Can't beat the real thing.
1959	The cold, crisp taste that so deeply satisfies.		1993	Always. Coca-Cola.
1961	Coca-Cola refreshes you best.			
1963	The big bold taste that's always just right.			
1963	Things go better with Coke.			
1963	Go better refreshed.			
1964	Coca-Cola gives that special zing. . . . refreshes best.			

Laboratory Applications

1. Which slogans are outdated? Why?

2. Which slogans persuade the reader to take action?

3. What slogans can you suggest to reflect Coca-Cola's positioning in the 1990s?

1965	Enjoy Coca-Cola.
1965	For extra fun—take more than one! Take an extra carton of Coke!
1966	Coca-Cola has the taste you never get tired of.

EXHIBIT • 1–2

The classifications of advertising

By target audience

Consumer advertising
Aimed at people who buy the product for their own or someone else's personal use

Business advertising
Aimed at people who buy or specify goods and services for use in business
  Industrial
  Aimed at people who buy or influence the purchase of industrial products
  Trade
  Aimed at middlemen (wholesalers and retailers) of goods and services who buy for resale to their customers
  Professional
  Aimed at people licensed to practice under a code of ethics or set of professional standards
  Agricultural (farm)
  Aimed at people in farming or the agriculture business

By geographic area

Local (retail) advertising
Advertising by businesses whose customers come from only one city or local trading area

Regional advertising
Advertising for products sold in one area or region, but not the whole country

National advertising
Advertising aimed at customers in several regions of the country

International advertising
Advertising directed at foreign markets

By medium

Print advertising
Newspaper, magazine

Broadcast (electronic) advertising
Radio, television

Out-of-home advertising
Outdoor, transit

Direct-mail advertising
Advertising sent through the mail

By purpose

Product advertising
Intended to promote goods and services

Nonproduct (corporate or institutional) advertising
Intended to promote the organization's mission or philosophy rather than a particular product

Commercial advertising
Intended to promote goods, services, or ideas with the expectation of making a profit

Noncommercial advertising
Sponsored by or for a charitable institution, civic group, or religious or political organization

Action advertising
Intended to bring about immediate action on the part of the reader

Awareness advertising
Attempts to build the image of a product or familiarity with the product's name and package

---

variety of **ideas**—economic, political, religious, and social. For the sake of simplicity, when we use the term **product**, we are referring to both goods and services.

For a message to be considered an ad, the sponsor must be *identified*. This seems obvious: Naturally, the sponsor usually wants to be identified—or why pay to advertise? What distinguishes advertising from *public relations* is that public relations activities, like *publicity*, aren't usually openly sponsored. We explore this subject further in Chapter 17.

Advertising reaches us through a channel of communication referred to as a **medium**. In addition to the traditional mass **media** (a plural form of *medium*)—radio, TV, newspapers, magazines, and billboards—advertising also uses other mediums such as direct mail, brochures, shopping carts, blimps, and videocassettes.

CLASSIFICATIONS OF ADVERTISING

Advertising can be classified by four main criteria: target audience, geographic area, medium, and purpose (see Exhibit 1–2).

EXHIBIT • 1-3

This ad promoting 3M Filing Systems is an example of industrial advertising aimed at individuals in business who might buy or influence the purchase of 3M's goods and services.

By Target Audience

Advertising is usually aimed at a particular segment of the population—the **target audience.** When you see an ad that doesn't appeal to you, it may be because the ad is not aimed at any of the groups you belong to. For example, a TV commercial for denture cream isn't relevant to young adults. They're not part of the target audience, so the ad isn't designed to appeal to them.

There are two main types of target audiences, *consumers* and *businesses.*

Consumer Advertising

Most ads in the mass media—TV, radio, newspapers, and magazines—are **consumer advertisements**. Sponsored by the manufacturer of the product or the dealer who sells the product, they are typically directed at **consumers**—people who buy the product for their own or someone else's personal use.

Business Advertising

The majority of consumer advertising appears in mass-consumer media. **Business advertising,** on the other hand, tends to be concentrated in specialized business publications or professional journals, in direct-mail pieces sent to businesses, or in trade shows. Since business advertising rarely uses the mass media, it is often invisible to consumers.

There are four types of business advertising: *industrial, trade, professional,* and *agricultural.*

Industrial advertising is aimed at individuals in business who buy or influence the purchase of **industrial products,** including goods and services used in the manufacture of other goods (plants, machinery, equipment) or that become part of other products (raw materials, semimanufactured goods, components). Industrial products also include goods or services used to conduct business—i.e., *capital goods* (office machines, computers, desks, operating supplies) or *business services* (insurance, bookkeeping, maintenance). The clever industrial ad in Exhibit 1–3 promotes a capital goods item—a 3M Filing System.

In this example of a trade advertisement, Lee jeans promotes its Lee Lites line to retailers, members of the clothing trade.

Lee Lites. A new line of lightweight denim.

Companies use **trade advertising** to obtain greater distribution of their products by developing more sales outlets or selling more products to existing outlets. For example, the ad in Exhibit 1–4 urges retailers to stock Lee Lites jeans since they're "just what the market ordered."

Professional advertising, aimed at teachers, accountants, doctors, dentists, architects, engineers, and lawyers, typically appears in official publications of professional societies (such as the *Archives of Ophthalmology* published by the American Medical Association). Professional advertising has three objectives: (1) to convince professional people to buy particular brands of equipment and supplies for use in their work; (2) to encourage professionals to recommend or prescribe a specific product or service to their clients or patients; and (3) to persuade the person to use the product personally.

By Geographic Area

A neighborhood store (or fine restaurant like that shown in Exhibit 1–5) usually uses **local advertising** in its immediate trading area because that's where the majority of its customers come from. Local advertisers face a variety of special challenges that we'll discuss more completely in Chapter 18.

On the other hand, a business that is part of a well-known U.S. or Canadian chain might use any of the four classifications of advertising based on geography—local, regional, national, or even international.

In recent years, the world has experienced dramatic political realignment, and many traditional trade barriers have disappeared. In Scandinavia you can see an ad for Crest toothpaste written in Norwegian. Sunkist advertises lemons in Japan. Visitors to Spain see print and TV ads for products advertised every day in the United States and Canada, such as Levi's or Coca-Cola (see Exhibit 1–6). As a result, the field of **international advertising**—advertising aimed at foreign markets—has grown so rapidly and become so important that we discuss global advertising issues wherever applicable throughout this book.

By Medium

Advertising can be classified on the basis of the *medium* used to transmit the message (e.g., radio, television, or newspaper). An **advertising medium** is any *paid* means used to present an advertisement to its target audience. Word-of-mouth, therefore, is not an advertising medium.

This ad for The Boulevard Restaurant plays off the concept of geography. It advertises a nonlocal environment (Mediterranean cuisine in a warm climate) to local patrons in Chicago—which is not particularly warm in the winter.

By Purpose

Advertising can also be classified on the basis of the sponsor's objectives. Some ads promote a good or service; others promote ideas. Some advertising is meant to generate profits for the advertiser; some is sponsored by nonprofit groups. Some ads try to spur the target audience to action, others to create awareness or understanding of the advertiser's good or service.

E X H I B I T • 1-6

Coca-Cola's trademark varies from country to country. But the overall look is retained through use of similar letter-forms and style, even with different alphabets.

1. Arabic   5. Spanish
2. French   6. Chinese
3. Japanese 7. Hebrew
4. Thai   8. Polish

Companies like Boeing may use *corporate advertising* for a variety of purposes; but typically the central aim is to comment on topics important to the public or to explain the firm's corporate mission. To be credible, corporate advertising should not attempt to sell a specific product or service.

Wed.(17), 2 kind., dakloos w. sloop, zkt. m. spoed opvang, liefst in bosrijke omgeving.

The headline for this *noncommercial* ad for the World Fund reads: "Widow (17), two children, homeless because of demolition of her dwelling place, is urgently looking for a place to stay, preferably in woody environment." Noncommercial advertising tries to convert the attitude of its readers and often seeks a direct response.

Product versus Nonproduct Advertising

Product advertising promotes goods and services. **Nonproduct advertising** sells ideas. A Citgo ad for its gasoline is a product ad. So are ads for banking, insurance, or legal services. But a Citgo ad that promotes the company's mission or philosophy (how the company protects the environment while drilling for oil), is considered **corporate, nonproduct,** or **institutional advertising.**

Corporate advertising can have various objectives: to counter public criticism or promote noncontroversial causes, such as support for the arts or charities. In the corporate ad shown in Exhibit 1–7, Boeing promotes the relevance of its work in space to our life on earth. Corporate advertising is the focus of Chapter 17.

Commercial versus Noncommercial Advertising

While **commercial advertising** seeks profits, **noncommercial advertising** is used around the world by governments and nonprofit organizations to seek donations, volunteer support, or a change in consumer behavior (see the Dutch ad in Exhibit 1–8). Chapter 18 discusses noncommercial advertising.

Action versus Awareness Advertising

In their book *Maxi-Marketing,* two advertising professionals, Stan Rapp and Tom Collins, categorize ads on the basis of expected consumer response. They

Action ads ask the reader to respond. This one uses a dotted border to clue readers that the ad is also a coupon—valuable only when the reader takes the action of redeeming it.

point out that some ads are intended to bring about immediate action on the part of the reader, whereas others have a longer-term goal.[2]

The objective of **awareness advertising,** for example, is to create interest in, and image for, a product and to influence readers or viewers to select a specific brand.

A direct-mail ad, on the other hand, exemplifies **action advertising** because it seeks an immediate, direct response from the reader. The ad in Exhibit 1–9 for "Lil Red" Eden Prairie Grocery features a humorous headline announcing a coupon that the reader can use immediately.

Most ads on TV and radio are awareness ads, but some are a mixture of awareness and action. For example, a 60-second TV commercial may devote the first 50 seconds to image building and the last 10 to a local phone number for immediate information.

TECHNOLOGY AND THE EVOLUTION OF ADVERTISING

As you can see, advertising takes many forms and has considerable influence on contemporary society and commerce. But this was not always true.

Thousands of years ago, people used primitive hand tools to produce goods. They lived in small, isolated communities where artisans and farmers bartered goods and services among themselves. Distribution was limited to how far people could walk and "advertising" to how loud they could shout.

Eventually, Greek and Roman merchants expanded contact with other societies. And with the development of more sophisticated tools, people achieved a higher level of production. These factors increased the demand for goods and created a need to advertise their availability. Merchants hung carved signs in front of their shops so passersby could see what products were being offered. Most people couldn't read, so the signs often used symbols (see Exhibit 1–10).

EXHIBIT • 1-10

An early form of advertising. Until the advent of public schooling, most people couldn't read—so signs featured symbols of the goods or services for sale, such as the jerkin on this tailor's sign in Williamsburg, Virginia.

Throughout history, technological developments dramatically affected advertising and communication. The popular phrase "The medium is the message," coined by Marshall McLuhan, refers to this connection between technology and communication.[3] McLuhan's legacy is the concept that technological advances have been responsible for fundamental changes in the way people communicate throughout history, and, as we examine the evolution of modern advertising, we'll see ample proof for his theory.

The Impact of Printing

The most important development in the history of advertising was the introduction of the printing press in the 1450s. Invented in Germany by Johannes Gutenberg, the press and its system of changeable metal letters revolutionized the way people lived and worked.

Prior to the invention of the printing press, most people were illiterate. Only monks and scholars could read and write; the average person had to memorize important information and communicate orally. Since oral communication could not be substantiated, people lived without documentable facts. And because dialects varied from region to region, most news never traveled more than 50 miles.[4]

The introduction of printing meant that facts could be established and substantiated. People no longer had to rely on their memories for data storage. Movable letters provided the flexibility to print in local dialects. Slow hand-transcription by monks gave way to more rapid, volume printing by a less-select group. Some entrepreneurs bought printing presses, mounted them in wagons, and traveled from town to town selling printing. This new technology made possible the first formats of advertising—posters, handbills, and signs—and enabled the development of the first mass medium—newspapers. In effect the cry of the vendor could now be multiplied many times and heard beyond the limits of the immediate neighborhood.[5]

In 1472, the first ad in English appeared: it was a handbill tacked on church doors in London announcing a prayer book for sale. Almost 200 years later, the first newspaper ad offered a reward for the return of 12 stolen horses. Soon newspapers had ads for coffee, chocolate, tea, real estate, and medicines— even "personals." These early ads were still directed to a limited number of people: customers of the coffeehouses where newspapers were read.

In the American colonies, the *Boston Newsletter* began carrying ads in 1704. Later, Benjamin Franklin, the father of advertising art, made ads more readable by using large headlines and considerable white space. In fact, Franklin was the first American known to use illustrations in ads.

The Impact of the Industrial Revolution

In the mid-1700s, the Industrial Revolution began in England, and by the early 1800s it reached North America. Machinery began to replace animal power. Manufacturers could mass-produce goods with uniform quality; and for the first time, it cost people less to buy a product than to make it themselves.

In order to manufacture a high volume of goods, however, producers needed mass consumption. They soon realized the tremendous value of advertising, which helped them sell to the frontier markets in the West and the growing industrial markets in the East.

In 1841, Volney B. Palmer, the earliest advertising agent in the United States, set up business in Philadelphia. He contracted with newspapers for large volumes of advertising space at discount rates and then resold the space to advertisers at a higher rate. The advertisers usually prepared the ads themselves. In 1890, N. W. Ayer & Sons, another Philadelphia firm, became the first to operate as ad agencies do today—planning, creating, and executing complete ad campaigns for media-paid commissions or fees from advertisers. Still operating, Ayer is the oldest ad agency in the United States.

The Communications Revolution

The technological advances of the Industrial Revolution created the greatest changes in advertising since the 1450s. Prior to the introduction of photography in 1839, products were depicted by handcrafted woodcuts or engraved metal drawings. Photography added credibility and a whole new world of creativity. Ads could show products, people, and places as they really were, rather than as an artist visualized them.

In the 1840s, manufacturers began using magazine ads to reach the mass market and stimulate mass consumption. Magazines made national advertising possible and allowed manufacturers to sell their products nationwide.

Other important communications devices invented in the late 19th and early 20th centuries—the telegraph, telephone, typewriter, phonograph, and motion pictures—enabled people to communicate as never before.

With development of a nationwide railroad system, the United States entered a period of spectacular economic growth. And in 1896, when the federal government inaugurated rural free delivery (RFD), direct-mail advertising and mail-order selling flourished. Manufacturers had an ever-increasing variety of products to sell—plus a way to deliver their advertising (via newspapers, magazines, and direct mail) and their goods to the public.

Social developments in the 19th century also affected the evolution of advertising. The United States experienced a rapid rise in population and, with the advent of public schooling, a 90 percent literacy rate. Manufacturers gained larger markets and advertisers a large reading public that could understand print ads.

The United States entered the 20th century as a great industrial nation with a national marketing system enhanced and propelled by advertising.

The Dawning of Responsibility

During the first two decades of the 1900s, advertising underwent an era of reexamination. After years of unsubstantiated product claims (see Exhibit 1–11), consumer resentment eventually focused on the advertising for patent medicines and health devices. The resulting consumer movement led to government regulation—and to industry efforts at self-regulation.

In the 1920s, after World War I, the era of salesmanship arrived. Full-color printing became the norm, and magazine advertisers employed it lavishly as shown by the 1922 ad in Exhibit 1–12.

On October 29, 1929, the stock market crashed, the Great Depression began, and advertising expenditures dropped drastically. However, perhaps out of desperation, false and misleading advertising continued to thrive. Several best-selling books exposed the advertising industry as an unscrupulous exploiter of consumers, giving birth to a new consumer movement and further government regulation.

Because of consumer sales resistance and corporate budget-cutting during the Depression, the advertising industry started using research to regain its credibility and improve its effectiveness. Daniel Starch, A. C. Nielsen, and George Gallup founded research groups to study consumer attitudes and

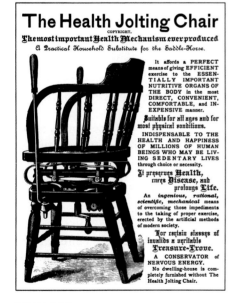

EXHIBIT • 1-11

By the 1880s, newspaper ads for health gimmicks and patent medicines were typical throughout the United States. As there were no U.S. government guidelines nor any organized system for regulating advertising, these ads came to be associated with the ancient Latin expression *caveat emptor* (let the buyer beware). The result was a consumer movement that led to increased legislation and extensive government regulation.

THE SATURDAY EVENING POST

EXHIBIT • 1–12

After World War I, the greater emotional impact of color was used by advertisers—despite the higher cost. This ad produced in 1922 is an early example.

preferences. By providing information on public opinion, the performance of ad messages, and sales of advertised products, these companies started a whole new business—the marketing research industry.

The Rise of Broadcast Advertising

As technology has invariably led to the growth of advertising, it has also opened the doors of opportunity to untold thousands of people. From its inception in 1920, radio rapidly became the nation's primary means of mass communication—and a powerful new advertising medium. World and national news could arrive direct from the scene, and a whole new world of family entertainment—music, drama, sports—became possible. Suddenly, national advertisers could reach huge audiences. In fact, the first radio shows were produced by the advertisers that sponsored them.

The greatest expansion of any medium occurred with the introduction of television broadcasting in 1941. Following World War II, television advertising grew rapidly, and today, television is the second largest advertising medium (after newspapers) in terms of total dollars spent by advertisers.

EXHIBIT • 1–13

EXHIBIT • 1–13

By the 1960s, ads shifted from listing product features to promoting a product's image. The "man in the Hathaway shirt" tripled Hathaway's annual sales and became a classic campaign of the era. The use of the eye-patched actor gave David Ogilvy his first big advertising hit and lent an aura of aristocratic British class and discriminating taste to the product's image.

The Gun is a $2,000 Purdey from England
(The shirt: A Sylex, Sea Island Cotton from Hathaway)

THE DEVELOPMENT OF MODERN ADVERTISING IN NORTH AMERICA

After World War II, as North America changed to a peacetime economy, manufacturers reverted to producing and marketing consumer products. And advertising expenditures increased phenomenally.

During the postwar prosperity of the late 1940s and early 50s, consumers tried to climb the social ladder by buying more products. Advertising entered its golden era, focusing on product features that implied social acceptance, style, luxury, and success.

Rosser Reeves of the Ted Bates advertising agency introduced the idea that every ad must point out the product's **USP—unique selling proposition—** those features that differentiated it from competitive products. As this idea caught on in more and more ads, consumers could hardly see what was "unique" any more. For example, Ford discovered that, despite massive advertising expenditures, consumers wouldn't accept another medium-priced, chromium-plated, "keep-up-with-the-Joneses" car—the Edsel (see Chapter 4).

The transition to the image era of the 1960s was a natural evolution. Advertising's emphasis shifted from product features to product image, or personality (see Exhibit 1–13). Cadillac became the image of luxury—the consummate symbol of success—surpassed only by the aristocratic Rolls-Royce.

The Positioning Era

In the early 1970s, Jack Trout and Al Ries wrote that just as the "me-too" (imitative) products of the 1950s killed the product era, the me-too images of the 60s killed the image era. The 1970s saw a new kind of advertising strategy, where the competitor's strengths became as important as the advertiser's. Trout and Ries were the greatest advocates of what they called the **positioning era.** Although they acknowledged the importance of product features and image, they insisted that what was really important was how the product ranked against the competition in the consumer's mind.

The most famous ads of the positioning era were Volkswagen ("Think small"), Avis ("We're only No. 2"), and 7UP ("The uncola"). Exhibit 1–14 shows Volkswagen's now classic "Think Small" ad. Many other manufacturers tried this approach with great success (see Chapter 4). Trout and Ries also pointed to product failures of the period—like Life Savers gum and RCA computers—and suggested that poor positioning was the reason.[6]

The "Me" Decade

The consumer movement of the 1970s received its greatest impetus from popular disillusionment following the Kennedy assassination, the Vietnam War, the Watergate scandals, and the sudden shortage of vital natural resources—all communicated instantly to the world via new satellite technology. These issues fostered cynicism and distrust of the establishment and everything traditional, and gave rise to a new twist in moral consciousness. On one hand, individual irresponsibility and self-indulgence were justified in the name of personal self-fulfillment. On the other, corporate self-fulfillment was challenged in the name of social accountability. All this led to another evolution in the style and the subjects of advertising.

By the mid-1980s, Americans had already experienced an avalanche of ads—especially in the toiletry and cosmetics industries—aimed at the "me" generation. ("L'Oreal. Because I'm worth it.") At the same time, the nation's largest industrial concerns were spending millions of dollars on corporate advertising to extol their social consciousness and good citizenship for cleaning up after themselves and protecting the environment.

ETHICAL DILEMMA   Truth in Advertising: Is It Puffed Up or Overblown?

Ron Jackson, CEO of Jackson/Riley & Co., a Cincinnati ad agency, claims that an integral part of selling is "emotion, romance, and the metaphor of ideas"—that is, puffery.

Fluff and puff are the bricks and mortar of most consumer advertising, or so it seems. Perhaps that's because the main factor that differentiates one product from another is advertising. Traditionally, puffery remains immune from legal constraints because it is considered opinion rather than fact. That means people aren't expected to believe it literally when Prudential says: "Own a piece of the rock!" But sometimes it's difficult to distinguish between puffery and truth. Although the Federal Trade Commission (FTC) contends reasonable people don't believe puffery, research consistently shows that many do.

Some companies venture into the gray area between truth and deception. For example, food and toy advertisers sometimes use special effects to exaggerate their products' qualities. Since the government began regulating toy commercials, however, some of the worst examples of puffery now occur in automotive advertising, where reality often takes a backseat to dramatization.

As a counterpoint to this problem, Della Femina Travisano & Partners created one of the auto industry's most memorable spokespersons—Joe Isuzu, a character famous for his inability to tell the truth. Jerry Della Femina said that his agency created Joe Isuzu to "get information to the consumer, which is usually fed in the worst way possible." Hal Riney, chairman of Riney & Partners, sees this "antitruth" approach as a possible solution to a problem that pervades the whole advertising industry. "We used up all our superlatives on lesser claims and made it difficult to come up with language that sounds believable when something really is different or special," he says.

While many people found the irreverent Isuzu commercials amusing, nobody laughed about the Volvo scandal. To make a point about Volvo's durability and safety in an accident, the company shot a commercial showing a line of cars being run over by Bear Foot, a monster truck. Only the Volvo survived intact. However, an investigation by the Texas attorney general's office found that the demonstration was fraudulent. Volvo later admitted that its production company artificially reinforced the Volvo's structure and cut the support pillars on competitors' cars.

Although both Volvo and its ad agency maintained their innocence, Volvo's reputation was crushed. The company had to repay investigative costs and run ads apologizing for the deception. Volvo's ad agency was forced to resign the account.

EXHIBIT • 1-14

Hailed by Jack Trout and Al Ries as "the most famous ad of the 60s," this Volkswagen ad co-opted the "small" position in consumers' minds, giving VW a leadership rank for many years.

Think small.

Our little car isn't so much of a novelty any more.
A couple of dozen college kids don't try to squeeze inside it.
The guy at the gas station doesn't ask where the gas goes.
Nobody even stares at our shape.
In fact, some people who drive our little flivver don't even think that about 27 miles to the gallon is going any great guns.
Or using five pints of oil instead of five quarts.
Or never needing anti-freeze.
Or racking up about 40,000 miles on a set of tires.
That's because once you get used to some of our economies, you don't even think about them any more.
Except when you squeeze into a small parking spot.
Or renew your small insurance. Or pay a small repair bill. Or trade in your old VW for a new one.
Think it over.

Some industry experts believe the Volvo debacle will cause advertisers to be more cautious about crossing the line between puffery and dishonesty. Rick Kurnit, partner at a law firm that works with ad agencies, says: "There is no doubt in my mind that post-Volvo, both the networks and the [Federal Trade Commission] will be focusing in on the demonstration issue." Sean Fitzpatrick, vice chairman of McCann-Erickson, adds, "If the cinematography is aiding you and convincing people that you can do things you can't do, then I'd say any reasonable person would say that's wrong. If nothing else, it's a matter of ethics."

Is it any wonder the public doubts advertisers' claims? The FTC rarely takes the lead in protecting consumers, and watchdog groups are frequently ineffective. Moreover, most people don't know that ad agencies must submit detailed affidavits verifying no tricks have been used in demonstration commercials. Naturally some advertisers are more scrupulous than others. According to a Honda spokesman, Honda uses a dramatization label "whenever we depict something in a commercial that could possibly be misconstrued." But as consumer cynicism grows, some industry experts fear the actions of a few may undermine the credibility of all advertisers. Donnie Deutsch, creative director at Deutsch, New York, says: "The public thinks all advertising is [bull] anyway . . . [even though] . . . there are thousands of things that are done right and legitimately."

Given the fierce competition in the marketplace and the lack of legal restraints, the question is not *whether* but *how much* puffery is allowable. Prudent consumers maintain a healthy skepticism about the advertising they see. They try to distinguish fact from fiction while keeping in mind the ancient admonition *caveat emptor:* let the buyer beware.

Questions

1. Do you think advertisers should be allowed to puff up their product claims using "emotion, romance, and the metaphor of ideas"? If advertisers were restricted to telling only the literal truth, how would that affect creativity in advertising?

2. If all puffery were outlawed, how would similar products (toothpaste, detergents, cereals, for example) differentiate themselves? Would it be morally preferable for some companies to go out of business rather than increase sales by puffery?

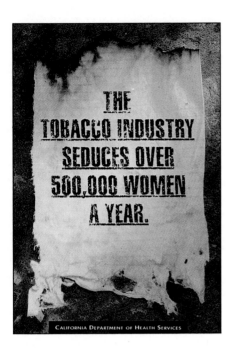

THE TOBACCO INDUSTRY SEDUCES OVER 500,000 WOMEN A YEAR.

CALIFORNIA DEPARTMENT OF HEALTH SERVICES

EXHIBIT • 1-15

Demarketing—slowing the demand for certain products—becomes a strategic tool for some noncommercial, issue-oriented advertisers.

During the energy shortages of the 1970s and 80s, a new marketing tactic called **demarketing** appeared. Producers of energy and energy-consuming goods used marketing and advertising techniques to *slow* demand for their products. Ads asked people to refrain from operating washers and dryers during the day when electricity demand peaked. In time, demarketing became a strategic tool for certain noncommercial, issue advertisers such as the California Department of Health Services, whose antismoking ad is shown in Exhibit 1–15. Some financial and health-care institutions also used demarketing to segment prospective customers. By actively discouraging some customers, for example, banks could concentrate on those who appeared most profitable.[7]

The Age of Marketing Warfare

In the 1980s, Trout and Ries published a new book, *Marketing Warfare,* in which they portrayed marketing as a war that businesspeople must be prepared to wage. Many of their ideas came from a classic book on military strategy written in 1831 by a Prussian general.

In *Marketing Warfare,* Trout and Ries outlined four strategic positions in the marketplace: *defensive, offensive, flanking,* and *guerrilla.* The **defensive strategy** belongs to the dominant company in a given market, which must defend itself against the onslaught of competitors aiming to knock it off the top of the mountain. The second- and third-place companies must use an **offensive strategy** to capture portions of number-one's market. The third strategy, adopted by middle companies in the hierarchy, is a **flanking strategy,** in which they point up the qualities that make them different from the top three. Finally, the remaining companies must adopt a **guerrilla strategy** to carve out small niches they can defend successfully in the larger marketplace. (For a more in-depth review of Trout and Ries's comparison of war and marketing strategies, see Chapter 7, Ad Lab 7–A.)

Toward the end of the 1980s, the economy slowed, and too many companies were chasing too few consumer dollars. The intensity of the advertising that followed provided additional evidence that marketing warfare strategies were enduring. For example, Coke and Pepsi's long-running battle heated up, with a series of counterpoint ads featuring a procession of celebrities choosing one cola or the other.

As the decade of the 90s began to unfold, a new form of advertising evolved. Based on comparative advertising, this new form, an intensified demarketing approach, sought to scare or shame buyers away from competitors' products. In one Chrysler commercial, for example, then-CEO Lee Iacocca harangued colleagues about Americans' propensity to overvalue Japanese cars and undervalue American ones.[8] The technique also found fertile ground in the political arena where negative, attack commercials and hit-mailers became standard fare in local, state, and national elections.

At the same time, a five-year study by the Ayer advertising agency found that consumers and producers were moving in opposite directions. Companies were under pressure to simplify and consolidate, while consumer markets were becoming increasingly diverse and fragmented. Fred Posner, Ayer's executive VP and director of research, urged marketers to redefine and reembrace the concept of branding (discussed in Chapter 5).[9]

Echoing the need to get back to basics, Hank Seiden, former chairman of Ketchum Advertising, denounced the glut of irrelevant and costly product commercials that were 99 percent show biz and 1 percent advertising. In an era when most sales are "conquest sales" (won at the expense of a competitor), he maintained that a "mean, lean sales point the advertiser believes in should come wrapped in a commercial without a trace of fat on it."[10]

Looking toward the 21st Century—The Information Age

The explosion of new technologies in the last decade affected advertising considerably. With cable television and satellite receivers, viewers can watch channels devoted to single types of programming, such as straight news, home shopping, sports, or comedy. This has transformed television from the most widespread of mass media to a more specialized, "narrow-casting" medium.[11] Now small companies and product marketers who appeal to a limited clientele can use television to reach audiences with select interests.

Another change in the TV world is the growing presence of videocassette recorders. Many consumers watch a video at home rather than go to a theater. Advertisers witness this trend with interest. Some videos now begin with an ad, filmed in a suitable cinematic style, promoting a product relevant to that particular movie's audience. In one expensive example, a woman going to the kitchen for a Pepsi encounters a series of hazards similar to the adventures of Indiana Jones. Again, this technological trend allows special-interest advertising through what was traditionally considered a mass medium.

Computer technology has an impact, too. Personal computers, modems, electronic mail, electronic bulletin boards, even facsimile machines give advertisers new media for reaching potential customers. But these options largely replace print media, and their advertising tends to be information- rather than image-oriented. Expanded access to computers benefits advertisers in many ways. As Chapter 16 will explain, now even the smallest companies can maintain computer databases for integrating their various marketing communications.

GROWTH AND STATUS OF INTERNATIONAL ADVERTISING

Although U.S. advertising expenditures in 1990 were $130 billion, or 47 percent of the world total,[12] advertising is no longer a peculiarly North American phenomenon. In the last 15 years, expenditures by foreign advertisers increased more rapidly than either U.S. or Canadian expenditures, thanks to improved economic conditions and a desire for expansion. Recent estimates of worldwide advertising expenditures outside the United States exceed $145.6 billion per year.[13] The emphasis on advertising in individual countries, though, depends on the country's level of development and its national attitude toward promotion. Typically, advertising expenditures are higher in countries with higher personal income.

Today, advertising is used worldwide to sell ideas, policies, and attitudes as well as products. From Procter & Gamble in Cincinnati to Fiat in Turin, Italy, major marketers believe in international advertising, and they back their convictions with sizable advertising budgets. As Exhibit 1–16 on page 22 shows, the top 10 worldwide advertisers are based in many different countries.

Communist countries, including China, once condemned advertising as an evil of capitalism. Now, with the collapse of the Soviet Union, East European countries encourage private enterprise and see the benefits of advertising. Although decades of propaganda conditioned communist consumers to distrust or ignore advertising, Western advertisers can gain attention in this market by featuring instructional as well as entertaining ads.[14]

As a communication form, global advertising contributes to the unification of the world and enhanced international understanding. With the continued

Top 10 international advertisers

Rank	Advertiser	Headquarters	Primary business	Countries in which spending was reported
1	Unilever NV	Rotterdam/London	Soaps	Argentina, Australia, Austria, Brazil, Britain, Canada, Denmark, France, Germany, Greece, India, Italy, Japan, Malaysia, Mexico, Netherlands, Pan Arabia, Portugal, Puerto Rico, South Africa, Spain, Switzerland, Taiwan, Thailand, Turkey, U.S.
2	Procter & Gamble Co.	Cincinnati	Soaps	Australia, Austria, Britain, Canada, France, Germany, Greece, India, Italy, Japan, Malaysia, Mexico, Netherlands, Pan Arabia,, Puerto Rico, Taiwan, Thailand, Turkey, U.S.
3	Nestlé SA	Vevey, Switzerland	Food	Argentina, Australia, Austria, Brazil, Britain, France, Germany, India, Japan, Malaysia, Mexico, Netherlands, Pan Arabia, Portugal, Puerto Rico, Spain, Switzerland, Taiwan, Thailand, U.S.
4	Renault SA	Paris, France	Automotive	Argentina, Austria, Britain, France, Germany, Italy, Netherlands, Pan Arabia, Portugal, Spain, Switzerland, Thailand, U.S.
5	Philip Morris Cos.	New York	Food	Argentina, Australia, Austria, Brazil, Britain, Canada, Denmark, France, Germany, Hong Kong, Japan, Malaysia, Mexico, Netherlands, Pan Arabia, Spain, Taiwan, Thailand, U.S.
6	Fiat SpA	Turin, Italy	Automotive	Brazil, Britain, Denmark, France, Germany, Italy, Netherlands, Portugal, Spain, Switzerland, U.S.
7	Matsushita Electric Industrial Co.	Osaka, Japan	Electronics	Brazil, Britain, Hong Kong, Japan, Malaysia, Pan Arabia, Taiwan, Thailand, U.S.
8	PSA Peugeot-Citroen SA	Paris, France	Automotive	Argentina, Austria, Britain, Denmark, France, Germany, Netherlands, Pan Arabia, Portugal, Spain, Switzerland, Thailand, U.S.
9	Nissan Motor Co.	Tokyo, Japan	Automotive	Australia, Britain, Germany, Japan, Mexico, Pan Arabia, Switzerland, Thailand, U.S.
10	Volkswagen AG	Wolfsburg, Germany	Automotive	Brazil, Britain, France, Germany, Mexico, South Africa, Spain, Sweden, Switzerland, Thailand, U.S.

evolution of technology and ideologies, international advertising will continue to flourish.

Advertising has come a long way from the simple sign on the bootmaker's shop. Today it is a powerful device that announces the availability and location of products, expresses their quality and value, imbues brands with personality, and simultaneously defines the personality of the people who buy them. In turn, advertising itself is shaped by the technology used to convey its message—in other words, the medium and the message have become virtually inseparable.

FUNCTIONS AND EFFECTS OF ADVERTISING

For any business with something to sell, advertising performs several functions, and its effects on that organization may be dramatic. Consider the beginnings of the Coca-Cola Company. Dr. Pemberton (pictured in Exhibit 1–17) and his partner, Frank M. Robinson, decided to write their product's name in a unique way. Later, the name and script were trademarked with the U.S. Patent Office to ensure their sole usage by the Coca-Cola Company in its advertising and packaging. This demonstrates perhaps one of the most basic marketing functions of advertising—*to identify products and differentiate them from others*. (Some of the many functions and effects of advertising are listed in Exhibit 1–18.)

As soon as Pemberton and Robinson named the product, they ran an ad to tell people about it and where they could get it. Within a year, as more soda fountains began to sell the product, handpainted oilcloth signs with "Coca-Cola" began to appear, attached to store awnings. Then the word *drink* was

EXHIBIT • 1–17

In 1886, John Pemberton started a fountain drink business based on his now-famous Coca-Cola formula. Ninety-nine years later, when the Coca-Cola Company announced a change in the original formula, consumers revolted and the world's favorite soft drink began to lose its coveted share of the market. The next year, on its 100th birthday, Coca-Cola had much to celebrate—the revival of Pemberton's original formula as "Coca-Cola Classic" had skyrocketed sales to levels well beyond its former top market position.

EXHIBIT • 1–18

Functions and effects of advertising as a marketing tool

- To identify products and differentiate them from others.
- To communicate information about the product, its features, and its location of sale.
- To induce consumers to try new products and to suggest reuse.
- To stimulate the distribution of a product.
- To build value, brand preference, and loyalty.
- To lower the overall cost of sales.

added to inform passersby that the the product was a soda fountain beverage. Here we see another basic function of advertising: *to communicate information about the product, its features, and its location of sale.*

In 1888, with Pemberton in ill health, Asa G. Candler bought the rights to Coca-Cola for $2,300. Candler was a promoter and a firm believer in advertising. He printed and distributed thousands of coupons offering a complimentary glass of Coca-Cola (see Exhibit 1–19). People who received free coupons tried the product and then tried it again. That's another reason for advertising: *to induce consumers to try new products and to suggest reuse.*

After more people tried the soft drink, liked it, and requested it, more pharmacies bought the product to sell to their customers. *Stimulating the distribution of a product* is yet another function of advertising.

Up to that time, Coca-Cola was sold only at soda fountains. One of the many purposes of advertising, though, is *to increase product usage.* In 1899, the first Coca-Cola bottling plant opened in Chattanooga, Tennessee. The second opened the following year in Atlanta. Now people could buy bottles of Coke to take with them and enjoy at home.

As with any popular product, imitators immediately appeared, and the battle against competitors has been continuous ever since. Another function of advertising is *to build value, brand preference, and loyalty.* Candler's use of an ongoing, consistent promotional campaign helped accomplish this.

In 1916, Coca-Cola introduced its famous bottle with the distinctive contour design. This helped identify Coke and differentiate it from competitors to such an extent that the bottle was registered as a trademark by the U.S. Patent Office. At the same time, the bottle enhanced the company's other promotional efforts and assured the public of Coke's standardized quality. Exhibit 1–20 (p. 28) portrays the evolution of the famous Coke bottle.

For more than a hundred years, Coca-Cola has used the media to communicate advertising messages to mass audiences. The purpose is to satisfy the most important function of advertising: *to lower the cost of sales.* The cost of reaching a thousand people through advertising is usually far less than the cost of reaching just one prospect through personal selling. The McGraw-Hill

Continued on page 28

EXHIBIT • 1–19

These coupons from the 1890s for a free glass of Coca-Cola were one component of the fledgling product's sales promotion program aimed at inducing customers to try and use the product.

Coca-Cola Illustrates the History
of Modern Advertising

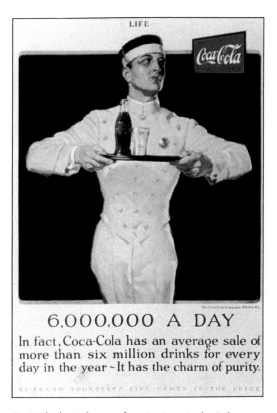

A. Coca-Cola was already widely distributed at soda fountains before cars became commonplace. The illustration in this 1905 ad associated Coca-Cola with the avant-garde—the wealthy few who could afford automobiles.

B. With the "charm of purity," a single Coke, one of 6 million per day, was served by a white-uniformed bellhop in this classic 1925 advertisement.

C. Coca-Cola discovered the benefits of merchandising very early. This 1934 tray pictured famous movie stars Maureen O'Sullivan and Johnny Weismuller (Tarzan).

D. While many ads of the 1930s showcased movie stars, later advertising, such as this 1943 ad, reflected life during wartime. Coke followed the troops. The company set up 64 bottling plants close to combat areas in North Africa, Europe, and the Pacific. Coca-Cola's president ordered that "every man in uniform gets a bottle of coke for 5¢ wherever he is and whatever it costs the company."

E. As Coca-Cola spread around the world, ads and news coverage in major American magazines continued to echo the themes of refreshment and availability. The *Time* magazine from the 1950s describes Coke as the world's friend.

F. "I'd like to teach the world to sing in perfect harmony. I'd like to buy the world a Coke and keep it company." A product such as Coca-Cola rarely changes, but society does. So advertising must change to reflect current lifestyles. This 1969 commercial, featuring children from around the world singing the Coke song (first three frames), was so popular that 20 years later, Coke invited the same singers back—with *their* children—to perform a "hilltop reunion."

G. Max Headroom, the first computerized celebrity presenter, was a popular symbol of New Coke for several years.

H. The "Always Coca-Cola" series of commercials reinterprets the "real thing" concept for the frenetic 90s—a dramatic departure using computer graphics, a mood-is-everything approach, and a variety of messages tailored to match each market segment. (Reproduced with permission from the Coca-Cola Company.)

I. Two weeks after Grandpa—played by Art Carney—buries a piece of Grandma's fruitcake and a magic pinecone in an empty Rockefeller Center planter, he and his grandson return to find the planter filled with one of the world's most beautiful Christmas visions: the glorious Rockefeller Center Christmas tree. This spot, which first aired in 1989, has become a Coca-Cola holiday classic.

J. To help celebrate the 350th anniversary of Montreal, Quebec, Coca-Cola borrows the swash from its own logo and its well-known wave emblem to create this billboard.

K. One of the sports stars Coca-Cola featured in recent years is basketball's Michael Jordan. His legendary jumping ability inspired this spot, titled "Moon Jordan," in which the goal of his rocket-like leap into outer space is to capture a stray bottle of Coca-Cola.

EXHIBIT • 1–20

With bottling, Coca-Cola overcame the limitations of fountain dispensing and gained worldwide distribution—the first in a series of now-classic marketing innovations. The bottle design of 1899 was changed in 1916. The unique, contour design became so recognizable it was trademarked 44 years later, an honor accorded only to a handful of other packages.

Laboratory reported in 1985 that the average face-to-face sales call cost a company well over $220.[15] Today the cost would be even higher. Multiply $220 by the more than 100 million people who watch the Super Bowl, and the cost comes to a mind-boggling $22 *billion*. However, for *only* $750,000, Coca-Cola can buy a 30-second TV commercial during the Super Bowl and reach the same 100 million people. In fact, through television, advertisers can talk to a *thousand* prospects for only $7.50—about 3 percent of what it costs to talk to one prospect through personal selling.

From this brief history of the Coca-Cola Company, we can see that advertising performs a variety of functions and may dramatically affect any business. As we'll see in this and subsequent chapters, advertising also plays an interesting and important role in our economy and society. Exhibit 1–21 is an ad that benefits French society by encouraging donations to fight cancer.

THE ECONOMIC IMPACT OF ADVERTISING

How important is advertising to a nation's economy? In 1992, advertising accounted for approximately 2.37 percent of the U.S. gross national product.[16] In relation to the total U.S. economy, this percentage is small. But as the French advertising pioneer Marcel Bleustein-Blanchet noted in the early 70s, it's no

EXHIBIT • 1–21

Advertising plays an important role in a country's society, as this French anti-cancer ad shows.

Contre le cancer, faites
un geste qui vient du cœur.

LA LIGUE

LIGUE NATIONALE CONTRE LE CANCER. BP 2000. PARIS 13.
POUR VAINCRE LE CANCER CONTINUONS LA LIGUE.

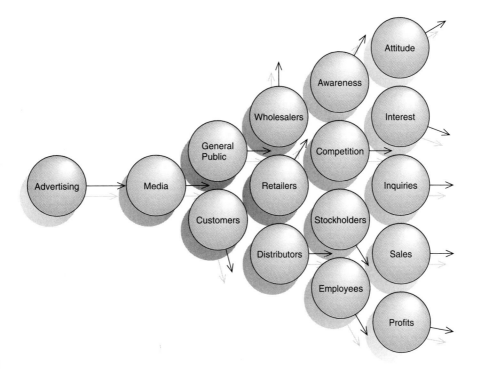

E X H I B I T • 1–22

The billiard-ball principle describes the chain reaction of economic events that takes place the moment a company begins to advertise. As in billiards, the magnitude of these events depends, to a great extent, on the force of the initial advertising impact.

coincidence that the level of advertising investment in every country is directly proportional to that country's standard of living.[17]

The economic effect of advertising is like the opening break shot in billiards, as shown in Exhibit 1–22. The moment a company begins to advertise, a chain reaction of economic events takes place. The extent of the chain reaction, although hard to measure, is definitely related to the force of the shot. But because it inevitably occurs at the same time as many other economic events, the direction of the chain reaction is often disputed.

For example, consider these questions about the effect of advertising. Does advertising affect the value of products? Does advertising raise or lower prices? Does advertising promote competition or discourage it? How does advertising affect the total demand for a product category? Does advertising make more consumer choices available or less? How does advertising influence the business cycle? These are just some of the many frequently asked (and difficult to answer) questions related to the chain reaction of economic events.

Effect on the Value of Products

Why do most people prefer Coca-Cola to some other cola? Why do more women prefer Estee Lauder to some other unadvertised, inexpensive perfume? Are the advertised products functionally better? Not necessarily. But advertising can add *psychic* value to a product in the consumer's mind.

In the mid-1960s, Dr. Ernest Dichter, a psychologist now known as the father of motivational research, supported the view that a product's *image*, which is produced partially by advertising and promotion, *is an inherent feature of the product itself.*[18] Subsequent studies concluded that even though an ad may say nothing verbally about the product's quality, the positive image conveyed by advertising may denote quality, make the product more desirable to the consumer, and thereby add value to the product.[19] This is why some people pay

EXHIBIT • 1–23

Research shows that the image of a product, which is produced partially by advertising and promotion, is an inherent feature of the product. Claims and promises become known over time, reassuring consumers of the product's reliability. As a result, people will pay more for Bufferin aspirin than for an unadvertised house brand about which they know little or nothing.

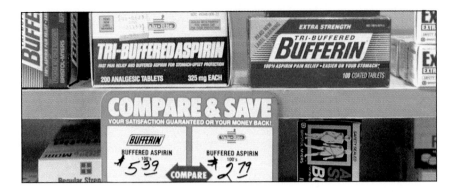

more for Bufferin than for an unadvertised house brand displayed right next to it (see Exhibit 1–23)—even though most buffered aspirin is functionally the same.

Advertising also creates the perception of added value by educating customers about new uses for products. Kleenex was originally advertised as a make-up remover; later it was promoted as a disposable handkerchief. Customers can also be educated about *how* to use a product. As shown in Exhibit 1–24, the Black & Decker Power Pro can be used for more than just picking up dust.

One advantage of the free market system is that consumers can choose the values they want in the products they buy. If low price is important, for example, they can buy an inexpensive economy car. If status and luxury are

EXHIBIT • 1–24

Advertising is a tool that helps prospects visualize the uses and capabilities of a product—like this dramatic demonstration of the Black & Decker Power Pro picking up an egg.

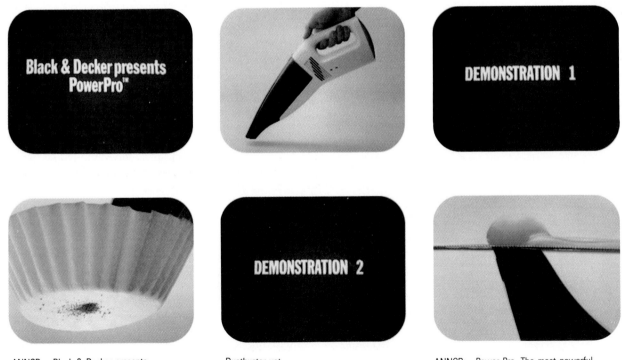

ANNCR: Black & Decker presents
Power Pro. The most powerful

Dustbuster yet.
SFX THROUGHOUT.

ANNCR: Power Pro. The most powerful
dustbuster yet.

important, they can buy a fancy sedan or racy sports car. Many of our wants are emotional, social, or psychological rather than functional. And one of the ways we communicate who we are (or want to be) is through the products we purchase and display. Advertising allows people in a free society the opportunity to satisfy those wants or needs.

Effect on Prices

If advertising adds value to products, it follows that advertising also adds cost. Right? And if companies stopped all that expensive advertising, products would cost less. Right?

Wrong.

Advertised products sometimes do cost more than unadvertised products. However, the opposite is also true. Recently, for example, the Federal Trade Commission and the Supreme Court ruled that because advertising has the competitive effect of keeping prices down, professional people such as attorneys, accountants, and physicians must be allowed to advertise.

Sweeping statements about advertising's positive or negative effect on prices are likely to be too simplistic. But we can make some important points.

- As one of the many costs of doing business, advertising is indeed paid for by the consumer who buys the product. The amount spent on advertising, though, is usually very small compared to total sales.
- Advertising is just one element of the mass-distribution system that enables many manufacturers to engage in mass production. The long, uninterrupted runs used in mass production lower the unit cost of products. These savings can then be passed on to consumers in the form of lower prices. In this indirect way, advertising helps lower prices.
- In industries subject to government price regulation (agriculture, utilities), advertising has historically had no effect on prices. In the 1980s, though, the government began deregulating many of these industries in an effort to restore free market pressures on prices. In these cases, advertising does affect price—often downward, sometimes upward.
- In retailing, price is a prominent element in many ads, so advertising tends to hold prices down. In manufacturing, companies use advertising to stress the features that make their products better, so advertising tends to support higher prices.

Effect on Competition

Some complain that small companies or industry newcomers can't compete with large firms' immense advertising budgets and eventually go out of business. They think advertising restricts competition.

Intense competition does tend to reduce the number of businesses in an industry. However, the firms eliminated by competition may be those that served the consumer least effectively.

In many cases, advertising by big companies has only a limited effect on small businesses because no advertiser is large enough to dominate the whole country. Regional oil companies, for example, compete very successfully with national oil companies on the local level—a fact portrayed in Exhibit 1–25. And nonadvertised store brands of food compete effectively with nationally advertised brands on the same shelves.

In industries characterized by heavy advertising expenditures, though, advertising does inhibit the entry of new competitors. In fact, in some markets, the original brands probably benefit greatly from this form of advertising

Very few advertisers are large enough to dominate the whole country. For example, many people believe that big oil companies are an international cartel. Union Oil created this ad to dispel that myth when the big oil companies were accused of "rigging" energy crises to raise prices. The ad pointed out that many local oil companies successfully compete for our gasoline dollars. As a result, American gas prices are among the lowest in the world.

barrier. But heavy spending on plants and machinery is also a barrier—usually a far more significant one.

Overly simplistic statements that attribute unreasonable power to advertising fail to acknowledge the importance of other influences on competition—such as product quality, price, convenience, and customer satisfaction—which are typically far more significant.

Effect on Consumer Demand

The question of advertising's effect on total consumer demand is extremely complex. Numerous studies show that promotional activity does affect aggregate consumption, but they don't agree on the extent. Many social and economic forces, including technological advances, the population's educational level, increases in population and per capita income, and revolutionary changes in lifestyle, are more significant.

For example, the demand for CD players, microwave dinners, and personal computers has expanded at a tremendous rate, thanks in part to advertising but more so to favorable market conditions. At the same time, advertising has done little to slow sales declines for such items as men's and women's hats, fur coats, and manual typewriters.

Advertising can help get new products off the ground by stimulating demand for a product class. But in declining markets, advertising can only hope to slow the rate of decline. In growing markets, advertisers generally compete for shares of that growth. In mature, static, or declining markets, they compete for each other's shares—"conquest sales."

Effect on Consumer Choice

For manufacturers, the best way to beat the competition is to make their product different. For example, look at the long list of car models, sizes, colors, and features used to attract different buyers. And as Exhibit 1–26 shows, grocery shelves may carry 15 to 20 different brands of breakfast cereals—something for everybody.

EXHIBIT • 1-26

EXHIBIT • 1-26

The competition for consumer dollars is fierce in the $6 billion ready-to-eat cereal business. Here, cereal boxes attract attention by featuring the same wordings, type styles, and visuals that appear in print advertising. In essence, the package may be the brand's best ad.

The freedom to advertise gives manufacturers an incentive to create new brands and improve old ones. When one brand reaches market dominance, smaller brands may disappear for a time. But the moment a better product comes along and is advertised skillfully, the tables suddenly turn, and the dominant brand rapidly loses to the new, better product.

Effect on the Business Cycle

The relationship between advertising and gross national product (GNP) has long been debated. Recently, John Kenneth Galbraith, a perennial critic of advertising, conceded that, by helping to maintain the flow of consumer demand, advertising helps sustain employment and income. He further maintains that, despite decline in the value of the dollar, the U.S. trade deficit persists because advertising and marketing activities create consumer preference for certain foreign products.[20]

Historically, when business cycles dip, worried executives cut advertising expenditures. That may help immediate short-term profits, but studies prove that businesses that continue to invest in advertising during a recession fare considerably better after the recession.[21] However, no study has ever shown that if everybody keeps advertising, the recessionary cycle will turn around.

We conclude that when business cycles are up, advertising contributes to the increase. When business cycles are down, advertising may act as a stabilizing force.

ECONOMIC IMPACT OF ADVERTISING IN PERSPECTIVE: THE ABUNDANCE PRINCIPLE

To individual businesses like Coca-Cola, the local car dealer, and the convenience store on the corner, advertising pays back more than it costs. If advertising didn't pay, no one would use it; and the various news and entertainment media, which depend on advertising for financial support, would all go out of business.

For the consumer, advertising costs less than most people think. The cost of a bottle of Coke includes about a penny for advertising. And the $15,000 price tag on a new car usually includes a manufacturer's advertising cost of less than $200.

To the economy as a whole, the importance of advertising may best be demonstrated by the **abundance principle.** This states that in an economy that produces more goods and services than can be consumed, advertising serves two important purposes: It keeps consumers informed of their alternatives, and it allows companies to compete more effectively for consumer dollars.

The U.S. and Canadian economies produce an enormous selection. Most supermarkets carry more than 10,000 different items. Each car manufacturer markets dozens of models. In both the U.S. and Canadian economies, many suppliers compete for the consumer dollar. This competition generally results in more and better products at similar or lower prices.

Advertising stimulates competition. Moreover, because North American consumers have more income to spend after their physical needs are satisfied, advertising also stimulates innovation and the sale of new products.

However, no amount of advertising can achieve long-term acceptance for products that do not meet consumer approval. Despite large advertising expenditures, less than a dozen of the 50 best-known cars developed this century are still sold today. Exhibit 1–27 shows one of those long-gone brands. Only 2 of

EXHIBIT • 1–27

Despite spending millions of dollars to advertise Studebaker as the "post-war leader in motor car style," the company is no longer in business. Neither are many other manufacturers familiar to our parents' generation.

Actual color photograph of 1947 Studebaker Champion Regal De Luxe 4-door sedan

This dream car is this year's style star...
the refreshingly different postwar Studebaker

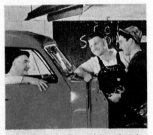

Three generations of Thorntons help to safeguard Studebaker quality—Seated, in this final assembly picture, is 64-year-old Russell E. Thornton. Alongside are his son, Everett V., and Everett's son, Kenneth. Members of this family, like many of their neighbors, have been Studebaker craftsmen for years. Russell Thornton has five sons in all at Studebaker.

Most people say that even the windows of this postwar Studebaker help to give it a special distinction.

The low-swung, roomy body gleams with more glass than you ever saw in a car before.

The effect is fascinating. But the practical result is enormously increased driving vision —alongside, behind and ahead.

You find the same useful end served by everything else that contributes to this Studebaker's eye appeal.

The car's whole design has a marvelous effect on the way it performs, handles and rides.

This Studebaker is the first car, too, with self-adjusting brakes. Its dash dials are glare-proofed by wartime aviation's "black light."

See for yourself how much safer and more enjoyable motoring can be, because of Studebaker's leadership in styling.

Drop in at a showroom for a look at Studebaker's new Champion, Commander and special long-wheelbase Land Cruiser.

STUDEBAKER
The postwar leader in motor car style

©The StudebakerCorp'n, South Bend27,Indiana,U.S.A.

the nation's 10 largest industrial firms in 1900 remain in the top 10 today despite massive advertising.

Advertising stimulates a healthy economy; it also helps create financially healthy consumers who are more informed, better educated, and more demanding. Consumers now demand that manufacturers be held accountable for their advertising. This has led to an unprecedented level of social and legal regulation, the subject of our next chapter.

Summary

Advertising is the nonpersonal communication of information, usually paid for and usually persuasive, about products, services, or ideas by identified sponsors through various media.

Advertising can be classified by target audience (consumer, industrial), by geography (local, international), by medium (radio, newspaper, television), or by function or purpose (product advertising, noncommercial advertising, action advertising).

In ancient times when most people could not read or write, advertisers used symbols on signs. As manufacturing and communication technologies developed, so did advertising. Printing was the first major technology to affect advertising; cable television and computers are the most recent. Since World War II, advertisers have attempted to differentiate products through positioning strategies and other techniques.

As a marketing tool, advertising serves several functions. It

- Identifies and differentiates products.
- Communicates information about the product.
- Induces trial of new products by new users and suggests repurchasing by existing users.
- Stimulates a product's distribution.
- Increases product use.

- Builds value, brand preference, and loyalty.
- Lowers the overall cost of sales.

Aside from marketing, advertising also serves several other functions in the economy and in society.

The economic impact of advertising can be likened to the opening shot in billiards—a chain reaction that affects the company as well as its competitors, customers, and the business community.

On a broader scale, advertising is often considered the trigger on a country's mass-distribution system, enabling manufacturers to produce the products people want in high volume, at low prices, with standardized quality. People disagree, however, about whether advertising adds value to products, makes products more or less expensive, encourages or discourages competition, affects total consumer demand, narrows or widens consumer choice, and affects national business cycles.

Although controversy surrounds most of these economic issues, few dispute the abundance principle, which states that, in an economy that produces more goods and services than can be consumed, advertising keeps consumers informed of their choices and helps companies compete more effectively.

Questions for Review and Discussion

1. How does advertising for the American Cancer Society compare with the standard definition of advertising?
2. Is an ad for an office computer industrial advertising, trade advertising, or professional advertising?
3. What is the difference between the media used for local advertising and for regional advertising?
4. How did the railroad affect the growth of advertising?
5. What examples can you think of (or conceive of) in which companies or organizations use a demarketing strategy?
6. What examples can you give to demonstrate the primary functions of advertising today?
7. As a consumer, will you save money buying at a store that doesn't advertise? Explain.
8. In what ways can advertising increase a product's value?
9. How would you explain the overall effect of advertising on consumer choice?
10. How would the advertising for a new shopping center affect your local economy? Are retailers in your area advertising more or less because of current economic conditions?

At Jeep, This Is A Stop Sign.

No matter how tough and unstoppable our 4x4s are designed to be, we hope that certain obstacles will bring them to a quick halt. Things like wildflowers, plants, and streams, for example.
As a founding member of "Tread Lightly!"—a non-profit organization

dedicated to protecting the environment from abusive off-road use—we know the importance of staying off unmarked trails.
We also know the importance of ecological engineering. Both our Grand Cherokee and the assembly plant where it's built have received

three national environmental awards for their pollution-prevention designs.
So the next time you get behind the wheel of a Jeep, think about the Earth. And obey all stop signs.

There's Only One Jeep®
A Division of the Chrysler Corporation.

Jeep is a registered trademark of Chrysler Corporation.

Always wear your seat belt.

The Social, Ethical, and Regulatory Aspects of Advertising

Objective: To identify and explain the social, ethical, and regulatory issues advertisers must consider. Society determines what is offensive, excessive, and irresponsible; governmental bodies determine what is deceptive and unfair. To be law abiding, ethical, and socially responsible, as well as effective, an advertiser must understand these issues.

After studying this chapter you will be able to:

- Identify common social criticisms of advertising.

- Debate advertising's effect on society.

- Differentiate between ethical dilemmas and ethical lapses.

- Explain how federal agencies regulate advertising to protect consumers and competing advertisers.

- Describe the role state and local governments play.

- Discuss recent court rulings that affect advertisers.

- Analyze how nongovernment organizations regulate advertising.

On a flight from New York to Chicago, John O'Toole, then chairman of Foote, Cone & Belding advertising agency, sat next to a woman who inquired what he did for a living. When he responded that he was in advertising, she stated somewhat scornfully, "I think advertising is destroying our language."

O'Toole debated whether to launch into his "case for national advertising as a preserver of clear, concise, colorful, and correct English." He refrained. Nor did this well-known poet tell his seatmate that advertising is "a portal for introducing new constructions and expressions into a constantly evolving language to enrich and renew it."

As he reported in a memo to his agency, O'Toole simply cited an institution that does a far more thorough job debasing the language:

> I didn't have to look beyond the vehicle we were in to find a first-class miscreant: the airline industry.
>
> I showed her this paragraph I had just read in the in-flight magazine.
>
> "TWA is required by the federal government to ensure compliance with the regulations concerning smoking on board its flights. For the comfort and safety of all, we earnestly solicit each passenger's cooperation in strictly observing these rules. Persistent disregard could result in the offending passenger's disembarkation."
>
> What I think they're saying, amidst all the passive and conditional gobbledygook (I like that one, too), is this:
>
> "The government makes us enforce the no-smoking rules. Please obey them or we'll have to throw you off the plane."
>
> Now being thrown off a plane, presumably in flight, is a disquieting prospect. So perhaps they deliberately obscured the thought with gratuitous verbiage to soften its impact. Whatever the motive, comprehension is the victim.
>
> Pompous as it sounds, *disembarkation* is a more accurate word to describe getting off an airplane than the one they normally use: *deplaning*. "We will be deplaning tonight," says the flight attendant, "through the forward exit." I have an image of passengers standing at the forward exit picking tiny planes off their persons and dropping them out into the darkness. We are not deplaning. Actually the plane is depeopling. But what's wrong with just "getting off"? Then there's the matter of redundancy in airline talk. "For your own personal safety and convenience," for example. Or, "Be sure your seat backs and tray tables are returned to their original upright positions."
>
> Compare that kind of language, which is the airline itself speaking, to the precision of advertising speaking for the airline: "Fly the friendly skies." "You're going to like us." "Doing what we do best."
>
> Anyone who concludes advertising is the offender deserves to be disembarked.[1]

Today articulate critics condemn advertising for sins and abuses far worse than misuse of language. In response, consumer groups, business organizations, and governmental bodies now regulate what advertisers say and do. ◆

THE SOCIAL IMPACT OF ADVERTISING

In this chapter, we address major social criticisms of advertising and contrast them with the benefits advertising offers. We examine the ethics of advertising and the social responsibility of advertisers. Finally, we discuss the regulatory methods government bodies, business organizations, the media, consumer groups, advertisers, and their agencies use to remedy abuses.

Social Criticisms

Advertising is the most visible activity of business. By inviting people to try their products, companies also invite public criticism and attack if their products don't measure up. Proponents of advertising say it's safer to buy advertised products because, when manufacturers put their company name and reputation

EXHIBIT • 2-1

This feature-laden ad for the Subaru SVX offers a host of implied promises.

"Hot" 60
(Open on car message. Voice-over scrolls by on the screen with various arrows and graphics.)
SFX. Music up and under.
Man (VO) I want a car. A car that moves. I've had my father's car. My older brother's car. A car that died pulling out of the lot. I want a car with power. Tell me it has 230 horse power like the super SVX. Tell me it'll produce 228 pound-feet of torque. I don't know what that means, but I like it. Tell me

it's built like a Subaru. I don't want any more mechanic friends. I have enough friends. Too many friends. Don't tell me how it'll handle on an open road. What's that? Tell me how it'll do in Chicago. Chicago on a lousy day. Tell me it has All-Wheel Drive like a Subaru SVX™ so it's good on Vermont snow, good on Miami rain, good on the road filled with drivers with their learner's permits. Don't tell me about wood paneling, about winning the

respect of my neighbors. They're my neighbors. They're not my heroes. Tell me it has special lash adjusters like the SVX. So there's no more valve adjustments. Tell me it has an air bag. And windows I can slide down when it rains and not get soaked. Like an SVX. Tell me. I have the money. I want to know what to drive.
(Fade to black)
Super. Subaru. What to Drive.

on the line, they try harder to fulfill their promises (particularly when they list benefits as in Exhibit 2–1).

Advertising is widely criticized for the role it plays in selling products and for its influence on society. It's important to understand the common criticisms, debunk the myths about advertising, and acknowledge the problems advertising does have.

Does Advertising Debase Our Language?

Defenders of traditional English think *advertising copy* (the text in ads) is too breezy, too informal, too casual, and therefore improper. They believe advertising has destroyed the dignity of the language.

Advertising research shows that people respond better to down-to-earth conversational language than to more dignified, formal writing. Good copywriters develop a style that is descriptive, colorful, and picturesque as well as warm, human, and personal. Because of the need for brevity, they use simple words that are lively, full of personality, and reflect the language usage and patterns of their target audience (see Exhibit 2–2).

Does Advertising Make Us Too Materialistic?

We all have needs and desires beyond the basics of food, clothing, and shelter. In a free society, people can choose the degree to which they indulge their desires, needs, and fantasies. Some people crave material possessions. Others desire less material goods and more cultural or spiritual enhancement in their lives. There are advertising sponsors at both ends of that spectrum. Advertisers promote natural products as well as convenience packaged goods; simple sandals as well as formal footwear; chamber music concerts as well as CD players. Given all the commercials for public services, one could just as well criticize advertising for making us too charitable. In other words, this criticism is analogous to shooting the messenger.

EXHIBIT • 2–2

The misuse of the English language in the body copy might appall grammarians, but this humorous, cleverly written ad won numerous awards from the advertising industry.

Does Advertising Make Us Buy Things We Don't Need?

Every year advertisers spend millions of dollars trying to convince people that some product will make them sexier, healthier, or more successful. But they can't *make* people buy a product they don't want (see Exhibit 2–3).

Wilson Bryan Key, who wrote several books on subliminal advertising, advances the theory that sexual messages are intentionally embedded in many ads in order to seduce consumers. But a multitude of academic studies have debunked this theory. There is absolutely no proof that such embedding either exists or has any effect.[2]

If it's so easy to convince people to buy, why do more products fail than succeed? Sociologist Michael Shudson points out that advertising's powers have been greatly exaggerated.[3] In fact, most Americans are highly skeptical of advertising. In one study, only about 20 percent of consumers surveyed indicated that advertising played the major role in their choices.[4]

Another aspect of the manipulation argument is that advertising *creates* artificial needs. Do people really *need* VCRs, frozen orange juice, or ballpoint pens? Robert Samuelson, writing in *Newsweek* magazine, made the case for the "sovereignty of the consumer."[5] He argued that, rather than corporate America controlling consumers through advertising, consumers control the marketplace by the choices they make with their discretionary income.

E X H I B I T • 2-3

The fallacy that people can be made to buy things they do not need is clearly portrayed in this ad by the American Association of Advertising Agencies.

Is Advertising Excessive?

In the United States, the average person is exposed to over 500 commercial messages a day. With so many products competing for attention (over 10,000 in the average supermarket), advertising professionals themselves worry about the negative impact of ad proliferation. But most Americans seem to accept this condition as the price for free television, freedom of the press, and a high standard of living.

Is Advertising Offensive or in Bad Taste?

Taste is highly subjective: What is bad taste to some is perfectly acceptable to others. And tastes change. What is considered offensive today may not be so tomorrow. People were outraged when the first ad for underarm deodorant appeared in a 1927 *Ladies Home Journal*; today no one questions such ads. And even with the AIDS scare, the three major networks still won't accept condom ads—although *USA Today*, the *New York Times*, and numerous network affiliates do.[6]

Today, grooming and personal hygiene products often use nudity in their ads. Where nudity is relevant to the product, people are less likely to regard it as obscene or offensive.[7] And in international markets, nudity in commercials is commonplace (see Exhibit 2–4). Ultimately, the market has the veto power—it can simply ignore material it considers offensive or in bad taste. If ads don't attract the target audience, the campaign will falter and die.

This Coppertone commercial shown in Brazil cannot be aired in many countries because it might offend many people and hurt product sales.

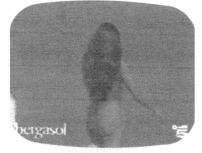

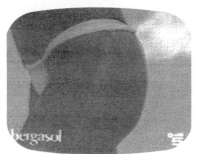

"Today with Bergasol you can get a quicker tan. . .
. . . without sunburns. Bergasol suncare

products are clinicially. . .
. . . tested to offer the highest safeness. With Bergasol you will be more quickly

tanned. . .
. . . and better protected. Bergasol, the quick and deep tan in complete safeness."

Does Advertising Perpetuate Stereotypes?

Advertisers have become increasingly sensitive to stereotyping minorities and women in their ads. Latinos, African-Americans, Italians, Chinese, Native Americans, and other minority group members are now portrayed more favorably in ads, not only because of pressure from watchdog groups, but because it's just good business—these consumers represent sizable target markets. Marilyn Kern-Foxworth, a Texas A & M professor and an expert on minorities in advertising, points out that positive role portrayal in some mainstream ads has had a positive effect on the self-esteem of black youth (see Exhibit 2–5).[8] As we'll see in Chapter 3, this positive trend has been helped by the emergence of new advertising agencies owned and staffed by minorities and aimed at reaching minority markets.

The image of women in advertising has also changed significantly in the past few years. More than 50 percent of all women now work outside the home, more than 10 million of them in professional and managerial careers (see Exhibit 2–6). Advertisers want to reach, not offend, this sizable market of upwardly mobile consumers.

Is Advertising Deceptive?

Critics define deceptiveness not only as false and misleading statements but also as false impressions conveyed, whether intentional or not. Ad Lab 2–A lists common deceptive practices.

For advertising to be effective, consumers must have confidence in it. So continued deception is self-defeating. Even meaningless—but legal—*puffery*

EXHIBIT • 2-5

Black athletes and musicians aren't the only suitable role models that can be portrayed in advertising. This ad series features prominent men in Jockey underwear—here, an agricultural economist.

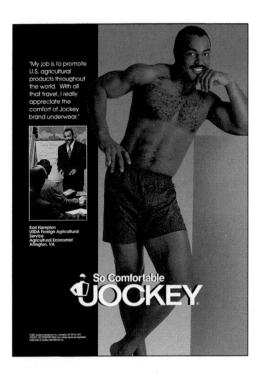

(claiming to be the "best," "greatest," or "premier") is sometimes believed and can therefore become deceptive.

Advertising puts the advertiser on record. Advertisers serve their interests best by being honest.

Social Benefits

Advertising benefits society in a number of ways. It encourages the development of new and better products; it gives consumers a wider variety of choices; it helps keep prices down; and it encourages competition. Advertising also

EXHIBIT • 2-6

Women and minorities in management positions are now pictured more and more in corporate and industrial ads.

AD LAB 2–A   Unfair and Deceptive Practices in Advertising

The courts have held that these acts constitute unfair or deceptive trade practices and are therefore illegal.

False Promises

Making an advertising promise that cannot be kept, such as "restores youth" or "prevents cancer."

Incomplete Description

Stating some, but not all, of a product's contents, such as advertising a "solid oak" desk without mentioning that only the top is solid oak and the rest is hardwood.

Misleading Comparisons

Making meaningless comparisons, such as "as good as a diamond," if the claim cannot be verified.

Bait-and-Switch Offers

Advertising an item at an unusually low price to bring people into the store and then "switching" them to a higher priced model by stating that the advertised product is "out of stock" or "poorly made."

Visual Distortions

Making a product look larger than it really is—for example, a TV commercial for a "giant steak" dinner special showing the steak on a miniature plate that makes it appear extra large, or showing a "deluxe" model that is not the same as the one offered at a "sale" price.

False Testimonials

Implying that a product has the endorsement of a celebrity or an authority who is not a bona fide user.

False Comparisons

Demonstrating one product as superior without giving the "inferior" item a chance or making comparisons with the least competitive product, such as comparing the road performance of a steel-belted radial with that of an "economy" tire.

Partial Disclosures

Stating what a product can do but not what it cannot do, such as claiming that an electrically powered automobile will go "60 miles per hour—without gasoline" and not mentioning that it needs an eight-hour battery recharge every 100 miles.

Small-Print Qualifications

Making a statement in large print ("Any new suit in stock— $50 off!") only to qualify or retract it in smaller type elsewhere in the ad ("With the purchase of a suit at the regular price").

Laboratory Application

What examples have you seen of deception?

subsidizes the media, supports freedom of the press, and provides a means of disseminating public information about health and social issues.

But advertising has been and still is misused. Advocates believe, though, that the abuse heaped on advertising is excessive and no longer warranted. They point out that, of all the advertising reviewed by the Federal Trade Commission in a typical year, 97 percent is found to be satisfactory.[9] In the end, it is up to both advertisers and consumers to ensure that advertising is used intelligently, ethically, and responsibly.

ADVERTISING ETHICS AND SOCIAL RESPONSIBILITY

Numerous laws determine what advertisers can and cannot do, but they also allow a significant amount of leeway. That's where ethics and social responsibility come into play. An advertiser can act unethically or socially irresponsibly and not break any laws. Attorney ads can use client testimonials and tobacco companies are free to sponsor rock concerts for college students. Ethical advertising means doing what the *advertiser* believes is morally right for a given situation. Social responsibility means doing what *society* views as best for the welfare of people in general or for a specific group of people.

Advertising Ethics

After the turn of the century, consumers, the government, and special-interest groups started becoming concerned about advertising practices, and advertisers began to develop higher standards of ethical conduct. To better understand the ethical issues advertisers wrestle with today, consider two topics: *ethical dilemmas* and *ethical lapses*.

Ethical Dilemmas

An **ethical dilemma** occurs when there are two conflicting but valid sides to an issue. How does an advertising person resolve an ethical dilemma? The best approach is to answer three questions: (1) Which course of action will produce the most good for the greatest number of people? (2) Will either course of action violate someone else's rights? (3) Will either course of action result in unfair treatment of any affected party?[10]

Consider the issue of *product placements* in TV programs—a shot of Quaker Oats Squares in "Roseanne" and IBM computers in "L.A. Law." Those products don't appear by chance, nor do the companies who make them pay to get them on the shows.[11] Paid product placements are illegal unless they're disclosed; but if they are disclosed, networks generally won't approve them.[12] Behind the scenes, though, some advertisers provide free products in return for free exposure. Critics say the practice hurts traditional advertisers who pay $100,000 or more for a 30-second spot. It's an ethical dilemma for both advertisers and broadcasters.

Ethical Lapses

An **ethical lapse** refers to a situation in which an advertiser makes a clearly unethical and sometimes illegal decision. Volvo, for example, tarnished its impeccable reputation when it rigged a commercial to make it appear that its cars could withstand being run over by a monster pickup truck. William Hoover, senior vice president for Volvo, said the company "feels pretty dumb."[13] An ethical dilemma involves an unresolved interpretation of an ethical issue; an ethical lapse is a clear case of unethical behavior.

Advertisers' Social Responsibility

Social responsibility is closely related to advertising ethics, but measures of social responsibility can change more rapidly than ethical positions. The AIDS scare caused many advertisers to tone down the use of sexual images in their ads. Concerned citizens, consumer advocates, and special-interest groups also pressure advertisers when the public's welfare is at risk. RJR Nabisco canceled plans for two new cigarette brands—Uptown, aimed at African-Americans, and Dakota, aimed at uneducated young women—in the heat of opposition from consumer-advocacy groups. And Lorillard (maker of Kent, Newport, and True cigarettes) was accused of being opportunistic when it announced plans to run yellow stripes on its print and billboard ads to show support for U.S. troops in the Persian Gulf. The Advocacy Group pointed out that "If [Lorillard was] genuinely interested in preserving and protecting human lives, they would quit marketing their lethal products to people."[14]

Environmental concerns are also inducing advertisers around the world to be more socially responsible. Many companies now advertise their socially responsible endeavors, as Castrol Motor Oil has done in its Australian ad in Exhibit 2–7.

EXHIBIT • 2–7

Companies spend huge sums developing products to meet environmental standards, and advertising can both announce and introduce such improvements.

Chevron demonstrated its sense of social responsibility with its long-running "People Do" ads. The first explained how the company delayed a gas pipeline project in Wyoming to avoid upsetting the mating season of local grouse.[15] And Wal-Mart launched a "green" campaign highlighting merchandise that is environmentally friendly.[16]

Most advertisers today strive to maintain high ethical standards and socially responsible advertising practices. Once a free-swinging, unchecked business activity, advertising is today a closely scrutinized and heavily regulated profession. Advertising's alleged past excesses and shortcomings (rightly or wrongly charged) have created layer upon layer of laws, regulations, and regulatory bodies. Consumer groups, governments, special-interest groups, and even other advertisers now review, check, control, and change advertising.

FEDERAL REGULATION OF ADVERTISING

In both the United States and Canada, the federal government imposes strict controls on advertisers through laws, regulations, and judicial interpretations. For example, in the United States, various federal agencies and departments regulate advertising: the Federal Trade Commission, the Food and Drug Administration, the Federal Communications Commission, the Patent and Trademark Office, the Library of Congress, and others (see Exhibit 2–8). Because their jurisdictions often overlap, an advertiser often has difficulty complying with their regulations.

EXHIBIT • 2-8

Federal regulators of advertising in the United States

Federal Trade Commission
Regulates all commerce between the states. Formed in 1914, the FTC is the leading federal regulatory agency for advertising practices and the subject of much criticism by the advertising profession.

Federal Communications Commission
Formed by the Communications Act of 1934, has jurisdiction over the radio, TV, telephone, and telegraph industries. It maintains indirect control over advertising through its authority to license or revoke the license of all broadcast stations.

Food and Drug Administration
Has authority over the advertising, labeling, packaging, and branding of all packaged goods and therapeutic devices. It requires full disclosure labels, regulates the use of descriptive words on packages, and has jurisdiction over the packaging of poisonous or otherwise hazardous products.

Patent and Trademark Office
Regulates registration of patents and trademarks. It enforces the Trade-Mark Act of 1947.

Library of Congress
Registers and protects all copyrighted material including ads, music, books, booklets, computer software, and other creative material.

Bureau of Alcohol, Tobacco, and Firearms
Has almost absolute authority over liquor advertising through its power to suspend, revoke, or deny renewal of manufacturing and sales permits for distillers, vintners, and brewers found to be in violation of regulations.

Office of Consumer Affairs
Is the chief consumer protection department in the federal government. Established in 1971, the OCA coordinates, maintains, and publicizes information on all federal activities in the field of consumer protection. Publications produced and circulated by the OCA include consumer education guidelines, monthly newsletters, and a consumer services column released to some 4,500 weekly newspapers.

U.S. Postal Service
Has authority to halt mail delivery to any firm or person guilty of misusing the mails. It maintains control over false and deceptive advertising, pornography, lottery offers, and deceptive guarantees.

Department of Agriculture
Closely monitors the distribution of misbranded or unregistered commercial poisons. The Department of Agriculture (USDA) works with the FTC to enforce regulations governing certain products. The USDA Grain Division has regulatory authority over false and deceptive advertising for seeds and grain products. The Grain Division can initiate action against violators.

Securities and Exchange Commission
Established in 1934, has jurisdiction over all advertising of stocks, bonds, and other securities sold via interstate commerce. The SEC requires that public offerings contain full disclosure of all pertinent information on the company and the securities offered so the prospective investor can make can informed buying decision. Disclosure must detail all risk factors that may affect the investment.

Department of Justice
Normally does not initiate legal action against persons or firms charged with violating the federal laws governing advertising. Instead, it enforces these laws by representing the federal government in the prosecution of cases referred by other federal agencies.

Consumer Product Safety Commission
Established in 1972 to develop and enforce standards for potentially hazardous consumer products. It derives its power from four acts: the Flammable Fabrics Act of 1954, the Federal Hazardous Substances Act of 1960, the Children Protection Act of 1966, and the Standard for the Flammability of Children's Sleepwear of 1972. It has jurisdiction over placement of warning statements in ads and other promotional materials for covered products. Its authority extends to household products, toys, and hazardous substances that cause accidental poisoning. The Consumer Product Safety Commission investigates product advertising and labeling violations brought to its attention by consumers and consumer protection groups. Continued violations by product makers are grounds for prosecution and punitive action by the Attorney General.

In Canada, the principal federal regulators are the Ministry of Consumer and Corporate Affairs Canada (CCAC), the Health Protection Branch of the Ministry of Health and Welfare Canada (HPB), and the Canadian Radio-Television and Telecommunications Commission (CRTC).[17] But the Canadian legal situation is considerably more complex than in the States due to the separate (and often concurrent) jurisdictions of paternalistic federal and provincial governments, the broad powers of government regulators, the vast array of self-regulatory codes, and the very nature of a bilingual and bicultural society. One simple example of this is the fact that federal laws require all packages and labels to be printed in both English and French throughout Canada.[18]

The U.S. Federal Trade Commission

The **Federal Trade Commission (FTC)** is the major U.S. regulator of national advertising for products sold in interstate commerce. Initially, the FTC just protected competitors from false advertising. But in 1938, Congress passed the Wheeler-Lee Amendment, which gave the FTC power to protect both consumers and competitors from *deceptive* and *unfair* advertising. Unfortunately, the definition of *deceptive* and *unfair* is controversial.

Defining Deception

Prior to 1983, the FTC interpreted deceptive advertising as having "the tendency or capacity to mislead substantial numbers of consumers in a material way." In 1983, FTC chairman James C. Miller III drafted a new definition he believed would prevent so many trivial violations. Miller defined **deceptive advertising** as any ad in which "there is a misrepresentation, omission, or other practice that is likely to mislead the consumer, acting reasonably in the circumstances, to the consumer's detriment."

This revised definition puts a greater burden on the FTC to prove that deception actually took place. Further, the FTC must show that consumer decisions were actually influenced in a material way. Finally, the new definition implies that an ad's effect on unthinking or ignorant consumers is relatively unimportant.

Critics worry that it will now be harder and more costly to win deceptive advertising cases.[19] They fear that advertisers will feel less restraint because they perceive the FTC as more lax. In spite of this criticism, the FTC remains a powerful regulator. The commission cracked down on half-hour TV ads (*infomercials*) that might deceive viewers into mistaking them for regular programming. They must be clearly identified as ads now.[20] The FTC also looks at environmental claims (such as biodegradable, degradable, photodegradable, and recyclable). To avoid confusing terminology, the National Association of Attorneys General recently requested that the FTC and EPA work jointly with the states to develop uniform national guidelines for environmental marketing claims.[21]

Defining Unfairness

Unfair advertising is *unfair* to the consumer although not necessarily deceptive. According to FTC policy, an ad may be called **unfair** when a consumer is "unjustifiably injured" or when there has been a "violation of public policy" (such as of other government statutes). Practices considered unfair are claims made without prior substantiation; claims that tend to exploit such vulnerable groups as children and the elderly; and instances in which the consumer cannot make a valid choice because the advertiser omits important information about the product or about competing products mentioned in the ad.[22]

In its 1984 case against International Harvester, the FTC found that the company's failure to warn of a safety problem was not deceptive but did constitute an unfair practice.[23] Advertising organizations argue that the word *unfair* is vague and "can mean whatever any given individual's value judgment may assign to it."[24] They lobbied Congress to eliminate the FTC's power to prosecute on unfairness grounds, but to date Congress has been unreceptive.

Investigating Suspected Violations

The FTC may decide to investigate an advertiser if it receives complaints from consumers, competitors, or the FTC's own staff members who monitor ads in various media. The FTC has broad powers to pursue suspected violators and demand information from them. Typically, the FTC looks for three kinds of information: *substantiation, endorsements,* and *affirmative disclosures.*

Substantiation   If a suspected violator cites survey findings, scientific studies, and the like, the FTC may ask to see the supporting data. Advertisers are expected to have supporting data in hand before running an ad, although the FTC does allow for postclaim evidence in some instances.[25] The FTC does not solicit substantiation from advertisers it is not investigating.

Identifying a celebrity's name with a
product requires full coordination and
agreement in advance.

Endorsements The FTC also scrutinizes ads that contain questionable endorsements or testimonials. The endorsers themselves (and the advertisers)
must be able to substantiate their claims. Celebrity endorsers can be held personally liable for misrepresenting a product or service.[26] (See Exhibit 2–9.)

Affirmative Disclosures Advertisers must make affirmative disclosure of their
product's limitations or deficiencies; for example, EPA mileage ratings for cars,
pesticide warnings, and statements that soft drinks containing saccharin may be
hazardous to one's health.

Remedies

When the FTC determines that an ad is deceptive or unfair, it may take three
courses of action: (1) negotiate with the advertiser for a consent decree, (2)
issue a cease-and-desist order, and/or (3) require corrective advertising.

Consent Decree A *consent decree* is a document the advertiser signs agreeing to
stop the objectionable advertising. Before signing the decree, the advertiser can
negotiate and bargain with the FTC over specific directives that will govern
subsequent advertising claims.

Cease-and-Desist Order If an advertiser doesn't sign a consent decree, the FTC may
issue a cease-and-desist order prohibiting further use of the ad. Before the
cease-and-desist order is final, a hearing is held before an administrative law
judge. (Exhibit 2–10 shows a flowchart of the FTC complaint procedure.) Most
advertisers sign the consent decree after the hearing and agree, without
admitting guilt, to halt the advertising. Only a small percentage appeal cease-
and-desist orders. Advertisers who violate either a consent decree or a cease-
and-desist order can be fined up to $10,000 per showing of the ad.

Corrective Advertising The FTC may also require corrective advertising. A portion of
the company's advertising for a period of time must be used to explain and

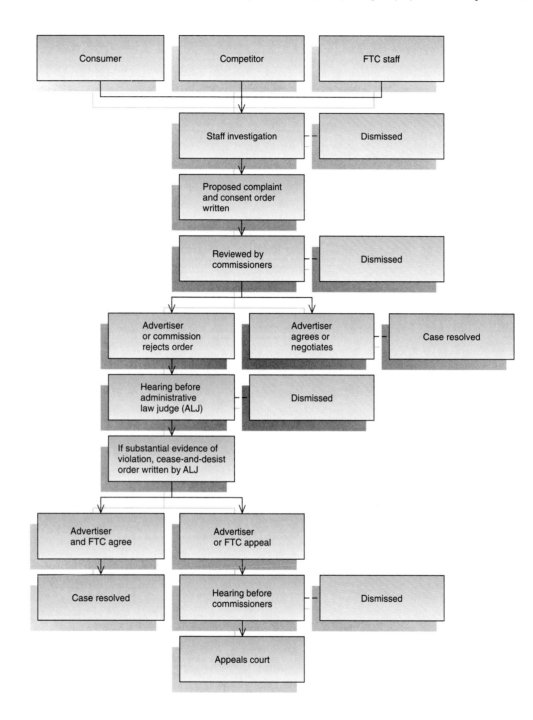

EXHIBIT • 2-10

Flowchart of the FTC complaint procedure.

correct the offending ads. A classic case of corrective advertising was Listerine's $10.2 million worth of ads stating, "Listerine will *not* help prevent colds or sore throats or lessen their severity."

To help other advertisers avoid such expensive punishment, the FTC will review advertising before it runs and give "advance clearance" in an advisory opinion. In addition, the FTC publishes *Industry Guides and Trade Regulation Rules*, which provide advertisers, agencies, and the media with ongoing information about FTC regulations.

False and Misleading Advertising in Canada

In Canada, the Competition Act of 1985, enforced by the CCAC, makes any public promotion an offense if it is "false or misleading in a material respect." For an offense to occur, it is not necessary for anyone to have been misled by the representation, only that it be false. The fact that it's an *offense* means it's a crime—an advertiser or agency could be indicted and, if convicted, go to jail for up to five years, pay a fine, or both.[27]

Food and Drug Administration, CCAC, and HPB

A unit of the Department of Health and Human Services, the **Food and Drug Administration (FDA)** has authority over labeling, packaging, and branding of packaged foods and therapeutic devices. The FDA requires manufacturers to disclose all ingredients on product labels, in all product advertising featured in stores, and in all accompanying or separately distributed product literature. The label must accurately state the weight or volume of the contents. Labels on therapeutic devices must give clear instructions for use. The FDA can require warning and caution statements on packages of poisonous or hazardous products. It regulates "cents off" and other promotional statements on package labels. The FDA also has jurisdiction over the use of words such as *giant* or *family* used to describe package sizes.

In response to the proliferation of consumer-oriented drug ads in the mid-80s, the FDA ruled that any ad for a brand-name drug must also include every piece of information in the package insert.[28] That meant advertisers would have to run lengthy commercials or use minuscule type in print ads. However, pharmaceutical companies found a way around the FDA ruling by not mentioning the brand name. Upjohn's successful ads for its antibaldness drug used only the Upjohn name, talked about baldness in general, and suggested that consumers see their doctors for further information.[29]

In 1987, the FDA lifted a long-standing ban on nutritional and health claims on food labels. Suddenly it was legal to use phrases like *high-fiber* or *low-cholesterol*. While the new policy boosted sales in many categories of packaged foods, it also led to exaggerated claims that outraged consumer groups and the FDA. As a result, President Bush signed the 1990 Nutritional Labeling and Education Act. Although the new law doesn't ban nutritional and health claims, the FDA established legal definitions for a wide range of terms, such as *light, low fat*, and *reduced calories*.[30] And it now requires labels to show food value for one serving alongside the total daily value as established by the National Research Council.

Perrier was one of the advertisers affected by the FDA's tougher stand. When the FDA learned that the French company's mineral water doesn't exactly go untouched from Mother Nature to consumers' lips, regulators forced Perrier to drop the words "naturally sparkling" from its labels.[31] As a result of increased FDA scrutiny, many advertisers are now more cautious about their health and nutritional claims, such as the California Milk Advisory Board's claim about butter in Exhibit 2–11.

In Canada, advertising for food and drugs is subject to intense regulation as a result of the Food and Drug Act of 1985. Regulations for packaging and nutrition labeling are extensive. All broadcast advertising for food products must meet strict, and sometimes arbitrary, rules and be precleared with the CCAC. Likewise, the HPB preapproves all broadcast ads for nonprescription drugs and cosmetics. It is illegal to make comparative therapeutic claims and also to advertise prescription drugs to the public.[32]

E X H I B I T • 2–11

The Food and Drug Administration (FDA) scrutinizes food ads that make nutritional claims. If this ad had claimed that butter has fewer calories than margarine, the California Milk Advisory Board would have to do some explaining to the FDA.

The federal Tobacco Products Control Act of 1985 makes it illegal to advertise any tobacco product in Canada—a law currently being challenged by tobacco marketers as a violation of their right to free commercial speech.[33]

Federal Communications Commission and the CRTC

The seven-member **Federal Communications Commission (FCC),** established by the Communications Act of 1934, has jurisdiction over the radio, television, telephone, and telegraph industries. The FCC's control over broadcast advertising is actually indirect, stemming from its authority to license broadcasters (or to take away their licenses). The FCC stringently controls the airing of obscenity and profanity, and it can restrict both advertising content and which products may be advertised on radio and TV. For example, the FCC required stations to run commercials about the harmful effects of smoking even before Congress banned cigarette advertising on TV and radio.

In the 1980s, the FCC decided that marketplace forces can do an adequate job of controlling broadcast media, so it dropped many of its rules and regulations for both radio and TV stations. The FCC no longer limits the amount of time that can be devoted to commercials, and stations no longer have to maintain detailed program and commercial logs. However, stations still keep records of commercial broadcasts so advertisers can be assured they ran.

New legislation gave the FCC additional teeth and may affect advertisers. The 1992 Cable Television Consumer Protection and Competition Act places new controls on the cable TV industry to encourage a more service-oriented attitude and to improve the balance between rates and escalating ad revenues.[34] The FCC can set subscriber rates for cable TV, so subscription revenues should slow while advertising rates rise.

Recent studies show a direct link between violence on TV and increased violent acts in public (a public health issue). Congress responded by enacting the 1992 Television Violence Act—a hint of what's to come. The act grants network and cable companies an exemption from antitrust laws if they agree on a self-regulation mechanism to police violence. Because networks and cable companies have been slow to respond and continue to deny that violence on TV is related to violence in life, government intervention is a real possibility.[35] Government regulation could easily affect the nature of future programming, lead to controls on who can buy advertising, and may even change the nature of advertising content.

Restrictions in Canada are even tighter. The federal government has exclusive jurisdiction over the entire Canadian broadcasting system. This enables the **Canadian Radio-Television and Telecommunications Commission (CRTC)** to regulate the quantity, and to some degree the quality, of radio and television advertising. This is done through licensing and by requiring preapproval for commercials for products such as food, drugs, patent medicines, and cosmetics to be sure the spots meet advertising codes.

Patent and Trademark Office and Canadian Trade-marks Office

A **trademark**, according to the U.S. Lanham Trade-Mark Act (1947), is "any word, name, symbol, or device or any combination thereof adopted and used by a manufacturer or merchant to identify his goods and distinguish them from those manufactured or sold by others." See Exhibit 2–12 for examples of important trademark terminology.

Ownership of a trademark may be designated in advertising or on a label, package, or letterhead by the word *Registered*, the symbol ®, or the symbol ™.

Trademark, brand
Initials, words, or symbols that identify one particular product or line of products from a single source

Trade name
Name under which a company does business; in some instances trade name and trademark may be identical (such as General Motors' GM)

MARK OF EXCELLENCE

House mark
A trademark used on all or most of the products of a particular company

Service mark
The name or symbol for a service as opposed to a product

Trade character
A person, animal, or other character used to identify a business

Certification mark
A mark guaranteeing the origin, trade, or quality of a product

Collective
A mark used to indicate membership in an organization

EXHIBIT • 2–12

Trademark terminology.

If someone uses a trademark owned by another and refuses to stop, the trademark owner can ask for a court order.

Ironically, advertising success can sometimes cause a trademark's demise. This is precisely what happened to famous trademarks like thermos, escalator, and cellophane. The owners lost their trademark rights when the courts declared the trademarks "generic," which means the name has come into common use and is now the dictionary name for the product.

Most trademark owners take precautions to prevent their trademarks from becoming generic. They separate the trademark from surrounding words and follow it with the generic name of the product (Band-Aid brand adhesive bandages, Scotch brand tape, Kleenex tissues, Jell-O brand gelatin).[36] They never refer to the trademark in the plural. Xerox even advertises the fact that its name is a registered trademark, as shown in Exhibit 2–13.

Canadian trademark law is similar to U.S. law, with some additional restrictions, since both countries are members of the international Union for the Protection of Industrial Property. In Canada, trademark registration is refused if the trademark is merely a person's name or surname, if it's clearly descriptive or deceptively misdescriptive of the wares or services, or if it's an official Canadian or British mark.[37]

Library of Congress and the Canadian Copyright Office

The **Library of Congress** registers and protects all copyrighted material, including advertising in the United States. A **copyright** issued to an advertiser grants the exclusive right to print, publish, or reproduce the protected ad for a

period of time equal to the life span of the copyright owner plus 50 years. An ad can be copyrighted only if it contains original copy or illustrations. Slogans, short phrases, and familiar symbols and designs cannot be copyrighted. Nor can an idea. Although a copyright prevents a whole ad from being legally used by another, it does not prevent others from using the general concept or idea of the ad or from paraphrasing the copy.

An advertiser that uses original creative written, musical, illustrative, or other material from an outside source without the express written consent of its creator is infringing on the copyright and may be subject to legal action. Advertisers and agencies must obtain permission before they use creative material—like music—from any outside source.

Copyright is indicated in an ad by the word *Copyright*, the abbreviation *Copr.*, or the copyright symbol © near the name of the advertiser. An ad with foreign or international copyright protection usually contains the year of copyright as well. Copyright marks also protect other forms of print advertising, including booklets, sales brochures, and catalogs.

Canadian law makes it unnecessary to use the copyright symbol or to register the copyright. Rights automatically accrue to the creator of the work—unless the work was commissioned by another, in which case the commissioner holds the copyright.[38]

STATE, PROVINCIAL, AND LOCAL REGULATION

Advertisers not only have to follow federal regulations; they are also subject to numerous state or provincial and local laws and local enforcement agencies. During the U.S. federal deregulation trend of the 1980s, state and local governments took a more active role. As a result, advertisers now have to keep a more diligent eye on state and local regulations when designing advertising for use in numerous states.

State Governments Also Regulate Truth in Advertising

State legislation governing advertising is often based on the "truth-in-advertising" model statute developed in 1911 by *Printer's Ink*, for many years the major trade paper of the industry. The statute holds that any maker of an ad found to contain "untrue, deceptive, or misleading" material is guilty of a misdemeanor. Today 46 states—all except Arkansas, Delaware, Mississippi, and New Mexico—enforce laws patterned after this statute.

All states also have what are referred to as "little FTC acts," or consumer protection laws, which govern unfair and deceptive business practices. Under such acts, states themselves can investigate and prosecute cases, and individual consumers can bring civil suits against businesses. To increase their clout, some states are teaming up on legal actions—most recently to challenge allegedly deceptive ad promotions in the airline, rental-car, and food-making industries. As William Howell, senior assistant attorney general in Florida points out, "Many of the food manufacturers could litigate some of the smaller states into the ground, but they might not be willing to fight it out against 10 states simultaneously."[39]

Different states have different regulations governing what can and cannot be advertised and what can be depicted in ads. Some states prohibit advertising for certain types of wine and liquor, and most states restrict the use of federal and state flags in advertising.

A successful state action may lead to changes in national campaigns. The New York attorney general's office found the Beef Industry Council's "Beef Gives Strength" campaign deceptive because eating beef alone cannot increase strength and endurance. As a result, the Council had to change its national campaign.[40]

Regulation by Provincial Governments

As in the United States, a dilemma faced by all Canadian national advertisers is conforming to the regulations of the various provinces. Each of the 10 provincial governments regulates consumer protection and trade practices differently. The legislation of Canada's largest province, Quebec, includes the Charter of the French Language which mandates that all advertising in Quebec be predominantly or—in the case of outdoor—solely in French.

The situation is further complicated by two court systems—federal and provincial—and two forms of law: British common law and the French *Code Civil*, a version of the Napoleonic Code. This means that national advertisers in Canada must think in terms of two distinct markets, each governed by a different set of rules.

For example, while advertising to children is severely restricted in all Canadian provinces (e.g., mandatory preapproval for all broadcast ads), Quebec prohibits *all* advertising directed to children under 13 years old. The Consumer Protection Office of Quebec actively enforces this prohibition. To determine if an ad is child-directed, it evaluates the context of all advertising presentations on the basis of three factors: the nature and purpose of the good being advertised (toys, candies, snack foods); the manner of presenting the message; and the time and place of presentation. Thus, marketers must be careful, even in the use of animation, since it might cause an ad to be construed as child-directed.[41]

Local Governments Regulate Local Businesses

Many cities and countries have consumer protection agencies to enforce laws regulating local advertising practices. The chief function of these agencies is to protect local consumers against unfair and misleading practices by area merchants.

The New York City Department of Consumer Affairs charged Sears with misleading advertising—such as advertising clothing discounts without explaining at what level prices started.[42] Instead of changing its ads and avoiding bad publicity, Sears sued New York City, insisting its ads comply with federal advertising laws and are protected by the First Amendment. According to New York's consumer-affairs commissioner, his office has negotiated advertising changes with more than a hundred retailers since the laws took effect 20 years ago, and all except Sears have complied.[43]

Local and municipal governments in Canada regulate aspects of advertising. They may license various business activities or place restrictions on how and where advertising is placed (outdoor signs, for example).[44]

RECENT COURT RULINGS AFFECTING ADVERTISERS

Recently, both federal and state courts made a number of significant rulings pertaining to advertising issues, including First Amendment rights, privacy rights, and comparative advertising.

First Amendment Rights

When it comes to free speech, the Supreme Court historically distinguished between "speech" and "commercial speech" (defined as speech that promotes a commercial transaction). However, in the last decade or so, it has made a series of decisions suggesting that truthful commercial speech is also entitled to full protection under the First Amendment.[45]

In 1977 the Court declared that state bar association bans on members' advertising violated the First Amendment. Now, a third of all lawyers advertise.[46] See Exhibit 2–14. A few states even permit client testimonials in lawyer ads. A Wisconsin personal injury and divorce lawyer said his firm gained 200 new clients after a $25,000 local TV ad campaign featuring client testimonials.[47] To help guard against deceptive and misleading legal ads, the American Bar Association issued advertising guidelines for attorneys.

In 1982, the Supreme Court upheld an FTC order allowing physicians and dentists to advertise. Since then, advertising by medical and dental organizations has exploded.

In 1993, the Supreme Court gave what some experts consider the biggest win in years to the advertising industry. It said the Cincinnati City Council violated

EXHIBIT • 2–14

Before 1977, lawyers were forbidden to advertise by the state bar associations, but today many lawyers advertise. Joel Hyatt, with 185 legal clinics in 22 states, spends about $5 million a year on TV advertising.

JOEL HYATT: His office was just across from the State House and he took all comers, big and small. His fees were so low, they alarmed his fellow lawyers. And on top of

that, Abraham Lincoln *advertised.* For the same reason Hyatt Legal Services does today: To bring the law closer to people. Lincoln always told you his fee up front. And

we do that today. Hyatt Legal Services. A good idea that just keeps getting better. I'm Joel Hyatt, and you have my word on it!

the First Amendment's protection of commercial speech when it banned news-racks of advertising brochures from city streets for "aesthetic and safety reasons" while permitting newspaper vending machines.[48]

Privacy Rights

Most advertisers know it's illegal to use a person's likeness in an ad without the individual's permission, but a recent court ruling states that even using a lookalike can violate that person's rights.

Jacqueline Kennedy Onassis sued Christian Dior and won on the grounds that the use of a lookalike without her permission constituted a violation of her right to privacy.[49] Other courts ruled that privacy rights continue even after a person's death.

Comparative Advertising

Advertisers use **comparative advertising** to claim superiority to competitors in some aspect. Such ads are legal so long as the comparison is truthful. In 1986, a federal appeals court in California upheld a $40 million damage award against now-bankrupt Jartran for ads that unfairly discredited U-Haul.[50] And in 1989, a Washington, D.C., court ordered Ralston Purina Company to pay $10.4 million in damages to Alpo Petfoods for misrepresenting Alpo's dog food.[51]

E X H I B I T • 2–15

Advertising regulations in selected countries of Western Europe.

	General regulations		Limitations on specific products
Country	Comparative advertising	Advertising to children	Alcoholic beverages
European Comm.	OK if data is accurate and verifiable	Ban on showing children in danger; exploiting their ignorance or credulity; or encouraging them to persuade adults to buy	TV advertising restricted
Austria	OK if based on objective, verifiable data	Direct appeal forbidden	Hard liquor banned on TV and radio
Belgium	Banned if denigrating	Follows EC guidelines	Strict labeling laws
Denmark	OK if accurate, relevant, and fair	Follows EC guidelines	Banned on radio and TV
France	OK if not disparaging	Generally follows EC guidelines, but stricter	Banned on TV and at sporting events; restrictions on ad content
Germany	Banned if denigrating	Voluntary restraints on direct appeals in radio and TV ads	Voluntary limits by industry
Italy	Direct comparisons restricted; indirect OK if substantiated	Ban on ads during cartoon programs	Follows EC guidelines
Netherlands	Indirect comparisons OK if complete, accurate, and not denigrating	Voluntary restraints on exploiting children's natural credulity	Strict industry regulations on ad content
Spain	Banned if denigrating or not objectively verifiable	Restricts exploitation	Some restrictions
Switzerland	OK if not denigrating; banned on TV	None	Banned on TV and radio; restricted in other media
United Kingdom	Banned if denigrating	Voluntary rules designed to protect children	Voluntary ban on TV advertising for hard liquor; content restrictions for other media

The 1988 Trademark Law Revision Act closes a loophole in the Lanham Act, which previously governed comparison ads but made no mention of misrepresenting another company's product. Under the new law, anyone who "misrepresents the nature, characteristics, qualities, or geographical origin of his or her or another person's goods, services, or commercial activities" is vulnerable to a civil action.[52]

In addition to being truthful, comparative ads must also make the comparison in terms of some objectively measurable characteristic. Wilkinson Sword encountered a million-dollar problem when it claimed its Ultra-Glide razor blade's lubricant strip was six-times smoother than Gillette's and preferred by men. Gillette sued and won.[53]

GOVERNMENTAL RESTRAINTS ON INTERNATIONAL ADVERTISERS

Foreign governments and cultures often regulate what ads say, show, or do. Many countries strongly regulate advertising claims and prohibit superlatives. In Germany, advertisers may use only scientifically provable superlatives. McCann-Erickson once had to translate the old Coca-Cola slogan, "Refreshes you best." The agency substituted "Refreshes you right" in Germany.

Many European countries also bar two-for-one offers, coupons, premiums, one-cent sales, box-top gimmicks, free tie-in offers, and the like. In Europe, companies may only advertise price cuts during "official sales periods," and advertisers typically need government approval before publishing a sale ad. Exhibit 2–15 lists the regulations some Western European countries impose on advertising.

Limitations on specific products		Media regulations	
Tobacco	Pharmaceuticals	Restricted or banned media	Limitations on commercials
Banned on TV	Prescription drugs banned on TV	None	May not exceed 15 percent of daily broadcast time
Banned on TV and radio	Greatly restricted by pharmaceutical law	Billboards heavily regulated; telephone advertising prohibited	Follows EC guidelines
Heavily restricted in all media; banned on TV and radio	Banned on radio and TV; restricted in other media	Billboards heavily regulated	Follows EC guidelines
Banned on TV and radio	Prescription drugs banned on TV and radio; prior government approval for others	Telemarketing banned; outdoor heavily restricted	Follows EC guidelines
Banned in all media except press and posters	Prescription drugs banned in public media; others require prior approval	Outdoor restricted locally	Follows EC guidelines
Banned on radio and TV	Permitted with strict regulations on content	None	Follows EC guidelines
Banned in all media	Prescription drug ads banned; copy clearance needed for others	Outdoor restricted by local ordinances	Follows EC guildelines; prohibits interruptive ads
Strict but voluntary regulation by industry	Prior approval by industry board; consumer ads for prescription drugs banned	Outdoor restricted by local ordinances	Follows EC guidelines
Restricted on TV	Prior government approval for OTC drugs; consumer ads for prescription drugs banned	Outdoor restricted locally	Regulation of content and duration of commercials
Banned on TV and radio; restricted in other media	Banned on TV and radio	Only commercial radio is local	No noncommercial advertising; restrictions on commercial length
Banned on TV and radio	Ban on ads for prescription drugs; strict regulations for OTC drugs	Local restrictions on outdoor; many restrictions on other media	Code of Advertising Standards

In Saudi Arabia, companies can't advertise alcohol or pork or even images of pigs, such as stuffed toys and piggy banks. Saudi Arabia also bans pictures of anything sacred. Ads may show only people with Arabic appearance and no women's faces. And the government bans all TV and radio advertising.[54]

The only solution to the myriad legal problems of international advertising is to retain a good local lawyer who specializes in advertising law.

NONGOVERNMENT REGULATION

Nongovernment organizations such as the Canadian Advertising Foundation and the American Association of Advertising Agencies (see Exhibit 2–16) also issue advertising guidelines. And advertisers face considerable nongovernment regulation by business-monitoring organizations, related trade associations, the media, consumer groups, and advertising agencies and associations.

The Better Business Bureau (BBB)

The largest of the American business-monitoring organizations is the **Better Business Bureau (BBB)**, established in 1916. Its national and local offices are funded by dues from over 100,000 member companies. It operates primarily at the local level to protect consumers against fraudulent and deceptive advertising and sales practices. When local bureaus contact violators and ask them to revise their advertising, most comply.

The BBB's files on violators are open to the public. Records of violators who do not comply are sent to appropriate government agencies for further action. The BBB often works with local law enforcement agencies to prosecute advertisers guilty of fraud and misrepresentation. Each year, the BBB investigates thousands of ads for possible violations of truth and accuracy.

The Council of Better Business Bureaus is the parent organization of the Better Business Bureau and part of the National Advertising Review Council. One of its functions is helping new industries develop standards for ethical and responsible advertising. It also provides ongoing information about advertising regulations and recent court and administrative rulings that affect advertising. In 1983, the National Advertising Division (NAD) of the Council of Better Business

EXHIBIT • 2-16

American Association of Advertising Agencies policy statement and guidelines for comparative advertising.

The Board of Directors of the American Association of Advertising Agencies recognizes that when used truthfully and fairly, comparative advertising provides the consumer with needed and useful information.

However, extreme caution should be exercised. The use of comparative advertising, by its very nature, can distort facts and, by implication, convey to the consumer information that misrepresents the truth.

Therefore, the Board believes that comparative advertising should follow certain guidelines:

1. The intent and connotation of the ad should be to inform and never to discredit or unfairly attack competitors, competing products, or services.
2. When a competitive product is named, it should be one that exists in the marketplace as significant competition.
3. The competition should be fairly and properly identified but never in a manner or tone of voice that degrades the competitive product or service.
4. The advertising should compare related or similar properties or ingredients of the product, dimension to dimension, feature to feature.
5. The identification should be for honest comparison purposes and not simply to upgrade by association.
6. If a competitive test is conducted, it should be done by an objective testing source, preferably an independent one, so that there will be no doubt as to the veracity of the test.
7. In all cases the test should be supportive of all claims made in the advertising that are based on the test.
8. The advertising should never use partial results or stress insignificant differences to cause the consumer to draw an improper conclusion.
9. The property being compared should be significant in terms of value or usefulness of the product to the consumer.
10. Comparatives delivered through the use of testimonials should not imply that the testimonial is more than one individual's thought unless that individual represents a sample of the majority viewpoint.

AD LAB 2-B   Advertising to Children: What You Can and Can't Do

Many people worry about advertising's effect on children. Watchdog groups believe that some toy commercials create unreasonable expectations through animation and other special effects. They are concerned about children being overexposed to sugary breakfast cereal and snack-food commercials. While kids don't buy the groceries, 78 percent of parents say their kids influence their cereal purchases. It's difficult for parents to teach good eating habits if they're constantly being undermined by TV commercials. Parents can simply turn off the TV, but kids should be able to watch their favorite programs without being exploited.

To protect children from unfair advertising techniques, TV networks established highly restrictive guidelines for children's advertising. Network censors closely scrutinize all ads submitted for Saturday morning programs in particular. However, many advertisers complain that network regulations are so precise they leave no room for creativity. For instance, only 10 seconds of a toy ad may contain animation and other special effects; the last 5 seconds must display all toys shown earlier and disclose whether they are sold separately and include batteries.

The Council of Better Business Bureaus also polices advertising directed to children. Staff members regularly monitor commercials on network children's shows and check ads in children's comics and magazines against the following guidelines:

1. Advertisers should always consider the audience's level of knowledge, sophistication, and maturity. Children have a limited ability to evaluate the credibility of what they see; advertisers have a special responsibility to protect children from their own susceptibilities.

2. Advertisers should not directly or indirectly stimulate unreasonable expectations of product quality or performance. Imaginative and make-believe play is an important part of a child's growing-up process; advertisers should be careful not to exploit that imaginative quality.

3. Advertisers should communicate truthfully and accurately knowing that children may learn practices from advertising that affect their health and well-being.

4. Advertisers should capitalize on advertising's potential to positively influence social behavior. Wherever possible, advertising should reflect positive and beneficial social standards such as friendships, kindness, honesty, justice, generosity, and respect for others.

5. Advertisers should contribute to the parent-child relationship in a constructive way. Although parents have the primary responsibility for providing guidance, many other influences affect a child's personal and social development.

Laboratory Applications

1. Are any of these guidelines too restrictive?
2. What additional guidelines would you suggest?

VO: Get ready for a toothpaste that tastes so great, kids will rush to brush. New Crest for Kids, with a flavor that is so different,

some kids call it berrylicious. No matter what they call it they'll rush to brush. And while they're enjoying the flavor they'll be

fighting cavities too. New Crest for Kids. It tastes so great they'll rush to brush.

Bureaus published guidelines for advertising to children, a particularly sensitive area (see Ad Lab 2–B).

National Advertising Review Council

The **National Advertising Review Council (NARC)** was established in 1971 by the Council of Better Business Bureaus, the American Association of Advertising Agencies, the American Advertising Federation, and the Association of

MISLEADING ADS CAN RUN BUT THEY CAN'T HIDE.

Member of Congress
Signature
Address

Name of Advertiser
When Advertising Appeared
Where Advertising Appeared (TV, Magazine, Etc.)

Why You Consider the Advertising Misleading

Mail to: The Director, NAD, 845 Third Avenue, New York, N.Y. 10022

The National Advertising Division of the Council of Better Business Bureaus continues to invite members of Congress to help us identify national advertisers who run misleading or false advertising.

Since 1971, the NAD has resolved more than 2,500 complaints. In over half of the cases, the advertising investigated has been modified or discontinued as a result.

If the NAD fails to achieve a resolution, the case is appealed to the National Advertising Review Board. In almost 20 years of operation, the NARB has never failed to resolve a case.

If you encounter an ad you believe is misleading, send us the information in writing. Your complaint will receive a quick reply and will be handled at no cost to the taxpayer. You will be informed of the results.

Let's continue to work together to protect the public. And to protect advertisers who tell the truth.

THE NATIONAL ADVERTISING DIVISION OF THE COUNCIL OF BETTER BUSINESS BUREAUS

EXHIBIT • 2–17

The NAD actively encourages consumers to register complaints about misleading or deceptive advertising. By voicing their disapproval, people can help the NAD protect both the public and those advertisers who do tell the truth.

National Advertisers. Its primary purpose is to promote and enforce standards of truth, accuracy, taste, morality, and social responsibility in advertising.

NARC is regarded as the most comprehensive and effective mechanism for regulating American advertising. A U.S. district court judge noted in a 1985 case that its "speed, informality, and modest cost," as well its expertise, give NARC special advantages over the court system in resolving advertising disputes.[55]

NARC Operating Arms

NARC has two operating arms: the **National Advertising Division (NAD)** of the Council of Better Business Bureaus and the **National Advertising Review Board (NARB).**

The NAD monitors advertising practices and reviews complaints about advertising from consumers and consumer groups, brand competitors, local Better Business Bureaus, NAD monitors, trade associations, and others. The NARB, the appeals board for NAD decisions, consists of a chairperson and 70 volunteer members: 39 national advertisers, 21 agency representatives, and 10 laypeople from the public sector.

The NAD/NARB Review Process

Most complaints filed with the NAD concern advertising that is untruthful or inaccurate. As shown in Exhibit 2–17, the NAD itself runs ads that include a complaint form.

When the NAD finds a valid complaint, it contacts the advertiser, specifying any claims to be substantiated. If substantiation is inadequate, the NAD requests modification or discontinuance of the claims. No investigation is conducted if the advertiser has discontinued the claims in question before the date of the challenger's complaint or if the claims are the subject of litigation.

If the NAD and an advertiser reach an impasse, either party has the right to review by a five-member NARB panel (consisting of three advertisers, one agency representative, and one layperson). The panel's decision is binding on the NAD and the challenger. If an advertiser refuses to comply with the panel's decision (something which has never yet occurred), the NARB refers the matter to an appropriate government body and so indicates in its public record. Exhibit 2–18 shows a flowchart of the NAD/NARB review process.

Very few cases make it to the NARB. Of 3000 NAD investigations conducted since 1971, only 70 were disputed and referred to the NARB for resolution.[56]

The NAD issues the monthly *NAD Case Reports* which includes all of its decisions from the previous month. The NARB issues its decisions as they are completed and also sponsors advisory panels to study specialized topics.

The Canadian Advertising Foundation (CAF)

The primary self-regulation mechanism in Canada is operated by the **Canadian Advertising Foundation (CAF)** with separate self-regulatory branches in English Canada and Quebec: the **Advertising Standards Council** and the **Conseil des normes.** The CAF administers the *Canadian Code of Advertising Standards* as well as a variety of other industry-approved codes designed to set and maintain standards of honesty, truth, accuracy, and fairness in the marketplace.[57] Some of these codes include the:

* *Broadcast Code for Advertising to Children*
* *CDC Advertising Standards*
* *Advertising Code of Standards for Cosmetics, Toiletries, and Fragrances*

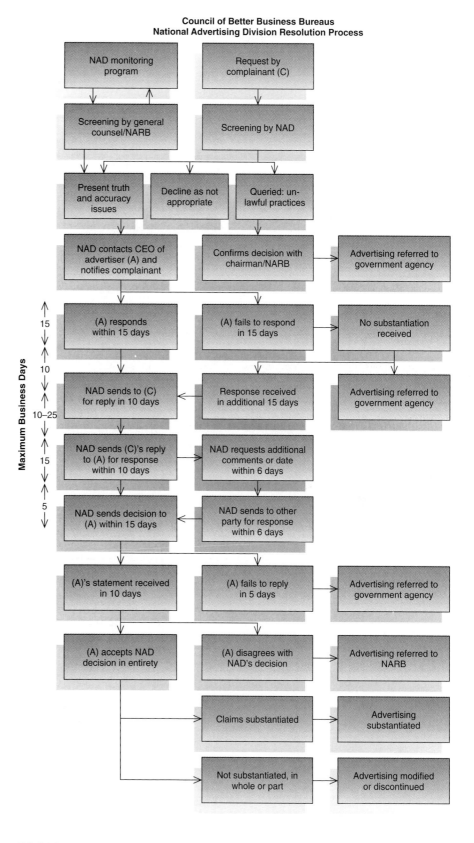

EXHIBIT • 2-18

Flowchart of the NAD/NARB review process.

- *Code of Consumer Advertising Practices for Non-Prescription Medicines*
- *Guidelines for Use of Comparative Advertising in Food Commercials*
- *Guidelines on Sex-Role Stereotyping*

The Advertising Standards Council reviews, investigates, and arbitrates complaints from consumers or competitors that any of the codes have been violated, and they may require an advertiser to withdraw or revise offending commercials. If an advertiser does not comply with the ASC's decision, the media carrying the ads will be notified, and they will typically remove the material themselves.

As Eric Gross, a leading advertising attorney in Toronto, points out, Canada is a conservative and resolutely fair-minded country. Advertisements which might seem commonplace in the United States, France, or Great Britain would not be aired in Canada. The government has traditionally been very paternalistic, tending to coddle consumers and limit their access to marketplace information, and there are many built-in safeguards against any kind of advertising abuses.[58]

Regulation by the Media

Almost all media review ads and reject material they regard as objectionable, even if it isn't deceptive. Many think the media are more effective than the government.

Television

Of all media, TV networks conduct the strictest review. Advertisers must submit all commercials intended for a network or affiliated station to the broadcast standards department of the network. Many commercials (in script or storyboard form) are returned with suggestions for changes or greater substantiation. Some ads are rejected outright for violating network policies, as discussed in Ad Lab 2–C on page 63.

The three major U.S. broadcast networks base their policies on the original National Association of Broadcasters Television Code. (The code was suspended by the NAB in 1983 following court invalidation of part of it for violating the Sherman Antitrust Act.) However, network policies vary enough that it's difficult to prepare universally acceptable commercials. Cable networks and local stations tend to be much less stringent, as demonstrated by their acceptance of condom ads.

Some TV advertisers use superimposed product disclaimers ("supers") to comply with network rules and regulations. Once limited primarily to aspirin commercials ("use only as directed") supers are now used by a variety of advertisers including Chrysler, AT&T, and American Express. But supers often pass by so quickly they can't be read. And some commercials got so cluttered with minuscule supers that network executives started ordering revisions to ensure legibility.[59]

The Canadian Broadcasting Corporation (CBC) is a government-subsidized radio and television network and the dominant force in Canadian broacasting. It has its own Code of Advertising Standards, but it and its French-Canadian branch, *Radio Canada*, often apply the code differently to reflect the standards of the differing communities they serve.[60]

Radio

The 19 U.S. radio networks, unlike TV networks, supply only a small percentage of their affiliates' programming so they have little or no say in what their affiliates advertise. A radio station is also less likely to return script or tape for changes. Station KLBJ in Austin, Texas, looks mainly at whether the advertising

AD LAB 2–C   The Issue of Issue Ads

The TV commercial depicts a dilapidated courtroom 25 years from now. Testifying in front of a teenage prosecutor and a jury of other youngsters, an old man tries to explain why nothing was done decades before to protect them from the ravages of deficit spending.

This commercial, produced and sponsored by W. R. Grace & Co., was rejected by all three networks. The networks claimed the ad violated their policies against "issue" advertising that advocates a particular point of view. Part of their concern stemmed from the Fairness Doctrine, which requires giving equal time to opposing points of view. But the networks also have a policy of rejecting advocacy ads if they feel the ads allow those with the most money to have their opinions heard. The Supreme Court ruled in 1973 that networks can reject paid editorial messages without violating the Communications Act or the First Amendment.

The Grace case prompted some commentators to point out that the networks may be too paranoid. The Grace commercial was accepted and aired by cable networks and independent stations as well as by some network affiliates. At one point in the controversy, 122 independent TV stations banded together and aired the commercial as a public-

service announcement, free of charge. CBS eventually accepted the ad after Grace made one minor change; ABC said it would accept the ad if it were resubmitted. NBC still refused to air it.

Corporations that wish to place issue ads on network TV argue that the airwaves belong to the public and that it is a violation of their First Amendment rights for the networks not to carry their ads.

The networks defend their position by citing the 1973 Supreme Court decision and by pointing out that they are fulfilling their obligations to free speech and public service through their news and public affairs programming.

Laboratory Applications

1. Should networks alter their policy on corporate issue advertising? In what way?
2. The FCC has repealed the Fairness Doctrine, but Congress is currently considering legislation that would make the doctrine law. Do you favor such legislation? Why or why not?

OLD MAN: I've already told you, it was all going to work out somehow. There was even talk of an amendment. But no one was willing to make the sacrifices. I'm afraid you're much too young to understand.

BOY: Maybe so. But I'm afraid the numbers speak for themselves. By 1986, for example,

the national debt had reached 2 trillion dollars. Didn't that frighten you?

ANNCR VO: No one really knows what another generation of unchecked federal deficits will bring.

OLD MAN: This frightens me.

BOY: No more questions.

OLD MAN: I have a question. Are you ever going to forgive us?

ANNCR VO: But we know this much. You can change the future. You have to. At W. R. Grace, we want all of us to stay one step ahead of a changing world.

is illegal, unethical, or immoral.[61] Radio stations are concerned that spots not offend listeners or detract from the rest of the programming. KLBJ won't air more than one spot per advertiser per hour to avoid irritating listeners. Radio stations usually reject taped commercials if the sound is distorted or too loud, or the overall production quality is poor.

Every radio station typically has its own unwritten guidelines, but they may be quite flexible. KDWB, a Minneapolis/St. Paul station with a large teenage audience turned down a psychic who wanted to buy advertising time, but allowed condom and other contraceptive ads after some serious internal debate.[62] KSDO in San Diego, a station with a business and information format, won't air commercials for X-rated movies or topless bars.[63]

Magazines

National magazines monitor all advertising, particularly those by new advertisers and for new products. Newer publications eager to sell space may not be so vigilant, but established magazines, like *Time* and *Newsweek*, are highly scrupulous. Many magazines will not accept advertising for certain types of products. *The New Yorker* won't accept discount retail store advertising, ads for feminine hygiene products, or self-medication products. *Reader's Digest* won't accept tobacco ads.

Some magazines test every product before accepting the advertising. *Good Housekeeping* rejects ads if its tests don't substantiate the advertiser's claims. Products that pass may feature the *Good Housekeeping* "Seal of Approval" on their labels and in advertising. *Parents Magazine* offers a similar product seal and warranty.

Newspapers

Newspapers also monitor and review advertising. Larger newspapers have clearance staffs that read every ad submitted; most smaller newspapers rely on the advertising manager, sales personnel, or proofreaders.

The general advertising policies set forth in *Newspaper Rates & Data* (Standard Rate & Data Service) include such restrictions as "No objectionable medical, personal, matrimonial, clairvoyant, or palmistry advertising accepted; no stock promotion or financial advertising, other than those securities of known value, will be accepted." Another rule prohibits ads that might easily be mistaken for regular reading material unless they feature the word *advertisement* or *advt.*

In addition, most papers have their own codes of acceptability—ranging from one page for small local papers to more than 50 pages for large dailies such as the *Los Angeles Times*. Some codes are quite specific. The *Detroit Free Press* won't accept classified ads containing such words as "affair" or "swinger." The *Kansas City Star and Times* requires advertisers who claim "the lowest price in town" to include a promise to meet or beat any lower price readers find elsewhere within 30 days.[64]

One problem advertisers face is that newspapers' codes are far from uniform. Handgun ads are prohibited by the *Boston Globe*, accepted by the *Chicago Tribune* if the guns are antique, and permitted by the *Orlando Sentinel* so long as the guns aren't automatic.[65] Newspapers do revise their policies from time to time. Many large papers now accept condom ads.

Regulation by Consumer Groups

Of all the regulatory forces governing advertising, consumer protection organizations are showing the greatest growth. Starting in the 1960s, the consumer movement became increasingly active in fighting fraudulent and deceptive advertising. Consumers demanded not only that products perform as advertised but also that more product information be provided so people can compare and make better buying decisions. The impact of the consumer movement gave rise to a new word: **consumerism**, social action to dramatize the rights of the buying public. Since then, one fact has become clear to both advertisers and agencies: The American consumer has the power to influence advertising practices.

Advertisers and agencies are paying more attention to product claims, especially those related to energy use (such as the estimated miles per gallon of a new car) and the nutritional value of processed foods. Consumerism fostered the growth of consumer advocate groups and regulatory agencies, and promoted more consumer research by advertisers, agencies, and the media in an effort to learn what consumers want—and how to provide it. Customer relations departments and investment in public goodwill ultimately pay off in improved consumer relations and sales.

Consumer Information Networks

Organizations like the Consumer Federation of America (CFA), the National Council of Senior Citizens, and the National Consumer League (1) serve as central clearinghouses for the exchange and dissemination of information among members; (2) help develop state, regional, and local consumer organizations; and (3) work with and provide services to national, regional, county, and municipal consumer groups.

Consumer interests also are served by several private, nonprofit testing organizations such as Consumers Union, Consumers' Research, and Underwriters Laboratories.

Consumer Advocates

Consumer advocate groups act on advertising complaints received from consumers and those that grow out of their own research.

They normally: (1) investigate the complaint; (2) if warranted, contact the advertiser and ask that the objectionable advertisement or practice be halted; (3) if the advertiser does not comply, release publicity or criticism about the offense to the media; (4) submit complaints with substantiating evidence to appropriate government agencies for further action; and (5) in some instances, file a lawsuit to obtain a cease-and-desist order, a fine, or other penalty against the violator.

Self-Regulation by Advertisers

Advertisers also regulate themselves. They have to; in today's competitive marketplace, consumer confidence is essential. Most large advertisers gather strong data to substantiate their claims. They maintain careful systems of advertising review to ensure that ads meet both their own standards and industry, media, and legal requirements. Most advertisers also reflect a sense of social responsibility in their advertising. Falstaff Brewing Company avoids implying that beer will give people "a lift." It also rejects appeals to adolescents and children and any references to sex.

Many industries maintain advertising codes that companies in the industry agree to follow. These codes also establish a basis for complaints. A member may ask the executive board of the association to review existing competitive conditions in terms of the industry's advertising code.

However, industry advertising codes are only as effective as the enforcement powers of the individual trade associations. And since enforcement may conflict with antitrust laws, trade associations usually use peer pressure rather than hearings or penalties.

Self-Regulations by Ad Agencies and Associations

Most ad agencies monitor their own practices. In addition, professional advertising associations oversee the activities of members to prevent problems that may trigger government intervention. Advertising publications actively report issues and actions before the courts to educate agencies and advertisers about possible legal infractions.

EXHIBIT • 2-19

"Advertising Principles of American Business" of the American Advertising Federation (AAF)

1. **Truth** Advertising shall reveal the truth, and shall reveal significant facts, the omission of which would mislead the public.

2. **Substantiation** Advertising claims shall be substantiated by evidence in possession of the advertiser and the advertising agency prior to making such claims.

3. **Comparisons** Advertising shall refrain from making false, misleading, or unsubstantiated statements or claims about a competitor or his products or service.

4. **Bait advertising** Advertising shall not offer products or services for sale unless such offer constitutes a bona fide effort to sell the advertised products or services and is not a device to switch consumers to other goods or services, usually higher priced.

5. **Guarantees and warranties** Advertising of guarantees and warranties shall be explicit, with sufficient information to apprise consumers of their principal terms and limitations or, when space or time restrictions preclude such disclosures, the advertisement shall clearly reveal where the full text of the guarantee or warranty can be examined before purchase.

6. **Price claims** Advertising shall avoid price claims that are false or misleading, or savings claims that do not offer provable savings.

7. **Testimonials** Advertising containing testimonials shall be limited to those of competent witnesses who are reflecting a real and honest opinion or experience.

8. **Taste and decency** Advertising shall be free of statements, illustrations, or implications that are offensive to good taste or public decency.

Advertising Agencies

Although advertisers supply information about a product or service to their agencies, agencies must research and verify product claims and comparative product data before using them in advertising. The media may require such documentation before accepting the advertising, and substantiation may be needed if government or consumer agencies challenge the claims.

Agencies can be held legally liable for fraudulent or misleading advertising claims (see the Ethical Dilemma in Chapter 8: "When Advertisers Dare to Compare"). For this reason, most major advertising agencies have in-house legal counsel and regularly submit their ads for review. If any aspect of the advertising is challenged, the agency asks its client to review the advertising and either confirm claims as truthful or replace unverified material.

Advertising Associations

Several associations monitor industrywide advertising practices. The **American Association of Advertising Agencies (AAAA)**, an association of the largest advertising agencies throughout the United States, controls agency practices by denying membership to any agency judged unethical. The AAAA *Standards of Practice and Creative Code* set advertising principles for member agencies.

The **American Advertising Federation (AAF)** helped to establish the FTC, and its early "vigilance" committees were the forerunners of the Better Business Bureau. The AAF "Advertising Principles of American Business," adopted in 1984, defines standards for truthful and responsible advertising (see Exhibit 2–19). Since most local advertising clubs belong to the AAF, this organization is very instrumental in influencing agencies and advertisers to abide by these principles.

The **Institute of Canadian Advertising** represents about 60 of the largest Canadian agencies. It works with its French-Canadian counterpart **(L'Association des agences de publicité du Québec)** and the **Association of Canadian Advertisers** to promote freedom of commercial speech in Canada, to deal with governments or other groups seeking to restrict advertising, and to negotiate radio and TV contracts with Canadian talent unions.[66]

The **Association of National Advertisers (ANA)** in the United States comprises 400 major manufacturing and service companies that are clients of member agencies of the AAAA. These companies, pledged to uphold the ANA code of advertising ethics, work with the ANA through a joint Committee for Improvement of Advertising Content.

Summary

As advertising proliferated, criticism of it intensified. Detractors say advertising debases the language, makes people too materialistic, and manipulates them into buying products they don't need. Further, they say, advertising is offensive, in bad taste, and even deceptive.

Proponents admit that advertising has been and sometimes still is misused. However, they point out that the criticism is often unjustified and excessive and that advertisers responded by avoiding stereotypes, controlling the proliferation of ads, and making ads more informative and entertaining. Advertisers know the best way to sell their products is to appeal to genuine consumer needs and be honest in their claims.

Under growing pressure from consumers, special-interest groups, and government regulation, advertisers developed higher standards of ethical conduct and social responsibility. Advertising is regulated by federal, state, and local government agencies; business-monitoring organizations, the media, and consumer groups; and by advertisers and the advertising industry themselves.

The FTC, the major U.S. federal regulator of advertising, determines whether ads are "deceptive" or "unfair." If the FTC finds the advertiser at fault, it may issue a cease-and-desist order to require corrective advertising. The major Canadian regulator is the Ministry of Consumer and Corporate Affairs (CCAC).

The FDA and the HPB keep an eye on advertising for food and drugs in addition to regulating product labels and packaging. The FCC and the CRTC have jurisdiction over the radio and television industries, but deregulation severely limited the FCC's control over advertising in these media. The Patent and Trademark Office governs ownership of U.S. trademarks, trade names, house marks, and similar distinctive features of companies and brands. The Library of Congress registers and protects copyrighted materials.

State, provincial, and local governments also enact consumer protection laws that regulate advertising. This is exceptionally complex in Canada.

The federal and state courts are involved in several advertising issues, including First Amendment protection of "commercial speech," professionals' right to advertise, infringements of the right to privacy, and lawsuits over comparative advertising.

Nongovernmental regulators include the Council of Better Business Bureaus, the National Advertising Division, and the Canadian Advertising Foundation. The NAD, the most effective U.S. nongovernment regulatory body, investigates complaints from consumers, brand competitors, or local Better Business Bureaus and suggests corrective measures. Advertisers that refuse to comply are referred to the National Advertising Review Board (NARB), which may uphold, modify, or reverse the NAD's findings.

Other sources of regulation include the print media and broadcasting codes and policies. Consumer organizations and advocates also control advertising by investigating and filing complaints against advertisers and by providing information to consumers. Finally, advertisers and agencies also regulate themselves.

Questions for Review and Discussion

1. Should advertising lead or reflect society? Explain.
2. Does advertising make us too materialistic?
3. Why are women and minorities upset about certain advertising? Is their displeasure reasonable?
4. Explain the difference between an ethical dilemma and an ethical lapse. How does an advertiser's ethics differ from an advertiser's social responsibility?
5. What is the relationship between the FTC and the advertising industry? Has the FTC overstepped its authority? Explain. Can you cite recent examples of FTC action against advertisers?
6. If you were to help the FDA draft guidelines for health claims in food ads, what items would you include?
7. How does "commercial speech" differ from free speech? Should this distinction be maintained, or should advertising be given the same First Amendment protection as other types of speech?
8. How do laws regarding advertising to children differ between the United States and Canada?
9. What is the value of comparative advertising? What are the drawbacks?
10. What is the importance of the NAD/NARB system to consumers and advertisers?

At Franklin Dallas, whenever we hear of a new business prospect, we send them one of these. We use it to subtly suggest that **they could get more impact from their advertising.** Even though we don't always get the business, clients seem to like them. We suspect they use them on their current agencies.

The Advertising Business: Agencies and Clients

Objective: To show how people and groups organize themselves to create and produce advertising. The advertising person may serve in a variety of roles and needs to understand the basic tasks of both the agency and the client, the role of the media and suppliers, how agencies acquire clients and make money, and the overall relationship between the agency and the client.

After studying this chapter you will be able to:

- Explain the organizations that participate in the advertising business and their relationship to one another.

- Define an advertising agency and describe the main types of agencies.

- Explain the roles people play in an advertising agency.

- Discuss how agencies get new clients and how they make money.

- Describe how different types of advertisers organize their advertising departments.

- Debate the pro's and con's of an in-house advertising agency.

- Discuss the factors that affect the client-agency relationship.

t wasn't an easy problem. But Jo Muse knew it was an unprecedented challenge—and a real opportunity.

His agency, Muse Cordero Chen in Los Angeles, was awarded a major piece of business from Nike, the worldwide leader in athletic shoes. Nike wanted to reach beyond its mainstream trade and consumer markets to the millions of ethnically diverse young people who wore its shoes. MCC was one of many new, growing ethnic specialty agencies, and it was hot.

MCC was already doing award-winning work for several clients including Honda and the California Department of Health. Jo was an African-American from Detroit. His partner Mavis Cordero was a Latina originally from Colombia, and David Chen was Chinese. MCC employees could read, speak, and write 19 different languages, and they could create ads aimed at the African-American, Spanish-speaking, and Asian communities.

The problem they faced was defining their market. Normal demographic classifications (age, sex, race, education) just didn't work because they don't account for cultural experience. And it was culture that really characterized the market they were after.

In the end, they did something new. They invented a new market segment: urban youth. And they defined it, not by demographics, but by attitude—a cultural attitude shaped by inner-city life. Their research uncovered that the attitude of urban youth crossed demographic lines and shaped the market's values: irreverence, fitness and athleticism, discipline.

Based on that attitude, MCC created a series of award-winning ads and commercials that not only sought to protect the urban youth market for Nike but also to empower it (see Exhibit 3–1). The ads were forthright, bold, even

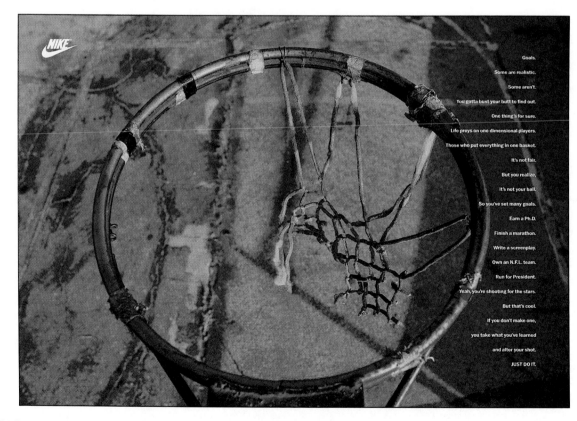

EXHIBIT • 3–1

Nike doesn't mince words in this ad by Muse, Cordero, Chen. Encouraging urban youth to shoot for the stars, the company uses basketball as an allegory for life: If you don't make a goal on the first try, don't quit. Learn from the experience and alter your shot. Just do it.

controversial. But Nike approved them, believing the ads not only promoted the brand but also made a positive social statement about urban youth. ◆

THE ADVERTISING INDUSTRY

People and organizations in many other industries—like shoe manufacturers—are also involved in the advertising business. That's because every successful company needs to use advertising. Advertising is a very large, complex, diversified industry involving many types of organizations and people.

The Organizations in Advertising

The advertising business is composed of four different groups. The two main ones are the advertisers and the agencies. The **advertisers** (or clients) are the companies—like Nike—that advertise themselves and their products. Advertisers range in size from huge multinational firms to small independent stores and in type from large service organizations to small industrial concerns. Assisting them is the second group—the **advertising agencies**—that plan, create, and prepare their clients' ad campaigns and promotional materials.

The third group, the **media**, sells time (in electronic media) and space (in print media) to carry the advertiser's message to the target audience. The last group, the **suppliers,** includes the photographers, illustrators, printers, typesetters, video production houses, and others who assist both advertisers and agencies in preparing advertising materials.

This chapter examines the advertisers and agencies—who they are, what they do, and how they work together. Subsequent chapters will deal with the media and the suppliers.

The People in Advertising

When most people think of advertising, they imagine the copywriters and art directors who work for ad agencies. But the majority of people in advertising are employed by the *advertisers*. Virtually every company has an advertising department, even if it's just one person.

The importance of a company's advertising department varies depending on the size of the company, the type of industry it operates in, the size of its advertising program, the role advertising plays in the company's marketing mix, and most of all, the involvement of top management.

Many people are involved in a company's advertising function:

1. Company presidents and top executives make advertising decisions.
2. Sales and marketing personnel provide input to the creative process, help choose the ad agency, and help evaluate proposed ad programs.
3. Artists and writers produce ads, brochures, and other materials.
4. Product engineers and designers give input to the creative process and provide information about competitive products.
5. Administrative people evaluate the cost of advertising programs and help determine ad budgets.
6. Clerical staff coordinate various advertising activities.

Large companies may have a separate advertising department employing many people and headed by an advertising manager who reports to a marketing director or marketing services manager (see Exhibit 3–2). These departments often resemble ad agencies in structure and function.

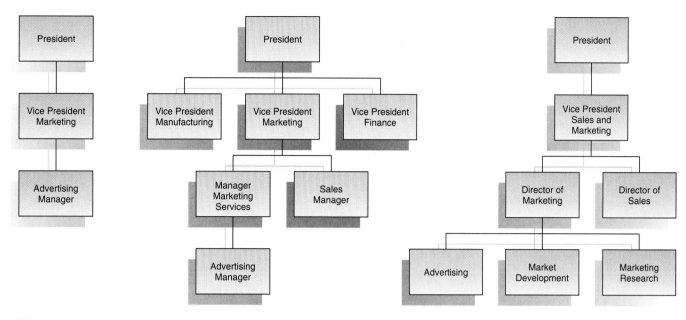

Many large companies have a separate advertising department able to perform a wide variety of functions. Small departments generally subcontract for creative and camera services; larger departments handle the majority of work on site.

WHAT ADVERTISING PEOPLE DO: FUNDAMENTAL TASKS

Advertisers and agencies must perform certain basic functions including *administration, planning, budgeting, coordination,* and *ad creation.*

Administration

Advertising managers organize and staff the department and recommend programs based on the company's marketing plans and budgets. They must thoroughly understand the major factors influencing the company's marketing activities. Advertising managers also analyze competitive advertising, evaluate their own ads, and establish procedures for handling inquiries.

Planning

Once or twice a year, advertising managers prepare formal proposals for management's approval. In the meantime, planning is a constant, ongoing process of defining and redefining goals and objectives, performing research, developing strategies, scheduling ads, and evaluating results. We discuss marketing and advertising plans in greater detail in Chapter 7.

Budgeting

The advertising manager formulates the annual budget and presents it to top management. The manager then sees that staff people adhere to the budget. Exhibit 3–3 shows which activities should be included in the budget.

Coordination

Business activities usually fall into three broad functional areas: production, finance, and marketing. Advertising, like sales, is a marketing activity. The

Chargeable		
• Space and time costs in regular media • Advertising consultants • Ad-pretesting services • Institutional advertising • Industry directory listings	• Readership or audience research • Media costs for consumer contests, premium and sampling promotions • Ad department travel and entertainment expenses • Ad department salaries • Advertising association dues	• Local cooperative advertising • Direct mail to consumers • Subscriptions to periodicals and services for ad department • Storage of advertising materials

Debatable		
• Catalogs for consumers • Classified telephone directories • Space in irregular publications • Advertising aids for salespeople • Financial advertising • Dealer help literature • Contributions to industry ad funds • Direct mail to dealers and jobbers • Office supplies • Point-of-sale material	• Window display installation costs • Charges for services performed by other departments • Catalogs for dealers • Test-marketing programs • Sample requests generated by advertising • Costs of exhibits except personnel • Ad department share of overhead • House organs for customers and dealers • Cost of cash value or sampling coupons	• Cost of contest entry blanks • Cross-advertising enclosures • Contest judging and handling fees • Depreciation of ad department equipment • Mobile exhibits • Employee fringe benefits • Catalogs for salespeople • Packaging consultants • Consumer contest awards

Not chargeable		
• Premium handling charges • House-to-house sample distribution • Packaging charges for premium promotions • Cost of merchandise for tie-in promotions • Product tags • Showrooms • Testing new labels and packages • Package design and artwork • Cost of non-self-liquidating premiums • Consumer education programs • Product publicity • Factory signs • House organs for salespeople	• Signs on company-owned vehicles • Instruction enclosures • Press clipping services • Market research (outside produced) • Samples of middlemen • Recruitment advertising • Price sheets • Public relation consultants • Coupon redemption costs • Corporate publicity • Market research (company produced) • Exhibit personnel • Gifts of company products	• Cost of deal merchandise • Share of corporate salaries • Cost of guarantee refunds • Share of legal expenses • Cost of detail or missionary people • Sponsoring recreational activities • Product research • House organs for employees • Entertaining customers and prospects • Scholarships • Plant tours • Annual reports • Outright charity donations

EXHIBIT • 3-3

The Black, White, and Gray Chart shows that some items belong in the advertising budget (white column); some don't (black); and some are questionable (gray column).

advertising manager must coordinate advertising activities with other marketing functions, as well as with production and finance activities. For example, sales and advertising people tell the production department which product and packaging features may improve customer satisfaction. They may consult with the accounting department for records on overhead, ad production, and media costs. And the legal department helps protect against trademark and copyright infringement and ensures ads are accurate and legal.

Advertising departments and agencies also supervise and coordinate outside advertising services such as the media and suppliers. The department or agency screens and analyzes the various services available, makes recommendations to management, and (usually) decides which services to use. The advertising manager then evaluates the work performed.

Creating Ads

The creative function, advertising's most visible task, consists of three main elements, all overseen by the advertising manager: copywriting, art direction, and production. The end product is a combination of words and pictures that depicts goods or services to prospective customers. We discuss the creative elements in more detail in Chapters 8 through 11.

THE ADVERTISING AGENCY

Why would a business like Nike hire an advertising agency? Couldn't it save money by hiring its own staff and creating its own ads. How does Muse Cordero Chen win such a large account? Must an agency's accounts be that big for it to make money? How do smaller agencies make money?

This section will shed some light on these issues and give a clearer understanding of why so many advertisers use agencies.

The Role of the Advertising Agency

The American Association of Advertising Agencies defines an **advertising agency** as an independent organization of creative people and businesspeople who specialize in developing and preparing advertising plans, advertisements, and other promotional tools. The agency purchases advertising space and time in various media on behalf of different advertisers, or sellers—its **clients**—to find customers for their goods and services.[1]

This definition offers clues as to why so many advertisers hire ad agencies. First, agencies are *independent*. They aren't owned by the advertiser, the media, or the suppliers, so they bring an outside, objective viewpoint to the advertiser's business—a state the advertiser can never attain.

The agency employs a combination of *businesspeople* and *creative people* including administrators, accountants, marketing executives, researchers, market and media analysts, writers, and artists. They have day-to-day contact with outside professional suppliers who create illustrations, take photos, set type, retouch art, shoot commercials, and record sound. They keep abreast of technological advances, price changes, and current production problems.

The agency provides yet another service by arranging and contracting for broadcast time and magazine or newspaper space. Because of its *media expertise,* the agency saves the client time and money.

Finally, good agencies have the savvy, skill, and competence to serve the needs of a variety of clients because of their daily exposure to a broad spectrum of marketing situations and problems. Ad Lab 3–A provides an overview of the ad agency business in the United States.

Agencies work for their clients, not for the media or the suppliers; their moral, ethical, financial, and even legal obligation is to their clients. Just as a well-run business seeks professional help from attorneys, accountants, bankers, or management specialists, advertisers use agencies because they can create more effective advertising (as promised in the agency ad in Exhibit 3–4)—and select more effective media—than the advertisers can. Today, almost all sizable advertisers rely on an ad agency for expert, objective counsel and unique creative skills—to be the guardian of their brands.[2]

Types of Agencies

Advertising agencies are normally classified by the range of services they offer and by the type of business they handle.

Full-Service Agencies

The modern **full-service advertising agency** supplies both advertising and nonadvertising services in all areas of communications and promotion. Adver-

AD LAB 3–A   How Big Is the Agency Business?

Advertising today is a worldwide business. In 1991, Tokyo (with $24.5 billion in billings) jumped ahead of New York (with $24.1 billion) as the world's advertising capital. London and Paris were third and fourth, respectively. Leading advertising centers in North America are New York, Los Angeles, Chicago, Toronto, and Montreal.

All U.S. and Canadian cities with at least 100,000 people have ad agencies. So do many smaller cities and towns. Of over 10,000 U.S. agencies, the top 500 represent about $54 billion in domestic billing (the amount of client money the agency spends on media and equivalent activities)—almost half of all U.S. advertising expenditures.

Interestingly, the top 10 U.S. agencies handle over 50 percent of the total volume of business done by the top 500 agencies—and that's just their U.S. billing. Their overseas operations often equal or exceed their U.S. billings.

The top 500 domestic ad agencies employ about 70,200 people. Agencies need fewer people than businesses in many other industries: five or six people can easily handle $1 million in annual billing. In agencies that bill $20 million or more a year, the ratio is even lower.

Basic information about ad agencies can be found in the *Standard Directory of Advertising Agencies* (the "Red Book"), which lists agencies; a related volume, the *Standard Directory of Advertisers,* which lists U.S. companies that advertise; and magazines such as *Advertising Age, Adweek,* and *Marketing* (Canada).

Laboratory Application

From your library, obtain a copy of the agency "Red Book." Are agencies in your town listed? If so, how many? If not, what town nearest you has agency listings. How many?

Top 10 TV U.S.-based consolidated agencies by worldwide gross income ($ millions)

Rank (income)	Agency	Worldwide gross income 1991*	Rank (billings)	Worldwide billings, 1991
1	Young & Rubicam, NY	$980.9	1	$7,331.4
2	Saatchi & Saatchi Advertising Worldwide, NY	829.2	2	5,665.7
3	McCann-Erickson Worldwide, NY	389.5	4	5,413.5
4	Ogilvy & Mather Worldwide, NY	794.9	3	5,520.7
5	BBDO Worldwide, NY	772.8	5	5,408.7
6	Lintus: Worldwide, NY	729.7	8	4,887.2
7	J. Walter Thompson Co., NY	727.0	6	5,048.8
8	DDB Needham Worldwide, NY	698.4	7	5,034.3
9	Backer Spielvogel Bates Worldwide, NY	698.4	10	4,266.3
10	Foote,Cone & Belding Communications	616.0	9	4,651.0

tising services include planning, creating, and producing ads, performing research, and selecting media. Nonadvertising functions run the gamut from packaging to public relations to producing sales promotion materials, annual reports, trade-show exhibits, and sales training materials.[3]

Full-service agencies may be *general consumer agencies* or *business* or *industrial agencies.*

General Consumer Agencies A **general agency** represents the widest variety of accounts, but it concentrates on consumer accounts—companies that make goods purchased chiefly by consumers (soaps, cereals, cars, pet foods, toiletries). Most of the ads are placed in consumer media—TV, radio, billboards, newspapers, and magazines—that are *commissionable* to the

EXHIBIT • 3-4

Creativity is one reason ad agencies are hired by clients. Agencies also use creativity in their own ads to attract fresh talent.

RESIST THE USUAL.
YOUNG&RUBICAM

EXHIBIT • 3-5

Young & Rubicam Canada, a general agency, couldn't resist the urge to run this ad to promote its un-"usual" creative nerve.

agency. General agencies get much of their income from commissions paid by the media for ads placed on behalf of clients.

General agencies include international superagencies and many other large firms in New York, Chicago, Los Angeles, Minneapolis, Montreal, and Toronto (Saatchi & Saatchi; Ogilvy & Mather; Foote, Cone & Belding; Ayer; Cossette Marketing-Communications; and Young & Rubicam) and thousands of smaller **entrepreneurial agencies** (Rubin/Postaer, Los Angeles; Ruhr/Paragon, Minneapolis; Geoffrey Roche & Associates, Toronto; BCP, Montreal; The Martin Agency, Richmond). See Exhibit 3–5.

Profit margins in entrepreneurial agencies are often slim, but they are more responsive to the smaller clients they serve, and their work is frequently startling in its creativity.[4] Some entrepreneurial agencies carve a niche for themselves by serving particular market segments. These include agencies that produce ethnic specialty ads like Muse Cordero Chen, Mendoza Dillon, Castor Spanish International, and Burrell Advertising (see Exhibit 3–6).

Industrial Agencies   An **industrial agency** represents clients that make goods sold to other businesses; for example, computer hardware and software, smelting furnaces, locomotives, and radium counters. Business and industrial advertising requires highly developed technical knowledge and the ability to translate that knowledge into precise and persuasive communications.

Most **industrial** (also called **business-to-business**) **advertising** is placed in trade magazines and other business publications. These media are commissionable, but because their circulation is smaller, their rates are far

1:45 a.m., October 12, 1991. Maverick's Flat, Los Angeles, California. The Accord Sedan. HONDA

EXHIBIT • 3-6

The number of ethnic specialty agencies is growing. Their ads typically feature an individual from the ethnic group being targeted or a symbol of the group's ethnic background such as the mural in this Honda ad by Muse Cordero Chen.

lower. Since commissions often don't cover the cost of the agency's services, industrial agencies frequently charge the client an additional service fee. Although expensive, especially for small advertisers, failure to obtain an industrial agency's expertise may carry an even higher price in lost marketing opportunities.[5]

Business and industrial agencies may be large international firms like Maclaren/Lintas in Toronto or like HCM/New York, which handles Ashland Chemical, IBM, and United Technologies. Or they may be smaller firms experienced in such special areas as recruitment (help wanted) advertising, health and medicine, or electronics (Exhibit 3–7 shows a Dutch industrial ad for Canon copiers).

Specialized Service Agencies

In the early 90s, specialization blossomed (see Ad Lab 3–B), fostering many small agency-type groups called *creative boutiques* and specialty businesses such as *media-buying services.*

Creative Boutiques Some talented specialists—like art directors, designers, and copywriters—set up their own creative services, or **creative boutiques.** They work for advertisers and occasionally subcontract to advertising agencies. Their mission is to develop exciting creative concepts and produce fresh, distinctive advertising messages. Creative Artists Agency, a Hollywood talent agency, recently acted as a creative boutique, using its pool of actors, directors, and cinematographers to create a series of commercials for Coca-Cola. But McCann-Erickson, which developed the "Always Coca-Cola" slogan, remains Coke's agency of record.[6]

Because advertising effectiveness depends on originality in concept, design, and writing, advertisers value this quality highly. However, boutiques, although economical, usually don't provide the marketing and sales expertise full-service agencies offer. So boutiques tend to be limited to the role of creative suppliers.

Media-Buying Services Some experienced media specialists set up organizations to purchase and package radio and TV time. The largest of these **media-buying services,** Western International Media in Los Angeles, places over $720 million

EXHIBIT • 3-7

A business-to-business ad for Canon Laser Copier 500.

worth of media advertising annually for clients such as Walt Disney, Arco, USAir, and Times-Mirror.[7]

Radio and TV time is "perishable." A 60-second radio spot at 8 P.M. can't be sold later. So radio and TV stations try to presell as much advertising time as possible, and they discount their rates for large buys. The media-buying service negotiates a special discount rate with radio and TV stations and then sells the time to ad agencies or advertisers.

As part of their service, media-buying firms provide their customers (both clients and agencies) with a detailed analysis of the media buy. Once the media package is sold, the buying service orders the spots, verifies performance, sees that stations "make good" for any missed spots, and even pays the media bills.

Compensation methods vary. Some services charge a set fee, others get a prescribed percentage of the money they save the client.

What Agency People Do

The American Association of Advertising Agencies (AAAA), the national organization of the advertising agency business, is the most responsible advocate for the industry. Its 750 agency members, representing only the largest and oldest agencies, place almost 80 percent of all national advertising handled by agencies in the United States.[8]

The AAAA *Service Standards* explains that an agency's purpose is to interpret to the public, or to desired segments of the public, information about a legally marketed product or service. How does an agency do this? First, the agency

AD LAB 3-B   The Challenge of the 90s: To Specialize or Aggregate?

Many ad agencies were infected by the 80s' merger mania. The biggest empire builder, London-based Saatchi & Saatchi PLC, rapidly became the world's largest agency by acquiring Compton Advertising, Dancer Fitzgerald Sample, and the giant Ted Bates Worldwide in addition to a host of firms in related communications fields.

But, the aggregation strategies used so extensively by so many companies—both advertisers and agencies—didn't always produce the desired results. With current economic realities and the recent wave of technological innovation, specialization is becoming the strategy of choice for the 90s. Now some of the biggest companies are spinning off divisions and focusing on their strengths.

Many agencies are debating which way to turn: specialize or aggregate. Some companies are specializing in the type of products or services they offer. Others specialize in particular markets or clients (like an agency that concentrates on industrial clients). Companies can now identify more market segments, and they have the tools to reach and serve those segments. For example, an ad agency can specialize in database marketing services.

As Larry Jones of Foote, Cone & Belding says, "Compressed margins mean that agencies must run very lean, so services are viewed very pragmatically. Depending on what a client's requirements are, agencies are staffing very much to fill those needs, rather than being 'full service.'" Also, many agencies are starting to unbundle certain services—like media buying.

On the other hand, Rance Crain, President of Crain Communication and Editor in Chief of *Advertising Age* magazine, forecasts that (media) advertising will soon become more integrated with other forms of marketing communications. In fact some agencies are becoming less specialized; they're changing their traditional focus from selling commissionable media advertising to providing clients with more integrated communications.

Ella Strubel, Senior Vice President, Corporate Communications for Leo Burnett, says a Burnett study found that consumers identified 102 different types of media as "advertising"—from TV to shopping bags. Burnett chose to aggregate its diversified services in order to offer an integrated communications strategy to its clients. (Chapter 16 will discuss integrated marketing communications.)

The days of mega-agencies appear to be over, and midsize companies ($100 million to $500 million) are in the most enviable position. They have all the options. They're small enough to aggregate with a larger company and large enough to acquire smaller agencies.

The vast majority of U.S. and Canadian agencies are small, with billings below $100 million. In general this group is doing well. According to *Advertising Age*, the U.S. billings of the bottom 450 agencies rose 6.8 percent last year, nearly six times faster than the 1.2 percent increase of the top 50 agencies. Many small agencies may aggregate through merger—being supported by the structure and financing of large agencies and enabling large agencies to enter niche markets with low overhead and excellent creative teams.

Laboratory Applications

1. Andy Berlin recently left the agency he helped build, Goodby, Berlin & Silverstein. He wanted to expand by opening offices in New York while his partners wanted to remain in San Francisco and focus on the agency's clients there. What points can you make in favor of each position?

2. If you were president of Saatchi & Saatchi, what issues would be most important if you decided to disaggregate the agency to stay viable in the 1990s?

studies the client's product to determine its strengths and weaknesses. Next, it analyzes the product's present and potential market. Then, using its knowledge of the channels of distribution, sales, and available media, the agency formulates a plan to carry the advertiser's message to consumers, wholesalers, dealers, or contractors. Finally the agency writes, designs, and produces ads and commercials, contracts for media space and time, verifies media insertions, and bills for services and media used.

The agency also works with the client's marketing staff to enhance the advertising's effect through package design, sales research and training, and production of sales literature and displays.[9]

To understand these functions, look at the people who were involved—directly or indirectly—in the creation, production, placement, and supervision of the Nike ad created by Muse Cordero Chen in Exhibit 3–8.

My dad's a gangster.
My dad's a father.
My dad runs around.
My dad runs 4 miles a day.
My dad says women are only good for one thing.
My dad says Black women are living jewels.
My dad sent me money.
My dad sent for me.
My dad says school's for fools.
My dad says knowledge is power.
Like father, like son?
Scold him.
Mold him.
Love him.
Don't let him quit.
If he's third string,
go to his games, anyway.
If he can't hit a curve ball,
don't sweat him.
If he's not doing well in school,
give him hell.
If he can recite a rap, word for word,
he can memorize a history lesson, date for date.
Be there for him.
And he'll be there for his brother.
JUST DO IT.

EXHIBIT • 3-8

Another of Muse Cordero Chen's startling ads for Nike, this one contrasts the perspective of two urban youths on dads, women, and life in the shadow of a city basketball court.

Account Management

Muse Cordero Chen's account management team is an essential part of the agency's organization. **Account executives (AEs)** are the liaison between the agency and the client. Responsible for formulating the advertising plan (discussed in Chapter 7), mustering the agency's services, and representing the client's point of view to the agency, the account executive is often caught in the middle. AEs must be entrepreneurial, tough, tactful, diplomatic, creative, communicative, persuasive, knowledgeable, sensitive, honest, and courageous—all at once. And they must be on time for meetings.[10]

Large agencies typically have many account executives who report to **management** (or **account**) **supervisors.** They in turn report to the agency's director of account (or client) services.

To survive, agencies must grow, and growth requires a steady flow of new projects. The best account and creative people always want to work for the "hot shops," the ones attracting new business and receiving awards for outstanding advertising. Sometimes agencies get new assignments when their existing clients develop new products. Sometimes clients seek out agencies whose work they are familiar with. Muse Cordero Chen receives 10 to 15 calls a week because it's well known for its Nike and Honda ads. (The ad in Exhibit 3–9 targets prospective clients to sell an agency's services.)

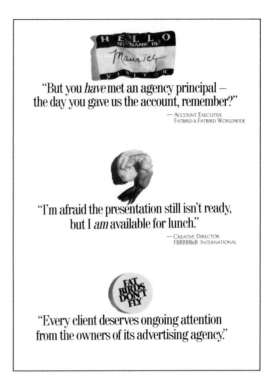

Research

Clients and agencies must give their *creatives* (artists and copywriters) all the
information they need to do a job because advertising is based on information.
Before creating any advertising, agencies research the uses and advantages of
the product, analyze current and potential customers, and try to determine what
will influence them to buy. Following the placement of ads, agencies use
research to investigate how the campaign fared. Chapters 5 and 6 discuss some
of the many types of research ad agencies conduct.

Account Planning: A New Discipline in the Agency Business

When Goodby, Berlin and Silverstein won the Porsche Cars North America
account, *Adweek* commented:

> In the end, what distinguished GBS was the sophistication of its account plan-
> ning . . . GBS conducted 1,000 interviews with current and prospective Porsche
> drivers.[11]

Account planning is a hybrid discipline that bridges the gap between
traditional agency research, account management, and creative departments.
The account planner acts as a surrogate for the consumer, representing the
consumer's point of view in the debate between the agency's creative team and
the client and encouraging ads that are creative, interesting, relevant, and on-
target.[12]

Account planners study consumers through interviews, phone surveys, and
focus groups. Then they help the creative team translate their findings into
imaginative, successful campaigns.[13] Berni Neal, who heads the account planning department at Muse Cordero Chen, literally spent many afternoons on
street corners in Los Angeles just talking to young people to understand their
attitudes, feelings, language, and habits. Then she could represent their
perspective in agency meetings with Nike.

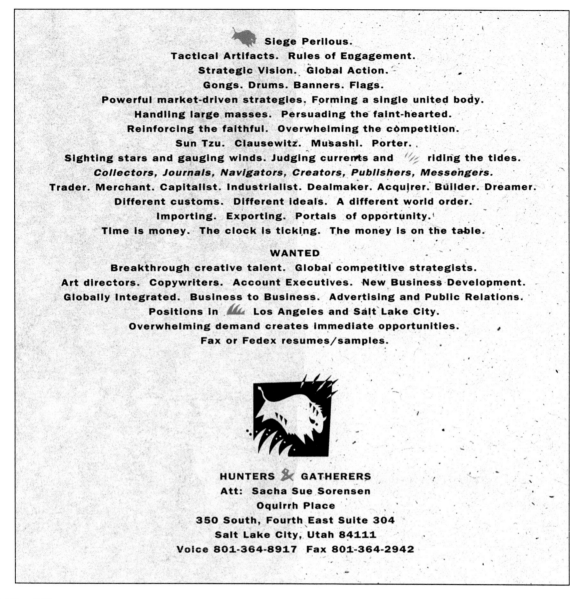

EXHIBIT • 3–10

A very creative help-wanted ad placed in a trade publication.

Creative Concepts

Most ads rely heavily on **copy**—the words that make up the headline and message. The people who create these words, called **copywriters,** must condense all that can be said about a product into a few salient and pertinent points. Copywriters work closely with the agency's artists and production staff. (See Chapter 8 for a full discussion of copywriting.)

The art department is composed of art directors, graphic designers, and production artists who illustrate how the ad's various components—the verbal and visual symbols—will fit together (discussed in Chapter 9).

Most large agencies have their own creative departments (see the ad in Exhibit 3–10, for a senior art director and copywriter.) Other shops purchase art services from independent studios or free-lance designers.

Advertising Production: Print and Broadcast

Once the ad is written, designed, and approved by the client, it is turned over to the agency's print production manager or broadcast producers and directors (discussed in Chapters 10 and 11).

For a print ad, the production department buys type, photos, illustrations, and other components and works with photoplatemakers, color separators, and other graphic arts suppliers. For a broadcast commercial, production personnel work from an approved script or storyboard. They use actors, camerapeople, and production specialists (studios, directors, editors), to produce a commercial on tape (for radio) or on film or videotape (for television).

Traffic

One of the greatest sins in an ad agency is a missed deadline. If Muse Cordero Chen misses the deadline for a monthly magazine read by Nike's youthful customers, the agency will have to wait another month to run the ad—much to Nike's displeasure.

The agency traffic department ensures the work flow is smooth and efficient. It coordinates all phases of production and checks to see that everything is completed on time for media deadlines. The traffic department is often the first stop for entry-level college graduates and is an excellent place to learn agency operations. (See Appendix C for information on careers in advertising.)

Additional Services

With the new trend toward integrating all marketing communications, some agencies employ specialists to provide a variety of additional services.[14] They may have a fully-staffed sales promotion department to produce dealer ads, window posters, point-of-purchase displays, dealer contest materials, and sales material. Or they may have public relations and direct-marketing specialists, home economics experts, package designers, or economists—depending on the nature and needs of their clients.

Agency Administration

Like any business, an agency needs management. In small agencies, administrative functions may be handled by the firm's principals. Large agencies often have accounting, personnel, data processing, purchasing, financial analysis, and insurance departments.

How Agencies Are Structured

An ad agency organizes its functions, operations, and personnel according to the types of accounts it serves, its size, and its geographic scope.

In small agencies (annual billings of less than $10 to $15 million), each employee may wear many hats (see Exhibit 3–11). The owner or president usually supervises daily business operations, client services, and new business development. Account executives and account supervisors generally handle day-to-day client contact. The AE may also do creative work and write copy. Artwork may be produced by an agency art director or purchased from an independent studio or free-lance designer. Most small agencies have a production and traffic department or an employee who fulfills these functions. They may have a media buyer, but in very small agencies the account executives also purchase media time and space.

EXHIBIT • 3-11

In small agencies, the agency head has more control over ad development and management.

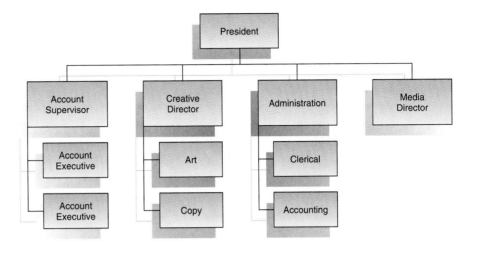

Medium and large agencies generally have a more formal organization and are usually structured in a *departmental* or *group system*. In the **departmental system,** the agency's functions—account services, creative services, marketing services, and administration—are handled by separate departments, as shown in Exhibit 3–12. The account executive handles client contact, the **creative department** writes and lays out ads, and media people select media.

In the **group system,** the agency is divided into a number of "little" agencies or groups (see Exhibit 3–13). Each group may serve one large account or, in many cases, three or four smaller ones. An account supervisor heads each group's staff of account executives, copywriters, art directors, a media director, and any other necessary specialists. A very large agency may have dozens of groups with separate production and traffic units for each.

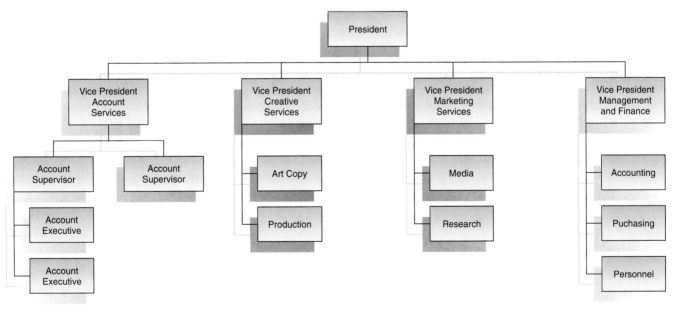

EXHIBIT • 3-12

In the departmental system, each function—account services, creative services, marketing services, and administration—is relatively independent and specialized. But departments can become too autonomous and inflexible.

EXHIBIT • 3-13

In the group system, small "agencies" or groups have all the personnel needed to serve that group's clients. This system helps huge agencies remain flexible.

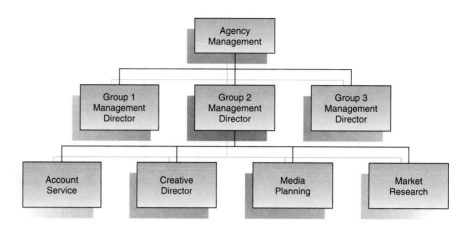

How Agencies Make Money

To survive, an agency must make a profit. But recent trends in the business—mergers of large "superagencies," lower media advertising budgets, shifts in emphasis from advertising to sales promotion, increased production costs, and the fragmentation of media vehicles—have all cut into agency profits.[15] Moreover, different clients demand different services, forcing agencies to develop various compensation methods.[16] Basically, agencies make money from three sources: *media commissions, markups,* and *fees* or *retainers.*

Media Commissions

Agencies save the media sales and collection expenses, so they allow agencies to retain a 15 percent **media commission** on the space or time they purchase for clients. (For outdoor advertising, the commission is usually 16⅔ percent.) If a magazine bills an agency $1,000 for an ad, the agency bills the advertiser $1,000. The advertiser pays the agency the total amount, and the agency sends $850 to the magazine, keeping its 15 percent commission ($150). For large accounts (over $10 million annual billing), the agency typically provides creative, media, and accounting and account management services—plus a host of other *"free"* services such as public relations or sales promotion assistance—for this commission. However, many agencies are now charging for what used to be free services.[17] For small accounts, commissions don't cover the cost of even basic services, so the agency may require additional fees.

Markups

To create a magazine ad, the agency normally buys type, photography, illustrations, and a variety of other services or materials from outside suppliers. The agency pays a set fee and adds a **markup** to the client's bill—typically 17.65 percent. When adding 17.65 percent to an invoice, the amount added becomes 15 percent of the new total.

By adding a markup of 17.65 percent to an $850 photography bill, the agency ends up with $150—15 percent of the total—the standard commission.

$$\$850 \times 17.65\% = \$150$$
$$\$850 + \quad \$150 \quad = \$1,000$$
$$\$1,000 \times \quad 15\% \quad = \$150$$

Some media—local newspapers, for example—allow a commission on the higher rates they charge national advertisers but not the lower rates they charge local advertisers. So agencies use a markup formula of 17.65. When a firm places an ad costing $1,000, the agency bills the firm $1,176.50, keeps the $176.50 markup, and remits the $1,000 to the medium.

Today many agencies find that the 17.65 percent markup doesn't cover their costs so they're increasing their markups to 20 to 25 percent. While this helps, agency profits are still under pressure, forcing many agencies to a fee system in place of, or in addition to, commissions and markups.

Fees

More and more clients expect agencies to solve problems rather than just place ads, so fees are becoming more common.[18]

There are two pricing methods in the fee system. With the **fee-commission** combination, the agency charges a basic monthly fee for all its services to the client and retains any media commissions earned. In the **straight fee** or **retainer** method, agencies charge for all their services and credit any media commissions earned to the client.

Today, accountability is a major issue in client-agency relationships. With a new type of agency compensation—the **incentive system**—the agency earns more if the campaign attains specific, agreed-on goals. DDB Needham, for example, offers its clients a "guaranteed results" program. If a campaign wins, the agency earns more; if it loses, the agency earns less. Kraft General Foods uses a rating system to reward its agencies based on performance: A-grades get an extra 3 percent commission; C-grades are put on review.[19]

How Agencies Get Clients

To succeed, advertising agencies need clients. Clients come from referrals, advertising, or solicitation, or because of the agency's reputation.

Referrals

Most good agencies get clients by referral—from existing clients, friends, or even other agencies. The head of one company asks another who's doing her ads, and the next week the agency gets a call. If a prospective client presents a conflict of interest with an existing client, the agency may refer the prospect to another agency.

Media reps frequently refer local advertisers to an agency they have a good relationship with, so it's important for agencies to maintain cordial relations with their existing clients, the media, and other agencies. Agencies often "put the word out" when they're looking for new business.

Soliciting and Advertising for New Business

Lesser-known agencies can't rely on referrals and must take a more aggressive approach. An agency may solicit new business by advertising, writing solicitation letters, making "cold" calls on prospective clients, or following up leads from sources in the business. Today, more agencies are advertising themselves. See the Martin/Williams agency ad in Exhibit 3–14.

One of an agency's principals usually solicits new business. But once a prospect is found, staffers may help prepare a presentation.

Clients Sure As Heck Aren't
Coming To Minneapolis For The Weather.

Many of our clients have migrated to us from places like Seattle, Dallas and Greensboro. Cities where the weather is a heck of a lot warmer than here.
So why do they come?
Because they've heard that some of the freshest advertising in the country is being created in Minneapolis.
And they know that fresh advertising can be like a shot of adrenaline for a brand that's struggling to establish itself or build market share.
And since we understand that our clients aren't exactly traveling to a garden spot, we work that much harder to make sure our advertising delivers on the promise.
Maybe it's time you made the trip to Minneapolis.
After all, are you going to let a little thing like weather stand between you and great advertising?

Martin/Williams

EXHIBIT • 3–14

This Martin/Williams ad implies that clients come to Minneapolis for the agency's creativity and expertise.

Reputation and Community Relations

Agencies frequently find that the best source of new business is a good reputation. Many agencies submit their best ads to competitions to win awards and gain notoriety. (Most of the ads in this text are award winners.) Some agencies work *pro bono* (for free) for charities or nonprofit organizations such as the American Indian College Fund (see Exhibit 3–15). Jo Muse contributes time to the Rebuild L.A. campaign, which started after the civic disorders of 1992.

Agencies may assist local politicians (a controversial practice in some areas) and become active in the arts, education, religion, or social circles. Some agencies sponsor seminars, others become active in advertising clubs or other professional organizations. All these activities help an agency become known and respected in its community.[20]

Presentations

Once an advertiser is interested in an agency, it may ask the agency to make a presentation—anything from a simple discussion of the agency's philosophy, experience, personnel, and track record to a full-blown audiovisual show complete with slides, films, sample commercials, or proposed campaigns.

Some advertisers ask for or imply that they want a **speculative presentation,** meaning they want to see what the agency will do for them before they sign on. But most agencies prefer to build their presentations around the work they've already done to demonstrate their capabilities without giving away their ideas. Invariably, the larger the client, the bigger the presentation.

The presentation process also allows the agency and the advertiser to get to know each other before they agree to work together. Advertising is a people business, so human qualities—mutual regard, trust, and communication—play an important role.

Most ads for nonprofit organizations are prepared on a *pro bono* basis.

THE ADVERTISERS (CLIENTS)

While every successful business uses advertising, the size and function of a company's advertising department depends on a variety of factors. And so does the way the department is organized and managed.

Large Advertisers

The advertising department's organizational structure depends on the unique circumstances of the company. Large companies tend to use two basic management structures: *centralized* and *decentralized*.

Centralized Organization

General Mills, one of the 20 largest national advertisers, operates a vast advertising and marketing services department with 350 employees and a $538 million annual advertising budget under its "Company of Champions" culture.[21]

General Mills' Marketing Services, located at corporate headquarters in Minneapolis, is really many departments within a department. As a **centralized advertising department,** it administers, plans, budgets, and coordinates the promotion of more than 50 brands. It also supervises 26 outside ad agencies and operates its own in-house agency for new or smaller brands.

Organized around functional specialties (market research, media, graphics, copy), Marketing Services consults with General Mills' brand managers and consolidates many of their expenditures for maximum efficiency. The media department, for example, is involved in all media plans and dollar allocations with the various marketing divisions. The production and art services department handles package design for all brands and graphics for the company's in-house agency. Marketing Services creates effective ad programs for a wide variety of products and brands from one central spot. See Exhibit 3–16.

Centralized advertising departments are common in large organizations because they are cost-effective and because they help maintain continuity in the company's communications programs. Typically, an advertising manager reports to a marketing vice president. Other than this consistent feature, companies organize the department in one of five ways:

1. By product or brand.
2. By subfunction of advertising (such as sales promotion, print production, TV/radio buying, and outdoor advertising).
3. By end user (consumer products, industrial products).
4. By media (radio, television, newspapers, and so forth).
5. By geography (western advertising, eastern advertising).

Decentralized Organization

As companies become larger, take on new brands or products, acquire subsidiaries, and establish divisions in different regions or different countries, a centralized advertising department becomes impractical. In a **decentralized** system, departments are assigned to divisions, subsidiaries, products, countries, regions, brands, or other categories that suit the company's needs. The general manager of each division is responsible for its advertising.

Procter & Gamble, a 157-year-old, $29-billion company, sells over 200 different consumer products internationally including such market leaders as Tide, Ivory soap, Pampers, Duncan Hines cake mixes, and Crest toothpaste.[22]

The nation's second-largest advertiser with expenditures exceeding $1.7 billion annually, P&G has eight consumer product divisions, five industrial product divisions, and four international divisions. Each division is set up almost like a separate company with its own research and development department, manufacturing plant, advertising department, sales force, and finance and accounting staff. Every brand within a division has a brand manager, two assistant brand managers, and one or two staff assistants. P&G believes this system ensures that each brand gets the single-minded drive and personal commitment necessary for success.[23]

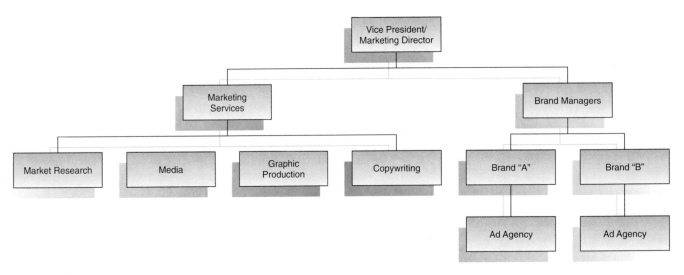

EXHIBIT • 3-16

General Mills has a centralized advertising department like the model above.

Each P&G brand manager has his or her own ad agency to develop and create the brand's media advertising. The division's advertising department helps coordinate sales promotion and merchandising programs across brands, and the corporate advertising department's media and research supervisors provide statistical information and guidance.

For new college grads, P&G's brand manager development program is known as the Marine Corps of marketing. Apprentice brand managers learn the statistics of their brand's performance, work on store displays, develop sales projections, help plan advertising budgets, and coordinate with other sections of the division's advertising department: media, copy, art and packaging, sampling and couponing, and legal. They learn how market research helps determine the package, scents, sizes, and colors people want, how product research improves the brand, and how the sales force tries to muscle more shelf space.

This decentralized brand manager system, a sacred cow at P&G for many years, was criticized in the 80s for no longer satisfying the needs of a rapidly changing marketplace and for being too product-oriented rather than market-oriented.[24] P&G reviewed the system and grafted onto it "category" **brand managers,** "future" brand managers (for products planned for the future), and regional marketing managers. Brand managers used to compete with each other under the old system; now the company uses teams that include manufacturing, sales, and research managers who all work together for the common good.[25] While the system is still decentralized, many activities are becoming centralized for economy, efficiency, and control.[26]

For large, multidivision companies, decentralized advertising is more flexible. Campaigns and media schedules can be adjusted faster and easier. New approaches and creative ideas can be introduced more easily, and sales results can be measured independently of other divisions. In effect, each division is its own marketing department, and the advertising manager reports to each division head (see Exhibit 3–17).

EXHIBIT • 3-17

In a decentralized department, each division is its own marketing department.

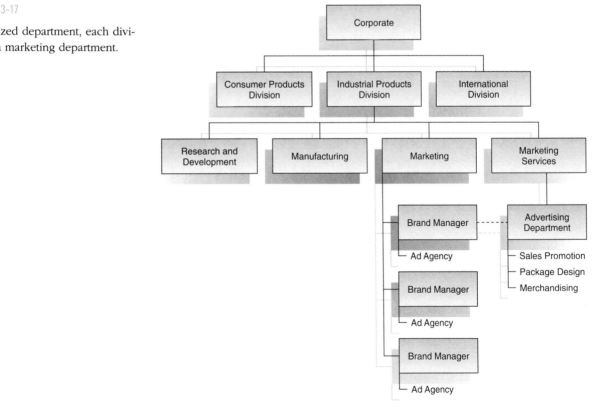

But decentralized departments tend to concentrate on their own budgets, problems, and promotions rather than the good of the firm as a whole. Ads may lack uniformity, diminishing the power of repetitive corporate advertising. Rivalry among brand managers may deteriorate into secrecy and jealousy. And some brand managers even resist using the same corporate logo.

Most companies blend centralized and decentralized structures to fit their own particular needs.

The In-House Agency

To save money and centralize their advertising, some companies set up a wholly-owned **in-house agency** (or *house agency*). The house agency does all the work of an independent full-service agency including creative tasks, production, media placement, publicity, and sales promotion. See Exhibit 3–18.

Advertisers with house agencies hope to save money by cutting overhead, keeping the media commission, and avoiding markups on outside purchases.

Advertisers think they get more attention from their house agencies. House agencies know the company's products and markets better and can focus all their resources to meet critical deadlines. To respond as fast, outside agencies often have to hire free-lance help for significant extra cost.

Many companies think management has better control of and more involvement in the advertising when it's done by company people—especially "single-business" companies whose products and services are similar.[27]

In spite of these advantages, companies may sacrifice considerably more than they gain. First, in-house agencies may provide flexibility at the expense of creativity.[28] Independent agencies offer experience, versatility, and diverse talent. In-house agencies have trouble attracting and keeping the best creative talent.

ETHICAL DILEMMA   The Conflict over Client-Agency Conflicts

Clients seem to believe the biblical maxim "No one can serve two masters." They become very concerned when their agencies work for competitors. John Powers, VP-director of marketing services at Eastman Kodak, says: "When we sign on with an agency, they say they want to be our full partners and increase our profits. How can they also increase my competition's profits and remain my partner?" It's no wonder that conflict with clients is becoming the number-one problem in the advertising business.

Part of the problem is the conflict over what constitutes a conflict. Everyone agrees that an agency shouldn't work on directly competing products like Cheerios and Wheaties. But should it handle Procter & Gamble's Sure deodorant and Colgate-Palmolive's Colgate toothpaste? The products don't compete, but the companies do. Many advertisers think indirect competition *does* represent a conflict and the client's perception is the litmus test.

Clients worry that agencies serving competitors might reveal confidential information. Kent Mitchell, VP-marketing services at General Foods, says, "Agencies working for you know your thinking, your tactical moves, and if you have worked together for a while, you've built up a certain amount of information about the industry you would like to protect." Clients also fear that an agency might not give equal time and talent to two competing accounts.

Ronald Coleman, president of the Business/Professional Advertising Association, echoes the belief that an "agency shouldn't get involved with any client that could be a competitor of an existing client." But that's easier said than done. Big, successful agencies attract big, successful clients, who have so many brands that conflict is virtually unavoidable.

Some clients are unyielding. P&G insists its agencies not do business with any competing company in any product category. McDonald's makes its agencies agree not to work for another fast-food account for a minimum of six months after resigning McDonald's business. Important clients like

EXHIBIT • 3-18
In-house agencies can produce very professional advertising like this ad for Anne Klein II.

these can make their demands stick. But is it ethical to ask an agency to commit all its resources and loyalty to a single account, particularly when the client spreads its business among a number of agencies?

For years, agencies experimented with ways to minimize conflicts. Some build "Chinese walls" between agency teams handling competing accounts. Others create separate offices. Still others divide into subsidiary businesses. But no solution addresses the underlying problem—lack of trust.

Clients and agencies both agree that the best approach to handling potential conflicts is to be straightforward and honest, but that often puts agencies in an impossible bind. What happens if one client develops a new product that will compete with another client's? Should the agency resign one of the accounts?

Fortunately, some clients are learning to coexist in an atmosphere of mutual trust. If more clients learn to have faith in their agencies, and if the agencies act ethically, perhaps

the conflict over conflicts will be replaced by better client-agency relationships.

Questions

1. Imagine you're the advertising manager for a successful brand of coffee and your ad agency accepts an assignment from a soft drink company. Is this a potential conflict? Would you fire the agency or lay down new ground rules?

2. Henry Kornhauser, CEO of Kornhauser & Calene, believes that conflicts shouldn't be as important as they are because each brand has its own character. He claims the key criteria should be: How good a job is the ad agency doing? How much thinking and idea generation is the account getting? And how are the brand's sales doing? Do you agree?

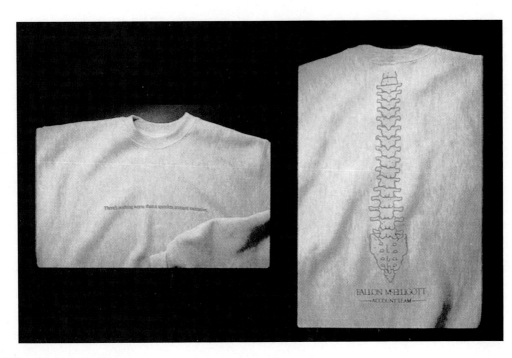

EXHIBIT • 3-19

This T-shirt by and for Fallon McElligott promotes the independent agency's creative "backbone," a characteristic in-house agencies may lack because management can override the in-house staff's decisions.

The biggest problem for in-house agencies is loss of objectivity. By reflecting the internal politics, policies, and views of corporate management, the advertising becomes company- rather than consumer-oriented. (See Exhibit 3–19.)

Small Advertisers

A small retailer—say, a hardware, clothing, or electronics store—may have one person in charge of advertising. That person, the **advertising manager,** performs all the administrative, planning, budgeting, and coordinating functions. He or she may lay out newspaper ads, write ad copy, and select the media. However, unless the manager is also a commercial artist or graphic designer, he or she won't design the actual ads, set type, or do pasteup.

A chain of stores might have a complete advertising department to handle production, media placement, and marketing support services. Such a department needs artists, copywriters, and production specialists. The department's head usually reports to a vice president or marketing manager, as shown in Exhibit 3–20. We cover the subject of local advertising in Chapter 18.

MANAGING INTERNATIONAL ADVERTISING

Companies advertising abroad face many challenges and opportunities. They must speak to an audience with a different value system, environment, and language. Foreign customers have different purchasing abilities, habits, and motivations than the average North American. Media customary for U.S. and Canadian advertisers may be unavailable or ineffective. And companies may need different advertising strategies too. But they also face a more basic problem: How to manage and produce the advertising? Should their domestic

EXHIBIT • 3-20

EXHIBIT • 3-20

Typical department structure for small advertisers with high volumes of work—such as grocery store chains.

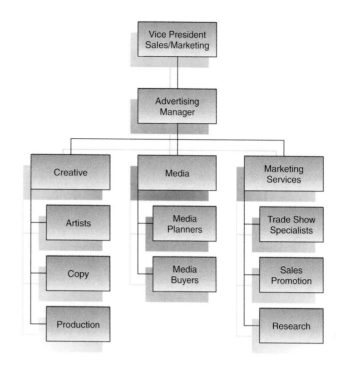

agency or in-house advertising department do it? Should they use a foreign agency or set up a foreign advertising department? To answer these questions, companies need to consider how their worldwide marketing operation is organized.

Worldwide Marketing Structures

Advertisers use three types of structures to market abroad—*international, multinational,* or *global*—and these terms are not interchangeable.

International Structure

Many advertisers break into **international marketing** by exporting the products they already produce. At first, the home office controls all foreign marketing and advertising—everything is centralized. But as the complexities of foreign operations expand, the pressure to decentralize grows.

As they get more involved, companies may form joint ventures or invest in foreign sales offices, warehouses, plants, manufacturing subsidiaries, and other facilities. The advertiser typically views such operations as "foreign marketing divisions"; the divisions become responsible for their own product lines, marketing operations, and profits.

Multinational Structure

As companies grow and prosper, they become true **multinational corporations.** They invest directly in many countries and make decisions based on choices available anywhere in the world.[29] They strive for full and integrated participation in world markets. Foreign sales often grow faster than domestic sales. Multinationals like Exxon and IBM earn about 50 percent of their sales abroad; Kodak and Xerox, about 25 percent. The top 25 U.S. multinational

Dentsu's creative director uses a traditional Japanese image (a large carp) in this ad for a Xerox color copier. Other cultures might find this image quite unappealing.

VO: Apply colors with an electronic palette. Increase the number. Change the size. Documents can have new colors. Just a little fantastic. XEROX's color copier Palette. Now on sale.

corporations get 42 percent of their revenues and 69 percent of their profits overseas.[30] Exhibit 3–21 shows the type of advertising Xerox uses in Japan.

A multinational typically exerts strong centralized control over all its marketing activities. Multinational organizations like Kodak sell in many countries, get strong direction and coordination from one central headquarters, and have a standardized product line and uniform marketing structure.

Global Structure

Multinationals that use the same advertising and marketing in all countries are **global corporations,** and they create *global brands.*

Coca-Cola is considered a global brand even though its advertising does vary from country to country. Its "General Assembly" commercial is available in 21 languages (see Exhibit 3–22).

Grey Advertising suggests three questions companies should ask before attempting a global advertising strategy: A "no" answer means the attempt will probably fail.[31]

- Has each country's market developed in the same way? (Many Europeans use clotheslines so they don't buy fabric softeners for dryers.)
- Are the consumer targets similar in different nations? (Japanese consumers like sophisticated, high-tech products, but many U.S. consumers fear them.)
- Do consumers share the same wants and needs? (Tang was successfully positioned as an orange juice substitute in the United States. But the French don't drink orange juice at breakfast, so Tang was repositioned as a daytime refreshment, as shown in Exhibit 3–23.).

Ultimately, the advertising direction a company takes depends on many variables, including breadth of product line, availability of qualified management, ability to use similar marketing techniques across countries, the costs of particular marketing strategies, as well as the decision to operate internationally, multinationally, or globally.

Selecting an Agency for International Advertising

Depending on their foreign marketing structure and business needs, advertisers can choose from several types of ad agencies—an international or global agency, a local foreign agency, an export agency, their normal domestic agency, or their house agency.

International and Global Agencies

Many multinational advertisers want a large agency with widespread offices or affiliates. So the largest agencies have established themselves in major foreign markets and shifted their focus from domestic advertising to international and global marketing. Several mega-agencies now wield significant clout in international media buying and worldwide advertising coordination. Exhibit 3–24 lists the 10 largest ad agencies worldwide.

An international agency's overseas offices usually employ multilingual, multinational creative specialists and administrators who can create distinct campaigns for different markets or one central campaign for a series of countries. Some advertisers hire various international agencies for different regions. Rolex uses J. Walter Thompson in 25 countries, Pimo in the Middle East, Ogilvy & Mather for Southeast Asia, and Intercom in South Africa.

EXHIBIT • 3-22

Coca-Cola's "General Assembly" commercial shows 1,000 teenagers from around the world joining together in a song of hope. Each of 16 versions begins with a teen from the target country singing in his or her own language. Coke's agency in each country can edit the commercial to focus on teens from that country.

GIRL SOLO: I am the future of the world.
I am the hope of my nation.
I am tomorrow's people.
I am the new inspiration and we've got a song to sing to you.

GROUP: (Under solo) Ooh.

GIRL SOLO: We've got a message to bring to you.

Please let there be for you and for me a tomorrow . . .

ALL TOGETHER: Tomorrow.
If we can agree, there'll be sweet harmony tomorrow, tomorrow . . .

GROUP: (Under solo) Aah.

GIRL SOLO: And we all will be there, Coca-Cola to share . . .

GROUP: Coca Cola to share . . .

GIRL SOLO: Feelings so real and so true.

GROUP: Feelings so real and so . . .

ALL TOGETHER: True.

GIRL SOLO: Promise us tomorrow and we'll build a better world for you.

GROUP: Build a better world for you.

EXHIBIT • 3-23

In France, Tang is positioned as a refreshing beverage, not as a breakfast drink. The youngster listens to his Tang "radio," which plays "raspberry taste on the Tang frequency." The copy below reads, Tang is "All ready. All new. All good."

EXHIBIT • 3-24

Top 10 agencies by worldwide billings

Agency	1992*
WPP Group (U.K.)	$2,813
Interpublic Group of Companies (U.S.)	1,989
Omnicom Group (U.S.)	1,806
Saatchi & Saatchi Co. (U.K.)	1,697
Dentsu Inc. (Japan)	1,387
Young & Rubicam (U.S.)	1,072
Euro RSCG (France)	951
Grey Advertising (U.S.)	735
Foote, Cone & Belding Communications (U.S.)	683
Hakuhodo (Japan)	661

*Dollars are in millions.

Local Foreign Agencies

An advertiser may use a local foreign agency to coordinate activities in a particular market because the foreign agency understands local attitudes and media. An advertiser that plans to promote the product differently to various markets may use several local agencies that understand the needs of those markets. However, it's difficult to coordinate various agencies.

Export Agencies

Some agencies specialize in creating ads for exporters. Such **export agencies** may work with domestic agencies or with clients of their own. Export agencies typically prepare ads for particular language groups or geographic areas. They employ writers and specialists familiar with the market and its media.

Domestic and House Agencies

Small companies exporting their products abroad may have their domestic agency prepare their first international ads, which many agencies do quite adequately. Some domestic agencies are affiliated with foreign shops that provide media counsel, translation services, or production assistance. Other domestic agencies join international **agency networks** to receive similar services and others such as arranging local press conferences or trade fairs. But a domestic agency may be inexperienced in international advertising.

Some companies, especially industrial firms, use their company advertising departments or house agencies for foreign advertising. However, like the domestic agency, in-house staff may lack expertise in foreign advertising.

THE CLIENT-AGENCY RELATIONSHIP

Many factors affect the success of a company's advertising program, but one consistent determinant is the nature of the relationship between the advertiser and its agency.[32]

Stages in the Client-Agency Relationship

Just as people and products have life cycles, so do relationships. In the advertising business, the life cycle of the agency-client relationship has four distinct stages: *prerelationship, development, maintenance,* and *termination*.[33]

The Prerelationship Stage

The **prerelationship stage** includes all the time before an agency and client officially do business. They may know each other by reputation, by previous ads, or through social contact. Initial perceptions usually determine if an agency is invited to "pitch" the account. Then, through the presentation process, the agency tries to give the best impression it can—because it is selling, and the client is buying. (The Checklist for Agency Review offers guidelines clients can use in selecting an agency.)

The Development Stage

Once the agency is appointed, the **development stage** begins. In this honeymoon period, the agency and the client are at the peak of their optimism and eager to develop a mutually profitable relationship. Expectations are at their highest, and both sides are most forgiving. During development, the rules of the relationship are established—either directly or nonverbally. The respective

---

CHECKLIST   Agency Review

Rate each agency on a scale from 1 (strongly negative) to 10 (strongly positive).

General Information

◇ Size compatible with our needs.
◇ Strength of management.
◇ Financial stability.
◇ Compatibility with other clients.
◇ Range of services.
◇ Cost of services; billing policies.

Marketing Information

◇ Ability to offer marketing counsel.
◇ Understanding of the markets we serve.
◇ Experience dealing in our market.
◇ Success record; case histories.

Creative Abilities

◇ Well-thought-out creativity; relevance to strategy.
◇ Art strength.
◇ Copy strength.
◇ Overall creative quality.
◇ Effectiveness compared to work of competitors.

Production

◇ Faithfulness to creative concept and execution.
◇ Diligence to schedules and budgets.
◇ Ability to control outside services.

Media

◇ Existence and soundness of media research.
◇ Effective and efficient media strategy.
◇ Ability to achieve objectives within budget.
◇ Strength at negotiating and executing schedules.

Personality

◇ Overall personality, philosophy, or position.
◇ Compatibility with client staff and management.
◇ Willingness to assign top people to account.

References

◇ Rating by current clients.
◇ Rating by past clients.
◇ Rating by media and financial sources.

---

roles get set quickly, the true personalities of all the players are discovered, and the agency's first work created. At this point, the agency's work is awaited with great expectation and judged very thoroughly. The agency also discovers how well the client pays its bills, how receptive the client is to new ideas, and how easy the client's staff is to work with. The first problems in the relationship occur during the development stage.

The Maintenance and Termination Stages

Maintenance is the day-to-day working relationship that, when successful, may go on for many years. Sunkist has used the same agency—Foote, Cone & Belding—for almost 90 years. Unfortunately, the average client-agency relationship is much shorter—usually seven or eight years.

At some point, an irreconcilable difference may occur, and the relationship must be terminated. It may simply be that one party or the other decides it is time to move on. In 1991, for example, several long-standing client-agency relationships were terminated: after 25 years, Wells Rich Green lost the Benson & Hedges account; Isuzu terminated Della Femina McNamee; and Ayer lost J. C. Penney.[34] The way the **termination** is handled will affect both sides for a long time and is an important factor in determining whether the two ever get back together. For example, after losing the Apple Computer account, Chiat/Day placed an ad thanking Apple for their many years together.

Factors Affecting the Client-Agency Relationship

Forces that influence the client-agency relationship include *chemistry, communication, conduct,* and *changes*—the four Cs.

Chemistry

The most critical factor is the personal chemistry between the client's and the agency's staff.[35] Agencies are very conscious of this factor and "wine and dine" their clients in hopes of improving it. Smart clients do the same.

Communication

Poor communication, a problem often cited by both agencies and advertisers, leads to misunderstandings about objectives, strategies, or tactics—and to poor advertising. Constant, open communication is key to a good relationship.[36]

Conduct

Dissatisfaction with agency performance is the most commonly cited reason for agency switches.[37] Does the client give the agency timely, accurate information? Does the agency understand the client's marketing problems and offer realistic alternatives? Does the work meet the client's expectations? Does the client appreciate good work? (For more on how clients hold up their end of the relationship, see the Checklist for Ways to Be a Better Client.)

CHECKLIST   Ways to Be a Better Client

◇ **Look for the big idea.** Concentrate first on positioning and brand personality. Don't allow a single ad—no matter how brilliant—to change your positioning or brand personality.

◇ **Learn the fine art of conducting a creative meeting.** Deal with the important issues first: strategy, consumer benefit, reason why.

◇ **Cultivate honesty.** Tell your agency the truth. Make sure your advertising tells the truth and implies the truth as well.

◇ **Be enthusiastic.** When you like the advertising, let the creative people know.

◇ **Be frank when you don't like the advertising.** Always give a reason for turning down an idea.

◇ **Be human.** React like a person, not a corporation. Laugh at a funny ad, even if it won't work.

◇ **Be willing to admit you aren't sure.** Don't let your agency pressure you. You may need time to absorb the agency's suggestions.

◇ **Insist on creative discipline.** Discipline helps creative people zero in on a target.

◇ **Keep the creative people involved in your business.** Successful copywriters want to know the latest market shares. Tell them what's happening, good and bad.

◇ **Don't insulate your top people from the creative people.** Agency creative people want to receive objectives directly from the top—not filtered through layers.

◇ **Make the agency feel responsible.** Tell the agency what you think is wrong, not how to fix it.

◇ **Don't be afraid to ask for great advertising.** Let your agency know you have confidence in the staff's ability to try new directions and take some risks.

◇ **Set objectives.** You must know where you want to go; set objectives for your advertising and your business.

◇ **Switch people, not agencies.** If there are problems, ask for new people to work on your account. You'll get a fresh approach without interrupting continuity.

◇ **Be sure the agency makes a profit on your account.** Don't demand more service than fees or commissions can cover. The agency should grow with the client.

◇ **Avoid insularity.** Force yourself to go beyond the comfortable world of your own lifestyle.

◇ **Care about being a client.** Creative people do their best work on accounts they like, for clients they like to work with.

◇ **Suggest work sessions.** Set up informal give-and-take discussions where copywriters can air ideas and you can talk about your objectives.

Changes

Changes occur in every relationship. Unfortunately, some of them damage the agency-client partnership. The client's market position may change. Client policy may change, or new management may arrive. Agencies may lose some of their creative staff. Client conflicts may arise if one agency buys another that handles competing accounts. Laws hold that an ad agency cannot represent a client's competition without the client's consent.[38] When Saatchi & Saatchi bought the Ted Bates agency, it suddenly became the world's largest advertising agency—but it also lost Bates's Colgate-Palmolive account because of the conflict with Saatchi & Saatchi's client Procter & Gamble.[39]

◆

Summary

The advertising business comprises two main groups: advertisers (clients) and agencies. In addition, there are media and suppliers. The advertising business employs creative people, product people, top executives, and clerical personnel.

All advertisers and agencies perform the functions of planning, budgeting, coordination with other departments or outside services, and creative supervision.

Advertising agencies are independent organizations of creative people and businesspeople who specialize in developing and preparing advertising plans, ads, and other promotional tools on behalf of clients.

Agencies can be classified by the range of services they offer and the types of business they handle. The two basic types are full-service agencies and specialized service agencies such as creative boutiques and media-buying services. Agencies may specialize in either consumer or industrial accounts. The people who work in agencies may be involved in research, account planning, creative services, traffic, media, account management, new business, administration, or a host of other activities.

Agencies may be organized into departments based on functional specialties or into groups that work as teams on various accounts. Agencies charge fees or retainers, receive commissions from the media, or mark up outside purchases made on behalf of their clients. Most agencies get clients through referral, advertising, community relations, or personal solicitation.

A client's advertising department may be centralized or decentralized. Each structure has advantages and disadvantages. The centralized organization is the most typical and may be structured by product, subfunction of advertising, end user, or geography. Decentralized departments are typical of large far-flung organizations with numerous divisions, subsidiaries, products, countries, regions, or brands.

Some advertising departments take responsibility for ad production, media placement, and other marketing support services. Some firms develop in-house agencies in hopes of saving money by keeping normal agency commissions for themselves. However, they sometimes save money but lose objectivity and creativity.

The client-agency relationship goes through a number of stages. Numerous factors affect the relationship, including chemistry, communication, conduct, and changes.

◆

Questions for Review and Discussion

1. What roles do the major organizations involved in the advertising business perform?

2. If a client has an advertising agency, does it still need an advertising manager? Why?

3. How can a full-service advertising agency help a manufacturer of industrial goods?

4. What are the most important points an advertiser should consider when selecting an agency?

5. Should an advertiser change agencies regularly? Why or why not?

6. What are the advantages and disadvantages of an in-house advertising agency?

7. How does an agency make money? What is the best way to compensate an agency? Explain.

8. How does the client-agency relationship evolve, and what can clients and agencies do to protect it?

9. What is the best structure for an international advertiser to use?

10. What methods can an advertiser or agency use to locate suppliers and evaluate their services?

Developing Marketing and Advertising Strategies

The success of any business depends on its ability to attract customers willing and able to buy its products and services. To do this, a business must find, understand, and communicate with potential customers where they live, work, and play. Part II examines the marketing process, the nature of consumers, the relationship between products and market groups, and the research and planning processes that make for marketing and advertising success.

Chapter 4, "The Importance of Marketing and Consumer Behavior to Advertising," describes products and markets and how advertisers use the marketing process to create effective advertising. The chapter presents the consumer as an acceptor or rejector of products and discusses how the consumer's complex decision-making process affects the design of advertising.

Chapter 5, "Market Segmentation and the Marketing Mix," discusses market segments, the aggregation of segments, and the influence of target marketing on a product company. It presents the elements of the marketing mix and discusses how advertisers use them to understand and improve a product concept.

Chapter 6, "Marketing and Advertising Research," points out the value of research in improving marketing and

advertising effectiveness. It describes how to organize and gather data and properly evaluate and report results. It also discusses the importance of research and the objectives and techniques of concept testing, pretesting, and post-testing.

Chapter 7, "Marketing and Advertising Planning," details the creation of effective marketing and advertising plans, particularly setting realistic and attainable objectives and developing creative strategies to achieve those objectives. The chapter presents both top-down and bottom-up marketing, as well as methods for allocating resources.

The Importance of Marketing and Consumer Behavior to Advertising

Objective: To highlight the importance of the marketing function in business and to define the important role advertising plays as a marketing communication tool by presenting the company and its products to the market. Since markets are made up of people, the successful advertising person must understand the relationship between marketing and the way consumers behave. It is that relationship that ideally shapes advertising.

After studying this chapter, you will be able to:

- Define marketing and explain its importance to advertisers.

- Discuss the concept of product utility and the relationship of utility to consumer needs.

- Explain what is meant by the expression, "The perception is the reality."

- Describe who the key participants are in the marketing process.

- Outline the consumer perception process.

- Discuss the interpersonal influences on consumer behavior.

- Explain how advertisers deal with the problem of cognitive dissonance.

One of the classic cases in marketing history occurred many years ago when, after nine years of development, Ford Motor Company introduced a new car touted as the "latest breakthrough" in engineering design. The car offered a host of features such as safety rim wheels, self-adjusting brakes, and an automatic transmission controlled by push buttons on the steering wheel. Ford spent over $250 million to design, engineer, and produce the car, eventually building 110,000 of them. Then Ford spent more than $30 million advertising it in print and electronic media. The company spared no effort—and certainly no expense—marketing this car that they had named after one of Mr. Ford's sons.

And yet, within two years, Ford stopped production, cutting its losses at $350 million. What went wrong? Why did the Edsel fail so miserably?

Did the car sell poorly because potential buyers didn't know about it? Not really; the Edsel was extensively advertised. Individual ads followed proven standards of effective copywriting and layout. And in keeping with the car's advanced design, Ford used innovative (for the time) print ads like the one in Exhibit 4–1.

If the advertising was not at fault, what was? Did the company rush into production without fully considering whether consumers wanted such a car? By that era's standards, Ford carefully analyzed the market at the beginning of the process. Prior to development and manufacturing, Ford's marketing research department surveyed potential customers for answers to these basic questions: Does the car-buying public want this car? Does it appeal to them? Do they need this car, or do other cars already fill the same need? At the price customers are able or willing to pay, can we cover the costs of manufacturing, distribution, advertising, and sales? After covering costs, can we still make an acceptable profit?

Ford Motor Company told us the Edsel was here to stay. The automaker was wrong. With a loss of $350 million in 1959 dollars, the Edsel was perhaps the largest single product marketing disaster in history.

Says you're going places

Slide onto the special seat reserved for the Edsel driver and glance out over that long, powerful hood. You get the feeling: *this is the way to look at the world.*

Just touch a Teletouch Drive button on the steering-wheel hub. The Edsel glides forward, gaining momentum instantly from America's most advanced engine. And you get the feeling:

this is the way to travel.

You're right. Only Edsel offers the originality, power and handling ease that clearly says you're going places.

Yet there's less than fifty dollars difference between Edsel and V-8's in the Low-Priced Three.*

So put away all your old ideas about cars and see your Edsel

Dealer for a demonstration drive. *Above: Edsel Citation Convertible. Engine: the E-475, with 10.5 to one compression ratio, 345 horsepower, 475 ft.-lb. torque. Transmission: Automatic with Teletouch Drive. Brakes: Self-adjusting.* *Based on comparisons of manufacturers' suggested retail delivered prices.*

EDSEL DIVISION · FORD MOTOR COMPANY

The EDSEL LOOK is here to stay—and 1959 cars will prove it!

1958 **EDSEL**

In 1954, when Ford first asked these questions, survey responses were only weakly affirmative. When Ford repeated the survey in 1956, results were even more negative. Unfortunately, top management ignored the survey results. They remained confident of their product's features and of their ability to pull the Edsel through the dealer network with $30 million in consumer advertising. The result was a costly failure.

The Edsel Syndrome

The Edsel story offers some good lessons. To succeed in business, a company's top managers must listen and respond to the marketplace. They must respect the importance of marketing and know how to weigh the data uncovered by their marketing people. Companies that ignore this run the risk of experiencing their own Edsels.

For those in the field of advertising, the Edsel story demonstrates another important principle—even superior advertising can't save a product that isn't marketed correctly. Many years afterward, an *Advertising Age* survey of advertising professionals voted Edsel the biggest product failure in history. One advertising person commented, "I happen to think that was a pretty good ad campaign. Mismarketing, to be sure. But okay advertising." The business world is not always so kind. All too often, advertising becomes the scapegoat for management's misfires. ◆

THE IMPORTANCE OF MARKETING TO ADVERTISING PEOPLE

The key to any company's success is its ability to attract and keep customers who are willing and able to pay for its goods and services. This means a business must be able to locate prospective customers—where they live, work, and play—and then be able to understand them and communicate with them.

All advertisers face a perennial challenge: how to effectively present their goods, services, and ideas through the media to buyers. But to do this, they must first comprehend the subtle relationship between the product and the marketplace. This relationship is the province of *marketing*. So, to begin, we examine the role of marketing in business—in order to more fully appreciate its importance to advertising.

Every business organization performs a number of diverse activities. Management typically classifies these activities into three broad functional divisions:

- Operations (production/manufacturing).
- Administration/finance.
- Marketing.

Students who major in business study a variety of subjects related to one or all of these general functions. For instance, courses in purchasing, quality control, and manufacturing relate to the operations function. Courses in accounting, industrial relations, and business law relate to the administration/ finance area. And while many students study advertising in a school of journalism or communications, advertising is actually a specialty area within the broad field of marketing. Other courses in marketing include market research, product distribution, inventory control, and sales management.

Unfortunately, marketing's role is often misunderstood and overlooked. For example, some people emphasize that a business can't survive without proper financing. And many point out that without production, there are no goods and services to sell. But how does a company know what products or services to produce? That's where marketing comes in.

Businesspeople use marketing research to determine if a demand even exists for a proposed product. Then, to obtain financing for the endeavor, an entrepreneur has to create a marketing plan acceptable to financing sources. In short, as important as finance and production are, marketing is still the only business function whose primary role is to attract revenues. And without revenue, a company cannot recover its initial investment or earn profits.

Advertising helps the organization achieve its marketing goals. So do marketing research, sales, product distribution, and inventory control. And these other marketing specialties all have a relationship to, and an impact on, the advertising a company employs. Therefore, an effective advertising specialist must have a broad understanding of the marketing environment in which advertising operates.

In the end, customers are people. Advertising professionals must understand how people act and think—and why they buy what they buy. This area of study is the province of another specialty—*consumer behavior.* By understanding consumer behavior, advertisers can perform their primary task of bringing products into consumers' consciousness.

The purpose of this chapter—in fact of this whole unit—is to define and outline the subject of marketing in order to clarify advertising's proper role in the marketing function and to introduce the underlying human factors that ultimately shape advertising.

WHAT IS MARKETING?

Over the years, as the field of marketing evolved, so has its definition. Typically, definitions depend on the perspective of the definer.[1] Since we need to understand the concept of *marketing* as it relates to the people who work in *advertising,* we define the term as follows:

Marketing is the process of planning and executing the conception, pricing, promotion, and distribution of ideas, goods, and services to create exchanges that satisfy the perceived needs, wants, and objectives of individuals and organizations.[2]

The first important element in this definition is the statement that marketing is a *process*—a series of actions or methods that take place sequentially. In the case of marketing, the process includes conceiving products, pricing them strategically, promoting them through sales and advertising activities, and making them available to customers through a distribution network. The ultimate goal of the marketing process is to earn a profit by uniting a product or service with customers who need or want it. As we'll see in Chapter 7, the marketing plan and the advertising plan formalize this process in written form and guide it in a prescribed sequence.

Needs and Utility

A second important element in the definition is its focus on the special relationship between a customer's needs and a product's problem-solving potential. Marketing theorists generally refer to this relationship as the product's **utility.** Utility extends to the product's ability to satisfy both functional needs and symbolic or psychological wants.[3] Ad Lab 4–A discusses the relationship between needs and utility.

In the initial stages of the process, marketers may use research to discover what needs and wants exist in the marketplace and to define the product's general characteristics in the light of economic, social, and political trends.

For example, a car manufacturer, noting that more families are having children, may decide to introduce a new station wagon. Additional research may then determine which group of consumers is most concerned with multi-passenger utility (e.g., baby boomers), how much they expect to spend on a car, and what other features are important to them (e.g., safety features). The

AD LAB 4–A   Understanding Needs and Utility

Superior quality by itself isn't enough to sell anything. Marketing people have to make the product available and promote its advantages, whether it's a new graphite tennis racket, a high-performance sports car, or even the prompt, friendly service of a bank.

Production and marketing, therefore, work together to create goods and services that satisfy consumers' needs. The power to satisfy those needs is called *utility*. Five types of functional utility are important to consumers; utility of form, task, possession, time, and place. In addition to these functional utilities, a product might provide psychic utility as well.

Companies create *form utility* whenever they produce a tangible good—like a bicycle. They provide *task utility* by performing a task for someone else. However, merely producing a bicycle—or repairing it—doesn't guarantee consumer satisfaction. Consumers must want the bicycle—or need the repair—or no need is satisfied, and no utility occurs. So marketing decisions guide the production, or *operations,* side of business too. What do consumers really want to purchase and why?

Even when a company provides form or task utility, marketers must consider how to give consumers possession. Consumers must be able to obtain the product and have the right to use or consume it. Money is typically exchanged for *possession utility*. An antique bicycle on display, but not for sale, may be just what a consumer wants. But if the consumer can't buy it, the bicycle has no possession utility.

Providing the consumer with the product *when* he or she wants it is known as *time utility*. Having an ample supply of bicycles, cars, or bank tellers at the time of consumer need is thus another marketing requirement.

Place utility—having the product available where the customer can get it—is also vital to business success. Customers won't travel very far out of their way to get bicycles or cars. They're even less likely to travel long distances for everyday needs. That's why banks have branches. That's why 24-hour convenience markets, which sell gasoline and basic food items, are so popular.

Finally, consumers gain another major type of utility, *psychic utility,* when a product offers symbolic or psychological need satisfaction such as status or sex appeal. Psychic utility is usually achieved through product promotion (i.e., advertising).

Product utility is an essential component of marketing success, whether it be psychic utility or the functional utilities of form, task, possession, time, and place.

Laboratory Application

Choose a product and describe in detail how it provides you with psychic utility and/or the functional utilities of form, task, possession, time, and place.

---

ultimate goal is to use this marketing information to shape a new product or service or to reshape an existing product to more fully satisfy the customer's needs and wants. The ad in Exhibit 4–2 illustrates the confidence an advertiser gains from research. The ad's "voice" speaks as if Ford knows the reader very well—"Curiosity runs in your family," "You're always searching for the new and unexpected," and "Your Explorer is ready." The audacity to make such statements comes from studying the market thoroughly, having complete confidence in the research, and using that information to shape the product and the advertising.

Businesspeople often give the marketing process short shrift or misunderstand how to use it. Many companies introduce a product without a clear idea of its utility to the customer. And the consequences of such a short-sighted policy can be severe.

Perception, Exchanges, and Satisfaction

The final part of the definition of marketing reads: ". . . . to create exchanges that satisfy the perceived needs, wants, and objectives of individuals and organizations." Three related concepts are presented here: *perception, exchanges,* and *satisfaction.*

Ford Motor Company introduced the Explorer in response to marketing research showing that families wanted a four-wheel drive vehicle with ample interior space and a variety of optional amenities.

Perception

Consider first the concept of *perception* and how it relates to marketing and advertising. Classic studies show that people take action only when they have a goal. More important, however, they must perceive the goal and accept it as such before they will act.[4] Herein lie the roots of effective marketing—and especially advertising. Advertisers must first help potential customers perceive the existence of the product (awareness) and its value in supplying a want or need (utility). Once customers are aware of the product and its value and establish the goal of satisfying their want or need, they may be motivated to act. And the greater the customer's need, the greater the potential value or utility of the need-satisfying product.

Advertising plays a key role in creating awareness of a product and a sense of value in customers' minds. By using unusual sound effects, brilliant light, or sensuous music, for example, a TV commercial can capture a customer's attention and stimulate his or her emotions toward the goal of need or want fulfillment.[5]

Exchanges

Now consider the concept of **exchange,** in which one thing of value is traded for another thing of value. Any business transaction in which one person sells something to someone else is an exchange.

People engaging in a business exchange often feel apprehensive about losing. They worry that the exchange may not be equal even when it is truly equitable. The perception of unfairness is more likely if the customer has little knowledge of or experience with the product. Under such conditions, the more knowledgeable party (in this case, the seller) must reassure the buyer that an equal exchange is possible. If the seller can provide the information and inspiration the buyer seeks, the two may agree that a *perceived equal-value exchange* exists. Without this perception, an exchange is unlikely.

E X H I B I T • 4-3

Lee Iacocca, former Chrysler chairman, became a celebrity by successfully guiding the car company out of debt. Here he makes his final appearance as the company's top executive and spokesperson introducing the newly engineered Chrysler cars.

One role of marketing is to discover whether potential customers are likely to perceive that an equal-value exchange is possible and which functional or symbolic needs, wants, and objectives relate to such perceptions. This information guides the company through another role of marketing—**product shaping**—designing and building products to solve the customer's problems. It also helps the company's promotional staff and advertising agency develop advertising appeals for the product.

U.S. car makers recently experienced turbulent times. At one point, Chrysler Corporation went bankrupt and needed a government bailout to stay in business. Chrysler president Lee Iacocca turned the company around by giving car buyers two things: the functional and psychic utilities they wanted in a car and the perception they were getting an equal-value exchange for their money. Appearing in a series of ads, Iacocca demonstrated that Chrysler products were "better engineered"—that the product had been changed to have the proper utility. Then, by being the first to offer a whopping six-year or 60,000-mile warranty, he gave consumers the perception their investment would be well protected. These two marketing moves had the desired effect. Consumers responded to Iacocca's appeal and within 36 months gave Chrysler the most profitable year in its history, allowing the company to repay its government loan ahead of schedule. For the 1990s, Iacocca introduced new engineering—the cab-forward design (see Exhibit 4-3).

Satisfaction

Even after an exchange occurs, the concept of satisfaction is still an issue. *Whenever* they use the product, customers must be satisfied that it meets their needs or they won't think an equal-value exchange took place. When products perform adequately or well, satisfied customers create more sales. Advertising reinforces satisfaction by giving customers the information they need to: (1) defend the product against skeptical peers, family members, and business associates, and (2) persuade other prospects to buy it. Of course, if a product performs poorly, the negative effect can be even more far-reaching. In fact, good advertising for a poor product may put the manufacturer out of business. The better the advertising, the more people who will try the product. And the more who try it, the more who will reject it and refuse to buy it again.[6]

The Evolution of Marketing Theory

Over the years, the concept of *marketing* has been shaped by the relationship between the availability of goods and the ability or desire of customers to own or use them.

Until a century ago, very few products were available compared to the number of consumers who wanted them. So businesses focused on making more products. Marketing simply transported and distributed these limited goods. Demand was so high that companies didn't have to promote their products like they do today. Marketers refer to this time as the **production-oriented period.**

As mass production developed, however, more goods and services became available, and the focus of marketing changed to selling. Companies used sales techniques to attract consumers to their goods and services and distract them from competing products. This **sales-oriented period** was marked by extravagant advertising claims and a business attitude expressed by the Latin phrase *caveat emptor* ("let the buyer beware"). Occasionally the government stepped in as referee to ensure that fair business practices prevailed.

The marketing exchange cycle consists of several steps: (1) Consumers express their wants through research studies or their actions at the cash register. (2) Marketers interpret this demand for management, which then funds and develops products to satisfy the needs. (3) Marketers develop and implement a system to make the products available and execute the exchange. The consumers buy or reject the new or altered product—thus expressing their wants or needs again. Marketing, therefore, begins and ends with the consumer.

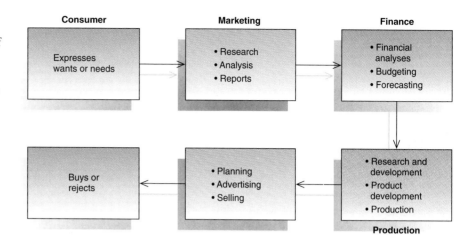

In the last half of the 20th century, as a deluge of products flooded the marketplace, business has found it more profitable to try to determine in advance what customers want and then develop goods and services to satisfy those desires. This is called the **marketing-oriented period.** A company steered by the marketing concept produces goods and services to meet customers' needs rather than trying to force customers to buy whatever the company wants to produce. Such companies are intensely interested in the consumer's point of view and allow that point of view to dictate many company decisions.

As Chapter 18 explains, even many nonprofit organizations operate under the marketing concept by seeking to develop services that satisfy their constituents' needs.

The Marketing Exchange Cycle

For firms operating under the marketing concept, the task of marketing is to manage the **marketing exchange cycle.** This responsibility is divided into three areas as shown in Exhibit 4–4:

1. Discovering, locating, and measuring the needs, attitudes, and desires of prospective customers.
2. Interpreting this information for management so goods and services may be improved and new ones developed.
3. Devising and implementing a system to make the good or service available, to inform prospective customers about the product's need-satisfying capabilities, and to execute the exchange.

As you can see, the cycle begins and ends with the consumer.

Where does advertising fit into this responsibility? Advertising is primarily concerned with the third phase in the marketing exchange cycle: informing consumers about the product and persuading them to buy it. Sometimes advertising may be directly involved in the exchange as in the case of mail-order advertising. But in any case, advertising cannot be effective unless a company coordinates all its marketing activities and performs them well.

The Key Participants in the Marketing Process

Satisfactory exchanges depend on three types of participants: *customers, markets* (groups of customers), and *marketers.*

Customers

Customers are the people or organizations who consume goods and services. They fall into three general categories: *current customers, prospective customers,* and *centers of influence.*

Current customers have already bought something from a business; in fact, they may buy it regularly. One way to measure a business's success is by the number of its current customers and their repeat purchases—i.e., their continuing goodwill. **Prospective customers** include people who are about to make an exchange or are considering it. If the exchange is made, a prospective customer becomes a current customer. **Centers of influence** are customers, prospective customers, or opinion leaders whose actions others respect and may emulate. A center of influence can often be the link to many prospective customers.

Markets

The second participant in the marketing process is the *market,* which is simply a group of current and prospective customers. A **market** comprises potential customers who share a common interest, need, or desire, who can use the good or service, and who can afford or are willing to pay for it. As we examine more fully in Chapter 5, a market rarely includes everybody. Companies advertise and sell to four broad classifications of markets:

1. **Consumer markets** include people who buy goods and services for their own use. Both Chrysler and Ford, for example, aim at the consumer market. But they also cater to different groups or segments within that market: single women, upscale young families, older retired people, outdoor sports enthusiasts, business executives, or people who live in a certain part of the country. Chapter 5 discusses some of the many ways to categorize consumer groups.

2. **Business markets** are composed of organizations that buy natural resources, component products, and services that they either resell or use to conduct their business or make another product. Two subtypes of business markets are *reseller markets* and *industrial markets.* **Reseller markets** buy products to resell them. Chrysler, for example, aims a portion of its marketing activities at a reseller market—its dealers. Likewise, a food manufacturer like Rosarito Mexican Foods first needs to convince food wholesalers and retail grocers to carry its brands, or they will never be sold to consumers. Reseller markets, therefore, are extremely important to most companies—even though most consumers are completely unaware of the marketing or advertising activities aimed at them.

   Industrial markets, which buy products needed to produce other goods and services, are also beyond the general consumer's view. Plant equipment and machinery manufacturers aim at industrial markets, as do office suppliers, computer companies, and telephone companies (see the ad in Exhibit 4–5). Chapter 5 lists additional types of industrial markets, categorizing them by such factors as their industry segment, geographic location, or size.

3. **Government markets** buy products to coordinate municipal, state, federal, and other government activities. Consider all the vehicles used by the post office; the weapons bought by the police and the military; and the desks, computers, and even pencils used by tax collectors. Some firms are immensely successful selling only to government markets.

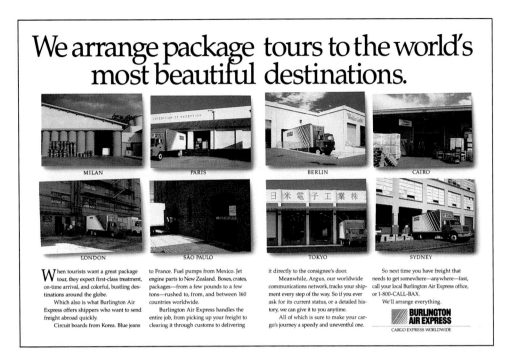

We arrange package tours to the world's most beautiful destinations.

MILAN   PARIS   BERLIN   CAIRO

LONDON   SÃO PAULO   TOKYO   SYDNEY

When tourists want a great package tour, they expect first-class treatment, on-time arrival, and colorful, bustling destinations around the globe.

Which also is what Burlington Air Express offers shippers who want to send freight abroad quickly.

Circuit boards from Korea. Blue jeans to France. Fuel pumps from Mexico. Jet engine parts to New Zealand. Boxes, crates, packages—from a few pounds to a few tons—rushed to, from, and between 160 countries worldwide.

Burlington Air Express handles the entire job, from picking up your freight to clearing it through customs to delivering it directly to the consignee's door.

Meanwhile, Argus, our worldwide communications network, tracks your shipment every step of the way. So if you ever ask for its current status, or a detailed history, we can give it to you anytime.

All of which is sure to make your cargo's journey a speedy and uneventful one.

So next time you have freight that needs to get somewhere—anywhere—fast, call your local Burlington Air Express office, or 1-800-CALL-BAX.

We'll arrange everything.

BURLINGTON AIR EXPRESS

CARGO EXPRESS WORLDWIDE

EXHIBIT • 4-5

This ad speaks to industrial markets and portrays Burlington Air Express as a full service worldwide shipper.

4. **International (or global) markets** include any of the other three markets located in foreign countries. Every country has consumers, resellers, industries, and governments. So what's the difference between the foreign market and the domestic U.S. or Canadian market for the same product? The answer is simply *environment*. The environment in France differs from that in Japan. The environment in Brazil differs from that in Saudi Arabia. And sometimes—as in the case of Switzerland—environments even vary widely within a single country. Targeting markets across national boundaries presents interesting challenges—and important opportunities—for contemporary advertisers, so we will deal with this subject wherever applicable throughout this book.

Marketers

The third participant in the marketing process is the *marketer*. **Marketers** include every person or organization that has goods, services, or ideas to sell. Manufacturers market tangible consumer and business products. Farmers market wheat; doctors market medical services; banks, stockbrokers, and insurance companies market financial products and services; and political organizations market philosophies and candidates. Marketers, of course, are also the individuals or organizations who use advertising.

HOW ADVERTISERS REACH THE MARKET

Now that we understand what marketing is, how the marketing exchange cycle works, and who the key participants in the marketing process are, let's briefly consider how marketers communicate with their markets. We look first at the nature of advertising as a science and an art and then at the basic process we humans use (whether through advertising or some other means) to communicate with one another.

The Art and Science of Advertising

Some people regard advertising as an art. Others consider it a science. Actually, advertising is a unique combination of the two. Talented, creative people with specialized knowledge in the **communicating arts** (writing and printing, drama and theatrical production, graphic design, photography, and so on) breathe life into advertising. The appropriateness of advertising creativity (the art), though, depends on how much marketers learn about people and groups of people from studies of the marketplace. Such studies, typically considered the province of the **behavioral** or **social sciences** (anthropology, sociology, psychology), provide necessary scientific data. How the marketer blends scientific data with art determines the strategy and the character of the advertising campaign. The richer and more accurate the data and the more communicative the art, the more successful the campaign.

In this and the next two chapters, we examine some of the scientific aspects of advertising strategy. And in Chapters 8 through 11, we see how this data, obtained scientifically, supports the creative processes.

The Marketing Communication Process

From our first cry at birth, our survival depends on our ability to inform or persuade others to take some action. And as we develop, we learn to listen and respond to others' messages. So to understand how marketers communicate, let's look first at how humans communicate.

The model in Exhibit 4–6 summarizes the series of events that take place when people share ideas. The communication process begins when one person *formulates* and *encodes* an idea as a message and sends it via some *medium* to another person. The person receiving the message must *decode* it, formulate a new idea, and then encode and send a new message. A message that acknowledges or responds to the original message constitutes *feedback*, which also affects the encoding of a new message.[7]

EXHIBIT • 4-6

In the human communication process, a sender converts a thought into real forms (language-based speech, writing, signaling), and transmits them via a medium to a receiver.

The receiver must convert the sender's language and actions (plus the effects of the medium) into a recognizable thought.

The cycle is complete when the receiver provides feedback to the sender, confirming whether both parties understand each other.

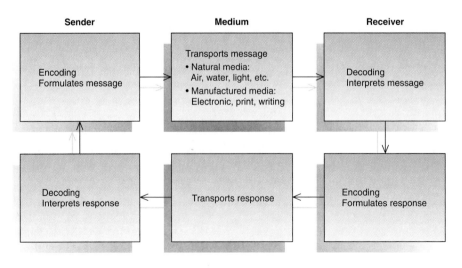

GUESS
WHAT
TYPE
BL   D
RICHM   ND
METR P LITAN
BL   D
SERVICE
REALLY
NEEDS.

Please help put an end to the shortage of type O blood in Richmond. Donate.
⬤ RICHMOND METROPOLITAN BLOOD SERVICE

EXHIBIT • 4-7

The missing "O"s—a technique that would be difficult to replicate in radio—serve to answer the question of this print ad for Richmond Metropolitan Blood Service and also increase the ad's memorability.

Because we all communicate regularly, we don't think about these complex processes. But the same basic sequence applies to marketing communications—so advertisers cannot afford to take this process for granted. Success depends on getting the message into the market's collective awareness.

Encoding

In the **encoding** stage, advertisers translate an idea or message into words and illustrations—or *symbols*. In abbreviated messages such as advertising, words and symbols are especially important. For symbols to work, sender and receiver must agree on their meaning.[8] For example, many car models use animals (cougar, jaguar, eagle) to represent the product because animals are accepted symbols of power, strength, or speed. Devising such symbols—encoding messages in terms that others will understand—is a major challenge of advertising.

The Medium

Another essential communication concept in marketing is the **medium,** the means or instrument by which the message is carried to the receiver. When a salesperson speaks, vocal chords vibrate air—the medium—which, in turn, vibrates the prospect's eardrums, creating the perception of sound and voice. The message is the spoken words.

As Marshall McLuhan observed nearly 30 years ago, the particular nature of any given medium affects the message dramatically, regardless of the message content. The salesperson's voice—that is, the vibrating air coming from the larynx—gives the presentation color, character, and emphasis. A radio commercial has no colors or graphics, but we still get a "picture" thanks to inflection, sound effects, and music. As McLuhan pointed out, since radio focuses intensely on just one sense—hearing—it can achieve great emotional "heat."[9] Likewise, only in a print ad could one omit certain letters to drive home a point (see Exhibit 4-7).

As a tool of marketing communication, each medium offers certain advantages and disadvantages in transmitting advertising messages. So as we shall see in Chapters 12 through 15, harnessing the particular attributes of a medium and recognizing its limitations are critical to the success of any advertising program.

Decoding

The way the message is **decoded**—interpreted by the receiver—is another challenge for the advertising person. We've all had the unpleasant experience of being misunderstood. And that, of course, is the last thing a marketer wants. Unfortunately, message interpretation is only partially determined by the words and the medium used. The unique characteristics of the *receivers* are also very important, and the sender often knows little or nothing about them. Attitudes, perceptions, personality, self-concept, and culture are just some of the many influences that affect the way people receive and respond to messages and how they behave as consumers in the marketplace.

Complicating this problem is the fact that the sender's advertising message must compete with hundreds of others every day. So the sender doesn't know *how* the message is received, or even *if* it's received, until some acknowledgment takes place.

Feedback

That's why feedback is so important. **Feedback** verifies that the message was received. In advertising, feedback may come in a variety of forms: redeemed coupons, telephone inquiries, visits to a store, requests for more information, sales, or responses to a survey. Dramatically low responses to an ad indicate a break in the communication process. Questions arise: Is the product wrong for the market? Is the message unclear? Are we using the right medium? Without feedback, these questions cannot be answered.

To better understand and anticipate how people will decode and respond to marketing communications, advertising professionals constantly monitor human perceptions, attitudes, motivations, and actions. This leads us into the broad subject of *consumer behavior*.

THE IMPORTANCE OF KNOWING THE CONSUMER

Do you know Joe Shields? Chances are you do. But, since he's fictitious, you may know him by another name. He's 22 years old, a little taller than average, good looking, and has curly, medium-length hair. Joe dresses casually but well, and he loves to have a good time. You've probably seen him cheering at football games, on the beach playing volleyball, or chatting with friends.

Joe has a strong personality. He plans to be a lawyer one day, which is no surprise. He is quite confident, somewhat opinionated, and has a way with words. Joe is not afraid to say what he wants, and he usually gets it. His friends look for his approval and tend to follow his lead. Joe's parents are pretty well-off. His dad develops real estate and seems to know everybody in town.

Currently a business major, Joe enjoys university life and is conscientious about his work. But that doesn't stop him from having a good time. He's not a loner or a homebody. Although he likes to party, he's not rowdy and at times can be serious and quiet.

Perhaps "casual" is the best way to describe Joe because even his personal relationships seem to be light and easy. Marriage and a family are a long way off, at least until after law school.

Do you recognize Joe? How well do you know him? Well enough to describe what kind of products he prefers? Do you think he eats out or cooks for himself? Does he ski? If so, what brands of gear does he buy? What radio stations does he listen to? What TV programs? Does he read the newspaper? If you were trying to advertise a sports car to Joe, what type of appeal would you use? What media?

Advertising people constantly try to keep individuals and groups of individuals (*markets*) interested in their products. To succeed, they need to understand what makes people like Joe Shields behave the way they do. The advertiser's goal is to get enough relevant market data to develop accurate profiles of buyers—to find the common ground (and symbols) for communication. This involves the study of **consumer behavior:** the activities, actions, and influencers of people who purchase and use goods and services to satisfy their personal or household needs and wants.[10] The behavior of **industrial buyers**—the people who purchase industrial goods and services for use in their business—is also very important. We examine this aspect of buying behavior in Chapter 5 as part of the discussion on market segmentation.

Consumer Behavior from the Advertising Perspective

Social scientists develop many sophisticated theories of consumer behavior. They give the marketing community a wealth of data and a variety of theoretical models to explain the sequence of behaviors involved in making a purchase decision. For our purposes, let's look at this information from the viewpoint of the advertiser.

Advertising's primary mission is to reach prospective customers like Joe Shields and influence their awareness, attitudes, and buying behavior. To do this, an advertiser must make the marketing communication process work efficiently.

The moment a medium delivers an advertising message to Joe Shields, Joe's mental computer runs a rapid evaluation program called the **consumer decision-making process.** This involves a series of subprocesses affected by a variety of influences. The conceptual model in Exhibit 4–8 presents the fundamental building blocks in the consumer decision-making process.

First, three **personal processes** govern the way Joe discerns raw data (*stimuli*) and translates them into feelings, thoughts, beliefs, and actions. These include the *perception,* the *learning,* and the *motivation processes.*

Second, an advertiser needs to understand how Joe's mental processes and behavior are affected by two sets of influences. **Interpersonal influences** include the consumer's *family, society,* and *culture.* **Nonpersonal influences**—factors often outside the consumer's control—include *time, place,* and *environment.* All these influences further affect the personal processes (perception, learning, motivation) mentioned above.

After dealing with these processes and influences, Joe faces the pivotal decision—to buy or not to buy. But taking that final step typically requires yet another process, the **evaluation of alternatives,** in which Joe chooses brands, sizes, styles, and colors. And even if Joe decides to buy, *postpurchase evaluation* will dramatically affect all his subsequent purchases.

Like the marketing communication process, the decision-making process is circular in nature. The advertiser who understands this process can develop messages more likely to reach and be understood by consumers.

Personal Processes in Consumer Behavior

The first task in promoting any new product is to create awareness—*perception*—that the product exists. The second is to provide enough information—*learning*—about the product for the prospective customer to make an informed decision. Finally, the marketer wants to be persuasive enough to stimulate the customer's desire—*motivation*—to satisfy his or her needs or wants by purchasing and repurchasing the product. These three personal processes of consumer behavior—perception, learning, and motivation—are extremely important to advertisers (see Exhibit 4–8).

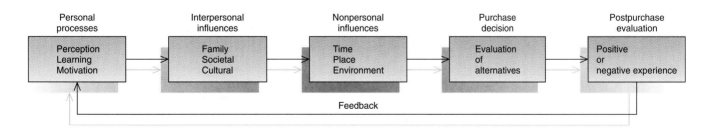

EXHIBIT • 4-8

The basic consumer decision-process comprises a set of fundamental steps that the consumer experiences during and after the purchase process. Advertising can affect the consumer's attitude at any point in this process. For the complete model of the process, see Exhibit 4–24 at the end of this chapter.

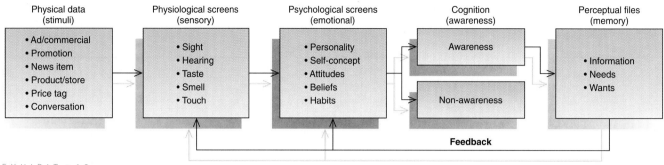

| Physical data (stimuli) | Physiological screens (sensory) | Psychological screens (emotional) | Cognition (awareness) | Perceptual files (memory) |

EXHIBIT • 4-9

The model of the consumer perception process portrays how the consumer perceives, accepts, and remembers an advertisement or other stimulus to buy.

By studying and understanding these mental processes, advertisers can better evaluate how people perceive their messages. They can determine what people think or know about their products, whether they have a particular attitude about them, and how prospective customers might develop the habit of purchasing them.

The Consumer Perception Process

The perception problem is the first and greatest problem advertisers face. Some marketers spend millions of dollars on national advertising, sales promotion, and point-of-purchase displays only to discover that many consumers don't remember their product or their promotion. The average adult is exposed to over 300 ads a day but notices only a handful and remembers even fewer.[11] How does this happen? The answer lies in the principle of perception. To understand these phenomena, let's look at what perception is and how the consumer perception process works.

Perception is our personalized way of sensing and comprehending the stimuli we are exposed to.[12] This definition suggests several key elements for understanding the consumer perception process, as shown in Exhibit 4–9.

Stimulus An outside **stimulus** is the physical data a person senses. When Joe Shields looks at a new automobile, the stimulus is the collection of paint, tires, glass, and steel. Likewise, when we look at a theater ad in the newspaper, we see type, art, and photography. That's the stimulus. So, for our purposes, assume that a stimulus is any ad, commercial, or promotion that confronts us.

A stimulus can appear in a variety of other forms: a window display at a local department store, the brightly colored labels on cans of Dole fruit cocktail, or even the price tag on a pair of skis at the Sport Chalet. These objects are all physical in nature. Like the ad shown in Exhibit 4–10, they stimulate our senses—with varying degrees of intensity—in ways that can be measured.

Perceptual Screens The second key element in the definition of perception is the personalized way of sensing the data—which brings us to the subject of *screens*. Before any data can be perceived, it must first penetrate a set of **perceptual screens,** the perceptual filters that messages must pass through.[13] There are two types of screens: *physiological* and *psychological.*

The **physiological screens** comprise the five senses—sight, hearing, touch, taste, and smell. They detect the incoming data and measure the

EXHIBIT • 4-10

In this ad, the "hidden" image is the logo for Colombian coffee—Juan Valdez and his faithful companion. DDB Needham Worldwide chose to design the ad as a color-blindness test to cleverly get across the message that consumers should look for the logo as a sign of quality. The ad will have difficulty penetrating the physiological screen of those who are truly red-green color blind.

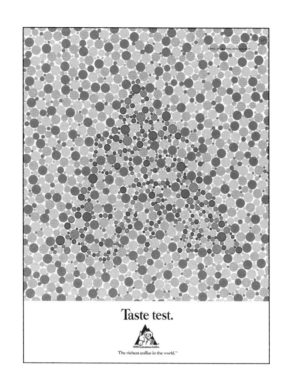

dimension and intensity of the physical stimulus. Obviously, a sight-impaired person can't read an ad in *Sports Illustrated*. If the type in a movie ad is too small for the average reader, it won't be read and perception will suffer. Similarly, if the music in a TV commercial for a furniture store is too loud, the viewer may change channels or even turn the TV off. Here, the advertiser's message is effectively screened out, perception will not occur, and the furniture will go unsold.

We are limited not only by the physical capacity of our senses but also by our feelings and interests. The consumer uses **psychological screens** to evaluate, filter, and personalize information according to subjective standards. More emotional in nature, these screens make evaluations based on criteria that include innate factors such as the consumer's personality and instinctive human needs, and learned factors such as self-concept, interests, attitudes, beliefs, past experience, and lifestyle. These screens help consumers formulate summary notions and concepts from sometimes unwieldy or complex data that may otherwise be too difficult to articulate. For example, perceptual screens help us accept or reject symbolic ideas such as the one suggested in Exhibit 4–11.

EXHIBIT • 4-11

In this ad for the U.S. Coast Guard, images replace words to symbolize the concepts of "float" or "sink"—two simple concepts that would be less communicative if expressed only in words.

EXHIBIT • 4-12

By challenging stereotypes in its advertising visuals, Maidenform reinforces the message that it understands women's varying needs —an appeal made credible by the fact that so few people see themselves fitting a stereotype.

VO: Somehow, women always seem to be portrayed like this. Or like this. Like this or like

this. Like this or like this. While there are many stereotypes of women, there aren't many

women who fit them. A simple truth known by all women, most men, and one lingerie company.

One study asked female consumers how they perceived the Maidenform brand. Many younger respondents described it as old-fashioned and conservative, a brand worn by older women as opposed to younger career women.[14] That was the respondents' reality. The product didn't fit their **self-concept—** the image we have of who we are and who we want to be. As a result, much of Maidenform's advertising didn't penetrate the younger consumers' screens. It went unnoticed, and future opportunities for sales to these women suffered. Maidenform's response was to use a bolder advertising approach to appeal to contemporary young women, while maintaining or not abandoning the older loyal Maidenform customer (as shown in Exhibit 4–12).

As the Maidenform example shows, advertisers face a major problem dealing with consumers' perceptual screens. As over-communicated consumers, we unconsciously screen out or modify many of the sensations that bombard us by rejecting those that conflict with our previous experiences, needs, desires, attitudes, and beliefs.[15] We simply focus on some things and ignore others. This is called **selective perception.** Hence, Goodyear Tire Stores may run many ads in the daily newspaper, but they won't penetrate the psychological screens of consumers who don't need new tires. Later these people will be unable to remember seeing the ads.[16]

Cognition   The third key element in our definition of perception is the concept of comprehension, or **cognition.** Once our senses detect the stimulus and allow it through the screens, we have an *awareness* of it. Since it relates to our previous experiences, we simultaneously *comprehend* and accept it. Now the act of perception has taken place.

This moment is an important experience for the consumer. Comprehension and acceptance of the stimulus make the perception come alive, placing it instantly in the consumer's reality zone.

Each of us has his or her own reality. For example, you may consider tacos advertised by Taco Bell to be "Mexican" food. That perception is your reality. But someone from Mexico might tell you that a fast-food taco bears little resemblance to an "authentic" Mexican taco. That person's reality, based on his or her perception, is considerably different. As a result, advertisers seek commonly shared perceptions of reality as a basis for their advertising messages (see Exhibit 4–13).

Bell bottom trousers epitomize the widely held perception of 70s fashion. Thus, they serve as a good metaphor for emphasizing the wide profit margins offered by Lee to retailers in the trade.

Our new price margins are the widest things we've offered since 1972.

Mental Files At the point of cognition, the consumer has to make a judgment—where to file the perception. The mind is like a memory bank, and the stored memories in our minds are called the **mental** (or *perceptual*) **files.** When we perceive new information, we must file it or we will instantly forget it. We file information both consciously and, more often, subconsciously.

We have files for our needs and wants, attitudes, preferences, beliefs, and habits. We even have files full of random information gleaned from past learning. Some of our files are very specific: for industries, products, services, brand names.

In today's highly communicative society, stimuli bombard our senses, and information crowds our mental files. To cope with the complexity of stimuli like advertising, we rank products and other data in our files by importance, price, quality, features, or a host of other descriptors. Unfortunately for many advertisers, consumers can rarely hold more than seven brand names in any one file—more often the number is one or two. The remainder either get discarded to some other file category or rejected altogether.[17] How many brands of coffee can you name, for example?

Because of our limited memory, we resist opening new files, and we avoid accepting new information inconsistent with what is already filed.[18] But once a new perception enters our files, the information from that perception alters the database on which our psychological screen feeds. Our mental files make major contributions to the screen-building process. For example, when middle-aged advertising media directors try to determine who reads *Rolling Stone* magazine (see Exhibit 4–14), they may first think of the draft resisters who fled to Canada during the Vietnam War. That perception may have been true 25 years ago but not today. The ad attempts to set them straight.

Since screens are such a major challenge to advertisers, it's important to understand what's in the consumer's mental files and, if possible, modify those files in favor of the advertiser's product. (See Ad Lab 4–B, "Positioning Strategy—Or How to Penetrate the Perceptual Screens.") That brings us to the second process in consumer behavior—learning.

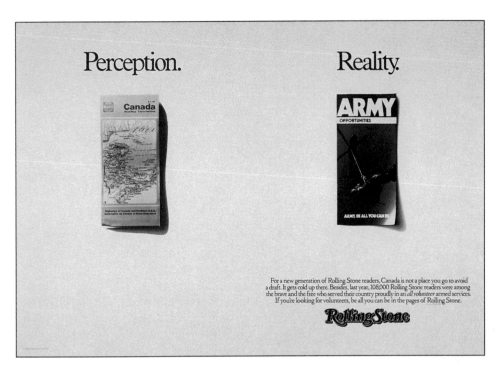

EXHIBIT • 4-14

If you were a teenager in the 60s—which many media directors were—this ad would stir your mental files and also tell you that the readers of *Rolling Stone* have changed since then.

The Consumer Learning Process

Each time we file a new perception in our minds it's an additional step in learning. In fact, many psychologists consider learning to be the most fundamental process in human behavior. But from the advertiser's perspective, perception is the most important because it precedes learning. In truth, perception and learning are a continuum, overlapping each other.

Like perception, learning works off the files and also contributes to them. Learning produces our habits and skills. It also contributes to the development of attitudes, beliefs, preferences, prejudices, emotions, and standards of conduct—all of which affect our perceptual screens and our eventual purchase decisions.

By definition, **learning** is a relatively permanent change in thought process or behavior that occurs as a result of reinforced experience. There are numerous theories of learning, but advertisers classify most into two broad categories—*cognitive theory* and *conditioning theory*—depending on the level of consumer involvement (high or low) required to make a purchase. **Cognitive theory** views learning as a mental process of memory, thinking, and the rational application of knowledge to practical problems. This theory may be an accurate description of the way people evaluate a complex purchase such as insurance, stocks and bonds, or industrial goods and services. **Conditioning theory**—also called *stimulus-response theory*—treats learning as a trial-and-error process and is more applicable to the less complex, basic purchases consumers make very day. Some *stimulus* triggers the consumer's need or want, which in turn creates the drive to *respond*. If the response the consumer selects reduces the drive, then satisfaction occurs, and the response is rewarded

AD LAB 4-B   Positioning Strategy—Or How to Penetrate the Perceptual Screens

Al Ries (chairman of the board) and Jack Trout (president) of Trout & Ries, Inc., are widely known for developing the "positioning" approach to advertising. Their book *Positioning: The Battle for Your Mind,* from which the following is adapted, has become an industry text. As a result, positioning has become a buzzword of marketing and advertising people not only in the United States and Canada but around the world.

Positioning is a simple principle that can best be demonstrated by asking yourself some basic questions. Who was the first person to fly solo across the North Atlantic? Right, Charles Lindbergh. Who was the second person to fly solo across the North Atlantic? Not so easy to answer, is it? Similarly, the first company to occupy the position in a prospect's mind is going to be awfully hard to dislodge: IBM in computers, Hertz in rental cars, Coke in cola.

Like a memory bank, the mind has a slot or position for each bit of information it has chosen to retain. In its operation, the mind is a lot like a computer. But there is one important difference. A computer has to accept what is put into it; the mind doesn't. In fact, quite the opposite. As a defense mechanism against the volume of today's communications, the mind screens and rejects much of the information it is offered. In general, the mind accepts new information only if it matches prior knowledge or experience. It filters out everything else.

For example, when a viewer sees a TV commercial that says, "NCR means computers," she doesn't accept it. IBM means computers; NCR means National Cash Register. The computer "position" in the minds of most people is filled by a company called IBM. For a competitive computer manufacturer to obtain a favorable position in the prospect's mind, it must relate its company to IBM's position.

To cope with advertising's complexity, people learn to rank products and brands. Imagine a series of ladders in the mind. On each step is a brand name, and each ladder represents a different product category. For advertisers to increase their brand preference, they must move up the ladder.

This is difficult, especially if the new category is not positioned against an old one. The mind has no room for the new and different unless it is related to the old. Therefore, for a truly new product, it's often better to tell the prospect what the product is not, rather than what it is.

The first automobile, for example, was called a horseless carriage, a name that positioned it against the existing mode of transportation. Current examples include words like *off-track betting, unleaded gasoline,* and *tubeless tires.*

Number-One Strategy

Successful marketers keep their eyes open to possibilities and strike before the product ladder is firmly fixed. The marketing leader usually moves the ladder into the consumer's mind with his or her brand nailed to the one and only rung.

Once there, what can a company do to keep its top-dog position? As long as a company owns the position, there's no point in running ads that scream "We're No. 1." It is much better to enhance the product category in prospects' minds. For many years, IBM ad campaigns typically ignored the competition and sold the value of computers—all computers, not just the company's models.

Number-Two Strategy

Most companies are in the number two, three, four, or even worse category. Nine times out of 10, these also-rans set out to attack the leader. The result is disaster.

In the communication jungle, the only hope is to be selective, to concentrate on narrow targets, and to practice segmentation. For example, Anheuser-Busch found an opening for a high-priced beer and filled it with Michelob. Advertisers must assess the competitors. They must locate weak points in their positions and then launch marketing attacks against them. Savin developed small, inexpensive copiers and took advantage of a weakness in the Xerox product line.

Simply stated, the first rule of positioning is this: You can't compete head-on with a company that has a strong, established position. You can go around, under, or over, but never head-to-head. The leader owns the high ground, the top position in the prospect's mind, the top rung of the product ladder.

Laboratory Applications

1. What type of car do you drive? What position does it occupy in its automotive category? Number one? Lower? What strategy would be most appropriate for advertising that model?

2. Find a magazine ad that appeals to you. First identify the product category. Then identify the strategy the advertiser used. Is it number one in its category? Or is it competing with number one? From what you know of the product and its position in the marketplace, is the strategy appropriate? Explain why or why not?

3. Think of several new concepts advertised by positioning them against old concepts. What slogans did they use?

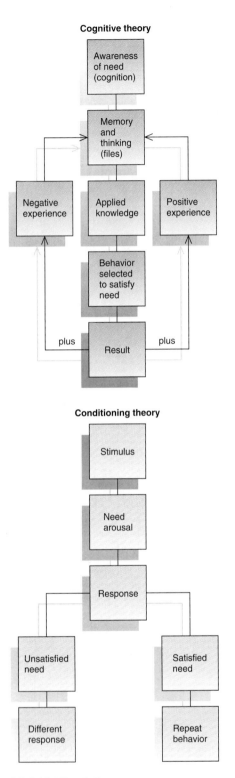

Cognitive theory

Awareness of need (cognition)

Memory and thinking (files)

Negative experience | Applied knowledge | Positive experience

Behavior selected to satisfy need

plus   plus

Result

Conditioning theory

Stimulus

Need arousal

Response

Unsatisfied need | Satisfied need

Different response | Repeat behavior

EXHIBIT · 4-15

Cognitive theory views learning as a mental process; *conditioning theory* treats learning as a trial-and-error process.

or reinforced. This produces repeat behavior the next time the drive is aroused, demonstrating that learning has taken place.[19] Exhibit 4–15 shows simple diagrams of these two theories.

Superior product performance, good service, and reminder advertising all provide purchase reinforcement. If learning is reinforced enough and repeat behavior is produced, a purchasing habit may result.

What if the purchase turns out to be unsatisfactory? Learning still takes place, but something else happens. As John O'Toole says, "The mightiest weapon consumers have, and the one manufacturers fear most, is their refusal to repurchase. Advertising is powerful in that it can get them to buy a product once. But if it doesn't please them, the heaviest media budget in the world won't get them to buy again."[20]

Good word of mouth works to create repeat purchases—leading to a purchasing habit. This is particularly important for businesses committed to long leases, large staffs, and many stores. Bad word of mouth, on the other hand, loses sales and cancels any chance of brand loyalty.

Repetition is important to learning. Just as a student prepares for an exam by repeating key information to memorize it, an advertiser must repeat key information to prospective and current customers so they remember the product's name and its benefits. Repeat messages help break through a customer's perceptual screens by rekindling memories of key information from prior ads. In Exhibit 4–16, Quebec-based Cossette Communications-Marketing used pairs of billboards for its client, Provigo grocery stores, each featuring a strong visual element similar to the other and positioned to be seen in succession. The repetition proved to be a highly successful awareness technique, producing $100 million in sales in just six months.[21]

Learning Produces Habits   The natural extension of learning is **habit,** an acquired or developed behavior pattern that becomes nearly or completely involuntary. The old cliché, "People are creatures of habit," is true.

Most consumer behavior is habitual for three interconnected reasons—it's safe, simple, and essential. First, regardless of how we learned to make our purchase decision (either through a cognitive or conditioning process), if we discover a quality product, brand, or service, we feel *safe* allowing ourselves to repurchase it through habit.

Second, habit is *simple and easy.* If we consider an alternative to our usual choice, we must think, evaluate, compare, and then decide. This is difficult, time-consuming, and risky.[22]

Finally, because habit is both safe and easy, we come to rely on it for daily living. Considering the number of purchases the average consumer makes every day, habit is *essential.* Imagine trying to rethink every purchase decision you make. It would be virtually impossible—not to mention impractical.

A major objective of many advertisers is to produce the phenomenon known as *brand loyalty,* a direct result of the habit of repurchasing. **Brand loyalty** is the consumer's conscious or unconscious decision—expressed through intention or behavior—to repurchase a brand continually.[23] This occurs because the consumer perceives that the brand offers the right product features, image, quality, or relationship at the right price.[24]

In the quest for brand loyalty, advertisers have three aims related to habits:

1. *Breaking habits:* get consumers to *unlearn* an existing purchase habit—that is, to stop buying their habitual brand and try a new one. Advertisers frequently offer incentives to lure customers away from old brands or stores.

2. *Acquiring habits:* help consumers learn to repurchase their brand or repatronize their establishment. For example, to get you started, record clubs offer free products the first month tied to a contract to purchase more later on.

Les histoires de Mario.

Le poisson de Provigo.

La beauté de Sarah.

Le concombre de Provigo.

EXHIBIT • 4-16

By repeating image elements on two successive billboards, Provigo, a grocery store chain in Canada, reinforces its message, creates reader involvement, and increases the probability that the passing motorist will remember it.

3. *Reinforcing habits:* remind current customers of the value of their original purchase and encourage them to continue purchasing. Many magazines, for example, offer special rates for regular subscribers.

Developing loyalty is a long-term objective of all marketers. Ironically, though, achieving brand loyalty today is more difficult due to consumers' increased sophistication and to the legions of habit-breaking, demarketing activities of competitive advertisers.[25]

Learning Produces Attitudes Attitudes and habits are two sides of the same coin. Habit is the behavioral side; attitude is the mental side. An **attitude** is the acquired mental position we hold in regard to some idea or object. It is the positive or negative evaluations, feelings, or action tendencies that we learn and cling to. To advertisers, gaining positive consumer attitudes is critical to success. Like habits, attitudes must be either capitalized on or changed. The Pepsi challenge campaign, for instance—with its comparison taste tests—aimed at changing the attitudes of Coca-Cola drinkers.

Learning Defines Needs and Wants The learning process is both instantaneous and long term. The moment we file a perception, some learning takes place. When we smell food cooking, we become aware we are hungry. As we collate the information in our mental files, comparing new perceptions with old ones, further learning takes place. The need may become a *want*. This leads us into the next personal process—motivation.

E X H I B I T • 4-17

The hierarchy of needs suggests that people resolve their needs according to a priority. Physiological and safety needs carry the greatest priority.

In advertising, the message must match the need of the market or the ad will fail.

Advertisers use marketing research to understand the level of need of their markets and use this information in determining the marketing mix.

Need	Product	Promotional appeal
Self-actualization	Golf clubs	"Time is to enjoy"
Esteem	Luxury car	"Be in control of the road"
Social	Pendant	"Show her you care"
Safety	Tires	"Bounces off hazards"
Physiological	Diet food	"Delicious without the fat"

The Consumer Motivation Process

Motivation refers to the underlying drives that contribute to our purchasing actions. These drives stem from the conscious or unconscious *goal* of satisfying our needs and wants. **Needs** are the basic, often instinctive, human forces that motivate us to do something. **Wants** are "needs" that we learn during our lifetime.[26]

Motivation cannot be directly observed. When we see people eat, we assume they are hungry, but we may be wrong. People eat for a variety of reasons besides hunger—they want to be sociable, it's time to eat, or they're bored or nervous.

Often a combination of motives underlies the decision-making process. The reasons (motives) some people stop shopping at Lucky Supermarket and switch to Von's may be that the Von's market is closer to home, that it has a wider selection of fresh produce, and (most likely) that they see other people like themselves shopping at Von's. Any one of these factors might be enough to make the shopper switch even if prices are lower at Lucky.

To better understand what motivates people, Abraham Maslow developed the classic model shown in Exhibit 4–17 called the **hierarchy of needs.** Maslow maintained that the lower, physiological and safety needs dominate human behavior and must be satisfied before the higher, socially acquired needs (or wants) become meaningful.[27]

The promise of satisfying a certain level of need establishes the basic promotional appeal for many advertisements. However, in such affluent societies as the United States, Canada, Western Europe, and Japan, most individuals pay little attention to physiological needs; they take satisfaction of these needs for granted. So, marketing and advertising campaigns portray the fulfillment of social, esteem, and self-actualization needs, and many offer the reward of better personal or love relationships (see Exhibit 4–18).

People with needs and wants are frequently unaware of them. For example, before the desktop computer, most people were completely unaware of any need or want for it. However, the moment a consumer consciously recognizes a product-related want or need, an interesting process begins. The consumer first evaluates the need or want and decides to either accept or reject it as worthy of action. Acceptance converts satisfaction of the want or need into a *goal,* which, in turn, creates the dedication—or the *motivation*—to reach a particular result. In contrast, rejection removes the necessity for action and thereby eliminates the goal and motivation to buy.

Advertising cannot serve simply as an awareness builder. It must do more. Advertising must stimulate a decision about wants and needs. An ad that effectively portrays a chicly-dressed model receiving enviable attention may

EXHIBIT • 4-18

The styling of this elegant Lineal Design pool chair is expressive of fine taste—an ideal product to own for someone seeking to feel a sense of achievement (an esteem need).

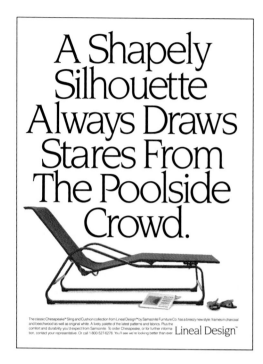

stimulate some men and women to recognize their need to be noticed and appreciated. If they accept this need, readers will formulate a goal: to shop for clothes that attract attention or recognition. If the ad clearly presents the name of the product or store, the advertiser may experience a sales increase.

Some people accuse advertisers of going too far in stimulating consumers' needs and wants. They assert that certain liquor ads, for example, contain concealed sexual images within the shadows and highlights of a glass, liquid, or ice cube. These people allege that embedded imagery plants the subconscious suggestion that liquor will resolve our need for a more active sex life. Are these claims true? Can decisions about needs and wants be encouraged by images and messages so well disguised that we can't see or hear them? For an answer, see Ad Lab 4–C, "Subliminal Manipulation: Fact or Fantasy?"

People usually are motivated by the benefit of satisfying some combination of two or more needs, and the needs may be both conscious and unconscious. *Motivation research* offers some insights into the underlying reasons for unexpected consumer behavior. We cover this subject more thoroughly in Chapter 6.

Before creating advertising messages, advertisers must carefully consider the goals that lead to consumer motivations. For example, Denny's Restaurants would make a costly mistake if its ads portrayed the benefit of a romantic interlude if the real goal of most Denny's customers is simply satisfying their need for a filling, low-priced meal.

Interpersonal Influences on Consumer Behavior

For the advertising professional, it's not enough just to know the personal behavioral processes of perception, learning, and motivation. Important **interpersonal influences** affect—and sometimes even dominate—these processes, and they also serve as guidelines and measuring sticks for consumer behavior. These interpersonal influences can best be categorized as the *family,* the *society,* and the *cultural environment* of the consumer.

AD LAB 4–C   Subliminal Manipulation: Fact or Fantasy?

Is it possible to manipulate people with subliminal advertising? This intriguing controversy started back in the 1950s when Vance Packard's best-seller, *The Hidden Persuaders*, described an experiment purporting to show that a message perceived, perhaps unconsciously, at levels below the "limen," or perceptual threshold, could motivate consumers.

In the six-week experiment, the words *Eat Popcorn* and *Drink Coca-Cola* were projected on the screen for 1/3,000 of a second during a showing of the movie *Picnic*. Sales allegedly jumped 57 percent for popcorn and 18 percent for Coca-Cola. As expected, this finding caused quite a stir. Some states passed laws to prevent the practice. However, this study has never been replicated successfully. One reason perhaps was that a number of factors may have affected the results of the experiment. For example, the movie shown during the experiment included many scenes of people eating and drinking in hot summer weather.

If subliminal advertising could persuade people "against their will," profound ethical questions would be raised. But researchers generally agree that this isn't possible. First, the threshold (or level) at which people perceive visual and aural stimuli varies greatly. Obviously, people with good eyesight perceive visual stimuli more easily than people who wear glasses. Furthermore, researchers can measure *galvanic skin response* (GSR)—changes in the electrical activity of the skin—when certain stimuli are introduced. But no GSR can be detected during supposed subliminal perception states. The conclusion, therefore, is that no message has been perceived. And even if a message were perceived, it could be easily distorted: "Drink Coke" might make a viewer "go smoke" or "think jokes."

The subliminal perception controversy was rekindled with the publication of books that accused advertising people of planting hidden sexual messages in print ads—particularly in the ice cubes portrayed in liquor advertising. *Subliminal Seduction* (subtitled "Here Are the Secret Ways Ad Men Arouse Your Desires to Sell Their Products") and *Media Sexploitation* include numerous examples of what the author (Wilson Bryan Key) believes are sexual symbols, four-letter words, and pornographic pictures buried in the otherwise bland content of various ads. He concludes that such "hidden persuaders" were carefully contrived by major advertisers and their agencies to seduce consumers at a subliminal level.

While Key's theories have been widely discredited by numerous academic studies, the fact is that virtually all photos used in national advertising are retouched, either by hand or electronically, to correct imperfections or add visual effects (see Chapter 10). At this point in the production process, some mischievous creativity could conceivably occur. A photo retoucher could, for example, add some carefully disguised sexual element into an ad which, when reduced to final size, would not be noticeable and would only be known to him or her. However, this would be considered highly unprofessional and unethical and, if discovered, would be cause for immediate termination of the offender. It would also seriously endanger the agency's relationship with its client.

As far as Key's idea of the insidious cunning of marketing decision makers goes, it is interesting to note that in more than 600 pages on the subject, he mentions not one individual who admits to, or even accuses others of, being involved in subliminal embedding.

Dr. Jack Haberstroh, professor in the School of Mass Communications at Virginia Commonwealth University, investigated Key's charge that S-E-X is embedded on the face of Ritz crackers. His research even included a visit to a Ritz cracker factory. He concludes that the charges of S-E-X written on Ritz crackers in particular and of subliminal advertising in general are "preposterous, absurd, ludicrous, and laughable."

Laboratory Applications

1. Would words with sexual connotations hidden in an advertisement motivate you to purchase a product? Why or why not?
2. Do you feel that appeals to the consumer's prurient interests can help sell products? If so, what kinds of products?

Family

Just think for a moment about where your attitudes and beliefs about ethical values, religion, work, gender roles, other ethnic groups, political philosophy, sexual behavior, right and wrong, and economics come from. They receive their initial direction in the family setting. From an early age, family communication affects our socialization as consumers—our attitudes toward many products and our purchasing habits.[28] This influence is usually strong and long-lasting. A child who learns that the "right" headache relief is Bayer aspirin and the "right" name for appliances is General Electric has his or her adult purchasing behavior pretty well formed.

EXHIBIT • 4-19

Contemporary social classes.
The groups outlined in this exhibit are just 10 of 50 Microvision lifestyle segments defined by National Decision Systems, a division of Equifax.

Upper Crust
Metropolitan families, very high income and education, manager/professionals; very high installment activity

Mid-Life Success
Families, very high education, managers/professionals, technical/sales, high income; super-high installment activity

Movers and Shakers
Singles, couples, students, and recent graduates, high education and income, managers/professionals, technical/sales; average credit activity, medium-high installment activity

Successful Singles
Young, single renters, older housing, ethnic mix, high education, medium income, managers/professionals; very high bankcard accounts, very high installment activity, very low retail activity

Stars and Stripes
Young, large school-age families, medium income and education, military, precision/craft; average credit activity

Social Security
Mature/seniors, metro fringe, singles and couples, medium income and education, mixed jobs; very low credit activity

Middle of the Road
School-age families, mixed education, medium income, mixed jobs; very high revolving activity, very high bankcard accounts

Trying Metro Times
Young, seniors, ethnic mix, low income, older housing, low education, renters, mixed jobs; low credit activity, medium-high retail activity

Low-Income Blues
Blacks, singles and families, older housing, low income and education, services, laborers; low credit activity, medium-high retail activity

University USA
Students, singles, dorms/group quarters, very low income, medium-high education, technical/sales; low credit activity, high percent new accounts

Recent research, however, indicates that the family influence is diminishing as working parents take a less active role in raising their children and youngsters look outside the family for social values.[29] As this happens, the influence of the social and cultural environment intensifies.

Society

The community we live in exerts a strong influence on all of us. When we affiliate with a particular societal division, or value the opinions of certain people, or identify with some special-interest group, it affects not only our views on life but also our perceptual screens and eventually the products we buy.

Societal Divisions Sociologists traditionally divided societies into social classes: upper, upper-middle, lower-middle, and so on. They believed that people in the same social class tended toward similar attitudes, status symbols, and spending patterns.

But today, this doesn't apply to most developed countries. North American society, especially, is extremely mobile—physically, socially, and economically. Americans, for example, believe strongly in "getting ahead," "being better than your peers," "moving up," and "winning greater admiration and self-esteem." As the famous U.S. Army campaign illustrates, advertisers often capitalize on this broad-based desire to "be all you can be."

Due to this mobility, to dramatic increases in immigration, and to the high divorce rate, social class boundaries have become quite muddled. Single parents, stockbrokers, immigrant shopkeepers, retired blue-collar workers, and bankers, for example, all see themselves as part of the great middle class.[30] So middle class just doesn't mean anything anymore. From the advertiser's point of view, social class no longer represents a functional or operational set of values.

To deal with these often bewildering changes, marketers seek new ways to classify societal divisions and new strategies for appealing to them. We discuss some of these in Chapter 5. Exhibit 4–19 outlines some of the more

EXHIBIT • 4-20

The reader who feels some kinship to the group of individuals pictured in this advertisement may very likely perceive them as a reference group.

contemporary classifications marketers use to describe society today: for example, Mid-Life Success, Movers and Shakers, Stars and Stripes, and University USA.

Reference Groups Most of us are concerned with how we appear to people whose opinions we value. We may even pattern our behavior after members of some groups we affiliate with. This is the significance of **reference groups**—people we try to emulate or whose approval concerns us. Reference groups can be personal (family, friends, co-workers) or impersonal (movie stars, professional athletes, business executives). A special reference group—our peers—exerts tremendous influence on what we believe and the way we behave. To win acceptance by our peers (fellow students, co-workers, colleagues), we may purchase a certain style of clothing, choose a particular place to live, and acquire habits that will earn their approval. The ad in Exhibit 4–20 indicates that one of the benefits gained from an exercise regimen is the camaraderie and approval of like-minded people—a reference group.

Often an individual is influenced in opposite directions by two reference groups and must choose between them. For example, a college student may feel pressure from some friends to join a Greek house and from others to live independently off-campus. A local apartment complex might successfully employ the appeal of reference groups in ads targeted to students.

Opinion Leaders An **opinion leader** is some person or organization whose beliefs or attitudes are respected by people who share an interest in some specific activity. All fields (sports, religion, economics, fashion, finance, politics) have opinion leaders. An opinion leader may be a knowledgeable friend or some expert we don't know personally but whose authority is credible. We reason, "If so-and-so believes Marker makes the best ski bindings, then it must be so. He knows more about the sport than I do." So the purchasing habits and testimonials of opinion leaders are important to advertisers.

When choosing an opinion leader as a spokesperson for a company or product, advertisers must understand the company's market thoroughly. For example, even though executives in the company may not relate to the spokesperson, the company must allow market tastes and interests to dictate its actions. A spokesperson who is out of sync with the market undermines his or her own credibility—and the company's. The ad in Exhibit 4–21, for example, illustrates a company seeking to relate to its target market through a cutting-edge professional—tennis star André Agassi.

Tennis star—and fashion maverick—
André Agassi is not just different. He's
better. And so, by implication, are
Donnay tennis rackets.

Culture and Subculture Culture has a tenacious influence on the consumer. Americans love to eat hot dogs, peanut butter, corn on the cob, and apple pie. Canada, Russia, Germany—every country has its own favorite specialties. And advertisers find it nearly impossible to change these tastes.

The United States and Canada embrace many subcultures, some of them quite large. They may be based on race, national origin, religion, language, or geographic proximity. The advertiser must understand these subcultures, since differences among them may affect responses to both products and advertising messages.

The United States, in particular, is a great melting pot of minority subcultures. According to the U.S. Census Bureau, 31 million African-Americans, 22 million Hispanics, and 7 million Asians lived in the United States in 1990—plus an unknown number of undocumented foreign nationals. In 1990, these three minority groups alone accounted for over 21 percent of the American population, and by the year 2000, they may account for more than 25 percent.[31] Canada has two major subcultures—anglophones and francophones—based on language (English and French) plus a mosaic of many other cultures based on ethnic and national origin.

Subcultures tend to transfer their beliefs and values from generation to generation. Racial, religious, and ethnic backgrounds affect consumers' preferences for styles of dress, food, beverages, transportation, personal-care products, and household furnishings, to name a few. As we saw in Chapter 3, many advertising agencies now specialize in minority markets as more advertisers recognize that an appeal tailored to minorities makes good business sense (see Exhibit 4–22).[32]

Just as in North America, the social environments in Italy, Indonesia, and Upper Volta are based on language, culture, literacy rate, religion, and lifestyle. Advertisers who market products globally can't ignore these customs.

In North America, advertising encourages us to keep our mouths clean, our breath fresh, and our teeth scrubbed. On the other hand, people in some

4:13 p.m., September 20, 1992. Courthouse Market, Route 3, King George, Virginia. The Accord Sedan.   HONDA

EXHIBIT • 4–22

As awareness of the opportunities presented by ethnic markets has grown, so has the number of ad agencies specializing in ads aimed at those market segments. Ethnic specialty ads typically feature an individual from the targeted group and usually appear in publications or on shows whose audiences are primarily from that ethnic background.

southern European countries consider it vain and improper to overindulge in toiletries. Consumers in the Netherlands and United Kingdom use three times as much toothpaste as those in Spain and Greece. To communicate effectively with Spanish consumers, who view toothpaste as a cosmetic product, advertisers use chic creative executions rather than dry, therapeutic pitches.[33]

In summary, many interpersonal factors influence us as consumers. They all have an important effect on our mental files, screen building, and subsequent purchase decisions. An awareness of these interpersonal influences helps marketers—domestic or international—create the strategies on which much advertising is based.

Nonpersonal Influences on Consumer Behavior

Numerous **nonpersonal influences** may also affect a consumer's final purchase decision. The most important nonpersonal influences—*time, place,* and *environment*—are typically beyond the consumer's control but not necessarily the advertiser's.

Time

The old saw, "timing is everything," certainly applies to marketing and advertising. A special three-day weekend sale may provide just the added incentive to break through customers' perceptual screens and bring them into a store. But running a commercial for that sale on Sunday evening would be a waste of advertising dollars.

Likewise, the consumer's particular need may be a function of time. Consumers don't need snow tires in the summer (although some off-season promotions do work). But if we unexpectedly get a flat on the highway, time is suddenly the most important consideration. As we see in our chapters on media, companies must plan all their marketing activities (including advertising) with the consumer's time clock in mind.

Place

Although Joe Shields, our imaginary college student, decides to purchase a product, he will still hesitate if he doesn't know where to buy it or if it isn't available in a convenient or preferred location. Similarly, if consumers believe a particular brand is a specialty good but it suddenly appears everywhere, their perception of the product's "specialness" may diminish. For these reasons, marketers carefully weigh consumer demand when deciding where to build stores or offer their products, and they devote much advertising time and space to communicating the convenience of location. *Place* is an important element of the marketing mix and will be discussed further in Chapter 5.

Environment

Many **environments**—ecological, social, political, technical, economic, household, and point-of-sale location, to mention a few—can affect the purchase decision. For example, during a recession, advertisers can't expect to penetrate the perceptual screens of consumers who don't have enough money to buy. And no matter how good the advertising or how inexpensive the price, NRA memberships aren't likely to be a hot item with members of the Audubon Society. On the other hand, an enticing display next to the cash register can improve sales of low-cost impulse items. Advertisers must consider the influence of the purchase environment on the consumer's decision processes.

International Environments

Global marketers are especially concerned with the purchase environment. In countries where people earn little, demand for expensive products is low. So the creative strategy of an automobile advertiser might be to target the small group of wealthy, upper-class consumers. In a country with a large middle class, the same advertiser might be better off mass marketing the car and positioning it as a middle-class product.

Likewise, the state of a country's technological development affects its economic and social conditions—and the prospects for advertisers of certain goods and services. For example, countries that don't manufacture computers might be poor markets for components such as disk drives and microprocessors. On the other hand, advertisers of low-priced, imported computers might do very well.

Finally, some foreign governments exert far greater control over their citizens and businesses than the U.S. and Canadian governments do. For example, until fairly recently, virtually no American-made products could be sold in many Eastern bloc countries or China. They simply weren't allowed. Political control often extends to which products companies may advertise and sell, which media they use, and what their ads say.

The political environment affects media availability as well. For example, the fall of communism in the Eastern bloc spurred the introduction of a Hungarian edition of *Playboy;* distribution of *The Wall Street Journal/Europe* in Hungary, Poland, and Yugoslavia; and sales of *USA Today International* in Hungary and in Poland.[34] Eastern Europeans, hungry for news from the West, provide a motivated market for these types of publications (see Exhibit 4–23).

In the European Community (EC), the Maastricht Treaty fostered a unified system of pan-European trade, finance, labor, and regulatory codes. Barriers to the flow of people, goods, and money within the EC have gradually fallen, making it easier than ever for advertisers to coordinate pan-European ad campaigns. U.S. and Canadian advertisers are well aware of the opportunity: a barrier-free EC means a $4 trillion market of 320 million consumers.

EXHIBIT • 4-23

The Wall Street Journal/Europe and *USA Today International* give advertisers new opportunities to reach the European market. These newspapers also publish Asian editions.

To better reach the changing European market, IBM started pan-European image advertising in the 1980s and followed up with its first pan-European product ad campaign in 1991. "The more Europe becomes integrated, the more important it is to have really consistent brands and advertising throughout the European Community," says Felix Bjorklund, IBM's European communications vice president. The pan-European approach also saved IBM money. By eliminating duplicate creative and production costs—only the language of the voice-overs varied—the company saved $2 million.[35]

The Purchase Decision and Postpurchase Evaluation

Now that we understand what all the elements are, let's examine the whole process involved in a typical purchase decision—the decision to buy a new blouse—made by a typical consumer—Joe Shields' younger sister, Christine. To help follow this process and see the interrelationship of the many behavioral factors we've discussed, study the complete model of the consumer decision-making process shown in Exhibit 4–24.

Christine lives at home and attends the local community college. Although she has a part-time job, she is still supported by her parents and therefore has to act conservatively when it comes to spending money.

One day, thumbing through *Elle,* Christine sees a warmly colored ad portraying an elegantly dressed young woman enjoying a candlelight dinner with an attractive man. The blouse catches Christine's attention. Its feminine tailoring, understated design, and rich silk fabric exude class—it's her kind of style. (See Ad Lab 4–D: "Applying Consumer Behavior Principles to Ad Making.") Christine's eyes drift across and down the page. The signature reads: "Escada at Saks Fifth Avenue."

In one split second her mind leaps from perception to motivation.

She wants it!

The next day she's at Saks. The ad has already done its work; the purchase decision process is well under way. At the point of making a purchase decision, though, consumers like Christine typically search, consider, and compare alternative brands.

While looking for the advertised blouse, Christine encounters a variety of alternative styles and labels by names she knows and trusts: Donna Karan, Liz Claiborne, Yves St. Laurent, Chanel.

Consumers evaluate alternatives (called the **evoked set**).[36] To do this, they establish **evaluative criteria,** the standards they use to judge the features and benefits of alternative products. Not all brands make it to the evoked set. In fact, based on their mental files, most consumers usually consider no more than four or five brands—which presents a real challenge to advertisers. If none of the alternatives meets the evaluative criteria, the consumer may reject the purchase entirely or postpone the decision.

Christine finds her "dream blouse." It doesn't look the same on the hanger as it did in the ad, however. And she's also found two others she likes—all attractive, all expensive. As she carries the blouses to the fitting room, she considers their unique qualities of style and design: "This one may be a little too dressy." "This one I could wear to parties." "This one would be okay for school, but I'm not sure about evening."

Christine compares the blouses, considering style, material, possible uses, and price (they are all within $15 of each other). She decides the advertised Escada really does make her look great. The purchase decision is complete when she signs on the dotted line (probably using her mother's charge card).

On the way home, Christine considers what she just did. The **postpurchase**

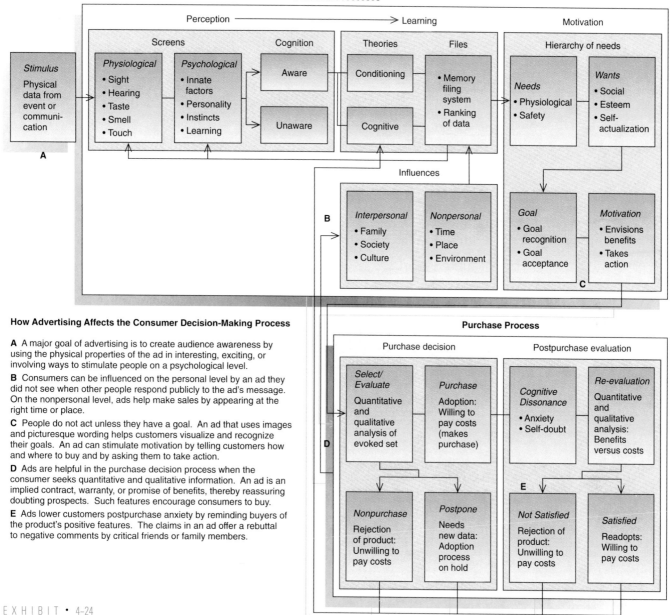

EXHIBIT · 4-24

The complete model of the consumer decision-making process.

How Advertising Affects the Consumer Decision-Making Process

A A major goal of advertising is to create audience awareness by using the physical properties of the ad in interesting, exciting, or involving ways to stimulate people on a psychological level.

B Consumers can be influenced on the personal level by an ad they did not see when other people respond publicly to the ad's message. On the nonpersonal level, ads help make sales by appearing at the right time or place.

C People do not act unless they have a goal. An ad that uses images and picturesque wording helps customers visualize and recognize their goals. An ad can stimulate motivation by telling customers how and where to buy and by asking them to take action.

D Ads are helpful in the purchase decision process when the consumer seeks quantitative and qualitative information. An ad is an implied contract, warranty, or promise of benefits, thereby reassuring doubting prospects. Such features encourage consumers to buy.

E Ads lower customers postpurchase anxiety by reminding buyers of the product's positive features. The claims in an ad offer a rebuttal to negative comments by critical friends or family members.

evaluation begins. She suddenly envisions her mother's negative reaction. Maybe she shouldn't have spent so much. She starts to worry—and to plan.

"It really is a lovely blouse, and it's very well made, and I'll get a lot of use out of it," she says to herself (to her mother).

A key feature of the postpurchase evaluation is *cognitive dissonance*. The **theory of cognitive dissonance**—also called **postpurchase dissonance**[37] —is that people strive to justify their behavior by reducing the dissonance, or inconsistency, between their cognitions (their perceptions or beliefs) and reality. In fact, research shows that, to combat dissonance, consumers like Christine are more likely to read ads about brands they've already purchased than about new products or competing brands.[38]

When Christine gets home, she pores over the ad in *Elle* one more time, then leaves the magazine on the coffee table open to that page (for her mother to

AD LAB 4-D   Applying Consumer Behavior Principles to Ad Making

When Jonathan's Uptown restaurant in Charlotte, North Carolina, chose Loeffler Ketchum Mountjoy to handle its advertising, agency staff worried. They would have to try to deliver two messages because Jonathan's featured two major benefits—fine dining and jazz music. They knew consumers become easily confused when advertisers try to communicate multiple messages simultaneously. In this case, "Is it a restaurant, or is it a jazz club?"

As with many ad campaigns, research played an important role for Jonathan's. After researching the advertising done by other restaurants in Charlotte, recounts art director Kathy Izard, agency staff realized that Jonathan's possessed something rare in restaurant advertising—the potential to establish a unique position. Jonathan's was a place to spend an entire evening.

With that position, both of Jonathan's features could be presented as part of one "big idea." Now agency staff could move forward to focus on ways to penetrate consumers' perceptual screens and get the consumer learning process working. One of the ads developed to accomplish the task is shown below.

Laboratory Applications

Study the visuals, the words, and the overall design of this ad. How do these elements help the ad accomplish the following tasks:

1. Penetrate consumer perceptual screens.
2. Stimulate consumer learning.
3. Utilize the consumer's existing perceptual files.
4. Stimulate consumer wants and needs to affect motivation.

discover). Then she phones her friend. She describes the purchase, emphasizing its value, the good use and enjoyment she will have wearing it, and how expensive it was.

During the postpurchase period, the consumer may enjoy the satisfaction of the purchase and thereby receive reinforcement for the decision. Or the purchase may turn out unsatisfactory for any reason. In either case, feedback from the postpurchase evaluation updates the consumer's mental files, affecting perceptions of the brand and similar purchase decisions in the future.

Joe and Christine Shields may each typify a particular group of consumers. Marketers are interested in defining target markets and developing effective marketing strategies for groups of consumers who share similar characteristics, needs, motives, and buying habits. These are the subjects of market segmentation and the marketing mix, the focus of Chapter 5.

Summary

Marketing is the process companies use to make a profit by satisfying their customers' needs for products. At the core of marketing is the perceived equal-value exchange. There are three phases in the marketing-exchange cycle: finding out who customers are and what they want; interpreting this information for management in order to shape products; and devising strategies to inform customers about the product's utility and to make it available.

Advertising is concerned with the third step in the marketing process. It is one of several tools marketers use to inform, persuade, and remind groups of customers, or markets, about their goods and services. Advertising effectiveness depends on the communication skill of the advertising person. It also depends on the extent to which firms correctly implement other marketing activities, such as market research and distribution.

There are three categories of participants in the marketing process: customers, markets, and marketers. To reach customers and markets, advertisers use the marketing communication process, an extension of the human communication process.

Because their job is to match people and products, advertisers are keenly interested in consumer buying behavior. Consumer advertising aims at motivating, modifying, or reinforcing consumer attitudes, perceptions, beliefs, and behavior. It must effectively blend data from the behavioral sciences (anthropology, sociology, psychology) with the communicating arts (writing, drama, graphics, photography). Advertisers study the behavioral characteristics of large groups of people to create advertising aimed at those groups.

Successful advertising people understand the complexity of human behavior. Consumer behavior is governed by three personal processes: perception, learning, and motivation. These processes determine how consumers see the world around them, how they learn information and habits, and how they actualize their personal needs and motives. Two sets of influences also affect consumer behavior. Interpersonal influences include the consumer's family, society, and culture. Nonpersonal influences include time, place, and environment. These factors combine to determine how the consumer behaves, and their influence may differ considerably from one country to another. By evaluating the effect of these factors on groups of consumers, advertisers may determine how best to create their messages.

Once customers or prospects are motivated to satisfy their needs and wants, the purchase process begins. Based on certain standards they have established in their own minds, they evaluate various alternative products—the evoked set. If none of the alternatives meets their evaluative criteria, they may reject the purchase or postpone it. If they do make the purchase, they may experience postpurchase dissonance in the form of self-doubt and concern. One of the most important roles of advertising is to help people cope with dissonance by reinforcing the correctness of their purchase decision. The result of the postpurchase evaluation will greatly affect the customer's attitude toward future purchases.

Questions for Review and Discussion

1. What is a process? Give an example of an advertising-related process.
2. What is utility, and how does it relate to advertising?
3. What is the significance of the perceived equal-value exchange?
4. What is a market, and what are the different types of markets?
5. How does an advertising person control or influence the communication process?
6. Which consumer behavior process presents the greatest problem to advertisers?
7. How does the learning process affect your behavior as a consumer?
8. What is the significance of Maslow's hierarchy of needs to advertisers?
9. What are some examples of how environmental influences might affect consumer behavior in international markets?
10. How does the theory of cognitive dissonance relate to advertising?

"Woman In Repose"

Levi's
JEANS FOR
WOMEN

Market Segmentation and the Marketing Mix: Matching Products to Markets

Objective: To describe how marketers use behavioral characteristics to cluster prospective customers into market segments. Since no product or service can please everybody, marketers need to select the specific target markets that offer the greatest potential for sales. By so doing, marketers can fine-tune their mix of product-related elements (the 4Ps), including advertising, to match the needs, wants, or desires of the target market.

After studying this chapter, you will be able to:

- Explain how the majority fallacy relates to market segmentation and advertising.

- Discuss the steps in the marketing process and how they are linked.

- Identify the methods used to segment consumer and business markets.

- Explain the process and the importance of aggregation to marketing.

- Discuss the target marketing process.

- Describe the elements of the marketing mix and their roles.

- Explain the role and importance of branding.

n its time, the trip was the most daring of adventures—17,000 miles and five months on a clipper ship from New York around South America to a rowdy frontier town aflame with gold fever. Imagine the awe and the excitement of Mr. Strauss, a young German immigrant, when he stepped off the ship in San Francisco in 1853.

Strauss came to San Francisco at the invitation of his brother-in-law, David Stern. Seeing the city's gold-boom economy, Stern sensed an opportunity for a thriving dry goods business. Strauss brought supplies for the business with him, including canvas for tents and Conestoga wagon covers.

By the time he reached San Francisco, though, Strauss had sold virtually all his merchandise to the other passengers—everything except the canvas. Before long, the inventive young entrepreneur came upon an idea for selling that as well.

"Should'a brought pants," the prospectors and gold miners told him. "Pants don't wear worth a hoot in the diggins!"

Strauss immediately took the heavy brown canvas to a tailor and created pants that he called "waist-high overalls." In fact, these were the world's first jeans, a term derived from the cotton trousers (called *genes* by the French) worn by ancient-day sailors from Genoa, Italy.

Word of the quality of "those pants of Levi's" spread quickly, and young Levi Strauss began turning out dozens of pairs. Exhausting his original supply of canvas, Levi switched to a sturdy serge fabric made in Nimes, France, called *serge de Nimes*. Later, the name of the fabric was conveniently shortened to "denim." And with the development of an indigo dye, the natural brown color turned to the now familiar deep blue.

While Levi's new product achieved rapid acceptance, prospectors found that the weight of gold nuggets caused the pockets to rip. Ever alert for ways to improve quality, Strauss was quick to adopt—and patent—the novel idea of riveting the pocket corners for added strength. To this day, rivets remain one of the hallmarks of the stiff, shrink-to-fit, button-fly pants, now known as Levi's "501" jeans (see Exhibit 5–1).

EXHIBIT • 5-1

This ad demonstrates the rugged Levi jeans of the post–Gold Rush days and promotes the unique feature that made the product famous—copper rivets.

Today, Levi Strauss & Co. is perceived as an American heritage. In keeping with that image, the company often demonstrates a strong sense of social responsibility such as this quilt commemorating Levi workers who died of AIDS-related illnesses.

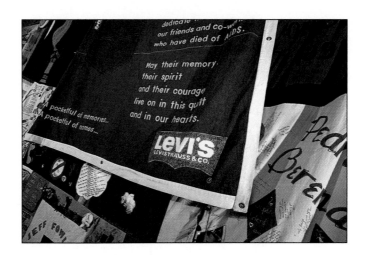

Young Levi achieved success beyond his wildest dreams. His pants, now sold in over 70 countries worldwide, became the flagship product of a diversified global company. Today, almost 150 years later, Levi's worldwide sales exceed $5.5 billion. The family-owned business Levi left to his nephews is the largest apparel company in the world, and a recognized trailblazer in corporate social responsibility (see Exhibit 5–2). Thanks to years of brilliant marketing and advertising—on a global scale—virtually everybody in the world knows Mr. Strauss's first name.[1] ◆

THE MAJORITY FALLACY

How does a company achieve that kind of familiarity? Obviously, advertising is a major factor. But who does Levi Strauss & Co. have to target to gain that level of awareness and credibility? Everybody? In the world?

From what you know about the success of Levi's products, how would you describe the company's target market?

If you answered "everybody," your reaction typifies the **majority fallacy**—a common misconception that to be successful a product or service must appeal to everybody or at least to the majority.

Today, sophisticated marketing and advertising people know this is just not true. When several (or many, in the case of apparel) products or services compete for the same customers, each may attract only a small fraction of the total market. A new competing product can often achieve deeper penetration and a stronger, more entrenched marketing position if it aims at just one group of customers rather than the entire population. Levi Strauss succeeded by selecting a very profitable market segment and diligently catering to it.

Given the widely differing needs, wants, and mental files of contemporary consumers, one product or service—be it an apparel brand or a financial institution—can't possibly appeal to or be purchased by "everybody." And no advertiser, not even the largest, has enough money to reach every prospect.[2]

THE PRODUCT MARKETING PROCESS

The **product marketing process** (the procedural side of the marketing exchange cycle discussed in Chapter 4) is the sequence of activities marketers perform to select markets and develop marketing mixes that eventually lead to exchanges. (see Exhibit 5–3). From the marketer's point of view, the product marketing process begins with a new product idea or with an existing good or service.

| Concept Stage | Market Segmentation Process | | Target Marketing Process | |

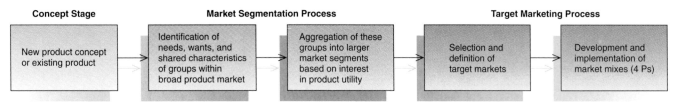

EXHIBIT • 5-3

The product marketing process consists of three stages: the concept, market segmentation, and target market stages.

But, marketers and advertisers face a dilemma. They must find groups of people with similar needs and tastes that can be satisfied by the product. And they must amass *enough* of these groups to make the product marketing process successful—and profitable. Realizing they can't appeal to everybody, marketers must turn to *market segmentation* and *target marketing* techniques—the subjects of this chapter.

THE MARKET SEGMENTATION PROCESS

Marketing and advertising people constantly scan the marketplace to see what needs and wants various consumer groups have and how they might be better satisfied. One of the techniques they use is **market segmentation,** a two-step strategic process of (1) *identifying* groups of people (or organizations) with certain shared characteristics within the broad markets for consumer or business products; and (2) *aggregating* (combining) these groups into larger market segments according to their mutual interest in the product's utility. This process gives a company a selection of market segments large enough to target. It also lays the foundation for developing a suitable mix of marketing activities—including advertising.

Because markets are diverse and consist of many segments, a company may differentiate products and marketing strategy for every segment, or it may concentrate all its marketing activities on only one or a few segments. Either task is far from simple. We saw how young Levi Strauss identified and targeted a single market segment and catered to it with specific products and services. The diverse markets Levi's serves today are really combinations of numerous smaller groups that share certain interests or product needs. Catering to all these needs—on a global level—requires a sophisticated marketing and communications system.

Identifying Consumer Market Segments: Finding the Right Niche

The concept of *shared characteristics* is critical to the market segmentation process. Marketing and advertising people know that, based on their needs, wants, and mental files, consumers leave many "footprints in the sand"—the variable characteristics of where they live and work, what they buy, and how they spend their leisure time, for example. By following these footprints, marketers can locate and define groups of consumers with similar needs and wants, create messages for them, and know how and where to send the messages. They try to find that particular "niche"—or space in the market—where the advertiser's product or service will fit (thus the buzzword *niche marketing*).

As Exhibit 5–4 shows, marketers group these variable characteristics into a variety of categories (*geographic, demographic, behavioristic,* and *psychographic*) to identify behavioral groups and segment consumer markets.

EXHIBIT • 5-4

Methods for segmenting consumer markets.

Variables	Typical breakdowns
Geographic	
Region	Pacific; Mountain; West North Central; West South Central; East North Central; East South Central; South Atlantic; Middle Atlantic; New England
County size	A, B, C, D
Climate	Northern, southern
City or SMSA size	Under 5,000; 5,000–19,999; 20,000–49,999; 50,000–99,999; 100,000–249,999; 250,000–499,999; 500,000–999,999; 1,000,000–3,999,999; 4,000,000 or over
Density	Urban, suburban, rural
Demographic	
Age	Under 6, 6–11, 12–19, 20–34, 35–49, 50–64, 65+
Sex	Male, female
Family size	1–2, 3–4, 5+
Family life cycle	Young, single; young, married, no children; young, married, youngest child under six; young, married, youngest child six or over; young, unmarried, with children; older, married with children; older, unmarried, with children; older, married, no children under 18; older, single; other
Income	Under $10,000; $10,000–20,000; $20,000–30,000; $30,000–40,000; $40,000–60,000; $60,000–100,000; $100,000 and over
Occupation	Professional and technical; managers, officials, and proprietors; clerical, sales; craftspeople, supervisors; operatives; farmers; retired; students; homemakers; unemployed
Education	Grade school or less; some high school; graduated high school; some college; graduated college
Religion	Catholic, Protestant, Jewish, other
Race	White, Black, Asian
Nationality	American, British, French, German, Scandinavian, Italian, Latin American, Middle Eastern, Japanese
Behavioristic	
Purchase occasion	Regular occasion, special occasion
Benefits sought	Economy, convenience, prestige
User status	Nonuser, ex-user, potential user, first-time user, regular user
Usage rate	Light user, medium user, heavy user
Loyalty status	None, medium, strong, absolute
Readiness stage	Unaware, aware, informed, interested, desirous, intending to buy
Marketing-factor sensitivity	Quality, price, service, advertising, sales promotion
Psychographic	
Societal divisions	Upper crust, movers and shakers, successful singles, social security, middle of the road, metro ethnic mix
Lifestyle	Straights, swingers, long-hairs
Personality	Compulsive, gregarious, authoritarian, ambitious

Geographic Segmentation

One of the simplest ways to segment markets is by **geographic** location. People in one region of the country—or the world—have needs, wants, and purchasing habits that differ from people in other regions. People in Sunbelt states, for example, buy more suntan lotion. Canadians buy special equipment for dealing with snow, ice, sleet, and subzero temperatures—products many Floridians never even heard of.

When marketers analyze geographic data, they study sales by region, coun-

EXHIBIT • 5-5

This commercial introduces Mott's Clamato Juice to a French-speaking regional market in Canada. The commercial demonstrates the product as an upscale drink.

(from frame)
RECIPE #7 How to get the better of your tennis partner.
MOTT'S MAN O. C.
How to get the better of your tennis partner. I have a trick.
First, break his concentration.
"Bob, did you see the bottle of Mott's Clamato?"

Second, create a psychological barrier.
"It's not easy to play when it's hot. Aren't you thirsty?"
Third, finish him off with a big glass of Mott's Clamato "Bob!"
He won't withstand the blow.
Ahhhh!!!

(from frame)
ADD SOME SPICE
ANNCR. V.O.
Mott's Clamato adds some spice!
MOTT'S MAN O.C.
"Mott's Clamato is like you, Bob; better on ice!"

try size, city size, specific locations, and types of stores. Many products sell well in urban areas but poorly in suburban or rural ones, and vice versa.

Even in local markets, geographic segmentation is important. For example, a local, progressive politician might send a mailer only to precincts where voters typically support liberal causes.

Demographic Segmentation

Demographics is the study of a population's numerical characteristics—sex, age, ethnicity, religion, education, occupation, income, and other quantifiable factors. For example, a company planning to target an area's Hispanic population might want to measure the group's size as well as its income and age distribution. Quebec's large French-speaking population presents such unique marketing opportunities that advertisers like Mott's Clamato Juice (see Exhibit 5–5) use special regional campaigns aimed at that demographic group.[3]

As Exhibit 5–6 demonstrates, people's responsibilities and incomes change as they grow older; and so do their interests in various product categories. Marketers need to study these changes because the human life cycle has a major effect on the market for many products.[4] In the 60s and 70s, for example, blue jeans were the basic uniform of all young males, and Levi's was the "in" brand. In the 80s, the baby boomer population grew older, and the number of young adults started to dwindle. The big market of men—now over 25 years old—needed professional clothes for work and wanted looser fitting clothes for relaxation. So they bought fewer jeans. Levi's needed to evolve the basic blue jean or risk losing this market forever. Levis responded by targeting its basic, 5-pocket, button-fly jeans to 15- to 24-year-olds. Then it developed more comfortable, looser-fitting jeans for men 25 to 34. And in 1986, Levi's introduced Dockers, a cotton casual slack targeted at men 25 to 54. The fastest growing brand in apparel industry history, Dockers now includes a whole family of casual clothing for men, women, and boys.

E X H I B I T • 5-6
Heavy usage patterns of various age groups.

Age	Name of age group	Merchandise purchased
0–5	Young children	Baby food, toys, nursery furniture, children's wear
6–19	Schoolchildren and teen-agers	Clothing, sporting goods, records and tapes, school supplies, fast food, soft drinks, candy, cosmetics, movies
20–34	Young adults	Cars, furniture, housing, food and beer, clothing, diamonds, home entertainment equipment, recreational equipment, purchases for younger age segments
35–49	Younger middle-aged	Larger homes, better cars, second cars, new furniture, computers, recreational equipment, jewelry, clothing, food and wine
50–64	Older middle-aged	Recreational items, purchases for young marrieds and infants, travel
65 and over	Senior adults	Medical services, travel, pharmaceuticals, purchases for younger age groups

Behavioristic Segmentation

Geographic and demographic data provide information about markets but little about the purchase behavior or psychological makeup of the people in those markets. And people in the same demographic or geographic segment often have widely differing product preferences.

One of the best ways to determine market segments is to cluster consumers into groups based on their attitude toward, use of, or response to actual products or product attributes. This is generally called **behavioristic segmentation.** Behavioral segments are determined by a number of variables, but the most important are *purchase occasion, benefits sought, user status,* or *usage rate.*

Purchase-Occasion Variables Buyers can be distinguished by *when* they buy or use a product or service—the **purchase occasion.** Air travelers, for example, fly for business or vacation. So one airline might promote business travel while

---

ETHICAL DILEMMA   Warning: Market Segmentation May Be Hazardous to Your Business

In early 1990, R. J. Reynolds Tobacco was poised to roll out a new product named Uptown. The idea of a light menthol cigarette in a sleek black and gold package held great promise—until Dr. Louis Sullivan, Secretary of Health and Human Services, openly accused Reynolds of "promoting a culture of cancer" among African-Americans. "This brand is cynically and deliberately targeted toward black Americans," Sullivan said. "I strongly urge you to cancel your plans to market a brand of cigarettes that is specifically targeted to black smokers," he added.

This unprecedented public attack by the nation's top health official caused an uproar in the black community. Reynolds scrapped its plans to test-market Uptown, incurred an estimated loss of $10 million, and protested loudly. "This represents a loss of choice for black smokers and a further erosion of the free enterprise system," executive vice president Peter Hoult said.

The advertising community was also up in arms. Sullivan had questioned the ethics of market segmentation, one of the industry's tried and true techniques. Advertisers feared the Uptown disaster would make it much more difficult to market products to minorities, women, and children.

Market segmentation is an accepted, precise, effective way for advertisers to target potential audiences. And it's becoming increasingly important in the tobacco industry. As the number of smokers steadily declines, cigarette makers respond by positioning brands to appeal to specific market segments.

Blacks represent a tempting target. The rate of smoking among blacks is declining more slowly than among whites and even increasing among young, poor, uneducated blacks. "We're an honest company; what do you say when the audience is going to be predominantly black?" a Reynolds spokesman said. But marketing specialists and antismoking

another promotes tourism. The purchase occasion can be affected by seasons (water skis, snow skis, raincoats), by frequency of need (regular or occasional), or by some fad-and-fade cycle (candy, computer games). A marketer who discovers common purchase occasions for certain groups or organizations has a potential target segment. One consulting firm, Advertiming, recommends appropriate timing of media advertising by correlating consumer purchase patterns with weather forecasts.[5]

Benefits-Sought Variables Consumers seek many **benefits** in the products they buy—high quality, low price, status, speed, sex appeal, good taste. For example, people buy Levi's Jeans for work, for play, or to make a fashion statement. Marketers can cluster consumer groups into segments based on the benefits being sought. **Benefit segmentation** is the prime objective of many consumer attitude studies and, as Exhibit 5–7 shows, the basis for many successful ad campaigns.

User-Status Variables Many markets can be segmented by the **user-status** of prospective customers (i.e., nonusers, new users, regular users, potential users, and ex-users). By targeting one or another of these groups, marketers develop new products for nonusers or new uses for old products.

Usage-Rate Variables It's usually easier to get a heavy user to increase usage than to get a light user to do so. In a process called **volume segmentation,** marketers measure **usage rates** to define consumers as light, medium, or heavy users of products. In many product categories, 20 percent of the population consumes 80 percent of the product. Marketers want to define who comprises that 20 percent and aim their advertising at them. For example, one-third of all households purchase 83 percent of Levi's annual products—worldwide! A company that markets dog food wants to attract heavy users—the 17 percent of the population that buys 87 percent of all dog food (see Exhibit 5–8).

By finding common characteristics among heavy users of their products, marketers can define product differences and focus their ad campaigns more effectively. For example, heavy users of bowling alleys are working-class men

activists agree: Reynolds' blatant declaration hurt its marketing effort.

The hue and cry that upset Reynolds' plan also harmed the black business community. Millions of Reynolds' ad dollars were lost to black-owned media. As *Philadelphia Magazine* publisher David Lipson points out, "It's a fact that blacks smoke a lot of cigarettes, and R. J. Reynolds wanted to design a product for the black market. What's wrong with that?"

The Association of National Advertisers insists that restricting the industry's right to target specific markets is censorship and a violation of First Amendment rights. Both sides clearly believe they're acting ethically, but troubling questions persist. Cigarettes are legal, but they're also deadly. On the other hand, no amount of advertising can force a person to smoke.

Market segmentation is a powerful advertising tool, and freedom of expression a cherished American right. But we need to seek a balance between rights, duties, freedom, and responsibility in order to achieve the greatest good for all the people.

Questions

1. Considering that all cigarette makers use market segmentation to focus their advertising, is it ethical to condemn one brand because of its audience?

2. Robert Schmidt, chairman of Levine, Huntley, Schmidt & Beaver, publicly announced, "We will never create any cigarette advertisements. There has to be some social conscience to an ad agency." Do you agree? Would you work on a cigarette account even if you believed smoking is harmful? Would you sacrifice your job over this principle?

EXHIBIT • 5-7

Benefit segmentation research helps advertisers recognize the audiences they must address. This ad speaks to two market segments: one that perceives Levi Dockers' benefits as a casual fashion statement and one interested in a dressier style, Dockers' dress slacks.

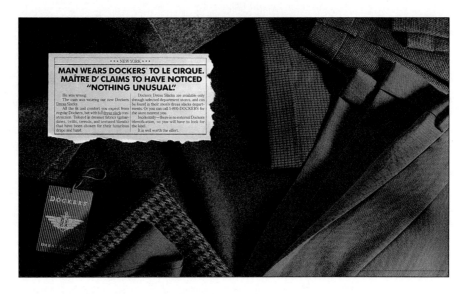

between 25 and 50 who watch more than three and a half hours of television a day and prefer sports programs. So a bowling equipment company would probably want to advertise on TV sports programs.

Marketers of one product sometimes find their customers are also heavy users of other products. If so, they can define their target markets in terms of the usage rates of the other products. Recent research from SRI International's VALS2 program (discussed in the next section) indicates that heavy users of home computers are also heavy users of foreign luxury cars, sports cars, backpacking equipment, binoculars, expensive bicycles, and literary magazines.[6]

Psychographic Segmentation

In many consumer product categories, customers are more likely to be swayed by appeals to their emotions and cultural values.[7] So some advertisers use

EXHIBIT • 5-8

Usage rates vary for different products. For example, of all households, 63 percent never buy vitamins (nonusers), 13 percent account for a third (34 percent) of vitamin sales (light users), and about a quarter of the households (24 percent) make two-thirds (66 percent) of the purchases (heavy users). Note the extreme difference between nonusers and heavy users of golf equipment.

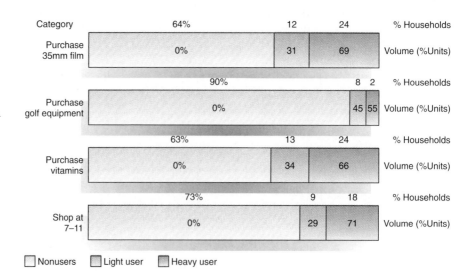

psychographic segmentation to define consumer markets. **Psychographics** groups people into homogeneous segments on the basis of their psychological makeup—their values, attitudes, personality, and lifestyle. It classifies people according to what they feel, what they believe, the way they live, and the products and services they use.[8]

Most of us want to be seen as a particular type of person, so we use brands that support that image. One study found that consumers thought GE brands attracted only conservative, older, business types. To change that image—and appeal to a broader range of consumers—GE adopted its now famous "Brings Good Things to Life" campaign.[9]

By discovering as many descriptive qualities of their prospects as possible, marketers end up with rich target market profiles that enable them to focus their marketing and advertising activities.

For years, marketers attempted to categorize consumers by personality and lifestyle types to find a common basis for determining advertising appeals. Monitor, a service developed by Yankelovich, Skelly and White, was the first major syndicated study of changing U.S. values.[10]

Another classification system, VALS (values and lifestyles), originated by SRI International, was quickly adopted by marketers across the country. In 1989, SRI updated the program, renaming it VALS2, and offered a new psychographic profile for segmenting U.S. consumers and predicting their purchase behavior (see Exhibit 5–9).[11]

The **Values and Lifestyles (VALS)** system breaks consumers into eight groups based on their financial resources and self-orientation. Each group exhibits distinctive behavior, decision-making patterns, and product consumption tendencies.

To reach some of the VALS2 lifestyle groups, radio is an excellent medium

EXHIBIT • 5-9

The VALS2® (Values and Lifestyles) classification system places consumers with abundant resources near the top of the chart and those with minimal resources near the bottom. Horizontally, the chart segments consumers by their basis for decision making: principles, status, or action. The boxes intersect to indicate that some categories may be considered together. For instance, a marketer may categorize Fulfilleds and Believers together.

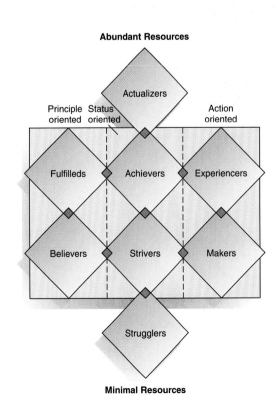

because it satisfies the news and/or entertainment needs of various groups of listeners. Conservative, blue-collar people with traditional values (the VALS2 Believer and Maker segments, which comprise 29 percent of the U.S. population) often choose country music stations. Higher-income men and women over 45 (the VALS2 Actualizer, Fulfilled, and Achiever categories) typically listen to news-and-talk radio. Since radio has no more than 12 unique formats, SRI's eight values and lifestyles typologies fit radio listenership reasonably well.[12]

Numerous advertising agencies jumped on the VALS bandwagon. Young & Rubicam used VALS for a variety of its clients, including Mercury Capri, Dr Pepper, Kodak Instant Cameras, and Merrill Lynch. By using VALS to understand their customers, advertisers hope to better establish an emotional bond between the brand and the consumer.

Limitations of Consumer Segmentation Methods

Every segmentation method has supporters and detractors. Advocates of VALS and other psychographic methods claim these methods help them address the emotional factors that motivate consumers. However, since the markets for many products comprise a broad cross-section of consumers, psychographics may offer little real value—especially when dealing with markets outside North America.[13] VALS and similar methods of classification are also faulted for oversimplifying consumer personalities and purchase behavior.[14]

Yet marketers do need to understand and monitor who their customers are, where they live, and what attitudes, lifestyles, and personalities they have. It helps them select potential target markets, match the attributes and image of their products with the types of consumers using the products, develop effective media plans, and budget their marketing dollars wisely.[15]

Identifying Business Market Segments

Business (or industrial) markets include manufacturers, utilities, government agencies, contractors, wholesalers, retailers, banks, insurance companies, and institutions that buy goods and services to help them in their own business. These include raw materials, parts, desks, office equipment, vehicles, or a variety of services used in conducting the business (see Exhibit 5–10). Products sold to business markets are often intended for resale to the public, as in the case of retail goods such as Levi's apparel.

Identifying target markets of prospective business customers is just as complex as identifying consumer market segments. But many of the variables used to identify consumer markets can also be used for business markets for example, geographic location, benefits sought, user status, usage rate, and purchase occasion.

Business markets also have special characteristics. They normally use a systematic purchasing procedure; they are classified by SIC code; they may be concentrated geographically; and they may have a relatively small number of buyers.[16] These characteristics have important implications for advertisers.

EXHIBIT • 5-10

Businesses often hire other businesses to conduct specific tasks, such as the accounting services advertised in this ad from Deloitte & Touche.

Business Purchasing Procedures

When businesspeople evaluate new products, they use a process far more complex and rigid than the consumer purchase process described in Chapter 4. Industrial marketers must design their advertising programs with this in mind.

Large firms have purchasing departments that act as professional buyers.

They evaluate the need for products, analyze proposed purchases, seek approvals from users and authorizations from managers, make requisitions, place orders, and supervise all product purchasing. It may take weeks, months, or even years to make a sale, especially when dealing with government agencies. Purchase decisions often depend on factors besides price or quality—delivery time, terms of sale, service requirements, dependability of supply, and others.[17] So marketers often stress these issues in their advertising and promotional appeals.

Industrial marketers often consider the purchase decision process of various segments before deciding on an appropriate target market. New companies, for instance, may target other small companies where the purchase decision can be made quickly. Or they may use commission-only reps to call on larger prospects that require more time.

Standard Industrial Classification

In the United States, the Department of Commerce classifies all businesses—and also collects and publishes data on them—by **Standard Industrial Classification (SIC) codes.** These codes are based on broad industry categories (food, tobacco, apparel, etc.) subdivided into major divisions, subgroups, and then detailed classes of firms in similar lines of business. Exhibit 5–11 shows a breakdown of SIC codes in the apparel industry. The federal government reports the number of firms, sales volumes, and number of employees, broken down by geographic areas, for each SIC code. SIC codes help companies segment markets and do research; and advertisers can obtain lists of companies in particular SIC groups for direct mailings.

Market Concentration

Many countries' markets for industrial goods are heavily concentrated in one region or several metropolitan areas. In the United States, for example, the industrial market is heavily concentrated in the midwest, the mid-Atlantic states, and California. Exhibit 5–12 shows that more than 50 percent of the manufacturing industry in the United States is located east of the Mississippi and north of the Mason-Dixon line. Market concentration greatly reduces the number of geographic targets.

Moreover, industrial marketers deal with a limited number of buyers. Less than 4 percent of U.S. companies employ nearly 60 percent of all production workers and account for over two-thirds of all manufacturing dollars.[18] Customer size is a critical basis for market segmentation. A firm may concentrate its marketing and advertising efforts on a few large customers or many more smaller ones. Steelcase, a manufacturer of office furniture, does both. Its sales force calls on major accounts; it uses dealers to resell its products to small purchasers.

Levi Strauss markets through three channels: independent department stores; specialty stores (like Miller's Outpost); and chain stores (like Sears and JC Penney). Its top 100 accounts provide 80 percent of the company's annual sales and are made through 13,000 retail outlets. Its remaining accounts (20 percent of sales) represent another 13,000 stores. Major accounts are served by sales reps from Levi's various divisions; smaller accounts by telemarketers and pan-divisional sales reps. Foote, Cone & Belding in San Francisco creates and coordinates advertising for all Levi Strauss divisions in the United States.

Business marketers can further segment markets by end users. For example, a firm may develop software for use in one specialized industry, such as

EXHIBIT • 5-11

A business marketer selling goods or services to firms in the apparel industry can use SIC codes in directories or on subscription databases to locate prospective companies.

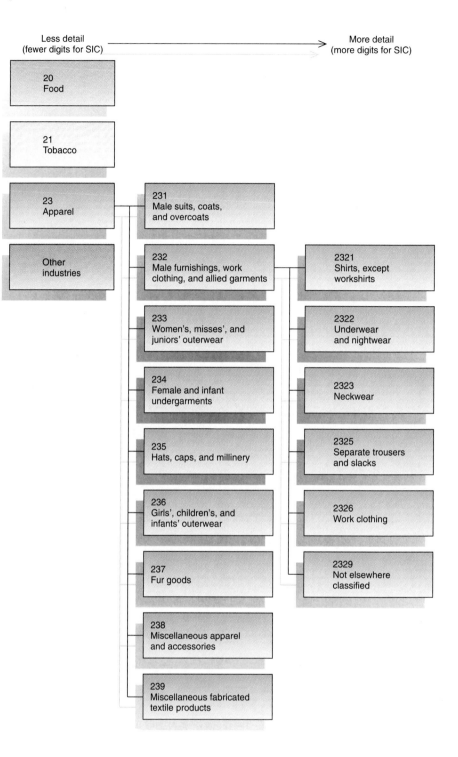

banking, or for general use in a variety of industries. That decision, of course, determines where ads should be placed.

Aggregating Market Segments

Once marketers group broad product-based markets by shared characteristics (geographic, demographic, behavioristic, or psychographic), they can proceed to the next step in the market segmentation process: (1) selecting groups that have a mutual interest in the product's utility and (2) reorganizing and aggregating (combining) them into larger market segments based on their potential for

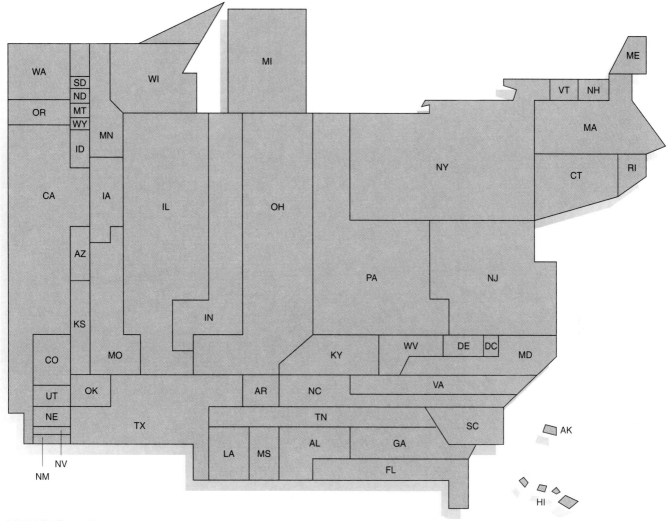

EXHIBIT • 5-12

The states in this map are represented in proportion to the value of their manufactured products.

sales and profit. Let's take a look at how this process might work for Levi Strauss in the U.S. market.

First, the company's management needs to know the market potential for jeans and casual pants in various market areas regionally and nationally; that is, they need to discover the **primary demand trend** of the total U.S. market for casual pants. To do this they use a variety of *marketing research* techniques (discussed in Chapter 6).

Then, management has to identify the needs, wants, and shared characteristics of the various groups within the casual apparel marketplace who live near the company's retail outlets. They may use the services of a large market segmentation company like National Decision Systems, which collects data on people's purchasing behavior and creates profiles of geographic markets across the country.

The company finds a huge market of prospective customers throughout the United States: students, blue-collar workers, young singles, professional people, housewives, and so on. It then measures and analyzes household groups in each major retail area by demographic, lifestyle, and purchasing characteristics, sorts them into 50 different geo-demographic segments, and refers to them with terms like those in Exhibit 5–13: Established Wealth, Movers & Shakers, Family Ties, Innercity Singles, and so on. Some households are comfortable financially;

National Decision Systems' MicroVision system classifies prospective customers in the Chicago area by census tract and labels each area by the shared characteristics of the residents.

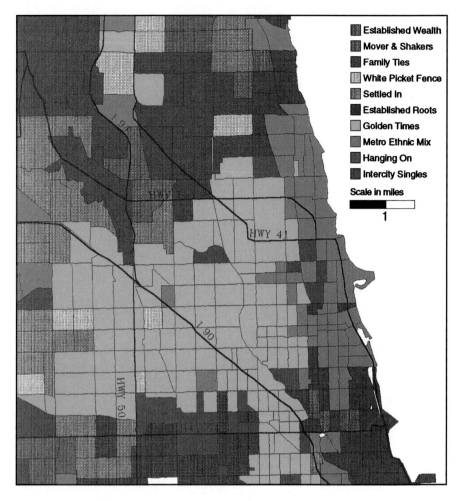

some are not. Some are working people; some are students. But all have apparel needs, and many might be interested in the style, cachet, and durability of the Levi's brand.

Selecting Groups Interested in Product Utility

Levi Strauss next selects groups that would like and be able to afford the utilities or benefits of Levi's apparel—suitability for work or play, comfort, style and fashion, low cost, durability, quality construction, convenient availability, etc. Groups interested in all these features make up the total possible market for Levi's pants.

Should the company try to appeal to all of these people, or just aim at some specialized segment? Part of the challenge of market segmentation is estimating the profits of the total market the company might realize if it (1) aims at the whole market or (2) caters only to a specific market segment. In highly competitive markets like apparel, it's wise to avoid the majority fallacy.

Combining Groups to Build Target Market Segments

The company needs to find groups that are relatively homogeneous (similar) and offer good potential for profit. Market data turn up a large number of demographic and lifestyle groups including ethnically diverse families, young singles, and seniors with lower education and income who often live in rented homes or apartments: On Their Own (3.4 percent), Back Country (6.0 percent), and Settled In (5.1 percent). Because of their minimal retail or credit activity, these groups are not prime targets for premium branded products sold in better department stores.

But other segments seem to offer greater potential—young to middle-aged households with medium to high incomes and average to high retail activity: Movers and Shakers (2.5 percent), Prosperous Ethnic Mix (2.8 percent), and Home Sweet Home (5.7 percent). By combining these (and similar groups) with the young professionals in the Good Step Forward (2.1 percent) and the Great Beginnings segments (3.6 percent), Levi Strauss can target a new and interesting market segment: young to middle-aged people on their way up. Nationally, that amounts to 20 million U.S. households. That's not everybody; but it's a large and potentially very profitable market segment. These people might like the style and comfort of Levi's 550s as well as the tradition of a brand they know and trust, and the company could develop a campaign to appeal to their particular needs, wants, and self-image.

THE TARGET MARKETING PROCESS

Once the aggregating process is complete, a company can proceed to the **target marketing process.** The way this is accomplished determines the content, look, and implementation of the company's advertising.

Target Market Selection

The first step in the target marketing process is to assess which of the newly created segments are large enough to offer the greatest profit potential and which can be most successfully penetrated. The company designates one or more segments as a **target market**—that group of segments the company wishes to appeal to, design products for, and aim its marketing activities toward.[19] It may designate another set of segments as a secondary target market and aim some of its resources at it.

Let's look at Levi Strauss & Co.'s most likely target market for loose-fitting jeans—young to middle-aged males with moderate to high income and education who like the style, comfort, and fashion of Levi's apparel. This group represents a significant percent of the total apparel market, a target that, if won, will generate substantial profits. Levi Strauss & Co. offers what these prospects need and want: the style and fashion of the jeans they grew up with, now updated to be more comfortable for the adult body (see Exhibit 5–14).

If Levi Strauss & Co. discovered that the 18–34, comfort-oriented segment wasn't large enough to be profitable, it would have to select a different target market. And its other marketing and advertising activities would have to change as well.

For an exercise, look at Ad Lab 5–A and consider how Reebok selected its target market.

The Marketing Mix: Matching Products to Markets

Now that Levi Strauss has a specific target market in sight, it must take steps to ensure it is ready to enter the marketplace.

Once a company defines its target market, it knows exactly where to focus its attention and resources. It can shape the product concept—even design special features for its target market (specific colors or special sizes). It can establish proper pricing. It can determine the need for location of stores or dealers, and it can prepare the most convincing advertising messages. In other words, the whole mix of marketing activities can be aimed at making the product attractive and accessible to the target market.

EXHIBIT • 5-14

Levi Strauss markets its loose-fitting jeans to the 18-to-36 aged comfort-oriented segment with moderate to high incomes and education who like the style, comfort, and fashionability of Levi's apparel.

AD LAB 5-A   Marketing Reebok: The Product Element and the Market Today

Reebok, a well-known brand of athletic shoe, was virtually unknown in 1980. Named after the swift, graceful African antelope, Reebok International was the newest name for one of Britain's oldest shoe manufacturers, Joseph W. Foster & Sons Athletic Shoes. Foster's first introduced the spiked track shoe around the turn of the century, and members of the 1924 British track team, highlighted in the film *Chariots of Fire,* all wore Foster running shoes.

In 1979, eager to enter the North American market, Reebok teamed up with Paul Fireman. Fireman's family had been in the camping and sporting goods business for some time, and he had been looking for a new and exciting product. Reebok looked like it.

As he sought to give Reebok a foothold in the marketplace, total U.S. industry sales were already reaching the $1 billion mark. Competition was formidable. Fireman had to find a way to compete with the big players—Nike, Converse, Adidas, and others. Nike had a 35 percent share of the market, followed by Adidas and Converse with about 10 percent each. Converse was the strongest company targeting the basketball segment. Nike was strongest with runners, the market Reebok's manufacturer had traditionally served.

How could Fireman's fledgling company compete against this kind of strength? Fireman had to examine the marketplace, studying basic marketing fundamentals such as the product life cycle, positioning, and the consumer decision-making process. He knew athletic shoes were scientifically designed for individual sports events. For example, a print ad from Nike pictured 10 athletic shoes used for 10 different sporting purposes: distance running, cross-country, sprinting, long jump, javelin throw, all-purpose running (two types), high jump, triple jump, shot put, and discus. At the same time, professional sports shoes were becoming popular with nonprofessionals—shoes for tennis, basketball, and jogging were sold in shoe stores, and markets such as aerobics, fitness, and walking were soon to follow.

Fireman realized he had a quality manufactured sports shoe with some unique features: attractive styling, a wide range of colors, a tradition of Olympic running shoes and British quality, the trademarked Foster Heel Cradle, special cooling mesh toe, water-repellent and air-breathing inner liner, and a dual-density midsole. Also he had to look ahead because the running shoe market was not a growing market like others. And he knew what he didn't have—a huge

As we discussed in Chapter 4, a product offers utility. In fact, a product generally offers a number of utilities—perceived by the consumer as a *bundle of values.* With this in mind, marketers and advertisers generally try to shape their basic, functional product into a total **product concept:** the consumer's perception of a product as a bundle of utilitarian and symbolic values that satisfy functional, social, psychological, economic, and other wants and needs.

Companies engage in many activities to enhance the product concept. Marketers categorize these activities under the broad headings of *product, price, place,* and *promotion*—the **Four Ps (4 Ps).**[20] The 4 Ps are the basic elements of the **marketing mix.** Every company tries to affect its product concept and improve sales by adding to, subtracting from, or modifying these four elements.

Advertising, one activity in the promotion element, is affected by two factors: the uncontrollable marketing environment in which the company operates (e.g., economy, seasonality, political and technological situation, culture), and controllable company decisions about the appropriate mix of other marketing activities.

The remainder of this chapter focuses on the relationship between advertising and the 4 Ps.

ADVERTISING AND THE PRODUCT ELEMENT

In developing a marketing mix, marketers generally start with the **product element.** Major activities typically include the way the product is designed and classified, positioned, branded, and packaged. Each of these affects the way the product is advertised.

Because life is not a spectator sport.

budget like his competitors and a complete distribution system.

Fireman sagely recognized that the athletic footwear market contained a sufficient number of market segments to support Reebok's current product line—his first offering to the U.S. public—and any new products he might create.

By 1986, Reebok led the U.S. athletic shoe market with a 31.2 percent share. By 1990, Reebok shared 59 percent of the market along with Nike and newcomer L.A. Gear.

Today, Reebok continues to defend its market position with a new line of casual sports shoes for men and women.

Laboratory Applications

1. What market segment, still untapped in 1980, eventually propelled Reebok to first place in athletic shoes? (Hint: The woman in the Reebok ad is wearing the appropriate outfit for the new market segment.)

2. How would you use the Olympic tradition and Foster's trademarked Heel Cradle to develop a positioning statement for Reebok?

Product Life Cycle

Marketers theorize that just as humans pass through stages in life from infancy to death, products (and especially product categories) also pass through a **product life cycle** (see Exhibit 5–15).[21] A product's position in the life cycle influences the kind of advertising used. The life cycle also hints at other factors in the marketing environment, for example, industry growth potential, competitive pressure, and ease of entry. There are four major stages in the product life cycle: *introduction, growth, maturity,* and *decline.*

For example, when a company introduces a major new product category, nobody knows about it. To educate consumers, the company has to stimulate **primary demand**—consumer demand for the whole product category, rather than for just its own brand. The ad for a CD-ROM player in Exhibit 5–16 pushes the new technology, rather than Sony's own brand.

When videocassette recorders were first introduced, advertisers had to first create enough consumer demand to *pull* the product through the channels of distribution. Promotional activities were designed to educate consumers about the new product and its category, stressing information about what VCRs were, how they worked, and the rewards of owning one. Other promotional efforts aimed at the retail trade—called **push strategy**—encouraged distributors and dealers to stock, display, and advertise the new products (see Chapter 16).

During the **introductory**—or *pioneering*—**phase** of any new product category, companies incur considerable costs for product development and for initial advertising and promotion to educate customers, build widespread dealer distribution, and encourage demand. In fact, a company may not earn a profit on a product until the growth stage, so it must be well capitalized to weather this period and continue advertising.

EXHIBIT • 5-15

A product's life cycle curve may vary, depending on the product category. Marketing objectives and strategies also change as the product proceeds from one stage to the next.

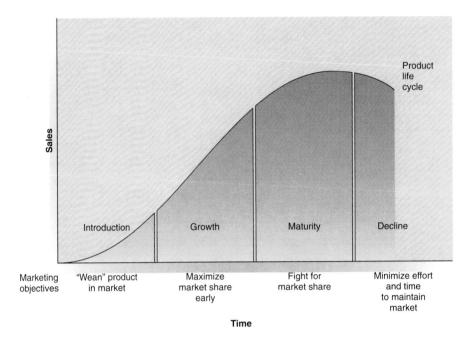

When sales volume begins to rise rapidly, the product enters the **growth stage.** This period is characterized by *market expansion,* as more and more customers, stimulated by mass advertising and word-of-mouth, make their first, second, and third purchases. Recognizing the growth opportunity, competitors jump into the market with competing brands. Sheer momentum now carries category sales upward, boosting sales of all brands. Advertising expenditures as a percent of total sales should decrease. At this point individual firms may realize their first substantial profits.

During the 1980s, for example, the demand for VCRs exploded, and sales quadrupled every year. By the end of the decade, over 66 percent of all U.S. homes (over 175 million people) had VCRs, and a variety of competitive brands—many with unfamiliar names—entered the market to cash in on the growth.[22]

In the **maturity stage,** as the marketplace becomes saturated with competing products and the number of new customers dwindles, industry sales reach a plateau. Competition intensifies, and profits diminish. Companies increase their promotional efforts but emphasize **selective demand** to impress customers with the subtle advantages of one brand over another. At this stage, companies increase sales only at the expense of competitors—*conquest sales.* The strategies of market segmentation, product positioning, and price promotion become

EXHIBIT • 5-16

This ad for Sony's CD-ROM player aims at increasing the overall—or primary—demand for the entire product category. The goal is to increase the total number of customers willing to buy, which in turn increases sales of individual brands. In a relatively new category (like CD-ROM technology), it's important for vanguard manufacturers and distributors to build primary demand as quickly as possible.

EXHIBIT 5-17

To extend a product's life cycle, companies redesign the product's features, expand its uses, change packaging, or run special promotions. Advertising is important for demonstrating and announcing these life-extending features.

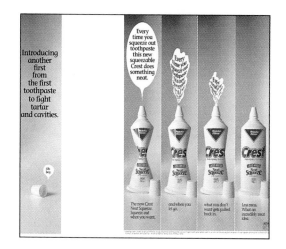

more important during this shakeout period as weak companies fall by the wayside and those remaining fight for small increases in market share.[23] By 1992, for example, VCRs were available in many configurations and at significantly lower prices. Ads stressed features and low prices, and the product became a staple of discount merchandisers.

Late in the maturity stage, as products approach the inevitable period of decline, companies frequently employ a variety of strategies to extend the product's life cycle. They may try to add new users, increase the frequency of use, develop new uses for the product, or change the size of packages, design new labels, or improve quality. For example, Procter & Gamble designed a "Neat Squeeze" package for its Crest toothpaste to extend the product's effective life (see Exhibit 5–17).

Finally, products enter the **decline stage** due to obsolescence, changing technology, or new consumer tastes. Companies may cease all promotion and phase the products out quickly, as in the case of the Edsel, or let them die slowly, like old brands of home movie film.

To prolong the maturity stage, they may also attempt to revitalize the product with new features and increased promotion. When successful college textbooks have been in the market for 20 or 30 years, sales inevitably begin to decline. Publishers often try to revitalize them by adding new authors, changing the look and feel of the book, significantly updating the content, and increasing promotional expenditures.

Product Classifications

The way a company classifies its product is important in defining both the product concept and the marketing mix. As Exhibit 5–18 shows, there are many ways to classify tangible goods: by markets, by the purchasing habits of the buyers, by physical attributes, and so on.

When most people speak of a *product,* they usually mean a physical entity— a *good.* Yet people also receive benefits when they buy insurance, annuities, or maintenance services. The fact is, a product may be either a tangible good or an intangible *service.*

A **service** is a bundle of benefits that may or may not be physical, that are temporary in nature, and that usually derive from completion of a task.[24] Thus we have *task utility* as described in Chapter 4. Rail service is transitory—used and priced on a time and distance basis. It offers the functional benefits of transporting people, livestock, and freight. But it can also offer psychological benefits as shown in Exhibit 5–19. The railroad relies on the use of *specialized*

EXHIBIT • 5-18

Product classifications

By market

Consumer goods
Products and services we use in our daily lives (food, clothing, furniture, automobiles).

Industrial goods
Products used by companies for the purpose of producing other products (raw materials, agricultural commodities, machinery, tools, equipment).

By rate of consumption and tangibility

Durable goods
Tangible products that are long lasting and infrequently replaced (cars, trucks, refrigerators, furniture).

Nondurable goods
Tangible products that may be consumed in one or a few uses and usually need to be replaced at regular intervals (food, soap, gasoline, oil).

Services
Activities, benefits, or satisfaction offered for sale (travel, haircuts, legal and medical services, massages).

By purchasing habits

Convenience goods
Purchases made frequently with a minimum of effort (cigarettes, food, newspapers).

Shopping goods
Infrequently purchased items for which greater time is spent comparing price, quality, style, warranty (furniture, cars, clothing, tires).

Specialty goods
Products with such unique characteristics that consumers will make special efforts to purchase them even if they're more expensive (fancy photographic equipment, special women's fashions, stereo components).

By physical description

Package goods
Cereals, hair tonics, and so forth.

Hard goods
Furniture, appliances.

Soft goods
Clothing, bedding.

Services
Nontangible products.

EXHIBIT • 5-19

In addition to offering functional benefits, an equipment-based service like Amtrak also offers psychological benefits, such as providing travelers with a more intimate view of the land.

Song: by Richie Havens
The way you see.
The way you see the miles passing by.

The way you look out on life.
Cities and mountains.
Shadows against the sky . . .

There's something about a train that's magic.
All Aboard Amtrak.

EXHIBIT • 5-20

Xerox displays its slogan "The Document Company," on its ads to reposition the company into a document-handling marketplace which is much broader than its original copier market.

equipment—vehicles able to pull huge loads over a unique track. This makes it an **equipment-based service.**

In contrast, an ad agency is a **people-based service;** it relies on the creative talents and marketing skills of individuals rather than on equipment. As one agency CEO said, "My inventory goes up and down the elevators twice a day."[25]

Product Positioning

Once an advertising person understands the product's stage in the life cycle and how it's classified, the first strategic decision can be made—how to **position** the product. Remember that consumers rank products in their mental files. Marketers try to determine what positions are open and then develop products that can occupy a number-one or number-two position.

Products may be positioned in many different ways. Generally, they are ranked by the way they are differentiated, by the benefits they offer, or by the particular market segment to which they appeal.[26] A product may even be positioned by the way it's classified (e.g., as a convenience good rather than a shopping good). As Exhibit 5–20 shows, Xerox—the one-time king of copiers—now positions itself as "The Document Company." This strategy is designed to *reposition* the company, moving from the narrow, mature, glutted, copier market to the broader, growing, document-handling market. With one stroke, Xerox redefines the business it is in, differentiates itself from the competition, and creates a new number-one position for itself.

Product Differentiation

Product differentiation is the competitive strategy of creating a product difference that appeals to the preferences of a distinct market segment. In advertising, nothing is more important than informing prospects how your product is different. For example, simply adding new colors might differentiate a product enough to attract a new set of customers. Not all product differences need be that obvious. Differences between products may be *perceptible, hidden,* or *induced*. Hank Seiden says every successful product has got to have a "Unique Advantage." Bob Pritikin humorously calls that differentiating quality the AMAZING, NEW![27]

Perceptible Differences

Differences between products that are visibly apparent to the consumer are called **perceptible differences.** For example, a red automobile is visibly different from a black one and may appeal to more people without increasing the manufacturing cost. Similarly, refrigerators are designed with right- and left-hand doors, single doors, and double doors.

Hidden Differences

Hidden differences are not so readily apparent. Trident gum looks and tastes the same as other brands but is differentiated by the use of artificial sweeteners. The same is true with many food products (caffeine-free colas) and automobiles (front-wheel drive). Imperceptible differences can enhance a product's desirability. But consumers need to know about them—a problem remedied by advertising.

Differentiating functionally similar products—such as oranges or lemons—can be very difficult. Sunkist's label creates an induced difference and implies a guarantee of value—factors that increase sales.

Induced Differences

For many product classes, such as aspirin, salt, gasoline, packaged foods, liquor, and financial services, advertising can create **induced differences.** The Mitsubishi Eclipse sports car outsells the Plymouth Laser although both cars are identical (both are manufactured by Diamond Star Motors, a joint venture between Chrysler and Mitsubishi). The Eclipse is differentiated through unique branding, distribution, dealer service, and advertising, all of which add **perceived value.** Banks, brokerage houses, and insurance companies use advertising and promotion to differentiate themselves because they offer virtually identical services and financial products.[28] Research showed that Canada's leading supplier of natural gas, Linde, was seen by its customers as part of a faceless industry. So Linde made a massive effort to make *customer service* a key differentiating factor.[29]

As Sunkist so successfully demonstrates (see Exhibit 5–21), the ability to create the perception of differences in functionally similar products and services makes the strategy of product differentiation very popular and the effective use of branding, advertising, and packaging very important.

Product Branding

The fundamental differentiating device for all products is the **brand**—the combination of name, words, symbols, or design that identifies the product and its source and differentiates it from competitive products. Without brands, consumers couldn't tell one product from another, and advertising them would be nearly impossible.

Decisions about branding strategy are difficult. A manufacturer may establish an **individual brand** for each product it produces. Unilever, for example, markets its toothpastes under the individual brand names Aim, Pepsodent, and Close-up. Such companies designate a distinct target market segment for each product and develop a separate personality and image for each brand.[30] However, as any advertising professional knows, this decision is very costly.

On the other hand, a company may use a **family brand** and market different products under the same umbrella name. When Heinz promotes its catsup products, it hopes to help its relishes too. This decision may be cost-effective, but one bad product in a line can hurt the whole family.

Since it is so expensive for manufacturers to market **national brands** (also called *manufacturer's brands*), some companies use a *private-labeling strategy.* They manufacture the product and sell it to **middlemen** (distributors or dealers) who put their own brand on the product. **Private brands,** typically sold at lower prices in large retail chain stores, include such familiar names as Kenmore, Craftsman, Cragmont, and Party Pride. In this case, the responsibility for creating brand image and familiarity rests with the distributor or retailer.

Branding decisions are critically important because the brands a company owns may be its most important capital asset.[31] Imagine the value of owning a brand name like Coca-Cola, Nike, Porsche, or Levi's. In fact, the value is so great that some companies pay a substantial fee for the right to use another company's brand name. Thus, we have **licensed brands** like Sunkist vitamins, Coca-Cola clothing, Porsche sunglasses, and Mickey Mouse watches.

Role of Branding

As products proliferate, the role of branding takes on added significance. For consumers, brands offer instant recognition and identification. More important, brands also promise consistent, reliable standards of quality, taste, size, durability, or even psychological satisfaction. This adds value to the product for both the consumer and the manufacturer.

Brand differentiation must be built on the differences in images, meanings, and associations.[32] In fact, the No Excuses line of clothing was first conceptualized as a brand—because of the potential for humorous associations—even before the marketer had a product to sell.[33] Ideally, when consumers see a brand on the shelf, they instantly comprehend the brand's promise and have confidence in its quality. Of course, they must be familiar with and accept the brand—a function of advertising effectiveness. Naturally, advertisers try to achieve brand preference and insistence or, as we point out in Chapter 4, *brand loyalty.*[34]

Over time, the goal of all brand advertising and promotion is to build greater *brand equity.* **Brand equity** is the totality of what consumers, distributors, dealers—even competitors—feel and think about the brand over an extended period of time. In short, it's the value of the brand's capital.

For the advertiser, the job of building brand equity requires time and money. Brand value and preference drive market share, but share points are usually won by the advertisers who spend the most.[35] Just as important, as shown in Exhibit 5–22, companies must maintain consistency in their message and tone by integrating all their communications—from packaging and advertising to promotion and publicity—in order to maintain and reinforce the brand's personality and image.

Product Packaging

The product's package is an integral component of the product element. But it is also a medium. In 1992, 15,886 new products were introduced into grocery and drugstores to compete for customer attention and dollars—a 3.1 percent increase over 1991.[36] Because of the emphasis on self-service, the package often determines the outcome of this competition.

Package designers (who sometimes work in agencies) must make the package exciting, appealing, and at the same time functional. The five considerations in package design are *identification, containment and protection, convenience, consumer appeal,* and *economy.* If handled in a unique and

EXHIBIT • 5-22

A company's overall image evolves over time through consistent images and buzz words presented in a variety of media. The images for Bass shoes paint an overall picture of comfortable outdoor shoes with "the look that never wears out."

creative manner, these functions may even become **copy points**—copywriting themes—in the product's advertising.

Identification

Packaging is such an important identification device that some companies use the same package and label design for years Why? Because the unique combination of trade name, trademark, or trade character—reinforced by the package design—quickly identifies the product's brand and differentiates it from competitors. For example, the traditional Coca-Cola bottle, shown in Exhibit 5–23, was so unique and popular that in 1992 the company began reintroducing it to U.S. markets. The company never stopped using it in many international markets since it differentiated Coke so well from other cola products.

Packages must offer high visibility and clear legibility just to penetrate shoppers' *physiological* screens. Product features must be easy to read, and color combinations must provide high contrast—all aimed at differentiating the product.[37]

This does not mean a package should be gaudy or garish. To penetrate the consumer's *psychological* screen, the package design must reflect the tone, image, and personality of the product concept. In fact, the package often reveals more about the product concept than the product itself; and, in many product categories (wine, cosmetics), the quality of the package is the primary determinant of the consumer's perception of the product's quality.

Containment, Protection, and Convenience

The basic purpose of any package is to hold and protect the product and make it easy to use. While marketers must design an interesting package, they must

EXHIBIT • 5-23

The famous Coca-Cola bottle with its unique, easy-to-hold shape faded from American markets as consumers were offered aluminum cans and plastic one-liter containers. In 1992, however, one of package design's classic examples of differentiation was returned to duty.

also ensure that it will keep the product fresh and protect its contents from shipping damage, water vapor (for frozen goods), grease, infestation, and odors. Consumers don't expect contaminated food, leaky packages, cut fingers, or tampering by criminals. And packages must adhere to the protection requirements established by both the government and trade associations.

Retailers want packages that are easy to stack and display; they also want a full range of sizes to fit their customers' needs. Consumers, likewise, want packages that are easy to open and store. So these are important design considerations. But convenience can't interfere with protection. Spouts make pouring easier, but they may also limit a package's physical strength.

Consumer Appeal

Consumer appeal in packaging is the result of many factors—size, color, material, and shape.

Certain colors have special meanings to consumers. (see Exhibit 5–24). General Foods, for example, changed the Sanka package to orange when it learned that its yellow label suggested weakness.

A package's shape, as Exhibit 5–25 demonstrates, also offers an opportunity for consumer appeal based on whimsy, humor, or romance. Containers of Janitor in a Drum and heart-shaped packages of Valentine's Day candy instantly tell what the product is and what it is used for.

Some companies design packages with a secondary use in mind. Kraft's cheese jar, once emptied, can be used for serving fruit juice. Some tins and bottles even become collectibles (Chivas Regal). These packages are really premiums that give the buyers extra value for the dollars they spend.

Economy

The costs of the features we discuss—protection, identification, convenience, and consumer appeal—add to basic production costs.

Sometimes a small increase in production costs may be more than offset by increased customer appeal. These benefits may make a considerable difference to the consumer and affect both the product concept and the way the product is advertised. For example, a variety of medicines now come in child-proof plastic bottles. And many companies advertise their packages as environmentally friendly.[38]

EXHIBIT • 5-24

Related products from Quaker Oats use color bars to indicate different flavors (blue for regular, magenta for raisin and spice flavor, etc.) and a consistent package color to create an overall product identity.

EXHIBIT • 5-25

The Certifiably Nuts packaging features little straitjackets and a whimsical message on the bottom of the point-of-purchase display, revealed only when the product is removed.

ADVERTISING AND THE PRICE ELEMENT

Many companies—especially small ones—request input from their advertising people about pricing strategies.[39] That's because the **price element** of the marketing mix influences consumer perceptions so dramatically.

Key Factors Influencing Price

Companies typically set their prices based on such factors as market demand for the product, costs of production and distribution, competition, and corporate objectives. Since price plays such an important role in advertising, we consider these factors briefly.

Market Demand

If the supply of a product is static, but the desire (or demand) for it increases, the price tends to rise. If demand drops below available supply, the price tends to fall; and this may dramatically affect advertising messages. See Exhibit 5–26.

In the recession of 1990–91, many auto manufacturers faced a glut of unsold new cars and declining customer demand. Several companies offered substantial factory rebates—in effect, a price cut—to motivate prospective buyers. Dealers immediately sold more cars. No amount of image or awareness advertising would have had the same effect. But, of course, advertising was essential to communicate the price cut.

Some marketing researchers theorize that for new durable-good products, advertising works with word-of-mouth communication to generate awareness of and belief in the product's attributes. Once consumers perceive that the product's value warrants the purchase price, sales occur. As product experience and information spread, the risks typically associated with new products diminish, which effectively increases the consumer's willingness to purchase at a higher price.[40] For advertisers, the implications of this theory are immense.

EXHIBIT • 5-26

This graph plots demand versus price and supply versus price. The demand curve shows the amounts demanded at various prices. The supply curve shows the amounts offered for sale at various prices. The point where the two curves cross is called the market clearing price, where demand and supply balance. It is the price that theoretically clears the market of supply.

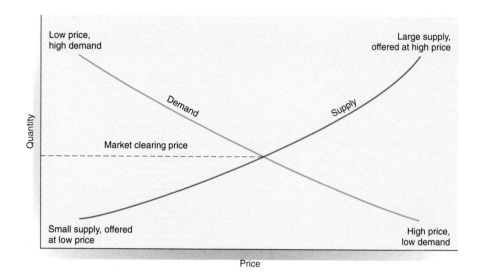

Production and Distribution Costs

The price of goods depends largely on the costs of production and distribution. As these costs increase, they must be passed on to the consumer or the company will be unable to meet its overhead and be forced out of business. Advertising can enhance a product's image in order to justify a higher price. (Interestingly, many premium-priced products are touted for the very fact that they cost more. L'Oréal successfully promotes the expense of its premium hair-care products with the line: "I'm worth it.")

Competition

Marketers believe that, in many product categories, consumers are less concerned with a product's actual price than with its perceived price relative to competitors. For the advertiser, maintaining that perception during periods of intense price competition and fluctuation is challenging and critically important. Protecting the company's perceived price position is the guidepost for many recommendations advertising managers offer.[41]

Corporate Objectives

A company's objectives also influence price. When introducing new products, companies often set a high price initially to recover development and start-up costs as quickly as possible. On the other hand, the objective may be to position the product as an inexpensive convenience item aimed at a broad target market. In this case, ads stress the product's economy.[42]

As products enter the maturity stage of their life cycle, corporate objectives tend to aim at increasing—or maintaining—market share. To accomplish this, competitive advertising and promotion heats up, and prices tend to drop.

Variable Influences

Prevailing economic conditions, consumer income and tastes, government regulations, marketing costs, and the supply of raw materials also influence prices and thus advertising. Marketing management must consider all these factors to determine an appropriate pricing strategy.

CHECKLIST   Strategies for Setting Prices

◇ *Competitive pricing strategy*. Prices set at or below competitors' prices. Ads show a variety of products with large, bold prices and boast, "We won't be undersold." Requires constant competitive monitoring; may invite retaliation.

◇ *Skimming strategy*. Initial prices set relatively high to recover the initial capital spent developing the product—or furnishing, decorating, stocking, and promoting a store. Ads feature quality, convenience, and service. As competition increases, prices might be lowered.

◇ *Penetration pricing*. Initial prices set low at first to penetrate the market quickly. As business develops, prices are gradually raised to a more profitable level. Initial ads feature low prices; later ads promote store services, quality products, wide selection, or convenience.

◇ *Promotional pricing*. Special low prices set to introduce new lines of equipment or to clear out old lines. Typical tactics include two-for-one specials or end-of-month sales. Designed to maintain traffic, stimulate demand, or make room for new merchandise.

◇ *Loss-leader pricing*. One piece of merchandise selected and advertised at a price well below cost to create store traffic and sell other regularly priced merchandise. Companies offering loss leaders must have the items in stock and be prepared to sell them without trying to "switch" customers to higher-priced items. Bait-and-switch advertising is illegal in many areas and unethical everywhere.

◇ *Prestige pricing*. Nonprice competition. The business offers the finest merchandise, the best service, free delivery, and friendly, knowledgeable clerks in plush, convenient surroundings. Ads may not even mention prices.

The Impact of Pricing Strategies on Advertising

A company has relatively few options for determining its price strategy, and these decisions depend on the desired product concept. Say you are opening a retail store. You plan to sell audio equipment, CD players, car stereos, and peripheral products. One of your first decisions is how to price your merchandise. Consider the alternatives listed in the Checklist of Strategies for Setting Prices. Each strategy will have a different effect on how you advertise.

Which of these strategies would you select for your new audio store? Why? What are the advantages and disadvantages of each? How would they affect your advertising? To understand Reebok's pricing strategy, see Ad Lab 5–B, "Marketing Reebok: The Price Element and the Market."

ADVERTISING AND THE PLACE ELEMENT

Every company must decide how and where its customers will buy its products. At the factory? From a door-to-door salesperson? In a store? Before the first ad can be created, the **place element**—or distribution—must be decided. Companies use two basic methods of distribution: direct or indirect.

Direct Distribution

When companies sell directly to end users or consumers, they employ **direct distribution**. Avon, for example, employs sales reps who work for the factory rather than a retailer and sell directly to consumers. Encyclopedia publishers, insurance companies, and many industrial concerns also often sell and distribute their products and services directly to customers without the use of wholesalers or retailers. In these cases, the advertising burden is carried entirely by the manufacturer without any assistance from other members of the distribution channel.

AD LAB 5–B   Marketing Reebok: The Price Element and the Market

Once Reebok selected its new target market and product concept in 1980, it decided on a premium pricing strategy aimed at the higher end of the aerobics market. Recall that total market revenues were $1 billion. By 1991, reported total market revenues reached $5.8 billion. Along with this growth came increased costs. Reebok's ad budget was $126 million in 1991, but sales growth was 13.7 percent that year. With continued growth, Reebok can be flexible in its pricing strategies for each line of shoe.

Laboratory Application

1. Review the Reebok story in Ad Lab 5–A and describe how the product's features justified the higher price to Reebok's target market of aerobics participants.

2. Visit two or three stores where Reeboks are sold. Can you determine the company's current pricing strategy or strategies?

Indirect Distribution

Manufacturers usually don't sell directly to end users or consumers. Most companies market their products through a *distribution channel* that includes a network of *middlemen*. A **middleman** is a business firm that operates between the producer and the consumer or industrial purchaser—someone who deals in trade rather than production.[43] Middlemen include both wholesalers and retailers, as well as manufacturers' representatives, brokers, jobbers, and distributors. (Note that gender has no bearing on the term *middleman*.) A **distribution channel** comprises all the firms and individuals that take title, or assist in taking title, to the product as it moves from the producer to the consumer.

Various types of indirect distribution channels make the massive flow of products available to customers more economically than manufacturers can through direct marketing. Appliance companies, for example, contract with exclusive regional distributors who buy the products from the factory and resell them to local dealers who, in turn, resell them to consumers. Many industrial companies market their products through reps or distributors to *original-equipment manufacturers (OEMs)*. These OEMs, in turn, may incorporate the product as a component in their own product, which is then sold to their customers.

The advertising a company uses depends on its method of distribution. Much of the advertising we see is not prepared or paid for by the manufacturer but by the distributor or retailer as in Exhibit 5–27. Members of a distribution channel give enormous promotional support to the manufacturers they represent.

As part of their marketing strategy, manufacturers must determine the amount of market coverage necessary for their products. Procter & Gamble, for example, defines adequate coverage for Crest toothpaste as virtually every supermarket, discount store, drugstore, and variety store. Other products might need only one dealer for every 50,000 people. Consumer goods manufacturers traditionally use three types of distribution strategies: *intensive, selective,* and *exclusive*.

(MUSIC: STIRRING THROUGHOUT)
ANNCR: To succeed in business, you don't need to be big. All you need is a dream. Just a dream and the passion to pursue it. And the dedication to see it through. And the talent to build on it. And the opportunity to use your talent. And a little luck. And some pencils. And pens. Maybe some typewriter ribbon and correction fluid. And some of those little yellow note pads with the sticky stuff on the back. And some computer paper. And some laser printers to put it in. And some desks to put the prints on. And a fax machine. And some of those #10 envelopes with the little windows in them so you can send out bills. And you can save a bundle on all of these things at Staples, The Office Superstore. Because Staples offers guaranteed lowest prices on over 5,000 basic business necessities. With such incredibly low prices, you can take all that money you save and put it into your dream, instead. Staples. The Office Superstore. Conveniently located in Cincinnati and Springdale or call for delivery at 1-800-333-3330. Dreams sold separately.

E X H I B I T • 5-27

With a little bit of humor, Staples gives tremendous promotional support to the brands it carries without ever mentioning a single one by name.

Intensive Distribution

Soft drinks, candy, Bic pens, Timex watches, and many other convenience goods are available to purchasers at every possible location because of **intensive distribution.** They are so widely available, consumers can buy them with a minimum of effort. The profit on each unit is usually very low, but the volume of sales is high. For this reason, the sales burden is usually carried by the manufacturer's national advertising programs. Ads appear in trade magazines to **push** the product into the retail "pipeline" and in mass media to stimulate consumers to **pull** the products through the pipeline. As a manufacturer modifies its strategy to more push or more pull, special promotions may be directed at the trade or at consumers to build brand volume (see Chapter 16).[44]

Selective Distribution

By limiting the number of outlets through **selective distribution,** manufacturers can cut their distribution and promotion costs. Many hardware tools are sold selectively through discount chains, home-improvement centers, and hardware stores. Levi Strauss sells through better department and chain stores. Manufacturers may use national advertising, but the sales burden is normally carried by the retailer. The manufacturer may share part of the retailer's advertising costs through a **cooperative advertising** program. For example, a Levi's retailer (see Exhibit 5–28) may receive substantial allowances from the manufacturer for advertising Levi's clothing in its local area. In return, the retailer agrees to display the manufacturer's products prominently.

Exclusive Distribution

Some manufacturers grant **exclusive distribution** rights to a wholesaler or retailer in one geographic region. For example, a town of 50,000 to 100,000 people will have only one Chrysler dealer and no Mercedes dealer. This is also common in high fashion, major appliances, and furniture lines. What is lost in market coverage is often gained in the ability to maintain a prestige image and premium prices. Exclusive distribution agreements also force manufacturers and retailers to cooperate closely in advertising and promotion programs.

Vertical Marketing Systems—The Growth of Franchising

To be efficient, members of a distribution channel need to cooperate closely with one another. This need gave rise to the development of the **vertical marketing system (VMS)**—a centrally programmed and managed distribution system that supplies or otherwise serves a group of stores or other businesses. A VMS profits from economies of scale and maximizes the marketing impact of all the stores in its chain.

There are many types of vertical marketing systems. But today, the greatest growth is in **franchising**—like McDonald's, Baskin Robbins, PIP Printing, or Futurekids (see Exhibit 5–29) in which dealers (or *franchisees*) pay a fee to operate under the guidelines and direction of the parent company or manufacturer (called the *franchisor*). An estimated 33 percent of all retail sales in the United States are made through franchise outlets.[45] This is an interesting statistic considering there are only 4,500 franchisors throughout the United States and Canada, compared to some 20 million businesses in the United States alone.[46] As a result, similar vertical marketing systems are developing in the health-care business—retail dentistry, urgent/primary-care centers, and freestanding day surgery clinics.[47]

Franchising and other vertical marketing systems offer both manufacturers and retailers numerous advantages: reduction of nonessential product offerings; streamlining of product and information flow; reduced duplication of efforts; standardization of record-keeping; centralized coordination of marketing

EXHIBIT • 5-28

Some retail advertising that also identifies a manufacturer's label may indicate a cooperative sharing of the advertising expense.

efforts; and substantial savings and continuity in advertising. Perhaps most important is consumer recognition: the moment a new McDonald's opens, the franchisee has instant customers. Moreover, a common store name and similar product inventories mean that a single newspaper ad can promote all of a chain's retailers in a particular trading area.[48]

As Exhibit 5–30 shows, many marketers—Burger King, Sir Speedy, Mailboxes, Etc.—find that franchising is the best way to introduce their services into global markets. Subway sandwich shops, for example, is the fastest growing franchise operation in North America with a total of 7,000 stores (400 in Canada). With a solid base at home, the company entered the 90s by aggres-

EXHIBIT • 5–30

Franchises are expanding their influence on an international level.

sively approaching new markets in Australia, Japan, Israel, Ireland, Mexico, Portugal, and South Korea.[49]

The European Economic Community, a large market of 340 million people, is rapidly opening to innovative marketers. As a result, franchising is starting to grow rapidly, especially in the United Kingdom, France, Germany, Spain, Belgium, and the Netherlands. While franchising is less regulated in Europe, advertising is more regulated. This again points out the need for local experts to manage the advertising function in foreign markets.[50]

Now that we've seen how advertising relates to the product, price, and place elements, let's look at the promotion element of which advertising is an integral part.

ADVERTISING AND THE PROMOTION ELEMENT

Once it determines product, price, and place, a company is ready to plan its promotional activities. Advertising is just one component of the promotion element. (See Ad Lab 5–C, "Marketing Reebok: Deciding on the Promotion Element.")

The **promotion element** includes all marketing-related communications between the seller and the buyer. A variety of marketing communication tools comprise the **promotional mix.** These tools can be grouped into *personal selling* and *nonpersonal selling* activities.

Personal selling includes all person-to-person contact with customers. **Nonpersonal selling** activities—which use some medium as an intermediary for communication—include *advertising, direct marketing, public relations, sales promotion,* and *collateral materials.* Today, successful marketing managers blend all these elements into an *integrated marketing communications program.* See Part V for a complete discussion of this subject.

Personal Selling

Some consumer products are sold by clerks in retail stores, others by salespeople who call on customers directly. Personal selling is very important in business-to-business marketing. It establishes a face-to-face situation in which the marketer can learn firsthand about customer wants and needs, and customers find it more difficult to say no.

Advertising

Advertising is sometimes called mass or nonpersonal selling. In an integrated marketing communication program, it informs, persuades, and reminds customers about particular products and services. In some cases—like mail order—advertising even closes the sale.

Certain products lend themselves to advertising more than others. The following factors are particularly important for advertising success:

- High primary demand trend.
- Chance for significant product differentiation.
- Hidden qualities highly important to consumers.
- Opportunity to use strong emotional appeals.
- Substantial sums available to support advertising.

Where these conditions exist, as in the cosmetics industry, companies spend large amounts on advertising, and the ratio of advertising to sales dollars is often quite high. For completely undifferentiated products, such as sugar, salt, and other raw materials or commodities, price is usually the primary influence, and

AD LAB 5–C   Marketing Reebok: Deciding on the Promotion Element

In its initial 1980 promotional program, Reebok gave samples to aerobics instructors, sold direct to dealers, and advertised in trade and consumer magazines.

Over the years, Reebok dramatically increased its ad budget; it is now one of the top 100 advertisers in the United States. In 1991 Reebok increased its U.S. advertising budget by 56 percent to more than $126 million; worldwide Reebok spent over $220 million.

With the success of its innovative Pump technology, Reebok tried to keep the lead in technology—even though it lost its sales lead to Nike in 1989. The company created a series of campaigns designed to catch the attention of various market segments. The ads pictured here, a three-page

insert in athletic enthusiast magazines, cleverly appeal to different market segments in their headlines and copy.

Laboratory Applications

1. Using geographic, demographic, psychographic, and behavioristic terms, how would you describe the target markets these ads appeal to? What specific elements in the ads lead you to your conclusions?

2. If you were a brand manager for Reebok, how would you use the promotion mix to create an integrated marketing communications program? Would you use public relations? Sales promotion? Collateral materials? How?

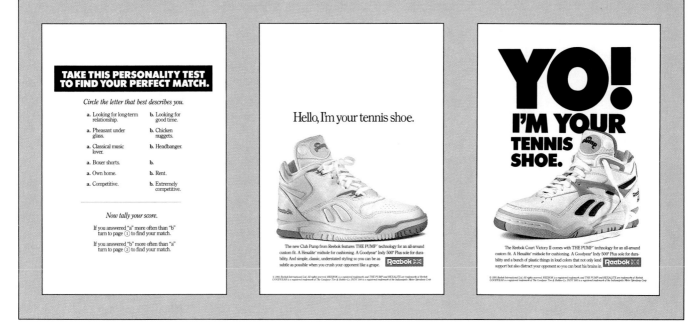

advertising is minimally important. Sunkist is an interesting exception. This farmers' cooperative successfully brands an undifferentiated commodity (citrus fruit) and markets it internationally.

Direct Marketing

Direct marketing is like taking the store to the customer. A mail-order house that communicates directly with consumers through ads and catalogs is one of many types of companies engaged in direct marketing. It builds and maintains its own database of customers and uses a variety of media to communicate with those customers.

Today, the field of direct marketing is growing rapidly as companies discover the benefits of control, cost efficiency, and accountability. For example, many companies like Levi Strauss use a **telemarketing** system (a direct-marketing technique) to increase productivity through person-to-person phone contact. By using the phone to follow up direct-mail advertising, companies can increase the response rate by 2.5 to 10 times.[51] Moreover, through telemarketing, a company like Levi Strauss can develop a valuable database of customers and prospects to use in future mailings and promotions.[52] We discuss this topic more thoroughly in Chapter 16.

Public Relations

Whereas advertising is paid-for communication, **public relations** usually has no clear or overt sponsorship. Many firms supplement (or replace) their advertising with public relations activities such as publicity (news releases, media advisements, feature stories) and special events (open houses, factory tours, VIP parties, grand openings) to inform various audiences about the company and its products and help build corporate credibility and image. Public relations, as we discuss in Chapter 17, is an extremely powerful tool that should always be integrated into a company's promotional mix.

Sales Promotion

Sales promotion, discussed in Chapter 16, is a broad category covering many nonmedia advertising activities such as trade deals, free samples, displays, trading stamps, sweepstakes, cents-off coupons, and premiums. *Reader's Digest,* for example, is famous for its annual sweepstakes designed to increase circulation. Manufacturers print and distribute over 300 billion coupons per year, but only 4 percent are ever redeemed. However, that 4 percent amounts to $2.5 to $3 billion annually.[53]

Collateral Materials

As mentioned in Chapter 3, **collateral** refers to the many accessory advertising materials companies prepare to integrate their advertising or public relations campaign: booklets, catalogs, brochures, films, trade-show exhibits, sales kits, annual reports, and point-of-purchase displays. These should always be designed to reinforce the company or brand image in the minds of customers.

THE MARKETING MIX IN PERSPECTIVE

With the target market designated and the various elements of the marketing mix determined, the company has a complete product concept and a strategic basis for marketing to that target. Now it can formalize its strategies and tactics in a written marketing and advertising plan. As part of the planning process, companies typically use a variety of marketing and advertising research procedures. In Chapter 6, we'll discuss these before dealing with the formal planning process in Chapter 7.

Summary

The majority fallacy refers to the common misconception that a product or service must appeal to the majority of people to be successful. In fact, by aiming at specific target market segments, new products usually compete better and achieve deeper market penetration.

The product marketing process is the sequence of activities marketers perform to select markets and develop marketing mixes.

Market segmentation is the process of identifying groups of people with certain shared characteristics within a broad product market and aggregating these groups into larger market segments according to their mutual interest in the product's utility. From these segments, companies can then select a target market. Marketers use a variety of methods to identify behavioral groups and segment markets. The most common are geographic, demographic, behavioristic, and psychographic.

Business markets are often segmented in the same way as consumer markets. In addition, they may be grouped by business purchasing procedures, by SIC code, or by market concentration.

In the target marketing process, companies designate specific segments to target and develop their mix of marketing activities. The product concept is the consumer's perception of the product as a bundle of utilitarian and symbolic need-satisfying values.

Every company can add, subtract, or modify four major elements in its marketing program to achieve a desired marketing mix. These elements, referred to as the 4 Ps, are product, price, place, and promotion.

The *product* element includes the way the product is designed and classified, positioned, branded, and packaged. Just as humans pass through a life cycle, so do products—and product categories. The stage of a product's life cycle may determine how it is advertised.

To satisfy the variety of consumer tastes and achieve competitive advantages, marketers build differences into their products. Even the product's package is a part of the product concept. The product concept may also be developed through unique positioning against competitive products.

Price refers to what and how a customer pays for a product. Companies use many common pricing strategies. Some products compete on the basis of price, but many do not.

The term *place* refers to how and where the product is distributed, bought, and sold. Companies may use direct or indirect methods of distribution. Consumer goods manufacturers use several types of distribution strategies.

Promotion refers to all marketing-related communications between the seller and the buyer. Tools of the promotional element include personal selling, advertising, direct marketing, public relations, sales promotion, and collateral materials. Marketers try to integrate all their marketing communications programs for greater effectiveness.

Questions for Review and Discussion

1. How does the majority fallacy relate to the subject of market segmentation?
2. How could you use VALS to develop the marketing strategy for a product of your choice?
3. How does the segmentation of business markets differ from that of consumer markets?
4. What is the most important factor to consider when determining the elements of the marketing mix?
5. What is the difference between a product and a product concept?

6. What are some examples of product positioning not discussed in this chapter?
7. What effect does the product life cycle have on the advertising a company employs?
8. What factors influence the price of a product?
9. How do the basic methods of distribution affect advertising?
10. What product characteristics encourage heavy advertising? Little advertising? Why?

POOR VISION IS NO EXCUSE FOR PICKING OUT AN UGLY PAIR OF GLASSES.

Marketing and Advertising Research: Inputs to the Planning Process

Objective: To examine how marketers and advertisers gain information about the marketplace and how they apply their findings to marketing and advertising decision making.

After studying this chapter, you will be able to:

- Discuss how research helps advertisers locate market segments and identify target markets.

- Explain the basic steps in the research process.

- Discuss the differences between formal and informal research and primary and secondary data.

- Explain the methodologies used in quantitative and qualitative research.

- Define and explain the concepts of validity and reliability.

- Recognize the issues and pitfalls in creating survey questionnaires.

- Debate the pros and cons of advertising testing.

t was a most unusual commercial for an antihistamine. But Dan believed it was just what the client needed to break through viewer boredom. The product—Claritin—was new to the over-the-counter (OTC) market. People didn't know the name, they didn't know the product, and they certainly didn't know the benefits it offered—effective allergy relief with no drowsiness. Moreover, Claritin faced two major, established competitors (Seldane and Hismanal) that had already carved up the nondrowsy antihistamine market for themselves.

Fortunately, in its two years on the market as a prescription drug, Claritin had sold well. And the client and agency had done a lot of research. They knew Claritin had the features allergy sufferers wanted—fast, effective, nondrowsy relief at an affordable price. From extensive clinical tests, they also knew Claritin didn't have the pharmacological problems of some of its competitors (although Canadian law, as well as business ethics, did not permit them to advertise this fact). They had to get people to try Claritin.

Claritin's agency was Cossette Communications-Marketing in Montreal, the largest domestically owned agency in Canada. And Daniel Rabinowicz was the agency's key person in charge of the Schering Canada business, the giant pharmaceutical company that developed Claritin and was preparing to launch it nationally. Dan marshalled the agency's top research, creative, and media people to come up with an unusual campaign for Claritin—one that would quickly penetrate consumers' perceptual screens and create instant awareness of the new product.

On the client side, Chuck McDonald was Schering's vice president of sales and marketing. Elyse Rowen was the OTC product manager in charge of Claritin. They agreed with Dan. Going up against a half dozen competitive products led by two strong market leaders, they had to use an unconventional approach and make an unprecedented assault on the marketplace—or they would never have a chance of recouping the millions that had been invested in research and development for Claritin.

They agreed to use TV. Media research convinced them that no other medium could get the product into the consumer's consciousness as fast.

The creative approach was, well, different. Instead of the typical "doctor" testimonial, a heavy metal rock singer making contorted facial expressions while twanging far-out discordant "music" on his lead guitar served as a metaphor for the pain and misery allergy sufferers experience. When Claritin came to the rescue, the image and sound of the rock guitarist shrank to nothingness (see Exhibit 6-1).

EXHIBIT • 6-1

Claritin's first commercial of a heavy metal rock musician was very memorable but received mixed reactions from the public, so the agency created new testimonial spots spoofing their own commercials.

"There's this TV ad that's driving me nuts."
SFX: Heavy metal guitar.
"It's this new antihistamine. . .
Uh. . . Claritin."
"He does something with his face. . ."

SFX: Heavy metal guitar.
"Claritin's great . . . it's the ad."
SFX: Heavy metal guitar.
"I think. I'm allergic to the commercial. . .
Quick gimme a Claritin."

VO: New Claritin. Fast, 24 hour relief of seasonal allergies that lets you stay alert. From the makers of ChlorTripolon.

EXHIBIT • 6-2

Cossette likened the distress of allergy sufferers to the misery of a jackhammer operator in one of its highly creative spots for Claritin.

VO: Having allergies can be this annoying.
SFX: Pneumatic Jack-Hammer throughout.
VO: Taking Claritin is this effective.

SFX: Sound of Jack-Hammer. . .
. . . diminishes.
SFX: Truck Horn.

VO: New Claritin. Fast, 24 hour relief of seasonal allergies that lets you stay alert. From
the makers of ChlorTripolon.

Awareness they got, but Chuck McDonald was not prepared for the subsequent barrage of letters. Half the viewers loved the commercials; the other half thought they were irritating and absolutely hated them. Schering debated whether to pull the commercials.

Cossette's research division, Impact Research, quickly ran a telephone posttest with a sample of 200 consumers to measure market reactions. Results were indeed negative. But rather than pulling the commercials, Cossette showed its creative moxie by using the research to spawn a new commercial: a series of real allergy sufferers talking about how much they hated the Claritin commercials—but loved the product.

Awareness soared. And so did trial. Schering and Cossette performed more research, and even more creative ads followed (see Exhibit 6–2). Claritin's sales rose; competitors' plummeted. Within two years, Claritin was a strong number two, and by 1993, it captured market leadership. By continuously researching the market and integrating that information with outstanding advertising creativity, Schering made Claritin second to none.[1] ◆

THE NEED FOR RESEARCH IN MARKETING AND ADVERTISING

Companies don't want to waste millions of dollars on advertising that their customers won't notice or respond to or in media their customers don't watch or read. Advertising is expensive. In the United States in 1991, for example, the cost of a single 30-second commercial on prime-time network TV average $122,200. That equates to an average of $9.74 to reach 1,000 TV households—more than double the cost in 1980. Likewise, a single, full-page color ad in a national magazine averages $18.44 to reach a thousand prospects.[2] That's too much money to risk on speculative information; and that's why advertising decision makers need research. Without it, they're forced to use intuition or guesswork. In today's fast-changing, highly-competitive, and global economy, this invites failure.[3]

Marketing Research

Marketing research refers to the systematic procedures used to gather, record, and analyze new information to help managers make marketing decisions.[4] (**Market research,** not to be confused with marketing research, is information gathering about a particular market or market segment.) For firms that operate under the marketing concept (discussed in Chapter 4), marketing research plays a key role in identifying consumer needs and market segments, developing new products and marketing strategies, and assessing the effectiveness of marketing programs and promotional activities. Marketing research is also useful in financial planning, economic forecasting, and quality control as well as in traditional marketing areas like advertising.

Companies today spend millions of dollars developing new products and bringing them to market. In the pharmaceutical business, for instance, a company like Schering may spend as much as $200 million on research and development before it can even bring a new drug to market. Major advertisers can't afford to risk that kind of money by ignoring research findings. They depend on sophisticated information. Worldwide companies currently spend an estimated $5 billion per year on marketing, advertising, and public opinion research. The top 50 U.S. research organizations—led by the global A.C. Nielsen company—account for close to 60 percent of this amount, much of it coming from foreign clients.[5]

Advertising Research

Before developing any campaign, an agency needs to know how consumers perceive the client's product (including its strong points and liabilities), how they perceive its competitors, and what image would be most credible. For that kind of information, companies need *advertising research.*

A subset of marketing research, **advertising research** is the systematic gathering and analysis of information to help develop or evaluate advertising strategies, ads and commercials, and media campaigns.

To develop media strategies, select media vehicles, and evaluate their results, advertisers use a subset of advertising research called **media research.** Agencies usually perform this type of research by subscribing to **syndicated research services** (A. C. Nielsen, Arbitron, Simmons, Standard Rate & Data Service, etc.) that monitor and publish information on the reach and effectiveness of media vehicles—radio, TV, newspapers, and so on—in every major geographic market in the United States and Canada. (We'll discuss these more in Part IV: Advertising Media.)

In this chapter, we explore the procedures and techniques used in marketing and advertising research. We consider the importance of research to the development of marketing and advertising plans and strategies, and we look at the ways research can be used to test the effectiveness of ads and campaigns both before and after they run.

STEPS IN THE RESEARCH PROCESS

There are five basic steps in the research process: situation analysis and problem definition, informal (exploratory) research, construction of research objectives, formal research, and interpretation and reporting of findings (see Exhibit 6–3).

Analyzing the Situation and Defining the Problem

The first step in the marketing research process is to analyze the situation to identify and define the problem. Many large firms have in-house research

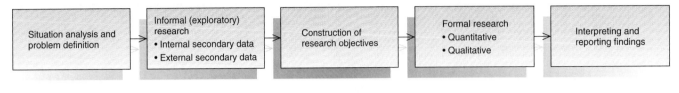

The marketing research process begins with evaluation of the company's situation and definition of the problem.

departments. At Schering Canada, for example, Robert West, the manager of marketing and sales services, develops and maintains a **marketing information system (MIS)**—a set of procedures and methods for generating a continuous, orderly flow of information for use in making marketing decisions. These systems ensure managers get the information they need when they need it.[6]

Most smaller firms don't have dedicated research departments, and their methods for obtaining marketing information are frequently inadequate. For them, the situation analysis is often difficult and time-consuming. Yet good research on the wrong problem is a waste of effort.

Conducting Informal (Exploratory) Research

The second step in the process is to use **informal** *(exploratory)* **research** to learn more about the market, the competition, and the business environment, and to better define the problem. Researchers may discuss the problem with informed sources inside the firm; with wholesalers, distributors, or retailers outside the firm; with customers; or even with competitors. They look for individuals who have the most information to offer.

There are two types of research data: *primary* and *secondary.* Information collected from the marketplace about a specific problem is called **primary data.** Acquiring primary data is expensive and time-consuming. So during the exploratory stage, researchers usually use **secondary data**—information previously collected or published, usually for some other purpose, either by the firm or by some other organization. This information is more readily available, either internally or externally, and can be gathered more quickly and inexpensively.

Assembling Internal Secondary Data

Company records are often a valuable source of secondary information. Useful **internal data** include product shipment figures, billings, warranty-card records, advertising expenditures, sales expenses, customer correspondence, and records of meetings with sales staffs.

A well-developed marketing information system can help researchers analyze sales data, review past tracking studies, and examine previous marketing research data.

Gathering External Secondary Data

Much information is available—usually at little or no cost—from the government, market research companies, trade associations, various trade publications, or even computerized databases. Ad Lab 6–A on page 178 lists sources of information on the vitamin market. Many of these sources are applicable to other markets as well.

Although secondary data are less costly and time-consuming to collect, the information may be obsolete, irrelevant, invalid, unreliable, or just overwhelming in amount.

Some of the most frequently used sources of secondary data include:

- Library reference materials (*Business Periodicals Index* and *Canadian Periodical Index* for business magazines, *Reader's Guide to Periodical Literature* for consumer magazines, *Public Information Service Bulletin,* the *New York Times Index,* and the *World Almanac* and *Book of Facts*).

- Government publications (the *Statistical Abstract of the United States* or *Statistics Canada Catalogue*).

- Trade association publications (annual fact books containing government data and information gathered by various industry groups listed in the *Directory of National Trade Associations* and the *Directory of Associations in Canada*).

- Research organization publications (literature from university bureaus of business research, Nielsen retail store audits, MRCA consumer purchase diaries, Standard Rate & Data Service, *Canadian Advertising Rates & Data*, all available on a subscription basis). See Exhibit 6–4.

- Consumer/business publications (*Business Week, Forbes, Fortune, American Demographics, Canadian Consumer, Canadian Business, Advertising Age, Computer Marketing, Marketing* [Canada], and thousands more).

- Computer database services (DIALOG Information Service, IQuest and Knowledge Index from CompuServe, Dow Jones News Retrieval Service, and Corporate Canada Online, available by subscription).

AD LAB 6-A   Using Marketing Research for New-Product Development

You are the advertising manager for a major manufacturer of prescription drug products. Management is interested in producing a line of vitamins for the over-the-counter market, and you must assess the opportunities available and evaluate the potential for obtaining profitable market share. Management also wants to know how quickly and thoroughly advertising can reach the appropriate market segments.

To obtain information on the vitamin market, you turn to four main sources: the government, trade and other organizations, the consumer and business press, and formal publications. Within these sources, you find a wealth of publications that supply relevant data.

General Reference Guidelines

Government *U.S. Government Organizational Manual, Federal Statistical Directory,* government reports and announcements, Statistics Canada.

Trade and Other Organizations *Encyclopedia of Associations, Directory of Associations in Canada.*

Consumer/Business Press *Business Publications Rates & Data, Consumer Magazine & Agri-Media Rates & Data, Canadian Advertising Rates & Data,* Media Measurement Service (Canada).

Publications *Business Periodicals Index, Funk & Scott Index of Corporations & Industries, Index Medicus, Thomas Register of American Corporations, Pharmaceuticals News Index, Reader's Guide to Periodical Literature.*

Issues Specific to the Vitamin Market

Nature of the product, vitamins and how they are used, new products, external issues influencing the market.

Government National Technical Information Service (Dept. of Commerce), National Center for Health Statistics (HHS).

Trade and Other Organizations Vitamin Information Bureau, American Dietetic Association, National Science Foundation.

Consumer/Business Press *Consumer Reports, Today's Health, Drug Topics, Prevention Magazine, American Druggist, Product Marketing.*

Publications *Journal of the AMA, New England Journal of Medicine, FDA Reports.*

Role of Government

Impact of existing and potential government rules and regulations.

Government Food & Drug Administration (HHS), reports of congressional committees.

Trade and Other Organizations The Proprietary Association, Pharmaceutical Manufacturing Association, consumer groups.

Consumer/Business Press Articles in business and drug trade magazines and medical journals.

Publications *Pharmaceutical News Index, FDA Reports.*

Consumer Behavior

Level of vitamin usage by consumers; consumers' perceptions and attitudes about vitamins.

Government National Technical Information Service (Dept. of Commerce), National Center for Health Statistics (HHS).

Using Secondary Data for International Markets

Unfortunately, the research profession is not as sophisticated or as organized in developing countries.[7] Available secondary research statistics may be outdated or invalid. When evaluating secondary data, advertising managers should ask the following questions: Who collected the data and why? What research techniques did they use? Would the source have any reason to bias the data? When was the data collected?

Regardless of the answers, international advertising managers should exercise caution when dealing with "facts" about foreign markets.

Trade and Other Organizations Consumer groups, Print Measurement Bureau (Canada).

Consumer/Business Press *Prevention Magazine*, readership studies of general consumer and trade magazines.

Publications *Findex Directory of Market Research Reports, Studies & Surveys*.

Competition

Nature of the competition and extent of leverage in the market.

Government Form 10-Ks (SEC).

Consumer/Business Press: Articles appearing in business and drug trade magazines.

Publications *Moody's Industrial Manual*, Standard & Poor's corporation records, *Value Line Investment Survey, Dun & Bradstreet Reports*, National Investment Library annual report, Disclosure, Inc., annual report, *Thomas Register of American Corporations, Canadian Trade Index*.

Market Trends and Developments

Size of the market and growth rate, major vitamin categories and relative growth, traditional distribution channels and major retail outlets, seasonal patterns or regional skews.

Government Census of Manufacturers (Dept. of Commerce), Survey of Manufacturers (Dept. of Commerce), current industrial reports (Dept. of Commerce), Statistics Canada.

Trade and Other Organizations The Proprietary Association, Pharmaceutical Manufacturers Association.

Consumer/Business Press *Product Marketing, Drug Topics, Supermarket Business, Canadian Business*, articles in business and drug trade magazines.

Publications *Standard & Poor's Industry Surveys, Pharmaceutical News Index*.

Advertising

Kinds and levels of advertising support, creative strategies employed by advertisers.

Consumer/Business Press *Advertising Age, Marketing Communications, Marketing* (Canada), *Info Press* (Canada).

Publications Leading national advertisers, Publishers Information Bureau.

Once your search is complete, the real job begins—understanding what you've collected!

Laboratory Application

Find an ad for a product in a field that you are familiar with and go to the largest library in your area (preferably your university or main city library). Identify at least two sources from each of the four categories that cite data relevant to the product. Use these data sources to answer the following questions:

1. How can the information you uncovered help improve the ad? Which of the four source categories proved most useful?

2. Which sources would be most helpful for selecting the best media? Be specific.

Establishing Research Objectives

Once the exploratory research phase is completed, the company may find it needs additional information from the marketplace. It may want to identify exactly who its customers are and clarify their perceptions of the company and the competition. To do so, the company first has to establish *specific research objectives*.

A concise, written statement of the research problem and objectives should be formulated at the beginning of any research project. In other words, a company must decide what it's after and correlate these objectives with its marketing and advertising plans.[8] For example, a department store might write its problem statement and research objectives as follows:

Market Share:
Our company's sales, while still increasing, seem to have lost momentum and are not producing the profit our shareholders expect. In the last year, our market share slipped 10 percent in the men's footwear department and 7 percent in the women's fine apparel department. Our studies indicate we are losing sales to other department stores in the same malls where our stores are located and that customers are confused about our position in the market.

Research Objectives:
We must answer the following questions: (1) Who are our customers? (2) Who are the customers of other department stores? (3) What do these customers like and dislike about us and about our competitors? (4) How are we currently perceived? and (5) What do we have to do to clarify and improve that perception?

This problem statement is specific and measurable, and the questions are related and relevant. Answers to these questions might provide a base for developing the company's positioning strategy. The positioning strategy, in turn, facilitates the development of marketing and advertising plans that will set the company's course for years to come.

Conducting Formal Research

When a company wants to collect primary data directly from the *field* (marketplace) about a specific problem or issue, it uses **formal research.** The two types of formal research are *quantitative* and *qualitative.*

Basic Methods of Quantitative Research

Advertising researchers use **quantitative research** to measure market situations in hard numbers. Three basic research methods used to collect quantitative data are *observation, experiment,* and *survey.*

Observation In the **observation method,** researchers monitor the actions of the person being studied. They may count the traffic that passes by a billboard, count a TV audience through instruments hooked to TV sets, or study consumer reactions to products displayed in the supermarket.

One recent development that facilitates observation is the **Universal Product Code (UPC)** label, an identifying series of linear bars with a 10-digit number. See Exhibit 6–5. By "reading" the codes with optical scanners, stores can tell which products are selling and how much. The UPC label not only ensures speed and accuracy at the checkout counter and timely inventory control, it also gives stores and manufacturers accurate data on which to evaluate alternative marketing plans, media vehicles, and promotional campaigns.[9]

At first, scanner data was so detailed and voluminous, it was too complex for many advertisers to handle. Now, thanks to personal computers and new software (like CoverStory from Information Resources), marketing and advertising managers can click a mouse and let the computer sift through data to find out how a product fared in different regions with different promotions facing different competitors. The software can even write a report in plain English.[10]

Companies can now use scanner data to learn how promotion affects purchasing. In one case, data indicated that a 40-cent coupon for toothpaste could create $147,000 in profits, but a 50-cent coupon on the same item would create a $348,000 loss.[11]

E X H I B I T • 6–5

The Universal Product Code on packaging is scanned at checkout counters. It improves checkout time and inventory control, and provides a wealth of accessible data for use in measuring advertising response.

Advertisers used to assume that changes in market share and brand position happen slowly. But observation methods show that the packaged-goods market is extremely complex and volatile. At the local level, weekly sales and share figures may fluctuate considerably, making it very difficult to measure advertising's short-term effectiveness.

Experiment To measure actual cause-and-effect relationships, researchers use the **experimental method.** An experiment is a scientific investigation in which a researcher alters the stimulus received by a test group and compares the results with that of a control group that did not receive the altered stimulus. This type of research is used primarily for test-marketing new products in isolated geographic areas and in testing new advertising campaigns prior to national introduction. For example, a new campaign might be run in one geographic area but not another. Sales in the two areas are then compared to determine the campaign's effectiveness. However, strict controls must be used so that the variable that causes the effect can be accurately determined. And because it's hard to control every marketing variable, this method is difficult and expensive to use.

Survey The most common method of gathering primary research data is the **survey.** The researcher hopes to obtain information on attitudes, opinions, or motivations by questioning current or prospective customers. (Political polls are a common type of survey.) Surveys can be conducted by *personal interview, telephone,* and *mail.* Each has distinct advantages and disadvantages, as shown in Exhibit 6–6.

Basic Methods of Qualitative Research

Quantitative methods can give a good statistical view, but advertisers also need *qualitative* research to understand the "why" of consumer behavior.

   Qualitative research seeks in-depth, open-ended responses, not yes or no answers, to get people to share their thoughts and feelings. However, no matter how skillfully posed, some questions are uncomfortable for consumers to answer. When asked why they bought a particular car, for instance, consumers might reply that it handles well or is dependable, but they won't give the real reason—that it makes them feel like a Hollywood star.[12]

   Qualitative research is used more often to give advertisers a general impression of the market, the consumer, or the product. Some advertisers refer to it as **motivation research.** The methods used in qualitative research are usually described as *projective* or *intensive techniques.*

EXHIBIT • 6-6

Comparison of data collection methods.

	Personal	Telephone	Mail
Costs	High	Medium	Low
Time required	Medium	Low	High
Sample size for a given budget	Small	Medium	Large
Data quantity per respondent	High	Medium	Low
Reaches widely dispersed sample	No	Maybe	Yes
Reaches special locations	Yes	Maybe	No
Interaction with respondents	Yes	Yes	No
Degree of interviewer bias	High	Medium	None
Severity of nonresponse bias	Low	Low	High
Presentation of visual stimuli	Yes	No	Maybe
Field worker training required	Yes	Yes	No

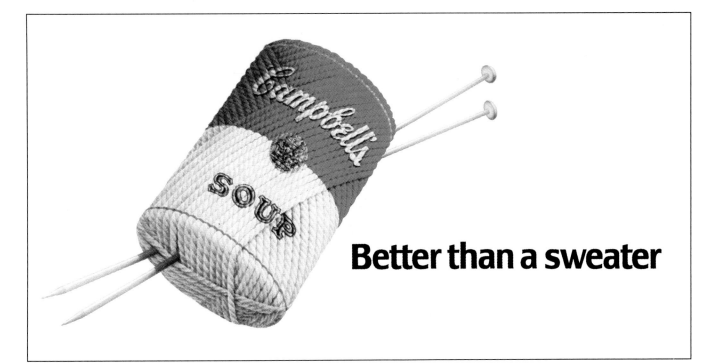

Better than a sweater

EXHIBIT • 6-7

Peter Hume, a "brand character" researcher and principal of the Canadian account planning firm Abraxas, informed Campbell's Soup of Canada that its ads promoting "zip" didn't match the brand image in consumers' minds. The new billboard shown here features a more "hearth-and-home" approach.

Projective Techniques To understand people's underlying or subconscious feelings, attitudes, opinions, needs, and motives, researchers use **projective techniques.** They ask indirect questions or involve consumers in a situation where they can express feelings about the problem or product. A researcher in Toronto used projective techniques to discover that people viewed Campbell soups as "cuddle-tum" food, as he called it. Campbell then revised its advertising from a "gives-you-zip" appeal to a "hearth-and-home" approach, as shown in Exhibit 6–7.

Projective techniques were adapted for marketing research after being used by psychologists for clinical diagnosis. Such techniques require highly experienced researchers.

Intensive Techniques **Intensive techniques** require great care when administering questions. In the **in-depth interview,** carefully planned but loosely structured questions help the interviewer probe respondents' deeper feelings. Schering uses in-depth interviews with physicians to ascertain what attributes doctors consider most important in the drugs they prescribe and to identify what brands they associate with different attributes.[13]

While in-depth interviews are helpful at discovering individual motivations, they are also expensive and time-consuming. And skilled interviewers are in short supply.

The **focus-group** is one of the most useful intensive research techniques. The company invites 8 to 10 people typical of the target market to a group session to discuss the product, the service, or the marketing situation. The session may last an hour or more. A trained moderator guides the often free-

EXHIBIT • 6-8

Focus groups are most effective when held in comfortable settings that encourage participants to discuss their attitudes and beliefs. The sessions are often monitored from behind a one-way mirror as seen here.

wheeling discussion, and the group interaction reveals the participants' true feelings or behavior toward the product. Focus-group meetings are usually recorded and may even be viewed or videotaped from behind a one-way mirror as shown in Exhibit 6–8. Focus groups aren't intended to represent a valid sample of the population. However, participants' responses can often be used to design a formal questionnaire. Focus groups can help put flesh on the skeleton of raw data.

In a series of focus-group studies, Chevrolet learned that consumers thought the company let them down by failing to build cars for the needs of modern Americans. As a result, Chevrolet launched its "Heartbeat of America" campaign to impart a distinct corporate identity and unify the image of its cars and trucks.[14]

Interpreting and Reporting the Findings

The final step in the research process involves interpreting and reporting the data. Research is very costly (see Exhibit 6–9), and its main purpose is to help solve problems. The final report must be comprehensible to the company's managers since they will use the information to implement solutions.

Tables and graphs are helpful, but they must be explained in words management can understand. Technical jargon (such as "multivariate analysis of variance model") should be avoided, and descriptions of the methodology, statistical analysis, and raw data should be confined to an appendix. The report

EXHIBIT • 6-9

The cost of professional research.

Type of research	Features	Cost
Telephone	500 20-minute interviews, with report	$15,000–$18,000
Mail	500 returns, with report—33 percent response rate	$8,000–$10,000
Intercept	500 interviews, four or five questions, with report	$15,000
Executive interviews (talking to business administrators)	20 interviews, with report	$2,500–$7,500
Focus group	One group, 8 to 10 people, with report and videotape	$2,500–$3,800

should state the problem and research objective, summarize the findings, and draw conclusions. The researcher's recommendations for management action should be described, and the report should be discussed in a formal presentation to allow for management feedback and to highlight important points.

CONSIDERATIONS IN CONDUCTING FORMAL QUANTITATIVE RESEARCH

Quantitative (descriptive) research requires formal design and rigorous standards for collecting and tabulating data to ensure its accuracy and usability. When conducting formal research certain issues must be considered.

Validity and Reliability

Assume you want to determine a market's attitude toward a proposed new toy; the market consists of 10 million individuals. You show a prototype of the toy to five people, and four say they like it, an 80 percent favorable attitude. Is that test *valid?* Hardly. For a test to be **valid,** results must reflect the true status of the market.[15] Five people aren't enough.

Moreover, if you repeated the test with five more people, you might get an entirely different response. In that case, your test also lacks *reliability*. For a test to be **reliable,** it must be repeatable—i.e., it must produce the same result each time it is administered. See Exhibit 6–10.

Validity and reliability depend on several key elements: the sampling methods used, the way the survey questionnaire is designed, and the methods used for data tabulation and analysis.

Sampling Theories

When a company wants to know what consumers think about its products or its image, it can't ask just everybody. So its research must reflect the **universe** (the entire target population) of prospective customers. Researchers select from the

EXHIBIT • 6-10

Using the analogy of a dartboard, the bull's-eye is the *actual* average of a value among a population (such as average age in the community). The left column shows high reliability, or *repeatability*—the ages of the sample members are fairly close. The right column shows low reliability; the sample consists of people of varying ages. The top row shows high validity. The marks are centered around the bull's-eye—they reflect the true status of the market. The bottom row shows low validity. In the lower left quadrant, a college fraternity gives similar answers (reliability), but their responses don't reflect the average of the total population.

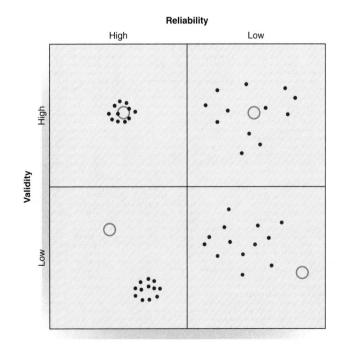

population a **sample**— a part of the relevant population—that they expect will give a representative minipicture of the population's true characteristics.[16] To accomplish this, they must make several basic decisions: who to survey, how many people to survey, and how to choose the respondents. The **sample unit,** those being surveyed, is very important.

To be considered adequate, a sample must be large enough to achieve precision or stability. As shown in Ad Lab 6–B, the larger the sample size, the more reliable the results. However, adequate sample size has nothing to do with the size of the population. Good reliability can be obtained with very small samples—a fraction of 1 percent of the population. There are two types of samples: *random probability samples* and *nonprobability samples;* both are derived from mathematical *theories of probability.*

Random probability samples offer the greatest accuracy because everyone in the universe has an equal chance of being selected.[17] For example, a

AD LAB 6–B   How Does Sampling Work?

By taking *samples* of the population, statisticians give marketing and advertising people the ability to analyze the behavior or attitudes of large masses of people. Then advertisers can predict the results of their advertising.

Statistics establish probabilities. The more information you have about a person, for example, the greater the probability you can predict his or her behavior. Sampling is a way to collect data. The more samples taken, the clearer the probabilities.

Sampling works like the dots in the photos shown here. The clarity of the image improves by using a greater number of dots. The clearest image has several hundred thousand dots (representative of a total population); the others have 2,000, 1,000, and 250 dots (representative of different samples of the population).

These pictures represent a specific type of sampling research called *area probability sampling*—the type often used by national polling organizations and market research firms to predict elections and other outcomes. If each dot represents a household within a neighborhood, the more households visited during the sampling period, the clearer the picture of the neighborhood's attitude—and the greater the chance of predicting the outcome.

Note that the 1,000-dot image is only twice as sharp as its

250-dot neighbor even though it has four times the number of dots. This is true with sampling too. To double the accuracy, researchers must *quadruple* the same size.

If you pull back, you see that the 1,000- and 250-dot images improve in clarity. You may not see a lot of detail, but you get a fairly reliable idea of what the child looks like. Similarly, a random sampling of only 1,200 homes can provide a reasonably accurate projection of how consumers will react to an ad, product, or service anywhere in the nation.

Laboratory Applications

1. Show the picture in this Ad Lab to 10 people and ask them if the child is a girl or a boy. Total the responses for each answer. Have a few classmates or friends show the picture to 10 other people and total the responses. Are their totals consistent with yours? In other words, was the initial sampling enough to accurately predict the response of the wider population? If not, how large a sample do you need?

2. How can sampling be used to determine the popularity of network TV shows? (Don't look at Chapter 14 for the answer.)

researcher who wants to know a community's opinion on a particular issue selects various members of the community at random. But this method has difficulties. Every unit (person) must be known, listed, and numbered so each has an equal chance of being selected, an often prohibitively expensive and sometimes impossible task especially with customers of nationally distributed products.

Nonprobability samples don't give every unit in the universe an equal chance of being included so there's no guarantee the sample is representative. As a result, researchers can't be as confident in the validity of the responses.[18] Nonetheless, researchers use nonprobability samples extensively because they're less expensive and time-consuming and because random sampling is often not feasible. Most marketing and advertising research studies use this method because they need general measures of the data. For example, the nonprobability method of interviewing shoppers in malls may be sufficient to determine the shopping preferences, image perceptions, and attitudes of customers.

How Questionnaires Are Designed

Constructing a good questionnaire requires considerable expertise. Much bias in research is blamed on poorly designed questionnaires. Typical problems include asking the wrong types of questions, asking too many questions, using the wrong form for a question (which makes it too difficult to answer or tabulate), and using the wrong choice of words. See Exhibit 6–11 for questions used in typical surveys.

Consider the simple question: "What kind of soap do you use?" The respondent doesn't know what the word *soap* means. Hand soap, shampoo, laundry detergent, dishwashing soap, cleansing cream, or dishwasher detergent? Does the word *kind* mean brand, size, or type? Finally, what constitutes *use?* What a person buys (it could be for someone else) or actually uses? In fact, one person probably *uses* several different *kinds*. It's impossible to answer the question accurately. Worse, if the question is answered, the researcher doesn't know what the answer signifies and will likely draw an incorrect conclusion. For these reasons, questionnaires must be pretested. (See the Checklist for Developing an Effective Questionnaire.)

CHECKLIST   Developing an Effective Questionnaire

◇ **List specific research objectives**. Don't spend money collecting irrelevant data.

◇ **Write short questionnaires**. Don't tax the respondent's patience; you may get careless or flip answers.

◇ **State questions clearly** so there is no chance for misunderstanding. Avoid generalities and ambiguities.

◇ **Write a rough draft first**, then polish it.

◇ **Use a short opening statement**. Include the interviewer's name, the name of the organization, and the purpose of the questionnaire.

◇ **Put the respondent at ease** by opening with one or two inoffensive, easily answered questions.

◇ **Ask general questions before more detailed ones**. Structure questions so they flow logically.

◇ **Avoid questions that suggest an answer or that could be considered leading**. They bias the results.

◇ **Include a few questions that cross-check earlier answers**. This helps ensure validity.

◇ **Put the demographic questions** (age, income, education) and any other personal questions at the end of the questionnaire.

◇ **Pretest the questionnaire** with 20 to 30 people to be sure the questions are interpreted correctly and that all the information sought is included.

EXHIBIT • 6-11

A personal questionnaire like this helps
determine shoppers' feelings toward a
chain of stores, its merchandise, and its
advertising.

1. Do you intend to shop at __(Store name)__ between now and Sunday?
   Yes   1   No   2   (If no, skip to queston 5)

2. Do you intend to buy something in particular or just to browse?
   Buy   1   Browse   2

3. Have you seen any of the items you intend to buy advertised by __(Store name)__ ?
   Yes   1   (continue)   No   2   (skip to question 5)

4. Where did you see these items advertised? Was it in a __(Store name)__ advertising flyer included with
   your newspaper, a __(Store name)__ flyer you received in the mail, on the pages of the newspaper itself,
   on TV, or somewhere else?

   Flyer in newspaper   _____
   Flyer in mail   _____
   Pages of newspaper   _____
   On TV   _____
   Somewhere else (specify)   _____
   Don't recall   _____

5. Please rate the __(Store name)__ advertising insert on the attributes listed below. Place an X in the box
   at the position that best reflects your opinion of how the insert rates on each attribute. Placing an X in
   the middle box usually means you are neutral. The closer you place the "X" to the left or right phrase
   or word, the more you believe it describes the __(Store name)__ insert.

Looks expensive							Looks cheap

   Looks expensive   Looks cheap
   Cleverly done   Unskillful
   Appealing   Unappealing
   Shows clothing   Does not show
   in an attractive   clothing in an
   manner   1   2   3   4   5   6   7   attractive manner

6. Please indicate all of the different types of people listed below you feel this __(Store name)__
   advertising insert is appealing to.

   Young people   _____   Quality-conscious people   _____
   Bargain hunters   _____   Low-income people   _____
   Conservative dressers   _____   Budget watchers   _____
   Fashion-conscious people _____   Older people   _____
   Rich people   _____   Middle-income people   _____
   Professionals   _____   Blue-collar people   _____
   High-income people   _____   Women   _____
   Men   _____   Office workers   _____
   Someone like me   _____   Smart dressers   _____
   Career-oriented women   _____   Other (specify) _____

Effective survey questions have three important attributes: *focus, brevity,* and
simplicity. They focus on the issue or topic of the survey. They are as brief as
possible while still conveying the intended meaning. And they are expressed
simply and clearly.[19]

There are many ways to ask the same question. Exhibit 6–12 lists four common types but there are many ways to ask questions within these four types.
Additional choices can be added to the multiple-choice format. Neutral
responses can be removed so the respondent has to answer either positive or
negative. And there is obvious bias in the dichotomous question.

Questions should elicit a response that is both accurate and useful. By testing
questionnaires on a small subsample, researchers can detect any confusion,
bias, or ambiguities.

EXHIBIT • 6-12

Different ways to phrase
research questions.

Type	Questions
Open-ended	How would you describe __(Store name's)__ advertising?
Dichotomous	Do you think __(Store name's)__ advertising is too attractive? _____ Yes _____ No
Multiple choice	What description best fits your opinion of __(Store name's)__ advertising? _____ Modern _____ Well done _____ Believable _____ Unconvincing _____ Old-fashioned
Semantic differential (scale)	Please indicate on the scale how you rate the quality of __(Store name's)__ advertising. ___ ___ ___ ___ 1 2 3 4 Poor Excellent

Data Tabulation and Analysis

Collected data must be validated, edited, coded, and tabulated. Answers must be checked to eliminate errors or inconsistencies. One person might answer two years, while another says 24 months; such responses must be changed to the same units for correct tabulation. Some questionnaires may be rejected because respondents' answers indicate they misunderstood the questions. Finally, the data must be counted and summarized. Small studies may be tabulated manually, but most are done by computers.

Many researchers want *cross-tabulations*—for example, product use by age group, education, or other important demographic information. Current software programs such as MINITAB® Statistical Software enable researchers to tabulate the data on a personal computer, then apply advanced statistical techniques to seek additional findings (see Exhibit 6–13).[20] Many cross-tabulations are possible; but researchers must use skill and imagination to select only those that show significant relationships. On small sample sizes, the level of confidence is dramatically reduced when additional cross-tabs are used.

Collecting Primary Data in International Markets

Research overseas is often more expensive than domestic research. But the advertiser must know if the message will work in foreign markets. (Maxwell House had to change its "great American coffee" campaign when it discovered that Germans have little respect for U.S. coffee.)

Advertisers need more than just facts about a particular country's culture. They need to understand and appreciate the special nuances of the country's cultural traits and habits—a difficult task for those who don't live there or speak the language. Knowledgeable international advertisers work with bilingual local marketing people—and conduct primary research when necessary.

For years, Mattel tried unsuccessfully to market the Barbie Doll in Japan. The company finally granted the manufacturing license to a Japanese company, Takara. Takara did its own research and found that most Japanese girls and their parents thought Barbie's breasts were too big and her legs too long. Takara modified the doll accordingly, changed the blue eyes to brown, and sold 2 million dolls in two years.

EXHIBIT • 6-13

EXHIBIT • 6-13

Release 8 of MINITAB® Statistical Software features a new menu interface and advanced statistical capabilities.

Conducting original research can be fraught with problems. First, the researcher must use the local language, and translation of questionnaires can be tricky. Second, in many cultures, people view strangers suspiciously and don't wish to talk about their personal lives. U.S. companies found that mail surveys and phone interviews don't work in Japan; they have to use expensive and time-consuming personal interviews.[21] Even so, Japanese respondents invariably answer all questions yes, meaning, "Yes, I heard the question." Only when asked to amplify will the person give a negative answer.

Despite these problems, it's still important for global advertisers to perform research. Competent research personnel are available in all developed countries, and major international research firms have local offices in most developing countries.

APPLYING RESEARCH TO MARKETING AND ADVERTISING STRATEGY

Companies use research to identify and uncover problems with their market share, evaluate their competitive strengths and weaknesses, and measure consumer attitudes. This information is vital to the development of a company's marketing or positioning strategy and its subsequent advertising plans.

Developing Marketing Strategy

Marketing research gives the advertiser and its agency the data they need to decide which strategies will enhance the product's image and lead to higher revenues and profits. Marketers use the marketing mix—product, place, price, and promotion—as their guide.

First they analyze the product and use research to answer some basic questions. What are the most important product benefits? What is the target market's perception of the product? What changes in the product's appearance and performance will increase sales? Answers may lead to product design and marketing decisions that directly affect the product's nature, content, and packaging.

Research also answers questions about the place element. Where do most customers live or work? What locations offer the best potential for new stores? How can store design and the use of floor space be improved to increase sales? Which distribution channels are most cost effective?

Research is critical to establish a realistic pricing strategy. Research reveals the range of prices for similar products, tells where customer demand is highest, and helps forecast financial trends—all of which affect pricing decisions.

Finally, research helps answer questions about the company's promotional strategy. How are the company's sales personnel perceived? Should the company advertise more? What sales promotion techniques will help increase market share? And so on.

Developing Advertising Strategy

Marketing research and advertising research often overlap as is apparent in the following four categories of advertising research:

1. Advertising strategy research (to define the product concept or select the target market, message-element, or media).
2. Creative concept research (to measure acceptability of different creative concepts).
3. Pretesting ads and commercials.
4. Posttesting ads, commercials, and campaigns (to evaluate a campaign after it runs).

Advertisers apply marketing research procedures to basic advertising strategy and concept development (Categories 1 and 2 in Exhibit 6–14).

Product Concept Definition

From their extensive consumer surveys and focus groups, Schering and Cossette determined that most Canadian allergy sufferers weren't completely satisfied with available antihistamines. Some had a sedating side effect that made them difficult to use during the workday. And some of the newer non-drowsy products had other problems: slowness in clearing from the body, weight gain, and dry mouth.

EXHIBIT • 6–14

Categories of research in advertising development.

	Category 1: Strategy determination	Category 2: Concept development	Category 3: Pretesting	Category 4: Posttesting
Timing	Before creative work begins	Before agency production begins	Before finished artwork and photography	After campaign has run
Research problem	Product concept definition Target market selection Message-element selection	Concept testing Name testing Slogan testing	Print pretesting Television storyboard pretesting Radio commercial pretesting	Advertising effectiveness Consumer attitude change Sales increases
Techniques	Consumer-attitude and usage studies	Free-association tests Qualitative interviews Statement-comparison tests	Consumer jury Matched samples Portfolio tests Storyboard test Mechanical devices Psychological rating scales	Aided recall Unaided recall Sales tests Inquiry tests Attitude tests

Research showed Claritin did not have the same negative side effects. Schering positioned Claritin as a fast-acting, long-lasting effective medication, and consumer use bore out the integrity of the product concept. Schering's Ethical Division of reps, who call on physicians throughout Canada, successfully informed doctors about Claritin, and more doctors started prescribing it. By 1990, Claritin's prescription sales surpassed both Seldane and Hismanal. In 1993, a major feature of Claritin's product concept was that it was "the antihistamine most recommended by doctors" (see Exhibit 6–15).

Target Market Selection

Allergy sufferers come from all walks of life and comprise approximately 25 percent of the population. Schering's research showed that the most attractive market of antihistamine users was 18 to 49 years old, a large target market in Canada.

With any new product, the biggest problem is invariably the budget. There is never enough money to attack all geographic markets effectively at the same time. So Cossette recommended the *dominance concept*—researching which markets are most important to product sales and selecting those where Schering could focus resources to achieve advertising dominance.

As a result of this study, Schering introduced Claritin first in the provinces of Alberta, British Columbia, Ontario, and the Maritimes, which accounted for approximately 67 percent of the Canadian population but 75 percent of the allergy market. After achieving success there, Claritin was introduced to the rest of Canada.

Message-Element Determination

Companies can find promising advertising messages by studying consumers' likes and dislikes in relation to brands and products.

For example, in 1993 AT&T developed a corporate campaign to communicate to consumers how innovative the company was at developing new high-tech products and services to improve people's lives. The company's agency was N.W. Ayer, the oldest advertising agency in the United States. Ayer conducted a series of qualitative consumer attitude studies and discovered numerous themes that might be used. Then the agency used concept testing to

EXHIBIT • 6-15

Claritin promised allergy sufferers they could thumb their nose at pollen. The product was the brand most recommended by doctors.

EXHIBIT • 6-16

AT&T developed animatic commercials to test the appeal of various future services it planned to advertise in its corporate campaign.

Anncr (VO): Have you ever paid a toll without slowing down?

Anncr (VO): Read a book from 1000 miles away?

Anncr (VO): Given dictation to a computer?

Anncr (VO): Or tucked your kid in from a phone booth?

determine which message-element options might prove most successful in the corporate effort. This was Category 2 research aimed at advertising-concept development.

Creative Concept Testing

Ayer prepared several tentative ad concepts in the form of *animatics*, rough commercials using stills instead of action. Each scene stressed a different service AT&T would offer consumers in the future such as sending faxes from the beach with a personal communicator, paying road tolls without slowing down, or buying concert tickets with a smart card (see Exhibit 6–16). The agency then conducted focus groups of volunteer consumers in its unique "developmental lab," which combines intensive qualitative interviews with certain quantitative techniques. While a discussion leader moderated the conversation, each group viewed the animatics. The groups' reactions were measured, taped, and observed by Ayer staff behind a one-way mirror.

Once the most appealing products and services were determined, Ayer had to develop a campaign to verbally and nonverbally express AT&T's benefits to the consumer. The theme it developed was simply: "YOU WILL." The commercials posed questions such as "Have you ever tucked your baby in from a phone booth?" Answer: "You will. And the company that will bring it to you . . . AT&T." This embodied the company's mission of being the world's leader in bringing people together, giving them easy access to each other and to the information and services they want and need—anytime, anywhere (see Exhibit 6–17).

EXHIBIT • 6-17

The "You will" campaign from AT&T received high marks from advertising critics—a result of good creativity and adequate testing.

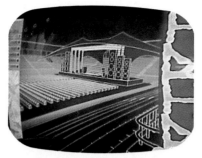

Anncr (VO): Have you ever paid a toll . . . without slowing down?
Anncr (VO): Bought concert tickets . . .
Second Girl: "There we go."

Third Girl: "Yeah, perfect."
Anncr (VO): Or tucked your baby in . . . from a phone booth?
Mother: "Hi, pretty girl."

Anncr (VO): You will.
Anncr (VO): And the company that will bring it to you . . . AT&T.

Testing and Evaluating Advertising

Advertising is often the largest single cost in a company's marketing budget. No wonder its effectiveness is a major concern! Companies can't stop advertising, nor do they want to. But they *do* want to know what they are getting for their money—and if their advertising is working.

Testing is the primary tool advertisers use to ensure their advertising dollars are being spent wisely. It can prevent costly errors—especially when judging which advertising strategy or medium is most effective. And it can give the advertiser some measure (besides sales results) of a campaign's value.

Objectives of Testing

Category 3 of advertising research—**pretesting**—increases the likelihood of preparing the most effective advertising messages. Pretesting helps advertisers detect and eliminate communication gaps or flaws in message content that may result in consumer indifference or negative response.[22] Schering didn't pretest its launch ads for Claritin and encountered a surprising reaction from the marketplace in the form of thousands of letters. But most negative response is more insidious; consumers simply turn the page or change the channel, thereby terminating the communication.

Posttesting, the fourth category of advertising research, determines the effectiveness of an ad or campaign *after* it runs and provides the advertiser with useful guidelines for future advertising.

Several variables are evaluated in pretesting including markets, motives, messages, media, budgeting, and scheduling. Many of these can be posttested too. However, in posttesting, the objective is to evaluate not diagnose.

Markets Advertisers may pretest advertising strategy and commercials with various market segments or audience groups. The advertiser may even decide to alter the strategy and target the campaign to a different market. In posttesting, advertisers want to know if the campaign succeeded in reaching its target markets. Changes in awareness or increases in market share are two indicators.

Motives Consumers' motives are outside of the advertiser's control, but the messages used to appeal to those motives are not. By pretesting ads, the advertiser can find ways to appeal to the consumer's needs and motives.

Messages Pretesting helps determine what a message says (from the customer's point of view) and how well it says it. Elements tested might be the headline, the text, the illustration, and the typography—or possibly the message concept, the information presented, or the symbolism. See Exhibit 6–18.

Through posttesting, the advertiser can determine to what extent the advertising message was seen, remembered, and believed. Changes in consumer attitude or perception indicate success as do consumers' ability to remember a campaign slogan or identify the sponsor.[23]

Media The cost of media advertising is soaring, and advertisers are demanding ever-greater accountability. Pretesting can influence four types of media decisions: classes of media, media subclasses, specific media vehicles, and units of space and time.

Media classes refer to the broad media categories: print, electronic, outdoor, and direct mail. **Media subclasses** are radio or TV, news magazines or business publications, and so on. The specific **media vehicle** is the particular

Survey workers interview consumers about the brands they use, if they recall seeing ads for the brands, which media the ads appeared in, and so forth. Because survey work is usually part-time, it is an ideal entry into the research field for marketing and advertising students.

program or publication. Exhibit 6–19 shows an ad for a print media vehicle—*Parade* magazine. **Media units** are half-page or full-page ads, 15- or 30-second spots, or 60-second commercials, and so forth.

After the campaign runs, posttesting can determine how effectively the media mix reached the target audience and communicated the desired message. Audience measurement is discussed in Chapters 12 through 14.

Budgeting How large should a company's advertising budget be? How much should be allocated to various markets and media? To specific products? Spending too little on advertising can be as hazardous as spending too much; but how much is too much? Advertisers use pretesting techniques to determine optimum spending levels before introducing national campaigns. (Chapter 7, "Marketing and Advertising Planning," provides further information on budgeting.)

Scheduling Advertisers can test consumer response to a product ad during different seasons of the year or days of the week. They can test whether frequent advertising is more effective than occasional or one-time insertions, or whether year-round advertising is more effective than advertising concentrated during a gift-buying season. (Chapter 12, "Media Planning and Selection," discusses the most commonly used types of media schedules.)

EXHIBIT · 6-19

This ad for *Parade* magazine uses the metaphor of high acceleration to imply a promise of quick results. With this media vehicle, advertisers can pinpoint geographic markets like a local newspaper but get the quality reproduction of a magazine. *Parade* is a syndicated weekly magazine inserted in the Sunday edition of daily papers.

Overall Results Finally, advertisers want to measure overall results to evaluate how well their advertising accomplished its objectives. *Posttesting* helps them determine whether and how to continue, what to change, and how much to spend in the future.

With all these tests, the researcher's greatest problem is deciding which and how many advertiser-controlled variables to measure and which consumer responses to survey.

Methods Used to Pretest Broadcast Ads

Although there is no infallible way to predict advertising success or failure, certain pretesting methods give the advertiser useful insights if properly applied. (See the Checklist of Methods for Pretesting Advertisements.)

Several methods are used specifically to pretest radio and TV commercials, and advertisers also use sales experiments and physiological testing techniques.

In **central location tests,** videotapes of test commercials are shown to respondents on a one-to-one basis, usually in shopping centers, and questions are asked before and after exposure. In **clutter tests,** test commercials are shown with other noncompetitive control commercials to determine their effectiveness, measure comprehension and attitude shifts, and detect weaknesses.

CHECKLIST   Methods for Pretesting Advertisements

Print Advertising

◇ **Direct questioning.** Asks specific questions about ads. Often used to test alternative ads in early stages of development.

◇ **Focus groups.** A moderated but free-wheeling discussion and interview conducted with four or more people.

◇ **Order-of-merit tests.** Respondents see two or more ads and arrange them in rank order.

◇ **Paired-comparison methods.** Respondents compare each ad in a group.

◇ **Portfolio tests.** One group sees a portfolio of test ads interspersed among other ads and editorial matter. Another group sees the portfolio without the test ads.

◇ **Mock magazines.** Test ads are "stripped into" a magazine, which is left with respondents for a specified time. (Also used as a posttesting technique.)

◇ **Perceptual meaning studies.** Respondents see ads in timed exposures.

◇ **Direct-mail tests.** Two or more alternative ads are mailed to different prospects on a mailing list to test which ad generates the largest volume of orders.

Broadcast Advertising

◇ **Central location projection tests.** Respondents see test commercial films in a central location like a shopping center.

◇ **Trailer tests.** Respondents see TV commercials in trailers at shopping centers and receive coupons for the advertised products; a matched sample of consumers just get the coupons. Researchers measure difference in coupon redemption.

◇ **Theater tests.** Electronic equipment enables respondents to indicate what they like and dislike as they view TV commercials in a theater setting.

◇ **Live telecast tests.** Test commercials are shown on closed-circuit or cable TV. Respondents are interviewed by phone and/or sales audits are conducted at stores in the viewing areas.

◇ **Sales experiments.** Alternative commercials run in two or more market areas.

Physiological Testing

◇ **Pupilometric devices.** Dilation of the subject's pupil is measured presumably to indicate the subject's reaction.

◇ **Eye-movement camera.** The route the subject's eye travels is superimposed over an ad to show the paths it takes and the areas that attracted and held attention.

◇ **Galvanometer.** Measures subject's sweat gland activity with a mild electrical current; presumably the more tension an ad creates, the more effective it is likely to be.

◇ **Voice-pitch analysis.** A consumer's response is taped and a computer used to measure changes in voice pitch caused by emotional responses.

◇ **Brain-pattern analysis.** A scanner monitors the reaction of the subject's brain.

Methods Used to Pretest Print Ads

Recent research shows that likability is the single best determinant of success.[24] So advertisers often pretest for likability using both qualitative and quantitative techniques. They also want to be sure the ads build the proper perception of the product—the desired product concept.

An advertiser can ask direct questions like: What does the advertising say to you? Does the advertising tell you anything new or different about the company? If so, what? Does the advertising reflect activities you would like to participate in? Is the advertising believable? What effect, if any, does it have on your perception of the merchandise offered? Do you find the ads likable?

The **direct questioning** method is designed to elicit a full range of responses from which researchers can infer how well advertising messages convey key copy points. Direct questioning is especially effective for testing alternative ads in the early stages of development. Respondents actually participate in the creative process when their reactions and input can best be acted on. In addition to direct questioning and focus groups, other techniques for pretesting print ads include order-of-merit tests, paired-comparison methods, portfolio tests, mock magazines, perceptual meaning studies, and direct-mail tests.

The Challenge of Pretesting

There is no best way to pretest advertising variables. Different methods test different aspects, and each has its own advantages and disadvantages—a formidable challenge for the advertiser.

Pretesting helps distinguish strong ads from weak ones. But since the test occurs in an artificial setting, respondents may assume the role of expert or critic and give answers that don't reflect their real buying behavior. They may invent opinions to satisfy the interviewer or be reluctant to admit they are influenced. Others try to please the interviewer by voting for the ads they think they *should* like.

Researchers encounter problems when asking people to rank ads. Respondents often rate the one or two that make the best first impression as the highest in all categories (the **halo effect**). Also, questions about the respondent's buying behavior may be the most interesting, but the least valid. Behavior *intent* may not become behavior *fact*.

Within the industry, some creative people mistrust commercial testing because they believe it stifles creativity. Marty Myers, director of creative services for a Toronto agency, says that "test commercials, animatics, photomatics, and their ilk are an expensive charade, a multimillion-dollar industry built on fear—the fear of the linear, literal advertising person or advertiser who needs numbers to bolster his decision, so that if the project goes awry, he can't be blamed." Yet Myers' own agency uses research extensively for brands such as Dial soap.[25]

Despite the variety of challenges to pretesting, the issue comes down to dollars. Small advertisers rarely pretest—but their risk isn't as great either. When advertisers risk millions of dollars on a new campaign, they *must* pretest to be sure the ad or commercial is interesting, believable, likable, and memorable—and that it supports the brand image.

Posttesting Techniques

Following the Claritin launch campaign, Schering was anxious to know to what extent people saw and paid attention to the campaign and how effective it was in communicating the product story. So Impact Research undertook a series of posttesting activities.

Posttesting is generally more costly and time-consuming than pretesting, but, unlike pretests, ads can be tested under actual market conditions. Advertisers can reap the benefits of pretesting *and* posttesting by running ads in a few select markets before launching a major nationwide campaign.

Advertisers use a variety of quantitative and qualitative methods in posttesting. The most common posttesting techniques fall into five broad categories: aided recall, unaided recall, attitude tests, inquiry tests, and sales tests. Each of these has distinct advantages and limitations. (See the Checklist of Methods for Posttesting Advertisements.)

Attitude tests measure a campaign's effectiveness in creating a favorable image for a company, its brand, or its products. Presumably favorable changes in attitude predispose consumers to buy the company's product.

Impact Research developed a proprietary posttest called TES (Tracking Efficiency Study) which it administers regularly for a variety of clients.[26] Using a small random probability sample of 200 people in each market, Impact researchers contact respondents by phone or door-to-door and ask a series of 8 to 10 questions to determine what ads or commercials they remember seeing, if they can identify the sponsor, what message elements they remember, and how well they liked the ads. From the responses, Impact develops statistics on the *real* reach and frequency of the campaign—that is, how many people *actually* saw the ads or commercials and how often (see Exhibit 6–20).

Nissan interviews 1,000 consumers every month to track brand awareness, familiarity with vehicle models, recall of commercials, and shifts in attitude or image perception. If a commercial fails, it can be spotted and pulled quickly.[27]

The Challenge of Posttesting

Each posttesting method has definite limitations.

Recall tests yield useful data on the effectiveness of various ad components, such as size, color, or attention-getting themes, as illustrated by the Starch scores in Exhibit 6–21. But they measure what has been noticed, read, or watched, not whether respondents actually buy the product.

Attitude tests are often a better measure of sales effectiveness than recall tests. An attitude change relates more closely to product purchase, and a measured change in attitude gives management the confidence to make informed, intelligent decisions about advertising plans.[28] Unfortunately, many people find it difficult to determine their attitudes and express them.

CHECKLIST   Methods for Posttesting Advertisements

◇ **Aided recall (recognition-readership).** To jog their memories, respondents are shown certain ads and then questioned whether their previous exposure was through reading, viewing, or listening.

◇ **Unaided recall.** Respondents are asked, without prompting, whether they saw or heard advertising messages.

◇ **Attitude tests.** Direct questions, semantic differential tests, or unstructured questions measure changes in respondents' attitudes after a campaign.

◇ **Inquiry tests.** Additional product information, product samples, or premiums are given to readers or viewers of an ad; ads generating the most responses are presumed to be the most effective.

◇ **Sales tests.** Measures of past sales compare advertising efforts with sales. Controlled experiments test different media in different markets. Consumer purchase tests measure retail sales from a given campaign. Store inventory audits measure retailers' stocks before and after a campaign.

Commercial:	"Dummy"
Advertiser:	XYZ
Market:	Toronto

Category: Television commercials for ... (category of product)
Period of exposure: From May 3 to June 15, 2001
Date of test: From June 15 to 18, 2001

Perceived noise level   %**

	%**
XYZ	29
ABC	16
LMN*	10
Others*	10
Can't specify	35
Total	100
Did not see TV adv.	25

* less than 5% mentions
** % Based on total mentions

Reach and frequency

	Potential	Actual	conversion %
GRP'S:	2602	968	37.2
Reach:	96%	59%	61.5
Freq.:	27.1	16.4	60.5
Freq. last 4 weeks.:		11.6	
Norm:		47%	
Seen to often:		21%	

Male	Female	18–34	35–64
58%	63%	68%	53%

Sponsor Identification   %

	%
XYZ	27%
ABC	7%
Others*	5%
Can't specify	61%
Total	100%
Norm:	48%

Male	Female	18–34	35–64
44%	35%	41%	38%

Appreciation   %

	%	
Very much	26%	81%
Somewhat	55%	
Not very much	6%	9%
Not at all	3%	
Can't specify	10%	
Norm:	71%	

Male	Female	18–34	35–64
76%	82%	84%	71%

Users vs non-users

	Users (n=72)	Non-users (n=145)
Noise level:	38%	24%
Reach:	53%	63%
	(n=38)	(n=91)
Frequency:	13.8	13.2
Sponsor Id.:	37%	23%
Appreciation:	82%	80%
Astute:	54%	53%

Top of mind awareness

XYZ	19
ABC	19
LMN	8
OPQ	5
RST	5
Others*	14
Can't specify	30
Total	100

Comprehension   %**

	%**
Gets rid of allergy symptoms	24
Buy the product	10
Nature is responsible for certain allergies	7
Relieves from discomfort caused by pollen	7
Good medication/effective	4
You can be friends with nature	3
Stop suffering	3
Others*	15
Can't specify	26
The "astute ones"	54
The "close but no cigars" ones	4
The "off the mark"	42

Appreciation   %**

	%**
Positive reasons	15
Humorous/funny	14
Like the animation/well done	11
Like the concept	10
Like the Jewish accent/the voice	7
Original/creative	7
Like the characters	4
Attention-getting	9
Others*	
Negative reasons	5
Do not like the Jewish accent	4
Not interested in the product	11
Others*	3
Can't specify	

EXHIBIT • 6-20

The TES study report from Impact Research tells advertisers how well their ads actually fared in the marketplace.

EXHIBIT • 6-21

Starch INRA Hooper, a leading firm in recall testing, reports three recognition scores: the percentage of readers who remember seeing the ad, who remember seeing or reading any part of the ad, and who read at least half the ad. This sample shows both overall readership and readership of the components (headline, visuals, copy).

Inquiry tests—in which consumers respond to an ad for information or free samples—enable the advertiser to test an ad's attention-getting value as well as its readability and understandability. They also permit fairly good control of the variables that motivate reader action, particularly if a split-run test is used (split runs are covered in Chapter 13). The inquiry test is also effective for testing small ads.

Unfortunately, inquiry tests are valid only for ads that elicit inquiries. Inquiries, though, may not reflect a sincere interest in the product, and responses may take months to receive.

The principal objective of most advertisers is to increase sales, so **sales tests** are a useful measure of advertising effectiveness when advertising is the dominant element, or the only variable, in the company's marketing plan. However, it is difficult to gauge if advertising is responsible since many other variables also affect sales (competitors' activities, the season of the year, and even the weather). Sales response may not be immediate, and sales tests, particularly field studies, are often costly and time-consuming. Finally, most sales tests measure results of campaigns, not individual ads or components of ads.

Summary

Marketing research is the systematic procedure used to gather, record, and analyze new information to help managers make decisions about the marketing of goods and services. Marketing research helps management identify consumer needs, develop new products and communication strategies, and assess the effectiveness of marketing programs and promotional activities.

Research involves several steps: analyzing the situation and defining the problem, conducting exploratory research by analyzing internal data and collecting external secondary data, setting research objectives, conducting research using quantitative or qualitative methods, and, finally, interpreting and reporting the findings.

Quantitative techniques include observation, experiment, and survey. Marketers use qualitative research to get a general impression of the market. The methods used include projective or intensive techniques.

The validity and reliability of quantitative surveys depend on the sampling methods used and the design of the survey questionnaire. The two sampling procedures used are random probability and nonprobability. Survey questions require focus, brevity, and simplicity.

In international markets, research is often more expensive and less reliable. But advertisers must use research to understand cultural traits and habits in overseas markets.

Advertising research helps advertisers develop strategies and test concepts, and research results help define the product concept, select the target market, and develop the primary advertising message elements.

Advertisers use testing to ensure that their advertising dollars are spent wisely. Pretesting helps detect and eliminate weaknesses before a campaign runs. Posttesting helps evaluate the effectiveness of an ad or campaign after it runs. Testing helps evaluate several variables including markets, motives, messages, media, budgets, and schedules.

Techniques used in pretesting include central location tests, clutter tests, and direct questioning. Pretesting has numerous problems including artificiality, consumer inaccuracy, and the halo effect of consumer responses.

The most commonly used posttesting techniques are aided recall, unaided recall, attitude tests, inquiry tests, and sales tests.

Questions for Review and Discussion

1. How important is research to advertisers? Why?

2. What example demonstrates the difference between marketing research and market research?

3. Which kind of research data is more expensive to collect, primary or secondary? Why?

4. Have you ever used observational research personally? How?

5. Do people use quantitative or qualitative research to evaluate movies? Explain.

6. Which of the major surveying methods is most costly? Why?

7. What research offers validity but not reliability? Give an example.

8. When could research help in the development of advertising strategy for an international advertiser? Give an example.

9. How could the halo effect bias a pretest for a soft drink ad?

10. How would you design a controlled experiment to test the advertising for a chain of men's stores?

Marketing and Advertising Planning

Objective: To describe the process of marketing and advertising planning. Marketers and advertisers need to know how to analyze situations, set realistic, attainable objectives, develop strategies to achieve them, and establish budgets for marketing communications.

After studying this chapter, you will be able to:

- Explain the role and the elements of a marketing plan.

- Describe how a marketing plan and advertising plan are related.

- Discuss the difference between objectives and strategies in marketing and advertising plans.

- Give examples of market-need and sales-target objectives.

- Discuss the suitability of top-down and bottom-up marketing and advertising planning.

- Explain how advertising budgets are determined.

- Describe how the share-of-market/ share-of-voice method can be used for new product introductions.

In the 1980s, Japanese cars were the stars of the automotive world. But in the 90s, a new player entered the scene—one as down-home American as fried chicken and corn on the cob.

It started a decade ago. Then GM chairman Roger Smith wanted to find better ways to manufacture and market cars by building partnerships between management and labor, company and supplier. GM had a mission: to produce a car that would be a powerful import fighter and build a car company that would be the best-liked in America—one that would share a special relationship with its customers.[1]

The company eschewed its Detroit roots for Spring Hill, Tennessee. There, in the rural foothills, it built the newest, most modern auto plant in America. Working with the target market of typical import buyers, the company designed the vehicle these customers wanted: small, economical, safe, attractive, comfortable, and affordable—the Saturn.

In partnership with its employees, the company discarded old assembly line methods and instead used teams to build its cars. Quality was paramount.

By 1987, Saturn officials started looking for an ad agency to introduce the first all-new American car since the Edsel. After an exhaustive search and 29 months before the first car would go on sale, they selected a San Francisco shop—Hal Riney & Partners.

Riney executives immediately began traveling to Saturn's headquarters to immerse themselves in the product plans and to undergo the orientation to Saturn culture given to all new employees.

Many key brand-building decisions were made well before the launch with contributions from Riney and a panel of 16 dealer advisers. Riney understood the need to position not just the car but the company as well. "Most people start and stop with the car," says Donald Hudler, Saturn VP-sales, service, and marketing. "We include image, perceptions, and the shopping, buying, and owning experience." With Riney's help, the company crafted Saturn's brand image meticulously.

Everything was carefully planned with an emphasis on straight talk. Red cars would be called red, not "raspberry red." Customers would not have to haggle with dealers over price, and dealers would be called retailers ("we're not in the deal business"). Even the models would be designated by letters or numbers rather than names. Riney didn't want anything detracting from the Saturn name and image. "The truth," Riney says, "is far better than anything we can make up. Saturn has to represent honesty and directness." Moreover, all communications had to be integrated and consistent.

Before producing any consumer advertising, the agency created several internal communications pieces about the company (see Exhibit 7–1). The short

EXHIBIT • 7-1

This 26-minute film entitled "Spring, in Spring Hill" used actual comments from real employees to tell what Saturn meant to them. The film was first used as an internal communication piece and later as a 30-minute commercial.

ALTON SMITH *has always loved cars. He first turned his backyard hobby into a full-time occupation in 1964, when he took a job on the line inspecting brake drums, fittings and gears. He remembers being gung-ho "because the guys depended on you." After nineteen years in the business, Alton talks about being gung-ho again. This time as a tool and die maker, building a brand new car called Saturn in Spring Hill, Tennessee.*

"…My best buddies in high school were twins. A couple of guys named Hugh and Hugo. We all had cars. And every Saturday we'd tear something down and put it back together just for the fun of it. So it's no big surprise that we all ended up in the car business.

But those guys wouldn't ever believe I just picked up and went to work for a car company that's never built a car before.

Well, what I'm doing now here at Saturn is something completely different.

Here, we don't have management and we don't have labor. We have teams. And we have what you call consensus. Everything's a group decision. **In the last seven months, I've only had a few days off here and there. But this is where I want to be. This is living heaven.**

You work through breaks and you work through lunch. You're here all hours and even sometimes Saturdays. And you don't mind. Because no one's making you do it. It's just that here you can build cars the way you know they ought to be built.

I know the competition's stiff. I was out in California for a family reunion and everything was an import. Hondas, Toyotas. Well, now we're going to give people something else to buy.

I wouldn't be working all these hours if I didn't think we could.…"

A DIFFERENT KIND *of* COMPANY. A DIFFERENT KIND *of* CAR.
If you'd like to know more about Saturn, and our new sedans and coupe, please call us at 1-800-522-5000.

© 1990 Saturn Corporation

EXHIBIT • 7-2

In lieu of listing the car's features, Saturn lets employees' personal stories represent the company and its philosophy.

film documented the start-up of the plant and revealed the incredible commitment of the Saturn workers. The company used the film to train new employees and help introduce itself to suppliers and the press. Dealers used it in presentations for bank loans and zoning variances. After the launch, Riney even ran it as an infomercial on cable TV. The film showed Saturn team members explaining in their own words—often emotionally—what the project was all about and what it meant to them.

When the agency began creating consumer ads, it took exactly the same tack: "A different kind of company. A different kind of car" (see Exhibit 7-2).

The cars were an immediate success—so much so that production couldn't keep up with demand. Riney had to create ads apologizing for delivery delays. By 1992, despite production restraints, Saturn sold 196,126 cars—more than twice as many as the year before—outselling Hyundai, Subaru, Mitsubishi, and Volkswagen. Touted by the critics for its high quality-to-price ratio, the company also finished third in the J. D. Power & Associates survey of new-car buyer satisfaction, right behind Lexus and Infiniti, which cost several times more than Saturn's frugal $10,000. With its fanatic devotion to integrated marketing communications, Riney helped Saturn build a brand.[2] And in 1993, thanks largely to its work on the Saturn account, Hal Riney & Partners was named Agency of the Year by *Advertising Age.* ◆

THE MARKETING PLAN

The Saturn story demonstrates that marketing success depends on careful planning. Yet, as many marketing experts point out, companies continue to waste millions on ineffectual advertising because of a woeful lack of planning.[3]

What is a marketing plan? And what is an advertising plan? What is the

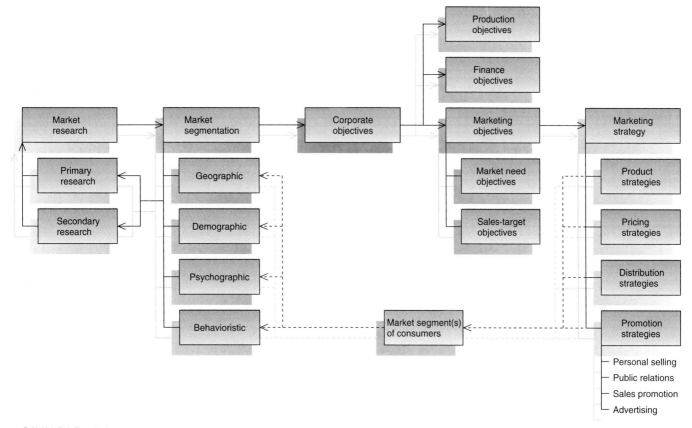

EXHIBIT • 7-3

Planning is a continuous process that blends the results of marketing research with company objectives to create sound strategies. These strategies are then applied to influence the market's buying patterns. Feedback from the market restarts the cycle.

difference, and what is their relationship? Let's deal with the first question first to better understand the overall success of Saturn's introduction.

What Is a Marketing Plan?

Since marketing is typically the company's only source of income, the marketing plan may well be a company's most important document.

The **marketing plan** serves a number of functions. In one written document, it assembles all the pertinent and current facts about the organization, the markets it serves, and its products, services, customers, competition, and so on. It forces all departments—product development, production, selling, advertising, credit, transportation—to focus on the customer. Finally, it sets goals and objectives for specified periods of time and lays out the strategies and tactics to achieve them. As the model in Exhibit 7–3 shows, planning is not a one-time event; it's a continuous process.

Effect of the Marketing Plan on Advertising

A marketing plan has a profound effect on the organization's advertising program. It helps managers analyze and improve all company operations, including past marketing and advertising programs. It dictates the role of advertising in the marketing mix. And it provides focus and guidance. It enables better implementation, control, and continuity of advertising programs, and it ensures the most efficient allocation of advertising dollars.[4]

Successful organizations do not separate advertising plans from marketing. They view each as a vital building block for success.[5]

Elements of the Marketing Plan

The written marketing plan must reflect the goals of the company's top management and be consistent with the company's capabilities. Depending on its scope, the plan may be long and complex or, in the case of a small firm or a single product line, very brief. Regardless of length, a basic marketing plan has four main sections: *situation analysis, marketing objectives, marketing strategy,* and *action programs.*

Extended marketing plans for large companies also include a section on measurement, control, and review; a section on resource allocation; and an executive overview at the beginning. Subjects that relate purely to marketing are beyond the scope of this text. However, Appendix A at the end of the text presents the basic outline of a complete marketing plan.

Situation Analysis

The **situation analysis** section is a *factual* statement of the organization's current situation and how it got there. Usually the longest portion of the marketing plan, it may be difficult and time-consuming to prepare. The situation analysis presents all relevant facts about the company's history, growth, products and services, sales volume, share of market, competitive status, markets served, distribution system, past advertising programs, results of marketing research studies, company capabilities, strengths and weaknesses, and any other pertinent information. The Checklist for Situation Analysis lists some of the most important elements to consider.

The situation analysis also includes information on key factors outside the company's control—for example, the economic, political, social, technological, or commercial environments the company operates in. To successfully plan for the future, company executives must agree on the accuracy of the data and its interpretation.[6]

Saturn entered a market disillusioned with Detroit's offerings. American cars were perceived as lacking the quality or value of Japanese and German competitors. Detroit's management and manufacturing systems were considered outmoded bureaucracies, and people were questioning the productivity of the American worker.[7] Roger Smith believed that Americans wanted to buy domestic cars but had to be given a good reason; and they were not interested in "business as usual."

Marketing Objectives

Once the situation analysis is completed and agreed on, the organization's management can determine specific marketing objectives. For example, in its efforts to recruit new soldiers every year, the U.S. Army sets specific numerical objectives—as well as quality objectives based on enlistees' mental aptitude and education—for the regular army, the reserve, and specific units (see Exhibit 7–4).

Marketing objectives must consider the amount of money the company has to invest in marketing and production, its knowledge of the marketplace, and the competitive environment. General Motors invested $5 billion in the Saturn project before the first car ever rolled out.[8]

Marketing objectives follow logically from a review of the company's current situation, management's prediction of future trends, and the hierarchy of com-

---

CHECKLIST   Situation Analysis

The Industry

◇ **Companies in industry**: dollar sales, strengths.

◇ **Growth patterns within industry**: primary demand curve, per capita consumption, growth potential.

◇ **History of industry**: technological advances, trends.

◇ **Characteristics of industry**: distribution patterns, industry control, promotional activity, geographic characteristics, profit patterns.

The Company

◇ **The company story**: history, size, growth, profitability, scope of business, competence, reputation, strengths, weaknesses.

The Product or Service

◇ **The product story**: development, quality, design, description, packaging, price structure, uses, reputation, strengths, weaknesses.

◇ **Product sales features**: exclusive, nonexclusive differentiating qualities, competitive position.

◇ **Product research**: technological breakthroughs, improvements planned.

Sales History

◇ **Sales and sales costs**: by product, model, sales districts.

◇ **Profit history**.

Share of Market

◇ **Sales history industrywide**: share of market in dollars and units.

◇ **Market potential**: industry trends, company trend, demand trends.

The Market

◇ **Who and where is market**: how was market segmented, how can it be segmented, what are consumer needs, attitudes, and characteristics? How, why, when, where do consumers buy?

◇ **Past advertising appeals**: successful or unsuccessful.

◇ **Who are our customers**: past and future? What characteristics do they have in common? What do they like about our product? What don't they like?

Distribution

◇ **History and evaluation**: how and where product is distributed, current trend.

◇ **Company's relationship**: with the distribution channel and its attitudes toward product/company.

◇ **Past policies**: trade advertising, deals, co-op programs.

◇ **Status**: trade literature, dealer promotions, point-of-purchase, displays.

Pricing Policies

◇ **Price history**: trends, relationship to needs of buyers, competitive price situation.

◇ **Past price objectives**: management attitudes, buyer attitudes, channel attitudes.

Competition

◇ **Who is the competition**: Primary, secondary, share of market, products, services, goals, attitudes. What is competition's growth history and size?

◇ **Strengths and competition**: sales features, product quality, size. Weaknesses of competition.

◇ **Marketing activities of competition**: advertising, promotion, distribution, sales force. Estimated budget.

Promotion

◇ **Successes and failures**: past promotion policy, sales force, advertising, publicity.

◇ **Promotion expenditures**: history, budget emphasis, relation to competition, trend.

◇ **Advertising programs**: review of strategies, themes, campaigns.

◇ **Sales force**: size, scope, ability, cost/sale.

---

pany objectives.[9] **Corporate objectives** are stated in terms of profit or return on investment—or net worth, earnings ratios, growth, or corporate reputation. **Marketing objectives**, which derive from corporate objectives, should relate to the needs of target markets and to specific sales goals. These are called general *market-need objectives* and specific *sales-target objectives*.[10]

Market-need objectives shift management's view of the organization from a producer of products or services to a satisfier of target market needs.[11] Saturn

The military services need to fill hundreds of different job specialties annually. Because budgets are limited, the advertising strategy is based on a forecast of essential openings in the coming year.

We Operate With Compassion. "Sometimes it's a toy, sometimes a reassuring touch, but I know I made a difference to a child. That's what I like about my job as an OR nurse in the Army. I can make a difference. Whether it's a child or an adult, military or civilian, every day is rewarding, every day is a challenge."

ARMY NURSE CORPS.   BE ALL YOU CAN BE.   1-800-USA-ARMY

exemplifies this view as do many consumer product companies. Revlon founder Charles Revson once said a cosmetic company's product is hope, not lipstick. An insurance company sells financial security not policies. What needs does Rollerblade want to satisfy with its ad in Exhibit 7–5?

Sales-target objectives are specific, quantitative, and realistic goals to be achieved within a specified time period. Saturn defined its goal as selling 75,000 cars nationwide in 1991, and 196,000 in 1992. These objectives were specific as to product and market, quantified as to time and amount, and—judging by the results—fairly realistic. In 1991, Saturn sold 74,493; and in 1992, 196,126. Only by setting specific objectives can management measure its marketing success. Saturn's objectives for 1993 were 235,000; and, for 1994, 300,000.[12]

Objectives may be expressed in a number of ways. Many companies use:

- Total sales volume.
- Sales volume by product, market segment, customer type.
- Market share in total or by product line.
- Growth rate of sales volume in total or by product line.
- Gross profit in total or by product line.

Other criteria include additions or deletions in the product line, creation of new distribution channels, development of new pricing policies, or retraining of field sales staff. Some firms even include such socially responsible objectives as preservation of natural resources, participation in community projects, and support of education.[13]

Marketing Strategy

The third major section of the marketing plan is the **marketing strategy**—how the company plans to accomplish its marketing objectives. In marketing terms,

EXHIBIT • 7-5

In this beautifully designed and written two-page magazine ad, Rollerblade offers a lot more than just skates—namely, freedom.

the objectives are what you want to accomplish, and the strategy is how you're going to do it. (See Ad Lab 7–A, "The Era of Marketing Warfare.")

For example, company executives have the objective of increasing the stock dividend. Their strategy for accomplishing this is to increase sales. To the marketing director, the chairman's strategy (increased sales) becomes an objective. The marketing director's strategy is to use advertising to persuade current customers to use the product more. That becomes the advertising agency's objective. The agency's strategy is to make the product more appealing to regular buyers by defining more use occasions.

A company's marketing strategy has a dramatic impact on its advertising. The marketing strategy affects the amount of advertising used, its creative thrust, and the media employed. Marketing strategy determines the objectives for advertising and provides the key to advertising strategy.

Selecting the Target Market   The first step in strategy development is to select the target market. As we discussed in Chapters 5 and 6, marketing managers use the processes of market segmentation and research to define their target market.

For instance, Saturn defined its target market as "college-educated import owners and intenders"—i.e., highly educated young adults (18–34) considering their first or second car purchase. These people were further defined as 40 percent male, 60 percent female, living in one- or two-person households, and seeking a vehicle with sporty styling, fun-to-drive performance, good fuel economy, a good warranty, and sound quality/reliability/dependability.[14] These are the same people who typically drive a Honda Civic, Toyota Corolla, or Nissan 240SX.

AD LAB 7–A   The Era of Marketing Warfare

Jack Trout and Al Ries's *Marketing Warfare* is based on the classic book on military strategy, *On War*, written in 1831 by a Prussian general, Carl von Clausewitz. The book outlines the principles behind all successful wars and two simple ideas dominate—*force* and the *superiority of the defense.*

The Strategic Square

How do the principles of warfare apply to marketing? It comes down to the "strategic square":

Out of every 100 companies

One should play defense	Two should play offense
Three should flank	And 94 should be guerrillas

Offensive Warfare

Colgate had a strong number-one position in toothpaste. But rival Procter & Gamble knew a thing or two about Carl von Clausewitz.

P&G launched Crest toothpaste not only with a massive $20 million advertising budget but also with the American Dental Association "seal of approval." Crest went over the top and is now the number-one selling toothpaste in the country.

But overtaking the leader is not that common. Most companies are happy if they can establish a profitable number-two position.

The rules for waging offensive marketing warfare are:

1. Consider the strength of the leader's position.
2. Launch the attack on as narrow a front as possible, preferably with single products.
3. Launch the attack at the leader's weakest position.

Defensive Warfare

Datril opened its war on Tylenol with a price attack. Johnson & Johnson immediately cut Tylenol's price, even before Datril started its price advertising. Result: It repelled the Datril attacks and inflicted heavy losses on the Bristol-Myers entry.

Here are the rules for defensive marketing warfare:

1. Participate only if you are a market leader.

2. Introduce new products and services before the competition does.
3. Block strong competitive moves by rapidly copying them.

Flanking Warfare

The third type of marketing warfare is where the action is for many companies. In practice, it means attacking the leader where the leader is weak, as Apple did successfully against IBM in the personal computer market.

Here are the principles of flanking marketing warfare:

1. Make good flanking moves into uncontested areas.
2. Use surprise. Too much research often wastes precious time.
3. Keep up the pursuit; too many companies quit after they're ahead.

Guerrilla Warfare

Most of America's companies should be waging guerrilla warfare.

The key attribute of successful guerrilla wars is flexibility. A guerrilla should abandon any product or market if the tide of battle changes.

Here are the principles of guerrilla marketing warfare.

1. Find a market segment small enough to defend.
2. No matter how successful you become, never act like the leader.
3. Be prepared to "bug out" at a moment's notice.

Bottom Up

Trout and Ries's subsequent book, *Bottom-Up Marketing* (discussed later in this chapter), continues the military analogy.

"Deep penetration on a narrow front is the key to winning a marketing war," they say. By this they mean that smaller companies should keep their product narrowly focused on a single concept. Too many companies "spread their forces over a wide front." In fact, most large corporations today face the problem of fending off focused attacks by smaller companies.

Laboratory Applications

1. Think of a successful product and explain its success in terms of marketing warfare.
2. Select a product and explain how marketing warfare strategy might be used to gain greater success.

Determining the Marketing Mix The second step in developing the marketing strategy is to determine a cost-effective marketing mix for *each* target market the company pursues. As we discussed in Chapter 5, the mix consists of a blend of the 4 Ps: *product, price, place,* and *promotion.*

Saturn carefully developed and manufactured a solidly engineered, driver-oriented product and supported it with a 24-hour roadside assistance program and a money-back guarantee for dissatisfied customers who returned their cars within 30 days or 1500 miles. Then, it set a no-haggle price well below Honda Civic and Toyota Corolla, and it allowed no factory rebates or dealer incentives—to reinforce its commitment to doing business differently.[15]

GM created a completely new automotive division and nationwide retail distribution system for Saturn—separate from the GM network. Finally, Saturn initiated a completely integrated marketing communications program including extensive training programs for retailer sales and service staffs (personal selling), innovative Media Days at the Spring Hill factory (publicity), and a full TV, magazine, and radio ad campaign to develop a distinct Saturn personality—not just for the car, but for the company itself (see Exhibit 7–6).

Companies have a wide variety of marketing strategy options. For example, a company might increase distribution, initiate new uses for a product, increase or change a product line, develop entirely new markets, or start discount pricing. Each option emphasizes one or more of the marketing mix elements.

EXHIBIT • 7-6

This ad portrays a real story of a couple discovering how Saturn is different—as a car and as a company.

Selection depends on the product's position in the market and its stage in the product life cycle.

Positioning Strategies David Ogilvy says that the first decision in marketing and advertising is also the most important: how to position the product. To Ogilvy, positioning means "what the product does and who it is for."[16] His agency (Ogilvy & Mather) developed the advertising for Dove soap. When Lever Bros. (now Unilever) introduced Dove in 1957, it decided to position the product as a complexion bar for women with dry skin. Every commercial still uses the same cleansing cream demonstration, and Dove is consistently the number-one brand in the $1.5 billion bar soap category.[17]

Companies usually have two choices in selecting a position. One is to pick a position similar to a competitor's and battle for the same customers. Another is to find a position not held by a competitor—a hole in the market—and fill it quickly, perhaps through product differentiation or market segmentation.

For example, a company might elect to position itself through price/quality differentiation. Like Karastan carpets, it could present a high-quality product concept by likening it to an investment (see Exhibit 7–7). Or, it might advertise good quality at an *amazingly* low price.

Saturn positioned itself as an American alternative to Japanese imports, offering comparable styling, performance, and quality at a lower price.

There are so many types of product differentiation, price/quality, positioning, and segmentation strategies, it's difficult to find the best one. Marketing and advertising managers need to work together to choose an evaluate alternatives.

EXHIBIT • 7-7

Karastan, a name known for quality, positions its carpets as an investment by presenting its ads as a stock certificate with a headline that equates its carpets with stocks, bonds, and retirement accounts.

Marketing Tactics (Action Programs)

A company's objectives indicate where it wants to go; the strategy indicates the intended route; and the **tactics** (or **action programs**) determine the short-term details. The tactics determine the specific actions to be taken—internally and externally—by whom and when.[18] Advertising campaigns live in the world of marketing tactics.

THE ADVERTISING PLAN

The **advertising plan** is a natural outgrowth of the marketing plan and is prepared in much the same way. Appendix B at the end of this text shows a complete outline for an advertising plan.

Review of the Marketing Plan

The advertising manager first reviews the marketing plan to understand where the company is going, how it intends to get there, and the role advertising will play in the marketing mix. The first section of the advertising plan, a situation analysis, briefly restates the company's current situation, target markets, long- and short-term marketing objectives, and decisions regarding market positioning and the marketing mix.

Setting Advertising Objectives

The advertising manager then determines what tasks advertising must take on. Unfortunately, some corporate executives—and advertising managers—state vague goals like "creating a favorable impression of the product in the marketplace in order to increase sales and maximize profits." As a result, no one understands what the advertising is intended to do, how much it costs to do it, or how to measure the results.

Understanding What Advertising Can Do

Everyone involved must understand what advertising can and can't do. Most advertising programs hope to encourage prospects to take action. However, it is unfair to assign advertising the whole responsibility for achieving sales.[19]

Sales goals are marketing objectives, not advertising objectives, and only a very small percentage of prospects act right away. Before customers can be persuaded to buy, a number of important steps must be accomplished. Most advertising seeks to inform, persuade, or remind its intended audience over an extended time about the company, good, service, or issue. See Exhibit 7–8. This is the type of advertising generally used by manufacturers (Sico Paint), retailers (Nordstrom), food processors (Kellogg's), insurance companies (Prudential), services (H&R Block), and associations (Greenpeace).

The Advertising Pyramid: A Guide to Setting Objectives

To understand the tasks advertising can perform, look at the pyramid in Exhibit 7–9. Before a new product is introduced, prospective customers are totally unaware. The first objective of any advertising is to create **awareness**—to acquaint some portion of the unaware people with the company, good, service, or brand.

EXHIBIT • 7-8

Sico is a Canadian paint manufacturer that uses outdoor advertising to remind prospects about the product's use and brand name.

EXHIBIT • 7-9

The advertising pyramid depicts the progression of effects advertising has on mass audiences—especially for new products. Compared to the large number of people advertising makes aware of the product (base of the pyramid), the number actually motivated to action is usually quite small.

The next task is to develop **comprehension**—to communicate enough information so some percentage of the aware group recognizes the product's purpose, image or position, and perhaps some of its features.

Next advertising needs to communicate enough information to develop **conviction**—to persuade a certain number of people to believe in the product's value. Of those who become convinced, some can be moved to **desire** the product. Finally, after accomplishing all the preceding steps, some percentage of those who desire the product will take **action**—request additional information, send in a coupon, visit a store, or buy it.

The pyramid is far from static. The advertiser works in three dimensions: time, dollars, and people. Advertising results take time, especially if the product is not purchased regularly.[20] Over time, as a company spends more on advertising, the number of people who become aware of the product increases. As more people comprehend the product, believe in it, and desire it, more take the final action of buying it.

Finally, **advertising objectives** should be specific as to time and degree so success can be measured by research studies and tests.[21]

Let's apply these principles to Saturn's advertising pyramid.

In 1992, Saturn introduced an entry level 2 + 2 coupe, the SC1. Specific advertising objectives for this car might have read as follows:

1. Within two years, communicate the existence and availability of the Saturn SC1 to 50 percent of the more than 500,000 people who annually buy foreign economy cars.

2. Inform two-thirds of this "aware" group that the Saturn is a technologically superior economy car with many design, safety, and performance features; that it is a brand new nameplate backed up with unmatched service, quality, and value; and that it is sold only through dedicated Saturn dealers.

3. Convince two-thirds of the "informed" group that the Saturn is a high-quality car, reliable, economical, and fun to drive.

4. Stimulate desire within two-thirds of the "convinced" group for a test-drive.

5. Motivate two-thirds of the "desire" group to visit a retailer and test-drive the SC1.

These advertising objectives are specific as to time and degree and are quantified like marketing objectives. Theoretically, at the end of the first year, a consumer attitude study could determine how many people are aware of the Saturn SC1, how many people understand the car's primary features, and so on. In other words, studies can measure the ad program's effectiveness.

Saturn's advertising accomplishes the objectives of creating awareness, comprehension, conviction, desire, and action; but once the customer is in the store, it's the retailer's responsibility to close the sale with effective selling and service.

By integrating all aspects of their marketing communications—from package and store design to personal selling, advertising, public relations, and sales promotion—companies hope to accelerate the pyramid process. For example, by using direct marketing or sales promotion devices—such as heavy sampling of a new product—marketers may convert people from being totally unaware one day to being users the next. But as we will discuss in Chapter 16, this can be extremely expensive.

The Inverted Pyramid: Satisfied Customers Build Brands

Once a certain percentage of people actually buy, a new advertising objective may be introduced: to stimulate reuse and build loyalty. As more people take action and develop a repurchasing habit, the marketer builds a new **inverted pyramid** (see Exhibit 7–10) on top of the original pyramid.

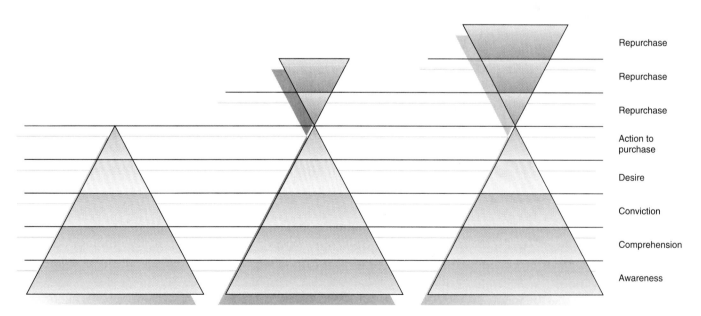

Repurchase

Repurchase

Repurchase

Action to purchase

Desire

Conviction

Comprehension

Awareness

EXHIBIT • 7–10

As people purchase and repurchase a product, the inverted pyramid grows larger, symbolizing the expanding volume of sales and customers. Established brands build the inverted pyramid by using advertising (and other marketing communications) to encourage and reinforce good word-of-mouth and brand loyalty.

The inverted pyramid is built by customer satisfaction and good word of mouth. The greater the satisfaction and the more people told about the product, the faster the inverted pyramid expands. At this point, **reinforcement advertising**—designed to build brand loyalty—reminds people of their successful experience with the product and suggests reuse. (See Ad Lab 7–B, "MaxiMarketing: How Small Advertisers Build the Inverted Pyramid.")

Models and theories tend to oversimplify the complex phenomenon of consumer behavior. But the pyramid models provide a simple way of understanding and defining some of the results that long-term media advertising can accomplish. (For more, see the Checklist for Developing Advertising Objectives.)

Advertising Strategy and the Creative Mix

The *advertising* (or *communications*) *objective* declares where the advertiser wants to be with respect to consumer awareness, attitude, and preference; the *advertising* (or *creative*) *strategy* describes how to get there.

Marketing strategy blends elements of the marketing mix (product, price, place, and promotion); promotional strategy (discussed in Chapter 5) integrates elements of the promotional mix (personal selling, advertising, public relations, sales promotion, and collateral). **Advertising strategy** blends the elements of the **creative mix**:

- The target audience.
- The product concept.
- The communications media.
- The advertising message.

CHECKLIST Developing Advertising Objectives

Does the advertising aim at *immediate sales?* If so, objectives might be:

◇ Perform the complete selling function.
◇ Close sales to prospects already partly sold.
◇ Announce a special reason for buying now (price, premium, and so forth).
◇ Remind people to buy.
◇ Tie in with special buying event.
◇ Stimulate impulse sales.

Does the advertising aim at *near-term sales?* If so, objectives might be:

◇ Create awareness.
◇ Enhance "brand image."
◇ Implant information or attitude.
◇ Combat or offset competitive claims.
◇ Correct false impressions, misinformation.
◇ Build familiarity and easy recognition.

Does the advertising aim at building a "long-range consumer franchise"? If so, objectives might be:

◇ Build confidence in company and brand.
◇ Build customer demand.
◇ Select preferred distributors and dealers.
◇ Secure universal distribution.
◇ Establish a "reputation platform" for launching new brands or product lines.
◇ Establish brand recognition and acceptance.

Does the advertising aim at helping *increase sales?* If so, objectives would be:

◇ Hold present customers.
◇ Convert other users to advertiser's brand.
◇ Cause people to specify advertiser's brand.
◇ Convert nonusers to users.
◇ Make steady customers out of occasional ones.
◇ Advertise new uses.
◇ Persuade customers to buy larger sizes or multiple units.
◇ Remind users to buy.
◇ Encourage greater frequency or quantity of use.

Does the advertising aim at some specific step that leads to a sale? If so, objectives might be:

◇ Persuade prospect to write for descriptive literature, return a coupon, enter a contest.
◇ Persuade prospect to visit a showroom, ask for a demonstration.
◇ Induce prospect to sample the product (trial offer).

How important are supplementary benefits of advertising? Objectives would be:

◇ Help salespeople open new accounts.
◇ Help salespeople get larger orders from wholesalers and retailers.
◇ Help salespeople get preferred display space.
◇ Give salespeople an entrée.
◇ Build morale of sales force.
◇ Impress the trade.

Should the advertising impart information needed to consummate sales and build customer satisfaction? If so, objectives may be to use:

◇ "Where to buy it" advertising.
◇ "How to use it" advertising.
◇ New models, features, package.
◇ New prices.
◇ Special terms, trade-in offers, and so forth.
◇ New policies (such as guarantees).

Should advertising build confidence and goodwill for the corporation? Targets may include:

◇ Customers and potential customers.
◇ The trade (distributors, dealers, retail people).
◇ Employees and potential employees.
◇ The financial community.
◇ The public at large.

What kind of images does the company wish to build?

◇ Product quality, dependability.
◇ Service.
◇ Family resemblance of diversified products.
◇ Corporate citizenship.
◇ Growth, progressiveness, technical leadership.

The Target Audience: Everyone Who Should Know

The **target audience,** the specific people the advertising will address, typically includes more segments than the target market. Advertisers need to know not just who the end-user is but also who makes the purchase and who influences the purchasing decision. Children often exert a strong influence on where the family eats. So while McDonald's target market is adults, its U.S. target audience

Two products from Quaker Oats use different product concepts to compete for a share of the same cereal market. The Life ad cleverly emphasizes good taste, while in the Plus Fiber ad, celebrity Wilford Brimley promotes the concept of a more healthful lifestyle.

includes children, and it spends much of its advertising budget on campaigns directed to kids.

The Product Concept: Presenting the Product

The "bundle of values" the advertiser presents to the consumer is the **product concept.** Both Quaker Oats Life cereal and Plus Fiber are similarly priced brands aimed at the U.S. ready-to-eat breakfast cereal market. However, the product concepts are completely different. Life is presented as a cereal kids will like; Plus Fiber (shown in Exhibit 7–11) as a healthy cereal for adult needs. (Ideally, the advertiser's view of the product concept matches the one held by consumers—although this is not always the case.)

When writing the advertising plan, the advertising manager must develop a simple statement to describe the product concept—that is, how the advertising will present the product. To create this statement, the advertiser first considers how the consumer perceives the product and then weighs this against the company's marketing strategy.

To help with this process, Foote, Cone & Belding developed the **FCB grid** shown in Exhibit 7–12, which depicts the degree and the kind of involvement the consumer brings to the purchase decision for different products. Some purchases, like cars, require a *high* degree of personal involvement. For others, like soap, involvement is *low.* And the kind of involvement may range from rational (*thinking*) to emotional or symbolic (*feeling*).

The Communications Media: The Message Delivery System

As an element of creative strategy, the **communications media** are all the various methods or vehicles that might transmit the advertiser's message. They

EXHIBIT • 7–12

The FCB grid classifies products and brands so advertisers can understand the nature of the purchase from the consumer's point of view. The grid has two dimensions. One moves from how demanding (high involvement) to how undemanding (low involvement) it is to make the purchase decision; the other looks at emotional aspects, from "think" (least emotional) to "feel" (most emotional).

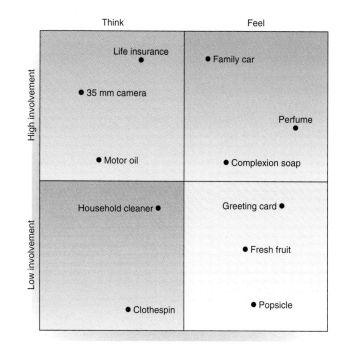

include traditional media such as radio, TV, newspapers, magazines, or billboards, and, in an integrated communications program, direct marketing, publicity, and sales promotion.

Introducing a new product is a daunting task, made even more acute if the advertiser's budget is lower than competitors'—as was the case with Saturn. Hal Riney & Partners invited the media to build a relationship with Saturn and then limited advertising media purchases to those that responded. As a result, Saturn got choice back-cover positions with magazines, economical placements on the Fox TV network, and—in a single deal with Patrick Media Group—became the largest brand advertiser on outdoor boards in California.[22]

The Advertising Message: What the Advertising Communicates

What the company plans to say in its ads and how it plans to say it—verbally and nonverbally—make up the **advertising message**. As we discuss in Chapter 8, the combination of copy, art, and production elements forms the message, and there are infinite ways to combine these elements. (See Ad Lab 7–C, "Creative Use of the Creative Mix," on pages 221–223.)

Riney broke new creative ground for Saturn. Rather than focusing on product features—standard fare in automotive advertising—Riney used Saturn employees and, later, customers to symbolize the company and its philosophy.[23] See Exhibit 7–13.

BOTTOM-UP MARKETING: HOW SMALL COMPANIES PLAN

The marketing and advertising planning processes we examined—analyzing the situation, establishing objectives, setting strategy, and determining tactics—are a proven method for large companies. Generally referred to as **top-down planning,** it is ideal for complex, bureaucratic organizations—allowing management at all levels to participate.

But how does a little company plan—particularly if it wants to become big? In a small company, everybody is both player and coach, and the day-to-day

E X H I B I T • 7–13

Schoolteacher Judith Reusswig didn't expect Saturn employees to attach a car to their answer to her letter. The true story became a famous metaphor for the relationship Saturn tries to establish with all its customers.

details seem to come first. However, there is a solution to this dilemma: **bottom-up marketing.**

Trout and Ries think the best way for a company to develop a competitive advantage is to focus on an ingenious tactic first and then develop it into a strategy. By reversing the normal process, advertisers sometimes make important discoveries.[24] Researchers at Vicks developed an effective, new liquid cold remedy but discovered that it put people to sleep. Rather than throwing out the research, Vicks positioned the formula as a nighttime cold remedy. NyQuil went on to become the most successful new product in Vicks' history and the number-one cold remedy.

The Tactic: A Singular, Competitive Mental Angle

By planning from the bottom up, entrepreneurs can find unique tactics to exploit. But advertisers should find just *one* tactic—not two or three or four. Once a tactic is discovered, the advertiser can build a strategy around it, focusing all elements of the marketing mix on the tactic.

Continued on page 226

AD LAB 7–C   Creative Use of the Creative Mix

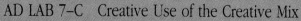

A. This beautiful poster for the Quebec recording industry association uses a play on words. The headline reads: "Quebec sings to you." But, spoken, it could also mean: "Quebec enchants you." Note how the poster design symbolizes the Quebec flag.

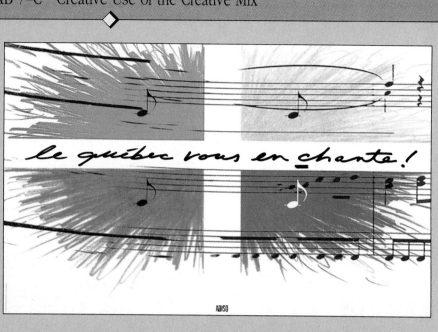

B. The Norwegian airline scored big points at the Cannes Film Festival in 1993 with this hilarious commercial about a man who thinks he'll surprise his wife only to be surprised by her parents—who had flown in for half-price on Braathens Safe.

AUDIO: Jolly Norwegian folk music throughout the entire film.

SUPER: Warning: We're flying your in-laws at half price. Braathens SAFE, the Norwegian airline.

AD LAB 7–C   Continued

C. The use of three-dimensional objects combined with the profiled cat on top of a billboard for the Humane Society of Missouri creates an eye-catching, real-life drama.

D. One of a series of fast-paced, MTV-style ads for Chevys Mexican Restaurant which highlight the restaurant's features—fresh tortillas and well-trained servers.

(Open on track) Several Chevys servers are running up some bleachers holding platters of chips and salsa.
ANNCR (VO): At Chevys all of our servers undergo rigorous physical training.
(Servers running through tires, doing various exercises.)
ANNCR (VO): They have to.
(Shots of the race. Servers, still holding platters, jump hurdles and run around obstacles.)

ANNCR (VO): Because at Chevys they'll rush our fresh tortilla chips to your table while they're still hot, within seconds. And with every basket of chips they'll bring salsa that's made fresh every hour. We call this Fresh Mex.
(Chevys waitresses as cheerleaders with pompons)
Super Fresh Mex.
ANNCR (VO): Like all great athletes, they make this look easy. Yeah. You try it sometime.

(Shots of a guy pole-vaulting with a tray and a relay race handoff. Servers go over a wall into a pit of water.)
Title: Chevys Fresh Mex
ANNCR (VO): Chevys Fresh Mex
(Last shot is of a guy shot-putting a basket of chips. It lands perfectly on a table where customers are sitting.)

Pont Neuf, Paris.

WE BRING CANADA TO *the* REST OF THE WORLD.

Paris is another of the 22 international destinations we serve, and one of seven cities in Europe. And we can get you there in the comfort of our award-winning Business Class.

Canadian is a registered trademark of Canadian Airlines International Ltd.

Canadian
Canadian Airlines International

E. At first glance this photo is very French—the Eiffel Tower and poodles. But wait, there's a Huskie in this magazine ad for Canadien, a clue that brings a different country to mind.

EXHIBIT • 7-14

Domino's tactic for rising above the many competing pizza restaurants was home delivery.

The combination of tactic and strategy creates a position in the consumer's mind. When Tom Monaghan thought of the tactic of delivering pizza to customers' homes, he focused his total strategy on this singular idea and ended up making a fortune with Domino's Pizza (see Exhibit 7–14).

The company's advertising plan is an excellent place to discover a competitive tactic. But opportunities are hard to spot because they often don't look like opportunities—they look like angles or gimmicks.

Small company managers are actually in an advantageous position. Surrounded with the details of the business, they are more likely to discover a good tactic that can be developed into a powerful strategy.

The Secret to Successful Planning

Whether the advertiser is a large corporation or small company, the key to successful planning is information. But the genius of business is in the interpretation of information—understanding what it means. This leads to direction. Once direction is established, planning becomes easier and more rewarding.

ALLOCATING FUNDS FOR ADVERTISING

In 1990, after eight years of unprecedented growth, the United States and Canada experienced the first throes of a recession. Interest rates were high, real estate sales dropped, construction of new homes slowed, defense spending was cut, and unemployment began to rise. To make matters worse, threats of war in the Mideast caused fear of higher fuel prices. Consumer confidence was sinking and with it retail sales.

As sales dropped, many executives ordered immediate cutbacks in advertising expenditures. Some cut their advertising budgets to zero. Two years later, when the government announced the recession was over, these same executives wondered why sales were still down and how their companies lost several percentage points in market share.

Money is the motor that drives every market and advertising plan. If you suddenly shut the motor off, the car may coast for a while, but before long, it stops running. No advertising or marketing plan is complete without a discussion of money. The advertising department has to convince management that advertising spending makes good business sense—even in an adverse economic climate (see Exhibit 7–15).

Advertising Is an Investment in Future Sales

Accountants and the Internal Revenue Service consider advertising a current business expense. Consequently, many executives treat advertising as a budget item to be trimmed or eliminated like other expense items when sales are either extremely high or extremely low. This is understandable but short-sighted.

The cost of a new plant or distribution warehouse is investment in the company's future ability to produce and distribute products. Similarly, advertising—as one element of the promotion mix—is an investment in future sales. While advertising is often used to stimulate immediate sales, its greatest power is in its cumulative long-range effect.

Advertising builds consumer preference and promotes goodwill. This, in turn, enhances the reputation and value of the company name and brand. And it encourages customers to make repeat purchases.

So while advertising is a current expense for accounting purposes, it is also a long-term capital investment. For management to see advertising as an investment, however, it must understand how advertising relates to sales and profits.

EXHIBIT • 7–15

In good times and bad, Procter & Gambel remains one of the leading advertisers in the United States. Why? Because it works.

AD LAB 7–D   How Economists View the Effect of Advertising on Sales

Normally, quantity sold depends on the number of dollars the company spends advertising the product. And within reasonable limits (if its advertising program is not too repugnant), the more dollars spent on advertising, the more a company will sell—up to a point. Yet, even the most enthusiastic ad agency admits, reluctantly, that it is possible to spend too much.

Management needs to know how much more it will be able to sell per additional dollar of advertising and when additional advertising dollars cease being effective. It needs to have, not a fixed number representing potential demand, but a graph or a statistical equation describing the relationship between sales and advertising.

In our illustration, most of the curve goes uphill as we move to the right (it has a positive slope). This means that additional advertising will continue to bring in business until (at a budget of x million dollars) people become so saturated by the message that it begins to repel them and turn them away from the product.

Even if the saturation level cannot be reached within the range of outlays the firm can afford, the curve is likely to level off, becoming flatter and flatter as the amount spent on advertising gets larger and larger and saturation is approached. The point at which the curve begins to flatten is the point at which returns from advertising begin to diminish. When the total advertising budget is small, even a $1

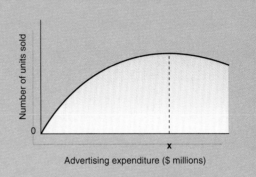

addition to the campaign may bring in as much as $10 in new sales. But when the market approaches saturation, each additional dollar may contribute only 30 cents in new sales.

Laboratory Applications

1. When would an advertising expenditure curve have a negative slope?
2. Economists suggest that the quantity sold depends on the number of dollars the company spends on advertising. Is that a safe assumption? Discuss.

Relationship of Advertising to Sales and Profits

There are many variables—both internal and external—that influence the effectiveness of a company's marketing and advertising efforts. However, methods to measure the relationship between advertising and sales and sales and profit are far from perfect. However, research does verify the following:

- In consumer goods marketing, increases in market share are more closely related to increases in the marketing budget than to price reductions—market share is a prime indicator of profitability.[25]
- Sales normally increase if there is additional advertising. At some point, however, the rate of return declines. (See Ad Lab 7–D, "How Economists View the Effect of Advertising on Sales.")
- Sales response to advertising may build over time, but the durability of advertising is brief, so a consistent investment is important.[26]
- There are minimum levels below which advertising expenditures will have no effect on sales.
- There will be some sales even if there is no advertising.
- There are saturation limits imposed by culture and competition above which no amount of advertising can increase sales.

To management, these facts might mean: Spend more until it stops working. In reality, the issue isn't that simple. Advertising isn't the only marketing activity that affects sales. A change in market share may occur because of quality perceptions, word of mouth, the introduction of new products, the opening of more attractive outlets, better personal selling, or seasonal changes in the business cycle.[27]

Furthermore, most companies don't have a clear-cut way to determine the relationship between sales and profit. What if the company sells a variety of products? Which advertising contributes to which product?

One thing remains clear. Since the response to advertising is spread out over an extended time, advertising should be viewed as a long-term investment in future profits. Like all expenditures, advertising should be evaluated for wastefulness. But historically, companies that make advertising the scapegoat during periods of economic fluctuation invariably end up discovering they lost substantial market share when the economy starts growing again.[28]

The Variable Environments of Business

Before attempting to determine advertising allocations, the advertising manager must consider the company's economic, political, social, and legal situation. General economic activity, social customs and attitudes, and tax laws affect total industry sales and corporate profits on sales. See Exhibit 7–16.

The manager must consider the institutional and competitive environments. What is the level of sales within the industry? How much are competitors spending? And what are they doing that might either help or hinder the company's marketing efforts?

Finally, the manager must consider the internal environment. Do the company's current policies and procedures allow it to fulfill the promises its advertising intends to make?

Methods of Allocating Funds

Most business executives will spend more money on advertising as long as they are assured it will mean more profit. However, the point of equilibrium is hard to predict in advance when advertising budgets are being developed.

Companies use a number of methods to determine how much to spend on advertising: percentage-of-sales, percentage-of-profit, unit-of-sale, competitive-parity, share-of-market, and task methods. (See the Checklist on Ways to Set Advertising Budgets.)

Some organizations rely on one technique, others use several. However, no technique is adequate for all situations. The three methods discussed here are used primarily for national advertising budgets. Retailers use other techniques which we discuss in Chapter 18.

Percentage-of-Sales Method

The **percentage-of-sales method** is one of the most popular techniques. It may be based on a percentage of last year's sales, anticipated sales for next year, or a combination of the two. Businesspeople like this method because it is the simplest, it doesn't cost them anything, it is related to revenue, and it is considered safe. The problem is knowing what percentage to use. As Exhibit 7–17 shows, even leaders in the same industry use different percentages.

Usually, the percentage is based on an industry average or on company experience. Unfortunately, it is too often determined arbitrarily. An industry average assumes that every company in the industry has similar objectives and

On January 1, the government is going to throw you a curve. (Nobody handles curves better than Porsche.)

Avoid being put in a corner with a new luxury tax. Buy a Porsche before January 1 and you'll be able to handle that corner just fine.

PORSCHE

E X H I B I T • 7–16

Many outside influences on business affect advertising strategy. Here, proposed taxation legislation influences a headline.

CHECKLIST   Ways to Set Advertising Budgets

◇ **Percentage of sales.** Advertising budget determined by allocating a percentage of last year's sales, anticipated sales for next year, or a combination of the two. The percentage is usually based on an industry average, company experience, or arbitrarily.

◇ **Percentage of profit.** Percentage is applied to profit—either past years' or anticipated.

◇ **Unit of sale.** Also called the *case-rate method*, specific dollar amount is set for each box, case, barrel, or carton produced. Used primarily in assessing members of horizontal cooperatives or trade associations.

◇ **Competitive parity.** Allocates dollars according to the amounts spent by major competitors. Also called *self-defense method*.

◇ **Share of market/share of voice.** Allocates dollars by maintaining a percentage share of total industry advertising comparable to or somewhat ahead of desired share of market. Often used for new-product introductions.

◇ **Objective/task method.** Also referred to as the *budget buildup method*, this method has three steps: defining objectives, determining strategy, and estimating the cost to execute that strategy.

◇ **Empirical research method.** By running a series of experimental tests in different markets with different budgets, companies determine which is the most efficient level.

◇ **Quantitative mathematical models.** Computer-based programs developed by major advertisers and agencies that rely on input of sophisticated data, history, and assumptions.

◇ **All available funds method.** Go-for-broke technique generally used by small firms with limited capital trying to introduce new products or services.

---

faces the same marketing problems. Company experience assumes that the market is highly static, which is rarely the case.

However, this method does have advantages. When applied against future sales, it often works well. It assumes that a certain number of dollars will be needed to sell a certain number of units. If the advertiser knows what the percentage is, the correlation between advertising and sales should remain constant, assuming the market is stable and competitors' advertising remains unchanged. Furthermore, management tends to think in terms of percentages, whether income or outgo. And since this method is common in the industry, it diminishes the likelihood of competitive warfare.

The greatest shortcoming of the percentage-of-sales method is that it violates a basic marketing principle. Marketing activities are supposed to *stimulate* demand and, thus, sales; marketing activities aren't supposed to occur as a *result* of sales. And if advertising automatically increases when sales increase and declines when sales decline, it ignores all other factors that might encourage an opposite move. It may also become a self-fulfilling prophecy.

Share-of-Market/Share-of-Voice Method

In markets with similar products, a high correlation usually exists between a company's share of the market and its share of industry advertising. Knowing this, some firms set a goal for a certain portion of the market and then apply the same percentage to their advertising budgets.

The **share-of-market/share-of-voice method**, developed by J. O. Peckham of the A. C. Nielsen Company, is a bold attempt to link advertising dollars with sales objectives.[29] According to Peckham, a company's best chance of holding its share of market is to keep a share of advertising (*voice*) somewhat ahead of its market share. For example, a company with a 30 percent share of the market should spend 35 percent of the industry's advertising dollars. (One shortcoming is that there's no guarantee competitors won't increase their advertising budgets.)

The share-of-market/share-of-voice method is commonly used for new prod-

EXHIBIT • 7-17

Advertising expenditures by the top 25 leading advertisers, 1991 ($ in millions).

Category	Rank	Company	U.S. advertising expenditures	U.S. sales	Advertising as percent of U.S. sales
Automotive	20	Chrysler Corp.	$ 531	$24,537	2.5
	9	Ford Motor Company	677	61,149	1.1
	3	General Motors Corp.	1,442	83,973	1.7
	12	Toyota Motor Corp.	632	N/A	
Beer, Wine & Liquor	22	Anheuser-Busch	508	12,634	4.0
Cigarettes	18	RJR Nabisco	571	12,546	4.6
Electronics & Appliances	25	Sony Corp.	439	8337	5.2
Entertainment & Media	23	Walt Disney Co.	489	4,882	1.0
	16	Time Warner	588	8,862	6.6
Food	19	General Mills	556	7,040	7.8
	17	Kellogg Co.	578	3,411	16.9
	14	Nestlé SA	601	8.098	7.4
	2	Philip Morris	2,046	37,890	5.3
Miscellaneous	10	Eastman Kodak	661	10,882	6.1
Personal Care	1	Procter & Gamble Co.	2,149	15,600	13.7
	15	Unilever NV	594	8,475	7.0
Pharmaceuticals, Remedies & Diets	24	American Home Products	447	4,878	9.1
	7	Johnson & Johnson	733	6,248	11.7
	11	Warner-Lambert	657	2,615	25.1
Restaurants	6	Grand Metropolitan	745	7,878	9.4
	8	McDonald's Corp.	695	3,710	18.7
	5	PepsiCo	903	15,168	6.0
Retailers	21	Kmart Corp.	527	33,520	1.6
	4	Sears, Roebuck & Co.	1,179	57,242	2.0
Telephone	13	AT&T	617	63,089	1.0

ucts.[30] According to Peckham's formula, when introducing a new product brand, the advertising budget for the first two years should be about one and a half times the brand's targeted share of the market in two years. This means that if the company's two-year sales goal is 10 percent of the market, it should spend about 15 percent of total industry advertising during the first two years.

One hazard of this method is the tendency to become complacent. Companies compete on more than one basis, and advertising is just one tool of the marketing mix. Simply maintaining a higher percentage of media exposure usually isn't enough to accomplish the desired results.[31] National packaged goods marketers sill spend 69 percent of their marketing budgets on consumer and trade promotion rather than consumer advertising.[32] Companies must be aware of *all* their competitors' marketing activities, not just advertising.

Objective/Task Method

The **objective/task** method, also known as the **budget buildup method,** gained considerable popularity and is now used by the majority of major national advertisers in the United States and Canada.[33] It considers advertising a marketing tool to generate sales.[34]

The task method has three steps: defining objectives, determining strategy, and estimating cost. After specific, quantitative marketing objectives have been set, the advertiser develops programs to attain them. If the objective is to increase the number of coffee cases sold by 10 percent, the advertiser determines which advertising approach will work best, how often ads must run, and which media to use. The cost of the program is determined and becomes the basis for the advertising budget. Of course, the company's financial position is always a consideration. If the cost is too high, objectives may have to be scaled back. After the campaign runs, if results are better or worse than anticipated, the next budget may need revision.

The task method forces companies to think in terms of accomplishing goals. Its effectiveness is most apparent when the results of particular ads or campaigns can be readily measured. Due to its nature, the task method is adaptable to changing market conditions, and it can be easily revised.

However, it is often difficult to determine in advance the amount of money needed to reach a specific goal. And techniques for measuring advertising effectiveness still have many weaknesses.

Additional Methods

Advertisers also use several other methods. The **empirical research method** uses experimentation to determine the best level of advertising expenditure. By running a series of tests in different markets with different budgets, companies determine which is the most efficient level of expenditure.[35]

Since the introduction of computers, **quantitative mathematical models** are being used for budgeting and allocating advertising dollars. Foote, Cone & Belding developed a response-curve database from tracking studies on more than 40 clients' products and services. The program analyzes media programs and estimates customer response.[36] Many other sophisticated techniques facilitate marketing and advertising planning, budget allocation across multiple product offerings, new-product introductions, and media analysis.[37] However, most are not easily understood by line executives, and each relies on data that may be unavailable or estimated.[38] While widely employed by major national advertisers, they require very sophisticated users and, for the most part, are still too expensive for the average business.

The Bottom Line

Unfortunately, all these methods rely on one of two fallacies. The first is that advertising is a *result* of sales. Advertisers know this is not true, and yet they continue to use the percentage-of-sales method.

The second fallacy is that advertising *creates* sales. In certain circumstances (where direct-action advertising is used) advertising closes the sale. But advertising's real role is to locate prospects, build brand equity, and stimulate demand. It may even stimulate inquiries. Salespeople likewise locate prospects and stimulate demand. They also close the sale. But only customers *create* sales. The customer makes the decision to buy, not the company.

The job of advertising is to influence perception by informing, persuading, and reminding. In that way, advertising *affects* sales. However, advertising is just one of many influences on consumer perception, and advertising managers must keep this in mind when preparing their plans and budgets.

Summary

The marketing plan may be the most important document a company possesses. It assembles all the pertinent and current facts about a company, the markets it serves, its products, and its competition. It sets specific goals and objectives to be attained and describes the precise strategies that will be used to achieve them. It musters the company's forces for the marketing battlefield and, in so doing, dictates the role of advertising in the marketing mix and provides focus for advertising creativity.

The marketing plan should contain four principal sections: situation analysis, marketing objectives, marketing strategy, and action programs. A company's marketing objectives should be logical deductions from an analysis of its current situation, its prediction of future trends, and its understanding of corporate objectives. They should relate to the needs of specific target markets and specify sales objectives. Sales-target objectives should be specific, quantitative, and realistic.

The first step in developing a marketing strategy is to select the target market. The second step is to determine a cost-effective marketing mix for each target market the company pursues. The marketing mix is determined by how the company uses the 4Ps—product, price, place, and promotion. Advertising is a promotional tool.

Advertising is a natural outgrowth of the marketing plan, and the advertising plan is prepared in much the same way as the marketing plan. It includes a section on analysis, advertising objectives, and strategy.

Advertising objectives may be expressed in terms of moving prospective customers up through the advertising pyramid (awareness, comprehension, conviction, desire, action). Or they may be expressed in terms of generating inquiries, coupon response, or attitude change.

The advertising (or creative) strategy is determined by the advertiser's use of the creative mix. The creative mix is composed of the target audience, product concept, communications media, and advertising message. The target audience includes the specific groups of people the advertising will address. The product concept refers to the bundle of product-related values the advertiser presents to the customer. The communications media are the vehicles used to transmit the advertiser's message. The advertising message is what the company plans to say and how it plans to say it. One way for small companies to accomplish the marketing and advertising planning task is to work from the bottom up—taking an ingenious tactic and building a strategy around it.

Several methods are used to allocate advertising funds. The most popular method is the percentage-of-sales approach. Others include the share-of-market/share-of-voice method and the objective/task method.

Questions for Review Discussion

1. What is a marketing plan and why is it a company's most important document?

2. What examples illustrate the difference between market-need objectives and sales-target objectives?

3. What basic elements should be included in any marketing plan?

4. How does one person's strategy become another person's objective? Give examples.

5. What is the most important consideration in developing any marketing strategy?

6. What are the elements of an advertising plan and an advertising strategy?

7. How can small companies use bottom-up marketing to become big companies?

8. What is the best method of allocating advertising funds for a real estate development? Why?

9. What types of companies tend to use the percentage-of-sales method? Why?

10. How could a packaged foods manufacturer use the share-of-market/share-of-voice method to determine its advertising budget?

III

Creating Advertisements and Commercials

After determining advertising objectives and strategies, the advertiser must develop a message strategy and create ads and commercials. Part III looks at ad creation from three sides: verbal (copywriting), nonverbal (art direction), and production (both print and electronic media).

Chapter 8, "Creative Copywriting," explains the process of developing advertising copy. It presents the copywriter's pyramid, a model for preparing effective advertising copy, and the "big idea," the key to creating ads that audiences remember. Key copywriting terms appear in easy-to-use charts, and a thorough explanation describes the fundamental structural elements of an ad.

Chapter 9, "Creative Art Direction," discusses art as a visual form of expression in advertising and describes its application to print and broadcast advertising and package design. The chapter defines terms and discusses steps in the layout of print advertising. Finally, the chapter describes the role of imagery in various types of radio and television commercials.

Chapter 10, "Creative Production: Print Media," depicts the complexity of print production and the dynamic impact of computerization. It discusses typography as a key communication device in advertising. The chapter explores the printing process in detail and the advantages and limitations of various printing methods. Finally, it shows how a successful ad is produced from concept through production.

Chapter 11, "Creative Production: Electronic Media," presents an overview of the techniques and equipment used in both radio and television commercials. Finally, the chapter examines how one well-known TV commercial came to life from initial concept through final production.

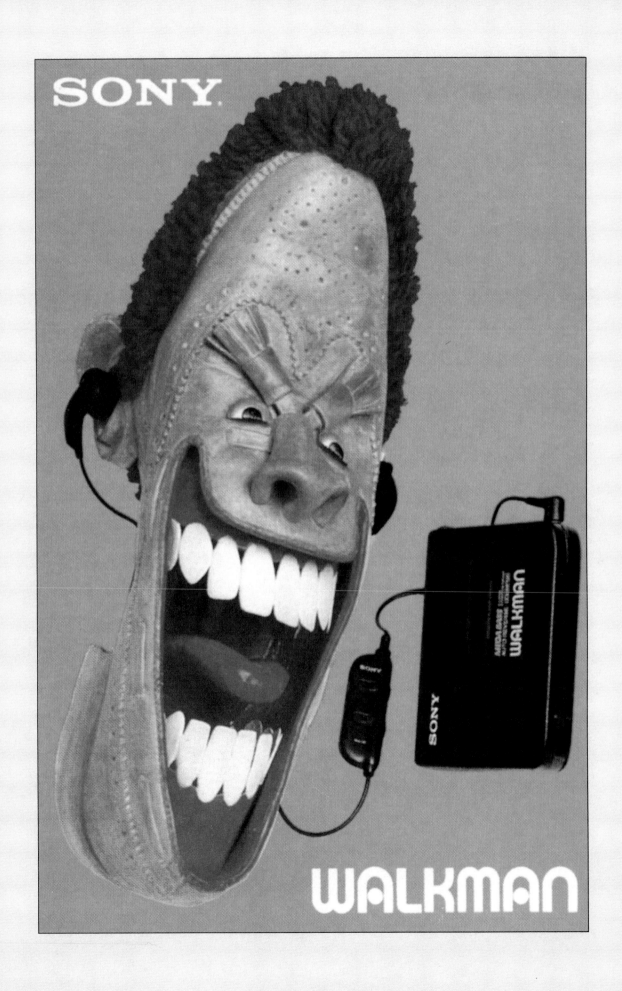

Our dishes have been
piling up for years.
Come to the Museum.
ROM Royal Ontario Museum

Creative Copywriting

Objective: To describe the role of the copywriter as a creator of advertising messages and a key member of an agency creative team. We discuss how research and planning guide what the copywriter writes; we explain key terms and concepts that allow writers to create effective copy for a variety of media; and we review common problems and pitfalls faced by writers.

After studying this chapter, you will be able to:

- Explain the importance of copywriting.

- Explain the role of the copywriter in relation to other members of the creative team.

- Discuss the five objectives of advertising copy and the role each plays in communicating the complete message.

- Describe the format elements of an ad and discuss how they relate to the objectives of advertising copywriting.

- Differentiate the types and the roles of various headlines and the elements that make up body copy.

- Discuss and debate the common pitfalls in writing copy.

- Explain the copywriting approval process.

One company's ads are a copywriter's dream—three to five columns wide, nearly all text, with no dominant photo or oversized headline. And they're as successful today as they were 20 years ago.

Donald Carr knew tires. While operating a small chain of tire stores in Los Angeles in the 1960s, he became convinced that tire marketing was about to change. As Carr recalls, "The tire industry was pretty stodgy. It was run by a lot of not-very-bright guys who sat around in Akron and told each other everything was wonderful. They didn't realize that Michelin and others were lurking offshore, waiting to eat their lunch. Which is exactly what happened."[1]

Phil Lansdale knew advertising. His reputation as a maverick began in 1929 when he opened his first ad agency in Los Angeles. His philosophy was straightforward: "I just try to make the company stand for something, and then I inform the people." And as for copywriting: ". . . details about the business are exciting—if you can find an interesting way to say it. After that, the important thing is to keep the message fresh."[2]

Lansdale and Carr teamed up and became partners. By pooling $50,000 each and combining their product knowledge with their marketing and advertising expertise, they created a fresh product concept for selling tires, a new way of operating the stores, and a fresh—some call it zany—advertising style. That was in 1969. Today, their chain is well known throughout the Southwest as 4day Tire Stores, a 54-store company grossing $130 million annually.

In the company's first decade, Phil Lansdale wrote more than 450 notable ads. Today, 4day's in-house advertising agency—Lansdale, Carr, and Baum—continues to generate newspaper ads based on the original product concept created in 1969. The ads exude a personality of their own. Their format includes such features as large amounts of type and unique, sketchy, line drawings with an "edge." Surprisingly, 4day ads appear up front in the newspaper, *not* in the sports section where tire dealers usually advertise. Today 4day's ads are *fun;* but in 1969 they were daring—for their gutsy, new marketing style and off-center creative bent.

Pete Lewis, the agency's president, points out that "although Phil passed away in 1990, his original spirit lives on in the writing and design of each 4day ad." This heritage inspires headlines with negative ideas most advertisers would never dare publish: "Why do our ads bury you with words?" and "Tire salesmanship, the lost art at 4day." And the body copy follows suit with text such as: "Before you're ready to buy, why should you read a tire ad? It tells you nothing worth remembering." Or: "Are we tire-ing you?" And even: "4day Tire Stores, the worst price cutters in town" (see Exhibit 8–1).

All this unusual talk is reinforced by intellectually zany cartoon visuals. "We continue to call Gene Holtan for illustrations," says Lewis. "He has been with us since the early days. Currently, we have over 700 illustrations in the drawer."

Above all, 4day ads prove one fact: words sell. ◆

COPYWRITING AND FORMULATING ADVERTISING STRATEGY

Encoding—the conversion of mental concepts into language-based symbols—is the job of the creative team, which includes the copywriter. He or she typically works with an art director under the supervision of a creative director (often a former copywriter). As one of the key people advertisers use to create (encode) advertising messages for the marketplace, the copywriter influences the form the communication takes (printed words, speech, gestures, action) and the medium used (print, broadcast). And, as you can see from Phil Lansdale's 4day ads, the copywriter's personality and conceptual skills play a significant role in an ad's overall character and ability to communicate.

The subject of this chapter, **copywriting,** focuses on the **verbal** element of the message strategy,—i.e., the words. Yet, words are only one part of the

EXHIBIT · 8–1

The personality of Phil Lansdale, the late creator and writer for hundreds of 4day Tire Stores ads, reveals itself in the choice of text and art. Wording like "bury you with words" and "our ads are so long-winded" blatantly dangles a major taboo—filibustering—in the reader's face. The ads become an inside joke for writers, begging the question "How will they get out of this one?" But the ad plays well with the buying mood of the market: ". . . as price cutters, we expect to get more for our money."

overall message strategy. A second element, the **nonverbal,** is the more visual and intuitive side of the message strategy. We discuss the nonverbal element later in this chapter and in Chapter 9, "Creative Art Direction." Working as a team, the creative director, art director, and copywriter bring together verbal and nonverbal elements to create effective ads and commercials.

While words carry the message in 4day's ads, behind the copywriter's choice of tone, words, and ideas lies an advertising strategy. Let's look at 4day's *advertising strategy* and see how its creative team translates that into a *message strategy* and finally into an effective ad. Then we'll discuss message strategy more completely. Recall that advertising (or creative) strategy consists of four elements: the *target audience*, the *product concept*, the *communications media*, and the *advertising message*.

What is 4day's target audience? 4day gained its early lead by serving the growing flood of Japanese imports. These cars needed smaller tires, so 4day stocked radials—a radically new concept at the time. Today, 4day continues to succeed because of its ability to identify and sell to other segments as well: women buyers, Cadillac and Mercedes owners, and even other tire dealers.

What is 4day's product concept? As the name symbolizes and the ads proudly announce, 4day stores are open only four days a week—Wednesday through Saturday. Doesn't this shorter week hurt sales? Not really. The average set of tires costs $250, so very few prospects buy on impulse. Most shop for the best price, then make an appointment for installation. Installers only work Wednesday through Saturday, so 4day keeps its overhead down and profits high. (Its 2 percent net profit exceeds the industry average of 1.4 percent.)

Further, 4day's managers dedicate Tuesdays to wholesale accounts. Because they sell so many tires, 4day has the buying clout to negotiate large discounts from manufacturers. In turn, 4day sells below retail to independent service stations and other dealers and still makes a profit.

What communication media does 4day use? 4day advertises in the daily newspaper only. Newspapers reach women, status car buyers, and small import owners—plus all shoppers who want to compare prices.

What is 4day's advertising message? In its simplest terms, **message strategy** is determined by what a company wants to say and how it wants to say it. 4day communicates its message with a *verbal* and *nonverbal* presentation that is simple, interesting, informative, entertaining, helpful, and, most of all, credible. 4day demystifies the buying process by explaining the nature of tires, displaying the company's guarantee and prices, and telling consumers where to call with questions or complaints (see Exhibit 8–2).

These four elements of the advertising (or creative) strategy—target, product, media, and message—must be thoroughly understood by the copywriter and other creative staff members. Now let's examine the elements of *message strategy* more closely.

Elements of Message Strategy

Usually written by the agency's account managers, a **message strategy** is a description of an ad campaign's overall approach and specific requirements, called *mandatories,* which include addresses, logos, slogans, and so on. A message strategy has three components:

- **Copy (verbal)**—guidelines for what to say; considerations that affect the choice of words; and type of medium(s) that will carry the message.
- **Art (nonverbal)**—overall nature of the ad's graphics; any visuals that must appear, and the medium(s) in which the ad will appear.

- **Production (mechanical)**—preferred production approach and mechanical outcome including budget and scheduling limitations (often governed by the medium involved).

If the advertising plan doesn't include a message strategy (often the case for smaller advertisers), the copywriter must develop one. He or she should collaborate with the art director if possible (or creative director, if there is one) and get approval from the client or agency account management. The fastest way to have an ad rejected is to write a brilliant piece of work that has nothing to do with the overall campaign strategy.

To develop the message strategy of a campaign, the creative team first needs to review the details of the marketing and advertising plan, analyze the facts, and study the market, the product, and the competition. (See the Checklist of Product Marketing Facts for Copywriters on p. 240.) All through this process, they need input and direction from agency account managers and from the client side (sales, marketing, product, or research managers).

Certain basic questions related to the product and the advertising strategy need to be asked and answered: How is the market segmented? How will the product be positioned? Who are the best prospects for the product? Is the target audience different from the target market? What is the key consumer benefit? What is the product's (or company's) current image? And what is the product's unique advantage?[3]

At this point, research data is important. Research helps the creative team identify the best prospects, the best mediums, and the most suitable consumer appeals and product claims.

Writing the Copy Platform

In developing the message strategy, the copywriter (or creative director) needs to create a **copy platform,** a document that serves as the creative team's guide for writing and producing the ad.[4] The copy platform is a written strategy statement of the most important issues to be considered in the ad or campaign—the *who, why, what, where, when* and the *how* of the ad:

1. **Who is the most likely prospect for the product?** The copy platform must define the prospect in terms of geographic, demographic, psychographic, and/or behavioristic qualities. If possible, it should describe the typical prospect's personality.

2. **Why?** Does the consumer have specific wants or needs the ad should appeal to? Advertisers use two broad categories of **appeals**. **Rational appeals** are directed at the consumer's practical, functional need for the product or service; **emotional appeals** at the consumer's psychological, social, or symbolic needs. For a sampling of specific appeals within these categories, see Exhibit 8–3. All these appeals help gain attention, create a personality for the product or service, and stimulate consumer interest, credibility, desire, and action.

3. **What product features satisfy the consumers' needs?** What factors

EXHIBIT • 8-3

Selected advertising appeals.

Rational	Emotional	
Cleanliness	Ambition	Pleasure of recreation
Dependability in quality	Appetite	Pride of personal appearance
Dependability in use	Avoidance of a laborious task	Pride of possession
Durability	Cooperation	Romance
Economy in purchase	Curiosity	Security
Economy of use	Devotion to others	Sex attraction
Efficiency in operation or use	Entertainment	Simplicity
Enhancement of earnings	Fear	Social achievement
Opportunity for more leisure time	Guilt	Social approval
	Health	Sport/play/physical activity
Protection of others	Home comfort	Style (beauty)
Rest or sleep	Humor	Sympathy for others
Safety	Personal comfort	Taste
Variety of selection		

CHECKLIST   Product Marketing Facts for Copywriters

◇ **Proprietary information**
Trade name.
Trademark.
Product symbol.
Other copyrighted or patented information.

◇ **History**
When was it created or invented?
Who introduced it?
Has it had other names?
Have there been product changes?
Is there any "romance" to it?

◇ **Research**
Is research available?
What research about the product does the supplier have?
Which research will be most useful for each medium?

◇ **Life cycle**
What is its life or use span?
What stage is it in now and what style of copy should be used for that stage?
What stages are competitors in?

◇ **Market position**
What is its share of the total market?
Does its market share suggest a positioning strategy?
What position does the company wish to occupy?

◇ **Competitive information**
Who are the competitors?
Does it have any advantages over them?
Does it have any disadvantages?
Are they all about the same?
Do rival products present problems that this one solves?

◇ **Product image**
How do people view the product?
What do they like about it?
What do they dislike about it?
Is it a luxury?
Is it a necessity?
Is it a habit?
Is it self-indulgent?
Do people have to have it but wish they didn't?

◇ **Customer use**
How is the product used?
Are there other possible uses?
How frequently is it bought?
What type of person uses the product?
Why is the product bought?
Personal use.
Gift.
Work.
What type of person uses the product most (heavy user)?

---

support the product claim? What is the product's position? What personality or image—of the product or the company—can be or has been created? What perceived strengths or weaknesses need to be dealt with?[5]

4. **Where and when will these messages be communicated?** What medium? What time of year? What area of the country?

5. **Finally, how should this be communicated?** What style, approach, or tone will the campaign use? And, generally, what will the copy say?

The answers to these questions help make up a copy platform. After writing the first ad, the copywriter should review the copy platform to see if the ad measures up. If it doesn't, the writer must start again.

Because all the elements of the message strategy—verbal, nonverbal, and mechanical—inevitably intertwine, they evolve simultaneously. Language affects imagery, and vice versa. However, the verbal elements are usually the starting point and foundation for most advertising campaigns.

THE ENCODING PROCESS

Copywriters thrive on the challenge and excitement of creating and writing advertising messages—the encoding process: But where to begin?

Encoding takes place on two levels—first in the mind, as an idea, and then on some medium, like paper. Let's take a brief look at both of these steps.

How much does the heavy user buy?

Where does the best customer live?

What kind of person is a heavy user or buyer?

◇ **Performance**

What does it do?

What might it be expected to do that it does not?

How does it work?

How is it made or produced?

What's in it?

    Raw materials.

    Special ingredients.

    Preservatives.

    Chemicals.

    Nutrients

What are its physical characteristics?

    Smell.

    Appearance.

    Color.

    Texture.

    Taste.

    Others.

◇ **Effectiveness**

Is there proof it has been tested and works well?

Do any government or other regulations need to be mentioned or observed?

How does it work compared to its competitors?

◇ **Manufacturing**

How is it made?

How long does it take?

How many steps in the process?

How about the people involved in making it?

Are there any special machines used?

Where is it made?

◇ **Distribution**

How widely is the product distributed?

Are there exclusive sellers?

Is there a ready supply or limited amount?

Is it available for a short season?

What channels of distributors must be reached?

◇ **Packaging**

Unit size or sizes offered.

Package shape.

Package design:

    Styling.

    Color.

    Special protection for product.

    A carrier for product.

Package label.

Conceptualization: Developing the Big Idea

For all creative people, the idea stage is always the toughest—and the most rewarding. It's the long, tedious, difficult task of assembling all the pertinent information, analyzing the problem, and searching for a key verbal or visual concept to communicate what needs to be said. It means establishing a mental idea or picture of the ad, commercial, or campaign before any copy is written or artwork begun.

This process, called **visualization** or **conceptualization,** is the most important step in creating the advertisement. It's the creative point where the search for the *big idea*—that flash of insight—takes place. The **big idea** is a bold, creative initiative that "synthesizes the purposes of the strategy, joins the product benefit with consumer desire in a fresh, involving way, brings the subject to life, and makes the reader or the audience stop, look, and listen."[6]

What's the difference between a *strategy* and a *big idea?* A strategy describes the direction the message should take. A big idea gives it life. For example, the copy platform for the Sunkist trade promotion in Exhibit 8–4 states the copy element of the message strategy under "Key Selling Point":

"You get everything you need to make the promotion a success. And it's so easy to implement."

But this would be a dull headline for an ad aimed at corporate cafeteria managers. It lacks what a big idea delivers: a set of multiple meanings that

FCB

COPY PLATFORM

Sunkist Foodservice Lemon Promotion Ad

Request

Sunkist has asked us to produce a 4/C, 1/2 page direct response coupon ad to sell their Sunkist Lemon Tap Promotion to Corporate Cafeterias.

Background

Corporate cafeterias are the number one growth segment in the foodservice industry. To attract this segment, Sunkist foodservice designed a turn-key promotion (a promotion that provides all the directions and materials to make the promotion a success). To sell the promotion initially, Sunkist sent out a direct mail piece which provided information on the promotion and included an order form postcard for requesting the kit. While 7% of the inventory was sold, sales didn't meet Sunkist's expectations. To boost sales, Sunkist has decided to advertise the promotion.

Description of Promotion

A free gift (a lemon tap and recipe booklet) is given to customers in exchange for ordering any food or drink garnished with a Sunkist lemon. Sunkist has assembled a complete promotional kit that helps to easily organize and implement the entire promotion, from start to finish.

Promotion's Value to the Cafeteria

Increases traffic and creates excitement for both cafeteria patrons and personnel.

Advertising Objectives

To motivate the target to buy the promotion via the ad's coupon.

Or, to at least call the Sunkist foodservice hotline and ask any questions.

Key Selling Point

You get everything you need to make the promotion a success. And it's so easy to implement.

Input

1. The ad must provide enough information about the promotion to eliminate any doubts or questions that would prevent the target from clipping the coupon and sending in the $30.00 for it.

2. The coupon is a vital part of the ad. Please refer to the attached copy of the return postcard for the information that the coupon should contain.

3. An 800 number must appear in the ad. The copy should read something like "To order or answer any questions, please call the Sunkist Foodservice hotline at 1-800-221-7318."

4. Foodservice operators like to see what they're buying. Therefore, the visual (or a visual) should show the essential elements of the promotion. Also, all artwork that's used for the promotion is available for us to pick-up.

Media

Publication: *Foodservice Director*

Issue Dates: July 15th & August 15th

EXHIBIT • 8-4

This copy platform from Foote, Cone & Belding provides the message strategy and sufficient background for the creative staff to develop the big idea for this promotion. The creative director (often a former writer) is usually responsible for developing the copy platform.

create interest, memorability, and, in some cases, drama. One possible big idea for the ad might be:

"Think of this kit as lemon-aid"

This concept could be the foundation for myriad word plays aimed at reinforcing the overall strategy. For example, "our twist makes your customer a winner" or "slice out the coupon" helps lighten the tone and reinforce the broader message.

While strategy requires deduction, a big idea requires inspiration.[7] The big idea in advertising is invariably a combination of art and copy. For example, some ads, like the one in Exhibit 8–5, use a specific word or phrase ("little reasons") to connect the text to the images (the visual of microbes).

To come up with big ideas, copywriters, the wordsmiths, of the team, often rely on *metaphors*—the likening of one process or thing to another by speaking of it as if it *were* the other. They borrow terminology commonly used to describe something else (the automobile was first called a "horseless carriage," a metaphor based on two words people already understood). Or they apply the attributes of one system to another (people often speak of money as if it were liquid—cash flow, liquid assets, spends money like water). A big idea is similar. 4day, for example, applies the concept of "inflation" to the economy and to tires.

To get their creative juices flowing, copywriters keep a tickler (or *swipe*) file of ads they've seen and liked that might stimulate a new idea. Experts suggest a variety of other techniques: cash in on their own experience with a product or the experience of others; talk with manufacturers and customers (and competitors' customers); study the product (from a different angle); review previous advertising; study competitors' ads (what are they *not* saying?); examine customer testimonials; solve the prospect's problem; brainstorm some outrageous approaches (what if airplanes flew underground?); sketch buzzwords on paper and tape them to the walls; focus on a single concept expressed simply; write from the heart (get emotional); put the subconscious mind to work to find a relevant metaphor; tell the truth (the unmitigated, whole truth); and develop variations on a successful ad.[8]

For advertisers, recognizing a big idea and evaluating it are almost as difficult as coming up with one.[9] David Ogilvy recommends asking five questions?

1. Did it make me gasp when I first saw it?
2. Do I wish I had thought of it myself?
3. Is it unique?

This ad for Aetna Health Plans forces a connection between the headline and the visual. When the audience makes the association, the result is more powerful than merely stating the concept in a headline.

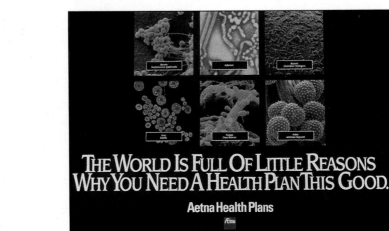

4. Does it fit the strategy to perfection?

5. Could it be used for 30 years?[10]

As Ogilvy points out, campaigns that have run five years or more are the superstars—the campaigns that keep on producing results and memorability: Dove soap (33 percent cleansing cream), Ivory soap (99 44/100 percent pure), Perdue Chickens ("It takes a tough man to make a tender chicken"), U.S. Army ("Be all you can be").

Choosing How to Convey the Big Idea

The next step in the encoding process involves choosing the symbols—the words, pictures, and sounds of the message—deciding how they'll be ordered to best communicate the big idea. The sequence of these symbols—their harmonious arrangement—is called **syntax.** For effective communication to occur, the creative team must be sure that the elements of an ad or commercial flow logically—that the syntax makes sense.

The arrangement of an ad's physical elements—visuals, text, etc.—is called the **format.** Copywriters typically announce most of the important principles, issues, or facts at the top of the ad while holding back the two most important facts—the who (the company providing the product) and the where (store site, telephone number)—until the end. This format appears in the Exhibit 8–6 ad for Sunlight, an environmentally friendly detergent sold in Switzerland.

THE COPYWRITER'S PYRAMID: A GUIDE TO FORMULATING COPY

Earlier we discussed the advertising pyramid as a model for setting advertising objectives based on how people typically behave. The **copywriter's pyramid**—related to the advertising pyramid—uses a similar, five-step structure, with only a slight variation in terminology (see Exhibit 8–7).

The purpose of copywriting is to persuade or remind people to take some

The headline in this Swiss Sunlight detergent ad makes the newsy claim "An end to superficial promises" at the top and saves the product's identity until last.

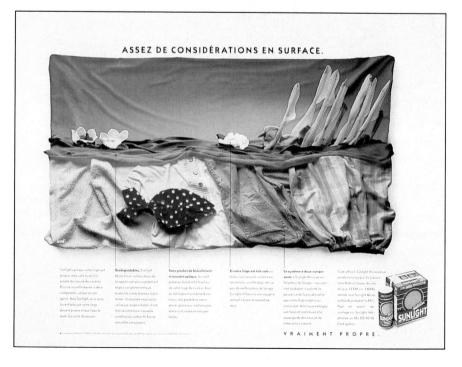

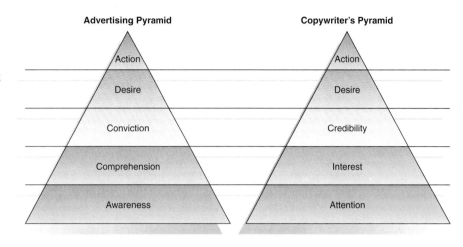

Advertising Pyramid

Action
Desire
Conviction
Comprehension
Awareness

Copywriter's Pyramid

Action
Desire
Credibility
Interest
Attention

E X H I B I T • 8-7

The copywriter's pyramid, like the advertising pyramid, offers an excellent, simple guide for establishing copywriting objectives.

Your Dog's Hearing Is 17 Times Better Than Your's.

So How Come He Doesn't Listen.

Luis Gomez • Master Dog Trainer • 212 866-7836

E X H I B I T • 8-8

Getting attention is a big hurdle, particularly in media that are dense with distractions. Newspaper ads and billboards rely heavily on the headline to carry much of the message. Here the headline carries the attention, interest, and credibility steps. Can you find the two punctuation errors in this award-winning ad?

action to satisfy a need or want. But first people need to be made aware of the problem or, if the problem is obvious, of a solution. To create awareness, the copywriter must first get people's *attention*—for example, by using large type and provocative visuals. Next, the copywriter must stimulate the prospect's *interest* in the product and build *credibility* for the product claims. Then the copywriter focuses on generating *desire* and finally on stimulating *action*. These five elements should be present in every ad or commercial.

When following the five steps of the copywriter's pyramid, the writer's words also help shape the various format elements of an ad—the headline, body copy, boxes and panels, slogans, and more.

Attention

An ad or commercial is a stimulus. It must break through consumers' physiological screens to create the kind of attention that leads to perception. *Attention,* therefore, is the first objective of any ad and the fundamental building block in the copywriter's pyramid.

Print ads often use the headline as the major attention-getting device. The ad in Exhibit 8–8 is *all* headline. It uses large type and a didactic statement to catch the eye, then a provocative question to engage the reader. Many other devices also help gain attention (in print media: dynamic visuals, unusual layout, vibrant color, or dominant ad size; in electronic media, special sound effects, music, animation, or unusual visual techniques).

Some factors are beyond the copywriter's control. The size of the ad—or length of the commercial—may influence how well or quickly it penetrates consumers' screens. Similarly, a TV spot's position in a cluster of commercials between shows—or an ad's position in a publication—may determine who sees it. The copywriter must take these factors into account before deciding on an attention-getting device.

The attention-getting device should create drama, power, impact, and intensity, and it must be appropriate—relate to the product, to the tone of the ad, and to the needs or interests of the intended audience.[11] This is especially true in business-to-business advertising. For example, a manufacturer of laboratory ovens used the headline: "The American work ethic is alive and well in Philadelphia," good news to patriots and local politicians, but not many of them buy laboratory ovens.[12]

Headlines that promise something but fail to deliver it in a credible manner won't make a sale; in fact, the advertiser may alienate a potential customer. Ads that use racy headlines or nude figures unrelated to the product or sales ideas often lose sales because prospects can't purchase the item that first attracted their attention.

Interest

Interest, the second step in the copywriter's pyramid, is extremely important. It carries the prospective customer—now excited from a successful attention step—to the more serious discussion in the body of the ad. It must keep the prospect's excitement alive as the information becomes more detailed and specific. To do this, the copywriter can answer a question asked in the attention step or add additional facts that relate to the headline.

The writer must focus on leading prospects from one step to the next. Research shows that people read what interests them and ignore what doesn't, so the writer must maintain prospects' interest at all times.[13] One way to do so is to relate to prospects' psychological screens—by talking to them about them, and about their problems, their needs, and how the product or service answers their needs. Copywriters use the word *you* frequently.

There are many effective ways to stimulate interest—a dramatic situation, a story, cartoons, or charts and tables. In radio, copywriters use sound effects or catchy dialogue between two characters. Television frequently uses quick cuts from one subject to another to maintain interest in the action—and the

---

ETHICAL DILEMMA   When Advertisers Dare to Compare

A recent judicial verdict hit the advertising agency industry where it hurts. Friedman-Benjamin, Inc., advertising agency for Wilkinson Sword, was held jointly liable with its client for claims that appeared in a series of *Ultra Glide* razor ads. Wilkinson claimed its *Ultra Glide* lubricant strip was "six times smoother" than ordinary strips, including Gillette's, and that men preferred it. Gillette sued, pointing to its own survey showing male preference for its *Atra Plus* product. On close examination, the court found that Wilkinson's own laboratory data didn't support its superiority claim. The court further ruled that Friedman-Benjamin was a knowing participant in Wilkinson's deceptive ads. Wilkinson and its agency had to pay Gillette almost a million dollars in damages.

The U.S. Trademark Law Revision of 1988 gives injured parties the right to sue an advertiser who misrepresents "another person's goods, services, or commercial activities."

"The potential for liability in damages has always been there," states Dan Jaffe, executive vice president of the Association of National Advertisers, "but now agencies know the potential is a reality."*

Advertisers and agencies use a number of defenses in these cases: (1) the legality of "puffery" in advertising; (2) the claim that company test data is the only information avail-

Consumer Reports, November 1992, p. 687.

able; or (3) the superiority of their testing methodology. Still, comparative advertising remains a strategy fraught with problems for advertising agencies. Why? Because they can be hit from two sides. Wilkinson Sword and its agency were sued by a competitor. Volvo and its agency were sued by the government—the Texas attorney general's office (see Ethical Dilemma in Chapter 1).

Clients are at risk too. Although direct comparisons create awareness for low-share brands, established products and services can lose sales because consumers often confuse the brands. Sales can fall as competitors improve their products based on information they read in the comparative ads. So there's no guarantee that comparative advertising will build brand equity for the advertiser.

Yet today's stiff competition encourages such cutthroat advertising. Bob Wolf, vice chairman of Chiat/Day Advertising, notes, "Comparative advertising has become really pointed and mean."

Some advertisers use unethical techniques—purposefully or inadvertently—to compare their products. One is to use questionable data. For example, Chevrolet ads talk about how many Ford owners are switching to Chevy trucks. Ford contends that Chevy's research techniques fail to meet professional standards. Plus, the ads ignore people who replace their Chevrolets with other brands. Seemingly objective data can lead to allegations of unfairness. As one marketing exec-

outcome—of the commercial. We discuss some of these techniques later in this chapter and in subsequent chapters on advertising production.

Credibility

The third step in the copywriter's pyramid is to establish *credibility* for the product or service. Customers today are sophisticated, skeptical, and cynical. They want to know that a product or service claim is backed up by facts. Comparison ads can build credibility, but they must be relevant to customers' needs—and fair.

Well-known presenters may lend credibility to commercials. For example, TV personality Ed McMahon represents a variety of products because of his personable, believable, down-to-earth style.

Advertisers often show independent test results to substantiate product claims. To work, such "proofs" must be valid, not just statistical manipulation. Advertisers and agencies must remember that many consumers have extensive product knowledge, even in specialized areas.

Desire

In the *desire* step, the writer encourages prospects to picture themselves enjoying the benefits of the product or service. Essentially, they are invited to experience the process of *visualization*.

---

utive says, "If you torture the numbers long enough, they'll talk."

In another case, a Sorrell Ridge TV campaign claimed that Smucker's preserves are made mostly from corn syrup, refined sugar, and a little fruit, while stressing that Sorrell's products are all fruit and fruit juice. The claim is true—but only if you ignore the fact that Smucker's has more than one product line. As Richard Smucker points out, Sorrell essentially made a fraudulent comparison because "We make an all-fruit product, but their comparisons are against our traditional fruit line."

Some comparative ads use subjective comparisons. Pepsi ads claim Diet Pepsi has the "taste that beats Diet Coke" and is "the undisputed champion" of taste. But these are hard claims to prove—or disprove.

It's difficult to separate truth from half truth. Even though all advertisers face clearance from TV network censors, networks can't keep up with changes in research methodologies. Disputed commercials often run for months while networks try to confirm their claims.

As a remedy, Coca-Cola proposed establishing an independent agent for adjudicating comparative claims. Networks, however, feel this will just add another level of bureaucracy, making clearances take even longer.

What is the future for comparative advertising? Industry experts believe that so long as competition increases, com-

parative advertising will flourish. And so long as ethical guidelines remain fuzzy, consumers will give up trying to separate truth from fiction. John Ruhaak, vice president of advertising for United Airlines, takes a slightly different tack. "If we try to juggle facts in our advertising rather than sell the value of our product," he says, "consumers won't believe our brands."

Observers hope that when advertisers—and their agencies—dare to compare, they'll flaunt their ethics as well.

Questions

1. Do you think Sorrell was unaware that Smucker's also had an all-fruit line of preserves? According to the Trademark Law Revision Act of 1988, can Smucker's challenge Sorrell-Ridge's claims in court? If you were a TV network censor, how much research would you conduct to make sure the Sorrell-Ridge ad was not misleading?

2. As a creative director at Friedman-Benjamin, would you ask for a transfer to another account or quit your job?

In newspaper and magazine ads, copywriters initiate visualization by using words and phrases like: "Picture yourself"; "Imagine"; "Be the first." In TV copywriting, the main character pulls a sparkling clean T-shirt from the washer, strikes a wide smile, and says "Yeah!" In radio, the announcer says, "You'll look your best."

The objective of the desire step is to hint at the possibilities and let the audience's mind take over. If prospects feel they're being led by the nose, they may feel insulted, resent the ad, and lose interest in the product. In some cases, writers maintain this delicate balance by having a secondary character nod yes while agreeing verbally with the main character and prattling off a few more product benefits. Having the secondary character carry the role of "dreamer" retains the integrity of the main character—the one audiences relate to best.

The desire step is one of the most difficult sections of the pyramid to write—and that may be why some copywriters omit it.

Action

The final step up the copywriter's pyramid is the *action* step. The purpose here is to motivate people to do something—to send in a coupon, call the number on the screen, or visit the store—or at least to agree with the advertiser.

This block of the pyramid reaches the smallest audience but those with the most to gain from the product's utility. So the last step is often the easiest. If the copy is clear about what readers need to do—whom to call, how to write, when to act—and commands them to act, chances are they *will* act (See Ad Lab 8–A: Applying the Copywriter's Pyramid to Print Advertising.)

The call to action may be *explicit:* "Fill out and mail today"; or *implicit:* "Fly the Friendly Skies." Either approach has the tone of a command. Some ads use coupons to get readers involved; others display toll-free phone or fax numbers in print and broadcast ads to make response more convenient. And direct mail pieces use mail-back cards or order forms with tear-off mail-back envelopes. Regardless of technique, ads should always request action.

HOW COPYWRITERS UTILIZE FORMATS

Now that we understand the objectives of good copy, let's examine the basic copywriting formats for print ads and broadcast scripts.

In print advertising, the key format elements are the *headline,* the *visual, subheads, body copy, boxes and panels, slogans, seals, logotypes (logos),* and *signatures.* As Exhibit 8–9 shows, copywriters can correlate the headline, visual, and subhead to the attention step of the copywriter's pyramid. The interest step typically corresponds to the subheadline and the first paragraph of body copy. Body copy handles credibility and desire, and the action step takes place with the logo, slogan, and signature block. We discuss these elements first and then look at the formats for radio and television commercials.

Headlines

Many advertisers consider the headline the most important element in a print ad. The term **headline** refers to the words in the leading position of the advertisement—the words that will be read first and that are situated to draw the most attention. That's why headlines usually appear in larger type than other parts of the ad.

AD LAB 8–A   Applying the Copywriter's Pyramid to Print Advertising

Notice how the five objectives of advertising copy apply to the ad shown below.

Attention: The left side of this ad uses a larger-than-life photo of the product and a how-to headline in interesting type—with lots of white space.

Interest: The second part of the heading ("to liters") completes the how-to statement in a clever and intriguing way so readers will want to find out more.

Credibility: The copy explains how the seemingly contradictory headline can be true. The free offer shows the manufacturer is interested in the reader's business, as does the offer of a chance to win a prize.

Desire: "You could end up a very happy camper" pro-

vides a positive prospect—allowing readers to envision an enjoyable weekend in the great outdoors.

Action: The copy urges readers to spend $8 or more on Stanley tools and to enter the contest.

Laboratory Applications

1. Find an ad that exhibits the five elements of the copywriter's pyramid. (Beware: The desire step may be hard to find.)

2. Why do so many good ads lack one or more of the five elements listed here? How do they overcome the omission?

Role of Headlines

To be effective, a headline must serve a set of functions—attract attention, engage the audience, be quickly understood, lead the audience into the body of the ad, and present the selling message.

Copywriter's Pyramid

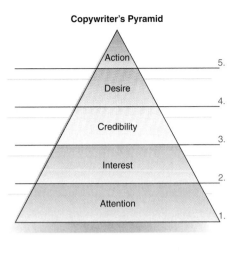

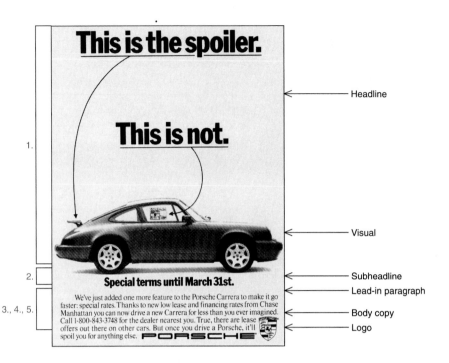

E X H I B I T • 8-9

An ad's success depends on the viewer's ability to absorb and learn its message. The copywriter's pyramid helps the copywriter present the conceptual elements of the message. The format elements (headlines, subheads, body text, captions) help segment the copy so audiences can decode the message more easily.

Initially, the headline must attract attention. One popular method is to occupy the entire top half of the ad with a headline written in large letters. This technique can be just as eye catching as a dramatic photograph or illustration.

Another goal of a headline is to engage and involve the reader, and to suggest a reason to read the rest of the ad. Saatchi and Saatchi/London prepared a series of ads for Seiko watches, official timekeepers of the XXV Olympiad. The one in Exhibit 8–10 uses a simple headline to capture readers' emotions and make them relate to the product.

This ad also serves to demonstrate another role of the headline—to engage the prospect *fast*. Surveys show that an ad has only four seconds to capture the reader's attention.[14] If the headline lacks immediacy, prospects turn their attention to another subject and pass the ad's message by.

Another task of the headline is to lead the reader into the body copy. In the Seiko ad, the headline also serves as the body copy. A more typical example is:

Headline: "What kind of man reads *Playboy?*"

Body copy: "He's a man who demands the best life has to offer."

Ideally, headlines present the complete selling idea. Research shows that, on average, three to five times as many people read the headline as read the body copy. So if the ad doesn't sell in the headline, the advertiser is wasting money.[15] Nike uses beautiful magazine and outdoor ads featuring just an athlete, the logo, and the memorable headline: "Just do it." Working off the visual, the headline creates the mood and tells the reader to take action (through implication, buy Nikes). Headlines help trigger a recognition response, which reinforces brand recognition and brand preference.

Headlines should offer a benefit—one that is apparent to the reader and easy to grasp; for example: "Picture Perfect Typing. Smith Corona"[16]

Finally, headlines should present product news. Consumers look for new products, new uses for old products, or improvements on old products. "Magic"

EXHIBIT • 8-10

EXHIBIT • 8-10

This ad captures readers feelings quickly by using the headline as the body copy, a growing trend.

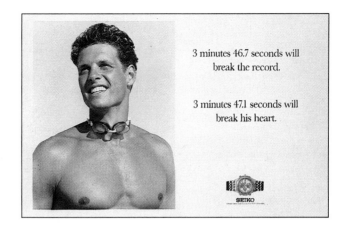

3 minutes 46.7 seconds will break the record.

3 minutes 47.1 seconds will break his heart.

SEIKO

words that imply newness can increase readership and should be used whenever applicable.[17] Some examples include: *free, now, amazing, suddenly, announcing, introducing, it's here, improved, at last, revolutionary, just arrived,* and *important development.* San Francisco advertising expert Robert Pritikin believes strongly in the product-news approach as a method of differentiation. He suggests that advertising people should always search for and promote what he calls the "Amazing New" aspect of the product.[18]

Variations on Writing Headlines

Headlines serve a variety of functions, but no one headline can serve all of them. So, copywriters use many variations depending on the requirements of the advertising strategy. Typically, they use the headline that presents the big idea most successfully. Let's take a closer look at some of the variations.

The need to capture attention and engage the prospect *fast* suggests that copywriters must cut to the chase. However, many successful headlines imply the story rather than telling it directly. The headline in Exhibit 8–11 builds interest because it sets up an idea that can be answered only by additional information—in this case, by the photograph.

Any well-prepared campaign targets audiences by demographic (age, sex, income, marital status) and psychographic criteria—because these people are the most likely to buy. Research data makes ad writing easier and helps focus the headline's message. It also provides the copywriter with a steady stream of buzzwords and concepts proven to stimulate an audience's mental files. But it doesn't always lead to a successful headline. Noted copywriter Stan Freeberg based a headline on psychographic data that showed some people were afraid to fly. The headline read: "Hey, you with the sweaty palms!" The campaign was short-lived since the headline reminded targeted customers of a very negative emotion.

Headlines that use strong grabbers (loud or grating sound effects, emotional words, or violent visuals) may also turn audiences off. And copywriters must be careful when identifying their target market in the headline because secondary markets—usually a planned source of additional revenue—may feel the ad does not apply to them. Copywriters must use great care when signaling target markets to respond.

Print ads often provide additional support to a television campaign; but to do so effectively, the copywriter must make sure the headline tells the whole story.[19] Finally, while brevity is the rule, David Ogilvy says advertisers should not be afraid of long headlines. His best headline, he says, contained 18 words:

EXHIBIT • 8-11

The visual and the headline combine to complete both the attention step and the big idea. The big idea—GE's lamps save the earth's light energy—appears in the lead-in paragraph. The last paragraph reinforces the big idea and also serves as the desire step; the word *someone* implies that the buyer of GE's lamps can save energy too.

"At 60 miles an hour, the loudest noise in the new Rolls-Royce comes from the electric clock."[20]

Types of Headlines

There are many ways to classify headlines—too many (one author came up with 23). For simplicity, we classify headlines by the type of information they carry: *benefit, provocative, news/information, question,* and *command.*

Benefit headlines promise the audience that experiencing the utility of the product or service will be rewarding. Information in the headline aids the customer's awareness of the product's benefits. Two good examples are "We'll give you a permanent without making waves in your budget" (Prime Cuts haircutting salon) and the German ad for Friki chicken shown in Exhibit 8–12, "We don't have antique chicken—Friki chickens are fresh!"

News/information headlines announce some news or promise some information. Sea World began its television announcement of a new baby whale with the black and white headline "It's a Girl."

Copywriters use **provocative headlines** to provoke the reader's curiosity—to stimulate questions and thoughts. To learn more, the reader must read the body copy. The danger, of course, is that the reader won't read on, and the headline won't sell anything. To avoid this, provocative headlines use visuals to clarify the message or provide some *story appeal.* For example, the headline in the Ray-Ban ad (Exhibit 8–13) undermines the reader's security by using the word *hazardous.* Thus engaged, the reader then looks to the ad copy for an answer.

A **question headline** asks a question, encouraging readers to search for the answer. An ad for 4day Tire Stores asks: "What makes our tire customers smarter & richer than others?" Question headlines are ideal for capturing audience attention and encouraging them to read the body of the ad.

But a question headline can be dangerous, too. If it asks a question the reader can answer quickly—or (even worse) negatively—the rest of the ad may

EXHIBIT • 8-12

The headline in this ad promises "We don't have antique chicken—Friki chickens are fresh!" The ad's format features the standard elements: headline, subhead (the kicker above the headline), body copy, and logo at the end. Distorted typesetting gets attention but dulls the immediacy of the message. The frame supports the action step.

not get read. Imagine a headline that reads: "Do you like food?" The reader answers, "Of course," and turns the page.

A good question headline piques the reader's curiosity and imagination.[21] The classic question headline, Miss Clairol's "Does she? Or doesn't she?" helped Clairol's hair-color products outsell competitors for years.

A **command headline** orders the reader to do something, so it might seem negative. But readers pay attention to such headlines. They motivate through fear or emotion—or because the reader understands their inherent correctness ("Drive safely. The life you save may be your own"). Other command headlines are less serious: "Listen to what you've been missing in cassette sound" (3M Company). And some make a request: "Please don't squeeze the Charmin" (bathroom tissue). One of the most successful command headlines of all time sold a lot of perfume: "Promise her anything but give her Arpege."

A good exercise for any copywriter is to create a checklist of basic headline categories and write several different types for each new project, remembering that many headline types are easily combined.

Subheads

The **subhead,** an additional smaller headline, may appear above the headline or below it. A subhead above the headline, called a **kicker,** is often underlined. Subheads may also appear in body copy.

Subheads are usually set smaller than the headline but larger than the body copy or text. Subheads generally appear in **boldface** (heavier) type or in a different ink color. Like a headline, the subhead transmits key sales points—fast! But the subhead usually carries less important information than the headline. Subheads are important for two reasons: most individuals read only the headline and subheads, and subheads usually support the interest step best.

Subheads are longer and more like sentences. They reinforce the headline

Last year, the U.S. Department of Transportation reported more traffic fatalities on normal weather days than on rainy and snowy days combined. Unfortunately, the sun's glare and haze can create a blind spot right where a driver needs visibility most: the front wind-shield. Ordinary sunglasses give drivers only partial protection from the sun's distractions. After all, they were designed more for viewing the curves on the beach than the ones on the road. That's exactly why we've developed Ray-Ban Sunglasses for Driving, sunglasses created specifically to help you keep your eyes on the road. With brown B-15 Top Gradient Mirror lenses and 100% UV protection, they're highly effective at screening out blue light. Which simply means they clear up road haze and sharpen detail without any color distortion. What's more, the top portion of the lens is mirrored to help reduce overhead glare, while the uncoated lower lens still gives you a crisp and clear view of the instrument panel. And unlike photochromic lenses that require ultra-violet sunlight to darken fully, Ray-Ban B-15 lenses always stay dark enough to reduce dangerous glare. All of which help make Ray-Ban Sunglasses for Driving the safest thing you could wear in your car next to a seat belt. Of course it doesn't hurt if the car you're driving is also designed for safety—like the Volvo 740, the Grand Prize in our Test-Drive Sweepstakes. To enter, just pick up an official entry form at your Ray-Ban dealer. And while you're there, test-wear a pair of Ray-Ban Sunglasses for Driving. They can turn 78° and sunny back into what it was always meant to be: a beautiful day for a drive.

78° And Not A Cloud In The Sky. What A Hazardous Day For A Drive.

Ray-Ban **Sunglasses For Driving.**

EXHIBIT • 8-13

This ad uses a provocative headline and features major format elements—visual, headline, body text, logo. The headline's reference to 78° and the word *hazardous* gets attention; the *lead-in paragraph* quotes a government study to hold interest; the *body copy* builds credibility with claims like "100% UV protection," attempts a trial close (action step) with its Test-Drive Sweepstakes offering, and includes the desire step promising that the Ray-Ban product can turn a sunny day into "a beautiful day for a drive."

and the ad's overall theme, and they serve as stepping stones from the headline to the body copy.

Body Copy

The advertiser tells the complete sales story in the **body copy,** or **text,** as it is sometimes called. The body copy comprises the interest, credibility, desire, and often even the action steps. Set in smaller type than headlines or subheads, the body copy is a logical continuation of the headline and subheads. Body copy covers the features, benefits, and utility of the product or service, and handles the sales appeal and the call for action.

In the body copy, the writer must speak to the reader's self-interest, explaining how the product or service satisfies the customer's need. The text may concentrate on one or several benefits. Copy should be written as if the writer were conversing with one person. In fact, copywriters often read their copy aloud to hear how it sounds—even if it's intended for print media. The ear is a powerful copywriting tool.

Experts tout the following techniques for writing effective body copy:

- Stress one major idea.
- Position the product clearly.
- Emphasize the consumer's ultimate benefit.

CHECKLIST   Writing Effective Copy

◇ **Make it easy on your reader.** Write short sentences. Use easy, familiar words.

◇ **Don't waste words.** Say what you have to say—nothing more, nothing less. Don't pad, but don't skimp.

◇ **Stick to the present tense, active voice**—it's crisper. Avoid the past tense and passive voice. Exceptions should be deliberate, for special effect.

◇ **Don't hesitate to use personal pronouns.** Remember, you're trying to talk to just *one* person, so talk as you would to a friend. Use "you" and "your."

◇ **Clichés are crutches.** Learn to get along without them. Bright, surprising words and phrases perk up readers, keep them reading.

◇ **Don't overpunctuate.** It kills copy flow. Excessive commas are the chief culprits. Don't give readers any excuse to jump ship.

◇ **Use contractions whenever possible.** They're fast, personal, natural. People talk in contractions. (Listen to yourself.)

◇ **Don't brag or boast.** Write from the reader's point of view, not your own. Avoid "we," "us," "our."

◇ **Be single-minded.** Don't try to do too much. If you chase more than one rabbit at a time, you'll catch none.

◇ **Write with flair.** Drum up excitement. Make sure the enthusiasm you feel comes through in the copy.

◇ **Read the copy aloud**—to see how it sounds and to catch errors. The written word is considerably different from the spoken word.

- Keep the brand name up front and reinforce it.
- Keep copy lean and tight. Tell the whole story and no more. When finished, stop.
- In radio and TV, support audio with video.[22]

Body Copy Styles

Experienced copywriters look for the technique and style with the greatest sales appeal for the idea being presented. (See the Checklist for Writing Effective Copy.) Common types of copy styles include *straight sell, institutional, narrative, dialogue/monologue, picture-caption,* and *device.*

In **straight-sell copy,** writers immediately explain or develop the headline and visual—or the pictures on the screen—in a straightforward, factual presentation. The straight-sell approach emphasizes and appeals to the prospect's *reason.* Since it ticks off the product's sales points in order of their importance, straight-sell copy is particularly advantageous for consumer products that require high personal involvement or that are difficult to use. Advertisers use the straight-sell technique extensively in direct-mail advertising and industrial or high-tech situations.

Advertisers use **institutional copy** to promote a philosophy or extol the merits of an organization rather than product features. Institutional copy paints a broad, simple overview of the company, its ideals and future. Often narrative in style and noncontroversial, it is intended to lend warmth to the organization's image. Banks, insurance companies, public utilities, and large manufacturing firms use institutional copy in both print and electronic media. However, David Ogilvy warns against the "self-serving, flatulent pomposity" that characterizes the copy in many corporate ads.[23]

Copywriters use **narrative copy** to tell a story. Ideal for the creative writer, narrative copy sets up a situation and then resolves it at the last minute by having the product or service come to the rescue. Recent ads for the Mitsubishi Home Theater system (Exhibit 8–14) start with a two-page spread that reads like

The insane laughter faded away behind me. To one side of the clearing sat a deserted house, as decomposed and forgotten as the people who'd once lived there.

The door opened, and I was in the front room, a room so dark I felt I could reach out and run my fingers through its inky stillness.

From outside the window came the sounds of the night. Owls. Crickets. And from across the room…drip, drip, drip.

My eyes, adjusting to the light, made out what appeared to be a coat hanging from a hat rack, but as the haze dissolved from my sight I saw that from the neck of the coat stared the lifeless face of Kuperman, his eyes frozen in horror. A shrieking laugh, as inescapable as a nightmare, rang out around me.

My heart, already shaking at the cage of my chest, exploded as a hand fell upon my shoulder.

"So how do you like the Mitsubishi Home Theater's surround sound?" asked the sales guy.

"Uhhh, great" I said, as I stumbled to the door of the showroom for a breath of fresh air.

▲ MITSUBISHI
TECHNICALLY, ANYTHING IS POSSIBLE

EXHIBIT • 8-14

This ad, without a headline, entices readers with an exciting story about "insane laughter," a deserted house, and a room so dark "I could reach out and run my fingers through its inky stillness."

a spy thriller or romance novel. Turn the page, and the story returns to real life. Here the copywriter successfully engages the reader in just a few seconds—a moment of escape that drives home the product's true benefit.

By using **dialogue/monologue copy,** the advertiser can add the believability that narrative copy sometimes lacks. The characters portrayed in a commercial or in a print ad do the selling in their own words through a testimonial or quasi-testimonial technique or through a comic-strip panel. In a series of ads for a London power utility (Exhibit 8–15), animated animals speak in everyday, *human* terms about their electrically-heated homes.

Beginning copywriters often have trouble writing this kind of copy unless they have some play-writing experience. Not everything people say is interesting. Poorly written dialogue copy can come off as dull or—even worse—hokey and unreal.

Sometimes it's easier to tell a story with illustrations and captions. A photo with **picture-caption copy** is particularly useful for products that have a number of different uses or come in a variety of styles or designs.

Another common technique, **device copy,** uses wordplays, humor, poetry, rhymes, great exaggeration, gags, and other tricks or gimmicks. Devices are often effective because they rely on metaphor. Many of the best ads use verbal devices, both in body copy and in headlines. An ad for the household lubricant, WD-40, for example, shows a close-up of the spray can aimed directly at the reader. The copy says: "Take a shot at tools with moving parts. . . . Anything that moves. WD-40. America's troubleshooter."

Humor is a popular form of device copy, particularly in broadcast advertising, as the radio commercial in Exhibit 8–16 shows. In fact, many creative directors use humor for its entertainment value. Humor can be effective when the advertiser needs high memorability in a short time or wants to destroy an outmoded attitude or use pattern. However, humor is also very subjective. It should always be used carefully and never in questionable taste. Some researchers believe humor can even be detrimental when used for serious services like finance and insurance.[24] (See the Checklist of Common Pitfalls in Writing Copy.)

EXHIBIT • 8-15

Frank The Tortoise's monologue copy employs sophisticated humor in this animated TV testimonial for London's power utility.

FRANK THE TORTOISE: Oh, it's good to come back into a warm flat after you've just done a run. And it's always nice to come into somewhere warm, if you've been freezin' to death outside on a ten mile

slog. Yea, it's easily controllable, um . . . and it n-needs to be easily controllable as well, because I don't have much time. I'm a very busy person so I have to have ev-everything (gulp) just as I need it.

Well they, they should, they should, be sort of fairly modern in design and they've got to be easily turn "off" and "onable".
ANNCR: For all your creature comforts. Heat Electric.

Formatting Body Copy

The keys to good body copy are simplicity, order, credibility, and clarity. Or, as John O'Toole says, prose should be "written clearly, informatively, interestingly, powerfully, persuasively, dramatically, memorably, and with effortless grace. That's all."[25] (Study the Copywriter's Portfolio on pages 260–262 for some good examples.)

Four basic format elements are used to construct body copy: the *lead-in paragraph, interior paragraphs, trial close,* and *close.*

Lead-In Paragraph The **lead-in paragraph** is a bridge between the headline, the subheads, and the sales ideas presented in the text. Like a subhead, the lead-in

EXHIBIT • 8-16

This humorous radio commercial sells by stating the product name in the first sentence. Like all good radio spots, the copywriting creates images—Silly Willy with big shoes, umbrella, and red nose in someone's living room. Calling the clown by his first name, Silly, clues the listener to the humorous mood.

MIKE: They say you can find anything in the NYNEX Yellow Pages. Well, today, under entertainers I found Silly Willy, the clown.
SILLY: Hi ho.
MIKE: Hi ho, Silly. Your ad promises a good time will be had by one and all.
SILLY: That's right, Mike. A silly willy good time.
MIKE: Tell me Silly, is it difficult playing to young audiences?
SILLY: Yeah, real difficult. Six-year-olds aren't exactly the most discerning critics, Mike. You poke yourself in the eye with an umbrella, they're in hysterics.
MIKE: I see.
SILLY: Real subtle stuff.
MIKE: Well, can you give us an idea of what you do in your act?
SILLY: I'm a clown Mike. I walk like a duck, I fall on my face. You want a free sample, go to a yogurt stand.
MIKE: Silly, forgive me for saying this, but you seem a little. . .

SILLY: Bitter, Mike?
MIKE: Uh, yes.
SILLY: Well, let's just say my life hasn't worked out exactly like I thought it would.
MIKE: I see, well thank you very much Silly.
SILLY: As a young man you dream of playing Hamlet at the Old Vic and where do you end up? In someone's living room wearing twenty-inch shoes and a bulbous red nose.
MIKE: Well, there you have it. The bitter-sweet comedy of Silly Willy.
SILLY: Bitter-sweet? Is that a smart crack or something?
MIKE: Further proof that if it's out there . . .
SILLY: Smart guy, huh?
MIKE: . . . it's in the NYNEX Yellow Pages.
SILLY: You're just like my wife. She ran off with Tubby Wubby, the bouncing clown.
MIKE: Why would anyone need another.
SILLY: I'll bounce him if I ever find him.

CHECKLIST   Common Pitfalls in Writing Copy

◇ **Obfuscation**
Avoid cumbersome and little-used words (like obfuscation) that nobody understands. Write simply in the everyday language people use in conversation. Use small words in short sentences. The longer the sentence, the harder it is to understand.

◇ **Filibustering**
Remember the importance of brevity. Filibusters should be confined to the Senate. Be complete but concise.

◇ **Clichés, Triteness, and Superlatives**
Overused expressions do nothing for copy. Most superlatives (greatest, large economy) and clichés (tried and true, a penny saved is a penny earned) erode consumer confidence and contribute to an out-of-date image.

◇ **Abstractness and Vagueness**
Abstract words, such as fine, really, and OK, have no specific meaning. They're unmeasurable, hard to evaluate, and easily misunderstood. Specific claims are more immediate and stronger.

◇ **"Me-Me-Me"**
Use the "you attitude" to appeal to the reader's self-interest." Talk about the customer's needs, hopes, wishes, and preferences. Talk about the customer—the most interesting person in the world.

◇ **No, Not Negativity**
Readers respond favorably to a positive viewpoint. Think and write negatively, and you will produce a negative response. Stress what things *are* or what they *can be*, avoid what they are not.

◇ **Euphemisms**
Copywriters use euphemisms (inoffensive, mild words for offensive, harsh, or blunt ones) to put a good face on an uncomfortable product or problem ("memorial gardens" for cemeteries, "irregularity" for constipation). Choose euphemisms carefully; they weaken messages, can be misleading, and may invite investigation by the Federal Trade Commission.

◇ **Defamation**
Avoid portraying real people in a bad light. The laws of defamation govern all advertising copy and prohibit making false statements or allegations about a person or holding a person up to contempt. *Libel* is the term for defamation in print advertising. *Slander* refers to defamation in broadcast advertising or verbal statements.

---

paragraph is part of the *interest* step—it must be engaging and able to convert a prospect's reading interest to product interest.

The lead-in paragraph may perform other functions as well. In short-copy ads (an increasing trend) and outdoor advertising, the lead-in paragraph may be the only paragraph. It may include the promise, the claim-support information, and the close. An ad for the Minneapolis Planetarium, for instance, shows a large cartoon of Buck Rogers under the headline: "The Buck Stops Here." The single paragraph of body copy reads "When you've had enough of science fiction, try some science fact at the Minneapolis Planetarium."

Interior Paragraphs   In the **interior paragraphs,** the copywriter's goal is to develop *credibility* by providing proof for claims and promises and to build *desire* by using language that stirs the imagination.

Building credibility often begins with a promise, but advertisers must be cautious. They should rely on research data, testimonials, and warranties to support their product promises. such proofs help avoid costly lawsuits, convince customers of the validity of the product, improve goodwill toward the advertiser, and stimulate sales.

Trial Close   Interspersed in the interior paragraphs should be requests for the order or suggestions to act now. Good copy asks for the order more than once; mail-order ads ask several times. Consumers often make the buying decision without reading all the body copy. The **trial close** gives them the option to make the buying decision early.

Close   Essentially, the close is the *action* step. A good **close** asks consumers to do something and tells them how to do it. Of course, not all ads sell products or

EXHIBIT • 8-17

This unique commercial uses the Nike slogan as the action step for a GTE service. The advantage? People are already familiar with the "Just do it" theme and the credibility of Nike, so the ad doesn't need to do much educating or credibility building for GTE. And Nike increases its name coverage at low cost.

VO: When we told NIKE how we could design a   run better, do you know what they told us?
communications network to actually help them   SFX: Silence.

services. Advertisers may want to change attitudes, explain their viewpoints, or ask for someone's vote.

The close can be *direct* or *indirect,* subtle suggestion or a direct command. English Leather's close is indirect—"My men wear English Leather or they wear nothing at all"—suggesting that men who want to please a woman will wear English Leather. A direct close seeks immediate response in the form of either a purchase, a store visit, or a request for further information. Exhibit 8–17 shows a direct close; it uses one company's slogan and close as the close for another company.

The close should simplify the audience's response, making it easy for them to order the merchandise, send for information, or visit a showroom. The close tells the audience where to shop or what to send. A business reply card or a toll-free phone number may be included. In fact, everything the audience needs to take action should be in the close or near it.

Boxes and Panels

Boxes and panels are great tools for the copywriter. In the information age, writers can access huge amounts of information to support their product's utility and demonstrate why customers need it. To avoid having the ad's text become a glut of testimonials, data, and off-the-issue discussions, copywriters segregate information of a secondary and supportive nature into boxes and panels next to the main body copy. This allows readers to first focus on the main issues and later study the detailed facts.

A **box** is copy with a line around all four sides. A **panel** is an elongated box that usually runs the whole length or width of an ad. Sometimes it may be shaded or completely black, with text or copy shown in reverse (white lettering). Boxes are useful for framing information the prospect must read (e.g., coupons, special offers, contest rules, and order blanks).

4day ads use boxes and panels well (see Exhibits 8–1 and 8–2). The main body text is situated toward the upper left while the right panel lists prices. At the bottom, boxes frame a variety of information—the guarantee, store locations, and the customer complaint procedure. If the body copy contained this much data, most prospects would find it too complex to read.

Continued on page 263

Copywriter's Portfolio

A. This ad solves a major copywriting challenge—how to organize the message for best audience comprehension. Copywriters generally divide overall information according to its complexity. Here the copywriter uses *straight-sell copy* to deliver the big idea, and *picture-caption copy* to break the information into easy-to-understand units.

B. This commercial for Schweppes uses a celebrity spokesperson, comedian John Cleese. The copywriter has to write monologue copy that suits the presenter's persona—or in this case a humorous character—without diminishing the product's image. Action on the screen must work appropriately with the stage props, sound effects, and dialogue as well as complement the product—a big challenge for any copywriter.

CLEESE: It's becoming ever more difficult to surround one's self with absolute, uncompromising quality.
(SFX: PFTTT!)
CLEESE: Which is why I take such extraordinary

pleasure in telling you about Schweppes.
(SFX: CLANGGG!)
CLEESE: With its unique Schweppervescence, and distinctively refreshing taste, it may be the last oasis of true excellence in an otherwise

vast desert of compromise.
(SFX: CRASH!)
CLEESE: Cheers!
ANNCR: Schweppes. The uncompromising line of classic soft drinks.

C. Typically, Hallmark commercials tell a story that demonstrates the product use and benefits. To do this effectively, the copywriter must establish believable actions and dialogue between fictitious characters.

SHEEHAN: Hey, Tony . . . who you taking to the dance?

TONY: Patti Harney.

JERRY: Oh man, Patti Harney?! She said "yes" and everything?

TONY: Well . . . no. I haven't really asked her yet. But I'm gonna.

SHEEHAN: In . . . person?

TONY: No way! I'll probably just call her on the phone.

FERGIE: Yeah, a phone call. I think that's what I'm gonna do.

TONY: So who are you going with, Jerry?

JERRY: Oh well . . . see there's this kid on my street—his name is Bill Shallcross—well, see he plays hockey with the brother of Rachelle Tasker, and she has gym class with Mande Moore, and Mande Moore has a locker next to Cheryl Berman, and Cheryl Berman's like really good friends with Nancy Eaglin. So she's gonna ask her.

TONY: Who?

JERRY: Cheryl's gonna ask Nancy . . . for me.

TONY: Oh . . . right.

FERGIE: Get a friend to ask for you . . . I think that's what I'm gonna do.

JERRY: What about you, Sheehan?

SHEEHAN: Well, I was thinking . . . what if you, uh . . . slipped a card into a girl's notebook?

JERRY: What do you mean . . . a card?

SHEEHAN: You know . . . a greeting card.

TONY: Like . . . a Hallmark card?

SHEEHAN: Exactly.

JERRY: You mean . . . you'd put it in writing?

SHEEHAN: Right.

JERRY: What if she hates you? She'd show it to everyone! It could even end up in the school newspaper!

TONY: Or in the girl's bathroom!

FERGIE: Or on the evening news!

JERRY: Evidence like that could ruin your reputation.

SHEEHAN: But . . . I don't have a reputation.

ALL: You will now! (Laughter)

GIRL: Danny? (Suddenly the laughter stops) Putting this card in my notebook . . . that was really neat. I'd love to go to the dance with you.

SHEEHAN: Uh, uh . . . okay. (Long Silence)

FERGIE: A card . . . I think that's what I'm gonna do.

D. It is easier to remember and relate to a product that has "character" or "personality." This magazine ad is one of a series that introduces us to "Mother," an older woman who represents an authority figure, serious about quality at Columbia sportswear.

E. Canadian Airlines uses a long-copy approach to demonstrate that, in spite of all the trees, they can still see the forest when it comes to serving business travelers.

Slogans

Many **slogans** (also called **theme lines** or **tag lines**) begin as successful headlines as did AT&T's "Reach out and touch someone." Through continuous use, they become standard statements, not just in advertising but for salespeople and company employees. Slogans become a battle cry for the company. In fact, the word *slogan* comes from the Gaelic term for *battle cry*.

Slogans have two basic purposes: to provide continuity to a series of ads in a campaign and to reduce an advertising message strategy to a brief, repeatable, and memorable positioning statement. DeBeers' ads, for example, still use the famous slogan: "Diamonds are forever." But First Interstate Bank's trite promise "We go the extra mile for you" lacks the creativity, freshness, and power to become a full-fledged slogan.

Because of their use in positioning a company or product, many slogans are developed at the same time the product or company name is coined (See Ad Lab 8–B: Creating Names for Products).

Slogans should be like old friends—recognized instantly year after year. Some slogans endure because they encapsulate a corporate philosophy: "At Zenith, the quality goes in before the name goes on."[26] Unfortunately, many slogans do not measure up to these lofty expectations; they fall into Ogilvy's category of "interchangeable fatuous bromides."[27]

Effective slogans are short, simple, memorable, easy to repeat, and most important, help differentiate the product or the company from its competitors. Rhyme, rhythm, and reason—not to mention alliteration—are valuable tricks of the trade for slogan writing.

Seals, Logotypes, and Signatures

A **seal** is awarded only when a product meets standards established by a particular institution or organization such as the Good Housekeeping Institute, Underwriters Laboratories, and Parents Institute. Since these organizations have credibility as recognized authorities, their seals provide an independent, valued endorsement for the advertiser's product.

The term *seal* is sometimes interpreted to mean the company seal or trademark. These are actually called logotypes. **Logotypes** (logos) and **signature cuts** (sig cuts) are special designs of the advertiser's company name or product name. They appear in all company ads and, like trademarks, give the product individuality and provide quick recognition at the point of purchase.

Developing Scripts for Electronic Media

We've seen how writers develop copy for print advertisements. Now let's take a look at writing for radio and television.

For electronic media, the fundamental elements—the five steps of the copywriting pyramid—remain the primary guides, but the copywriting formats differ. Radio and television writers prepare *scripts* and *storyboards*. We discuss each, along with the challenges they present, next.

Writing Radio Copy

A **script** format resembles a two-column list. On the left side, speakers' names are arranged in a vertical sequence along with descriptions of any sound effects

AD LAB 8-B   Creating Names for Products

Copywriters often help develop names for companies or products. Here's how they do it.

Personal Names

Products can be named after a real person (Orville Redenbacher gourmet popcorn, Honda cars). However people have similar names, and names can be copied. Fictitious names, like Bartles & Jaymes, help avoid this problem.

Geographic Names

A geographic name used arbitrarily (like Newport cigarettes) can function as a trademark. However, a name that identifies a product's place of origin or suggests where the product may have come from (like Detroit Auto Works) cannot be trademarked.

Coined or Invented Names

The most distinctive names are often coined. Kodak was coined by George Eastman because he wanted a name beginning and ending with an infrequently used letter. Kleenex, Xerox, Acura, and Compaq have an advantage because they are short, pronounceable, and arbitrary. Today, computer programs can generate unique coined names for both companies and products such as Exxon.

Initials or Numbers

Except for IBM computers, RCA televisions, and A-1 steak sauce, initials and numbers usually don't make good product names because they don't say anything about the product. For example, what kind of product is a Harris 5500?

Company Name

Company names are sometimes used as brand names—Texaco, Gulf, Shell. But most companies develop different names for their products to avoid confusion and create greater value for their brand.

Foreign Words

Perfume companies often use French words to project an image of romance (Vol de Nuit). Auto manufacturers use foreign words to add mystery and intrigue (Cordova, Biarritz). Restaurants use them to identify the kind of food they serve (Del Taco, L'Auberge, La Scala).

Licensed Names

Companies (and individuals) may license names for their marketability (Snoopy toothbrushes, Sunkist vitamins, and Elizabeth Taylor perfumes), but licensing is expensive and restrictive.

Arbitrary Dictionary Words

Many successful products have dictionary names (Roach Motel, Hefty trash bags, Gap apparel). Dictionary words unrelated to the product description are more easily protected. They may also give the product an image. Fragrance advertisers often use steamy advertising and shock-value names—Obsession, Poison, Opium—to pique consumer interest.

Laboratory Applications

1. Look through publications for an example of each category of product name (other than the names mentioned here). Which category is easiest to find? Which is most difficult?

2. Find a product in a popular magazine that you believe is poorly named. Identify the category for the product name. Choose two other categories that might be better for renaming the product.

3. If you were opening a hair salon or a restaurant, what would you call it? Why?

---

and music. The wider column on the right contains the dialogue the characters or announcers will speak—called the **audio**. Exhibit 8–18 shows an actual radio script used by an advertising agency.

Copywriters first need to understand radio as a medium. Radio provides entertainment or news to listeners who are busy doing something else—driving, washing dishes, reading the paper, or even studying. To be heard, an advertising message must be catchy, interesting, and unforgettable. Radio listeners usually decide within five to eight seconds if they're going to pay attention. Research indicates the primary determinant is the product category.[28]

EXHIBIT • 8-18

An actual radio script for Western Union prepared by Scali, McCabe and Sloves. The quality of a final commercial is really determined by how well the announcer (actor) reads the script—tone, inflection, personality—and how well the sound engineers edit the spot and sweeten it with music and sound effects.

SCALI, McCABE, SLOVES, INC.

Client	Western Union	Product	Telegrams
		Date	1/17/91
Job No.	R-QWAT-9106	Length	:60
Code No.	"Valentines"		
Title		Air Date	

Broadcast Manuscript

SWEET, ROMANTIC MUSIC.

ANNCR: Valentine's Day is coming up. And you, you romantic devil, may be thinking about getting that special lady in your life one of those cute heart-shaped boxes of candy. 12,897 calories she can paste directly to her thighs. Bad idea. Okay. So, maybe you send her flowers. But they last what an hour and a half? And you know they are a bit of a cliche. But if you really want to impress your lady, send her something that's bright yellow and very personal. A Western Union Telegram. Women have been known to paste these things on their mirrors, sleep with them under their pillows and keep them around longer than the guys who sent them. And each one is unique. Because it expresses your feelings. Now if you need a little help in that area, how about this? "O' my love is like a red, red rose/That's newly sprung in June/O'my love is like a melodie /That's sweetly played in tune." Signed Harold. You like it? Take it. The guy who wrote it's dead. To send a Western Union Telegram call 1-800-325-6000. She'll love you for it. Western Union Telegram. When the words are for keeps.

5797p/54

Therefore, to attract and hold listeners' attention—particularly those not attracted to a product category—radio copy must be intrusive.

Intrusive, yes; offensive, no. An insensitive choice of words, overzealous effort to attract listeners with irritating everyday sounds (car horn, alarm clock, screeching tires), or characters that sound exotic, odd, or dumb can cause listener resentment and ultimately loss of sales.

Motel 6 ads show how effective a personal, relaxed, and cheerful style can be. Other guidelines include the following:

- If the commercial doesn't offer humor, offer drama.
- Mention the advertiser's name early and often—at least three times.
- Without visual enhancements like TV, consider spelling out a tricky company or product name at least once.
- Be conversational. Use easy-to-pronounce words and short sentences. Avoid tongue twisters.
- Keep the message simple. Omit unneeded words.
- Concentrate on one main selling point. Make the big idea crystal clear.
- Paint pictures with the words. Use descriptive language.
- Choose familiar sounds such as ice tinkling in a glass, birds chirping, or a door shutting to help your narrative or dialogue create a visual image.
- Stress action words rather than passive words. Use more verbs than adjectives.
- Emphasize product benefits repeatedly and with variations.
- Ask for the order. Try to get the listener to do something.

CHECKLIST   Creating Effective Radio Commercials

◇ **Identify sound effects.** A sound effect is effective only when the listener knows what it means.

◇ **Don't be afraid to use music as a sound effect.** Commercials work if the meaning of the music is clear.

◇ **If you use a sound effect, build your commercial around it.** It pays to build the message around the relationship between the sound effect and the product.

◇ **Allow enough time.** Radio ads need time to set a scene and establish a premise. A 30-second commercial that nobody remembers has zero efficiency. Fight for 60-second commercials.

◇ **Consider not using sound effects.** A distinctive voice or a powerful message straightforwardly spoken can be more effective than noises from the tape library.

◇ **Beware of comedy.** Professional comedians devote their lives to their art. It's rare for anyone else to sit down at a typewriter and match their skill.

◇ **If you insist on being funny, begin with an outrageous premise.** The best comic radio commercials begin with a totally ridiculous premise from which all subsequent developments logically follow.

◇ **Keep it simple.** Radio is a good medium for building awareness of a brand. It's a rotten medium for registering long lists of copy points or making complex arguments.

◇ **What one thing is most important about your product?** That's what your commercial should spend 60 seconds talking about.

◇ **Radio is a local medium.** Adjust your commercials to the language of your listeners and to the time of day they'll be broadcast.

◇ **Presentation counts a lot.** Most radio scripts—even great ones—look boring on paper. Acting, timing, vocal quirks, and sound effects make them come alive.

One of the most challenging aspects of writing for broadcast media is making the script fit the time slot.[29] The copywriter should read the script out loud for timing. With electronic compression, recorded radio ads can now include 10 to 30 percent more copy than text read live. Still, the following is a good rule of thumb:

10 seconds: 20–25 words.

20 seconds: 25–45 words.

30 seconds: 55–60 words.

60 seconds: 100–120 words.

For more ideas, see the Checklist for Creating Effective Radio Commercials.

Writing Television Copy

Radio's basic two-column script format also works for television. But in a TV script, the right side is titled "Audio" and the left side "Video." The audio column lists the spoken copy, the sound effects, and the music. The video column describes the nature of the visuals and general production information—camera angles, action, scenery, and stage directions. Exhibit 8–19 shows a script for an AT&T commercial. (Abbreviations such as CU for Close Up and ECU Extreme Close Up are art direction terms discussed in Chapter 9.)

Once the basic script has been conceived, the writer and art director prepare a *storyboard* (discussed in Chapter 9). The typical storyboard is a preprinted sheet with 8 to 20 blank television screens (frames). An artist sketches **video** scenes in each frame; the audio portion and video instructions are typed underneath. Storyboards help both agency and client personnel visualize the commercial, estimate costs, discover any weaknesses in concept, gain management approval, and guide the actual shooting. But storyboards just approximate what the final commercial will look like.

EXHIBIT • 8-19

This script for the AT&T calling card reinforces the decision of those who never left AT&T for a competitor. The frustration of the man trying to make a long-distance call on a competitive carrier while double-parked comes through the script—even without seeing the commercial. And the spot acts as a warning for anyone considering the competition.

NW Ayer Incorporated
1345 Avenue Of The Americas, New York, N.Y. 10105

CLIENT AT&T	PROGRAM
PRODUCT Testimonial	FACILITIES
TITLE Meter Maid	DATE 3/27/90
NUMBER AXLL 9099 AS PRODUCED	LENGTH :30

VIDEO	AUDIO
OPEN ON MCU OF MAN GETTING OUT OF CAR THAT HE JUST DOUBLE PARKED ON A BUSY STREET.	MUSIC UNDER THROUGHOUT. MAN VO: This is gonna be a piece of cake right?
CUT TO MLS OF MAN RUNNING TO CURB.	Pull over, make a fast call.
CUT TO MCU OF MAN DIALING ON PAY PHONE.	But I'm using this other long distance company. Now, ...
CUT TO CU OF POLICE TRAFFIC VEHICLE.	First, they have me ...
CUT TO MCU OF MAN DIALING PHONE.	dialing all these numbers just to get them. Then I gotta dial the ...
CUT TO ECU OF TRAFFIC VEHICLE SIREN.	number I'm calling.
CUT TO CU OF MAN LOOKING FRUSTRATED.	MAN UNDER: You call this easy?
CUT TO ECU OF MAN ON PHONE.	MAN VO: Then I still have to dial all these other numbers.
CUT TO MS OF TRAFFIC VEHICLE. CUT TO CU OF METER MAID.	MAN UNDER: Come on, I'm double parked.
CUT TO CU SHOTS OF MAN ON PHONE.	MAN VO: So yeah, I make the call. MAN UNDER: Thank you.
CUT TO SHOT OF METER MAID WRITING TICKET.	MAN VO: To the tune of 35 bucks.
CUT TO MS OF MAN RUNNING OUT OF BOOTH.	CLIFF ROBERTSON VO: With the AT&T card, calling is easy.
CUT TO PC SCREEN WITH NAMES.	Another reason people are coming back to AT&T.
CUT TO AT&T LOGO. SUPER: The Right Choice. 1 800 225-7466	Aren't you glad you ...
CUT TO MLS OF MAN PICKING UP TICKET OFF CAR WINDOW.	never left.

F-440 Rev 10/

Broadcast commercials are demanding to make. They must be credible, believable, and relevant. And even zany commercials must exude quality in their creation and production—implying the product has quality too. Because credibility and believability must be achieved using both words and pictures, the art director's work is very important. However, the copywriter sets the tone of the commercial, establishes the language that determines which visual to use, and pinpoints when the visual should appear.

Research shows the following techniques work best:

- The opening should be a short, compelling attention getter— a visual surprise, compelling in action, drama, humor, or human interest.
- Demonstrations should be interesting and believable—authentic and true to life; they should never appear to be a camera trick.
- The commercial should be ethical, in good taste, and not offend local mores.
- Commercials should be entertaining (to hold the viewers' attention), but the entertainment shouldn't interfere with the message.

EXHIBIT · 8–20

This commercial for Lubriderm Lotion is a well-crafted example of copywriting and creativity. The woman and setting are meta-phors for smooth, feminine skin while the alligator represents dry, scaly skin. The announcer's copy is understated, a modest approach that melds well with the visual and the music.

SFX: Music.
VO: A quick reminder. Lubriderm Lotion restores

lost moisture to heal your dry skin and protect it. Remember, the one created for dermatolo-

gists is the one that heals and protects. Lubriderm. See you later, alligator.

- The general structure of the commercial and the copy should be simple and easy to follow. The video should carry most of the weight, but the audio must support it.
- Characters become the living symbol of the product—they should be appealing, believable, and most of all, relevant.[30]

To illustrate these principles, let's look at a commercial. Many people want smooth, soft skin and consider a patch of rough, flaky skin anywhere on their body a disappointment. If you were the copywriter for Lubriderm skin lotion, how would you approach this somewhat touchy, negative subject?

The creative staff of J. Walter Thompson devised the well-crafted, artistic solution shown in Exhibit 8–20. The alligator is a winning big idea for Lubriderm—it brings together all the elements that make an ad successful. The gator's scaly sheath is a metaphor for rough, flaky skin. Its appearance ignites our survival instincts—we pay attention, fast. The alligator also complements the concept of smoothness. The lovely woman in the scene, the personification of smooth, feminine skin, seems smoother in the presence of the alligator. The swing of the animal's back and tail echoes the graceful curves of the two simple pieces of furniture on the set, and its slow stride keeps the beat of a casual, light jazz tune.

This commercial uses many successful techniques. It opens with an attention-getting big idea that is visually surprising, compelling, dramatic, and interesting. It's also a demonstration: the alligator shows scaly, prickly skin; we see it straight—no camera tricks; and the woman demonstrates a winning confidence with her relaxed facial expression and willingness to touch the alligator as it passes by—an implication of the confidence Lubriderm can bring.

This commercial is simple, easy to follow, and tasteful. Draped in white, the woman resembles a Greek goddess. The scene is idyllic. The alligator is not violent, the music is pleasant, and the announcer's soft voice speaks only 34 simple words of copy.

The ad follows the copywriter's pyramid well. The alligator captures attention visually while the first words act like an attention-getting headline, "A quick reminder." The ad commands us to listen and sets up the interest step that offers this claim: "Lubriderm restores lost moisture to heal your dry skin and protect it." Now for the credibility step: "Remember, the one created for dermatologists is the one that heals and protects." If dermatologists like it, it must be good, right? And then a quick trial close, "Lubriderm." And then, the desire step helps us envision the primary product benefit and adds a touch of humor: "See you later, alligator."

Take a moment to appreciate the fine delivery of this commercial and then compare it with others you've seen. How many are so concise, simple, and credible?

WRITING COPY FOR INTERNATIONAL MARKETS

Manufacturers are involved in developing a message strategy for foreign markets. When Galleries Lafayette tried to market fake furs in the United States, the company took out a two-page ad in *Elle* magazine and pitched the product as it would have in France—as an up-market, haute couture garment. But U.S. consumers don't think of fake furs in those terms, and the company did not sell much in the United States.[31]

Advertisers must base their appeals on the foreign consumer's purchasing abilities, habits, and motivations. Language is one important factor, but so are national advertising regulations, as we discussed in Chapter 2.

Foreign Audiences May Have Different Purchasing Habits

Advertising messages—foreign or domestic—must address markets that can afford to buy the product. In low-income countries, housing ads that stress luxury qualities will draw only a small audience. In a market with many financially pressed middle-class consumers, messages stressing the house's functional or economical aspects will be most effective.

How and *when* consumers normally make purchases are also important considerations. Most important, though, is *who* makes the buying decision. In North America and Europe, spouses usually exercise about the same control over purchasing decisions. In Latin American countries, the husband often controls major decisions. In the United States, even children may have a strong influence (especially in the choice of breakfast cereals, snacks, toothpastes, and fast-food chains), but this is much less common in foreign markets.

These differences vary from country to country and product to product, and advertisers must consider these issues carefully before creating ads or buying media. One company introduced a new detergent in Holland by advertising solely in one magazine for children under 10. The company offered a miniature sports car as an in-pack premium. The success of the introduction showed that, in this case at least, children did influence the buying decision.

Consumer Motives and Appeals

Advertisers also need to understand the personal motivations, national pride, social roles, and differences in taste and attitude in each market. Selling deodorant in Japan is difficult because most Japanese don't think they have body odor—and they don't, thanks to their low-protein diet. A commercial for Feel Free deodorant, therefore, positioned the product as youthful, chic, and convenient rather than as an odor fighter. The advertiser showed a young girl on her way out for a date suddenly remembering her deodorant and using it quickly before leaving.

Some lower-income, less-developed nations respect and desire North American products but fear and resent the national influence and power these products represent. While this is rarely a problem for Canadian advertisers, U.S. advertisers must be careful to avoid irritating national sensitivity.

This clever international business ad for Canon copiers would work in virtually any market and any language. Instead of crediting the photographer for shooting this beautiful picture, the company credits him for making a photocopy of it on the Canon color copier.

Social roles play an important part in determining whom the ads should address. In Saudi Arabia, for example, husbands traditionally make the purchasing decision for durable goods such as cameras and cars (women don't drive), and women decide which food, toiletries, clothing, and household furnishings to buy. Shopping is a social affair, and Saudi Arabians almost always shop in groups. So an ad campaign stressing peer approval might be more appropriate than one emphasizing individual growth or self-indulgence.[32]

Differences in taste and attitude aren't so apparent or important in business-to-business advertising. Businesspeople's problems are fairly universal, as are the advertising appeals to solve them. Differences in approach come down to a region's economics. The ad in Exhibit 8–21 illustrates the universality of industrial advertising messages.

The Question of Language and Campaign Transfer

The most important consideration for copywriters and creative directors is language. In Western Europe, people speak at least 15 different languages and more than twice as many dialects—a potentially enormous problem for U.S. and Canadian advertisers entering the European market. A similar problem exists in Asia, Africa, and, to a lesser extent, South America.

International advertisers have debated the transferability of campaigns for years. One side believes it's too expensive to create a unique campaign for each national group. They simply translate one campaign into the necessary language, as shown in Exhibit 8–22. Other advertisers believe this approach never works well and the only way to ensure success is to create a special campaign

EXHIBIT • 8-22

In global advertising, a single basic ad is used and is translated into the languages of the various countries where it will run. This global campaign for Visa ran simultaneously in dozens of countries.

for each market. Still others feel both solutions are uneconomical and unnecessary. They run their ads in English worldwide.

None of these solutions is always correct. Advertisers need not create different campaigns for every country. Moreover, they have to weigh the economics of various promotional strategies. Advertisers must look at each situation individually.

Regardless of strategy, translation remains a basic issue. Classic examples of mistranslations and faulty word choices abound in international advertising. Braniff Airlines once advertised its comfortable leather seats in terms that Spanish readers understood as an invitation to sit naked. And a faulty Spanish translation for Perdue chickens read, "It takes a sexually excited man to make a chick affectionate."[33]

A poorly chosen or badly translated product name can undercut advertising credibility in foreign markets. Ford, for example, had to change the name of a product after initially introducing it in Brazil under its U.S. name, Pinto. In Portuguese, Pinto means "small male appendage." Even Coke suffered linguistic problems. Its product name was once widely translated into Chinese characters that sounded like "Coca-Cola" but meant "bite the wax tadpole."[34]

People in the United States, Canada, England, Australia, and South Africa all speak English, but with wide variations in vocabulary, word usage, and syntax. Similarly, the French spoken in France, Canada, Vietnam, and Belgium may be as different as the English spoken by a British aristocrat and a Tennessee mountaineer. Language variations exist even within single countries. The Japanese use five lingual "gears," ranging from haughty to servile, depending on the speaker's and the listener's respective stations in life. Japanese translators must know when to change gears.

Advertisers must follow some basic rules in using translators:

- The translator *must* be an effective copywriter. In the United States and Canada, most people speak English, yet relatively few are good writers and even fewer good copywriters. Too often advertisers simply let a translation service rewrite their ads in a foreign language. That's not a good solution.

- The translator must understand the product, its features, and its market. It is always better to use a translator who is a product or market specialist rather than a generalist.
- Translators should translate into their native tongue, and they should live in the country where the ad will appear. Only in this way can the advertiser be sure the translator has a current understanding of the country's social attitudes, culture, and idiomatic use of the language.
- The advertiser should give the translator easily translatable English copy. Double meanings and idiomatic expressions—which make English such a rich language for advertising—rarely translate well. They only make the translator's job more difficult.

Finally, remember the Italian proverb, *Tradutori, traditori* ("Translators are traitors"). There is no greater insult to a national market than to misuse its language. The translation must be accurate, *and* it must also be good copy.

English is rapidly becoming the universal language for corporate ad campaigns directed to international businesspeople. However, some industrial firms, baffled by the translation problem, also print their technical literature and brochures in English. This approach can incite nationalistic feelings against the company. Worse yet, it automatically limits a product's use to people who read and understand technical English. It also increases the probability of misunderstanding and, thus, additional ill will toward the company.

Legal Restraints on International Advertisers

Finally, all advertising creativity, including what the ads say, show, or do, is at the mercy of foreign governments and cultures. As we discussed in Chapter 2, many countries strongly regulate advertising claims and prohibit superlatives. Many European countries bar sales promotion techniques common in North America—two-for-one offers, coupons, premiums, one-cent sales, etc. And in Europe, companies may only advertise price cuts during "official sales periods" or risk extremely high fines. Further, advertisers typically need government approval before publishing a sale ad in Europe.

THE COPYWRITING PROCESS

To develop text for ads and commercials—whether for domestic or international markets—copywriters rely on tools of the writer's trade, and their work undergoes a sequence of editing and approval.

Tools of the Trade

In times past, copywriters used pencils, pads, markers, typewriters, and red or blue editing pens. First drafts were often done in pen or pencil, then typed, edited, retyped, and reedited. Today, computers are standard equipment for all agencies and most free-lancers. Copywriters use mostly IBM compatibles and Macintosh, dot matrix or laser printers, and word-processing software (Microsoft Word, WordPerfect, MacWrite, and Write Now among others). Better programs offer a complete thesaurus, spell checker, and a variety of style sheet templates for editing, formatting, and file storage. In addition, computers can access on-line bulletin boards and databases and transfer ad text directly into typesetting and page-making.

The Approval Process

As with any creative endeavor, the copywriter's work is always subject to approval. The larger the agency and the larger the client, the more formidable this process becomes (see Exhibit 8–23). Copy is first approved by the creative department's senior copywriters and creative directors. Then the agency's account management team reviews it for political or sensitive issues—and may well take a few whacks at "improving" it. Next, the client's product managers and marketing staff review it, often changing a word or two or, in some cases, rejecting the whole approach. Both the agency's and client's legal departments scrutinize the copy for potential pitfalls that could pose a legal or unfair practices problem. Finally, the company's top executives usually see—and critique—the final concept and text.

The biggest challenge in the approval process is keeping approvers from corrupting the style, or character, of the ad. The copywriter and creative team work hard to achieve a certain tone, a sensitive use of language, a choice of unique buzzwords, and particular visuals to establish a cohesive style. Then a group of nonwriters and nonartists have the opportunity to change it all. Agency people—especially creative types—can get terribly frustrated, and some passively allow managers to change the ad at will. Unfortunately, a passive attitude ensures a poorly constructed ad. The creative team must gracefully "educate" noncreatives about the role of each tactic or technique. Writers must be flexible—able to accept or carefully rebut inevitable critiques, additions, and deletions—and remain keen enough to recognize and adopt valid changes or corrections. Editors' changes are so common that good writers develop thick skins. Under these circumstances, maintaining artistic purity is extremely difficult and requires patience, flexibility, maturity, and the ability to articulate an important point of view.

The discipline of writing is so fundamental to many aspects of advertising, no single chapter on the topic of copywriting can ever be complete. For that reason, we'll continue to discuss certain copywriting issues in subsequent chapters on advertising production and media.

EXHIBIT • 8-23

The copy approval process begins within the agency and ends with approval by key executives of the client company. Each review usually requires some rewrite and a presentation to the next level of approvers. When the agency and the advertiser are large companies, the process can be time-consuming and require long lead times.

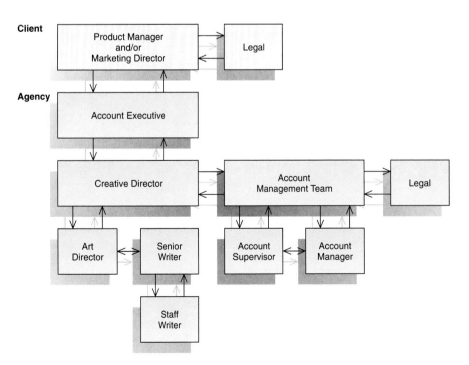

Summary

Copy is the verbal and art the nonverbal, or visual, presentation of the message strategy. Before beginning, the copywriter (usually under the guidance of a creative director) must understand the intended marketing and advertising strategies. The creative team, which includes the copywriter, should develop a brief written copy platform that tells what the copy will say and how it will support the message strategy.

Once the copy platform is established, the search for the big idea begins—the most important step in creating an ad. The big idea is the creative flash that adds meaning, interest, memorability, and drama to the strategy statement. It is the essence of the ad or commercial.

To create effective advertising, creative people use the copywriter's pyramid—similar to the advertising pyramid—as a model to gain attention, create interest, achieve credibility, heighten desire, and stimulate action.

The key copy format elements in print advertising are headlines, subheads, body copy, boxes and panels, slogans, seals, logotypes, and signatures. In electronic media, copy is normally spoken dialogue that is prepared using a script; it is referred to as the audio portion of the commercial. The copy may be delivered as a voice-over by an unseen announcer or on camera by an announcer, spokesperson, or actor.

The advertising pyramid and the format elements come together in creating effective print ads—the headline carries the attention step, the subhead and first line of body copy hold the interest step, and the body copy contains the credibility, desire, and action steps.

Many types of headlines and copy styles are used in print advertising. There are five basic types of advertising headlines: benefit, provocative, news/information, question, and command. Copy styles also fall into several categories: straight sell, institutional, narrative, dialogue/monologue, picture caption, and device.

Radio commercials must be intrusive to catch and hold the attention of people who are usually doing something else. Radio copy must be more conversational than print copy and should paint word pictures for listeners to see in their mind's eye.

Television copywriters use scripts and storyboards to communicate the verbal and nonverbal ideas of a commercial. When writing TV ads, the creative team must strive for credibility, relevance, and consistency in tone. While TV ads should be entertaining, the entertainment should not interfere with the selling message.

When writing copy for international markets, advertisers must consider the different purchasing habits of foreign consumers, the variations in language, and the legal restrictions imposed by foreign governments or cultures.

Today, virtually all copywriters use word processing software, which makes computer literacy a must. As advertising copy goes through the editing process, copywriters must be prepared for an inevitable—and sometimes lengthy—succession of edits and reedits from agency and client managers and legal departments. Copywriters must be more than creative; they must be patient, flexible, mature, and able to exercise great self-control.

Questions for Review and Discussion

1. Select an ad in this chapter and describe what you believe to be the advertiser's message strategy.

2. Continuing from question 1, how well has the advertiser followed the steps up the copywriter's pyramid? Explain.

3. Select a magazine ad you like. What functions do various format elements in the ad provide?

4. What are the basic functions of a headline?

5. Choose an ad you don't like. How would you rewrite the headline using three different styles?

6. Find an ad with a desire step. What is its function, and what is your opinion of it?

7. Using any one of the ads you've already selected, what issues do you believe the advertiser considered in writing the copy platform? Discuss.

8. What are some of the most effective methods for making copy interesting?

9. Find an international advertisement or commercial you like. What is the message strategy? Can you discern the copy style? Do you think the copy and headline reflect the strategy? What do you like about the ad? Why?

10. What guidelines can you cite for preparing an ad in a foreign language?

Creative Art Direction

Objective: To present the role of *art*—as both a creative process and a visual element—in print, radio, and television advertising and in package design. Artists include a variety of specialists who follow specific procedures for conceptualizing, designing, and producing advertising materials. To be successful, advertising people must be conversant in the commercial art terms used in the business. They must also develop an aesthetic sensitivity to be able to recognize, create, evaluate, or recommend quality work.

After studying this chapter, you will be able to:

- Define *art* as the term applies to advertising.
- Describe the roles of the various types of artists in the advertising business.
- Explain the use of advertising layouts and the steps in creating them.
- Understand the purpose and use of visuals in advertising.
- Evaluate the role of art in package design.
- Explain the art director's role in radio commercials.
- Define the basic terms that appear in television and radio scripts.
- Discuss the advantages of the major types of television commercials.

For 17 years, Timberland Company's award-winning ads featured witty copy and beautifully lit studio shots of its all-weather gear. One ad pictured a column of water rolling out of a spigot onto the golden-rough, natural leather toe of a Timberland boot. The headline: "For long wear and rugged good looks, just add water." But Timberland wanted a new direction for the 90s.

John Doyle, an art director for Boston-based Mullen Advertising, was assigned to the job. Doyle chose to break with the studio look and take the client's products outdoors into nature's expansive settings and full spectrum of light. "We wanted people to be visually transported to a different place," says Doyle, "where they could feel the environment and the elements."

The big idea—Timber Land, an imaginary place that played off the company's name—became the focus for the campaign. Timber Land would be a utopian setting of extraordinary landscapes and crystalline waters where the mountains dramatically disappeared into the clouds. Great creativity, as well as photographic skill, would be needed to express such a wondrous place.

Doyle was familiar with the work of New York photographer Eric Meola, a master at capturing the look and feel of monumental subject matter. Doyle hired him, noting that Meola's "shots are so intriguing, a viewer is compelled to spend time with them—which is just what we needed for this campaign."

They spent 44 days shooting in Alaska, Arizona, and Scotland. In the process, they auditioned over 200 models, struggled through blinding snow gusts, and rented six planes to stage shots at the 7,000-foot level of Mount McKinley. After all this effort, Meola and Doyle captured just nine shots of Timber Land that they deemed usable—just enough to start the campaign.

Now, with the photos in hand, Doyle had to finalize the ads. Brainstorming with copywriter Paul Silverman produced a lot of ideas but only a few were real winners.

Finally it all came together. Meola's stunning wide-angle shots across lakes, plains, and mountainous landscapes with a lone person in the foreground were capped by Silverman's headlines: "Timberland. Because the earth is two-thirds water"; and "Timberland. Where the elements of design are the elements themselves." Doyle's elegant design included a special typeface whose character added the suggestion of quality to the spacious design (see Exhibit 9–1).

EXHIBIT • 9-1

Timberland's ad campaign for its boots represents a departure from the studio photography and witty headlines typical of this product category. Here the reader is offered the adventure of traveling to a new and wondrous utopia—Timber Land. The mood and tone of this pristine environment serve as a metaphor for the quality and image of the advertised product.

This was it—the look and concept that expressed the mystique of Timber Land, the place. And the image that would carry Timberland, the company, successfully into the new decade.[1]

The nonverbal aspect of an ad or commercial carries half the burden of encoding the message. The appearance of an ad often determines—to a great extent—the way it *feels* to the viewer. That mood, in turn, flavors the message. The advertiser hopes the artistic elements will make the ad as understandable and believable as possible. In this chapter, therefore, we discuss advertising concepts from the standpoint of the visual details: the art in advertising—what it is, where it comes from, how it's done. ◆

WHAT IS ART?

In its broadest sense, the term **art** refers to a system of principles that guides us in creating beauty. But mention the word *art*, and most people immediately think of visual art—a painting or photograph. In print advertising, such images are called the **visual** and usually consist of a reproduction of a photograph, a computer-generated image, or a hand-rendered illustration. However, the visual is not the only kind of art in a print ad.

In advertising, art shapes the message into a complete communication that appeals to the senses as well as the mind. So *art* refers to the whole presentation—visual, verbal, and aural—of the commercial or advertisement. In a print ad, for example, the *artful* selection of words not only communicates facts about the product but also stimulates positive feelings for the product. When artfully designed and crafted, a typeface not only makes reading easier, it also evokes a mood—a sense of the formal, the regal, or the casual. By creatively arranging format elements—surrounding the text with lines, boxes, shades, and colors, and relating those to one another in size and proportion—the designer can further enhance the ad's message. Art also shapes the *style* of photography and illustration. An intimate style uses soft focus and close views, a documentary style portrays the scene without pictorial enhancements, and a dramatic style features unusual viewing angles, distorted color, or blurred action images.

In short, if *copy* is the spoken (or written) language of an ad, *art* is the body language. TV uses both sight and sound to attract and involve viewers. Art directors even help write radio commercials to create visual *word pictures* in the minds of the listeners. The particular blend of writing, visual designs, and sounds makes up an ad's expressive character. So while the quality of the art may sometimes be inferior, every ad uses *art*. And **art direction** is the act or process of managing the visual presentation of the ad.

As writers, visual artists, musicians, and film directors know, creative elements are identifiable but often difficult to define. In advertising the principles of balance, proportion, and movement are guides for uniting images, type, sounds, colors, and qualities of the medium into a single communication. The artist understands these principles and uses them to organize sounds, images, and words so they relate to and enhance one another. (See the Checklist of Artistic Principles on page 280).

THE ROLE OF ART IN CREATING PRINT ADVERTISING

Timberland's ad campaign stands out because of its strong adherence to and vivid presentation of the *big idea*—a factor common to all good advertising. This big idea demanded rare artistic vision. But to be relevant to the audience and to the objectives of the company, John Doyle had to execute the concept with brilliance and precision.

This ad, another of the award-winning series for Timberland, required uncommon vision and attention to detail. Art director and designer John Doyle found just the right creative collaborators, settings, and models to pierce the reader's physiological and psychological screens and beguile the prospect into venturing out to a spacious new environment.

Designing the Print Ad

The term **design** refers to how the art director and graphic artist (or graphic designer) conceptually choose and structure the artistic elements that make up an ad's appearance or set its tone. A designer sets a *style*—the individual manner in which a thought or image is expressed—by consistently choosing particular artistic elements and blending them in a unique way.

The Timberland design truly enhances the message. Note how the ad in Exhibit 9–2 exudes a feeling of *space*. How is this done?

First, the sheer size of the photograph captures attention, drawing readers immediately to the subject—a man launching his boat across a broad expanse of water. All the important elements—the man, boat, shoes, and Timberland label—appear in one area, keeping the other parts of the ad simple and enhancing the sense of spaciousness.

Sparse text gives the ad breathability. The copy is set in a neat, easy-to-read, four-column format with lots of white space. Art and copy elements break out into the margins on either side of the ad and further enhance the feeling of spaciousness. The shoes placed on the surface of the picture plane and the landscape disappearing back toward the horizon give the ad a three-dimensional effect. This quality of *space* gives the ad unity and balance in spite of the number and diversity of elements.

A variety of artists, working under the art director, may produce initial layouts of the ad concept. In collaboration with copywriters, artists draw on their expertise in graphic design—including photography, typography, and illustration—to create the most effective ad or brochure.

The Use of Layouts

A **layout** is an overall orderly arrangement of all the format elements of an ad—headline, subheads, visual(s), copy, captions, trademarks, slogans, and signature.

CHECKLIST   Artistic Principles

Balance

The **optical center** is the reference point that determines the layout's balance. The optical center is about one-eighth of a page above the physical center of the page. Balance is achieved through the arrangement of elements on the page—the left side of the optical center versus the right, above the optical center versus below.

◊ **Formal balance.** Perfect symmetry is the key to formal balance: *matched elements* on either side of a line dissecting the ad have equal optical weight. This technique strikes a dignified, stable, conservative image.

◊ **Informal balance.** A visually balanced ad has elements of different size, shape, color intensity, or darkness at different distances from the optical center. Like a teeter-totter, an object of greater optical weight near the center can be balanced by an object of less weight farther from the center. Many ads use informal balance to make the ad more interesting, imaginative, and exciting.

Movement

Movement is the principle of design that causes the audience to read the material in the desired sequence. It can be achieved through a variety of techniques.

◊ People or animals can be positioned so that *their* eyes direct *the reader's* eyes to the next important element.

◊ Devices such as pointing fingers, boxes, lines, or arrows (or moving the actors or the camera or changing scenes) direct attention from element to element.

◊ Design can take advantage of readers' natural tendency to start at the top left corner of the page and proceed in a Z motion to the lower right.

◊ Comic-strip sequence and pictures with captions force the reader to start at the beginning and follow the sequence in order to grasp the message.

◊ Use of white space and color emphasizes a body of type or an illustration. Eyes will go from a dark element to a light one, or from color to noncolor.

◊ Size itself attracts attention because readers are drawn to the biggest and most dominant element on the page, then to smaller elements.

Proportion

◊ Elements should be accorded space based on their importance to the entire ad. Attention-getting elements are usually

---

The layout serves several purposes. First, as a physical presentation of what the ad will look like, it helps both the agency and the client develop and evaluate the ad's final look and feel. It gives the client, usually not an artist, a tangible item to correct, change, comment on, and approve (see Exhibit 9–3).

Second, the layout helps the creative team develop the ad's psychological elements—the nonverbal and symbolic components. The "look" of the ad should elicit an image or mood that reflects and enhances the advertiser and the product. Many retail stores—groceries, for example—use a cluttered, busy layout with rows of items listed alongside large, boldface prices. Such bargain basement advertising creates the image of large volumes of merchandise available at no-frill, giveaway prices. On the other hand, stores that offer better-quality merchandise, service, and status (at higher prices) usually use large, alluringly beautiful illustrations, often in color, small blocks of copy, and ample white space. Many of these ads don't even mention price.

Both styles of design communicate store image, but each uses design formats differently. Therefore, when designing the initial ad layout, the art director must be very sensitive to the desired image of the product or business and use a format that projects that image. In the Timberland ads, image was the primary reason for combining a dominant, spacious photograph with sparse, elegant copy. The ad instantly makes a highly credible impression on its target audience, and this adds value to the brand.

given more space. Avoid the monotony of giving equal amounts of space to each element.

White Space (Isolation)

◇ **White space** is the part of the ad not occupied by other elements (note that white space may be some color other than white). White space helps focus attention on an isolated element—it makes the copy appear to be in a spotlight. White space is an important contributor to the ad's overall image.

Contrast

◇ An effective way of drawing attention to a particular element is to use **contrast** in color, size, or style; for example, a *reverse* ad (white letters against a dark background) or a black-and-white ad with a red border.

Clarity and Simplicity

◇ Any elements that can be eliminated without damaging the overall effect should be cut. Too many type styles, type that is too small, too many reverses, illustrations, or boxed items, and unnecessary copy make for an overly complex layout and an ad that is hard to read.

Unity

◇ **Unity** means that an ad's many different elements must relate to one another in such a way that the ad gives a singular, harmonious impression. Balance, movement, proportion, contrast, and color may all contribute to unity of design. Many other techniques can be used.

Type styles from the same family.
Borders around ads to hold elements together.
Overlapping one picture or element on another.
Judicious use of white space.
Graphic tools such as boxes, arrows, or tints.

Continuity

◇ **Continuity** is the relationship of one ad to the rest of the campaign. This is achieved by using the same design format, style, and tone; the same spokesperson; or the same graphic element, logo, cartoon character, or catchy slogan.

EXHIBIT • 9-3

An agency sketches a series of layouts to conceptualize an ad. Once approved, the layout is a blueprint for those producing the finished ad: artists, photographers, copywriters. In the rough layout shown here, the headline and writing on the bottle are hand lettered, the artwork is a simple drawing, and lines simulate body text.

AD LAB 9–A   The Role of the Advertising Artist

All the people employed in advertising art are called **artists** or **commercial artists,** but they may perform entirely different tasks. Surprisingly, some can't even draw well; instead, they're trained for different artistic specialties.

Art Directors

Art directors are responsible for the visual presentation of the ad. Along with a copywriter, they develop the initial concept. They may do initial sketches or layouts, but from that point on, they might not touch the ad again. Their primary responsibility is to supervise the ad's progress to completion.

The best art directors are good at presenting ideas in both words and pictures. They are usually experienced graphic designers with a good understanding of consumers. They may have a large or small staff, depending on the organization. Or they may be free-lancers (independent contractors), and do more of the work themselves.

Graphic Designers

Graphic designers are precision specialists preoccupied with shape and form. In advertising they arrange the various graphic elements (type, illustrations, photos, white space) in the most attractive and effective way possible. While they may work on ads, they usually design and produce collateral materials, such as posters, brochures, and annual reports.

In an agency, the art director often acts as the designer. Sometimes, however, a separate designer is used to offer a unique touch to a particular ad.

Illustrators

Illustrators paint or draw the visuals in an ad.

Illustrators frequently specialize in one type of illustrating, such as automotive, fashion, or furniture.

Very few agencies or advertisers retain full-time illustrators; most advertising illustrators free-lance. Typically, agencies hire different illustrators for different jobs, depending on an ad's particular needs, look, and feel.

Photographers

Similar to the illustrator, the **advertising photographer** creates a nonverbal expression that reinforces the verbal

Third, once the best design is chosen, the layout serves as a blueprint. It shows the size and placement of each element in the ad; it tells the copywriter how much copy to write; it suggests the size and style of the image to the illustrator or photographer; and it helps the art director specify the type. Also, once the production manager knows the dimensions of the ad, the number of photos, the amount of typesetting, and the use of art elements such as color and illustrations, he or she can accurately determine the cost of producing the ad (see Ad Lab 9–A: "The Role of the Advertising Artist").

The Advertising Design Process

The design process serves as both a creative and an approval process. And each phase in the design process serves a particular purpose.

There are two phases in the design process for print advertising. In the conceptual phase, the designer uses *thumbnails, roughs, dummies,* and *comprehensives*—in other words, *nonfinal art*—to establish the ad's look and feel. In the prepress (or production art) phase, the artist prepares a *mechanical*—the final artwork with the actual type in place along with all the visuals the publisher or printer will need to reproduce or print the ad. We'll discuss each of these steps briefly.

message. Photographers use the tools of photography—cameras, lenses, and lights—to create images. They select interesting angles, arrange subjects in new ways, carefully control the lighting, and use many other techniques to enhance the subject's image quality.

A studio photographer uses high-powered lights to photograph products in front of a background or as part of an arranged setting. A location photographer generally shoots in real-life settings like those in the Timberland ads. Many photographers specialize—in cars, celebrities, fashion, food, equipment, or architecture.

Agencies and advertisers rarely employ staff photographers. They generally hire free-lancers by the hour or pay a fee for the assignment. Photographers also sell **stock photography**—photos on file from prior shootings that can be used for other jobs.

Production Artists

Production (or **pasteup**) **artists** assemble the various elements of an ad and mechanically put them together the way the art director or designer indicates. Good production artists are fast, precise, and knowledgeable about the whole production process (described in Chapter 10). In addition, production artists today must be computer literate; they must know how to use a variety of software programs for page making, drawing, painting, and photo scanning.

Most designers and art directors start their careers as production artists and work their way up. It's very difficult work, but it is also very important, for this is where an ad actually comes together in its finished form.

Laboratory Applications

1. Look at the Toronto Zoo ad in the Art Director's Portfolio on page 294 and explain which advertising artists were probably involved in its creation and what the responsibility of each artist was.

2. Which ad in the Art Director's Portfolio do you think needed the fewest artists? How many?

Thumbnail Sketches

The **thumbnail sketch**—or, simply, thumbnail—is a small, very rough, rapidly produced drawing used to try out ideas. The artist uses it to visualize a number of layout approaches without wasting time on details; the best sketches are then developed further. Because thumbnails are so basic—lines drawn to indicate text and boxes sometimes used to indicate visuals—they're more useful to agency people than to clients. There are two forms of thumbnails. Some art directors prefer to sketch their ideas in miniature on tracing paper or foolscap—approximately one-fourth to one-eighth the size of the finished ad, as shown in Exhibit 9–4A. Others like to use a full 8½″ × 11″ (or larger) sheet for each sketch, tearing pages off and starting again after each try.

Rough Layout

In a **rough**, the artist draws to the actual size of the ad. As shown in Exhibit 9–4B, headlines and subheads suggest the final type style, illustrations and photographs are sketched in, and body copy is simulated with lines. Roughs *are* presented to clients—particularly cost-conscious ones.

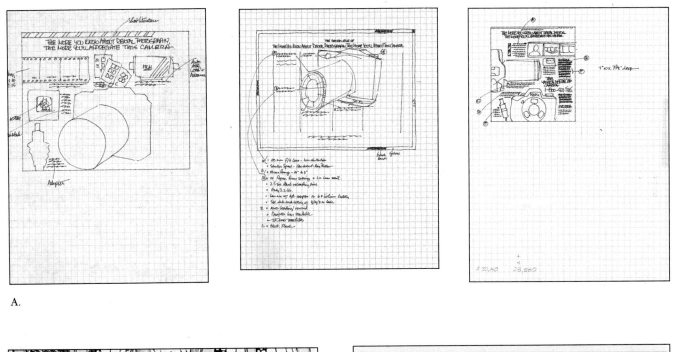

A.

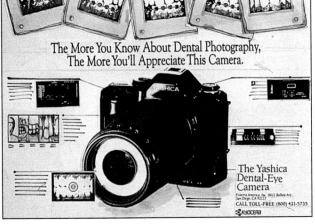

B.

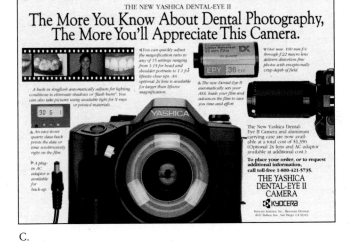

C.

EXHIBIT • 9-4

A. Thumbnails are small sketches used to try out various layouts. They are a fast, inexpensive way to visualize the copy platform.
B. The rough layout is a larger sketch done to actual size.
C. The finished ad for Kyocera's Yashica Dental-Eye camera, as well as the layouts, was produced by Tom Michael and Bob Hines of Market Design in Solana Beach, California.

Comprehensive

The **comprehensive layout,** or comp, a highly refined facsimile of the finished ad, allows the advertiser to judge how the finished ad will look. A comp is generally quite elaborate, with colored photos, press-on lettering, photostats of subvisuals, and a glossy spray-coat. Today, art and computer suppliers offer complete systems for making ad comps. Generally, copy for the comp is typeset on computer and positioned with the visuals, and the ad is printed as a full color proof. When the process reaches the comp stage, all visuals should be final.

Dummy

A **dummy** is a form of rough design generally used to present the hand-held look and feel of brochures, multipage materials, or point-of-purchase displays. Like ads, dummies may be done as thumbnails, roughs, or comps. The artist assembles the dummy by hand, using color markers and computer proofs, mounting them on sturdy paper, and then cutting and folding them to size. A dummy for a brochure, for example, is put together, page by page, to look exactly like the finished product and may be as polished as a comp.

The Mechanical (Pasteup)

In print advertising, the type and visuals must be placed into their exact position for reproduction by a printer. Many agencies still make traditional **mechanicals** where black type and line art are pasted in place on a piece of white artboard—called a *pasteup*—with overlay sheets indicating the hue and positioning of color. Printers refer to the mechanical or pasteup as *camera-ready art* because they photograph it using a large production camera before starting the reproduction process—creating color keys, prints, and films of the finished ad. Today, however, most designers do this work on the computer. The art goes directly from disk to an output device that makes negatives for the printing process—completely bypassing the need for a mechanical. (See Chapter 10, "Creative Production: Print Media," for a more in-depth discussion.)

Any time during the design process—until the printing press lays ink on paper—changes can be made on the art. However, the expense grows tenfold with each step from roughs to mechanicals to printing.

Which Design Format Works Best?

Recent readership studies indicate that 85 percent of ads don't even get looked at.[2] These studies also show virtually *no* relationship between the level of spending and how well an ad is recalled. But the quality of the advertising *is* important.[3] Ads must achieve attention and interest, which, in print, is greatly influenced by an ad's design.

Traditionally, the highest-scoring print ads have a standard, poster-style format with a single, dominant visual that occupies between 60 and 70 percent of the ad's total area.[4] In fact, some research shows that ads scoring in the top third for stopping power devote an average of 82 percent of their space to the visual.[5] Next in ranking are ads that have one large picture and two smaller ones. The visuals are intended to stop the reader and arouse interest, so their content must be interesting.

Headlines also stop the reader and may actually contribute more to long-term memory than the visual. Research shows that short headlines with one line are best but a second line is acceptable. The total headline area should fill only 10 to 15 percent of the ad, so the type need not be particularly large. Headlines may appear above or below the visual, depending on the situation. David Ogilvy believes that when the headline appears below the illustration, as in Exhibit 9–5, the ad gains about 10 percent more readership.[6]

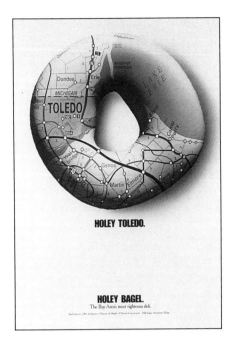

This ad for Holey Bagel uses a poster-style presentation with the dominant visual headline, and white space underneath taking up 60 to 70 percent of the total space.

Research also shows that readership drops considerably if ads have more than 50 words. So to attract a large number of readers, copy blocks should be kept to less than 20 percent of the ad. However, with many products, the more you tell the more you sell.[7] Long copy works—when it's *appropriate.*

Finally, most people who read ads also want to know who placed the ad. Company signatures or logos need not be particularly large or occupy more than 5 to 10 percent of the area. For best results, signatures or logos should be placed in the lower right-hand corner or across the bottom of the ad.

The Advertising Visual

The artists who paint, sketch, and draw in advertising are called **illustrators.** The artists who produce pictures with a camera are called **photographers.** Together they are responsible for all the visuals, or pictures, we see in advertising.

Purpose of the Visual

Most prospects look at the picture, read the headline, and read the body copy, in that order.[8] If any one of these elements fails, the ad's impact diminishes. Since the visual carries so much responsibility for an ad's success, it must be attention-getting, offer relevant story appeal, and accomplish most of the following tasks:

- Capture the reader's attention.
- Identify the subject of the ad.
- Qualify readers by stopping those who are legitimate prospects.
- Arouse the reader's interest in the headline.
- Create a favorable impression of the product or advertiser.
- Clarify claims made by the copy.
- Help convince the reader of the truth of those claims.
- Emphasize the product's unique features.
- Provide continuity for all ads in the campaign by using a unified visual technique in each individual ad.[9]

Determining the Chief Focus for Visuals

Timberland ads are dominated by a large, single visual that demonstrates the environment in which the product is used rather than the product itself. More important, the visuals capture a mood and create a feeling—a context for the consumer's perception of the product.

Selecting the focus for advertising visuals is a major step in the creative process. It often determines how well the big idea is executed. Print advertising uses many standard subjects for ad visuals, typically more product-related than the Timberland approach. The 10 most common include:

1. **The package containing the product.** Especially important for packaged goods, it helps the consumer identify the product on the grocery shelf.
2. **The product alone.** This doesn't work well for nonpackaged goods.
3. **The product in use.** Automobile ads invariably show a car in use while talking about the ride, the luxury, the handling, or the economy. Cosmetic ads usually show the product in use with a close-up photo of a beautiful

This French ad creates the feeling that TBS boat shoes can endure the most turbulent conditions ("Try to imagine what shoes should be like in a wet and tilting world"). The lower portion of the ad, with its neatly justified block of type, highlights product features and the solid look of the square TBS logo.

woman. Timberland ads also show the products in use; they're just too small to see in the totality of the visual.

4. **How to use the product.** Recipe ads featuring a new way to use food products historically pull very high readership scores.

5. **Product features.** Computer software ads frequently show a photograph of the monitor screen so the prospect can see how the software features are displayed. The French ad in Exhibit 9–6 uses illustrations to highlight the key features of the soles of TBS boat shoes.

6. **Comparison of products.** The advertiser compares its product's features to a competitor's.

7. **User benefit.** When Sylvania introduced its new 10-bulb flash cartridge, it illustrated user benefit with 10 photos of the Mona Lisa. The headline keyed the humor: "Now you have two more chances to get it right." It's especially difficult to illustrate intangible user benefits. However, marketers know that the best way to get customers' attention is to show how the product will benefit them.

8. **Humor.** If used well, humor can make an entertaining and lasting impression, but it can destroy credibility if used incorrectly.

9. **Testimonial.** "Before and after" endorsements by celebrities or actual users are very effective for weight-loss products, skin-care lotions, and body-building courses.

10. **Negative appeal.** Sometimes, visuals point out what happens if you *don't* use the product. As Exhibit 9–7 shows, negative ideas can spark interest.

Choosing the Visual

An infinite number of pictures can be used to communicate the benefits of a product or service. The kind of picture used is often determined during the visualization process (see Ad Lab 9–B, "Techniques for Creating Advertising.

EXHIBIT • 9-7

This ad uses a negative headline to stir attention and reinforce the idea that the agency can create media attention. Negative appeals are so rare, advertisers who use them stand out. But over time, consumers often forget the point of the original message and continue to associate a negative feeling with the product or service—a factor that can hurt sales over the long haul.

AD LAB 9–B   Techniques for Creating Advertising Visuals

Visuals in an ad help consumers envision a fact or concept—with immediacy. The style and size of the visual depends on several factors: its role in the ad, cost, technical limitations, production time, effect desired, printing requirements, and the availability of the necessary professionals.

Two types of visuals are used in advertising: *photographs* and *illustrations* (drawn, painted, or computerized).

Photography

A good photograph usually makes several important contributions to an ad.

Provides Realism Good color photography can give an exciting, realistic look to all kinds of products, from up-close views of high-tech products to wide landscape vistas.

Photographs—especially news-type photos—put the reader at the scene. Knowing the photographer had to be there, the reader becomes personally involved in the action.

Brings the "Cartoon Effect" to Life Photography lends realism to unusual or cartoonish subjects. A drawing of the famous eye-patched Hathaway man would have lacked the realism and story appeal of the actual man.

Adds Mood, Beauty, and Sensitivity Photography can deliver a mood or a tremendous emotional wallop—like a photo-

graph of an abused child. And it also offers beauty.

Offers Speed, Flexibility, and Economy An illustration usually takes considerably longer to complete than a photograph. Many photos can be taken and developed overnight.

Using photography is relatively simple. The photographer shoots a variety of poses at various angles and with various light settings. Then, in the case of print photography, the negatives are printed actual size on a contact sheet unretouched. With a magnifying glass, the art director finds and proofs the most suitable photo. Most color photos are shot as transparencies (slides), and the art director uses a light table or slide viewer to make selections.

Photography can be economical. Photos can be cropped to any size or shape and retouched by computer or with a paintbrush or airbrush to improve the image. Also, stock photography houses have tens of thousands of photos, and they're usually cheaper than hiring a photographer.

Cautions, Though When photos are commissioned or bought by an advertiser or agency, any individuals who appear in the picture must sign a standard model release (available from many stationery stores), which gives the advertiser permission to use their picture.

In addition, copyright laws state that *the image belongs to the artist* (photographers and illustrators included); hence, it's customary to pay for *each use*. The price a photographer charges usually depends on the intended use, frequency of use, and size of the market—not to mention the renown of the photographer.

Visuals"). But frequently the visual is not determined until the art director or designer actually lays out the ad. Advertising managers and art directors often keep checklists handy (as well as an extensive file, or *morgue,* of noteworthy ads, photos, and illustrations) to serve as idea ticklers.

What if a restaurant wants to advertise its caviar? How exciting is a picture of a can of caviar? Should the caviar appear on a plate or fork? Should the can be opened or closed? The Hong Kong restaurant ad in Exhibit 9–8 shows an interesting solution.

Selecting an appropriate photo or visual is a difficult creative task. (See the Art Director's Portfolio on page 292 for several examples of dynamic, creative ads.) Art directors deal with several basic issues:

- Is a visual needed for effective communication?
- Should the visual be black-and-white or color? Is this a budgetary decision?
- What should the subject of the picture be? Is that subject relevant to the advertiser's creative strategy?
- Should the ad use an illustration or a photograph?
- What technical and budgetary issues must be considered?

Illustration

Hand-drawn or painted illustrations offer different benefits. Some things cannot be photographed: certain concepts and past and future events. Likewise, a line drawing may more clearly portray a product or instill the proper mood. Illustrations may also be used to exaggerate a subject.

Illustrators are limited only by their own skill. Unlike photographers who must capture a scene (either in nature or with expensive staging), the illustrator can create the desired image and still add personal style.

Illustrators use a number of techniques (or media) to produce illustrations, including (1) pencil, crayon, and charcoal; (2) ink and ink wash; (3) scratchboard; (4) airbrush; (5) oil, acrylic, tempera, and watercolor, and (6) computers.

Line Drawings Line drawings use lines to depict an image. Ideal for sharp and clearly detailed subjects, line drawings are usually created in black and white, with no shades of gray. The mediums used include pencil, crayon, and charcoal, which are known for their dry, scratchy appearance; and ink and markers, which can appear wet. Sometimes referred to as pen-and-ink drawings, line drawings are less costly to reproduce than drawings with tonal values. Technical drawings and cartoons are frequently done as line drawings. Line drawings are usually inexpensive and often the least time-consuming type of illustration.

Wash Drawings When tones and grays are desired, a wash drawing might be used. Ink is applied in various shades of one color using a brush filled with varying degrees of

ink and water. There are two types of wash drawings. A *tight* drawing is detailed, realistic, and done with both a pen and a brush. A *loose* wash drawing is more impressionistic and done with a brush only; this is used by fashion and furniture illustrators in newspaper advertising.

Scratchboard Using special paper with a soft, chalky surface called scratchboard, the illustrator applies black ink to the area that will carry the illustration. Then, using a sharp object for scratching—ideally a stylus meant for scratchboard—the ink is removed, leaving a white line. This technique gives the impression of extremely fine workmanship and requires many hours of meticulous craftsmanship.

Other Illustrative Techniques Numerous other illustrative techniques can be employed. Airbrush creates fine shadings and edges rather than lines; and oil, tempera, and watercolor illustrations appear to be wet. Computer-generated drawings can be created to resemble other mediums: ink line drawings, graphic renderings (featuring flat fields of colors or patterns with lines and text on top), airbrush, and photographs (using digitized photography).

Laboratory Applications

1. Select five ads from the text and describe which visual technique is used for each and how effective it is.
2. Select an ad from the text and propose a different visual from the one used. Describe the rationale for your choice.

EXHIBIT • 9-8

This ad for the Mandarin/Oriental hotel restaurant in Hong Kong is a smorgasbord of visuals that draws the reader to the ad and its relatively small headline. The visuals educate and entice the reader while reinforcing the message.

- Should the ad use an illustration or a photograph?
- What technical and budgetary issues must be considered?

As an exercise, thumb through any chapter in this book and study one of the ads. Ask yourself the questions listed above as they apply to the ad you chose. On any day, in any agency, top art directors perform this exercise routinely.

Art Direction and International Markets

Philosophers often refer to the arts as a kind of "international language" where the nonverbal elements translate freely regardless of culture. A nice idea but, in advertising, a very costly one. Although most people see a particular color the same way, they usually ascribe different meanings to that color depending on their culture. When designing ads for use in other countries, the art director must be familiar with each country's artistic preferences and peculiarities.

Some consider color to be indicative of emotion: someone "has the blues" or is "green with envy." But as mentioned in Ad Lab 9-C, "The Psychological Impact of Color," the response to color can also be determined by culture. The emblems of national pride—the Canadian Maple Leaf, "the Red-White-and-

AD LAB 9–C   The Psychological Impact of Color

Reaction to color, says leading package designer Walter Margulies, is generally based on a person's national origin or culture. For example, warm colors are red, yellow, and orange; they tend to stimulate, excite, and create an active response. People from warmer climes, apparently, are most responsive to those colors.

Violet and "leaf green" fall on the line between warm and cool. They can be either, depending on the shade.

Here are some more of Margulies's observations:

Red

Symbol of blood and fire. Second to blue as people's favorite color but more versatile, the hottest color with highest "action quotient." Appropriate for soups, frozen foods, and meats. Conveys strong masculine appeal—shaving cream.

Brown

Another masculine color associated with earth, woods, mellowness, age, warmth, comfort—the essential male; used to sell anything (even cosmetics)—Revlon's Braggi.

Yellow

High impact to catch consumer's eye, particularly when used with black, good for corn, lemon, or suntan products.

Green

Symbol of health and freshness; popular for mint products, and soft drinks—7UP.

Blue

Coldest color with most appeal; effective for frozen foods (ice impression); if used with lighter tints becomes "sweet"—Yoplait yogurt, Lowenbrau beer, Wondra flour.

Black

Conveys sophistication, high-end merchandise, and is used to stimulate purchase of expensive products; good as background and foil for other colors.

Orange

Most "edible" color, especially in brown-tinged shades; evokes autumn and good things to eat.

Laboratory Applications

1. Explain the moods or feelings that are stimulated by three color ads or packages illustrated in this text.
2. Choose two ads in the Art Director's Portfolio and explain the contribution color makes to each.

Blue" of the United States, or the Tricolor of France—are nonverbal signals able to stir patriotic emotions, thoughts, and actions. However, these same symbols could hurt sales. For example, a promotion using colors similar to those of the U.S. and French flags could easily fail in Southeast Asia, where some people still have painful memories of wars fought against the U.S. and France.

An **icon,** a pictorial image representing some idea or thing, can have a meaning that cuts across national boundaries and reflects the tastes and attitudes of a group of cultures.

An ad with a snake—an icon for the devil and eroticism in many western cultures—could easily lose sales in North American markets. But in the Far East, where the snake represents renewal (by shedding its skin), the same visual might work as a dynamic and successful expression of a product's staying power.

On a more personal level, a culture's icons can express social roles. When an agency calls a casting company or talent agent in search of a model, the agency, in essence, seeks an icon. It hopes the model will effectively symbolize the product's benefits or help the target market relate better to the ad. A model considered attractive in one culture will not necessarily seem so in another, however.

Continued on page 295

Art Director's Portfolio

A. An important consideration for advertising artists is the relationship between the *figure*—the subject(s) in the forefront—and the *field,* the area or pattern that fills the background. This Wamsutta ad uses the flatness of the sheet's surface to fill the entire visual area from edge to edge. The sheet itself serves as the field. The type appears to float above the pattern of the sheet and, thus, takes the position of the figure.

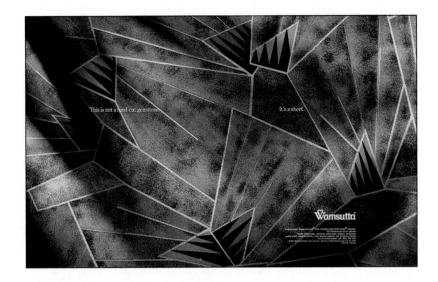

B. Since the advent of photography, people view traditional painting with less reverence. Illustration, a cousin of fine art painting, is used extensively today to portray things we cannot see in life—images of microbes interacting, surrealistic mindscapes, the Yellow Pages fingers limping down the sidewalk covered with bandaged wounds, and, in this example, *Blue Boy* wearing Lee's Euro Rider jeans. Richard Hess, the illustrator and a very successful art director, was one of the first to introduce traditional-looking illustrations with untraditional content. In this ad, art director Arty Tan balances the illustration's power by letting the white space of the neighboring page dominate rather than using a distractingly large headline.

C. In times past, a quality fountain pen was the highest level of writing technology. Today, the practical ballpoint is everywhere, but legends do live on. In this ad for Waterman Pens, the art director builds the feeling of tradition and quality using a variety of art elements. The visual—a photograph—features masculine colors (brown, orange, golds) and the luxury of wood trim. The field behind the text and image of the pen exudes the classic look of parchment paper. The text is set in a personable serif type and laid out in a spacious manner. And the pen, silver with gold trim, features classic styling associated with turn-of-the-century elegance. These artistic choices make a total statement of enduring quality and elegance.

D. The artist's handcrafted lettering and illustrations give this ad for Egg Beaters a down-home flavor. The soft edge and rounded corners of the warmly colored photo exude a comfortable, fuzzy feeling. And the fine-line drawings add to the traditional ambiance, harking back to simpler times and farm-fresh wholesomeness.

E. In this poster for the Toronto Zoo, the illustrator can portray the ugliness of the warthog in a positive manner—a feat difficult for photography. The illustration is important to the poster's success because it attracts the eye, serves as an integral part of the message, and adds color and personality.

F. In contrast to the other ads in this portfolio, the one for SSR Travels strives to be low-tech in appearance and execution. Like the others in the series, it uses the look of a wood block print as a field to frame the photographic visual. The textured screen in the visual adds to the overall tactile feeling that seems to lie across the ad. The irregular but positive-feeling headline type ("SSR's holiday villages. . . . The alternative for all") adds to the handmade look and tells readers that SSR Travels can help its customers travel off the beaten track.

EXHIBIT • 9-9

By placing hockey skates alongside the footwear traditionally worn in the orient, Canadian Airlines demonstrates—in symbolic fashion—that it flies Canadians to the Far East.

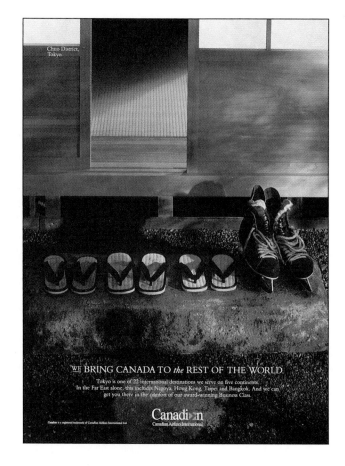

Catchy, current phrases popular in a local culture are often used for advertising. But even if the idea translates verbally into another language—which is rarely the case—the art director may still have difficulty using the same imagery. Advertisers working in global markets must pretest art and design concepts with natives of each country (see Exhibit 9–9).

THE ROLE OF ART IN PACKAGE DESIGN

In 1990, U.S. companies spent more than $70 billion on package design—as much as they spent on media advertising.[10] Many businesses spend *more* money on packaging. With today's trend toward self-service, packages play a major role in both advertising and selling.

Packaging encompasses the physical appearance of the container and includes design, color, shape, labeling, and materials. In designing a package, consideration should be given to three factors: its stand-out appeal, how it communicates verbally and nonverbally, and the prestige or image desired.

Like advertising, packaging communicates both verbally and nonverbally. For example, one bread manufacturer decided that a green wrapping would connote freshness. But customers associated it with mold!

Research shows that consumers respond to packaging intuitively. After buying a product, consumers must still be "sold" on it. So packaging design can be as powerful a tool as advertising in building a product's brand image.[11]

Packaging establishes a brand's personality and prestige. Therefore, the package designer must consider what consumers regard as prestigious. This is especially important for so-called nonrational products—such as health and beauty aids, perfume, sports accessories, and confection gifts—in which fancy, whim, and mystique all operate in place of rational choice.[12]

EXHIBIT • 9-10

The brand identity and package design system for Pasta La Bella includes a variety of products and sizes.

To sell products off the shelf, packages must use shape, color, size, interesting visuals, or even texture to deliver a marketing message, give product information, and indicate in-use application (see Exhibit 9–10).[13] In some cases the package design might even include the display shelf. Packages should continue promoting the product in the home, reinforcing the brand's image, so they should open and close with minimal effort and be easy to handle.[14]

Packaging Forms and Materials

Packages come as wrappers, cartons, boxes, crates, cans, bottles, jars, tubes, barrels, drums, and pallets. Packages are made of many substances—from paper and steel ("tin" cans) to wood, glass, and burlap. Newer packaging materials include plastic-coated papers, ceramics, and even straw. Metal foils that protect the contents and add to the attractiveness of the package are becoming common. Improvements in packaging include amber-green glass bottles that protect the contents from damage by light and heavy-duty, gray computer disk jackets that reflect heat and protect the disk from damage.[15] The plastic film pouch for food products has become a substitute for tin cans and is more flexible, light, and compact.

With the public's growing concern for the environment, especially in international markets, recyclable tin-coated steel and aluminum packages are enjoying a resurgence in popularity. Similarly, the popular aerosol spray can is rapidly becoming free of fluorocarbons in order to protect the ozone layer.[16] Because European countries are so densely populated, their regulations requiring environmentally friendly packaging are far more stringent than in North America. Such regulations add to the cost of doing business overseas.

Packaging Specialists

Management ultimately makes the final design decisions about packages and labels. However, because packaging is so closely related to advertising and uses similar techniques, the advertising department and the ad agency may play an important role in package development. Many ad agencies design labels and packages and prepare the copy that goes on them. Often they coordinate this work with the overall theme of the ad campaign. Manufacturers who once viewed packaging as a facet of production now see it as a form of promotion.

Packaging problems are so complex that many advertisers use **packaging specialists.** Such specialists fall into one of three categories:

1. Outside package consulting firms, staffed by experienced designers and artists, that provide complete package design.
2. Design departments of larger corporations that have their own staff to work on packaging and that probably help design the product as well.
3. Container manufacturers that sell metal, paper, plastic, or other packaging materials and often help with package design as a service to their customers.

When Should a Package Be Changed?

There are many reasons to change a package: product alteration or improvement, substitution in packaging materials, competitive pressure, environmental concerns, changes in legislation, or the need to increase brand recognition as illustrated in Exhibit 9–11.

Package design must communicate product value. Advertisers spend millions researching and promoting new images. And packages have to reflect a contemporary brand image consistent with constantly changing consumer perceptions.[17]

However, a decision to stay with the present packaging may be the best strategy, so marketers should always exercise caution. And designers often change packaging very gradually to avoid confusing consumers.

THE ROLE OF ART IN RADIO AND TELEVISION ADVERTISING

When they received a flood of calls from amputees, the executives at Du Pont Corporation knew their new commercial was a success.

Created by BBDO Worldwide from an inspiration by a Du Pont department head, the ad featured Bill Demby, a Vietnam veteran who had lost his legs in a rocket attack. In the TV spot, shown in Exhibit 9–12, Demby is on his way to play basketball in an urban neighborhood. As he pulls off his sweatpants, attention focuses on his two artificial legs. As Demby freely dashes, jumps, scrambles, and shoots, the voice-over describes that he is wearing the "Seattle Foot," a prosthesis designed by the Prosthetics Research Study in Seattle, Washington. Suddenly, Demby falls. Play stops. He's offered a helping hand but jumps right up, and the rapid-fire action begins again. As the spot ends, an out-of-breath player calls out: "Hey, Bill, you've been practicing!"

Developing the Artistic Concept for Commercials

Creating the concept for a radio or TV commercial is similar to creating the concept for print ads. The first step is to determine the big idea. Next, the art director and copywriter must decide what commercial format to use. For example, should a celebrity present the message, or should the ad dramatize the product's benefits with a semi-fictional story? The next step is to write a script containing the necessary copy or dialogue plus a basic description of any music, sound effects, and/or camera views.

In both radio and television, the art director assists the copywriter in script development; but in television, artistic development is much more extensive.

EXHIBIT • 9–11

Callahan Seeds redesigned its packaging to improve the product's image and to increase brand recognition.

A. The original package artwork before the advertising agency, The Majestic Group, created new art.
B. Two of many thumbnails.
C. Two of several roughs presented to the client.
D. The final package designs. Farmers reported they hesitated to destroy emptied bags because they looked "so nice."

A.

B.   C.

D.

Using the TV script, the art director creates a series of **storyboard roughs** to present the artistic approach, the action sequences, and the style of the commercial (see Exhibit 9–13). When the storyboard meets approval, it serves as a guide for the final production phase.

Getting through these first phases, though, can be the toughest. For BBDO, the biggest challenge for the Du Pont commercial was finding the main "actor." BBDO staff wanted the credibility of a real Vietnam veteran with his own Seattle Foot. But he also had to be telegenic, physically strong, and able to display athletic skills. "You'd be surprised how difficult a task that proved to be," says Cathy Mendel, BBDO account supervisor. "After exhausting all the traditional casting sources," she recalls, "we finally looked at participants in the Disabled Games. That's where we found Bill Demby."

Normally the concepts and characters we witness every day on radio and TV are born in the minds of the men and women who conceive the original commercial—the art director, the copywriter, and the creative director.

If the concept is to create a dramatic scene, the script may call for an actor to play the part of a fictitious character. Or the team may decide it wants to use a

EXHIBIT • 9-12

In this ad, the story line is a framework within which to portray the value of the product and demonstrate its ruggedness. The story itself began without a specific person in mind, but Bill Demby—a real-life beneficiary of the product—helped make the product's utility come alive.

(Music under)
ANNCR: When Bill Demby was in Vietnam, he dreamed of coming home and playing a little basketball.
MAN: Hey, Bill!

ANNCR: A dream that all but died when he lost both legs to a Vietcong rocket. But then researchers discovered that a Du Pont plastic could help make truly lifelike artificial limbs.
(SFX: sounds of game in progress)

ANNCR: Now Bill's back, and some say he hasn't lost a step. At Du Pont, we make things that make a difference.
MAN: Hey, Bill, you've been practicing!
ANNCR: Better things for better living.

well-known celebrity to lend credibility to the product. As was true with Bill Demby, casting these characters involves major deliberation.

In casting, the most important consideration is relevance to the product. For example, agencies don't use a comic to sell financial products—or mortuary services. And in spite of Bill Cosby's success for advertisers such as Jell-O, Ford, McDonald's, and Coca-Cola, some experts don't even believe in using celebrities. David Ogilvy, for example, thinks viewers remember the celebrity more than the product.[18]

As the concept evolves, the creative team will define the characters' personalities in a detailed, written brief. These descriptions serve as guides in casting sessions when prospective actors audition for the roles. Sometimes, agencies discover a Tony and Sharon (of Taster's Choice fame)—solid, memorable characters who go beyond a simple role and actually create a personality or image for the product.

Formats for Radio and Television Commercials

A major challenge for the creative team in radio and television advertising is deciding on the format. Similar to print advertising, the format for a broadcast ad serves as a template for arranging message elements into a pattern. Once the

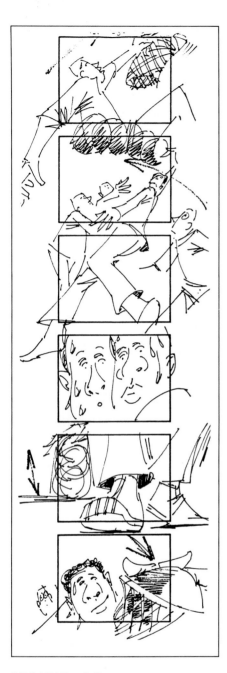

This commercial revolves around a single character, Bill Demby, and how a Du Pont product contributes to "better living" for him. One of the "arts" of TV and radio advertising is choosing a viable character who can make the product credible and appealing. This impressionistic storyboard helped depict his story and the action that would be incorporated into the ad.

art director and copywriter establish the big idea, they must determine the commercial's format; then they can develop the script.

Although radio and TV commercials can't always be rigidly classified, a wide variety of styles have been successful. Some of these are listed in Ad Lab 9–D, "Creative Ways to Sell on Radio." Hank Seiden, vice chairman of Jordan, McGrath, Case & Taylor, developed the Execution Spectrum—24 "basic" formats or techniques that range from frivolous to serious (see Exhibit 9–14).[19] Here, we'll consider eight common commercial formats that can be used in either radio or television: *straight announcement, presenter, testimonial, demonstration, musical, slice of life, lifestyle,* and *animation.* Note that most of these overlap with Seiden's categories.

Straight Announcement

The **straight announcement** is the oldest and simplest type of radio or TV commercial and probably the easiest to write. One person delivers the sales message—usually a radio or TV announcer—typically with no special sound effects. Music, if any, plays in the background. Straight announcements are popular because they are adaptable to almost any product or situation. In radio, a straight announcement can also be designed as an **integrated commercial**—that is, it can be woven into a show or tailored to a given program.

For TV, an announcer may deliver the sales message **on-camera**—directly into the camera—or off-screen, as a **voice-over**, while a demonstration, slide, or film shows on-screen. The appeal may be either "hard sell" or relaxed. If the script is well written and the announcer convincing, straight announcements can be very effective. Since they don't require elaborate production facilities, they save money, too.

Straight announcements are giving way to more creative concepts. But they are still commonly used on late-night TV programs, by local advertisers, and by nonprofit or political organizations.

Presenter

A familiar format for broadcast commercials and an outgrowth of the straight announcement, the **presenter commercial** uses one person or character to present the product and carry the sales message. Some presenters are celebrities, like Lynn Redgrave for Weight Watchers or Ray Charles for Pepsi-Cola. Other times, they are corporate officers of the sponsor, like Lee Iacocca, former chairman of Chrysler. Other sponsors, like Bank of America, use a noncelebrity actor who delivers a straight pitch rather than playing a particular role. Research shows that attractive presenters are more credible; audiences tend to trust them, like them, and believe in their "expertise."[20]

In radio, a **radio personality**—talk show host, disk jockey, or celebrity like Sally Jessie Raphael—may ad lib an ad message live in his or her own style. Done well, such commercials can be very successful. However, the advertiser surrenders control to the personality. The main risk, outside of occasional blunders, is that the personality may criticize the product. Even so, this sometimes lends realism that is otherwise hard to achieve. The personality gets a *highlight sheet* listing the product's or the company's features, the main points to stress, and the phrases or company slogans to repeat. But he or she can choose the specific wording and mode of delivery.

AD LAB 9–D   Creative Ways to Sell on Radio

Product demo The commercial tells how a product is used or the purposes it serves.

Voice power A unique voice gives the ad power.

Electronic sound Synthetic sound-making machines create a memorable product-sound association.

Customer interview A spokesperson and customer discuss the product advantages spontaneously.

Humorous fake interview The customer interview is done in a lighter vein.

Hyperbole or exaggerated statement Overstatement arouses interest in legitimate product claims that might otherwise pass unnoticed; often a spoof.

Fourth dimension Time and events are compressed into a brief spot involving the listener in future projections.

Hot property Commercial adapts a current sensation—a hit show, performer, or song.

Comedian power Established comedians do commercials in their own unique style, implying celebrity endorsement.

Historical fantasy Situation with revived historical characters is used to convey product message.

Sound picture Recognizable sounds involve the listener by stimulating imagination.

Demographics Music or references appeal to a particular segment of the population, such as an age or interest group.

Imagery transfer Musical logo or other sound reinforces the memory of a television campaign.

Celebrity interview Famous person endorses the product in an informal manner.

Product song Music and words combine to create a musical logo, selling the product in the style of popular music.

Editing genius Many different situations, voices, types of music, and sounds are combined in a series of quick cuts.

Improvisation Performers work out the dialogue extemporaneously for an assigned situation; may be postedited.

Laboratory Applications

1. Select three familiar radio commercials and discuss which creative techniques they use.

2. Select a familiar radio commercial and discuss how a different creative technique would increase its effectiveness.

Testimonial

Whether the "product" is a political candidate or a bar of soap, people are often persuaded by the opinions of individuals they respect. The true **testimonial**—where a satisfied user tells how effective the product is—can be highly credible in both TV and radio advertising. Celebrities may gain attention, but they must be believable and not distract attention from the product.

Actually, people from all walks of life endorse products—from known personalities to unknowns and nonprofessionals. Which type of person to use depends on the product and the strategy.

Satisfied customers are the best sources for testimonials. While they may be shy of the microphone or camera, their natural sincerity is usually persuasive.

EXHIBIT • 9-14

The Execution Spectrum, used by Ketchum Advertising for clients as part of its Spectrum Analysis, shows 24 different execution formats—ranging in style from frivolous to serious—for both print and electronic advertising.

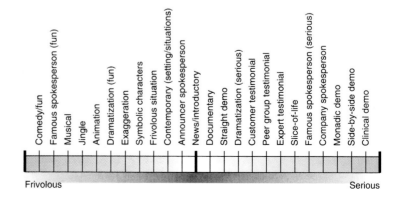

Ogilvy suggests shooting candid testimonials when the subjects don't know they're being filmed.[21] But advertisers must always be sure to get their permission before use.

Demonstration

A **demonstration** convinces an audience better and faster than an oral message.[22] Memorable demonstrations have shown the advantages of car tires, ballpoint pens, and paper towels, to mention just a few. Naturally, it's easier to demonstrate the product on TV than on radio, but some advertisers have used radio to create humorous, tongue-in-cheek demonstrations.

Products may be demonstrated in use, in competition, or before and after. These techniques help viewers visualize the product's performance if they should own it. Therefore, the demonstration should be as clear, simple, graphic, and relevant as possible—and interesting.

Musical

The **musical commercials,** or **jingles,** we see and hear on radio and TV are among the best—and worst—ad messages produced. Done well, they can bring enormous success—well beyond the average nonmusical commercial. Done poorly, they can waste the advertising budget.

Musical commercials have several variations. The entire message may be sung; jingles may be interspersed throughout the spoken copy; or orchestras may play symphonic or popular arrangements. Many producers use consistent musical themes for background color or to close the commercial. After

---

ETHICAL DILEMMA   Imitation or Plagiarism—What's the Difference?

When two companies run strikingly similar ads, is it imitation, plagiarism, or coincidence? It depends on your point of view. In the mid-1980s, a commercial by Rubin Postaer & Associates for American Honda ended with the picture frame turned sideways while the subject, a Honda, blasted off like a rocket. Five years later, Leo Burnett Advertising created a commercial featuring astronaut Scott Carpenter and his son comparing an Oldsmobile to a spaceship. At the end, the Olds turned sideways and blasted off—just like the Honda. Larry Postaer, creative director at the Honda agency, claimed, "That was a direct steal from us." But Burnett executives denied pilfering the visual. Burnett president Rick Fizdale said he wasn't even familiar with the Honda ad.

That's been the historical pattern of the debate: angry accusations followed by denials, and then everything blows over until next time. Some advertisers try to ignore the problem by convincing themselves that being copied is actually good. Hugh Thrasher, executive VP of marketing for Motel 6, says of his often-imitated Tom Bodett commercials: "We think these copycat ads just remind people of the originality of our concept." Others like Nancy Shalek, president

of LA.'s Shalek Agency, maintain, "If you haven't been ripped off, you're really in trouble."

The debate won't end soon. Part of the problem is that creative advertising is essentially derivative, popular movies, books, and music providing the basis for countless ads. As Millie Olson, executive creative director at Ketchum Advertising, San Francisco, points out, "We try to follow the trends and speak the language people are speaking."

The moment a genuine breakthrough occurs, everybody jumps on the bandwagon. Some of the best—and most imitated—recent campaigns include the shaky-camera spots for AT&T and the humorous caricature spots created by Joe Sedelmaier for Alaska Airlines. It's easy to copy these ads' style because plagiarism is almost impossible to prove. The only rule seems to be: make enough changes to avoid being so obvious that you draw flak from the originator.

Surprisingly, clients are avoiding the debate over copycat advertising. Perhaps that's because they're more comfortable with well-worn ideas than with bold, original concepts. The attitude seems to be that ads are just tools of the trade. If it works for the competition, why not use it?

numerous repetitions of the advertiser's theme, the listener begins to associate the music with the product. This is called a **musical logotype.**

Advertisers have three sources of music. They can buy the use of a tune from the copyright owner, which is usually expensive. They can use a melody in the public domain, which is free. Or they can hire a composer to write an original tune. Some original tunes, including Coke's song "I'd like to teach the world to sing" mentioned in Chapter 1, have become popular hits.

Slice of Life (Problem Solution)

The **slice of life** commercial is a little drama that portrays a fictional real-life situation. It usually starts with just plain folks, played by professional actors, discussing some problem. The situation is usually tense, full of stress—for example, the need to get a package delivered overnight for an important meeting. Often, the situation deals with something of a personal nature—bad breath, loose dentures, dandruff, B.O., or yellow laundry. A relative or a co-worker drops the hint, the product is tried, and the next scene shows the result—a happier, cleaner, more fragrant person off with a new date. The drama always concludes with a successful trial. Played with the proper drama, such commercials can get attention and create interest. While they are often irritating to viewers and hated by copywriters, their messages still break through the psychological screens and sell.[23]

The key to effective slice-of-life commercials is simplicity. The ad should concentrate on one product benefit and make it memorable. Often, a **mnemonic device** can dramatize the product benefit and trigger instant recall.

The real crux of the problem is that imitation is an accepted part of the business, at least unofficially. Many art directors and writers collect competitive ads for use as inspiration. Advertising is such a highly collaborative process that it's often difficult to determine each individual's creative contribution. With personal responsibility so unclear, it becomes easier to ignore professional ethics.

But every so often, someone creates an ad that goes beyond the "gray zone." One campaign promoted Mint Condition, a new candy for smokers. The ad showed a cowboy on a horse coming toward the reader. In the foreground were two flip-top boxes of mints; the theme under them read: "Come to Mint Condition." Visually, it was a dead ringer for a classic Marlboro ad right down to the typeface. Mint Condition's president, Joel Gayner, defended the ads, saying they "make something even more original by changing it three degrees." Philip Morris's lawyers weren't amused by the parody and considered an infringement suit.

Even flagrant infringement cases are very hard to win because ideas aren't protected by copyright laws, and creative advertising is an idea business. That's why some industry leaders are passionate about the need for personal ethics. As Jim Golden, executive producer of DMH MacGuffin, says, "All we have in this business are creativity and ideas. The moment someone infringes on that, they're reaching into the very core of the business and ripping it out." Ultimately, if the problem is ever to be solved, advertisers must stop "borrowing" ideas from each other and demand greater creativity from themselves.

Questions

1. Some art directors claim that "independent invention" explains why many ads look the same. Is that possible? If so, does it excuse running imitative advertising—or should the originator of an idea be the only one allowed to use it?

2. Should clients be more concerned about the ethics of copycat advertising? What would you do if a client asked you to copy an ad that was already running?

Users of Imperial Margarine suddenly discover crowns on their heads, for example; or the doorbell rings for the Avon representative.

Joe Sedelmaier, a Chicago television commercial producer, developed a unique, recognizable style of humor out of the slice-of-life form.[24] He turns Everyman's trials of daily life into caricatures. He builds sympathy for his beaten-down characters, and then offers a solution, as in the Alaska Airlines commercial in Exhibit 9–15.

A variation on the slice-of-life technique makes the believability almost painful to watch. Anacin, for example, combined the slice-of-life and testimonial forms by showing highly believable, depressing headache complaints from a sooty coal miner, a weather-beaten farmer, and a plain-looking housewife—all actors, of course. Such ads, which approach the cinema verité art form with their natural lighting, subdued colors, erratic motion, extreme close-ups, and grainy film quality, have been used by a variety of advertisers, including AT&T, Home Savings, and Hospital Corporation of America.[25]

Believability is difficult to achieve. People don't really talk about "ring around the collar," so the actors must be highly credible to put the fantasy across. That's why most local advertisers don't—and shouldn't—use the slice-of-life technique. Creating that believability takes very professional talent and money. (Chapter 11 presents a "tasteful" slice-of-life commercial in the Creative Department: From Concept through Production of a Television Commercial.) In all cases, the story should be relevant to the product and simply told.

Lifestyle

To present the user rather than the product, advertisers may use the **lifestyle** technique. For example, Levi's targets its 501 Jeans messages to young, contemporary men by showing characters working in a variety of occupations and participating in a variety of pasttimes. Likewise, beer and soft-drink advertisers frequently target their messages to active, outdoorsy, young people, focusing on who drinks the brand rather than on specific product advantages.

Animation

Cartoons, puppet characters, and animated demonstrations are very effective in communicating difficult messages and in reaching specialized markets such as children. The way in which aspirin or other medications affect the human system is difficult to explain. Animated pictures of headaches and stomachs, however, can simplify the subject and make a demonstration understandable.

Today, computer-generated graphics animate television commercials for everything from high-tech products to bathroom cleaner. (This will be more fully discussed in Chapter 11, "Creative Production: Electronic Media.") TRW, for instance, used state-of-the-art computerized animation to enhance the message that TRW is future-oriented. Computer animation requires a great deal of faith on the part of advertisers; since most of this very expensive work is done on the computer, there's nothing to see until the animation is well developed.[26]

Basic Mechanics of Storyboard Development

After the creative team selects the big idea and the format for a television commercial, the art director and the writer develop the script. As we discussed in Chapter 8, the script describes the video on the left side and the audio on the right. Television is so visually powerful and expressive, the art director's role is particularly important.[27] Art directors must be able to work with a variety of professionals—producers, directors, technicians, and artists—to successfully develop and produce a commercial.

EXHIBIT • 9-15

This classic TV commercial produced by Joe Sedelmaier for Alaska Airlines uses a humorous *slice-of-life* format. Here, Everyman confronts the insult of being searched before boarding a plane. The Livingston agency's rough storyboard suggests a good-looking, tall character. But Sedelmaier's character, a short, stocky man, serves as a metaphor for that feeling of insignificance many passengers experience in the inspection line.

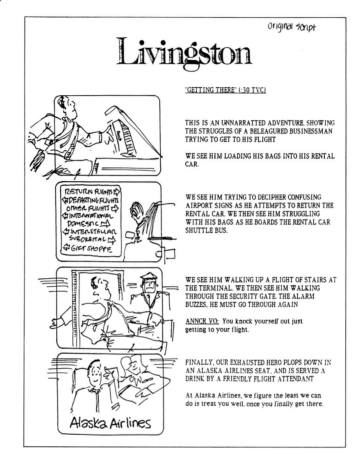

Getting There
30 seconds
(SFX: Sound of bus pulling up and screeching to a stop)
Fade up on a packed bus speeding into an airport and stopping.
(SFX: Sounds of people bumping into each other, music begins)
Quick cuts of man being thrown forward, other passengers falling out the bus door, and with the man on a crowded people-mover in the airport struggling with his bag.

(SFX: Alarm rings every time he falls)
Dissolve to man going through the security gate and triggering the alarm. Cut to him going through again, cut to him, jacket off, trying again. Cut to him trying again without vest and tie. Cut to naked man behind a screen being searched with a metal detector.
VO: You knock yourself out just getting to your flight.
Dissolve to the very disheveled man on another crowded people-mover tucking in his shirt and struggling with his bags.

VO: That's why . . .
Dissolve to Alaska Airlines ticket agent handing the man his ticket.
VO: . . . at Alaska Airlines, we figure the least we can do is treat you well once you finally get here.
Dissolve to the worn-out man finally in his seat. He smiles as the stewardess takes his jacket and hands him some orange juice. Dissolve to Alaska Airlines plane in the sky.

EXHIBIT • 9-16

Cut, Zoom, and Wipe, Please! (Common abbreviations used in TV scripts).

CU: Close-up. Very close shot of person or object.

ECU: Extreme close-up. A more extreme version of the above. Sometimes designated as BCU (big close-up) or TCU (tight close-up).

MCU: Medium close-up. Emphasizes the subject but includes other objects nearby.

MS: Medium shot. Wide-angle shot of subject but not whole set.

FS: Full shot. Entire set or object.

LS: Long shot. Full view of scene to give effect of distance.

DOLLY: Move camera toward or away from subject. Dolly in (DI), dolly out (DO), or dolly back (DB).

PAN: Scan from one side to the other.

ZOOM: Move in or out from the subject without blurring.

SUPER: Superimpose one image on another—as showing lettering over a scene.

DISS: Dissolve (also DSS). Fade out one scene while fading in another.

CUT: Instant change of one picture to another.

WIPE: Gradually erase picture from screen. (Many varied effects are possible.)

VO: Voice-over. An off-screen voice, usually the announcer's.

SFX: Sound effects.

DAU: Down and under. Sound effects fade as voice comes on.

UAO: Up and over. Voice fades as sound effects come on.

THE ROLE OF ART DIRECTION IN PERSPECTIVE

Storyboard Design

Once the basic script is completed, the art director must turn the video portion of the script into real images. This is done with a **storyboard,** a sheet pre-printed with a series of 8 to 20 blank windows (frames) in the shape of television screens. Below each frame is room to place the text of the commercial including the sound effects and camera views as noted by abbreviations like those in Exhibit 9–17.

Through a process similar to laying out a print ad—thumbnail, rough, comp—the artist carefully designs how each scene should appear, arranging actors, scenery, props, lighting, and camera angles to maximize impact, beauty, and mood. The storyboard helps visualize the commercial's tone and sequence of action, discover any conceptual weaknesses, and make presentations for management approval. It also serves as a guide for filming.

Even when designed to the level of a comp, though, the storyboard is, at best, only an approximation. Actual production often results in many changes in lighting, camera angle, focal point, and emphasis. The camera sees many things that the artist couldn't visualize, and vice versa (see Chapter 11, "Creative Production: Electronic Media," for more details on working with storyboards).

Animatic—The Video Comp

During the last decade, TV production and media costs soared, pressuring agencies to pretest their commercials before final production. To supplement the storyboard or pretest a concept, therefore, a commercial may be taped in rough form using the writers and artists as actors.[28] Or an **animatic** may be shot—a film strip composed of the sketches in the storyboard accompanied by the audio portion of the commercial synchronized on tape.

However, even an animatic now costs $10,000 or more to produce. But computers are having a cost-saving impact. Peter Farago of Farago Advertising, for example, developed a Macintosh-based random-access computerized editing system that enables the agency to create moving pictures on the screen (after scanning storyboard sketches into the computer), lay sound behind them, and transfer the entire package onto videotape to send to the client.[29]

This system cuts the cost to produce testable material from about $11,000 to $1,100. "We're doing video comps, if you will, on a Macintosh," says Farago.[30] Currently, Macintosh Quicktime software allows agencies to convert videotape sequences into digital codes for the computer, store them on disk, and place them into word processing and presentation software. This technology is being adopted by more and more agencies as they look for ways to serve their clients' creative needs better for less money.

Upon approval of the storyboard and/or the animatic, the commercial is ready for production, a subject we cover in detail in Chapter 11, "Creative Production: Electronic Media."

Many "rules" of good design—whether for print or electronic media—express current thought and experience. But rules won't create a great looking ad, an exciting commercial, or an outstanding package design. To do the job well, the art director needs to push—to bend and sometimes break rules—while still maintaining standards of good taste. That's a ticklish task. But art direction is not science, and that's why they call it art.

Summary

Every ad uses art. In advertising, art refers to the whole visual presentation of the commercial or ad including how the words in the ad are arranged, the size and style of type, whether photographs or illustrations are used, and how actors are placed in a TV commercial.

The many types of artists involved in advertising include art directors, graphic designers, illustrators, and production artists, to name a few. Each is trained to handle a particular specialty.

For print advertising, the first work from the art department is a rough design of the ad's layout. The layout has four purposes: it shows where the parts of the ad are to be placed; it is an inexpensive way to explore creative ideas; it helps the creative team check the ad's psychological or symbolic function; and it serves as a blueprint for the production process.

Several steps are used to develop an ad's design: thumbnail sketch, rough layout, and comprehensive layout. The mechanical is the final art ready for reproduction. Brochures and other multipage materials use a three-dimensional rough called a dummy. For television, the rough design is referred to as a storyboard.

In print advertising, the visual has a great deal of responsibility for an ad's success. The picture may be used to capture the reader's attention, identify the subject of the ad, create a favorable impression, or for a host of other reasons.

The two basic devices for illustrating an ad are photography and drawings. Photography can make several important contributions: realism; a feeling of immediacy; a feeling of live action; the special enhancement of mood, beauty, and sensitivity; and speed, flexibility, and economy. Drawn illustrations do many of these things, too, and may be used if the artist feels they can achieve greater impact than photos. The chief focus for visuals may be the product in a variety of settings, or a user benefit, a humorous situation, a testimonial, or even some negative appeal.

Art direction for international markets requires an indepth knowledge of the foreign culture. Even if the translation of verbal message works well, the icons and images may not.

Today companies spend as much money on packaging as on advertising primarily because of increased emphasis on self-service. Some factors to consider in packaging design include how the package communicates verbally and nonverbally, the prestige desired, and ease of use. Companies change their package designs to align the package more closely with the product's marketing strategy, emphasize the product's benefits, emphasize the product's name, or take advantage of new materials.

In radio and TV advertising, art also plays an important role and includes concept development, character definition, set and scene design, costuming, lighting, scripting, and camera angles—everything having to do with the visual value of the commercial.

Common formats for radio and TV commercials include straight announcement, presenter, testimonial, demonstration, musical, slice of life, lifestyle, and animation. The art director must work with writers and artists to develop the artistic qualities of the big idea, the format, and the storyboard. The storyboard, the basic rough design of a TV commercial, includes sketches of the scenes along with the script. To supplement the storyboard and pretest a commercial, an animatic may be used.

Questions for Review and Discussion

1. Choose any television commercial shown in this text. How would you describe the "art" in that commercial?
2. Select a print ad of your choice. What type of artists probably developed and finalized its look and visuals?
3. What is a layout? What is its purpose?
4. What color stimulates sales best? Why?
5. What is a mechanical? How is it used?
6. What color is white space?
7. What is the purpose of a picture in an advertisement? When would you not use a visual?
8. What is a storyboard, and what is its role?
9. How is an art director important to the creation of a radio commercial?
10. What television spots typify the eight major types of television commercials?

Creative Production: Print Media

Objective: To introduce the creative and technically complex field of print production. With their dynamic effect on the production process, computers are giving advertisers many more options to save money and time, and enhance production quality. Yet advertisers still need a basic knowledge of typology and printing.

After studying this chapter, you will be able to:

- Discuss the role of computers in the print production process.

- Explain the production process ads and brochures go through from concept through final production.

- Describe the characteristics of the five major type groups.

- Understand how type is structured and measured.

- Discuss how materials for printing are prepared for the press.

- Define common printing terms like sheetwise and work & turn.

- Debate the advantages of the major printing methods used today.

They finally decided to let Raphaële do it—with Bob's help.

Steve Makransky, art director at Young & Rubicam, had the big idea for a business-to-business campaign for NYNEX, one-stop supplier for the Fortune 500 companies with sophisticated communications or computer networking problems.

The ads were going to appear in special-interest sports publications like *Tennis* and *Golf Digest*, magazines read by top business executives and corporate CEOs who attend sporting events and belong to the country club set. The goal: to promote the idea that NYNEX was more than just a local phone company for New York and New England. Steve and his writing partner would tie into the sporting theme with a series of ads featuring stunning visuals and teasing word-play headlines.

The big idea was: "With us it's not a game" above a picture that—at first glance—appeared to be a city skyline. But on second glance, the eye would spot something awry—chess pieces the size of skyscrapers? Nifty idea. But it presented a real problem—how to do it.

They considered using an illustration first, but the client rejected the idea; it wasn't realistic enough. Photography was the next logical choice. But because the subject was a *concept*, not a real object, a photo would need heavy modification. They turned to a special-effects photographer. His suggestion: construct a model city. How long would it take? Too long. At what cost? Too much. They had to look elsewhere.

During the conceptual phase, the creative team easily envisioned the cityscape, and Makransky easily sketched out the idea. But to actually produce the image was another matter entirely—a common problem in advertising. The production process is where every ingenious creative approach—every vision—crashes head-on into physical reality.

They considered a third approach: Transfer images of buildings onto heat-sensitive materials that could then be shrinkwrapped onto the chess pieces. They could photograph the chess pieces and then photocomposite them onto a stock photo of the city. A step in the right direction but still not good enough to work in real life. Wrapped around the chess pieces, the images warped so badly they became totally unbelievable.

At that time, Alistair Gillett was Y&R's senior vice president and top art buyer. He remembered a Budweiser campaign with striking images created by a retoucher using sophisticated computer imaging. Gillett fired off a call to Houston, Texas, and contacted Raphaële. A transplanted French woman, she owned Raphaële Digital Transparencies and a secret, multimillion-dollar mainframe computer system named "Bob." Alistair explained the job to her, and Raphaële promised she and Bob could deliver the desired image. All she needed was the shot of the cityscape and the photos of the chess pieces.

Makransky worked with photographer Bill White, shooting each white ivory chess piece from eight different angles. For the cityscape, the agency reviewed a wide variety of **stock photos**—pictures already photographed for a different purpose and available for lease. They selected a beautiful business skyline of downtown Dallas by photographer Marc Siegel.

With the photos in hand, Raphaële first used a scanner to digitize each image of the chess pieces and the cityscape. Then she edited out the buildings where the chess pieces were to fit, cloned a section of blue sky, and dropped it into the space where the buildings had been.

Next, she digitally mounted and wrapped the textured images of the buildings around the images of chess pieces. To do this she created a three-dimensional computer model of each chess piece. Using specially designed software, the computer wrapped the building textures around each model and even put reflections in the windows to match the new surrounding environ-

ment. To complete the effect, Raphaële overlaid shadows and light from the
photos of the original chess pieces onto the buildings. The entire process—
including minor adjustments requested by the agency—took about five weeks
from beginning to end.

The final image was output as an 11″ × 14″ transparency and shipped to the
agency for completion. The finished full-page ad appears in Exhibit 10–1. The
effect was so stunning, it was later adapted to a full-page, black-and-white
newspaper ad and run in *The Wall Street Journal* and *The New York Times*. But
without the new, sophisticated production technologies available to advertisers
today, it never would have happened. ◆

THE PRODUCTION PROCESS

The average reader of ads has little idea of the intricate, detailed, technical
stages printed ads and promotional materials go through from start to finish. But
experienced advertising people do—especially art directors, designers, and
print production managers. In fact, they pay very close attention to every detail.
They know the details give an ad added impact and completeness. And when
an approved design goes into production, they have to remain vigilant because
the entire advertising effort can be radically affected by the outcome.

Role of the Production Manager

Every print ad represents the outcome of a highly complex process: reproduction of often-unusual visuals in full color; precise specification and placement of
type; and the checking, approving, duplicating, and shipping of printing materials to newspapers and magazines in time to meet their deadlines. These tasks
are the responsibility of the production manager.

The term **print production** refers to the systematic process an approved ad
or brochure design goes through from concept to final printing. Print production managers ensure that original designs are successfully printed. They must

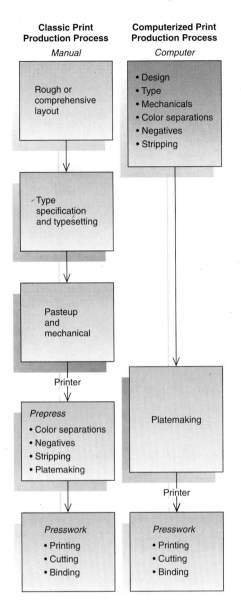

Classic Print Production Process
Manual

Rough or comprehensive layout

Type specification and typesetting

Pasteup and mechanical

Printer

Prepress
• Color separations
• Negatives
• Stripping
• Platemaking

Presswork
• Printing
• Cutting
• Binding

Computerized Print Production Process
Computer

• Design
• Type
• Mechanicals
• Color separations
• Negatives
• Stripping

Platemaking

Printer

Presswork
• Printing
• Cutting
• Binding

EXHIBIT • 10-2

Classic and computerized print production processes.

translate the rough or comprehensive design into a final assembly of black-and-white artwork called a **mechanical** or **pasteup** (or set of mechanicals). Then they make sure the mechanical is converted into a correct set of negatives for the printer to use to make printing plates. Printers use high-contrast, black-and-white photographic film negatives to place an image on the printing plate, so artwork must be photographed in black and white only. To create full-color printed images, the printer must make four plates—one to print each of four colors: magenta (red-violet), cyan (blue-green), yellow, and black. Each plate must be made from black-and-white artwork ready for the printer's camera to shoot. (We discuss this process more thoroughly under the heading "Printing in Color.") Production managers may observe the initial printing to be sure the final impression is not too light or dark, or the colors aren't distorted.

Although computers are revolutionizing the print production process, many companies still rely on traditional manual methods (see Exhibit 10–2).

When production people fail to follow a designer's layout correctly, they can destroy an ad's power, beauty, and effectiveness. If type spacing is too wide, lines too thick, photographs unretouched, or inappropriate illustration techniques chosen, readers will perceive a lack of harmony and have difficulty gliding across the ad. Improper printing processes, papers, or inks can also weaken an ad's appearance, increase costs, and even lead to reprinting. If an advertiser mistakenly uses oil-based inks to print promotional information on cereal boxes, for instance, rather than the lawfully required vegetable-based inks, the entire job will have to be scrapped and reprinted. Print production managers can lose tens of thousands of their client's or agency's dollars—and sometimes their jobs—by ignoring the details of print production.

A basic knowledge of production procedures can save a lot of money and disappointment.

Impact of Computers on Print Production

Enormous technological progress is taking place in graphic arts due to the revolutionary application of computers and electronics. As the model in Exhibit 10–2 shows, by using computer graphics or imaging programs on either large ($100,000 range) or small, affordable (less than $10,000) computers, today's graphic artist or designer can do much of the work previously performed by hand retouchers and pasteup artists. In fact, small IBM PC and Macintosh-based systems are ideal for **desktop publishing**—the process that enables individuals with desktop computers to prepare, and occasionally even print, moderate-quality ads, documents, and publications. On the screen the artist can see an entire page layout with illustrations and photos and easily alter any of them in a few minutes. With manual pasteup, such alteration could take hours or even days.

Larger, more costly minicomputer systems—such as the Hell ScriptMaster, Scitex, and Crosfield workstation—present even more opportunities and benefits. With a wide range of electronic options, these systems are the top guns of high-quality image enhancements and **prepress production**—the process of converting page art and visuals into the materials (generally film negatives and color separations) needed for printing.[1] Computers offer great flexibility. Artists can make changes quickly, they can get high-quality proofs immediately, and, with sophisticated software, they can flip, twist, rotate, or reverse images instantly. Finally, these systems produce high-quality output, whether paper for the printer to photograph or film negatives. Exhibit 10–3 shows various configurations of desktop publishing and related computer equipment used to produce prints or negatives. As we mentioned in Chapter 9, the desktop computer approach is also useful for creating TV storyboards.[2]

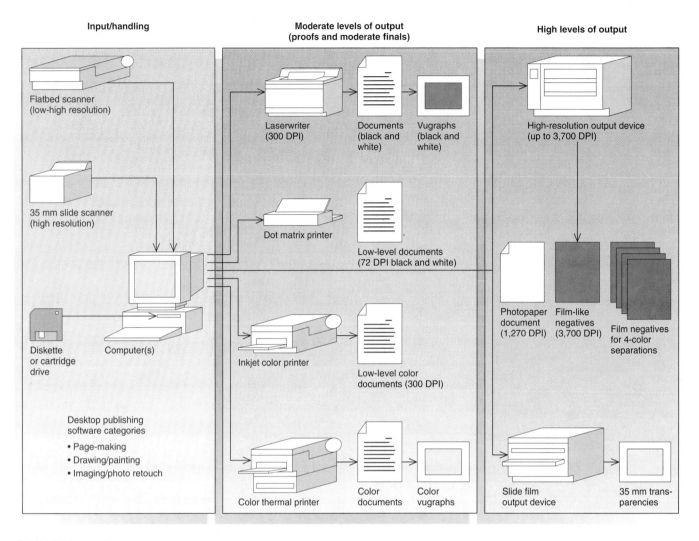

| Input/handling | Moderate levels of output (proofs and moderate finals) | High levels of output |

EXHIBIT • 10-3

Typical desktop publishing configurations. Once images are electronically scanned, specialized software lets artists manipulate images, set type, and create layouts. Moderately priced laser and low-priced dot-matrix printers produce color and black-and-white proofs of the ad. An expensive, high-resolution printer produces the highly detailed, accurate negatives used in printing.

Sophisticated graphics software is now available for personal computers for page making (QuarkXpress® and Aldus PageMaker®), painting and drawing (Aldus FreeHand®, Adobe Illustrator®), and image manipulation (ColorStudio® and Adobe Photoshop®). And moderate cost makes such software accessible to free-lancers, small businesses, and agency creative departments.[3] Personal computer graphics programs allow users a wide choice of classic and designer-type styles at low cost. Today, smaller shops—like Dahlin Smith White in Salt Lake City, Utah, creators of the ad in Exhibit 10–4—require only a couple of Macintosh II or Quadra series computers to produce camera-ready art on disk ready for printing.[4] The file can then be output by a high-resolution photo-typesetter as paper mechanicals or final negatives, saving time and money. Despite their speed, computers can actually *lengthen* design time. However, this extra time is more than compensated for because essential production steps take place simultaneously.[5]

Now even nonartists have the tools to do simple to moderately difficult drawings, charts, and photo-retouching. However, these systems can't turn an unskilled artist into a skilled one. Today's graphic artist, illustrator, and retoucher must be computer literate and highly experienced in a number of art and page-making programs—in addition to having a thorough knowledge of aesthetics, rendering, and design.

PLANNING PRINT PRODUCTION

Once the agency and client approve the design and copy, the ad or brochure falls under the supervision of the print production manager and a staff of production artists and assistants. In smaller agencies and in-house art departments, the art director may also oversee print production.

The print production department specifies the style and size of the typefaces to be used. If the shop doesn't have its own typesetting machines or computer systems, it orders type from a typesetting company. Type may be positioned electronically or output onto paper and glued on an artboard (usually a thick posterboard with a smooth, matte, or glossy surface) within an area the size of the final printed image. If an additional color is to be printed, another artboard marked to the same dimensions is used for the second image. Sometimes, the second image is glued onto a clear plastic **overlay** that lies on top of the first image (called the **base art**). The production artist first places crossmarks in the corners of the base art and, then, on the transparent overlay, superimposes additional crossmarks precisely over those on the base art. This registers the exact position as shown in Exhibit 10–5. When the printer makes the two plates, each pasteup (mechanical) has to be photographed separately. An overlay is removed and photographed separately from the base art. Then each plate is printed one after the other in its own color (printing the second set of registration marks over the first set), and the final printed piece comes together into a single page featuring both colors.

Artwork for a publication ad usually must be **camera-ready**—suitable for the newspaper's or magazine's printer to photograph to make negatives and plates. With computerization, many agencies just send a disk, and the publisher converts the computer image to negatives. Magazines often provide specific instructions and measurements for each of the ad sizes they offer.

When preparing a brochure, the print production manager may also get bids from several printers and order the printing. The production manager must be sure the printer understands all the technical instructions.

The production manager must decide early on which is most important for a particular project: speed, quality, or economy. The answer determines the production methods used and personnel employed. Typically, the manager must sacrifice one in favor of the other two. If cost is more important than quality, a high-grade copying machine can resize artwork more economically than a huge, wall-mounted production camera. If speed is most important, rush fees (which can easily triple costs) and overnight deliveries may be justifiable.

Working backward from publication **closing dates** (deadlines), the production manager decides when each step of the work must be completed. Deadlines can vary from months to hours. Generally, the manager tries to build extra time into each step because every word, art element, and most of the aesthetic choices may need last-minute change. The production manager informs the art director and copywriter of the opportunities and limitations of various production techniques and keeps them abreast of the job's progress.

Finally, the production manager must check all proofs for errors and obtain approvals from agency and client executives before releasing the ads to pub-

E X H I B I T • 10-4

Produced completely within the Dahlin Smith White agency (except for final negatives), this ad shows how the computer can keep smaller agencies on the cutting edge of creativity.

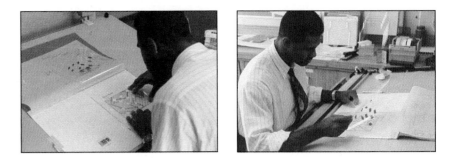

A mechanical (or pasteup) combines the main image (or base art) with one or more clear plastic overlay sheets (sometimes called a *rubylith* or *amberlith* overlay). Each overlay allows placement of a different color, and each may be photographed separately. In the printing process, the colors print one after the other on the same page to make up the total image.

lications. Proofing is a time-consuming task because not everyone is available when the work is ready for approval.

For the production process to run smoothly, everybody concerned must understand the procedure. Consider the problem of errors. The later in the process they're discovered, the more expensive they are to fix. Changing a single comma after copy is typeset may cost as much as $50, or $500 once negatives are made, or $5,000 if the job is already printed.[6]

The production process requires good planning, and those involved must understand art, graphics, typography, platemaking, printing, and color.

TYPOGRAPHY

Typography is the art of selecting and setting type. Because almost every ad has some reading matter, type has tremendous importance. Typefaces affect an ad's appearance, design, and readability. Although good type selection can't compensate for a weak headline, poor body copy, or an inappropriate illustration, it can create interest and attract readers.

Designers and production artists *must* know typography. The graphic designer typically chooses the typeface and suggests it in the rough art. When the artwork enters production, the production artist makes sure each typeface fits the rough layout in the proper proportion, size, and placement. Then he or she must correctly size and fit the type on the pasteup. Imagine the challenge of selecting type for the Celestial Seasonings ad in Exhibit 10-6.

Successful print ads—as well as brochures and other promotional pieces—embody a particular personality, mood, or tone. One ad may feature a visual of a skier in action, another a still shot of technical equipment. To complement the tone or mood of the visual, art directors carefully select type styles to enhance the desired personality of the product or ad.

To make their ads unique and exclusive, some advertisers even commission a new type design. The Volvo ad in Exhibit 10-7, for example, shows a bold, sans serif typeface designed by its agency's creative director.

Other advertisers strive for uniformity. Some tailor their typography to blend with the magazines or newspapers it appears in. This gives the ad an editorial look and, the advertiser hopes, enhanced credibility (or at least interest).

In the end, type choices help meet the objectives and strategy of the campaign by creating a link between the mood of the ad and the target audience's mental files and attitude.

Type Selection

The artful use of typefaces requires knowledge and experience. And in most cases, artists acquire this expertise only through long study and trial and error.

While the designer may suggest type styles in the rough art and choose which typefaces to use, it's up to the production artist to make the type fit properly for a dynamic final look. Imagine the challenge of sizing and fitting the various styles of type in this Celestial Seasonings ad.

Volvo owns the type style used in the headline of this ad. Such exclusivity helps keep Volvo advertising distinct and consistent—valuable assets for a company seeking differentiation and strong product identity.

As a result, among local advertisers, type selection is often the most overlooked aspect of advertising creativity.

Graphic artists need to know the five major type groups, the artistic variations within a family of type, and the structure of type. Ad Lab 10–A, "The Characteristics of Type" describes these and other type-related topics. As a general guide, advertisers should consider four important concepts when selecting type: readability, appropriateness, harmony or appearance, and emphasis. We discuss each of these briefly.

Readability

The most important consideration in selecting a typeface is readability. As David Ogilvy says, good typography helps people read; bad typography prevents them from doing so.[7] General factors that contribute to readability include the type's style, boldness, and size; the length of the line; and the spacing between words, lines, and paragraphs. An ad is meant to be read, and reduced readability kills interest. Difficult-to-read typefaces should be used infrequently and only to create special effects.

Large, bold, simply designed typefaces are the easiest to read. However, the amount of space in the ad and the amount of copy that must be written limit the use of these type forms. The length of the line of copy can also affect the readability. Newspaper columns are usually less than 2 inches wide; magazine columns, slightly wider. For ads, columns of copy should be less than 3 inches (18 picas) wide.

Continued on page 318

AD LAB 10–A   The Characteristics of Type

To understand the nature of typography, we need to look at how type is classified, how it's measured, and how it's set.

Classes of Type

There are two classes of type used in advertising.

Display type is larger and heavier than text type; useful in headlines, subheads, logos, addresses, and for emphasis.

Text type is smaller and finer, used in body copy.

Type Groups

Roman (serif) type is the most popular type group due to its readability and warm personality (you are reading serif type right now); distinguished by small lines or tails called **serifs** that finish the ends of the main strokes and by variations in the thickness of the strokes; comes in a wide variety of designs and sizes.

Gothic (sans serif) type is the second most popular type group; also referred to as **block** or **contemporary;** characterized by lack of serifs (hence the name *sans serif*) and relatively uniform thickness of the strokes; not as readable as roman but widely used because the simple, clean lines give a slick, modern appearance. (See Figure A.)

Square serif type is a combination of sans serif and roman typefaces; has serifs but letter strokes have uniform thickness.

FIGURE·A

Cursive or script type resembles handwriting; letters often connect and may convey a feeling of femininity, formality, classicism, or beauty; difficult to read; used primarily in headlines, formal announcements, and cosmetic and fashion ads.

Ornamental type—novel designs with a high level of embellishment and decorativeness; adds a "special effects" quality but often difficult to read.

Type Families

A **type family** is made up of related typefaces. The roman typeface you are reading now is called ITC Garamond Light. Within a family, the basic design remains the same but varies in the proportion, weight, and the slant of the characters. The type may be light, medium, bold, extra bold, condensed, extended, and italic. Variations enable the typographer to provide contrast and emphasis without changing the family. (See Figure B.)

A **font** is a complete assortment of capitals, small capitals, lowercase letters, numerals, and punctuation marks for a particular typeface and size.

FIGURE·B

Measuring Type

Type characters have height, width, weight, and, for some ornamental typefaces, depth. They also come in shapes called a case. And with the advent of computers, type also comes in a variety of resolutions.

Size is the height of a character (or letter) measured in points (72 points to the inch) from the bottom of the descenders to the top of the ascenders. (See Figure C.)

The **set width** of a letter, known as an **em** space, is usually based on the maximum width and proportions of the capital letter "M" for that particular typeface. Set width of the letter "N" is called an **en** space.

Capital letters are **uppercase,** small letters **lowercase** (in the "hot type" era, compositors stacked the case containing the capital letters above the one with the small letters). It's easiest to read a combination of uppercase and lowercase. Type may be set in all caps (for emphasis) or in **common-case** (caps and small caps).

Resolution refers to the fineness of the type. The goals of fine typesetting are readability, clarity, and smoothness of appearance. Type on a computer screen is usually 72 to 78 dots per inch (dpi). A dot-matrix printer outputs type at 144 dpi, a laser printer at 300 dpi. The preferred level of quality for magazines and brochures begins at 1,000 dpi; advertisers often use resolutions of 2,400 to 3,750 dpi.

Laboratory Applications

Use the various figures and terms in this Ad Lab to answer the following:

1. Describe the class, group, family, and size of the type used in the chapter title, "Creative Production: Print Media," that appears on the first page of this chapter.

2. Do the same for the captions that appear below the exhibits in this book.

Text type

6 POINT   SIZE of type

8 POINT   SIZE of type

9 POINT   SIZE of type

10 POINT   SIZE of type

12 POINT   SIZE of type

14 POINT   SIZE of type

Display type

16 POINT   SIZE of type

18 POINT   SIZE of type

20 POINT   SIZE of type

24 POINT   SIZE of type

30 POINT   SIZE of type

36 POINT   SIZE of type

FIGURE • C

Spacing between lines also influences an ad's readability. Space between lines of type allows for **descenders** (the part of the letter that extends downward as in the letters j, g, p) and **ascenders** (the part of the letter that extends upward as in the letters b, d, k). When this is the only space between lines, type is said to be "set solid." Sometimes an art director adds extra space between lines (called **leading** and pronounced *ledding*) to give a more "airy" feeling to the copy. The name comes from the thin lead strips that used to be inserted between lines of metal type.

Kerning—spreading or narrowing the spaces between letters—also improves an ad's appearance and readability. The narrower the kerning, the more type can fit into the available space. Narrow kerning is effective in headlines because people read large type faster when the letters are close together. But narrow kerning is hard to read if overdone or in smaller type sizes.

Appropriateness

A typeface must be appropriate to the product being advertised. Each typeface and size conveys a mood and feeling quite apart from the meanings of the words themselves. Some typefaces suggest ruggedness and masculinity, others delicateness and femininity. One typeface whispers "luxury," another screams "bargain!" A typeface that looks old-fashioned would generally be inappropriate for an electronic watch.

Harmony/Appearance

Advertising novices often mix too many typefaces, creating disharmony and clutter. Type should harmonize with the other elements of an ad—including the illustration and layout. Skilled artists choose typefaces in the same family or faces that are closely related in appearance.

Emphasis

Contrast creates emphasis. Artists often use more than one type style or mix italic and roman, small and large type, lowercase and uppercase. But they must be careful not to emphasize *all* elements or they won't emphasize *any*.

Copy Casting and Type Specification

Production people must know how to fit type into a set space. Computers can change type's vertical and horizontal size and adjust copy automatically within an assigned space.

But artists who don't use a computer and plan to have someone else set the type use a process called **copy casting** to forecast the total block of space the type will occupy in relation to the typeface's letter size and proportions. This is an important task because type is expensive to buy and costly to change. There are two ways to fit copy: the *word-count method* and the **character-count method.**

With the **word-count method,** the words in the copy are counted and then divided by the number of words per square inch that can be set in a particular type style and size, as given in a standard table.

The **character-count method** is more accurate. Someone counts the number of characters (letters, word spaces, and punctuation marks) in the copy, finds the average number of characters per *pica* for each typeface and size, and determines how much space the copy will fill.

Points

Type's depth (or height) is measured in **points.** There are 72 points to the inch, so one point equals 1/72 of an inch. The height of a line of type is measured from the bottom of a character's *descender* (j, g, p) to the top of its *ascender* (b, d, k).

The most common type sizes in advertising are 6, 8, 10, 11, 12, 13, 14, 18, 24, 36, 42, 60, 72, 84, 96, and 120 points. However, with computerized photo-typesetting equipment, any type size is possible (generally, in half-point increments). Smaller sizes, 6 through 14 points, are used for text type; this text is set in 10-point type. Larger sizes are used for display (headline) type.

Picas

The **pica** is the traditional unit of measurement for the width of lines of type. There are six picas to the inch and 12 points to the pica.

The width of a single letter depends on the style of the typeface, whether it is regular or bold, extended, or condensed, and the proportions of the letter. Type manufacturers and typesetting houses supply specimen books listing the number of characters per pica for each type style and size.

Specifying Type

The production manager and production artist also need to know how to **specify** type—i.e., write instructions for typesetters. Type specifications—a set of numbers and abbreviations—must be written beside the copy and usually accompanied by a layout. When specifying type, the art director or type director gives the typeface by name, the type size and leading, the width of the line of type in picas, and the justification desired. For example, the type you're reading now—10 point ITC Garamond Light on 12 points of space (2-point leading) on a justified line 28 picas long—would be specified like this:

$$\frac{10}{12} \text{ ITC Garamond Light} \times [28 \text{ picas}]$$

The brackets tell the typesetter to *justify* the type—set it flush to the margins on both the left and the right. Using only the left bracket tells the typesetter to line up the type on the left side only and leave the right side ragged looking. Using only the right one means to line all the type flush to the right side. Reversing the brackets—e.g.,]27 picas[—tells the typesetter to center the type.

Additional specifications must be given for each section that requires a different style, size, or alignment.

The art directors, type directors, or print production staff normally handle type specification. However, copywriters and account executives should understand the basics of type specification and copy casting since copy is often written to fit a particular space.

Typesetters—skilled specialists who work at phototypesetting machines—are a rapidly vanishing group. Desktop computers now allow almost anyone to fit type quickly and easily. Moreover, they do more tasks, and cost less to buy and maintain.

But desktop publishers also need to know how to measure type so they can instruct the computer how to fit it.

Typesetting Methods

Technology has revolutionized typesetting methods. Old "hot-type" composition (letters formed by pouring molten lead into brass molds) is obsolete. In today's "cold-type" era, letters are imprinted directly onto photosensitized film or paper.

Photocomposition

The dominant method of setting type for advertising materials is **photocomposition**—a combination of computer technology, electronics, and photography. Photocomposition offers an almost unlimited number of typefaces and sizes, faster reproduction at relatively low cost, and excellent clarity and sharpness.

The basic function of all phototypesetting machines is to expose photosensitive paper or film to a projected image of the character. The most commonly used equipment today operates by cathode-ray tube (CRT) technology or by laser scanning.

CRT Typesetters The first digital, computer-style typesetters, these machines use an electron beam to write digitized letterforms onto a cathode ray tube (CRT). The type image on the CRT is then projected onto photosensitive paper or film.[8] These machines can store hundreds of fonts and run at extremely high speeds. Digital typesetters replaced original photo-optic machines, and now desktop publishing systems are replacing them.

Laser Typesetters With the new computer-laser technology, type fonts and software programs can be stored digitally in a computer. As the computer turns the laser on and off, the laser beam "writes" onto paper or film. High-end machines use photosensitive paper and films producing resolutions of 1,270 dots per inch (dpi) on paper and 2,700 to 3,500 dpi on films (see the discussion of resolution in Ad Lab 10–A). Low-end laser printers attach to personal computers and work like plain-paper copiers, melting a black plastic dust to shape the letters. The resolution on these printers, from 300 to 1,000 dpi, is suitable for low- and moderate-level artwork like sales letters, flyers, and advertising coupon books. Laser printers are fast, reliable, and versatile, and they can also output graphics and half-tone pictures.

THE PRINTING PROCESS

Few advertisers have the necessary capital equipment and personnel to produce printed materials themselves. Instead, they hire outside print production companies who work at their direction. These suppliers may include a typesetting house, a color separator, a photoplatemaker, a printer, or a duplicating house (for newspaper material). Before printing, though, they must prepare materials for the press.

Preparing materials for the Press (Prepress)

Today's modern, high-speed presses—letterpress, rotogravure, or offset lithography—require printing plates. Printers use a process called **photoplatemaking** to create the printable surface on the plates.

Photoplatemaking begins by photographing a mechanical or pasteup to make a negative. The negative is laid onto a photosensitive metal plate, and the image is exposed onto the plate with ultraviolet light. The plate is then used for printing.

E X H I B I T • 10–8

Because the printing process lays ink onto paper in solid patches and lines, gray tones must be simulated. This is done using halftones—a technique where black dots share space with the white background to create the illusion of continuous shades. The enlarged halftone segment above demonstrates how the dots overlap in the darker areas and the white space begins to dominate in the lighter areas. The effect creates the appearance of dark transitioning to light.

Before the plate can be made, though, the artwork has to be prepared properly.

Line Films

Photographic paper (like a snapshot made with a camera) produces images in continuous tones from black to white with shades of gray in between. But the printing process uses only areas of solid ink and areas of no ink. Printers use **orthographic film,** a high-contrast film yielding only black-and-white images, no gray tones. So to be camera-ready, artwork has to be made without color and in black-and-white. All's fine if the artwork is simply typeset copy, pen-and-ink drawings, or charcoal illustrations. The artwork is simply photographed to create a **line film.** From that, a **line plate** is produced for printing.

However, a photograph or other illustration requiring graduations in tone cannot be reproduced on orthographic film or a plate without using an additional process—a *halftone screen.*

Halftones

While line plates print lines and solid areas (like type), halftone plates print *dots.* The key element is the **halftone screen,** which breaks up continuous-tone artwork into tiny dots. The screen itself is glass or plastic, crisscrossed with fine opaque lines at right angles like a window screen. It is placed in the camera between the lens and the negative. The artwork is photographed, and the resulting combination of dots, when printed, produces the illusion of shading like in a photograph. In the dark areas of the image, the dots bump into each other and make the paper appear nearly black. In the gray areas, the size of the black dots equals the amount of white paper showing through, and in the white areas, the black dots are surrounded by a lot of white or are almost completely missing (see Exhibit 10–8). The human eye, seeing minute dots of ink, mixes them with the amount of white paper showing through and perceives them as gradations of tone.

The fineness of the halftone screen determines the quality of the illusion. A fine screen has more lines and thus produces more dots per square inch. Screens generally range from 50 to 150 lines to the inch each way. Coarser screens are used to print on coarse, ink-absorbent paper because the ink spreads when it hits the paper and fills in white areas. Fine-quality, glossy magazine paper can take fine-screen halftones because the compressed chalk surface doesn't let the ink spread into the white areas. As Exhibit 10–9 shows, with a coarse screen the dots can be seen quite easily with the naked eye.

Different types of screens with unique and interesting irregularities are used to create special effects. See Exhibit 10–10.

When shooting halftones, printers often **flash** the film, a technique for lightening the darker areas to keep them from plugging up with ink during the printing process and looking blotchy.

Stripping

For each color to be printed, the printer must make a single negative of all the line and halftone artwork. Because negatives are usually smaller than plates, they are mounted onto orange paper or plastic sheets that serve as masks. These extend beyond the size of the actual negative and hook up with registration pins at the edge of the light table. The printer uses a process called **stripping** to mount the negatives onto these sheets of masking material and to

65-line screen

100-line screen

150-line screen

EXHIBIT • 10-9

Halftone screens help the printer control ink flow when trying to emulate the continuous tone quality of photos. On newsprint, where the ink soaks in and spreads, a coarse 65-line screen gives the ink some room between the dots. A finer, 150-line screen gives a better appearance, but it works best with magazine-quality paper that has a compressed chalk coating to keep ink from spreading.

register the negative within the dimensions of the plate along with any "sister" negatives used to print the other colors. Once stripping is complete, the plate is **burned**—exposed to an ultraviolet arc light. Dark areas of the negative block the light, transparent areas let light through to burn the image on the plate.

Thinking like a Printer

Advertising designers can save everyone's time and money by understanding the realities of printing and thinking like a printer. Early on they need to know what kind of press the job will be run on. Different presses accommodate different sheet sizes. Although bigger presses require bigger plates and bigger startup costs, the way the image area is used can make a larger press less expensive. But using too large a press wastes expensive paper.

Advertising designers also need to understand **imposition**—how the image to be printed imposes itself (fits) on the sheet of paper. Because printing is such a competitive business, a printer must find ways to get as many images onto one sheet of paper as possible in order to give the best bids and get the work. So imposition is extremely important. There are two kinds of imposition: sheetwise and work & turn.

Sheetwise Imposition

Say you are printing an eight-page brochure. In **sheetwise imposition**, half the pages would print on one side of the sheet and the other half on the reverse.

Work & Turn Imposition

In **work & turn imposition,** 16 page images would print on one side of the sheet (eight front and eight back pages). After the first side runs, the sheets are flipped over to the blank side, and the run continues using the same plate and colors. The images of each page are registered so they can be cut and folded to make two complete sets of pages in sequence.

Advantages of Work & Turn

Imagine you have to print the outside and inside of a brochure in two colors using a press that runs two colors simultaneously (two-color press). One printer has only smaller presses and is forced to use sheetwise imposition. The other printer has a larger press, with larger startup costs, but is able to run the job using work & turn (see Exhibit 10–11).

The printer with the smaller press faces three disadvantages. First, the outside of the brochure must run on one side of the sheet and the inside on the other. Since it's a two-color job, this means two plates must be made for *each* side of the sheet (a total of four). In contrast, work & turn imposition requires only one plate for each color (a total of two).

Second, the printer may be forced to waste paper because the image may fill up the maximum printing area on one axis but not the other. With work & turn, only half the plates are needed so there is less stripping, fewer negatives, and less handling, usually compensating for the cost of any wasted paper. In addition, a run with two images often uses the paper's maximum image area more efficiently.

Two-color texture

Random line

Mezzo tint

Wavy line (dry brush)

EXHIBIT • 10-10

Special screens lend an artistic look to photos. Whether the screens use lines, scratches, or some other technique, they work on the same principle as the half-tone dot screen.

Third, the small press is stopped halfway through so that last two plates can be mounted. With work & turn, the press isn't actually stopped, just put in neutral for a few minutes while the paper is turned over.

Traps

Designers also need to know how the artwork *traps*. A **trap** occurs where the edge of one color or shade overlaps its neighbor by a small fraction of an inch to assure that the white paper underneath doesn't show through. Proper trapping is crucial for an ad to project a quality image. If the production artist fails to trap the artwork properly, the printer has to slightly overexpose one negative (sometimes called a *fatty*) or slightly underexpose another (a *skinny*) (see Exhibit 10–12).

To save money and avoid trapping problems, designers often plan for the typesetting to **overprint**—print on top of—the background color with black ink. But when printing colored type over a different background color, the background color must let white show through so that the true color of the colored type won't be distorted. Called a **reverse knockout,** this requires careful trapping.

For full color ads, it's often wise to overprint text in black ink. When ads or brochures reprint, advertisers often make type changes. If the text overprints, the advertiser needs only to change the black negative and plate. If the text is any other color, all the negatives, stripping, and plating would have to be changed.

Bleeds

Finally, designers also need to consider **bleeds**—colors, type, or visuals that run off the edge of the page. Production artists must plan to leave at least a quarter inch of color outside the image area to accommodate variations in the printing and cutting process.

Methods of Printing

The objective of all printing methods is to transfer an image from one surface to another. Printed advertising materials are reproduced today by four major methods: letterpress, rotogravure, offset lithography, and screen printing.

Letterpress

For many years, letterpress was the universal method of printing. Johannes Guttenberg and Ben Franklin both used forms of letterpress. It was used for newspapers and magazines that needed reasonable quality with sharp contrast.

With **letterpress,** printing is done from a metal or plastic printing plate on a large round drum or cylinder. The process is similar to a rubber stamp. Like a stamp, the image to be transferred is backward ("wrong reading") on the plate. The ink is applied to a raised (relief) surface on the plate and then transferred to the paper.

With the advent of newer, higher-quality methods, very little letterpress printing is done in North America anymore.

E X H I B I T • 10-11

Imagine a printer has to print an 11″ × 17″ brochure (A) with a quarter-inch bleed on all four sides. Which imposition is best? A press that only handles paper up to 13″ × 20″ (B) requires sheetwise imposition and two plates (one for each side). A press that can handle a sheet up to 23″ × 29″ (C) could use work & turn imposition, which requires only one plate. If the press can run sheets 25″ × 35″ (D) and the press run is more than a few thousand brochures, the images can run "four up" for greater profit and use work & turn imposition. Short runs of a few hundred sheets are usually run on the smallest press possible.

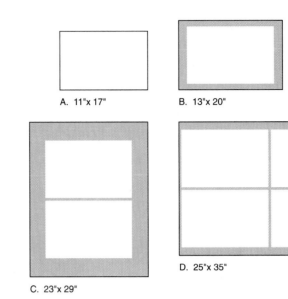

A. 11"x 17"   B. 13"x 20"

C. 23"x 29"

D. 25"x 35"

E X H I B I T • 10-12

Black ink can overprint a background color (*far left*). However, art or text printed in a color other than black should have no background color underneath. For example, if a blue letter "A" were to appear on a red field of color, a white reverse knockout would keep the blue from being affected by the red (*second from left*). If the blue letter "A" and the reverse knockout aren't properly aligned or the blue letter is smaller than the white knockout, the letters will not trap, and white paper will show between the two colors (*far right*).

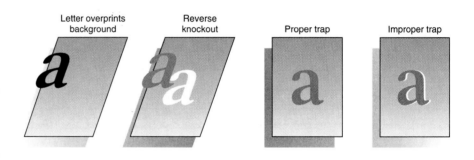

Letter overprints background   Reverse knockout   Proper trap   Improper trap

Rotogravure

Rotogravure is noted for good reproduction of color on both newsprint and quality paper and for its ability to stand up to long press runs. The process used in **rotogravure** differs from letterpress in several ways. First, two separate films are made—one for type and line illustrations and the other for halftones. The negatives are combined into a single film "positive." In the gravure process, even type and line art are screened.

The rotogravure process prints from depressed areas in the surface. Like letterpress, the image is backward ("wrong reading"). The design is etched or electromechanically engraved into a metal plate or cylinder, leaving microscopic depressions. Ink left in the tiny depressions transfers to the paper by pressure and suction (see Exhibit 10–13).

Preparing the printing plates or cylinders is time-consuming and costly, so rotogravure is practical and economical only for long press runs. Sunday newspaper supplements, mail-order catalogs, some major magazines, packaging, and other materials requiring a great number of photographs work well with this method.

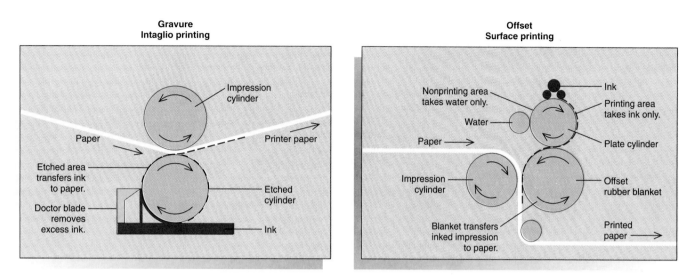

EXHIBIT • 10-13

The four major printing processes include letterpress, rotogravure, offset lithography, and screen printing. The most popular in advertising today, rotogravure and offset lithography, are shown here.

Offset Lithography

Today, **offset lithography** is the most popular printing process in North America. The printing plates cost less, printing can be done on almost any quality paper, and preparation time is short. Because the process is photographic, it meshes well with the most popular form of typesetting, photocomposition. Advertisers simply provide pasted-up art for the printer's camera (*camera-ready materials*) or film for the platemaker.

To the naked eye, the image on a lithographic printing plate appears to be flat instead of raised, as in letterpress, or depressed, as in rotogravure. And the image is "right reading."

The underlying principle in lithography is that oil and water don't mix. To start, a photograph is made of the material to be printed. The negative is then laid on top of a zinc or aluminum printing plate and exposed to light. Chemicals are applied to the plate after exposure, and the image takes the form of a greasy coating. The plate is then attached to a cylinder on a rotary printing press, and water is applied with a roller. The greasy image repels the water, the blank portions of the plate retain it. As the plate is covered with an oily ink, the moist, blank portions of the plate repel the ink. The greasy-coated image retains the ink for transfer to an intermediate rubber surface called a **blanket,** which comes in contact with the paper and prints the image (see Exhibit 10–13).

Lithography is used extensively for inexpensive advertising materials prepared at "instant" printing shops. Most newspapers and magazines use this process on high-speed offset presses. (They are called offset presses because the image is "offset" onto the blanket and then onto the paper; the paper and the plate never touch.) Exhibit 10–14 shows a high-speed, five-color offset press widely used today. Likewise, most books (including this one), direct-mail materials, and catalogs are printed by offset. And because it's suitable for printing on metal, most packaging materials, including cans, are also printed by lithography.

The high-speed Heidelberg five-color offset press prints magazine-quality publications and advertising materials. The first four units are used for four-color process printing. The fifth can add a protective coat of clear varnish over the printing page or lay down a fifth color (some art directors may want a "company blue," a specific color of ink rather than a combination of process colors).

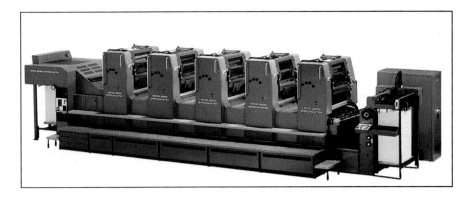

Screen Printing (Serigraphy)

Signs and billboards are examples of **screen printing.** Billboards use sheets of paper too large for many printing presses. Also, the quantities needed, especially for local campaigns, are so small it is often uneconomical to use other printing processes.

Screen printing, an old process based on the stencil principle, requires no plates. A special screen is stretched tightly on a frame. The frame is placed on the surface the message or image is to print on. A stencil, either hand cut from film or photographically prepared, is used to block out areas that won't be printed. Ink is squeezed through the screen by a squeegee (rubber rollers) sliding across the surface, transferring the image onto the paper or other surface. For printing in color, a separate stencil is made for each color.

Printing stencils used to be made from silk—hence the old term **silk screen.** Now they're made of nylon or stainless steel mesh. Today, automatic presses make silk-screening economical for even longer runs.

Printing in Color

An advertiser who wants to print an ad or a brochure in blue, green, and black needs three different plates (one for each color), and the job is referred to as a *three-color job.* Approved roughs usually indicate the number and nature of the colors.

Four-color process is the method for printing full-color ads with tonal values, such as photographs and paintings. This process can simulate nearly all colors by combining **process red** (also called magenta), **process blue** (cyan), **process yellow** (yellow), and black (which provides greater detail and density as well as shades of gray).

Designs that don't need four colors are printed in blended inks rather than process colors. For example, it would take two process colors (magenta and yellow) to make red or three process colors (magenta, yellow, and cyan) to make burgundy. When printing a brochure in black and burgundy, it's cheaper to use only two ink colors rather than black plus three process colors. So the printer would use black plus a burgundy colored ink.

A PANTONE® color, one of a spectrum of colors that makes up the PANTONE MATCHING SYSTEM® (**PMS**), is a single ink premixed according to a formula and numbered. They are displayed in swatchbooks featuring over 100 colors in solid blocks, screened blocks, and on a variety of materials (see Exhibit 10–15).[9]

Each printing process can print color, but a printing plate can print only one color at a time. For a job printed in full color, the printer must prepare four different printing plates—one for each process color plus black.

EXHIBIT • 10-15

EXHIBIT • 10-15

The PANTONE MATCHING SYSTEM® offers designers and production artists a way to identify a specific color according to a system of numbers rather than by a generic name such as "burgundy" or "reddish brown." The advertiser chooses a color's number from a swatch book, and the production artist designates that number on the mechanicals.

Four separate halftone negatives are needed to make a set of four-color plates: one for yellow, magenta, cyan, and black. Each of the resulting negatives appears in black and white; the set is called the **color separation.**

Until recently, most color separations were done using a photographic process. The original color photograph was photographed through each of four filters and a halftone screen. One filter let only magenta pass through, another only cyan, and so on. The halftone screen was rotated to a different angle for each separation so the dots did not completely overlap, allowing all four colors to show. If all the dots were superimposed, the image would appear as a dirty black (all the colors added together print as black).

Today electronic scanners can perform four-color separations and screening in one process, along with enlargement or reduction. Scanners are complete computerized color prepress systems capable of positioning illustrations and text as well as enabling electronic retouching.[10] In a single operation, an operator can change the density of highlights and shadows, modify contrast, change color, or remove an area or a whole piece. All this can be accomplished in several minutes instead of the hours or days previously needed for camera work and hand etching.

Regardless of the separation method used, when properly printed, tiny clusters of halftone dots in various colors, sizes, and shapes give the eye the optical illusion of seeing the colors of the original photograph or painting. In printing, the process color inks are somewhat transparent, so two or three colors can overlap to create another color. For example, green is reproduced by overlapping yellow and cyan dots. (See Creative Department: From Concept through Production of a Magazine Advertisement, p. 328.)

Selecting Papers for Printing

When preparing materials for printing, it is important to know the kind of paper the ad will print on. Some advertisers print their ads on higher quality paper than newspapers or magazines regularly use. Then they ship the printed material to the publication for insertion or binding.

Continued on page 334

◆

Creative Department

Marketing Considerations

As a strategic defense against the recent introduction of a dry soup mix by Campbell Soup, the Thomas J. Lipton Company introduced a new product of its own, Lipton International Soup Classics. Designed to fit the contemporary consumer lifestyle, the product was a high-quality, single-serving convenience food. It could serve as an integral part of a light meal (e.g., salad, cheese, soup), as an appetizer for a formal dinner, or as a nutritious between-meal snack. Available in five creamy recipes, the product could satisfy a wide range of tastes. The Soup Classics were distinctively packaged in black cartons with dramatic product photos prominently positioned to display the soup's creamy texture and large, freeze-dried pieces of meat or vegetables. Distribution took place first in the East, followed by the central and western regions and, finally the South.

Creative Concepts

Lipton wanted to target upscale audiences in its primary market areas. Its advertising agency, Young & Rubicam, suggested showing both the distinctive packaging and the appetite appeal of the product in one shot. Since the package face displayed a picture of the product, the art director, Gary Goldstein, proposed a *trompe l'oeil* (optical illusion) layout where a beauty shot of a spoon in a steaming bowl of soup would replace the straight product shot. The idea even included having the spoon extend beyond the edge of the package— making the soup look ready-to-eat right off the front of the box (see A).

A. Rough layout.

Shooting the Ad

To achieve the desired look, the concept required at least four photographs: one main visual of the package itself, one for the soup, one for the steam, and one for the row of other flavors. Working with a tight layout and acetates, the photographer carefully positioned the package shot and the soup shot so that the perspective and lighting would match. The hot soup shot was slightly overexposed to capture the steam, which was an important element both for the *tromp l'oeil* and the appetite appeal.

Preparing for Production

The creative department reviewed the film (shot in an 8 × 10 format) based on the original layout. Four *chromes* were selected, each having the color density needed for high-quality, four-color reproduction. Then a composite print was created to show the client for approval. Subsequently, a mechanical retouching and stripping guide was developed from stats of the photos and type and shown to the agency art buyer and print producer for their input. During a preproduction meeting, it was decided that it would be best to retouch this job on an electronic pagination system. Once client approval was obtained, the mechanical was given to the color separator, Potomac Color Industries, along with a timetable and the original transparencies. Reviewing the task with the separator, the following directions were developed:

1. Utilize the steam from chrome D (B) and photocompose into main visual (C). The steam should be transparent, allowing the background package to come through.
2. Photocompose the soup bowl (D) into main visual. Create a shadow of the spoon in chrome A on the surface of the table.

B. Chrome D, showing steam.

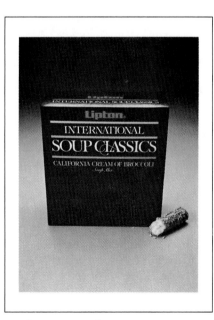

C. The main visual.

D. Chrome A, showing soup bowl.

E. Chrome B, showing package shots.

3. Photocompose the package shots from chrome B (E) into the main visual.
4. Color balance all packages and the background of the main visual.

A cost estimate was requested, and once approved, the job proceeded.

Production

First, each transparency was scanned into the electronic system, converting each of the images to digitized pixels. Next, at the computer workstation, the retoucher superimposed the bowl of soup on the main package shot and then added the steam to this composition. Behind the steam, the color had to be corrected very carefully to make the whole composition believable. Moreover, the steam itself was extended to break over the headline. A little soup was added to the spoon, and the drop shadow was created beneath the spoon.

From the computer's memory bank, the system was able to use a variety of selected applications as needed in the process, such as cloning, imaging, photocomposing, silhouetting, and vignetting.

When all adjustments had been made and the electronic retouching was finalized, Chromalins (slick, color reproductions) were sent to the agency for review and evaluation. After approval, the digitized film data with all corrections was stored in the computer for later disposition.

Typesetting

While this photo was in process, type had to be set for the ad. The art director and the copywriter, Marvin Waldman, submitted the rough layout and the approved copy to the agency type director. Together they selected a suitable type style for the ad. The type director then determined the size of the headline and carefully marked up the copy for the style of typeface, spacing, and size (see F).

The layout and copy were sent to the typographer, who set the headline and body copy with photodisplay equipment. From the film put out by this equipment, a photomechanical of the ad was created according to the rough layout. The copywriter, art director, and type director then proofed the mechanical for

F. Marked copy for typesetter.

G. Photomechanical.

errors and made whatever aesthetic or technical adjustments were required. The ad was then submitted to the client in this form for approval (see G).

When all adjustments and corrections in copy and artwork had been determined, the mechanical was returned to the typographer. The corrections were made, and the new photomechanical was then used to make a negative line film for delivery to the photoplatemaker.

Photoplatemaking

Once the corrected film data of the main visual was retrieved from the computer, four-color screened film was manufactured. A line negative of the typographic elements was then incorporated with these screened separations. From the negative, four-color offset plates were made and placed on the press. A set of proofs and progressive proofs showing the single colors was pulled off the press and sent to the agency for approval (see H). Minor corrections were handled by sending the job back to the computer or by hand through a process called dot etching on the offset film masters.

H. Progressive proofs (color separations).

Yellow

Magenta

Yellow and magenta

Cyan

Yellow, magenta, and cyan

Black

After client and agency product group approval, the master films were duplicated by the platemaker, and the necessary quantity of films, proofs, and progressive proofs were sent to each of the publications involved. The proofs were then used by the publications as a guide for color at the press to be sure that a faithful reproduction would be achieved (see I.).

I. Completed ad.

Advertisers use three categories of paper: *writing, text,* and *cover stock.* Letters and other direct-mail pieces commonly use **writing paper.** Bond writing paper is the most durable and the most frequently used.

The many different types of **text paper**—news stock, antique finish, machine finish, English finish, and coated—range from less expensive, very porous, coarse papers used for newspapers to smooth, expensive, heavier papers used for magazines, industrial brochures, and fine-quality annual reports.

Because it's thicker, tougher, and more durable, **cover paper** is useful for softcover book covers and some direct-mail pieces. It comes in many finishes and textures.

Preparing Materials for Print Media

Most local newspapers and magazines help advertisers produce their ads—frequently for free. The local business provides copy and illustrations, and the newspaper's production department takes care of the rest. However, such ads, often done quickly by low-level artists, rarely create a high-quality *look* and *feel* for the advertiser.

Advertisers who want better quality and more control hire agencies. Agencies know that one poorly made ad could hurt their reputation for creativity and quality so they prepare their own materials rather than relying on the media.

Many ads run in a number of publications at the same time, and the advertiser must provide prints or negatives for each one.

To find out what material each publication needs, advertisers consult the Standard Rate & Data Service *Print Media Production Data* directory, which gives the printing specifications and mechanical measurements (dimensions of ad space) of every major publication. (See Exhibit 10–16.)

EXHIBIT • 10–16

Standard Rate & Data Service publishes an extensive set of volumes listing the advertising specifications and measurements for every major advertising medium. This sample is for *Outdoor & Travel Photography* magazine.

OUTDOOR & TRAVEL PHOTOGRAPHY
A Harris Publications, Inc. Publication

Location ID: 18 PCLS 39   Mid 050225-000
Published quarterly by Harris Publications, Inc., 1115 Broadway, New York, NY 10010. Phone 212-807-7100. FAX: 212-627-4678.

1. PERSONNEL
Assoc Pub—Elaine T. Sexton, 212-807-7100; FAX: 212-627-4678

2. GENERAL REQUIREMENTS
Printing Process: Offset Full Run
Trim Size: 8 x 10-7/8.
Binding Method: Saddle Stitched.

AD PAGE DIMENSIONS			
1 pg	7 x 10	1/3 v	2-1/4 x 10
2/3 v	4-5/8 x 10	1/3 h	4-3/4 x 4-3/4
1/2 v	4-3/4 x 7	1/4	3-3/8 x 4-3/4
1/2 h	7 x 4-3/4	1/6 v	2-1/4 x 4-3/4

3. BLEED
BLEED AD PAGE DIMENSIONS
1 pg .... 8-1/8 x 11-1/4
LIVE MATTER 7 x 10

4. MATERIAL SPECIFICATIONS
SWOP Standards Apply.
Preferred Material: Positives, (Right Reading Emulsion side down).
Negatives, (Right Reading Emulsion side up).
PROOFING
Progressives 4 sets.
Rotation of colors: Black, cyan, magenta, yellow.
Inking TEXT: Type of ink 4A Standard Process; Paper weight 70 lb.; Paper stock type Machine Coated Stock.
Ink proofing: R.O.P. Head to foot; Black & White Head to foot; Black/Color Head to foot; 4-color Head to foot; Cover Head to foot.

7. ISSUE AND CLOSING DATES
Published quarterly.

Issue:	On sale	Closing (+)	(*)
Aug (Fall)	8/26	6/25	7/2
Oct (OTP buyers guide)	10/8	8/6	8/13
Nov (Winter)	11/26	9/24	10/1
Mar (Spring)	3/3	12/30	1/7
May (Summer)	5/26	3/24	3/31
Aug	8/25	6/23	6/30

(+) Space
(*) Material

For rotogravure printing, advertisers send color-separated film positives; for offset lithography, *photographic copies* of the mechanical and screened art. Such photographic copies may be **photoprints** (a screened print or a Velox) or color-separated contact **film negatives**, depending on the publication's requirements. Publications then make their own printing plates.

The print production process is very complex and, with expanding technology, highly technical. But it offers many new and exciting opportunities for those interested in the printing side of the advertising business.

Summary

The production process in print advertising is critical; if it is not handled correctly, an otherwise beautiful ad can be destroyed. Computerized prepress systems facilitate the production process —and make it more complex. A fundamental understanding of production techniques can save advertisers a lot of money and disappointment.

The print production manager ensures that the final ad reflects what the art director intended and that it meets time, quality, and budget constraints.

A typeface affects an ad's appearance, design, and legibility. There are two broad classes of type: display and text. In addition, typefaces can be classified by their similarity of design. The major type groups are roman, sans serif, square serif, cursive or script, and ornamental. Within each group are many type families. In a type family, the basic design remains the same, but the type varies in weight, slant, and size.

Type is measured in points and picas. Points measure the vertical size of type. There are 72 points to an inch. Picas measure the horizontal width of a single line of type. There are six picas to an inch. Type is also referred to as *uppercase* (capital letters), *lowercase* (small letters), and *commoncase* (large and small capitals).

Four important points should be considered when selecting type: readability, appropriateness, harmony or appearance, and emphasis. The process of determining how much type will fit a specified area is called *copy casting*. There are several methods used to cast copy today.

There are also several methods used to set type. The most important of these are the various photocomposition techniques including cathode-ray tube (CRT) techniques and laser exposure.

Printing processes have changed greatly in recent decades. Today, the most common types are offset lithography, rotogravure, and screen printing. Each method has advantages and disadvantages.

Preparing plates for printing involves exposing an image to a sensitized metal plate. Two types of images are used for printing: line images and halftone images. Line images print only two tonal values—black and white. Halftone images, like illustrations or photographs, simulate gradations of tone by using various sizes of black dots.

When full color is required, four halftone plates are used, one for each process color plus black. The colored dots print in tiny clusters, creating the illusion of full color.

For efficiency and economy, advertisers should understand impositioning and know how to select paper.

Questions for Review and Discussion

1. What effect have computers had on the print production process?
2. What is the primary role of the print production manager?
3. What are the characteristics of the five major type groups?
4. What does *copy casting* mean? Explain how it is done.
5. What is the importance of these terms: readability, appropriateness, harmony/appearance, emphasis?
6. What terms describe how type is measured? What do they mean?
7. What are the major differences between rotogravure and offset lithography?
8. What is a halftone? Why is it important, and how is it produced?
9. How are color photographs printed? What are the potential problems with printing color?
10. What do the terms *sheetwise, work & turn, traps*, and *bleeds* mean to a printer?

Polaroid.
REMEMBER IT WITH
POLAROID.

Creative Production:
Electronic Media

Objective: To present an overview of how radio and television commercials are produced. As in print production, computers are having a dynamic effect. Many techniques available today save money and time, and enhance production quality.

After studying this chapter, you will be able to:

- Discuss the difference between producing commercials for radio and television.

- Explain the process TV and radio commercials go through from concept through final production.

- Describe the major types of radio and TV commercials.

- Understand how to save money in television production.

- Discuss the opportunities for special effects in television.

- Define common electronic production terms.

- Debate the advantages of film or videotape.

n 1985, the Dallas-based chain of economy motels lost $20 million. It had no marketing department and no ad campaign. Its occupancy rate was 59 percent and sinking. Then it was sold in a leveraged buyout. New owners Kohlberg, Kravis, Roberts & Co. brought in new management, a new agency, and a folksy radio announcer from Homer, Alaska.

They added a few amenities, started building and acquiring more properties, and launched an aggressive nationwide campaign. They didn't use TV, newspapers, or magazines—just radio. Within a year, things changed dramatically.

Announcer Tom Bodett told listeners "We don't put a chocolate on your pillow like those big, fancy chains. . . . We'll only charge you about $20 . . . and we'll leave the light on for you." He convinced the car-driving public to pull into a clean, friendly Motel 6.

By 1988, his laid-back, folksy humor and the endearing, award-winning ads written and placed by The Richards Group (see Exhibit 11–1) contributed to a 73 percent occupancy rate and a record 12.6 million rooms sold. Today, thanks to radio, Motel 6 is the nation's largest chain of budget motels.[1] ◆

THE VALUE OF TALENT IN PRODUCING COMMERCIALS

Both radio and TV commercials need good **talent**—the actors, announcers, disk jockeys, celebrities, singers, and dancers who deliver the commercial message to the target audience.

Once the basic creative elements—the big idea and the script—are finalized, the next step is picking the *talent*.

EXHIBIT • 11–1

A simple radio script featuring the low-key, folksy humor of Tom Bodett enabled Motel 6 to turn its financial fortunes around.

ANNCR: Hi. Tom Bodett for Motel 6 with a few words about roughin' it. Well when you stay at Motel 6 you'll have to turn the bed down all by yourself, and go without that little piece of chocolate those fancy hotels leave on your pillow. Well I know it's a lot to ask, but for around 20 bucks, the lowest prices of any national chain, well you can't expect the moon now can you? After all, you do get a clean comfortable room, free TV, movies and local calls. And no service charge on long distance calls. No, we won't bring meals to your room on a silver cart, but that doesn't mean you can't get room service. Since local calls are free, just look up a pizza joint that delivers and give 'em a buzz. They'll bring that large pepperoni pineapple right to your door. So if you can tough it out all in the name of savin' a few bucks, well Motel 6 is where you oughta stay. We've got over 420 locations coast to coast. Just call 505-891-6161 for reservations. I'm Tom Bodett for Motel 6 and we'll leave the light on for you.

Because talent is a form of icon, the selection process is very important. The advertiser and the agency consider a number of factors before arriving at a decision: the person's reputation, acting skills and creativity, intelligence and style of thinking, and such natural assets as physical appearance, tone of voice, or way of moving. The unusual effect of Tom Bodett's vocal style proves how valuable good talent can be. Celebrity presenters such as Cher, Michael Jordan, Ray Charles, and Cheryl Tiegs, successfully contribute the aura of their persona along with a highly credible message. Indeed, many actors and professional sports figures earn more from commercials than they do from their "real" careers.

THE RADIO PRODUCTION PROCESS

Radio commercials—called *spots*—are among the quickest, simplest, and least expensive ads to produce. In fact, many stations provide free production services for local advertisers.

Some commercials are simply read live by the announcer, in which case the station gets a script and any recorded music to be used. However, the material must be accurately timed. A live commercial script should run about 100 to 120 words per minute, enabling the announcer to speak at a normal, conversational pace.

The disadvantage of live commercials is that announcers may be inconsistent in their delivery, and sound effects are quite limited. Uniform delivery requires a recorded commercial. The process of producing a recorded commercial includes *preproduction, production,* and *postproduction* (or finishing) phases (see Exhibit 11–2).

Preproduction

In the **preproduction** phase, the advertiser and agency perform a variety of tasks that allow production to run smoothly, on time, and within budget. An agency may assign a radio producer from its staff or hire a free-lance producer. The radio producer estimates costs and prepares a budget for the advertiser's

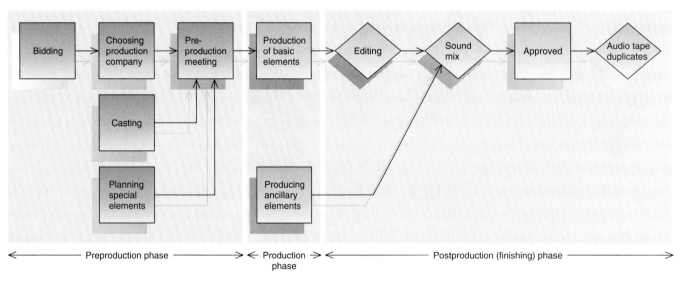

EXHIBIT • 11–2

Radio commercials have three production phases. The preproduction and finishing phases are usually the most complex. Preplanning and postproduction editing and mixing typically require far more time than the actual recording session.

dB-SPL

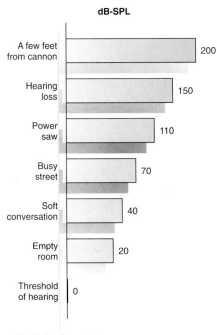

A few feet from cannon	200
Hearing loss	150
Power saw	110
Busy street	70
Soft conversation	40
Empty room	20
Threshold of hearing	0

EXHIBIT • 11-3

The range of human perception of sound, measured in decibels.

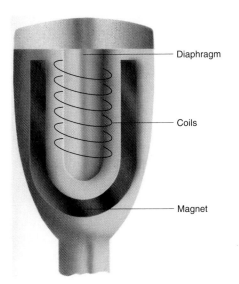

— Diaphragm

— Coils

— Magnet

EXHIBIT • 11-4

In a moving-coil microphone, sound vibrations cause the coil to move through a magnetic field, creating an electrical signal. The resulting electrical energy goes to an amplifier and then to an audio console for mixing and channeling to other equipment such as tape recorders or loudspeakers.

approval. For recorded commercials, the producer selects a studio and a casting director.

For greater control of the production process and high-quality sound reproduction, most ad agencies use independent recording studios. The best studios have experienced sound directors and technicians, close ties to well-known talent, and the latest recording equipment.

During the preproduction phase, the casting director searches for the right talent. If the script calls for music, the producer decides whether to use prerecorded music or hire a composer. The producer may also hire a music director, musicians, and singers, often after listening to audition tapes. Sound effects can be created or prerecorded.

Finally, a director supervises rehearsals until everything is ready for recording.

Production: Cutting the Spot

Sound recording and mixing take place at a **session.** Here, the voice and music talent perform in the studio using microphones. The sound engineer and director use an *audio console* in a control room to set the recording levels and channel sound data to the recording equipment—taking care to keep the levels of pitch and loudness within acceptable levels for broadcast.

The Nature of Sound

When air molecules vibrate, they form alternating rings of compressed and rarefied (decompressed) air, and we hear *sound*. One compressed section of air with one decompressed section makes up one **cycle,** and this is measured on the *hertz* scale. The greater the number of cycles hitting the eardrum per second, the higher the hertz, and the higher the sound's **pitch.** Most humans hear low pitches like rumbling sounds beginning at the 40-hertz (Hz) area and stop hearing high sounds like whistles at just above 15 kilohertz (1 kilohertz equals 1,000 cycles per second). The hertz cycles represent the number of high and low pressures passing by in a second, but they do *not* represent loudness.

Loudness is measured in **decibels**—the *volume* of air compressed in each cycle. Sounds become louder when air pressure is increased. (See Exhibit 11–3.) Pressures greater than 150 decibels can cause hearing loss.

The Use of Microphones

Microphones (or *mikes*) capture sound for radio and television commercials. All mikes, regardless of design, convert sound energy into electrical impulses, but each one does so in a slightly different way. Professionals use three basic types: *moving coil, condenser,* and *ribbon.* One major consideration in microphone selection is *impedance*—how a microphone's electronics and materials impede (slow) the flow of electrical impulses. If impedance is low, pulses flow more quickly, and the sound is less likely to be affected by electrical noise such as "hums" and static. The low-impedance, moving-coil mike shown in Exhibit 11–4 is the most widely used in broadcasting today.[2]

Professionals also categorize microphones by their *field of sensitivity.* An **omnidirectional microphone** captures sound from all directions; it has a spherical screen that protrudes from the shaft of the mike. A **unidirectional microphone** captures sound from one direction only and generally has a nonprotruding flat screen or one recessed into the end of the microphone's shaft. A **bidirectional microphone** captures sounds from two opposite directions simultaneously; it has a large, flat, two-sided screen protruding from the shaft.

Mikes can be further refined for particular approaches. The unidirectional **shotgun microphone** captures sound from long distances and is ideal for sporting events where the sound crew needs to capture players talking on the field. The small, unobtrusive **lavalier microphone,** used on TV and radio talk shows, hooks onto a person's lapel, shirt, or tie.

Studio technicians and engineers carefully select, disperse, and aim the appropriate microphones to capture the full spectrum of sounds. For radio, they usually hang the mikes from booms and place them slightly above the speaker's face. Or they may place a single mike on a stand directly in front of the announcer. For television and film, mikes may be *boomed* over the actors' heads out of the camera's view. When setting up a number of microphones, technicians separate them by about three times the space between the voice talent and his or her microphone to avoid the squeal of feedback.

The Studio, the Sound Booth, and the Control Room

The talent performs in a **studio,** which has sound-dampening wall surfaces, a carpeted floor, microphones, a window to the control room, and a variety of wall plugs for connecting equipment and instruments to the control room.

Standard items in the sound studio are the microphones, headphone sets, and speakers. An announcer wears headphones to keep verbal instructions from the control room from entering and interrupting the sound environment in the studio. Singers wear headphones to hear instructions from the director in the control room and to monitor prerecorded, instrumental tracks as they sing (thereby keeping the music track from being recorded onto the voice track).

The studio may have a separate **sound booth**—a small windowed room or partitioned area—to isolate drums or louder back-up talent so the sound technicians can better balance the overall group of sounds.

The producer, director, and sound engineer sit in the **control room** where they monitor and control all the sounds generated in the sound studio. They work at an **audio console** (also called a **board**), the central "switchboard" for channeling sounds to the appropriate recording devices. The board also serves as a sound mixer, blending both live and prerecorded sounds for immediate or delayed broadcast. The board connects to a range of recording and playback units including multitracking, reel-to-reel or cartridge ("cart") tape recorders, and compact disc (CD) recorders. A turntable may be used to mix music and sound effects unavailable on modern recording mediums.

The audio console features a number of switching and volume controls. Toggle switches, called **keys,** send the sounds either to the active program line or to an audition line (generally used for reviewing sounds for possible use on the program line). A set of **potentiometers** (also called *pots*)—relatively large dials or sliding linear buttons—control the volume of each device. The **gain** controls the overall master volume. **Volume unit meters** (*VU meters*) ensure that the total sound is not too weak or too loud (when overly loud, sound becomes fuzzy). VU meters have a digital indicator or a needle that moves from left to right as sound gets louder.

The board plays a role in both recording and postproduction. Disk jockeys often run live radio programs from a control room using a board. They mix sounds from carts and CDs into the program line along with their voices. Radio station producers use the same technique to record radio commercials. However, radio stations generally use tapes with 4 and 8 tracks on one side; professional sound studios use special tape decks that record 16 to 32 tracks on one side. Sound studios can blend many tracks together to create a very

EXHIBIT • 11-5

A sophisticated audio console manipulates sound electronically, making sounds sharper or fuzzier, with more echo, or more treble or bass. Ideal for recording radio and TV commercials, its multitrack mixing and sound enhancement capabilities are most useful during the postproduction phase.

powerful commercial. Professional studios often use enormous audio consoles, like the smaller one shown in Exhibit 11–5, with keys, linear sliding pots, and VU meters for all 32 tracks. Such consoles often require two sound engineers.

Postproduction: Finishing the Spot

After recording the commercial several times, a selection is made from the best *takes*. The sound engineer usually records music, sound effects, and vocals separately and then mixes and *sweetens* during the **postproduction** (or finishing) **phase.** Once completed, the final recording is referred to as the **master tape.**

From the Master tape, the engineer makes duplicates called **dubs,** records them onto ¼-inch magnetic tape, and sends them to radio stations for broadcast.

A radio spot is relatively simple to produce compared to the enormous complexity of television.

PRODUCING TELEVISION COMMERCIALS

Imagine you are the creative director for an agency. Your assignment is to create a TV commercial that will: (1) introduce a new line of beachwear, (2) communicate the California surfer mystique, (3) incorporate the bright colors and splash graphics of the company's well-recognized print ads, (4) punch the company name and brand hard enough to get national awareness, (5) stay true to grass-roots surfers, the traditional customers, while appealing to nonsurfing young people, and (6) get the spot noticed in the fast-paced, highly graphic MTV visual environment. You have 30 seconds.

Graphic designer Mike Salisbury got that assignment from Gotcha surfwear.[3] Fortunately Salisbury had been designing Gotcha's print ads ever since the company's founding in a Laguna Beach garage back in 1978. So it was natural to turn to Salisbury when Gotcha decided to move into TV—especially since Gotcha wanted its TV commercials to maintain the authenticity of the print campaign.

EXHIBIT • 11-6

The complex, colorful images featured in Gotcha's print ads also appear in its TV commercials. Technically complex, the TV spots incorporate live-action film, animation, and special effects.

By 1990, the little surfwear company was doing over $100 million in annual sales. Although Gotcha was no longer an "underground" company, it wasn't in a position to launch a nationwide network TV campaign. But MTV was affordable, and its demographics perfectly matched Gotcha's market—young males in their teens. Further, MTV's highly graphic visual environment seemed a good setting for the style Salisbury used in the company's print ads. See Exhibit 11–6.

Translating this concept to television, though, was no simple task. The company wanted a graphically interesting, fast-paced, hard-hitting approach that wouldn't alienate its loyal surfer customers. Gotcha wanted to show the fashions in a thoroughly modern California lifestyle setting—to update the surfing film look of the 60s—and to capture the contemporary look of beach culture. The footage from Gotcha's own surfing film two years earlier was a good beginning. But Salisbury ended up using a lot more. By the time he finished, he used every major production technique available.

Advertisers spend hundreds of millions of dollars to produce more than 50,000 television commercials every year.[4] For a local advertiser, a simple spot may cost from $1,000 to $20,000. National quality spots cost considerably more; the average is well over $125,000.[5]

As technology expands the production possibilities, costs and complexity result in greater specialization. Major agencies used to maintain complete production facilities in-house. Not anymore. Now they use outside producers, directors, production companies, and other technical suppliers. And they constantly seek more economical sites for location and studio shooting—often in Canada.[6]

As a result of specialization, advertising agency producers must be generalists, able to work with a variety of technicians to bring a spot's creative essence to life. They must have knowledge of the video and filmmaking craft—as well as the suppliers. And they must have the savvy to budget and spend vast amounts of money wisely. (Interestingly, women now outnumber men in this profession.)[7]

Today, virtually everybody involved in advertising must understand basic TV production concepts—the most common and most effective types of commercials, the basic terms and techniques, and the production process.

CHECKLIST   Creating Effective TV Commercials

◇ **Create a pertinent, relevant, unforced opening.** This permits a smooth transition to the rest of the commercial.

◇ **Use a situation that lends itself naturally to the sales story.** Avoid extraneous, distracting gimmicks.

◇ **Develop a plot that is high in human interest.**

◇ **Create a situation the viewer can easily identify with.**

◇ **Keep the number of elements in the commercial to a minimum.**

◇ **Present a simple sequence of ideas.**

◇ **Use short sentences with short, realistic, conversational words.** Be sure the script avoids "ad talk."

◇ **Let the words interpret the picture and prepare the viewer for the next scene.**

◇ **Write concise audio copy.** Fewer words are needed for TV than for radio. Fewer than two words per second is

effective for demonstrations. Sixty-second commercials with 101 to 110 words are most effective; those with more than 170 words are least effective.

◇ **Synchronize audio and video.**

◇ **Run scenes five or six seconds on average.** In general, no scene should run less than three seconds.

◇ **Avoid static scenes—use movement.**

◇ **Offer a variety of scenes without "jumping."**

◇ **Handle presenters properly.** See that they are identified, compatible, authoritative, pleasing, and nondistracting.

◇ **Ensure that the general video treatment is interesting and the commercial looks fresh and new.**

Students of advertising should also know these concepts to understand how commercials are made, why production is so expensive, and what methods they can use to cut costs without sacrificing quality or effectiveness. The Checklist for Creating Effective TV Commercials is a good place to start.

Techniques for Producing Television Commercials

Three major categories of production techniques are used today: *live action, animation,* and *special effects.* Mike Salisbury used all of them for Gotcha.

Live Action

Live-action portrays people and things in lifelike, everyday situations like typical slice-of-life TV commercials.

Salisbury used live-action shots to illustrate the California beach scene. To grab the attention of the 15-year-old male audience, one commercial opens with a live shot of a bikini-clad model. Throughout the commercials, as shown in Exhibit 11–7, scenes of surfers, crashing waves, vans with surfboards, and couples on beach blankets were interspersed with other effects in rapid-fire order to create the motion and impact typical of the MTV style.

Live action is the most realistic, but it lacks the distinctiveness of animation or special-effects—so Salisbury incorporated these methods too.

Animation

Animation—cartoons, dancing puppets, and demonstrations in which inanimate objects come to life—can effectively communicate difficult messages or reach special markets such as children. For example, it's hard to explain how aspirin and other medications affect the human system, so advertisers use animated pictures of heads and stomachs to make the demonstration understandable.

SALISBURY COMMUNICATIONS

EXHIBIT • 11–7

Storyboards incorporating actual photographs of live-action beach and surfing scenes showed Gotcha executives how the finished commercials would look and feel.

Advertisers began using animated TV commercials in the 1950s; today many are done by computer. This computer-animated commercial introduces Cool Mint Listerine.

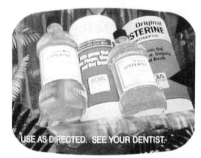

It kills germs. Just like it always did.
It fights plaque. . .
and the gum disease. . . Gingivitis.
Just like it always did.
Now it does one thing it never did.
Introducing Cool Mint Listerine.
With an exhilarating. . . cool minty taste.
New Cool Mint Listerine Antiseptic.
Works like Listerine,
tastes like cool mint.

Traditional animation techniques use *cartoons, photo animation, stop-motion photography,* and *video animation.*

Cartoons Commercials featuring **cartoons** often have the highest viewer interest, the longest life, and therefore the lowest cost per showing. However, many viewers consider them childlike, and initial production is very expensive. A fully animated commercial, for example, can easily cost $150,000 to $200,000.[8] Animators draw illustrations of each step in the action and photograph them one frame at a time. The film, projected at 24 frames per second, gives the illusion of movement.

Cartoons are sometimes supplemented by live action, especially for a serious purchase decision when product benefits must be described.

Photo Animation **Photo animation,** which uses still photography instead of illustrations or puppets, makes titles appear to move. This low-budget technique creates the illusion of animation.

Stop-Motion Photography In **stop-motion photography,** objects and creatures come to life—walk, run, dance, and do tricks. One of the best-known examples is the charming "claymation" campaign originally created for the California Raisin Advisory Board and later used for a variety of advertisers including Claritin (discussed in Chapter 6). Created by Will Vinton Productions using plasticene clay, the claymation characters are flexible figures with movable parts that can be bent to simulate walking or dancing. Each frame of film is shot individually, then the frames are assembled. The effect is smooth and natural, combining the whimsy of animation with the substance of live action. At 24 frames per second, 1,440 frames must be shot for each minute of raisin dancing.[9] Stop-motion is typically used with other famous puppet and doll characters like the Pillsbury Doughboy and the Snuggles bear.

Video Animation Today, advertisers use computer-generated graphics to animate TV commercials for everything from high-tech products to mouthwash (see Exhibit 11–8). However, this very expensive technique requires a great deal of faith on the part of advertisers. Most work is done on the computer, and the client sees little or nothing until the animation is well under way.

For Gotcha, Salisbury's initial ideas for film animation were too expensive, so he decided to use computer-generated graphics. He wanted to frame a live shot in a border of wiggling leaves, so he created the collage of leaves shown in Exhibit 11–9 and shot it on videotape. Then he created a second collage, repositioning the leaves slightly, and shot that. By toggling between the two tapes running simultaneously, the leaves seemed to wiggle. He recorded the leaves onto another tape called a *B-roll.* Then he ran the B-roll at the same time as the live-action tape, combining the two into a final shot.

Special Effects

Much video animation and most **special effects,** such as moving titles and whirling logos, can be done with a joystick. All major video production companies today use dedicated **digital video effects units (DVEs)** that can manipulate graphics on the screen in a variety of ways—fades, wipes, zooms, rotation, and so on.

Salisbury shot a fish graphic to video and imported it into the DVE. Then he digitally altered the graphic into two different shapes and, with the joystick, moved them across the screen to produce the swimming effect.[10] See Exhibit 11–10. The resulting psychedelic effect incorporates images used in Gotcha's surfwear fashions.

E X H I B I T • 11-9

To create a border of wiggling leaves for a Gotcha commercial, two different collages of leaves were videotaped. Computerized editing equipment allowed rapid switching from one collage to the other, creating the illusion that the leaves were wiggling. The live-action tape was then superimposed on this border.

E X H I B I T • 11-10

Sophisticated video equipment enables the creators of the Gotcha commercials to manipulate graphics. Here, the animators create the illusion of fish and other animals "swimming" through the basic scene. Though entertaining and effective, special effects can also be expensive.

Computers can also digitally manipulate music and sound. Sound designer Hein Hoven used the sound of windshield wipers as the underlying rhythm combined with a synthesized ballad music underscore and a discernible hiss of water to create a seductively intrusive sound for an AT&T spot.[11]

Special effects entertain viewers and win advertising awards. But if the sales message is complex or based on logic, another technique might be better. However, no technique should so enthrall viewers that they pay more attention to it than to the product—or the strategic message. Further, more than one fantasy or mnemonic device—Energizer bunny, jolly green giant, or Imperial crown—might confuse audiences. Fantasies must relate to the product's claims and be repeated heavily to make a strong impression on the viewer.[12]

The Television Production Process

The process of producing a TV commercial always involves three stages, as shown in Exhibit 11–11:

1. Preproduction—all the work prior to the actual day of filming.
2. Production—the actual day (or days) the commercial is filmed or videotaped.
3. Postproduction (or finishing)—all the work done after the day of shooting to edit and finish the commercial.

Each step has a dramatic impact on cost and quality. For a look at how all three affect the end product, read Creative Department: From Concept through Production of a Television Commercial (pp. 356–359).

Preproduction

Proper planning before production can save advertisers a lot of money.[13]

Casting must be completely settled before the day of shooting. Children and

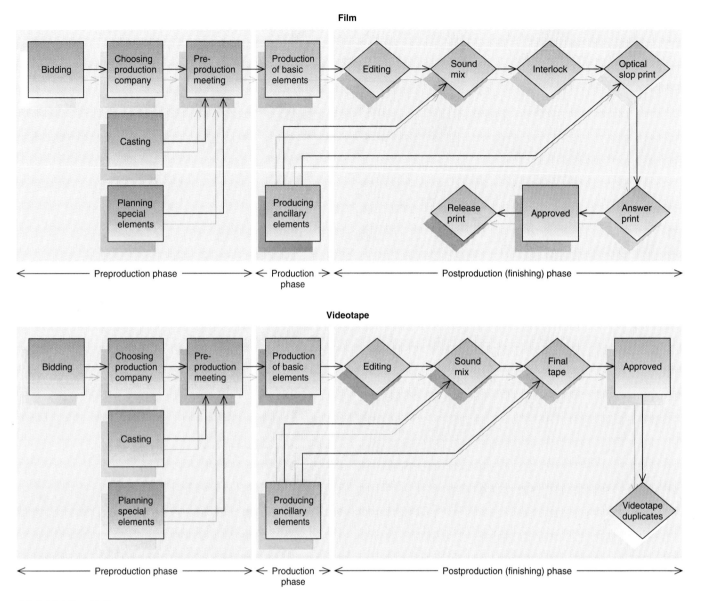

Film

Videotape

EXHIBIT • 11–11

The production process for film and videotape commercials is similar to radio spots. They differ in the finishing phase. Computerized video editing speeds up this phase considerably.

animals are unpredictable and often cause production delays. Rehearsals before production are a must.

Once the advertiser approves a storyboard and budget, the production process begins. The commercial is a group effort; the team includes a writer, art director, producer, director, and sometimes a musical composer and choreographer. The producer (either in-house or free-lance) is responsible for completing the job on schedule and within budget.

The agency producer usually sends copies of the storyboard to three studios for competitive bids. The bids include the services of a director, camera operators, electricians, and other technicians. The studio may do the film or tape editing or it may be done elsewhere. Exhibit 11–12 shows a typical advertising agency contract.

Commercial production contract form. A radio or TV commercial involves many specialists. A signed written contract spells out who will do what—and for how much.

WARWICK BAKER & FIORE INC.

ADVERTISING
100 AVENUE OF THE AMERICAS, NEW YORK, NY 10013
(212) 941-4200 FAX: (212) 941-4277
A PARTNER IN ALLIANCE INTERNATIONAL

DATE: _____
JOB #: _____

This will confirm our understanding and serve as a complete agreement between you and us (sometimes herein referred to as "Agency"), for our client, _____, for the production and delivery of _____ commercial motion picture film(s) and/or tape(s) subject to our approval and acceptance and in accordance with scripts and/or storyboards supplied by us, and in compliance with the attached "Film/Tape Commercial Production Specifications and Quotations" for use under any circumstances, on the following terms and conditions:

1. (a) Code number(s), title(s), and product(s) to be inscribed on the negative leader of each film or at the beginning of each tape.

CODE #	TITLE	LENGTH	PRODUCT

(b) Film(s)/tape(s) to be photographed in ☐ 35mm ☐ 16mm ☐ B/W ☐ Color suitable for television use.

2. Film(s)/tape(s) to be produced at mutually agreeable locations and studios.

3. You will be responsible for supplying every item and element for the above production as specified in the attached "Film/Tape Commercial Production Specifications and Quotations" sheet. You are hereby directed to use _____ as your subcontractor for the editing and completion of the commercials.

4. **Production Schedule:** It is agreed that the essential dates are as follows:

Photography: # of 35mm Film(s)/Master(s):

Answer Print(s)/Master(s):   # of 3/4" Videocassettes:

5. **Delivery:** Upon completion of the commercial(s), you will deliver all material as indicated on the attached "Proof of Performance & Delivery" sheet.

6. **Price:**

Shooting through dailies:	$
Editing through completion:	$
Duplicating master(s):	$
TOTAL CONTRACT PRICE:	$

Weather contingency: out-of-pocket costs up to $ _____ (any excess costs to be borne by you). The above prices do not include agency commission or sales tax. You will add total sales tax to your final invoice, if applicable. You agree to look solely to Agency for payment.

7. **Payment Schedule:**
   1/3 upon signing of this agreement
   1/3 upon completion of photography
   1/3 upon delivery of the film/tape materials and your final billing

8. Time of Production and Delivery are of the essence.

9. This agreement, with "Proof of Performance & Delivery" and "Film/Tape Commercial Production Specifications and Quotations" attached hereto constitutes the entire understanding between the parties and there are no other agreements or understandings, written or oral, in effect between the parties relating to the subject matter hereof. This agreement may not be modified or terminated orally.

10. Final 1/3   payment will not be made unless we have heard from the subcontracted editor that he has received payment.

11. All provisions and clauses on the reverse side hereof are part of this contract.

WARWICK BAKER & FIORE INC.

For and on behalf of: _____

By: _____

Agreed and Accepted:

_____
(Contractor)

By: _____

_____   _____
(Title)   (Date)

When the studio is chosen, the cast is selected and an announcer, if needed, is chosen. Next, the set is built, and the crew and cast rehearse under the director's supervision.

In the case of Gotcha, a very unusual event took place. Salisbury had a difficult time communicating his concept in storyboard form. His clients, unfamiliar with storyboards, couldn't visualize what he intended. So Salisbury did something radical. He booked a production crew and spent a day at the beach shooting scenes in 16 mm film. He pulled color still shots that he pasted next to his storyboard sketches. The next time he showed the storyboard, the client got excited—and the concept was approved. Now Salisbury booked the studios and the specialists he needed. He shot the live action in 16 mm film, which could be converted to video for editing and special effects.

The cost of studios, cast, crew, and equipment makes shooting days very expensive. Although delays must be avoided, some factors—like bad weather—are uncontrollable. Locations near home are best; extra days on location are extremely expensive.

In the preproduction phase, the producer and director must consider all these factors. Every aspect of the commercial's production should be discussed, decided, and approved by the client, agency, and production company prior to the shooting day.

During this period, preproduction meetings are necessary between the producer, the agency account representative, the writer, the art director, the studio director, possibly the advertiser, and anyone else important to the production. They should iron out any last-minute problems and make final decisions about the scenes, the actors, or the announcer. They should review everything—music, sets, the action, lighting, and camera angles. A finished 60-second film commercial takes only 90 feet of film, but the shooting often requires several days and 3,000 to 5,000 feet of film.

Recording of the sound track may occur before, during, or after actual production. Recording sound in advance ensures that the commercial will be neither too long nor too short; it also helps when the subject has to move or dance to a specific rhythm.

Production: The Shoot

The actual shooting day (or days) can be very long and tedious. The crew may take several hours just to light the set to the director's liking. Today producers can use technology to control sound, lighting, and staging.

Quiet on the Set: Sound As in radio, sound is extremely important to any TV commercial. The ring of a high-pitched bell, with proper timing, can make a smile seem brighter, add extra sparkle to a glass, or announce when a character experiences a smart idea.

ETHICAL DILEMMA   In Political Advertising, the Nays Have It

U.S. politics is often a brutish affair with candidates hurling defamatory and sometimes ruthless accusations at one another. Radio and television stations broadcast these confrontations coast to coast. In debates, when one candidate gets a good "dig" in at the other, the studio audience cheers—as do the partisans watching at home.

Negative political advertising may have reached its zenith during the 1980s—for several reasons. Complex issues like foreign, economic, and trade policies are far more difficult to communicate and grasp than simplistic 30-second commercials focusing on an opponent's behavior. Negative advertising is intrusive; it cuts through the commercial clutter. But most important, candidates' political consultants think negative ads work.

Michael Dukakis learned this lesson in the 1988 presidential campaign. Bush ads portrayed Dukakis as soft on crime and successfully exploited pollution, tax, and patriotism issues against him. Dukakis failed to respond immediately; when he did, it was too little, too late. Bush won.

Some think negative political ads not only destroy opponents but also discourage people from voting. And recent studies suggest that negative advertising doesn't really work

well, it just makes people more cynical about the political process. One study concludes that voters respond better to ads that simply give positive information about a candidate.

However, the same study also indicates that negative advertising is effective for unknown challengers running against well-known incumbents. New candidates have a tough time gaining media attention unless they attack incumbents, and attack hard.

Political media consultant Roger Ailes, the reputed master of negativity, makes a salient point. "There's nothing wrong with negative advertising as long as it's accurate and fair. It's perfectly right to discuss an opponent." Unfortunately, political candidates and their consultants don't define "accurate and fair" very objectively.

Is Ailes' point well taken? If a challenger doesn't call an incumbent's record into question, who will? If the challenger doesn't disagree with the incumbent's policies, why run? If the incumbent is harassing female employees, taking boondoggle trips, bouncing checks, or simply voting contrary to constituents' interests, shouldn't the challenger point this out—in every way possible? But the challenger who does risks being accused of "negative" campaigning.

Procedures for recording and controlling music and sounds are similar to those used in radio. Microphones capture sound; recorders transfer and store the sound on a medium like magnetic tape. Then, with the use of a multichannel control board, a sound engineer manipulates sounds for effect and records them onto film, video, or a playback system synchronized with film.

But the original recording is the key to success—for two reasons. First, the original sound recording is synchronized with the original visual recording, and with the action and the emotion expressed by the actors. Re-creation never quite matches the timing or feeling of the original.

Second, before it reaches its final form, the original recording undergoes rerecording many times—with some loss of fidelity each time. So high-quality sound-recording equipment is mandatory. And any extraneous sounds must be eliminated. Hence the well-known order: "Quiet on the set!"

Lights The director and the cinematographer must deal with a variety of light sources. For example, a scene with a person standing close to a window may have three light sources: daylight through the window; high-intensity studio lighting for brightening the subject and the room's interior; and a regular table lamp serving as a prop. All these shed different types of light that could adversely affect the scene. To control this effect, technicians need to measure the light and then style it to suit the scene.

Experienced **cinematographers**—motion picture photographers—can guess the range and intensity of light by briefly studying its source. However, they use light meters to determine how to set the camera's lens **aperture**—the opening that controls the amount of light that reaches the film or videotape. To record the correct color and brightness, all light sources must be in balance. Too

---

The lessons of the 80s may be having an effect. In the 1992 presidential election, much of the focus shifted from advertising to public relations. Although President Bush openly taunted Clinton with inferences of draft dodging, pot smoking, and antiwar activism, Clinton continued to emphasize the positive aspects of his background and eventually won. (Of course, he too attacked Bush's record—especially on the economy and domestic issues.)

Most political consultants believe candidates will continue to use negative advertising simply because there are no regulations to stop them. When it comes to political campaigning, the First Amendment guarantee of free speech is interpreted very liberally. Furthermore, the American Association of Political Consultants has yet to discipline a single member for violating its Code of Ethics. As Democratic pollster Paul Maslin says: "The weapons [are] so powerful, that if you don't use them, you will lose them, because the other side will use them on you."

Some recent polls indicate that negative advertising harms both of the candidates and their credibility. This may be one reason voters so often feel they're choosing between the lesser of two evils. Politicians have the power to influence the course of the world's history. Eventually, candidates, voters—and the media—must realize that elections are too important to be decided by negative advertising.

Questions

1. Is it unethical for a political candidate's ads to reveal an opponent's drinking problems and drunk driving arrests?

2. How do you define "accurate and fair" as a guideline for political advertising?

3. Bob Garfield, editorialist for *Advertising Age,* proposed that all political ads carry the following disclaimer: "This has been a paid political announcement. The station is compelled by law to run it, but we have no right and no means to verify its accuracy or untruthfulness. We encourage you to seek other sources for more complete information. *Warning: Political advertising can legally distort the truth.*"
Do you agree? If so, why?

EXHIBIT • 11-13

This light meter can measure both incidental and reflected light by changing the bubble unit on the top. It helps photographers arrange and aim light sources, set the camera's lens aperture, and select filters.

EXHIBIT • 11-14

Temperature Kelvin (K) for Different Light Sources

Source	Color temperature
Candle flame	1,500°K
60-watt household bulb	2,800
Film-studio lights	3,200
Photoflood lights	3,400
Sunset in Los Angeles	3,000
Noon summer sunlight	5,400
Hydrargyrum medium arc-length iodide (HMI) lamp	5,600

much light can overexpose film or cause *flares* and *burn-ins* on video equipment; light that is too low may fail to produce any image at all. Unbalanced light may cause color shifts as well. Photographers measure light for its *intensity* (brightness) and for its *temperature* (color).

An **incident light meter** pointed at a light source measures the intensity—or volume—of light the source is emitting and indicates the correct aperture setting for the type of film being used. A **reflected light meter** measures the volume of light *reflected by* the subject. Some light meters, as shown in Exhibit 11–13, measure both incidental and reflected light.

Once intensity is determined, the photographer needs to measure the light's temperature or color range. Because light is electromagnetic energy—like heat—it can be measured by degrees on the *Kelvin scale* using a **color light meter.** A color light meter tells the photographer if the scene is too blue, green, or red in relation to daylight or tungsten film. This is important, because various light sources can discolor an image, making it greener or redder than it appears to the eye. Daylight, considered *white light,* measures 5,400 degrees Kelvin. Red light ranges from 2,500 to 3,300 degrees and blue light 3,300 to 4,200 degrees.

White light—like from the sun—contains all the degrees Kelvin that humans can see. People see individual colors when white light hits a material that absorbs all of the light *except* for one color, which is reflected to the eye. A leaf appears green because it absorbs all other colors and reflects only the green wavelength.

Most manufactured light sources generate light that is not white. Fluorescent lighting appears green to video cameras and film. Incandescent bulbs emit light in the red range.

Theater, film, and video production lamps create the higher intensities of manufactured light but in differing Kelvin ranges, as shown in Exhibit 11–14. High-intensity lights may be quartz-halogen (approximately 3,200 degrees Kelvin) or arc lamps (approximately 5,600 degrees Kelvin). Quartz-halogens emit a redder light; arc lamps emit a wavelength nearest to daylight.

Cinematographers make sure the lighting on the set is consistent in temperature. When light sources vary in temperature—and/or intensity—some may have to be turned off or filtered as shown in Exhibit 11–15. For video, the camera operator aims the camera at a white card and quickly adjusts the dials to shift the discolored image back to a true white.

Lighting also has to be styled. The arrangement of lights—whether in the studio, the studio lot, or on location—establishes a visual mood. Intense light from a single source gives a harsh appearance and may be used to create anxiety in the viewer. By using filters, warmer lights, diffusion screens, and reflectors, the cinematographer can create a reddish, more consistent, soft illumination—and a more romantic mood. The director works with the art director, the cinematographer, and the lighting engineer to choose the most appropriate placement, types, and intensities.

Standard terms for different types of lighting are shown in Exhibit 11–16. The **keylight** is the primary light to fall on the subject. **Fill light,** which is much dimmer, brightens shadow areas enough to reveal details. **Backlight,** placed directly behind or behind and above the subject and aimed toward the camera, outlines the subject and sets it apart from the background. And **special-effects lighting** enhances and distorts a scene to make it more visually exciting.

The careful and skillful combination of lighting adds artistic and emotional appeal.

Camera Professional film cameras used for making TV commercials shoot 16 mm, 35 mm, and 65 mm film, the diagonal measurement of a single film frame.

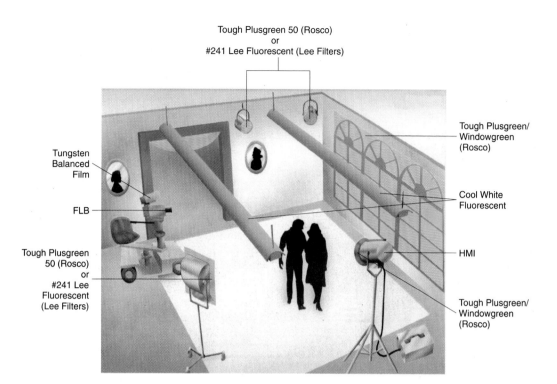

Tough Plusgreen 50 (Rosco)
or
#241 Lee Fluorescent (Lee Filters)

Tungsten Balanced Film

FLB

Tough Plusgreen 50 (Rosco) or #241 Lee Fluorescent (Lee Filters)

Tough Plusgreen/ Windowgreen (Rosco)

Cool White Fluorescent

HMI

Tough Plusgreen/ Windowgreen (Rosco)

E X H I B I T • 11–15

In filmmaking, an array of lens filters and light gels work together to balance the color temperature of the light with the type of film in the camera. In this example, Rosco filters make tungsten lights (which generate a reddish light) greener so that they are in balance with the light generated by the fluorescent lighting, which is also greenish. In addition, the camera uses film made to handle indoor light (from tungsten light bulbs) in order to make the artificial light record as white as possible.

Major brands such as Arriflex and Panaflex (shown in Exhibit 11–17) offer a variety of models for synchronized sound on high-speed shots. Some cameras can convert to a hand-held mode and may offer video assists for simultaneous video viewing.

Producers of local TV commercials used to shoot with the grainier but less expensive 16 mm film; national spots were shot on 35 mm for extra quality and precision. While film is still widely used for national spots—because of the "atmosphere" it brings to an image—most local spots are now shot on video.

Video cameras can be classified by their functions. Heavy duty studio video cameras mounted on a stand with wheels can carry a number of accessories, one of the most important being the lens-mounted *teleprompter*. The **teleprompter's** two-way mirror allows the camera to see a spokesperson through the back of the mirror while he or she reads moving text reflected off the front. Professional video cameras are significantly larger than home units and feature shoulder mounts and sound-recording units.

Unlike film cameras, studio video cameras are tied to a control room by large cables. In the control room, multiple video screens and sound channels are wired to a control panel. Specialized technicians keep the cameras and control rooms operating. Working at the control panel, the director switches from one camera to another and simultaneously sets the input and output levels of sound and visuals for recording and editing on a number of recording systems. Control

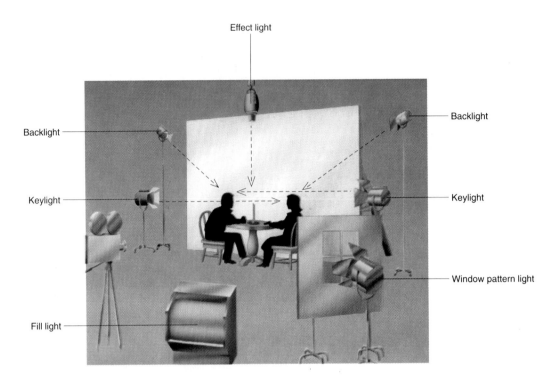

EXHIBIT • 11–16

Different types of lighting can enhance a scene and create special moods. Here, strong keylights light up the actors. The fainter light of the window screen casts a window-shaped pattern onto the background. The effect light above enhances the reflected glow of the candle on the table top. To bystanders the scene appears very bright, but when the camera's aperture is set properly, the film sees a darker, more shadowy play of lights and darks.

panels also have special-effects devices (DVEs) for creating text or visual effects on screen.

Action (Staging and Talent) Staging for a commercial may be done in the isolation of a studio, outside on a studio lot, or on location. The studio offers the greatest degree of control.

Most film and video studios have heavy soundproofing to eliminate outside noises such as sirens and low-flying aircraft. Inside, corrugated wall surfaces dampen echoes on the set. The studios are lightproof, which allows for complete lighting control. Special equipment is easier to use in the controlled environment of a studio. But studio lighting can make a scene appear artificial.

For scenes requiring large amounts of space, historic or unique architecture, scenery, and the full effect of outdoor lighting, the studio *lot* offers the best control. The **lot** is outside acreage shielded from stray, off-site sounds. The lot is convenient to the studio's carpentry shop, and sets can be left standing until the completion of all shootings and retakes. Usually the lot is also near the studio's postproduction facility. Unique equipment is easier to handle on the studio lot than on location. Unfortunately, natural events such as rain can still create costly delays.

Although it adds realism, location shooting is generally a technical and logistical nightmare. Every location has natural and manufactured features that create obstacles. Natural lighting is strong, creating bright highlights that contrast with harsh shadows. Large, reflective screens and high-intensity lights, like those shown in Exhibit 11–18, are required to brighten up shadows for a more even-toned exposure. Energy sources for lighting and equipment may be

This Panaflex studio camera holds film in the canister above and has a video view-finder that can be plugged into a TV screen for simultaneous viewing.

insufficient on location, requiring long cabling and mobile generators. And natural events such as rain and fog can cause costly interruptions. But since sets don't have to be built, location shooting can be ideal for low-budget commercials.

Shooting on location sets up special challenges for directors using video. A truck, van, motor home, or a trailer is wired for video and sound control recording. Inside, a row of TV *monitors* and a multichannel control panel direct the recording from one or more cameras running simultaneously.

Reflector screens and high-intensity lights make it possible to even out the existing light of a film location.

EXHIBIT • 11–19

The academy leader mixed with live-action shots at the beginning of the Gotcha commercial immediately communicated the sponsor's name. The "dial" on the left side of the image spells out both *Gotcha* (around the perimeter) and *Danger* (in the center letters).

Whether at the studio or on location, most scenes require several "takes" for the **talent** (actors) to get them right. Lighting may need readjusting as unexpected shadows pop up. The director usually wants two or three good takes of every scene. In addition, each scene is shot from two or three different angles: one to establish the characters, one to show only the speakers, and one to show the listener's reaction.

Scenes aren't necessarily shot in order. Those with no synchronized sound are usually shot last since they don't require the full crew.

It may take a long time between scenes to move the camera, reset the lights, reposition the talent, and pick up the action, sound, and look to match the other scenes. Each action must match what comes before—and after. Commercials with disconcerting jumps destroy credibility.

Once all the scenes are "in the can," the commercial enters the *postproduction* phase, or finishing. Some reshooting may be necessary if the commercial can't be fit together smoothly or if the client wants to change something.

Postproduction

In the **postproduction** phase, the film editor, sound mixer, and director actually put the commercial together.

Mike Salisbury created the Gotcha commercials almost entirely in the postproduction stage. Everybody agreed on the need to establish the Gotcha name early and often, so each commercial started with an *academy leader*—like the countdown at the beginning of a reel of movie film—that spelled out the name G-O-T-C-H-A, one letter at a time. Line art for each frame was created on a Macintosh computer using Adobe Graphics software, then colored and shot on video. Using the on-line edit bay at Master Communication in Los Angeles, Salisbury married the academy leader graphics to live-action footage to create a dynamic, attention-getting opening like the one shown in Exhibit 11–19.

Salisbury and editor Robert Master had several types of tapes: live action, graphic footage, and sound and music. In the edit session, they used computers to mix and match elements from each and record to the master tape. As shown in Exhibit 11–20, editors can switch from tape to tape and add effects such as wipes and dissolves—all electronically. Salisbury spent 72 hours editing four Gotcha commercials, considerably less than he would have needed for film editing and lab work.

Many professionals, however, still prefer film. When working with film, the visual portion of the commercial first appears on one piece of celluloid without the extra effects of dissolves, titles, or **supers** (words superimposed on the picture). The sound portion of the film is assembled on another piece of celluloid. This is the **work print** stage (also called the **rough cut** or **interlock**). At this time, scenes may be substituted, music and sound effects added, or other last-minute changes made.

External sound is recorded next. This includes the actors' voices, the announcer, the music track, the singers, and the sound effects. The sound engineer records the musicians and singers, as well as the announcer's voice-over narrative. Prerecorded stock music may be bought and integrated into the commercial. The mixing also includes any sound effects such as doorbells ringing or doors slamming.

Once sound editing is complete, the finished sound is put on one piece of celluloid. That, combined with the almost-completed visual celluloid, yields the **mixed interlock.** The joining of these two, along with all the required optical effects and titles, results in the **answer print.** This is the final commercial. If approved, **dupes** (copies) are made for delivery to the networks or TV stations.

E X H I B I T • 11–20

In the postproduction phase for the Gotcha commercials, Mike Salisbury and Robert Master saved a lot of time and money by using computerized video and sound editing.

The Film versus Tape Debate

Today, live TV commercials are rare. Even those that look live are usually videotaped, and most national commercials are shot on color film. Film projects a soft texture that live broadcasts and videotape do not have. Because film is the oldest method, producers have a large pool of skilled talent to choose from. Also, film is extremely flexible and versatile. It is suitable for numerous optical effects, slow motion, distance shots, mood shots, fast action, and animation. Duplicate film prints are also cheaper than videotape dupes.

A 1- or ¾-inch magnetic videotape offers a more brilliant picture and better fidelity. It looks more realistic and appears to have a "live" quality. Tape is also more consistent in quality than film stock. The chief advantage of tape is that it provides immediate playback so scenes can be checked and redone while the props and actors are still together on the set. Moreover, computerization has cut editing time up to 90 percent. Videotape can be replayed almost forever, but a film commercial can be run only about 25 times.

Today, many directors shoot their commercials on film for texture and sensitive mood lighting, but then, like Mike Salisbury, they dub the processed film onto videotape for editing. This process is more costly, but it gives them faster finishing and the opportunity to see optical effects instantly. Some directors, however, still prefer to edit on film because of the wider range of effects possible, thereby achieving a higher level of "creative story telling." (For an additional example of creative story telling, see Creative Department: From Concept through Production of a Television Commercial.)

Continued on page 360

◆

Creative Department

Marketing Background

Taster's Choice, introduced by Nestlé in 1967, was the first nationally distributed freeze-dried coffee. Advertising positioned Taster's Choice as the instant coffee that "tastes closest to fresh brewed, because freeze-drying locks in the coffee's flavor." Nestlé gave the product a premium image—and a premium price. Sales rose rapidly.

But by the late 80s, competitors were outspending Taster's Choice four to one in advertising and promotion. Rather than watch its market share continue to erode, Nestlé decided to jettison its focus on the product and develop a more emotionally driven campaign.

Creative Strategy

Nestlé's ad agency, McCann-Erickson, started by conducting an Emotional Bonding test among instant-coffee drinkers. This test, which the agency developed, helps identify the emotional components that "bond" consumers to brands, making them loyal to one or two products. Typical Taster's Choice users were found to be discriminating, self-assured, and sophisticated.

Nestlé wanted to try a totally new advertising approach, something its main competitors, Folgers and Maxwell House, had never done. The client and agency agreed that romance was conspicuously absent in coffee advertising. Adding a touch of romance to the brand's sophisticated image, they hoped, would make the advertising for Taster's Choice distinctive.

Creative Concept

Meanwhile, in England, Nestlé U.K. was promoting a premium instant coffee with a McCann-Erickson campaign. The unusual series of ads featured a couple whose relationship developed in each episode. This technique, rare enough in Great Britain and virtually unknown in the United States, was increasing sales by 20 to 30 percent.

The serial campaign technique seemed to fit perfectly with the creative strategy Nestlé and McCann-Erickson decided on for the U.S. markets, so they tested it on American consumers. They used the first commercial in the British campaign but replaced the British announcer with an American one. The commercial tested surprisingly well. Viewers recalled both the store and the product, and they believed that Taster's Choice would be appropriate for more discriminating, sophisticated coffee drinkers.

Storyboard, Script, and Production Estimate

Confident the spots would be successful, Nestlé asked the agency to estimate the cost of producing the first two commercials in the series. Nestlé also wanted a bid on two lengths: 45 seconds and 30 seconds.

The British originals were 40 seconds long. Revising them to 45 seconds was easy; the extra 5 seconds was used to lengthen the dramatic pauses, increasing

the romantic tension between the two characters (see the storyboards). Reducing the originals to 30 seconds was more difficult. Each line of dialogue was critical to the character and plot development. Finally, McCann-Erickson cut 10 seconds by using fewer words to convey the same thought and by eliminating a few scenes.

Bidding and preproducing the commercial were relatively easy. The client and the agency decided to use the same actor and actress, the same director, and the same production company as the British campaign. They also decided to produce the commercials in London.

Preproduction

Because the critical casting decisions had already been made, preproduction focused on finding the "other women," who each have a line in the first two episodes. Finding two actresses in London who could speak English with an American accent was a challenge. "Americanizing" the set, props, wardrobe, and lead actor's accent was equally challenging. The client and the agency decided to leave the lead actress's accent British, however, to give the commercials an air of sophistication.

Shooting the Commercials

Each scene had to be shot once from the actor's point of view and once from the actress's. The two leads were hired for only three days, so shooting had to proceed at a breakneck pace. Two days were spent filming them in scenes together, and one day was spent filming each of them in their scenes with the "other women."

Dailies to Distribution Prints

After each day of shooting, the director and McCann-Erickson representatives reviewed the "dailies" to ensure that the lighting, sound, and other creative aspects were correct. The director then cut together his recommended edits and sent them to the agency. Simultaneously, he shipped the original film to the United States. It took a week to clear customs.

After reviewing the director's cut, the agency's creative department edited its own version of the first two commercials. The agency account group reviewed the rough cuts and asked for minor revisions. Once these changes were made, the rough cuts were presented to Nestlé. After Nestlé's revisions were made, the rough cuts were finished. A voice-over was added, colors were adjusted, the cuts between scenes were made smoother, and finished music was added. Nestlé approved the finished spots.

The commercials were transferred from film to videotape, duplicated, and shipped to the networks.

Campaign Results

After six months, the first two episodes generated more positive consumer mail and phone calls than any other Nestlé campaign. Television, print, and radio stories on the campaign generated unprecedented levels of positive publicity for Taster's Choice. Even though both Folgers and Maxwell House cut their price, Taster's Choice sales rose. Shown here is the most recent spot in the series. Sharon joins Tony in Paris—and brings the Taster's Choice.

McCANN-ERICKSON

Client: Nestle Beverage Co.	Title: "Paris"	Art Director: Matt Lester
Product: Taster's Choice	Time: 45 Seconds	Writer: Irwin Warren
Comml. No.: NEXC 3405	Date Aired: 5/3/93	Producer: Dorothy Franklin

SFX: TRAFFIC NOISE

TONY: I got your telegram.

SHARON: I just had to come to Paris.

SHARON: I knew there was something you just couldn't live without.

TONY: Taster's Choice

AVO: Savor the sophisticated taste...

AVO: of Taster's Choice

TONY: It's wonderful...the view...

TONY: the Taster's Choice.

SHARON: Is that all?

TONY: No

Costs

Many factors contribute to the rising cost of commercial production.[14]

- Inadequate planning and lack of preparation.
- Unnecessary production luxuries.
- Use of children and animals.
- Superstar talent and directors.
- Large casts.
- Night or weekend filming.
- Animation.
- Involved opticals, special effects, stop-motion photography.
- Location shooting.
- Both location and studio shooting for one commercial.
- Expensive set decoration or construction.
- Special photographic equipment.
- Additional shooting days.
- Major script changes during a shoot.
- Hierarchy of decisionmakers, approvers, and lawyers.

There's an old saw about too many cooks. In advertising, too many approvers may make an exceptionally expensive stew out of a reasonably economical commercial.

Summary

Producing radio and television commercials is similar. They use the same basic formats, follow the same pattern of development, and share the same need for good *talent*—the people who deliver the commercial's message.

Since talent is a form of icon, talent selection is a very important process. Many factors are considered, including: the talent's reputation, acting skill or creativity, intelligence and style of thinking, and natural assets such as physical appearance, tone of voice, or way of moving. Most important is the talent's relationship with the public.

Radio commercials are among the quickest, simplest, and least expensive ads to produce. They may be produced at local radio stations or at independent production studios. The process of producing a recorded commercial includes the preproduction, production, and postproduction (or finishing) phases.

At a recording session, the sounds of music, voices, and effects are picked up by microphones and recorded on audio tape. The pitch of sound is measured on the hertz scale, while loudness is measured in decibels. Many types of microphones are used today, but the most common one for broadcast commercials is the low-impedance, moving-coil mike. In a recording session, the talent works from a sound booth, and the director and editor work at an audio console in a control room to record, mix, and fine-tune the spot. The final commercial is dubbed onto ¼-inch tape for distribution.

Producing television commercials is expensive; in recent years these costs have soared. People in advertising must be familiar with the production process or risk wasting thousands of dollars.

Three major techniques used for producing television commercials are live action, animation, and special effects. Animation techniques include cartoons, photo animation, stop-motion photography, and video animation. The computer has dramatically affected the use of special effects.

Producing a television commercial involves the same three stages as radio: preproduction, production, and postproduction. The preproduction stage includes all the work prior to the actual day of filming—casting, arranging for locations, estimating costs, finding props and costumes, and other work. During the production stage, the commercial is filmed or videotaped. Here, the control of light and sound is important. Postproduction, the work done after shooting, includes editing, processing film, recording sound effects, mixing, and duplicating final films or tapes.

Most national commercials are still shot on film. Film is extremely flexible and versatile, it can be used for numerous optical effects, and film prints are cheaper than videotape dubs. In recent years, many more commercials—especially local ones—have been shot on tape. Videotape offers a more brilliant picture and better fidelity than film, it looks more realistic, and tape quality is more consistent than film stock. The chief advantage of tape is that it provides immediate playback and greatly speeds the editing process.

Questions for Review and Discussion

1. Why should advertising people understand broadcast production techniques?
2. What is the role and importance of talent? Explain.
3. What do the terms *hertz* and *decibel* refer to?
4. If you wanted to record the action sounds of a football game, what kind of microphone would you use?
5. What are the advantages and disadvantages of animation?
6. What leads to the greatest waste of money in broadcast commercial production? Explain.
7. At what stage of production do all the elements of a commercial come together?
8. When is it better to use film?
9. What are the advantages of videotape?
10. How can an advertiser cut the cost of TV production?

IV

Advertising Media

Advertising media are the channels of communication through which advertising messages are conveyed. Choosing media for an advertising campaign is a critical task, requiring a sound knowledge of the benefits each channel provides for the products being advertised and the audiences being targeted.

Chapter 12, "Media Planning and Selection," introduces the media plan and the changing role of media planners today. It discusses how target audiences are determined and objectives are established for reaching those audiences. The chapter explains the elements of media strategy, how to select specific media vehicles, and how to schedule their use.

Chapter 13, "Print Media," discusses the advantages and disadvantages of advertising in newspapers and magazines and considers the importance of such factors as flexibility, audience selectivity, reproduction quality, and circulation.

Chapter 14, "Electronic Media," presents the yardsticks advertisers use to measure the merits of advertising on television and radio. The chapter discusses the opportunities presented by both broadcast and cable TV, as well as radio's principal feature of high reach and frequency at efficient cost.

Chapter 15, "Direct Mail, Outdoor, Transit, and Supplementary Media," offers the advantages and disadvantages of advertising through direct mail and various out-of-home media. The chapter discusses direct mail's effectiveness and expense, and it covers outdoor media's much less expensive channels such as poster panels, bulletins, and transit advertising. Finally, the chapter discusses such supplementary media as specialty advertising, trade shows, and Yellow Pages directories.

"You're fired," said the **MANAGER** to the oh-so-typical jeans ad. "For three good reasons; you're sexist, you're sexist and you're sexist. And if you give me a moment, I'm sure I'll think of a fourth."

MANAGER
Jeans

Blz. 73, catalogus <u>la Redoute.</u>

Media Planning and Selection

Objective: To show how communication media help advertisers achieve marketing and advertising objectives. To get their messages to the right people in the right place at the right time in a highly fragmented, complex, global marketplace, media planners follow the same procedures as marketing and advertising planners: setting objectives, formulating strategies, and devising tactics. To make sound decisions, media planners today must possess an uncommon blend of marketing savvy, analytical skill, and creativity.

After studying this chapter, you will be able to:

- Describe how a media plan accomplishes marketing and advertising objectives.

- Define reach and frequency.

- Tell how reach, frequency, and continuity are related.

- Calculate gross rating points (GRPs) and cost per thousand (CPM).

- Name some of the secondary research sources available to planners and describe how they are used.

- Explain the media mix.

- Describe different types of advertising schedules and the purposes for each.

EXHIBIT • 12-1

To give a coherent look to all Del Monte ads, McCann-Erickson used several consistent elements: extra bold, sans serif headline type, a close-up photo of the product package, and the "We grow natural taste" slogan beside the logo.

Something had to be done—the situation was threatening the company's market share and its future profitability. It was time to take action.

McCann-Erickson knew that its client's ad budget was not going to grow. But the cost for television—the client's primary medium—was rising. Continuing to buy television time on a flat budget would result in a disastrous loss of market share. It was time to radically overhaul the entire advertising program—especially the media plan.

Television, as an industry, was changing. TV audiences were watching more local programming and more cable channels. So while costs were escalating, TV's effectiveness was dropping.

The client was Del Monte Foods, the 100-year-old manufacturer of canned fruits, vegetables, and snacks. It faced a major decision. Should it stay the course and continue advertising on TV as it had done so successfully for decades? Or should it listen to its agency and jump ship to a new medium? Either decision involved monumental risks.

After much analysis, thorough debate—and some soul searching—the company's in-house media team agreed with McCann-Erickson. They pulled the plug on television and shifted the lion's share of their ad budget to magazines.

It certainly made sense financially. Magazine advertising rates were becoming more and more negotiable. Del Monte's parent company—RJR Nabisco—could contribute its buying clout and corporate discounts. And with magazines, Del Monte could maintain a continuous presence in the marketplace—a great advantage over television.

But a media plan must offer more than cost savings. It must also be effective by reaching the desired audience with the right message. The lush color of magazines could present Del Monte's food in an appealing way, giving readers the positive perception of succulent taste. New recipes and serving suggestions —difficult to communicate well on TV—would be the focus of ads in magazines such as *Good Housekeeping, Woman's Day,* and *People.*

McCann designed a series of ads with a consistent graphic format so consumers would instantly recognize them. (See Exhibit 12–1.) With this graphic consistency and a deep media schedule (frequent appearances in lots of magazines), McCann felt it could build preference for the overall brand name while simultaneously promoting Del Monte's individual products.

As Exhibit 12–2 shows, Del Monte's shift from TV to magazines was dramatic. Del Monte used to spend more than two thirds of its $30.1 million media budget on network television. Within three years, the numbers flip-flopped. Now Del Monte spends 90 percent of its media budget on magazines.

The effect on sales was equally dramatic. Del Monte's sales grew 10 percent in a category that grew only 5 percent during the same period, and all four Del Monte categories (vegetables, fruits, snack cups, and stewed tomatoes) increased market share. Yet, Del Monte actually *decreased* its media expenditures by $7.7 million! In short, Del Monte spent its limited budget efficiently and effectively through sound media planning and selection.

EXHIBIT • 12-2

Del Monte's dramatic media shift (in thousands of dollars).

Year	Magazines	Television	Total
1	$ 8,723.0	$20,504.5	$30,142.9
2	14,206.5	8,094.1	26,627.3
3	22,349.1	2,362.9	25,502.4
4	21,962.7	479.9	22,442.6

What's Del Monte's plan for the future? To stick to the general magazines that target women 25 to 54 years old, and to use different categories of magazines for more specific product usage, such as gourmet magazines to deliver recipe messages, and young family-oriented magazines for snack food products. Will the company return to television? Only on a selective basis for new product launches or other strategic needs.[1] ◆

MEDIA PLANNING: AN OVERVIEW

Media planners need as much creativity as senior art directors and copywriters. This chapter shows that sound media decisions are an integral part of the overall marketing communications framework.

The purpose of **media planning** is to conceive, analyze, and select channels of communication that will direct the advertising message to the right people in the right place at the right time. It involves many decisions:

- Where should we advertise? (In what countries, regions, cities, or parts of town?)
- Which media vehicles should we use?
- When during the year should we concentrate our advertising?
- How often should we run the advertising?
- What opportunities are there for integrating other communications?

The People Who Plan Media Strategy

Media planners work in several kinds of department structures. The three most common include:

1. **Advertising agency media departments.** Full-service ad agencies have departments that perform various media functions for their clients. Many large agencies separate the *media planning function* from the *media buying function*. Media planners play a more strategic role, deciding where and how often ads will run. Media buyers execute the plans, negotiating price and placement, and buying space and time from print and electronic media. Today these traditional roles are evolving into planner/buyer generalists who may focus on a particular area such as print.
2. **Independent media buying services.** Volume media specialists often buy advertising space and time at lower bulk rates and then sell it, at a higher rate or for a handling commission, to advertisers or ad agencies that don't have a fully staffed media department.
3. **In-house media departments.** Some advertisers have departments that plan and buy for the company or supervise the media work of an ad agency or independent media buying service.

The Challenge

People in media planning are low profile compared to their counterparts in creative and account service departments. But one media planner can be responsible for millions of dollars of a client's money. Joe De Deo, president of Young & Rubicam, predicts that media will become even more critical as the complexity of the field increases. "Media will come into prominence, particularly on an international basis in the 90s," he says. "Clients are putting pressure on agencies to be more than efficient. They want creative buys."[2]

What is making media planning so much more complicated than it was just 5 or 10 years ago?

Increasing Media Options

For one thing, there are more media to choose from today, and each medium offers an increasing number of choices.

"When I started 20 years ago, there were three networks, two independents, and eight big magazines," says Stacey Lippman, director of corporate media at Chiat/Day. "It was an easy, easy job. It's not easy anymore. There's too much to keep track of and too many things to explore."[3]

TV is now fragmented into network, syndicated, and local television, as well as network and local cable. Specialized magazines now aim at every possible population segment. Even national magazines publish editions for particular regions or demographic groups. In addition, nontraditional media from video-tape and theater-screen advertising to blimps, balloons, and shopping carts widen the scope of choices. Ad Lab 12–A describes other nontraditional media.

Increasing Fragmentation of the Audience

Audience fragmentation also complicates the media planner's job. Readers and viewers now choose from many media options, essentially acting like programmers, selectively reading only parts of magazines or newspapers, watching only segments of programs, and listening to many different radio stations. This makes it very difficult to find the consumer in the marketplace.[4]

Increasing Costs

Costs are increasing for almost all media. In the last decade, the cost of exposing 1,000 people to each of the major media (called **cost per thousand** and abbreviated as **CPM**) rose faster than inflation. Rising costs make media planning more challenging than ever, especially for advertisers with small budgets. Advertisers today demand more proof that their money is wisely spent and put more pressure on the media planner to justify each decision.

Increasing Complexity in the Way Media Buys Are Made

Buying and selling media is not the straightforward process it once was. In the battle for additional sales, many print and broadcast media companies developed "value-added" programs to provide additional benefits.[5] In addition to selling space or time at rate card prices, these companies also offer reprints, special sections, even sponsorships, and mailing lists (see Exhibit 12–3). To get a bigger share of the advertiser's budget, larger companies now bundle the various stations, publications, or properties they own and offer them together as further incentive. International Data Group (IDG), which publishes *PC World* and *Computer World* magazines, offers a Marketing Access Program (MAP) that gives major advertisers access to IDG's research subsidiary, its world exposition unit (for trade shows), and its book company.[6] Television networks are working with professional sports associations to develop integrated marketing programs for sports and event sponsors.[7]

To some advertising people, the term *value-added* is a nebulous euphemism for discounts. But as cost-conscious clients try to squeeze every ounce of impact from their advertising dollars, media planners must learn how to evaluate and

EXHIBIT • 12-3

The most attractive value-added options.

According to advertisers	According to agencies
1. Targeted promotional mailings	1. Research surveys
2. Research surveys	2. Free list rental
3. Advertorials	3. Targeted promotional mailings
4. Free list rental	4. Special editorial sections
5. Focus groups	5. Postcard mailings
6. Special editorial sections	6. Advertorials
7. Postcard mailings	7. Exclusive event sponsorship
8. Telemarketing services	8. Convention, seminar, or trade show tie-ins

execute these complex deals. Such packages often employ vehicles outside traditional media planning, such as public relations, promotion, and direct marketing. Placing a value on these deals is difficult because the nonmedia elements are hard to quantify. Perrier sponsored the 1989 U.S. Open tennis tournament. The media buy included everything from logos on packages of tennis balls to tickets to the event, to ads in *Tennis* magazine, to hospitality tents. How do you assign a value to all these things?

The trend toward integrating marketing communications is resulting in a new breed of media planner—a "renaissance" planner—younger, computer savvy,

AD LAB 12–A   Off-the-Wall Media That Pull Customers off the Fence

Advertising can be found everywhere these days, even places where we least expect it.

Videotapes

Advertisers either sponsor videos, such as Mr. Boston's *Official Bartender's Guide* and Red Lobster Inns' *Eat to Win*, or place ads on videos of popular films.

Aerial Banners and Lights

Banners carrying ad messages can be pulled by low-flying planes. After dark, traveling aerial lights can display messages of up to 90 characters. Slow-flying helicopters can carry 40'-by-80' signs lit by thousands of bulbs.

Blimps

In addition to Goodyear, blimps now carry ads for Citibank, Coca-Cola, and Fuji Film, among others. Computer-run lighting systems allow the blimps to advertise at night.

In-Flight Ads

Many airlines' in-flight audio and video entertainment runs ads. The travel industry and advertisers that want to reach business fliers are the primary users.

Parking Meters

In Calgary, Alberta, or Baltimore, Maryland, parking meters carry signs on top advertising national products and local businesses. Currently being developed are solar-powered meters with liquid crystal displays for ad messages.

Electronic Billboards

Most modern sports stadiums and arenas sell ad space on giant electronic displays.

Inflatables

Giant inflatable beer cans, mascots, cereal boxes, and other items are used for advertising purposes.

Litter Receptacles

Some major cities offer ad space on concrete litter receptacles at major commercial intersections.

Taxicab Advertising

In addition to the familiar ads on the roofs and backs of taxis, some companies sell ad space inside, facing the riders. One sophisticated system has an electronic message scrolling across a screen in the rider's view.

and schooled in marketing disciplines beyond traditional media. George Hayes, McCann-Erickson's senior VP-media director, points out that the good media specialist today is actually "a real advertising generalist."[8] For an in-depth discussion of integrated marketing communications, see Chapter 16.

In this chapter, we examine how media planners develop a basic plan, devise strategies to carry out the plan, and schedule media buys. But first we need to see how media planning fits into the overall marketing plan.

THE ROLE OF MEDIA IN THE MARKETING FRAMEWORK

Before media planning begins—indeed, before advertising is even considered—companies must establish an overall marketing plan for their products, brands, or services.

Marketing Objectives and Strategy

As we saw in Chapter 7, the marketing plan defines the market need and the company's sales objectives and details strategies for attaining those objectives. As Exhibit 12–4 shows, objectives and strategies result from a marketing situation analysis, which uncovers both problems and opportunities. Marketing objectives may focus on solving a problem ("regaining sales volume lost to

Milk Cartons

Government agencies and other noncommercial advertisers use the sides of milk cartons to advertise issues important to the public, such as missing children and recycling.

Laboratory Applications

1. How effective are off-the-wall media?
2. What other off-the-wall media can you think of?

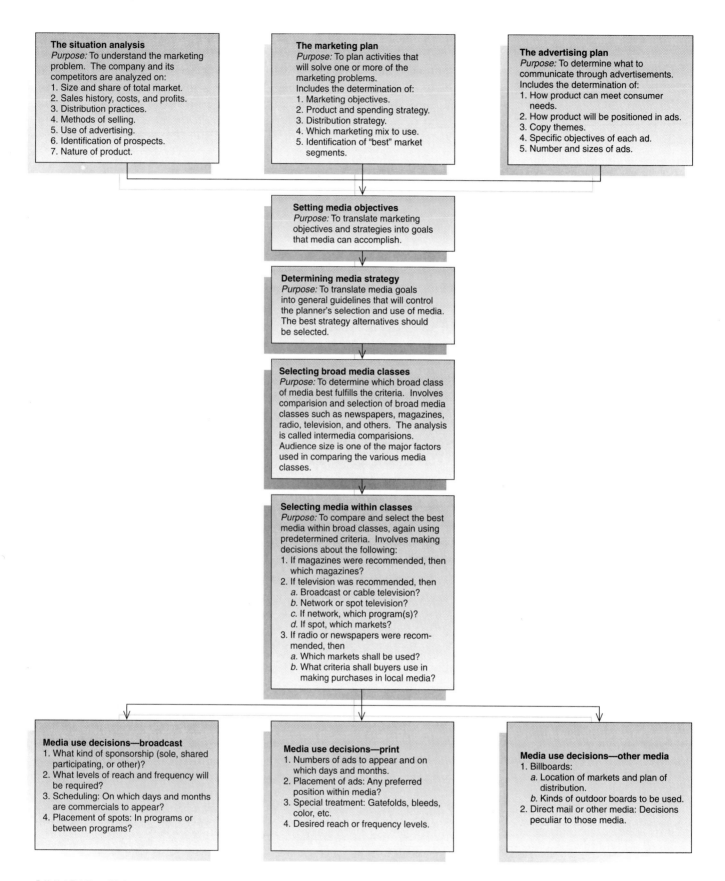

The situation analysis
Purpose: To understand the marketing problem. The company and its competitors are analyzed on:
1. Size and share of total market.
2. Sales history, costs, and profits.
3. Distribution practices.
4. Methods of selling.
5. Use of advertising.
6. Identification of prospects.
7. Nature of product.

The marketing plan
Purpose: To plan activities that will solve one or more of the marketing problems.
Includes the determination of:
1. Marketing objectives.
2. Product and spending strategy.
3. Distribution strategy.
4. Which marketing mix to use.
5. Identification of "best" market segments.

The advertising plan
Purpose: To determine what to communicate through advertisements.
Includes the determination of:
1. How product can meet consumer needs.
2. How product will be positioned in ads.
3. Copy themes.
4. Specific objectives of each ad.
5. Number and sizes of ads.

Setting media objectives
Purpose: To translate marketing objectives and strategies into goals that media can accomplish.

Determining media strategy
Purpose: To translate media goals into general guidelines that will control the planner's selection and use of media. The best strategy alternatives should be selected.

Selecting broad media classes
Purpose: To determine which broad class of media best fulfills the criteria. Involves comparision and selection of broad media classes such as newspapers, magazines, radio, television, and others. The analysis is called intermedia comparisions. Audience size is one of the major factors used in comparing the various media classes.

Selecting media within classes
Purpose: To compare and select the best media within broad classes, again using predetermined criteria. Involves making decisions about the following:
1. If magazines were recommended, then which magazines?
2. If television was recommended, then
   a. Broadcast or cable television?
   b. Network or spot television?
   c. If network, which program(s)?
   d. If spot, which markets?
3. If radio or newspapers were recommended, then
   a. Which markets shall be used?
   b. What criteria shall buyers use in making purchases in local media?

Media use decisions—broadcast
1. What kind of sponsorship (sole, shared participating, or other)?
2. What levels of reach and frequency will be required?
3. Scheduling: On which days and months are commercials to appear?
4. Placement of spots: In programs or between programs?

Media use decisions—print
1. Numbers of ads to appear and on which days and months.
2. Placement of ads: Any preferred position within media?
3. Special treatment: Gatefolds, bleeds, color, etc.
4. Desired reach or frequency levels.

Media use decisions—other media
1. Billboards:
   a. Location of markets and plan of distribution.
   b. Kinds of outdoor boards to be used.
2. Direct mail or other media: Decisions peculiar to those media.

EXHIBIT • 12–4

This diagram outlines the scope of media planning activities.

major competitive introductions over the past year") or seizing an opportunity ("increasing share in the male buyer segment of the frozen food market").

Marketing strategies lay out the steps for meeting these objectives by blending the four Ps of the marketing mix. A company whose marketing objective is to increase sales of a particular brand in a certain part of the country can adapt the product to suit regional tastes (product), lower the price to compete with local brands (price), gain greater shelf space in retail outlets (place), and reposition the product through intensive trade and consumer advertising (promotion). Advertising is just one of the strategic tools a company can use to achieve its marketing objectives.

Advertising Objectives and Strategy

The objectives and strategies of an advertising plan unfold from the marketing plan. But advertising objectives focus on communication goals for example,

- Increasing brand preference by 8 percent in the South during the next year.
- Increasing intent to purchase the brand among men ages 18 to 24 by 10 percent within the next year.

To accomplish these objectives, companies devise advertising strategies that employ the elements of the creative mix—the product concept, the target audience, the advertising message, and the communication media.

The media department makes sure the advertising message (developed by the creative department) gets to the correct target audience (established by the marketing managers and account executives) effectively (as measured by the research department). Media planners go through the same process of setting objectives, devising strategies, and defining tactics.

DEFINING MEDIA OBJECTIVES

Media objectives translate the advertising strategy into goals that media can accomplish. Exhibit 12–5 shows general media objectives for a new food product. They explain who the target audience is and why; where messages will be delivered and when; and how much advertising weight needs to be delivered.

Media objectives have two major components: *audience objectives* and *message-distribution objectives*.

Audience Objectives

The whole media effort is futile if ads fail to reach the right people, so **audience objectives** define the specific types of people the advertiser wants to reach. In Exhibit 12–5, the target audience is homemakers with large families who live in urban areas across the country.

The target audience may consist of people in a specific income, educational, occupational, social, or ethnic group—any of the segmentation groups we discussed in Chapter 5. And they may not be the product's actual consumers.

Del Monte, for example, had to defend its decision to switch from TV to print ads with the trade—the retailers who carry Del Monte products. Why? If these people construed the loss of TV advertising as a loss of advertising support, they might not give Del Monte products as much shelf space.

So Del Monte's ad campaign targeted the trade—as well as consumers—emphasizing the company's leadership in the product category. As Exhibit 12–6

EXHIBIT • 12-5

How media objectives are expressed.

> *ACME Advertising*
>
> Client: Econo Foods
> Product/Brand: Chirpee's Cheap Chips
> Project: Media Plan, First year introduction
>
> ### *Media Objectives*
>
> 1. To target large families with emphasis on the homemaker—the family's food purchaser.
> 2. To concentrate the greatest weight of advertising in urban areas where prepared foods traditionally have greater sales and where new ideas normally gain quicker acceptance.
> 3. To provide extra weight during the announcement period and then continuity throughout the year with a fairly consistent level of advertising impressions.
> 4. To deliver advertising impressions to every region in relation to regional food store sales.
> 5. To use media that will reinforce the copy strategy's emphasis on convenience, ease of preparation, taste, and economy.
> 6. To attain the highest advertising frequency possible once the need for broad coverage and the demands of the copy platform have been met.

EXHIBIT • 12-6

To ease retailers' worries about abandoning TV advertising, Del Monte designed a campaign for people in the trade. Rather than setting advertising objectives such as brand recognition (as they would for consumers), Del Monte's trade communications emphasized the company's leadership, consumer loyalty, and retailer support.

shows, the trade ads used the same bold graphics as the consumer ads. This way, retailers could associate Del Monte brands with the magazine ads used in the consumer campaign. Says Del Monte vice president of corporate communications Dee Ann Campbell, "We basically said to them, 'You sell this magazine in your store, and you sell our products in your store, and the combination of the two is going to work all month long.'"

Del Monte's media objectives for the consumer market were quite different. The consumer target audience is often determined from the marketer's past research or through studies conducted to identify present and future users. Media planners also rely on secondary research such as Simmons Market Research Bureau (SMRB) or Mediamark Research, Inc. (MRI) (see Exhibit 12–7). These syndicated reports give demographic profiles of heavy and light users of various products and enable planners to define the target audience. The reports also specify which kinds of TV programs or magazines heavy and light users watch and read, which helps planners select media with large audiences of heavy users. Planners select media **vehicles,** particular magazines or broadcast programs, according to how well they "deliver" or expose the message to an audience that closely parallels the desired target audience.

Message-Distribution Objectives

Distribution objectives define where, when, and how often advertising should appear. In other words, how much of the target audience should be exposed to the advertising, where, and how often? To answer these questions, a media planner must understand such concepts as *reach, frequency, gross rating points,* and *continuity.*

Reach

The term **reach** refers to the total number of *different* people or households exposed to an ad or campaign during a given period of time, usually four weeks. For example, if 80 percent of 10,000 people in the target market hear a commercial on radio station KKO at least once during a four-week period, the reach is 8,000 people. Reach measures the *unduplicated* extent of audience exposure to a media vehicle. It may be expressed as a percentage of the total market (80 percent) or as a raw number (8,000).

EXHIBIT • 12-7

A media planner's toolbox.

Secondary sources of information help media
planners do their jobs, for example:

- Simmons Market Research Bureau (SMRB) and
  Mediamark Research, Inc. (MRI): report data
  on product, brand, and media usage by both
  demographic and lifestyle characteristics.
- Broadcast Advertisers Reports (BAR), Leading
  National Advertisers (LNA), and Media
  Records: report advertisers' expenditures by
  brand, media type, market, and time period.
- Standard Rate & Data Service (SRDS): provides information on media rates, format,
  production requirements, and audience.
- Audit Bureau of Circulations (ABC): verifies
  circulation figures of publishers.

This number, however, doesn't take into account the *quality* of the exposure. Some people exposed to the message still won't be aware of it. Since one goal of advertising is to penetrate the consumer's screens, reach isn't the best measure of media success. The term **effective reach** indicates quality of exposure. It measures the number, or percentage, of the audience who have been exposed to the message enough times to be aware of it.

Frequency

Frequency refers to the number of times the same person or household is exposed to a communication vehicle—radio spot or magazine ad, for example —in a specified time span. Across a total audience, frequency is calculated as the average number of times individuals or homes are exposed to the vehicle. The figure is used to measure the *intensity* of a specific media schedule.

For example, suppose 4,000 people listen to a radio commercial three times during a four-week period and another 4,000 people listen to it five times. The **average frequency** is:

$$\text{Average frequency} = \text{Total exposure} \div \text{Audience reach}$$
$$= (4{,}000 \times 3) + (4{,}000 \times 5) \div 8{,}000$$
$$= 32{,}000 \div 8{,}000$$
$$= 4$$

For the 8,000 listeners reached, the average frequency or number of exposures was four. Frequency is an important planning tool because it measures the exposure repetitions possible from a specific media schedule—and *repetition is the key to memory*.

Media planners use the term **effective frequency** to express the correct frequency for a given message in a given medium. Effective frequency establishes the average number of times a person must see or hear a message before becoming aware of it. Then it establishes the point at which further exposures would be a waste. Effective frequency falls between a minimum level that achieves message awareness and a maximum level that becomes overexposure, which leads to "wearout"—i.e., it starts to irritate consumers.

Conventional wisdom considers effective frequency to be four to seven contacts over a four-week period, but no magic number works for every commercial and every product. There are many factors to consider. For popular products—dishwashers, CD players, and diet plans—consumers only need to see an ad two times before they absorb all the information. Product categories in which consumers show less interest—instant cereal, insurance, and laundry detergent—require more exposure.[9]

Other factors also influence effective frequency: the complexity of the message, the size of the ad or length of the commercial, the ad's entertainment value, and the volume of competing ads. All must be considered to determine effective frequency levels.[10]

Message Weight

Sometimes media planners want to determine the **message weight** of the media plan—the size of the audience for a set of ads or an entire campaign. Advertisers calculate message weight by adding the audience size for each ad and disregarding any overlap or duplication. There are two ways to express message weight: *gross impressions* and *gross rating points*.

Gross Impressions   The total number of exposures generated by a media plan, called its **gross impressions,** is calculated by multiplying the number of people who receive a message by the number of times they receive it. In the radio example used earlier, there were 32,000 gross impressions.

Gross Rating Points Gross impressions can run into the millions, so a more convenient way to express this information is in **gross rating points (GRPs).** A single rating point represents 1 percent of the audience.

GRPs can be computed two ways. One is to divide the total number of impressions by the size of the target population and multiply by 100. In our radio example, the total gross impressions was 32,000, and the target audience was 10,000 people. So gross rating points are:

$$\text{Gross rating points} = (\text{Total gross impressions} \div \text{Target audience}) \times 100$$
$$= (32{,}000 \div 10{,}000) \times 100$$
$$= 320 \text{ GRPs}$$

Another way to calculate GRPs is to multiply the percent of reach by the average frequency. In our example, 80 percent of the radio households heard the commercial an average of four times during the four-week period:

$$\text{Reach} \times \text{Frequency} = \text{GRPs}$$
$$80 \times 4 = 320 \text{ GRPs}$$

GRPs describe the total message weight of a media schedule, without regard to audience duplication, over a given period of time. For broadcast media, GRPs are often calculated for a week or a month; in print media, they're calculated for the number of ads in a campaign; and for outdoor advertising, they're calculated on the basis of daily exposure.

Continuity

Continuity refers to the length of time an advertising message or campaign will run over a given period of time. A media planner for a new product might decide that after a heavy introduction period of, say, four weeks, the campaign needs to maintain continuity for an additional 16 weeks but on fewer stations. Frequency is important to *create* memory, continuity is important to *sustain* it. The principal media objectives of reach, frequency, and continuity all depend on the advertiser's budget. Budgets are limited, and so are media objectives.

Once the advertiser determines the media objectives—that is, the optimum levels of reach, frequency, message weight, and continuity—the media planner can develop a strategy.

DEVELOPING A MEDIA STRATEGY: THE MEDIA MIX

The **media strategy** describes how the advertiser will achieve the stated media objectives: which media will be used, where, how often, and when.

Advertisers develop marketing and advertising strategies by blending the elements of the marketing mix and then the elements of the creative mix. Similarly, an advertiser develops media strategy by blending the *elements of the media mix.*

Elements of the Media Mix

To develop an effective media strategy, media planners use the **Four Ms (4Ms)** of the **media mix**—markets, money, media, and methodology—as described in Exhibit 12–8.

Markets
The various targets for communications: business, trade, or consumer;
geographic emphasis; segmentation considerations.
Money
How budget will be allocated between media, geographic regions, target audiences.
Media
Integrates all media options: classes, subclasses, vehicles, etc., including publicity,
sales promotion, direct marketing, collateral.
Methodology
Mechanical considerations (size of units, color) and the overall scheduling
strategy to achieve the reach, frequency, and continuity objectives.

EXHIBIT • 12–8

The 4Ms of the media mix.

Markets

As an element of the media mix, **markets** refers to the various possible targets of a media plan. The media plan may have to reach both trade and consumer audiences; global, national, or regional audiences; or certain ethnic or socio-economic groups.

Money

The media planner will have to decide how much to budget and where to allocate funds: how much for print media, how much in TV, how much to each geographic area. The media planner recommends spending more here and less there, using a combination of marketing savvy and analytical skill.

Media

In this context, **media** includes *all* communications vehicles available to a marketer, including broad media classes and subclasses such as radio, TV, newspaper, magazines, outdoor, direct mail, as well as various supplemental media and ancillary activities such as sales promotion, direct marketing, public relations and publicity, special events, and collateral materials.

Media planners should encourage companies to integrate all their marketing communications. They should look at the media element, not just analytically, but creatively to achieve the company's objectives.

Methodology

Methodology includes mechanical considerations (size of time or space units, color, B/W, position in the medium, etc.) and overall scheduling strategy to achieve the reach, frequency, and continuity objectives. Here again, the media planner faces a host of options and trade-offs within a limited budget.

Influencing Factors in Media Strategy Decisions

The 4Ms are elements within the media planner's control. However, media decisions are greatly influenced by a variety of factors outside the media planner's control. These include: the scope of the media plan; the sales potential of different markets; competitive strategies and budget considerations; the availability of different media vehicles; the nature of the medium and the mood of the message; message size and length; and consumer purchase patterns.

Scope of the Media Plan

The location and makeup of the target audience strongly influences the breadth of the media plan, thereby affecting decisions regarding the *market,* the *money,* and the *media* elements.

Domestic Markets

A media planner normally limits advertising to areas where the product is available. A *local* plan may be used if the product is available in only one city or if that market has been chosen for introduction or test-marketing. We'll explore the subject of local advertising further in Chapter 18.

A *regional* plan may cover several adjoining metropolitan areas, an entire state or province, or several neighboring states and employ a combination of local media, regional editions of national magazines, or spot TV and radio. The advertiser may have to accommodate sectional differences in taste or preference. Canadian purchase patterns are quite different in francophone (French-speaking) and anglophone (English-speaking) provinces. In the United States, Midwesterners buy more instant coffee than New Englanders. These factors affect how and where media money is spent.

Advertisers who want to reach an entire country use a *national* plan including network TV and radio, full-circulation national magazines and newspapers, and nationally syndicated Sunday newspaper supplements. Exhibit 12–9 shows local and national advertising expenditures in the United States.

Global Markets

North American advertisers adapt quickly to foreign styles of advertising but not to foreign media. Governments around the world own and control most broadcast media, and many do not permit commercials. Others limit advertising to a certain number of minutes per hour or per day.

In countries that do allow TV advertising, advertisers face another problem. How many people own televisions sets, and who are they? Most Europeans own TVs, but in less-developed nations only upper-income consumers have them. So advertisers must use a different media mix.

One way to develop an international media plan is to formulate individual national plans first. But that's tougher than it sounds. Reliable information about media isn't as available overseas, circulation figures aren't necessarily audited, audience demographics may be sketchy, and even ad rates may be unreliable.[11]

Because of the media variations in each country, global advertisers often entrust national media plans to in-country media specialists rather than run the risk of faulty, centralized media planning.

Gauging the Sales Potential of Different Markets

The *market* and *money* elements of the media mix also depend on the sales potential of each area. National advertisers use this factor to determine where to allocate their advertising dollars. There are several ways planners can determine an area's sales potential.

EXHIBIT • 12-9
Expenditures for advertising in the
United States.

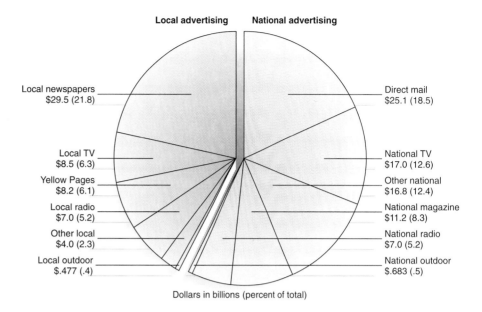

Dollars in billions (percent of total)

The Brand Development Index

The **brand development index (BDI)** indicates the sales potential of a
particular brand in a specific market area. It compares the percentage of the
brand's total U.S. sales in an area to the percentage of the total U.S. population
in that area. The larger the brand's sales relative to the area's percentage of U.S.
population, the higher the BDI, and the greater the brand's sales potential. BDI
is calculated as:

$$\text{BDI} = \frac{\text{Percent of the brand's total U.S. sales in the area}}{\text{Percent of total U.S. population in the area}} \times 100$$

Suppose sales of a brand in Los Angeles are 1.58 percent of the brand's total
U.S. sales and the population of Los Angeles is 2 percent of the U.S. total. The
BDI for Los Angeles is:

$$\frac{1.58}{2} \times 100 = 79$$

An index number of 100 means the brand's performance balances with the size
of the area's population. A low BDI index number (below 100) indicates
potential for the brand is not strong.

The Category Development Index

The **category development index (CDI)** works on the same concept as the
BDI and is calculated in much the same way to determine the potential of the
whole product category. Thus, we calculate CDI using the following formula:

$$\text{CDI} = \frac{\text{Percent of the product category's total U.S. sales in the area}}{\text{Percent of total U.S. population in the area}} \times 100$$

If category sales in Los Angeles are 4.92 percent of total U.S. category sales,
the CDI in Los Angeles would be:

$$\text{Los Angeles CDI} = (4.92 \div 2) \times 100 = 246$$

EXHIBIT • 12-10

Media buyers compare the Brand Development Index (BDI) with the Category Development Index (CDI) for their products to better understand which markets will respond best to advertising. Advertising can be expected to work well when BDI and CDI are both high, but probably not when both are low.

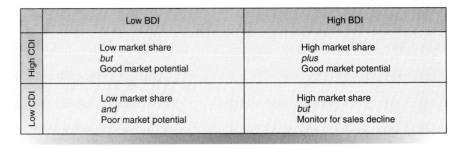

		Low BDI	High BDI
High CDI		Low market share *but* Good market potential	High market share *plus* Good market potential
Low CDI		Low market share *and* Poor market potential	High market share *but* Monitor for sales decline

The BDI and CDI combination can help the planner determine a media strategy for the market. (See Exhibit 12–10.) In our example, low BDI and high CDI in Los Angeles indicate that the product category has high potential but the brand is not selling well. This could represent either a problem or an opportunity. If the brand has been on the market for some time, the low BDI raises a red flag—some marketing problems are standing in the way of brand sales. But if the brand is relatively new, the low BDI may not be alarming. In fact, the high CDI may indicate the brand can grow substantially, given more time and more media and marketing support. At this point, the media planner should assess the company's *share of voice* (discussed in Chapter 7) and budget accordingly.

Competitive Strategy and Budget Considerations

Advertisers always consider what competitors are doing, particularly if they have larger advertising budgets. Several services report competitive advertising expenditures in the different media. By knowing the size of competitors' budgets, what media they're using, the regionality and seasonality of their sales, and any new product tests and introductions, advertisers can better plan a counterstrategy.[12]

Again the media planner should analyze the company's *share of voice* in the marketplace. If an advertiser's budget is much smaller than the competition's, the brand could get lost in the shuffle. Advertisers should bypass media that competitors dominate and choose media that offer a strong position. One agency introduced Stresstabs vitamins with an entirely print campaign to avoid what was then a large arena of TV advertising. The target audience was exposed to their message more efficiently and effectively in print.[13]

But it makes sense to use media similar to the competition if the target audiences are the same or if competitors are not using their media effectively.

Media Availability and Economics: The Global Marketer's Headache

North Americans are blessed—or cursed—with an incredible array of media choices, locally and nationally. Such is not the case in other areas of the world.

Every country has communication media, but they are not always available for commercial use—especially radio and television. And coverage may be quite limited. Lower literacy rates and education levels in some countries restrict the coverage of print media. Where income levels are low, television ownership is also low. These factors tend to segment markets by media coverage.

In countries with national newspapers, circulation may be limited to upper-class, well-educated people. On the other hand, both Pepsi and Coke reach lower-income markets successfully through radio. In some developing countries, stores and bars blare radios into the street for passersby to hear. Auto manufacturers successfully use TV and magazine advertising to reach the upper class. And cinema advertising can reach whole urban populations where TV ownership is low because motion picture attendance in such countries is very high. The Checklist for International Media Planning outlines some basic considerations for media buyers entering international markets.

Advertisers may want to use international media, but effective ones are scarce. International advertisers often use local media in the countries where they do business, so they have to produce ads in the language(s) of each country (and some countries have more than one official language).

Finally, there's the problem of **spillover media**—local media that a substantial number of consumers in a neighboring country inadvertently receive. For example, French media may spill over into Belgium and Switzerland. Media tend to spill over into countries lacking indigenous-language publications, particularly specialty publications. English and German media enjoy a large circulation in Scandinavian countries, for example.

According to a study by the Foote, Cone & Belding advertising agency, spillover media pose a threat for the multinational advertiser because they expose readers to multiple ad campaigns. If the advertiser runs both international and local campaigns for the same products, discrepancies in product positioning, pricing, or advertising messages could confuse potential buyers. Advertisers' local subsidiaries or distributors need to coordinate local and international ad campaigns to preclude such confusion. On the positive side, spillover media offer potential cost savings through regional campaigns.

Nature of the Medium and Mood of the Message

An important influence on the media element of the mix is how well a medium works with the style or mood of the message.

Advertising messages differ in many ways. Some are simple, dogmatic messages: "AT&T: The right choice." Others make emotional appeals to people's needs for safety, security, social approval, love, beauty, or fun: "What a luxury car should be" (Lincoln). Many advertisers use a reason-why approach to explain their product's advantages: "Twice the Room. Twice the Comfort. Twice the Value. Embassy Suites. Twice the Hotel."

Complex messages require more space or time for explanation. Ads announcing a new product or product concept are unfamiliar to consumers. Each circumstance affects the media selection and the *methodology* element of the media mix.

A new or highly complex message, like the Norfolk Southern commercial in Exhibit 12–11, may require greater frequency and exposure to be understood and remembered. A simple, dogmatic message like AT&T's may require a surge at the beginning, then low frequency and greater reach.

Reason-why messages may be complex to understand at first. But once understood, pulsing advertising exposures at irregular intervals are often sufficient. Emotionally oriented messages are usually more effective spaced at regular intervals to create continuing feeling about the product.

Message Size, Length, and Position Considerations

The mechanics of different media affect the methodology element of the media mix. For example, in print, a full-page ad attracts more attention than a quarter-

CHECKLIST   International Media Planning

Basic Considerations (Who Does What?)

◇ **What is the client's policy regarding supervision and placement of advertising?** When, where, and to what degree is client and/or client branch office abroad involved?

◇ **Which client office is in charge of the campaign?** North American headquarters or foreign office or both? Who else has to be consulted? In what areas (creative or media selection and so forth)?

◇ **Is there a predetermined media mix to be used?** Can international as well as foreign media be used?

◇ **Who arranges for translation of copy if foreign media are to be used?**
  ◇ Client headquarters in North America.
  ◇ Client office in foreign country.
  ◇ Agency headquarters in North America.
  ◇ Foreign media rep in North America.

◇ **Who approves translated copy?**

◇ **Who checks on acceptability of ad copy in foreign country?** Certain ads need approval by foreign governments.

◇ **What is the advertising placement procedure?**
  ◇ From agency branch office in foreign country directly to foreign media.
  ◇ From North American agency to American-based foreign media rep to foreign media.

◇ From North American agency to American-based international media.

◇ From North American agency to affiliated agency abroad to foreign media.

◇ **What are the pros and cons of each of these approaches?** Is media commission to be split with foreign agency branch or affiliate office? Can campaign be run from North America? Does the client save ad taxes by placing from North America? In what currency does client want to pay?

◇ **Who receives checking copies?**

◇ **Will advance payment be made to avoid currency fluctuation possibilities?**

◇ **Who bills?** What currency? Who approves payment?

Budget Considerations

◇ **Is budget predetermined by client?**

◇ **Is budget based on local branch or distributor recommendation?**

◇ **Is budget based on agency recommendation?**

◇ **Is budget related to sales in the foreign market?**

◇ **What is the budget period?**

◇ **What is the budget breakdown for media,** including ad

EXHIBIT • 12–11

This TV campaign for Norfolk Southern, titled "Horse of a Different Color," is a complex message. Computer-generated images of the horse—the key element of the logo—pass through several transformations to symbolize the variety of services and benefits offered. Understated or complex commercials such as this must be aired with greater frequency than simple, bold messages.

(MUSIC & SFX) To grow stronger, America depends on its bounty.

Both natural and. . . man made. Finding new ways to get these

goods to market more efficiently and . . . reliably is the noble pur-

suit of . . . Norfolk Southern. The Thoroughbred of Transportation.

taxes, translation, production and research costs?

◇ What are the tie-ins with local distributors, if any?

Market Considerations

◇ What is your geographical target area?
  ◇ Africa and Middle East.
  ◇ Asia, including Australasia.
  ◇ Europe, including Eastern Europe.
  ◇ Latin America.
◇ What are the major market factors in these areas?
  ◇ Local competition.
  ◇ GNP growth over past four years and expected future growth.
  ◇ Membership of country in a common market or free trade association.
  ◇ Literacy rate.
  ◇ Attitude toward North American products or services.
  ◇ Social and religious customs.
◇ What is basic target audience?
  ◇ Management executives in business and industry.
  ◇ Managers and buyers in certain businesses.
  ◇ Military and government officials.
  ◇ Consumers; potential buyers of foreign market goods.

Media Considerations

◇ Availability of media to cover market: Are the desired media available in the particular area?
◇ Foreign media and/or international media: Should the campaign be in the press and language of a particular country, or should it be a combination of the two types?
◇ What media does the competition use?
◇ Does medium fit?
  ◇ Optimum audience quality and quantity.
  ◇ Desired image, editorial content, and design.
  ◇ Suitable paper and color availability.
  ◇ Justifiable rates and CPM (do not forget taxes on advertising, which can vary by medium).
  ◇ Discount availability.
  ◇ Type of circulation audit.
  ◇ Availability of special issues or editorial tie-ins.
◇ What are the closing dates at North American rep and at the publication headquarters abroad?
◇ What is the agency commission (when placed locally abroad at the agency, commission is sometimes less than when placed in North America)?
◇ For how long are contracted rates protected?
◇ Does the publication have a North American representative to help with media evaluation and ad placement?

page ad and a full-color ad more than a black-and-white one. With limited advertising budgets, color and larger units of space or time cost dearly in terms of reach and frequency. (See Exhibit 12–12).

Is it better for a small advertiser to run a full-page ad once a month or a quarter-page ad once a week? Should TV advertisers use 60-second commercials or a lot of 15- and 30-second ones? There are no simple answers. The planner has to consider the nature of the message—some simply require more time and space to be explained. Competitive activity often dictates more message units. The product itself may demand the prestige of a full page or full color. The need for high frequency may mean smaller units. It's often better to run several small ads consistently than one large ad occasionally.

Other considerations involve where to position the ad. Preferred positions for magazine ads are front and back covers; for TV, sponsorship of prime-time shows. Special positions and sponsorships cost more, so the media planner must weigh the additional costs against loss of reach and frequency.

A. Readership scores for ads of various sizes. Readership is the greatest for four-color, two-page ads, but increased readership may not offset the additional cost in some publications.

B. Readership scores for ads with various degrees of color.

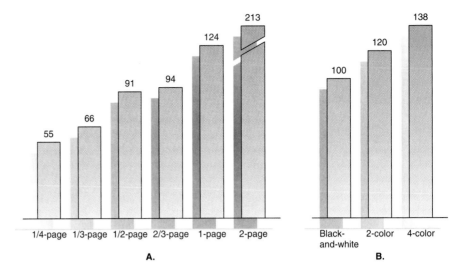

A.

B.

Consumer Purchase Patterns

Finally, the customer's product purchasing behavior affects every element of the media mix. The media planner must consider how, when, and where the product is typically purchased and repurchased. Products with short purchase cycles (convenience foods and paper towels) require more constant levels of advertising than products purchased infrequently (refrigerators and furniture). Short purchase cycles call for relatively high frequency and high continuity.

Stating the Media Strategy

A written statement of the media strategy is an integral part of any media plan. Without one, it's difficult for client and agency management to analyze the logic and consistency of the recommended media schedule.

Generally, the strategy statement should start with a brief definition of the target audiences (the market element) and the priorities for weighting them. And it should outline specific reach and frequency goals. It should explain the nature of the message and indicate which media types will be used, how, and why (the media element), should provide a budget for each medium (the money element) including the cost of production and any collateral materials. Finally, it should state the intended size of message units, any position or timing considerations (the methodology element), and the effect of budget restrictions.

MEDIA TACTICS: SELECTING AND SCHEDULING MEDIA VEHICLES

Once the general media strategy is determined, the media planner can select and schedule media vehicles. The planner usually evaluates each medium's value on a set of specific criteria (see Ad Lab 12–B). Some are quantitative; others depend on the planner's opinions. Both are important in the evaluation process.

Criteria for Selecting Individual Media Vehicles

In evaluating specific media vehicles, the planner considers several factors: overall campaign objectives and strategy; size and characteristics of each medium's audience; attention, exposure, and motivational value of each medium; and cost efficiency. See Exhibit 12–13.

AD LAB 12–B   Media Selection: As the Creative Person Sees It

	Creative advantages	Creative disadvantages
Newspapers	Almost any ad size available. Black and white still one of the most powerful color combinations. Sense of immediacy. Quick response; easy accountability. Local emphasis. Changes possible at short notice.	Loss of fidelity, especially in halftone illustrations. Difficulty controlling ad position on page.
Magazines	High-quality reproduction. Prestige factor. Accurate demographic information available. Graphic opportunities (use of white space, benday screen, reverse type). Color.	Not as large as newspapers or posters. Long closing dates, limited flexibility. Lack of immediacy. Tendency to cluster ads. Possible difficulties securing favorable position.
Television	Combination of sight, sound, movement. A single message at a time. Viewer empathy. Opportunity to demonstrate the product. Believability: "What you see is what you get."	No time to convey a lot of information. Air clutter (almost 25 percent of broadcasting is nonprogramming material). Intrusiveness (TV tops list of consumers' complaints).
Radio	Opportunity to explore sound. Favorable to humor. Intimacy. Loyal following (the average person listens regularly to only about two stations). Ability to change message quickly.	Lack of visual excitement. Wavering attention span. Inadequate data on listening habits (when is the "listener" really listening?). Fleeting nature of message.
Direct mail	Graphic, flexible production. Can use three-dimensional effect (folding, die-cuts, pop-ups). Measurable. As scientific as any other form of advertising. Highly personal.	State, federal, and postal regulations affect creativity. Censorship unpredictable. Formula thinking encouraged by "proven" direct-mail track records.
Outdoor/Transit	Graphic opportunities. Color. Large size. High-fidelity reproduction. Simple, direct approach. Possibility of an entirely visual message.	A one-line medium with limited opportunity to expand on the message. Limited audience research, especially in transit advertising.
Point of sale	Opportunities for three-dimensional effects, movement, sound, new production techniques.	Difficulty pinpointing audience. Retailers use material improperly.

Laboratory Application

1. If you wanted a set of complementary media to cover all the creative advantages, which mix would you select?
2. What creative disadvantages and advantages can you add to the list?

Overall Campaign Objectives and Strategy

The media planner's first job is to review the nature of the product or service, the intended objectives and strategies, and the primary and secondary target markets and audiences.

The characteristics of the product may suggest a suitable choice. A product with a distinct personality or image—such as a fine perfume—might be advertised in media that reinforces this image. The media planner considers how consumers regard various magazines and TV programs—feminine or masculine, highbrow or lowbrow, serious or frivolous—and determines whether they're appropriate for the brand.

The content and editorial policy of the media vehicle and its compatibility with the product are important considerations. *Tennis* magazine is a poor

	Spot television	Network TV	Cable TV	Spot radio	Network radio	Consumer magazines	Business publications	Farm publications	Sunday supplements	Daily newspapers	Weekly newspapers	Direct mail	Outdoor	Transit	Point of purchase
Audience considerations															
Attentiveness of audience	⊖	⊖	⊖	⊖	⊖	⊖	⊖	⊖	⊖	⊖	⊖	⊖	○	○	○
Interest of audience	⊖	◐	◐	⊖	⊖	◐	◐	◐	◐	◐	◐	◐	○	○	○
Offers selectivity to advertiser	○	○	✓	⊖	⊖	◐	◐	◐	○	○	○	◐	○	○	○
Avoids waste	○	○	⊖	○	○	◐	◐	◐	⊖	○	○	◐	○	○	○
Offers involvement	⊖	⊖	⊖	⊖	⊖	⊖	◐	◐	⊖	⊖	◐	○	○	○	⊖
Offers prestige	⊖	◐	⊖	○	⊖	◐	◐	⊖	⊖	⊖	◐	○	○	○	○
Good quality of audience data	⊖	⊖	⊖	⊖	⊖	◐	◐	◐	◐	◐	○	⊖	○	○	○
Timing factors															
Offers repetition	○	○	○	○	○	⊖	⊖	⊖	○	⊖	○	✓	○	○	⊖
Avoids irritation	○	○	○	○	⊖	⊖	⊖	⊖	⊖	⊖	⊖	⊖	⊖	⊖	⊖
Offers frequency	○	○	○	○	⊖	⊖	⊖	⊖	○	⊖	○	⊖	◐	◐	⊖
Offers frequency of issuance	○	○	○	○	○	✓	✓	○	○	⊖	○	✓	—	—	—
Offers flexibility in scheduling	○	○	○	○	○	✓	✓	○	○	⊖	○	✓	—	—	—
Avoids perishability	○	○	○	○	○	◐	◐	◐	⊖	○	⊖	◐	○	○	○
Allows long message	⊖	⊖	◐	⊖	⊖	◐	◐	◐	◐	◐	◐	◐	○	○	○

Note: ○ = Weak; ⊖ = Medium; ◐ = Strong; — = Not a factor for this medium; ✓ = Varies from one vehicle to another within the medium.

EXHIBIT • 12-13

Comparative evaluation of advertising media.

vehicle for cigarette or alcohol ads even though its demographic profile and image might match the desired target audience.

Consumers use a particular media vehicle because they gain a "reward": self-improvement, financial advice, career improvement, or simply news and entertainment. Advertising is most effective when it positions a product as part of a solution the consumer seeks. Otherwise consumers may see it as an intrusion.[14]

If the marketing objective is to gain greater product distribution, the planner should select media that influence potential dealers. If the goal is to stimulate sales of a nationally distributed product in isolated markets, ads should be placed in the local and regional media that penetrate those markets. Pricing strategy influences media choices too. A premium-priced product should use prestigious or "class" media to support its market image.

The media planner determines the characteristics most relevant to the acceptance, purchase, and use of the product and matches them to the characteristics of various media audiences.

Characteristics of Media Audiences

An **audience** is the total number of people or households exposed to a medium. The planner needs to know how closely the medium's audience matches the profile of the target market and how interested such people are in the publication or program. A product intended for a Hispanic audience must appear in the medium that exposes Hispanics to the message most efficiently (see Exhibit 12–14). Data on the size and characteristics of audiences for

	Spot television	Network TV	Cable TV	Spot radio	Network radio	Consumer magazines	Business publications	Farm publications	Sunday supplements	Daily newspapers	Weekly newspapers	Direct mail	Outdoor	Transit	Point of purchase
Geographic considerations															
Offers geographic selectivity	●	○	●	●	○	◐	◐	◐	●	●	●	●	◐	◐	●
Offers proximity to point of sale	○	○	○	○	○	○	○	○	○	○	○	◐	◐	◐	●
Provides for local dealer "tags"	◐	○	●	◐	○	◐	◐	◐	●	●	●	●	◐	◐	●
Creative considerations															
Permits demonstration	●	●	●	○	○	◐	◐	◐	◐	◐	◐	●	○	○	●
Provides impact	●	●	●	◐	◐	◐	◐	◐	◐	◐	◐	●	○	○	◐
Permits relation to editorial matter	◐	◐	◐	○	◐	●	●	●	◐	◐	◐	●	—	—	—
Mechanical and production factors															
Ease of insertion	◐	●	◐	◐	●	●	●	●	◐	◐	○	●	◐	◐	○
High reproduction quality	◐	◐	◐	◐	◐	●	●	●	●	✓	✓	●	✓	✓	●
Flexibility of format	◐	◐	◐	◐	◐	●	●	●	○	—	—	●	◐	○	○
Financial considerations															
Low total cost	◐	○	◐	◐	○	○	○	○	◐	●	●	○	◐	◐	◐
High efficiency	◐	●	●	●	◐	◐	◐	◐	◐	◐	○	●	●	●	○

EXHIBIT • 12–13

(continued)

particular vehicles is readily available. Simmons Market Research Bureau provides research data on age, income, occupational status, and other characteristics of a wide range of magazine readers. Simmons also publishes demographic and psychographic data on product usage among a varied group of consumers.

The *content* of the medium usually determines the type of people in the audience. Some radio stations emphasize in-depth news or sports; others, jazz, rock, or classical music. Each type of programming attracts a different audience.

Exposure, Attention, and Motivation Value of Media Vehicles

The media planner has to select media that will not only achieve the desired *exposure* to the target audience, but also attract *attention* and *motivate* people to act. This is no easy task, and there's little reliable data to work with.

Exposure To understand the concept of **exposure value,** think of how many people an ad "sees" rather than the other way around. How many of a magazine's 3 million readers will an ad actually see? How many of a TV program's 10 million viewers will a commercial actually see?

Even though someone reads a particular magazine or watches a certain program, he or she doesn't necessarily see the ads. Some people read only one article, set the magazine aside, and never pick it up again. Many people change channels during a commercial or leave to get a snack. Comparing the exposure value of different media vehicles is very difficult. Without statistics, media planners have to use their best judgment—based on experience.

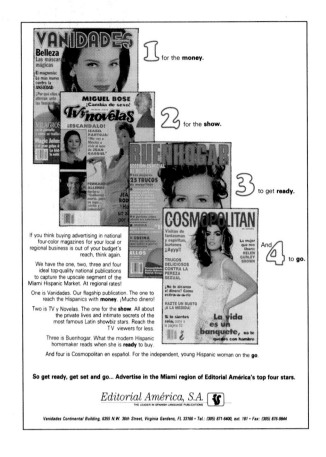

The deputy director of media services at D'Arcy Massius Benton & Bowles
outlined five basic factors that affect the probability of ad exposure:[15]

1. The senses used to perceive messages from the medium.
2. How much and what kind of attention the medium requires.
3. Whether the medium is an information source or diversion.
4. Whether the medium or program aims at a general or a specialized audience.
5. The placement of the ad in the vehicle (within or between broadcast programs; adjacent to editorial material or other print ads).

Attention Degree of attention is another consideration. Consumers with no
interest in motorcycles or cosmetics won't remember the ads. But someone in
the market for a new car tends to notice every new-car ad.

Exposure value relates only to the medium; **attention value** relates to the
advertising message and copy as well. Special-interest media, such as boating
magazines, offer good attention value to a marine product. But what kind of
attention value does the daily newspaper offer such a product? Do sailors think
about boats while reading the newspaper? Much research still needs to be done,
but six factors are known to affect attention value:[16]

1. Audience involvement with editorial content or program material.
2. Specialization of audience interest or identification.
3. Number of competitive advertisers (the fewer, the better).
4. Audience familiarity with advertiser's campaign.
5. Quality of advertising reproduction.
6. Timeliness of advertising exposure.

EXHIBIT • 12–15

Advertisers buy space in magazines because the editorial content, color, and fine reproduction can actually motivate ad readers.

Motivation These same factors affect a medium's **motivation value,** but in different ways. Familiarity with the advertiser's campaign may affect attention significantly but motivation very little. The attention factor of good-quality reproduction and timeliness can also motivate someone (see Exhibit 12–15).

Media planners analyze these values by assigning numerical values to their personal opinions of a medium's strengths and weaknesses. Then, using either a simple or complex weighting formula, they add them up. They use similar weighting methods to evaluate other factors, such as the relative importance of age demographics versus income characteristics.

Cost Efficiency of Media Vehicles

Finally media planners analyze the cost efficiency of each medium. A common term used in media planning and buying is **cost per thousand,** or **CPM.** If a daily newspaper has 300,000 subscribers and charges $5,000 for a full-page ad, the cost per thousand would be computed as:

$$CPM = \$5{,}000 \div (300{,}000 \div 1{,}000) = \$16.67$$

However, media planners are more interested in **cost efficiency**—the cost of exposing the message to the target audience rather than to the total circulation. If the target audience is males ages 18 to 49, and 40 percent (100,000) of a weekly newspaper's readers fit in this category, the CPM would be:

$$\$3{,}000 \div (100{,}000 \div 1{,}000) = \$30$$

A daily newspaper might turn out to be more cost-efficient if 60 percent of its readers (180,000) belong to the target audience:

$$\$5{,}000 \div (180{,}000 \div 1{,}000) = \$27.78$$

Comparing different media by CPMs, while important, does not take into account each medium's other advantages and disadvantages. The media planner must evaluate all the criteria to determine:

1. How much of each medium's audience matches the target audience;
2. How each medium satisfies the needs of the campaign's objectives and strategy; and
3. How well each medium offers attention, exposure, and motivation.

EXHIBIT • 12–16

Kodak invites comparison by putting pictures of this park in Amsterdam in front of the actual park. The "headline" translates as *Kodacolor Gold. True-to-life colors.*

After such an evaluation, a planner can decide whether a daily or weekly newspaper is a better buy.

Economics of Foreign Media

As we pointed out in Chapter 1, a major purpose of media advertising is to communicate with customers less expensively than by personal selling. In some underdeveloped countries, however, it's cheaper to send people out with baskets of samples. For mass marketers in North America, this kind of personal contact is impossible.

In North America legislation and labor costs inhibit the growth of outdoor advertising. In many foreign markets, outdoor enjoys far greater coverage because it costs less to have people paint the signs and there is less government restriction. Almost every street in Mexico seems to have a "Disfrute Coca-Cola" sign. In Nigeria, billboards with the slogan "Guiness gives you power" next to the bulging biceps of an African arm made Guiness stout ale a best seller despite an 80 percent illiteracy rate. Exhibit 12–16 shows outdoor ads for Kodak film in Amsterdam.

Cost inhibits the growth of TV in many foreign markets, but some countries are beginning to sell advertising time to help foot the bill. As more countries allow commercial broadcasts, and as international satellite channels gain a bigger foothold, TV advertising will grow. As labor rates rise, media planners may use fewer print and outdoor ads as well as less personal selling.

The Synergy of Mixed Media

When Del Monte felt it had maximized its print schedule, the company ran an aggressive outdoor campaign during the summer of 1990. Del Monte wanted to increase its brand visibility by taking advantage of summer's heavier traffic. Outdoor also brought Del Monte's ads closer to the point of sale. By strategically placing the billboards, Del Monte positioned its advertising to expose consumers on their way to the grocery store.

Media planners have to decide whether to use a single medium or several. A combination of media is called a **mixed media approach** (*media mix* for short). There are numerous reasons for using mixed media:

EXHIBIT • 12-17

Mixed media campaigns create a synergistic effect. This campaign integrates TV spots, print advertising, public relations activities, and a number of promotional programs to build a strong tie with target markets.

- To reach people unavailable through only one medium.
- To provide additional repeat exposure in a less expensive secondary medium after attaining optimum reach in the first.
- To use the intrinsic values of an additional medium to extend the creative effectiveness of the ad campaign (such as music on radio along with long copy in print).
- To deliver coupons in print media when the primary vehicle is broadcast.
- To produce **synergy,** where the total effect appears to be greater than the sum of its parts.

Ben Givauden of the Givauden Agency in New York appreciates the "synergy" between newspapers and magazines. "Newspapers can be used to detonate an idea, with magazines following up for the harder sell." He says newspapers offer in-depth circulation, whereas magazines offer retentive value.[17]

In 1992, General Electric used a mixed media campaign for its lighting products (see Exhibit 12–17). Designed to promote both GE and the NBC fall TV programs ("Win with GE and be on NBC"), the promotion used a combination of network television spots, print advertising, Sunday supplement inserts, in-store displays in over 150,000 stores, and a highly creative publicity program. Special NBC *Fall Preview Guides* with an instant-win game card and discount coupons were distributed in millions of packages of GE lighting products. By using an integrated, mixed-media approach, the campaign produced "unprecedented" consumer awareness and dealer support. It had synergy.[18]

Methods for Scheduling Media

After selecting the appropriate media vehicles, the media planner decides how many space or time units of each vehicle to buy and schedules them for release over a period of time. The major goal is to schedule advertising when consumers are most apt to buy.

Continuous, Flighting, and Pulsing Schedules

To build continuity in a campaign, planners use three principal scheduling methods: *continuous, flighting,* and *pulsing.* See Exhibit 12–18.

In a **continuous schedule,** advertising runs steadily and varies little over the campaign period. It's the best way to build continuity. Advertisers usually follow this scheduling pattern for products consumers purchase regularly. For example, a commercial is scheduled on radio stations WTKO and WRBI for an initial four-week period. Then, to maintain continuity in the campaign, additional spots run continuously every week throughout the year on station WRBI.

Flighting alternates periods of advertising with periods of no advertising. This intermittent schedule makes sense for products and services that experience large fluctuations in demand throughout the year (tax services, lawn care products, and cold remedies). The advertiser might introduce the product with a four-week *flight* and then schedule three additional four-week flights to run during seasonal periods later in the year.

The third alternative, **pulsing,** mixes continuous and flighting strategies. The advertiser maintains a low level of advertising all year but uses periodic **pulses** to "heavy-up" during peak selling periods. This strategy is appropriate for products like soft drinks, for example, that are consumed all year but more heavily in the summer.

Michael Drexler, executive vice president of media at Bozell, Jacobs, Kenyon & Eckhardt, compares pulsing to flicking a light switch on and off: "If I flip it on and off fast enough, you may never know the light is off."[19]

Additional Scheduling Patterns

As the consumer's purchasing cycle gets longer, pulsing becomes more appropriate. For high-ticket items that require careful consideration, **bursting**—running the same commercial every half hour on the same network in prime time—can be effective. A variation is **roadblocking,** buying airtime on all three networks simultaneously. Chrysler used this technique to give viewers the impression that the advertiser was all over the place, even if the ad only showed

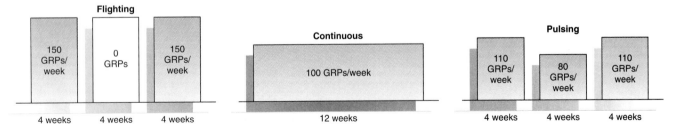

EXHIBIT • 12-18

Three ways to schedule the same number of total GRPs: flighting, continuous, and pulsing.

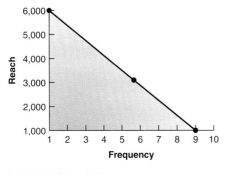

EXHIBIT • 12-19

Reach and frequency have an inverse relationship. For the same budget, an advertiser can reach 6,000 people 1 time, 3,000 people 5.5 times, or 1,000 people 9 times.

for a few nights. Ramada Inns used a scheduling tactic called **blinking** to stretch its slim ad budget. It advertised on Sundays to reach traveling salespeople while they were still at home anticipating the forthcoming week.[20]

Maximizing Reach, Frequency, and Continuity: The Art of Media Planning

Good media planning is an art. The media planner must get the most effective exposure on a limited budget. As Exhibit 12–19 shows, the objectives of reach, frequency, and continuity have an inverse relationship. To achieve greater reach, some frequency has to be sacrificed, and so on. Exhibit 12–20 gives guidelines for determining the best reach, frequency, and continuity combinations. Research shows that all three are critical.

1. Continuity is important because advertising is quickly forgotten. To achieve continuity, advertisers must commit dollars over a continuous period of time.
2. Repeated exposures are needed to impress a message on a large proportion of consumers.
3. Frequency is the key to remembering. As the number of exposures increases, both the number of people who remember it and the length of time they remember it increase.
4. An intensive burst of advertising will cause a very large number of people to remember (at least for a short time).
5. Fewer exposures per prospect in a comparatively large group promote greater memory than more exposures per prospect in a smaller group. At some point, reach is more important than frequency in promoting memory.
6. With additional exposures per prospect, the dollar efficiency of advertising decreases. At some point, reach is more important than additional frequency.

The Use of Computers in Media Selection and Scheduling

Computers have been an important part of media planning since the early 1970s. They perform the tedious number crunching needed to compute GRPs, CPMs, reach, frequency, and so on. And they can save time and money. Ogilvy & Mather found it could plan TV, radio, and print co-op budgets for each of client Ford's 1,000 dealers with only three people and a software system. The year before, it took 70 staffers working for a week and a half.[21]

Computers make the media planner's job easier. For example, with data on audience demographics of radio stations in Pittsburgh, the computer can rank the stations on how closely their audience profile matches a product's target audience. With information on the Pittsburgh stations' ad rates, ratings, and so on, the computer can produce several alternate radio advertising schedules that fit the ad budget. As each radio buy is made, the computer can track how much of the budget has been spent, the cost per rating point, and the CPM by daypart.

Media planners use three main types of computer programs. The older **linear programming model** creates a complete media schedule that maximizes exposure within a given budget. However, no linear model is fully practical because there are too many real-world variables.[22]

A second program, the **simulation model,** estimates the ability of the chosen media vehicles to expose target individuals to a message. Simulation programs don't plan media schedules; they evaluate individual vehicles' target audience, cost efficiency, and so on. Specialized simulation models can calculate optimum timing for an ad campaign.

Finally, **formula models** calculate reach, frequency, and other statistics for different media vehicles and rank the vehicles according to selected parameters:

EXHIBIT • 12–20

Guidelines for determining the reach, frequency, continuity, and pulsing combination.

Considerations	Objectives			
	Reach	Frequency	Continuity	Pulsing
Needs				
New or highly complex message, strive for:		✓		
Dogmatic message, surge at beginning, then:	✓			
Reason-why messages, high frequency at first, then use:				✓
With emotionally oriented messages, strive for:			✓	
When message is so creative or product so newsworthy that it forces attention, seek:	✓			
When message is dull or product indistinguishable, strive for:		✓		
Consumer purchase patterns				
To influence brand choice of regularly purchased products, use:		✓	✓	
As purchase cycle lengthens, use:		✓		✓
To influence erratic purchase cycles, strive for:				✓
To influence consumer attitudes toward impulse purchases, seek:		✓	✓	
For products requiring great deliberation, alternate between:	✓	✓		
To reinforce consumer loyalty, concentrate on:	✓		✓	
To influence seasonal purchases, anticipate peak periods with:	✓	✓		
Budget levels				
Low budget, use:				✓
Higher budgets, strive for:			✓	
Competitive activity				
Heavy competitive advertising, concentrate on:		✓		
When competitive budgets are larger, use:				✓
Marketing objectives				
For new, mass-market product introductions:	✓			
To expand share of market with new uses for product, strive for:	✓			
For direct response from advertising, use:		✓		✓
To create awareness and recognition of corporate status, use:	✓		✓	

the best reach, the best frequency, and so on. With any of these models, the computer instantly recalculates results whenever a factor changes.

Since the advent of microcomputers in the early 1980s, software programs for media planning have proliferated. Some are highly customized. J. Walter Thompson U.S.A.'s special program helps 20th Century Fox plan newspaper buys for its film ads. Other general programs, like Media Management Plus, help plan, buy, and manage all forms of advertising media. Computer users can also access giant databases or subscribe to services that provide data on CDs or floppy disks.

But even with technological timesavers and short cuts, it's still up to the media planner to know the product, know the market, know the media, and make the call. Computers *can't* decide which medium or environment is best for the message. They can't evaluate the content of a magazine or the image of a TV program. They can't judge whether the numbers they're fed are valid or reliable, and they can't interpret the meaning of the numbers. Computers help in the planning process, but they can't take the place of people as long as subjective judgment is an important part of the process.

Summary

Media planning directs the advertising message to the right people at the right time. It involves many decisions, such as where to advertise, when to advertise, which media to use, and how often to use them. Media planners need as much creativity as art directors and copywriters. And like good art and copy ideas, media decisions should be based on sound marketing principles and research, not just on experience and intuition.

The media function involves two basic processes: media planning and media selection. Media planning begins by defining the specific types of people the advertising message will be directed to, then setting goals or objectives for communicating with those audiences. The target audience is often determined from the marketer's past research, through special research studies, or through secondary research sources such as Simmons Market Research Bureau and Mediamark Research (MRI). Once the target audience is determined, the planner sets message distribution objectives that specify where, when, and how often the advertising should appear. These objectives may be expressed in terms of reach, frequency, impressions, gross rating points, and continuity.

In developing the appropriate media strategy, the planner develops the best blend of the 4Ms—markets, media, money, and methodology. The planner must consider many variables: the scope of the media plan, which is determined by the location and makeup of the target audience; the sales potential of different markets; competitive strategies and budget considerations; the nature of the medium and the mood of the message; the size, length, and position of the message in the selected media; and consumer purchase patterns. Foreign media are not always available for commercial messages.

After the media strategy is developed, the planner must select specific media vehicles. Some criteria used to make this decision are quantitative, others qualitative, but both are important in the evaluation process. Factors that influence the selection process include campaign objectives and strategy; the size and characteristics of each medium's audience; geographic coverage; the attention, exposure, and motivation value of each medium; cost efficiency; and the advisability of a mixed media approach.

Once media vehicles are selected, the media planner decides on scheduling—how many of each medium's space or time units to buy over what period of time. A media campaign can run continuously or in erratic pulses. These decisions are affected by consumer purchase patterns, the product's seasonality, and the balance of reach, frequency, and continuity that meets the planner's media objectives and budget.

The media planner must use money wisely to maximize the campaign's effectiveness.

Questions for Review and Discussion

1. What major factors contribute to the increased complexity of media planning?
2. What must media planners consider before they begin planning?
3. What secondary research sources are available to planners?
4. What is the "right" frequency for a given message?
5. How are GRPs and CPMs calculated?
6. What are the 4Ms of the media mix, and how are they determined?
7. What major factors influence the choice of individual media vehicles?
8. Why do advertisers use a mixed media approach?
9. What are the principal methods used to schedule media?
10. How are reach, frequency, and continuity related?

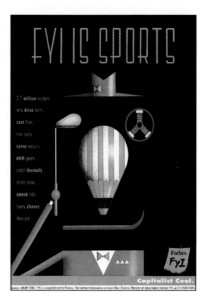

Print Media

Objective: To explain how print advertising enhances the advertiser's media mix. Newspapers and magazines, with their unique qualities, can complement broadcast, direct mail, and other media. By using print wisely, advertisers can greatly expand the impact of their campaigns and still stay on budget.

After studying this chapter, you will be able to:

- Explain the advantages and disadvantages of magazine advertising.

- Discuss several categories of magazines.

- Explain the advantages and disadvantages of newspaper advertising.

- Describe how newspapers are categorized.

- Define the major types of newspaper advertising.

- Discuss how rates are determined for print media.

- List several sources of print media data.

he entire campaign was to be upscale and intelligent, with just a touch of wry humor. The messages were to deal with banking—a fact that would influence the ad's sophisticated tone and placement.

Continental Bank had discontinued its consumer division and was now devoting all of its energy and resources to building its business accounts. To be successful, it would have to inform and convince business executives that, by specializing in their needs, the bank could more effectively serve the business community.

"Some of the ideas they wanted to communicate were very complex," says Bob Barrie, art director of Fallon McElligott in Minneapolis. "We needed to grab attention with interesting visuals and headlines, but, to be effective in business advertising, we also had to deliver a relevant message."

"Advertising people tend to think that bankers don't have a sense of humor," says Barrie. But he feels that banking executives are people too and therefore banking ads should be no less entertaining or human than consumer ads. With that thought in mind, Barrie and copywriters Rob Kilpatrick and Jamie Barrett used intriguing visual metaphors to express the bank's new focus.

A foot about to slip on a banana peel illustrates the dangers of economic fickleness; an octopus represents the typically unfocused structure of many banks; and, as Exhibit 13–1 shows, a row of dominoes ready to topple demonstrates the effect of a wrong business decision. The copy was carefully written to avoid the pomposity of other bank ads. It conveyed that Continental had serious information to offer its business customers but, at the same time, didn't take itself too seriously. For example, the dominoes ad talks about managing an asset portfolio: "You move one innocent-looking little piece and . . . oops, there goes your entire set-up."

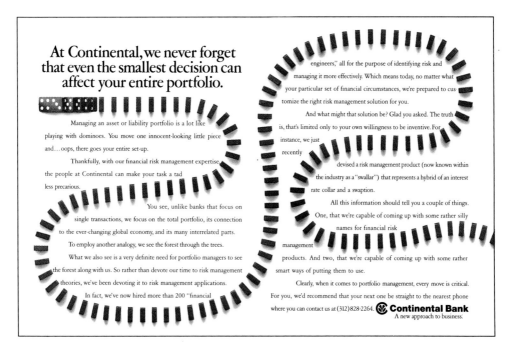

EXHIBIT • 13–1

Continental Bank uses simple symbols and humorous copy to communicate the concept of interconnectivity in financial portfolio management. Other ads in the series featured equally witty copy.

The campaign had to reach the target audience—corporate financial decision-makers. Broadcast media—radio and television—reach too broad a market. Newspapers have the same problem; *The Wall Street Journal* and *Barron's* reach the right people but, like most other papers, aren't upscale enough in their makeup or appearance, and don't carry color ads. So magazines became the medium of choice. The bank could reproduce full-color images on high-grade, glossy paper, and its ads would be in the company of other upscale companies advertising in the same magazines.

The agency placed two-page, full-color ads in *Business Week, Sports Illustrated, Forbes,* and *Fortune* magazines, all of which have substantial circulation in the business community. The response was immediately positive. The campaign logged exceptionally high readership scores and resulted in a surge of new business for Continental Bank.[1] ◆

USING MAGAZINES IN THE CREATIVE MIX

One of the great features of magazines is that they allow an advertiser to reach a select target audience with a high-quality presentation. Continental Bank is just one of many leading companies that uses magazines as an important element of their creative mix (see Exhibit 13–2). Of course, each medium offers a different set of advantages to different advertisers. Through a series of Checklists and Ad Labs in this and subsequent chapters, we will present the pros and cons of each.

One of the primary benefits of magazine advertising is permanence. Magazines may sit on a coffee table or shelf for months and be reread many times. In fact, market research indicates that magazines are typically looked at by a number of individuals on several occasions. As the Checklist: Pros and Cons of Magazine Advertising describes, magazines offer a host of other features too: flexible design options, lush color, and superb reproduction quality, in addition to authority, prestige, excellent audience selectivity, and cost efficiency. See Ad Lab 13–A: Magazines and the Marketing Mix.

Special Possibilities with Magazines

Magazines also offer advertisers a wide variety of creative possibilities through various technical or mechanical features: *bleed pages, cover positions, inserts* and *gatefolds,* and special-size ads such as *junior pages* and *island halfs.* We discuss these elements briefly below.

When the dark or colored background of the ad extends to the edge of the page, it is said to "bleed" off the page. (See the Liberty Scarf ad in the Portfolio of Award-Winning Magazine Advertisements later in this chapter.) Most magazines offer **bleed pages,** but they charge a 10 to 15 percent premium for them. The advantages of bleeds include greater flexibility in expressing the advertising idea, a slightly larger printing area, and a more dramatic impact.

If a company plans to advertise in a particular magazine consistently, it may seek a highly desirable **cover position.** Few publishers sell ads on the front cover, commonly called the *first cover.* They do sell the inside front, inside back, and outside back covers (the *second, third,* and *fourth covers,* respectively) usually through multiple-insertion contracts at a substantial premium.

A less expensive way to use magazine space is to place the ad in unusual places on the page or dramatically across spreads. A **junior unit** is a large ad (60 percent of the page) in the middle of a page surrounded with editorial matter. Similar to junior units are **island halves,** except more editorial matter surrounds them. The island sometimes costs more than a regular half-page; but,

E X H I B I T • 13-2

Top 10 Magazine Advertisers in the United States.

Rank	Advertiser	Magazine ad expenditures, 1991*
1	General Motors Corp.	$250.4
2	Philip Morris Cos.	215.1
3	Ford Motor Co.	149.6
4	Procter & Gamble Co.	142.9
5	Chrysler Motor Corp.	106.7
6	Toyota Motor Corp.	105.4
7	Grand Metropolitan	83.3
8	Unilever NV	81.0
9	Nestlé SA	77.1
10	Time Warner	66.9

* Dollars in millions.

CHECKLIST   The Pros and Cons of Magazine Advertising

The Pros

◇ **Flexibility** in readership and advertising; magazines cover the full range of prospects, they have a wide choice of regional and national coverage, and a variety of lengths, approaches, and editorial tones.

◇ **Color** gives readers visual pleasure, and color reproduction is best in slick magazines. Color enhances image and identifies the package. In short, it sells.

◇ **Authority and believability** enhance the commercial message. TV, radio, and newspapers offer lots of information but little knowledge or meaning; magazines often offer all three.*

◇ **Permanence**, or long shelf life; magazines give the reader more opportunity to appraise ads in detail, allowing a more complete education/sales message and the opportunity to communicate the total corporate personality.

◇ **Prestige** for products advertised in certain upscale or specialty magazines like *Architectural Digest* and *Connoisseur.*

◇ **Audience selectivity** is more efficient in magazines than any other medium except direct mail. The predictable, specialized editorial environment selects the audience and enables advertisers to pinpoint their sales campaigns; for example, golfers (*Golf Digest*), businesspeople (*Business Week*), twentysomething males (*Details*), or teenage girls (*Seventeen*).

◇ **Cost efficiency** because wasted circulation is minimized, and new *print networks* give advertisers reduced prices for advertising in two or more network publications.

◇ **Selling power** of magazines has been proven, and results are measurable.

◇ **Reader loyalty** that sometimes borders on fanaticism.

◇ **Extensive "pass-along" readership**; nonsubscribers read the magazine after subscribers finish it.

◇ **Merchandising assistance**; advertisers can generate reprints and merchandising materials that help them get more mileage out of their advertising campaigns.

The Cons

◇ **Lack of immediacy** that advertisers can get with newspapers or radio.

◇ **Shallow geographic coverage** especially on the local level, and they don't offer the national reach of broadcast media.

◇ **Inability to deliver mass audiences** at a low price. Magazines are very costly for reaching broad masses of people.

◇ **Inability to deliver high-frequency** since most magazines come out only monthly or weekly. However, the advertiser can build frequency faster than reach by adding numerous small-audience magazines to the schedule.

◇ **Long lead time** required for ad insertion—sometimes 2 to 3 months.

◇ **Heavy advertising competition**; the largest circulation magazines have 52 percent advertising to 48 percent editorial content.†

◇ **High cost per thousand**; average black-and-white cost per thousand in national consumer magazines ranges from $5 to $12 or more; some trade publications with highly selective audiences have a CPM of more than $20 for a black-and-white page.

◇ **Declining circulations**, especially in single-copy sales, is an industrywide trend that limits the reach of an advertiser's message.

* Stephen H. Martin, "Magazines: A Medium to Watch," *Marketing and Media Decisions*, August 1985, p. 79.
† *Hall's Magazine Reports*, Magazine Publishers of America, January 1990.

because it dominates the page, many advertisers consider the extra charge worth it. Exhibit 13–3 shows other space combinations that create impact.

Sometimes, rather than buying a standard advertising page, an advertiser uses an **insert.** The advertiser prints the ad on special, high-quality paper stock to add weight and drama to the message, and then ships the finished ads to the publisher for insertion into the magazine at a special price. Another option is multiple-page inserts. Calvin Klein promoted its jeans in a 116-page insert in *Vanity Fair.* Almost half as thick as the magazine itself, the insert reportedly cost more than $1 million. It contained 107 pictures of scantily clad models portraying the hedonistic life of a rock band. There was no copy other than the Calvin Klein logo. But the copy written about the insert in major daily newspapers and national magazines gave the ad enormous publicity value.[2] Adver-

AD LAB 13–A   Magazines and the Marketing Mix

Read the Checklist: Pros and Cons of Magazine Advertising and see if you can apply that information to the following situation.

You manage an elegant restaurant in Los Angeles and you want to build the business by promoting the special ambience your restaurant offers. So you plan to give away a free long-stemmed rose with each entrée.

Laboratory Applications

1. Is a magazine the best way to advertise this special? If no, explain why. If so, explain why and include which type of magazine would be best.
2. Since you wish to build the restaurant's image, how can magazine advertising help you?

tising inserts may be devoted exclusively to one company's product, or they may be sponsored by the magazine and have a combination of ads and special editorial content consistent with the magazine's focus.

A **gatefold** is a special kind of insert. The paper is extra long so the extreme left and right sides have to be folded into the center to match the size of the other pages. When the reader opens the magazine, the folded page swings out like a gate to present the ad. It may occupy the cover position or the centerfold. Gatefolds make spectacular and impressive announcements. Not all magazines provide gatefolds, and they are always sold at a substantial premium.

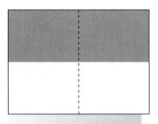
Facing horizontal half-pages to dominate a spread

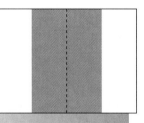
Vertical halves across the gutter with the same objective

Checkerboard facing a half-page ad

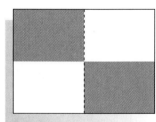
Staggered horizontal half-pages

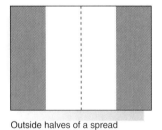
Outside halves of a spread

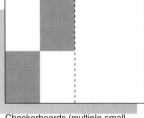
Checkerboards (multiple small space units on a single page)

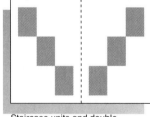
Staircase units and double staircases on facing pages

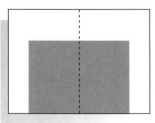
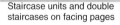
Island spread

EXHIBIT • 13-3

An ad's position on the page influences its effectiveness. The size and shape of the ad often determine where it will fall on the page. This chart shows eight two-page spreads and most of the possible positions the ads can take depending on their size and shape.

UNLIKE most ALMANACS, WE
PROMISE YOU SUNSHINE 365 DAYS a YEAR.

EXHIBIT • 13-4

This Sunkist ad aims its message at those in restaurants and institutions who buy and sell fruit, particularly grapefruit.

How Magazines Are Categorized

In the jargon of the trade, magazines are called *books,* and advertisers commonly categorize them by *content, geography,* and *size.*

Content

Over the last three decades, one of the most dramatic developments in publishing has been the emergence of magazines with special appeal and content. Although specialized editorial content doesn't guarantee success, it has given many *books* good prospects for long-term growth.

The broadest classifications of content are *consumer magazines, farm magazines,* and *business magazines.* Each may be broken down into hundreds of categories.

- **Consumer magazines,** purchased for entertainment, information, or both, are edited for consumers—who buy products for their own personal consumption: e.g., *Time, Newsweek, Sports Illustrated, Skiing, Glamour, Good Housekeeping, Chatelaine,* and *National Geographic.* The Portfolio of Award-Winning Magazine Advertisements shows the range of creativity in consumer magazine advertising.
- **Farm publications** are directed to farmers and their families or to companies that manufacture or sell agricultural equipment, supplies, and services: e.g., *Farm Journal, Progressive Farmer, Prairie Farmer,* and *Successful Farming.*
- **Business magazines,** by far the largest category, target business readers. They include *trade publications* for retailers, wholesalers, and other distributors; *industrial magazines* for businesspeople involved in manufacturing; and *professional magazines* for lawyers, physicians, dentists, architects, teachers, and other professionals. The ad in Exhibit 13–4 appeared in a trade magazine for institutional food buyers.

Geography

Regardless of content, a magazine may also be classified as local, regional, or national. Today most major U.S. cities have a *local city magazine:* e.g., *San Diego Magazine, New York, Los Angeles, Chicago, Philadelphia, Palm Springs Life,* and *Crain's Chicago Business.* Their readership is usually upscale, professional people interested in the arts, fashion, culture, and business.

Regional publications are targeted to a specific area of the country, such as the West or the South: e.g., *Sunset, Southern Living, InfoPress* (a regional business publication for Quebec's French-speaking advertising community). In addition, national magazines sometimes provide special market runs for specific geographic regions. *Time, U.S. News & World Report, Newsweek, Woman's Day,* and *Sports Illustrated* offer advertisers the opportunity to buy a single major market. Exhibit 13–5 on page 403 shows the 10 major geographic editions of *Reader's Digest.*

National magazines range from those with enormous circulations, such as *TV Guide* with a circulation of more than 16.3 million, to lesser-known national magazines with circulations under 100,000, such as *Modern Drummer* and *Volleyball Monthly.*[3] The largest circulation magazine in the United States today is *Modern Maturity,* distributed to the 21 *million* members of the American Association of Retired Persons.

Continued on page 403

◆

Portfolio of Award-Winning Magazine Advertisements

A. Magazines allow for elegant design as seen in the montage look of this visual.

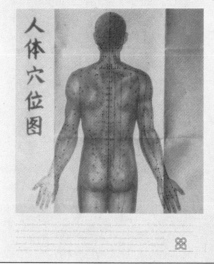

B. Photography's ability to capture dramatic lighting and details is transferable to magazines.

C. Magazines offer a full range of techniques like bleeds and large solid areas of color.

D. Magazines help the art direction—the body language of an ad—show through. This ad recaptures the look of 1777.

E. Magazines capture the soft quality in this ad without losing the brightness of color.

F. Large areas of white with limited areas of color do well in magazines.

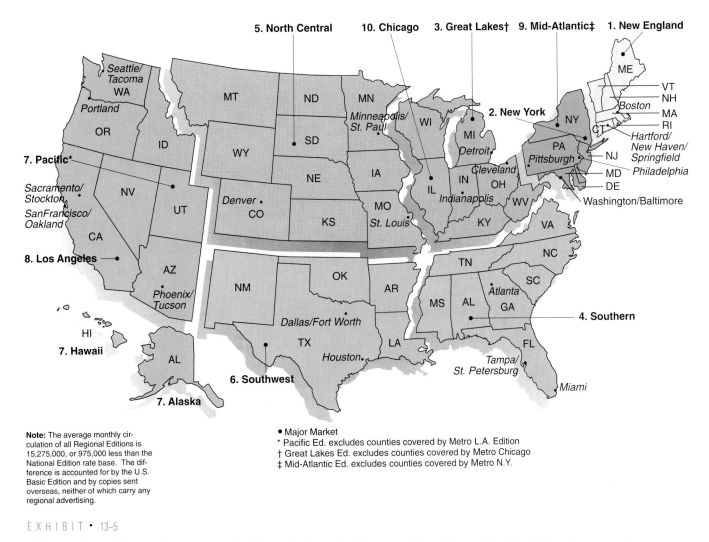

5. North Central   10. Chicago   3. Great Lakes†   9. Mid-Atlantic‡   1. New England

Note: The average monthly circulation of all Regional Editions is 15,275,000, or 975,000 less than the National Edition rate base. The difference is accounted for by the U.S. Basic Edition and by copies sent overseas, neither of which carry any regional advertising.

• Major Market
* Pacific Ed. excludes counties covered by Metro L.A. Edition
† Great Lakes Ed. excludes counties covered by Metro Chicago
‡ Mid-Atlantic Ed. excludes counties covered by Metro N.Y.

E X H I B I T • 13-5

Advertisers benefit from selecting regional editions similar to the 10 geographic editions of *Reader's Digest* shown on the map above. Regional binding and mailing allows advertisers to buy ad space for only the amount of distribution they need.

Size

It doesn't take a genius to figure out that magazines come in different shapes and sizes, but might take one to figure out how to get one ad to run in different-sized magazines and still look the same. Magazine sizes run the gamut from very large to very small, which makes production standardization an occasional nightmare. The most common magazine sizes are:

Size Classification	Magazine	Approximate size of full-page ad
Large	*Life*	4 col. × 170 lines* (9⅜ × 12⅛ inches)
Flat	*Time, Newsweek*	3 col. × 140 lines (7 × 10 inches)
Standard	*National Geographic*	2 col. × 119 lines (6 × 8½ inches)
Small or pocket	*Reader's Digest, TV Guide*	2 col. × 91 lines (4½ × 6½ inches)

* 1 line = 1/14 inch

HOW TO BUY MAGAZINE SPACE

Advertising media buyers consider a wide range of factors when analyzing which magazines to include in a media buy—circulation, readership, cost, mechanical requirements, and ad closing dates. Therefore, they must thoroughly understand the magazine's circulation and rate card information.

Understanding Magazine Circulation

The first step in analyzing a publication's potential effectiveness is to assess the magazine's audience. The buyer studies circulation statistics, primary and secondary readership figures, and the number of subscription and vendor sales. The buyer also considers any special merchandising services the magazine might offer.

Guaranteed versus Delivered Circulation

A magazine's rate structure is based on its circulation. The *rate base* is the circulation figure on which the publisher bases its rates; the **guaranteed circulation** figure is the number of copies the publisher expects to circulate. The latter is particularly meaningful for advertisers because they buy space with the assurance of reaching a certain number of people. Since some copies counted as guaranteed circulation may be sold on newsstands, the publisher may not reach its guaranteed circulation figure. If this *delivered figure* is not reached, the publisher must provide a refund. For that reason, most guaranteed circulation figures are stated safely below the average circulation that is actually delivered.

Advertising people often speak of guaranteed circulation as *audited* circulation. Most agency media buyers expect publications to verify their circulation figures. So publishers pay thousands of dollars each year for a **circulation audit**—a thorough analysis of the circulation procedures, outlets of distribution, and other distribution factors—by companies such as Audit Bureau of Circulations (ABC). An audit report breaks total circulation into a number of demographic categories (males, females, managers, trades, professions, etc.). Directories such as the Standard Rate Data Service (SDRS) feature the logo of the auditing company in each listing for an audited magazine.

Primary and Secondary Readership

Data from the ABC or other verified reports tell the media buyer the magazine's total circulation. Called **primary circulation,** it represents the number of people who buy the publication either by subscription or at the newsstand. **Secondary readership,** or **pass-along readership,** can be very important to some magazines—in some cases more than six different people read the same copy of a publication. Consider how many people read one copy of *Time* in a doctor's waiting room. Multiplying the average pass-along readership by, say, a million subscribers can give a magazine a substantial audience beyond its primary readers.

Vertical and Horizontal Publications

There are two readership classifications of business publications: *vertical* and *horizontal.* Advertisers choose one or the other depending on how deeply they want to penetrate a particular industry or how widely they want to spread the message across various industries. Apple Computer, for example, advertises in both horizontal and vertical publications.

EXHIBIT · 13-6

Purchasing magazine is a horizontal publication read by purchasing agents in a variety of different businesses and industries.

A **vertical publication** covers a specific industry in all its aspects. For example, Cahners Publishing produces *Restaurants & Institutions* strictly for restaurateurs and food service operators. The magazine's editorial content includes everything from news of the restaurant industry to institutional-size recipes.

Horizontal publications, in contrast, deal with a particular job function across a variety of industries. *Packaging* magazine addresses issues of concern to package engineers and designers. Readers of *Purchasing* work in purchasing management in many different industries. (See Exhibit 13–6.)

Subscription and Vendor Sales

Media buyers also want to know a magazine's ratio of subscriptions to newsstand sales. Today, subscriptions account for the majority of magazine sales. Newsstands (which also encompass bookstore chains) are still a major outlet for single-copy sales, but no outlet can handle more than a fraction of the magazines available. Display space is limited, and retailers sometimes complain that distributors make them take publications they don't want in order to get others they do.

From the advertiser's point of view, newsstand sales are impressive because they indicate that the purchaser really wants the magazine and is not merely subscribing out of habit. According to the Magazine Publishers Association, revenues from single-copy sales account for 34 percent of total revenues for a representative sampling of leading magazines. Some publications are sold entirely through newsstands; others, such as most trade publications, are distributed entirely by subscription.

Paid and Controlled Circulation

Business publications may be distributed on either a *paid circulation* or *controlled circulation* basis. A paid basis means the recipient must pay the subscription price to receive it. *Business Week* is a **paid circulation** business magazine.

In **controlled** circulation, the publisher mails the magazine *free* to a select list of individuals who the publisher thinks can influence the purchase of advertised products. Managers of corporate video departments receive *Corporate Video Decisions.* To receive a controlled circulation publication, these people must indicate in writing a desire to receive it and must give their professional designation or occupation. Ordinarily, to qualify for the subscription list, they must also include information about their job title, function, and purchasing duties. Dues-paying members of organizations often get free subscriptions. Members of the National Association for Female Executives receive free copies of *Executive Female.*

Advertisers don't want to pay to reach subscribers who aren't interested in what they're selling. Publishers of paid circulation magazines say subscribers who pay are more likely to read a publication than those who receive it free. But controlled circulation magazines can reach good prospects for the goods and services they advertise. Publishers say, by giving the publication away, they get good coverage of the market with little or no effect on readership.

Merchandising Services: Added Value

Magazines—and newspapers too—often provide liberal *added value* services. They may prepare mailings for the advertiser to notify dealers of an impending ad. They may also send countertop cards stating "As advertised in" for retailers to use in their stores. Many magazines also provide:

- Special free promotions to stores
- Marketing services that help readers find local outlets through a central phone number.
- Response cards that allow readers to request an advertiser's brochures and catalogs.
- Aid in handling sales force, broker, wholesaler, and retailer meetings.
- Advance editions for the trade.
- Research into brand preference, consumer attitudes, and market conditions.

If a publication's basic factors—editorial, circulation, readership—are strong, these additional services can increase the effectiveness of its ads.[4]

Reading Rate Cards

Magazine rate cards follow a standard format (see Exhibit 13–7). This helps advertisers determine costs, discounts, mechanical requirements, issue and closing dates, special editions, and additional costs for features like color, inserts, bleed pages, split runs, or preferred positions.

Typical rate card from *People* magazine details whom to contact, rates for space, standard sizes accepted, and volume discounts.

Rates

As we discussed in Chapter 12, one way to compare magazines is to look at how much it costs to reach a thousand people based on the magazine's rates for a one-time, full-page, black-and-white ad. This cost per thousand (CPM) figure is computed by dividing the B/W page rate by the number of *thousands* of subscribers:

$$\frac{\text{Page rate}}{(\text{Circulation}/1{,}000)} = \text{CPM}$$

If the magazine's black-and-white page rate is $10,000 and it has a circulation of 500,000:

$$\frac{\$10{,}000}{(500{,}000/1{,}000)} = \frac{10{,}000}{500} = \$20\,\text{CPM}$$

Consider this comparison. In 1990, the page rate for a one-time, black-and-white ad in *Flying* magazine was $12,560 on total paid circulation of 321,801; *Plane & Pilot* offered the same ad for $4,270 on total paid circulation of 103,670. Both aviation publications claimed substantial pass-along readership. Which was the better buy?

Exhibit 13–8 lists the circulations, readership, and color page rates for 18 leading consumer magazines. Using these data, you can calculate which national buys offer the best CPMs.

Discounts

Newspapers and magazines often give discounts based on frequency and volume. *Frequency discounts* are based on the number of ad insertions, usually within a year; *volume discounts* are based on the total amount of space bought

Magazine	Total paid circulation	Readers per copy			Page cost for four-color ad
		Men	Women	Total	
Modern Maturity	21,033,000	.62	1.03	1.65	$218,215
Reader's Digest	16,602,000	1.27	1.72	2.99	124,730
TV Guide	16,334,000	1.29	1.59	2.88	112,900
National Geographic	8,571,000	1.93	1.76	3.69	139,280
Better Homes and Gardens	8,078,000	3.12	1.04	4.16	119,000
Family Circle	5,195,000	.67	3.82	4.49	82,165
Ladies' Home Journal	5,083,000	.49	3.31	3.80	78,200
Good Housekeeping	4,880,000	.96	5.08	6.04	103,190
Time	4,515,000	2.12	1.83	3.95	120,130
Woman's Day	4,358,000	.44	4.04	4.48	73,075
Redbook	3,846,000	.49	2.90	3.39	71,530
Sports Illustrated	3,739,000	4.64	1.43	6.07	113,220
National Enquirer	3,705,000	1.90	2.96	4.86	47,200
Playboy	3,347,000	3.02	.87	3.89	65,280
Star	3,206,000	1.02	1.99	3.01	37,300
People Weekly	3,203,000	4.28	6.99	11.28	91,165
Newsweek	3,173,000	3.94	2.89	6.83	100,980
Cosmopolitan	2,512,000	.89	4.26	5.15	58,435

AD LAB 13–B   Innovations in Magazine Advertising

Magazines work closely with advertisers to develop new technologies for presenting ideas and products. From these efforts have come such innovations as fragrance strips, color strips, and pop-ups.

Developed in the early 1980s, **fragrance strips** have become a great favorite with perfume advertisers. With the *Scentstrip,* readers can sample a scent by opening a sealed insert tucked into a magazine. Despite some consumer complaints, Scentstrips are incredibly popular. Odors are useful for other products as well—a Rolls-Royce ad in *Architectural Digest* carried a Scentstrip bearing the essence of leather.

Cosmetics manufacturers can insert **color strip** samples of eye shadow, blusher, lipstick, and makeup that readers can try immediately. Color strips are expensive to produce, but many advertisers think the cost is worth it.

Another costly innovation is the **pop-up ad,** as shown. Corporate advertisers such as Honeywell and TransAmerica were among the first to try this eye-catching approach; product ads, such as a pop-up Dodge Dakota, followed.

Other intriguing approaches include **3-D ads** (complete with 3-D glasses), other forms of product samples (facial tissues and paper towels), and unusual shapes and sizes for inserts. An ad for Sarah Lee cheesecake used a single heavy-stock page with what appeared to be a bite taken out of a large-as-life cheesecake slice. A half-page insert for Gleem toothpaste featured a metallic graphic of a mirror with the slogan "Check Your Mirror."

Researchers are probing the possibilities of holographic ads and ads that "talk" when readers pass a device across the

HFC, Direct Mail/DDB Needham Worldwide

page. Already ads can "sing"—liquor companies include microchips that play Christmas carols in their December magazine ads, and Camel cigarette ads played "Happy Birthday" on the brand's 75th anniversary.

Such innovative approaches not only attract readers' attention but also *involve* them in the experience by appealing to more than just the visual sense.

Laboratory Application

What kinds of products besides perfumes and cars could Scentstrips be used to advertise?

---

during a specific period. Most magazines also offer *cash discounts* (usually 2 percent), and some offer discounts on the purchase of four or more consecutive pages in a single issue. With the recent decline in magazine advertising, many publications offer other discounts as well—such as the "added value" services mentioned earlier.[5] In fact, more than half of all magazine publishers now negotiate their rates. Some offer discounts up to 50 percent. Industry observers expect this rate-cutting trend to continue.[6]

Premium Rates

Magazines charge extra for special features. Color normally costs 25 to 60 percent more than black-and-white. Some publications, such as *Money,* even offer metallic and aluminum-based inks and special colors (beyond the four typically used in color printing) by special arrangement. Bleed pages add as much as 20 percent to regular rates, although the typical increase is about 15 percent.

Second and third cover rates (the inside covers) typically cost less than the fourth (back) cover. Cover rates usually include color, whether the ad is run in color or not. *Newsweek* charges $100,980 for a normal color page, but $108,050 for second and third covers and $138,505 for the fourth cover.

Magazines charge different rates for ads in geographic or demographic issues. *Geographic* editions target geographic markets; *demographic* editions reach readers who share a demographic trait, such as age, income level, or professional status. *Time* offers one-page four-color ads (one-time insertion) in Boston for $10,779 (166,000 circulation), in Texas for $12,698 (210,000 circulation), to college students for $21,100 (413,042 circulation), and to the 50 largest metropolitan markets for $107,200 (3.1 million circulation). Advertisers pay more for geographic or demographic editions with broader reach. For some additional ideas on creativity, see Ad Lab 13–B: Innovations in Magazine Advertising.

Issue and Closing Dates

Three dates affect magazine purchases:

Cover date—the date printed on the cover.

On-sale date—the date the magazine is actually issued.

Closing date—the date all ad material must be in the publisher's hands for inclusion in a specific issue. Lead time may be as much as three months.

USING NEWSPAPERS IN THE CREATIVE MIX

EXHIBIT • 13-9

Newspaper ad for a Minneapolis hair salon was one of a series that used stock images to suggest the problems of "bad haircuts." Inexpensive to produce, the campaign was extremely successful.

Sometimes—just sometimes—a client will give an agency the freedom to really flex its creative muscles. When that happens, the results can be astounding. Such was the case when a small haircutting salon in Minneapolis asked one of the leading creative shops in the country for help.

The client's only requirement was that the agency put the client's name on the ads. Fallon McElligott had to create an awareness campaign for the little barber shop with the funny name—7 South 8th for Hair—and still leave enough in reserve to place the ads with sufficient frequency.

"This was a very easy campaign to create, really painless," says Jarl Olsen, the copywriter at Fallon McElligott. "The whole thing took less than a day to plan."

They decided to run the campaign in local newspapers because of their ability to reach a large audience quickly at reasonable cost. Newspapers also turned out to be best for getting across the campaign's simple, straightforward message.

"We wanted to generate some talk value, so we used something everyone could laugh at. We were all over the board," says Olsen, "and all of the ideas were weird."

Random scrawlings eventually led to the ad shown in Exhibit 13–9, featuring the snake-haired Medusa and a single line of copy: "A bad haircut is a real can of worms." The rest of the campaign spun off that original idea.

"We sat around trying to think of bad haircuts," Olsen recalls with a laugh. "We thought of several, but we could only think of a few copy lines that made any sense." The ads had stock photos of famous bad haircuts, a witty line of copy, and the salon's name and address. Another in the series features a picture of former President Richard Nixon over the headline: "You can't cover up a bad haircut."

The campaign took the city by storm. The ads appeared all over Minneapolis in newspapers and later in local magazines and on posters.

"These ads were everywhere," says Olsen, "and everyone was talking about them. Other shops were cutting the ads out and sticking their own logos on them. I called 7 South 8th to tell them about it. They laughed and said they knew. They thought it was funny."[7]

CHECKLIST   The Pros and Cons of Newspaper Advertising

The Pros

◇ **Mass medium** penetrating every segment of society. Almost all consumers read the newspaper.

◇ **Local medium with broad reach.** Covers a specific geographic area that comprises both a market and a community of people sharing common concerns and interest.

◇ **Comprehensive** in scope, covering an extraordinary variety of topics and interests.

◇ **Geographic selectivity** is possible with special zoned editions for specific neighborhoods or communities.

◇ **Timeliness** because they primarily cover today's news and are read in one day.

◇ **Credibility.** Studies show that newspaper ads rank highest in believability. TV commercials are a distant second.

◇ **Selective attention** from the relatively small number of active prospects who, on any given day, are interested in what the advertiser is trying to tell them or sell them.

◇ **Creative flexibility.** An ad's physical size and shape can be chosen and varied to give the degree of dominance or repetition that suits the advertiser's purpose. The advertiser can use black-and-white, color, Sunday magazines, or custom inserts.

◇ **An active medium** rather than a passive one and a **permanent record.** Readers turn the pages, clip and save, write in the margins, and sort through the contents.

The Cons

◇ **Lack of selectivity** of specific socioeconomic groups. Most newspapers reach broad, diverse groups of readers which may not match the advertiser's objectives.

◇ **Short life span.** Unless readers clip and save the ad or coupon, it may be lost forever.

◇ **Low production quality.** Coarse newsprint generally produces a less impressive image than the slick, smooth paper stock of magazines, and many newspapers can't print color.

◇ **Clutter.** Each ad competes with editorial content and every other ad on the same page or spread.

◇ **Advertisers lack control** over where ad will appear unless they pay a preferred position premium.

◇ **Overlapping circulation.** Some people read more than one newspaper. Advertisers may be paying for readers their ads already reached in a different paper.

The Pros and Cons of Newspaper Advertising

The 7 South 8th story demonstrates how small stores, with even smaller budgets, can benefit from creative newspaper advertising. Creative advertising gives the advertiser a chance to be heard, to present an offer. Print ads in general and newspapers in particular provide a unique, flexible medium for advertisers to express their creativity—especially stores that rely on local customers.

Newspapers offer many advantages. One of the most important is timeliness—an ad can appear very quickly, sometimes in just one day. Newspapers also offer geographic targeting, a broad range of markets, reasonable cost, and more. But newspapers suffer from lack of selectivity, poor production quality, and clutter.

Knowing the advantages and disadvantages of different media is important to an advertiser's success. See if you can use the information in the Checklist: Pros and Cons of Newspaper Advertising to answer the questions in Ad Lab 13–C: Newspapers and the Creative Mix.

Who Uses Newspapers?

Newspapers are the dominant medium in terms of advertising volume, receiving more than 26 percent of the dollars spent by advertisers in the United States.[8]

Consider these important facts:

• More than 113 million U.S. adults read daily papers each weekday; nearly two out of three Americans read a paper every day.

AD LAB 13–C   Newspapers and the Creative Mix

Study the Checklist: Pros and Cons of Newspaper Advertising, and see if you can apply that information to the following situation.

You're the product manager for a major brand of bar soap and you wish to go nationwide with an ad featuring a coupon.

Laboratory Applications

1. Which newspaper would be best?
   a. A weekly
   b. A daily
2. If you use a daily, in what section of the paper would you want your ad to appear?
3. If you decided on the Sunday supplement, which of the following would you choose and why:
   a. *Parade* Magazine?
   b. Color coupon supplement?

- The typical daily newspaper reader spends an average of 45 minutes a day reading one or more newspapers and 62 minutes a week reading a Sunday paper.
- An average of 2.1 persons read each of the more than 62 million daily papers circulated in the United States each day.
- In 1989, there were 1,626 daily newspapers in the United States with a total circulation of 62.6 million. In 1990, the nation's 7,550 weekly newspapers had a combined circulation of more than 55 million.
- U.S. advertising volume in daily newspapers increased by 3.8 percent in 1989, with total sales of more than $32 billion—$5 billion more than its nearest competitor.[9]

Although the newspaper is the major community-serving medium for both news and advertising, more and more national advertisers are shifting to radio and television. As a result, radio and TV carry most of the national advertising in the United States, while 88 percent of newspaper advertising revenue comes from local advertising. As Exhibit 13–10 shows, retailers are the primary national newspaper advertisers.

EXHIBIT • 13–10

Top 10 newspaper advertisers in the United States.

Rank	Advertiser	Newspaper ad expenditures, 1991*
1	May Department Stores Co.	$155.2
2	R. H. Macy & Co.	139.2
3	Federated Department Stores	91.8
4	Sears, Roebuck & Co.	88.7
5	Circuit City Stores	73.3
6	Carter Hawley Hale Stores	70.5
7	AMR Corp.	68.7
8	American Stores Inc.	57.2
9	Delta Air Lines	53.6
10	Dayton Hudson Corp	46.0

* Dollars in millions.

How Newspapers Are Categorized

Newspapers can be classified by frequency of delivery, physical size, or the type of audience they reach.

Frequency of Delivery

On the basis of frequency, advertisers can use two basic types: *dailies* and *weeklies*. A **daily newspaper** is published as either a morning or evening edition at least five times a week, Monday through Friday.

Of the 1,626 dailies in the United States, 1,125 are evening papers and 530 are morning papers. (The total exceeds 1,626 because 29 consider themselves morning *and* evening papers, or "all-day" newspapers).[10] Morning editions tend to have broader geographic circulation and a larger male readership; evening editions are read more by women. Despite these general characteristics, each daily paper has its own circulation traits, determined by the geographic region it serves and the demographic makeup of its readers.

Weekly newspapers characteristically serve readers in small urban or suburban areas of farm communities. With their emphasis on local news and advertising, they are becoming the fastest-growing class of newspapers. Weekly newspapers offer relief from unsettling national and international crises by offering news of familiar names and local personalities, hometown sports, entertainment, and social coverage.

A weekly newspaper's cost per thousand (CPM) is often higher than a daily paper's, but a weekly has a longer life and is often exposed to more readers per copy.

Physical Size

There are two basic newspaper formats: *standard size* and *tabloid*. The **standard-size newspaper** is about 22 inches deep and 13 inches wide and is divided into six columns. The **tabloid newspaper** is generally about half the size—about 14 inches deep and 11 inches wide. National tabloid newspapers like the *National Enquirer, The Star,* and the *Globe,* use sensational news stories to fight for single-copy sales. Other tabloids, such as the *New York Daily News,* emphasize straight news and features.

Placing ads used to be a complex task because papers varied greatly in their dimensions, number of columns, and methods of calculating ad space. But in 1984, the newspaper industry introduced a new **standard advertising unit (SAU)** system that uses inches, or **column inches,** as the main unit of measure. The SAU system standardized the newspaper column width of 2$\frac{1}{16}$ inches; an SAU column inch is 2$\frac{1}{16}$ inches wide by 1 inch deep. Previously, the standard unit of measure was *agate lines,* or **lines,** each a column wide and $\frac{1}{14}$ inch deep. The SAU system also standardizes page and ad sizes, as shown in Exhibit 13–11. There are now 56 standard ad sizes for standard papers and 32 for tabloids, each with a defined width and depth. Previously, newspapers used about 400 different ad sizes. Virtually all dailies converted to the SAU system—some at great expense—and so did most weeklies.

Specialized Audience

Some dailies and weeklies serve special-interest audiences, a fact not lost on advertisers. Their specialized news and features enable them to achieve high readership. They generally contain advertising oriented to their special audiences, and they may have unique advertising regulations.

EXHIBIT • 13-11

EXHIBIT • 13-11

The SAU Grid shows the various standardized sizes for ads in tabloid-size and standard-size newspapers.

The Expanded SAU® Standard Advertising Unit System

Depth in Inches	1 COL. 2-1/16"	2 COL. 4-1/4"	3 COL. 6-7/16"	4 COL. 8-5/8"	5 COL. 10-13/16"	6 COL. 13"
FD*	1xFD*	2xFD*	3xFD*	4xFD*	5xFD*	6xFD*
18"	1x18	2x18	3x18	4x18	5x18	6x18
15.75"	1x15.75	2x15.75	3x15.75	4x15.75	5x15.75	
14"	1x14	2x14	3x14	4x14	N 5x14	6x14
13"	1x13	2x13	3x13	4x13	5x13	
10.5"	1x10.5	2x10.5	3x10.5	4x10.5	5x10.5	6x10.5
7"	1x7	2x7	3x7	4x7	5x7	6x7
5.25"	1x5.25	2x5.25	3x5.25	4x5.25		
3.5"	1x3.5	2x3.5				
3"	1x3	2x3				
2"	1x2	2x2				
1.5"	1x1.5					
1"	1x1					

1 Column 2-1/16"
2 Columns 4-1/4"
3 Columns 6-7/16"
4 Columns 8-5/8"
5 Columns 10-13/16"
6 Columns 13"

Double Truck 26-3/4"
(There are four suggested double truck sizes:)
13xFD*   13x18
13x14   13x10.5

*FD (Full Depth) can be 21" or deeper. Depths for each broadsheet newspaper are indicated in the Standard Rate and Data Service. All broadsheet newspapers can accept 22" ads, and may float them if their depth is greater than 21".

Tabloids: Size 5 x 14 is a full page tabloid for long cut-off papers. Mid cut-off papers can handle this size with minimal reduction. The N size, measuring 9⅜ x 14, represents the full page size for tabloids such as the New York Daily News and News-day, and other short cut-off newspapers. The five 13 inch deep sizes are for tabloids printed on 55 inch wide presses such as the Philadelphia News. See individual SRDS listings for tabloid sections of broadsheet newspapers.

Printed in U.S.A. 11/93

Some serve specific ethnic markets. Today more than 200 dailies and weeklies, such as the Ft. Worth, Texas, *Times* and the New York *Amsterdam News,* are oriented to the African-American community. Others serve foreign-language groups, such as Spanish, German, Polish, Chinese, or Armenian readers. In the United States, newspapers are printed in 43 languages other than English.

Specialized newspapers also serve business and financial audiences. *The Wall Street Journal,* the leading national business and financial daily, enjoys circulation of nearly 2 million. Other papers cater to fraternal, labor union, or professional organizations, and some to religious groups or hobbyists. There are even weekly newspapers for stamp and coin collectors.

And more than 1 million people in the armed services overseas receive the daily and Sunday European and Pacific editions of the leading U.S. military newspaper, *Stars and Stripes*.

Other Types of Newspapers

In the United States, there are 847 Sunday newspapers—mostly Sunday editions of daily papers—with a combined circulation of 62 million.[11] Sunday newspapers generally combine standard news coverage with other special functions, such as:

- Increased classified advertising volume.
- Greater advertising and news volume.
- In-depth coverage of business, sports, real estate, literature and the arts, entertainment, and travel.
- Review and analysis of the past week's events.
- Expanded editorial and opinion sections.

Most Sunday newspapers also feature a newspaper-distributed magazine, or **Sunday supplement.** Some publish their own supplement, such as "Los Angeles Magazine" of the *Los Angeles Times*. Others subscribe to syndicated supplements, which are compiled, edited, and printed by a central organization and shipped to individual papers for insertion.

Printed on rotogravure on heavier, coated paper stock, Sunday supplements are more conducive to color printing, making them attractive to national advertisers who want better reproduction quality.

Another type of newspaper, the **independent shopping guide** or free community newspaper, offers advertisers local saturation. Sometimes called *pennysavers* or *shoppers,* most newspapers of this type carry little news and practically no features. Instead, they feature free distribution and extensive advertising pages targeted at essentially the same audience as the weekly newspapers—urban and suburban community readers. Shoppers may be published weekly, biweekly, or monthly. Readership is often high, and the publisher uses hand delivery or direct mail to achieve maximum saturation. In the Long Island, New York, area, 83 percent of those receiving the papers read them regularly, and 91 percent said they got information they couldn't get from other newspapers.[12]

North Americans also read national newspapers including the *Globe-Mail, USA Today,* and the *Christian Science Monitor. USA Today* has a national circulation of 1.4 million, second only to *The Wall Street Journal* in national distribution and first among U.S. general-interest dailies, surpassing the *New York Daily News*. In the mid-80s, *USA Today* became the number-one print vehicle for automotive ads due to its high-quality color reproduction.[13]

Types of Newspaper Advertising

The major classifications of newspaper advertising are *display, classified, public notices,* and *preprinted inserts*. Advertisers use the different types of ads to achieve various advertising goals.

Display Advertising

Display advertising differs from **classified advertising** in that it includes not only copy, but illustrations or photographs, headlines, and other visual components—like the ads for 7 South 8th for Hair, discussed earlier. Classified ads

This ad for the classified section of the *Village Voice* represents the two major types of newspaper advertising. First, it's a **display ad** having a visual, sig cut, and a logo. Its visual shows the second form of advertisement—a **classified ad**—limited to a "situated wanted" header, a few lines of block type, and a telephone number. The witty copy shows how the power of good writing can make any newspaper ad memorable.

usually include only copy. The ad for the *Village Voice* newspaper in Exhibit 13–12 is a display ad aimed at promoting the use of classified ads.

Display ads vary in size and appear in all sections of the newspaper except page one, the editorial page, the obituary page, the classified section, and the first page of major sections.

Display ads can be black-and-white or color, with or without pictures. Most local display advertising is either black-and-white or multicolored with a few basic colors. One common variation of the display ad, the **reading notice**, looks like editorial matter and sometimes costs more than normal display advertising. Many newspapers accept reading notices, but to prevent readers from mistaking them for editorial matter, the word *advertisement* appears at the top.

Retailers often run newspaper ads through **cooperative** (or co-op) **programs** sponsored by the manufacturers whose products they sell. The manufacturer pays fully or partially to create and run the ad, which features the local retailer's name and logo.

Classified Advertising

Classified advertisements are a distinctive feature of newspapers. They provide a community marketplace for goods, services, and opportunities of every type—from real estate and new-car sales to employment and business opportunities. They are also a significant source of ad revenues. In fact, a newspaper's profitability usually depends on a healthy classified section.

Classified ads usually appear under subheads that describe the class of goods or the need the ads seek to satisfy. For example, people look for a job under the "Help Wanted" classification or for an employee under "Situations Wanted." Most employment, housing, and automotive advertising appears in the form of classified advertising.

Classified rates are typically based on the number of lines the ad occupies and the number of times the ad runs. They may also vary depending on whether the ad is for real estate, employment, or some other category.

Some newspapers also accept **classified display advertising.** These ads run in the classified section of the newspaper but feature larger-size type, photos, art borders, abundant white space, and sometimes even color.

Public Notices

For a nominal fee, newspapers carry legal notices of changes in business and personal relationships, public governmental reports, notices by private citizens and organizations, and financial reports. These ads follow a preset format.

Preprinted Inserts

Like magazines, newspapers also carry **preprinted inserts.** The advertiser prints the inserts and delivers them to the newspaper plant for insertion into a specific edition either by machine or by the newsdealers. Insert sizes range from a typical newspaper page to a piece no larger than a double postcard; formats include catalogs, brochures, mail-back devices, and perforated coupons.

Some large metropolitan dailies allow advertisers to limit their inserts to specific circulation zones. A retail advertiser that wants to reach only those shoppers in its immediate trading area can place an insert in the local-zone editions. Retail stores, auto dealers, large national advertisers, and others find it less costly to distribute their circulars this way than to mail or deliver them door-to-door.

HOW TO BUY NEWSPAPER SPACE

Buying newspaper space follows the same basic procedure as buying magazine space. To get the most from the advertising budget, the media buyer must know the characteristics of a newspaper's readership—the median age, sex, occupation, income, educational level, and buying habits of the typical reader.

Understanding Readership and Circulation

Readership information is available in standardized form from various sources such as Simmons Market Research Bureau and Scarborough Research Corporation. In addition, most large papers provide extensive readership data, including information on various geographic editions.

In single-newspaper cities, reader demographics will reflect a cross-section of the general population. In cities with two or more newspapers, however, these characteristics may vary widely. The *Los Angeles Times* is directed to a broad cross-section of the community and *La Opinion* to the area's large Hispanic population. Each newspaper has a significantly different audience—which colors its overall attractiveness to different types of advertisers.

The time of day a newspaper is published can also affect readership. An advertiser may have to decide between advertising a bedding sale in a morning newspaper that has a 60 percent male readership or an evening newspaper with high female readership. Each alternative has its advantages. The morning paper can advertise the sale for that day and attract immediate shoppers, while an ad in the evening paper can motivate a husband and wife together to come to the sale the following day.

In addition to understanding the newspaper's basic readership, advertisers must also know the extent of its circulation. The paper's total circulation includes both subscribers and single-copy newsstand buyers as well as secondary readers—people who read a paper that someone else bought. Only by analyzing the paper's total circulation can advertisers estimate how far their newspaper advertising dollars will go.

Rate Card

The newspaper **rate card** is similar to the magazine rate card—it lists advertising rates, mechanical and copy requirements, deadlines, and other information. Because rates vary greatly, advertisers should calculate which papers deliver the most readers for their money, and weigh that information against the readership.

Local versus National Rates

Most newspapers charge local and national advertisers different rates. The national rate averages 75 percent higher, but some papers charge as much as 254 percent more.[14] Newspapers attribute higher rates to the added costs they incur serving national advertisers. For instance, an ad agency usually places national advertising and receives a 15 percent commission from the paper. Some papers serve agencies through media representatives, who also receive a commission. If the advertising comes from another city or state, then additional costs, such as long-distance telephone calls, are involved.

But the dual rate system is still quite controversial among advertisers. In fact, many national advertisers rebel against the high rates and take their business elsewhere—only about 3 percent of national ad dollars now go to newspapers, and that proportion may shrink even further.[15] In response to declining national advertising revenue, newspapers have begun experimenting with simplified billing systems and discount rates for their national clients. One group of 258 papers joined forces to offer packaged goods advertisers an average 30 percent discount on ads that were a quarter page size or larger and that ran 13 times. This special rate was still 25 percent above local rates but lower than the usual 62 percent differential.[16] Smaller groups of papers also joined forces to test other discount plans in an attempt to lure back national accounts.

Flat Rates and Discount Rates

Local advertisers can sometimes earn even lower rates by buying larger or repeated amounts of space at **volume discounts,** but not all newspapers offer such discounts. Many national papers charge **flat rates,** which means they allow no discounts for large or repeated space buys, and a few newspapers offer a single flat rate to both national and local advertisers.

Newspapers that offer volume discounts have an **open rate**—their highest rate for a one-time insertion—and **contract rates,** whereby local advertisers can obtain discounts of up to 70 percent by signing a contract for frequent or bulk space purchases. *Bulk discounts* offer advertisers decreasing rates (calculated by multiplying the number of inches by the cost per inch) as the number of inches used increases. Advertisers earn *frequency discounts* by running a given ad repeatedly in a specific time period. Similarly, advertisers can sometimes get **earned rates**- a discount applied retroactively as the volume of advertising increases through the year. More than 1,000 newspapers also participate in Newsplan, a Newspaper Advertising Bureau program that gives national and regional advertisers discounts for purchasing six or more pages per year. Exhibit 13–13 shows a rate card for the *Boston Globe* listing various contract rates.

Short Rate

An advertiser who contracts to buy a specific amount of space during a one-year period at a discount rate and then fails to do so is charged a **short rate.** The short rate is actually the publisher's earned rate for a lesser number of inches. The short rate is computed by determining the difference between the rate contracted for and the earned rate for the actual inches run. Conversely, an advertiser who buys more inches than the number contracted for may be

---

The Boston Globe

P. O. Box 2373, 135 Morrissey Blvd., Boston, MA 02107-2378.
Phone 617-929-2200, TWX, 710-333-0294. Fax: 617-929-2014.

AD·SAU.
SAU
newsplan — DISCOUNTS FOR CONTINUITY
ABC Coupon Distribution Verification Service
The Audit Bureau (ACB)

Location ID: 1 NSNL MA   Mid 016696-000
MORNING, SATURDAY AND SUNDAY MORNING.
Member: INAME; NAB, Inc; ABC Coupon Distribution Verification Service; ACB, Inc.

1. PERSONNEL
Pub—Wm. O. Taylor.
Adv Dir—Oliver H.P. Rodman.
Display Adv Mgr—George E. Harden.

2. REPRESENTATIVES and/or BRANCH OFFICES
Newspapers First.
Canada—American Publishers' Representatives Ltd.
Europe—Colin Turner Group, LTD.

3. COMMISSION AND CASH DISCOUNT
15% agency discount; 2%—20th of following month.

4. POLICY-ALL CLASSIFICATIONS
30-day notice given of any rate revision.
Alcoholic beverage and cigarette advertising accepted.

ADVERTISING RATES
Effective July 1, 1990.
Received June 5, 1990.

5. BLACK/WHITE RATES

	Morn.	Sun.
SAU open, per inch	211.00	245.00

Saturday and/or Holidays will be billed at 90% of ads morning rate. Sunday ad may repeat once within 6 days 97.00 per col. inch, (same copy). Morning full rate as may repeat once in the daily paper within 6 days at 97.00 per col. inch, (same copy). Combination ad will count toward bulk contract.
Inches charged full depth: col. 21; pg. 126.

BULK CONTRACT RATES

	Morn.	Sun.
31″	208.00	242.00
63″	205.00	239.00
126″	201.00	233.00
250″	198.00	230.00
500″	194.00	228.00
750″	193.00	226.00
1,200″	192.00	224.00

	Morn.	Sun.
1,600″	189.00	222.00
3,200″	186.00	220.00
6,500″	181.00	218.00
9,000″	179.00	214.00
12,500″	177.00	209.00
18,000″	174.00	204.00
25,000″	170.00	197.00
31,000″	165.00	191.00
36,000″	163.00	189.00
41,000″	161.00	187.00
46,000″	159.00	185.00
51,000″	157.00	183.00
56,000″	155.00	181.00
61,000″	153.00	179.00
71,000″	151.00	175.00
76,000″	149.00	173.00
81,000″	147.00	170.00
86,000″	145.00	168.00
91,000″	143.00	166.00

APPLICATION OF DISCOUNTS
Must be signed in advance to qualify for volume or frequency discounts. All advertising will be accumulated against the contract. Contracts not fulfilled will receive a short rate billing. A refund will be available if lower rate is earned. Ads will be rated at the contract level in each type or class of advertising.

NEWSPLAN—SAU

Pages	% Disc.	Morn.	Sun.	Inches
6	8.21	193.00	226.00	756
13	10.11	189.00	222.00	1,638
26	12.02	186.00	220.00	3,276
52	13.78	181.00	218.00	6,552
78	14.95	179.00	214.00	9,828

See Newsplan Contract and Copy Regulations—items 1, 2, 3, 4, 6, 8, 9, 10, 11, 12, 13, 15, 17.

7. COLOR RATES AND DATA

	Daily		Sunday	
	b/w 1 c	b/w 4 c	b/w 1 c	b/w 4 c
Open	2,800.00	3,500.00	3,100.00	3,900.00
2-5 times	2,660.00	3,325.00	2,945.00	3,705.00
11-12 times	2,520.00	3,150.00	2,790.00	3,510.00
12-17 times	2,380.00	2,975.00	2,635.00	3,315.00

	Daily		Sunday	
	b/w 1 c	b/w 4 c	b/w 1 c	b/w 4 c
18-23 times	2,240.00	2,800.00	2,480.00	3,120.00
24-29 times	2,100.00	2,625.00	2,325.00	2,925.00
30 or more times	1,960.00	2,450.00	2,170.00	2,730.00

Reservations, 7 days in advance of insertion date.
Closing dates: Complete material or cancellation 7 days in advance.

9. SPLIT RUN
50/50 only: minimum size 45 col. inches. Both ads must be same dimensions and same products. Premium of 200.00 daily; 300.00 Sunday.
STRIP ADS: Min. 6 cols. x 1″ deep. 51.00 per col. inch extra Morning or Sunday. Chargeable on any Strip Ad measuring less than 6 cols. x 7″.

11. SPECIAL DAYS/PAGES/FEATURES
Best Food Day: Wednesday.
Health & Science, Monday; Business Extra, Tuesday; Calendar Section, Money-A Guide to Personal Finance, Thursday; At Home, Sports Plus, Friday.
Books, Home & Garden, Living, Arts, Travel, Learning, Theatre, Hobby pages Business: Sunday.

12. R.O.P. DEPTH REQUIREMENTS
Minimum depth requirements: 1 col. 1/2″; 2 col. 2″; 3 col. 5-1/4″; 4 col. 5-1/4″; 5 col. 7″; 6 col. 7″. Ads exceeding 18″ in depth floated in full depth. Reading matter not placed over ads greater than 18″ deep.

13. CONTRACT AND COPY REGULATIONS
See Contents page for location of regulations—items 1, 2, 3, 5, 6, 7, 8, 9, 10, 11, 12, 13, 14, 15, 16, 17, 18, 19, 20, 22, 23, 24, 25, 26, 27, 28, 29.

14. CLOSING TIMES
Published Morning, Saturday and Sunday.

Day	Time	Closes	Day	Time	Closes
Mon	3 pm	Sat	Fri	3 pm	Wed
Tue	3 pm	Sun	Sat	3 pm	Thu
Wed	3 pm	Thu	Sun	10 am	Wed
Thu	3 pm	Tue			

SPECIAL SECTIONS

Day			Time	Closes
Amusements (Sun.)			5 pm	Wed
Books (Sun.)			5 pm	Wed
Hobbies (Sun.)			5 pm	Wed
Home & Garden & Living (Sun.)			5 pm	Wed
Travel, Resort (Sun.)			5 pm	Wed

15. MECHANICAL MEASUREMENTS
Also see SRDS Print Media Production Data.
PRINTING PROCESS: Offset.
6 col; ea 2-1/16″; 1/8″ betw col.
Inches charged full depth: col. 21; pg. 126.

16. SPECIAL CLASSIFICATIONS/RATES
Amusement—general rate applies.
Book publishers billed at 90% of ad's, morning or Sunday contract or open rate.
Financial: 17.00 per col. inch premium for ads ordered first NY Stock page. Stamp and Hobby Page—general rate applies.
Travel-Transportation-Travel Agents, Sunday:

	Per col. inch
Open or 1 Sunday	225.00
126″	214.00
250″	208.00
500″ or 52 Sundays	204.00
	Per col. inch
750″	201.00
1,200″	199.00
1,600″	195.00
3,200″	192.00
6,500″	186.00
9,000″	182.00
12,500″	179.00
18,000″	175.00

Any Sunday Travel ad may repeat 1 time in a daily with 6 days at 97.00 per col. inch (same copy).
Resort (Sunday Resort Section):

	Per col. inch
Open or 1 Sunday	195.00
126″ or 10 Sundays	180.00
250″ or 20 Sundays	173.00
500″ or 52 Sundays	163.00
750″	160.00
1,200″	158.00
1,600″	157.00
3,200″	156.00

Minimum 1/2 inch. Contract required to earn other than open rate. May repeat 1 time within week (same copy) 97.00 per col. inch.

POSITION CHARGES
Page 2, Death Notices or Public Notices only, Morning, per col. inch 242.00; Sunday, per col. inch 275.00.
Min. 1 col. x 1″ deep; max. 1 col. x 3-1/2″ deep.
No solid reverse, bold type or screened lines accepted. No display advertising or Reading notices accepted on page 1. No display advertising accepted on page 3 or comic page, daily.

17. CLASSIFIED RATES
For complete data refer to classified rate section.

18. COMICS
POLICY—ALL CLASSIFICATIONS
When orders are placed through Metro-Puck Comics Network—see that listing.
Effective July 1, 1990.
Received June 5, 1990.
COLOR RATES AND DATA
Black & 3 colors:

1 page	17,970.00
2/3 page	13,843.00
1/2 page (h)	8,988.00
1/3 page	6,924.00
1/6 page	4,855.00

EXHIBIT · 13–13

This typical newspaper rate card for the *Boston Globe* is similar to that for magazines and breaks out the variety of ad sizes and their costs.

entitled to a rebate or credit because the earned rate for the additional advertising space is lower.

Combination Rates

Combination rates are often available for placing a given ad in (1) morning and evening editions of the same newspaper; (2) two or more newspapers owned by the same publisher; and (3) in some cases, two or more newspapers affiliated in a syndicate or newspaper group. Publishers sometimes offer advertisers combination rates for placing a given ad in consecutive Saturday and Sunday editions of the same newspaper. At one time, some newspapers required advertisers to buy combinations, but courts declared this practice illegal, and combinations are now optional.

Run of Paper (ROP)

ROP advertising rates entitle a newspaper to place a given ad on any newspaper page or in any position it desires—in other words, where space permits. Although the advertiser has no control over where the ad appears in the paper, most newspapers try to place an ad in the position the advertiser requests. ROP rates are lower than those for preferred positions.

Preferred Position

An advertiser can ensure a choice position for an ad by paying a higher **preferred position** rate. A tire manufacturer or retailer may pay the preferred rate to ensure a position in the sports section.

There also are preferred positions on the newspaper page. The preferred position near the top of a page or on the top of a column next to reading matter is called **full position.** It's usually surrounded by reading matter and may cost the advertiser 25 to 50 percent more than ROP rates. Slightly less desirable, but also a preferred position, is placement *next to reading matter* (NR), which generally costs the advertiser 10 to 20 percent more than ROP rates.

Color Advertising

Color advertising is available in many newspapers on an ROP basis (see Exhibit 13–14). Because of their high-speed presses and porous paper stock, newspapers are not noted for high-quality color printing. So advertisers frequently preprint ads using processes known as HiFi color and Spectacolor. The ad is printed on a roll, and the roll is fed into the press by the newspaper, which prints its own material on the blank side. Some national advertisers preprint their color ads on the type of paper used in magazine supplements. The cost of a color ad is usually based on the black-and-white rate with an extra charge for each additional color.

Split Runs

Many newspapers (and magazines) offer **split runs.** The advertiser runs two ads of identical size but different content for the same product in the same or different press runs on the same day. This way, the advertiser tests the pulling power of each ad. Newspapers set a minimum space requirement and charge extra for this service.

Co-op Insertions

As an aid to national advertisers, the **Newspaper Advertising Bureau (NAB)** offers the **Newspaper Co-op Network (NCN).** With this system, salespeople from participating newspapers help advertisers line up retailers for dealer-listing ads. The national advertiser produces the ad and includes a blank space for each paper to insert local retailers' names. The system also helps manufac-turers manage local advertising tie-ins to national campaigns and themes. Before the development of NCN, national advertisers had to place ads and recruit local dealers individually—a process that required hundreds of phone calls and a lot of paperwork. Now an insertion in up to 1,500 daily newspapers entails only a few phone calls.[17]

The Newspaper Association of America plans to launch a one-order one-bill system for national advertising by the beginning of 1994. Advertisers using this system can make multimarket newspaper buys by placing one order and paying one bill, instead of having to contact—and pay—each paper individually; and costs will be standardized on a CPM-based rate structure.[18]

Insertion Orders and Tear Sheets

When advertisers place an ad, they submit an **insertion order** to the news-paper (see Exhibit 13–15) stating the date(s) on which the ad is to run and its size, the desired position, the rate, and the type of artwork—mechanicals, Velox prints (halftones), or photostats—accompanying the order.

An insertion order serves as a contract between the advertiser (or its agency) and the publication. If an advertiser fails to pay the agency, the agency still must pay the publication. To avoid this liability, many agencies now place a dis-

Agencies use an insertion order to place print ads in newspapers and magazines. That way all the particulars about the ad—size, run date, desired position, and so on—are put in writing to avoid any misunderstanding.

McDONALD DAVIS & ASSOCIATES
250 W. Coventry Court
Milwaukee, WI 53217
414 228-1990

INSERTION ORDER

Date	12/8/93
Insertion Order #	
Job #	24-062
Ad #	See Below
Client Name	Vista Del Mar Inn
Space Reserved	12/8/93
Revision Number	
Pub Phone #	(915) 546-6260
Pub Fax #	(915) 546-6404
Material Due Date	FRI 12/17/92 - Noon
Repeat Ad Last Ran	

Publication Address:
El Paso Times
Times Plaza
El Paso, TX 79901-1470
Attn: Joe Thompson

Materials To:
Same as Above

Issue Date	Space:	Ad Title/No.	Net Cost	Gross Cost
Sun 12/20/93	2 col. x 6"	"Grand Opening Special" BUD-41-062	538.56	633.60
Sun 1/3/93	2 col. x 6"	"Grand Opening Special" BUD-41-062	538.56	633.60
Sun 1/10/94	2 col. x 6"	"Now Open" BUD-46-062	538.56	633.60
Sun 1/17/94	2 col. x 6"	"Overnight" BUD-47-062	538.56	633.60

If rates are not correct, please notify agency at once.   **TOTALS:** | $2,154.24 | $2,534.40 |

*** NOTE: Do NOT place advertisements on same or facing page with ALCOHOL or TOBACCO Advertisements or the OBITUARIES. ***

Position Request:	Main News, Far Forward, Right Hand Page
Rate:	$52.80 gross/col. in.
Monthly Cost:	Dec: $538.56 Net Jan: $1,615.68 Net	Reason for Revision:

TWO TEARSHEETS FOR EACH AD MUST BE SENT TO MDA. NO INVOICES WILL BE PAID WITHOUT TEARSHEETS !!

| Accepted by (Publication) Please sign & return | Ordered by (MDA): Andrew Fleury |

| Accounting/2 | Bill | Pay | Publication | | Traffic/2 | | Media | | A.E. | |

---

claimer on their insertion orders stating that the agency is acting solely as an *agent for a disclosed principal*—a middleman for the advertiser—and is therefore *not* liable for the payment. Some publications refuse to accept insertion orders with disclaimers unless payment accompanies the order. This controversy heated up in 1991 when the 4A's recommended to its agency members that they no longer accept sole liability for their client's bills.[19]

When a newspaper creates ad copy and art, it gives the advertiser a **proof copy** to check. In contrast, most national advertising arrives at the newspaper with the art, copy, and layout in final form. The agency or advertiser must receive verification that the ad ran, so the newspaper tears out the page on which the ad appeared and sends it to the agency or advertiser. Today most **tear sheets** for national advertisers are handled through a private central office—the Advertising Checking Bureau.

When a tear sheet arrives, the advertiser examines it to make sure the ad ran according to instructions—in the right section and page position, and with the correct reproduction. If the ad did *not* run per instructions, the agency or advertiser is usually due an adjustment—a discount or even a free rerun.

PRINT: A WORLDWIDE MEDIUM

Every country has newspapers and magazines. Advertisers in foreign markets generally use either international or local media, depending on their campaign objectives and intended audience. Whether at home or abroad, advertisers must study the audience and remember the basics of print advertising, some of which are enumerated in the Checklist of What Works Best in Print.

Several large U.S. publishers, including Time, McGraw-Hill, and Scientific American, circulate international editions of their magazines abroad. The *Inter-*

CHECKLIST   What Works Best in Print

◇ **Use simple layouts.** One big picture works better than several small pictures. Avoid cluttered pages. (Layouts that resemble the magazine's editorial format are well read.)

◇ **Always put a caption under a photograph.** Twice as many people read picture captions as body copy. The picture caption can be an ad by itself.

◇ **Don't be afraid of long copy.** People who read beyond the headline are good prospects. If your product is expensive—like a car, a vacation, or an industrial product—prospects are hungry for information. Consider long copy if you have a complex story to tell, many different product points to make, or an expensive product or service to sell.

◇ **Avoid negative headlines.** People are literal minded and may remember only the negatives. Sell the positive benefits in your product—not that it won't harm or that some defect has been solved. Look for emotional words that attract and motivate, like *free* and *new* and *love.*

◇ **Don't be afraid of long headlines.** On average, long headlines sell more merchandise than short ones.

◇ **Look for story appeal.** After the headline, a striking visual is the most effective way to get a reader's attention. Try for story appeal—the kind of visual that makes the reader ask: "What's going on here?"

◇ **Photographs are better than drawings.** Photography increases recall an average of 26 percent over artwork.

◇ **Look at your ad in its editorial environment.** Ask to see your ad pasted into the magazine in which it will appear—or, for newspapers, photostated in the same tone as the newspaper page. Beautifully mounted layouts are deceptive. The reader will never see your ad printed on high-gloss paper, with a big white border, mounted on a board. It is misleading for you to look at it this way.

◇ **Develop a single advertising format.** An overall format for all print advertising can double recognition. This rule holds a special meaning for industrial advertisers. One format will help readers see your ad as coming from one large corporation, rather than several small companies.

◇ **Before-and-after photographs make a point better than words.** If you can, show a visual contrast—a change in the situation or a demonstration of product superiority.

◇ **Do not print copy in reverse type.** It may look attractive, but it reduces readability. For the same reason, don't print copy on top of an illustration.

◇ **Make each ad a complete sale.** Your message must be contained in the headline. React to the overall impression as the reader will. Only advertisers read all their advertisements. Any ad in a series must stand on its own. Every one must make a complete sale. Assume it will be the only ad for your product a reader will ever see.

---

national *Herald Tribune, The Wall Street Journal,* and London's *Financial Times* are widely read in Asia, Europe, and the Middle East.

Well-educated, upper-income consumers read these publications, which are typically printed in English, so they are the closest to global media for reaching this audience. The *Reader's Digest*—no doubt the oldest international mass-audience medium—reaches 170 foreign countries. Yet, because the Reader's Digest Association prints the magazine in local languages and tailors it to each country, advertisers often view the magazine as a local medium.

The number of international business, trade, or specialty publications is growing. Switzerland's *European Business* and Belgium's *Electronic Product News,* both English-language magazines, are distributed throughout Europe.

Political changes in the former Soviet Union and Eastern bloc countries are spurring many new trade publications. Most are published locally in association with foreign publishers. In 1990, McGraw-Hill launched Russian-language editions of *Aviation Week & Space Technology* and *Business Week.* And International Data Group launched several trade publications in the former Soviet Union and Eastern bloc countries including *PC World USSR* and *Computerworld Poland.*[20]

In the past, international advertising media consisted mainly of newspapers and magazines. Today Superchannel and Sky Channel pan-European satellite-to-cable broadcast options are beginning to supplement print media. We will discuss this more in the next chapter, Electronic Media.

SOURCES OF PRINT MEDIA INFORMATION

To make informed media buying decisions, advertisers and their agencies need information about newspapers and magazines. Publications provide information about their readership, circulation, rates, advertising policies, and editorial focus. In addition, media planners also consult the following sources:

- **Audit Bureau of Circulations (ABC).** The **Audit Bureau of Circulations** was formed in 1914 to verify circulation and other marketing data on magazines and newspapers. Each publication submits a semiannual statement, which is checked by specially trained ABC field auditors. The publisher supplies data on paid circulation (for a specified period) for its regional, metropolitan, and demographic editions, broken down by subscription, single-copy sales, and average paid circulation. The ABC also analyzes new and renewal subscriptions by price, duration, sales channel, and type of promotion.

- **Simmons Market Research Bureau.** SMRB is a well-respected syndicated research organization that publishes magazine readership studies. Its annual *Study of Media and Markets* report provides data on the purchase behavior and demographics of readers based on personal interviews. In addition, SMRB publishes the *National College Study* and the *Simmons Teen-Age Research Study* twice a year.[21]

- **Mediamark Research Inc.** MRI also conducts personal interviews to determine readership patterns. In addition to reporting the audiences and readership demographics for leading consumer magazines and national newspapers, MRI publishes annual studies on the affluent market, business-purchase decision makers, and the top 10 local markets.[22]

- **Newspaper Advertising Bureau.** The **Newspaper Advertising Bureau** of the American Newspaper Publishers Association is the promotional arm of the nation's newspaper industry. The bureau provides its newspaper members with market information by conducting field research and collecting case histories.

- **Magazine Publishers Association (MPA).** The **Magazine Publishers Association** has a total membership of more than 230 publishers, representing 1,200 magazines. This trade group makes available the circulation figures of all ABC member magazines (general and farm) from 1914 to date, with annual figures related to population. It estimates the number of consumer magazine copies sold by year from 1943, and it lists the 100 leading ABC magazines according to circulation.

- **Standard Rate & Data Service (SRDS). Standard Rate & Data Service** publishes *Newspaper Rates and Data, Consumer Magazine and Agri-Media Rates and Data,* and *Business Publication Rates and Data,* as well as other monthly directories so advertisers and their agencies don't have to obtain rate cards for every publication.

- **Audience studies provided by publications.** Newspapers and magazines also offer media planners many other types of statistical reports including reader income, demographic profiles, percentages of different kinds of advertising carried, and more. Exhibit 13–16 is an example from *Runner's World* magazine.

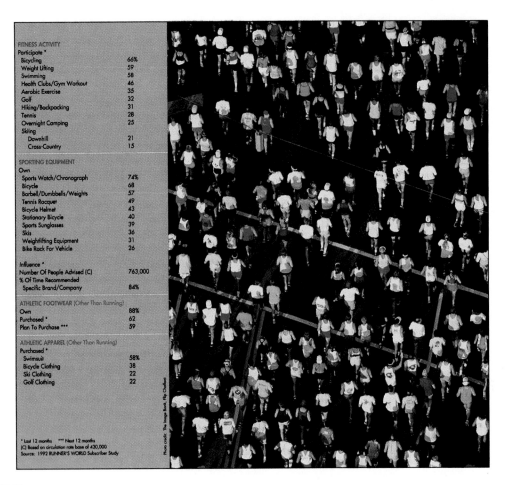

FITNESS ACTIVITY	
Participate *	
Bicycling	66%
Weight Lifting	59
Swimming	58
Health Clubs/Gym Workout	46
Aerobic Exercise	35
Golf	32
Hiking/Backpacking	31
Tennis	28
Overnight Camping	25
Skiing	
Downhill	21
Cross-Country	15
SPORTING EQUIPMENT	
Own	
Sports Watch/Chronograph	74%
Bicycle	68
Barbell/Dumbbells/Weights	57
Tennis Racquet	49
Bicycle Helmet	43
Stationary Bicycle	40
Sports Sunglasses	39
Skis	36
Weightlifting Equipment	31
Bike Rack For Vehicle	26
Influence *	
Number Of People Advised (C)	763,000
% Of Time Recommended	
Specific Brand/Company	84%
ATHLETIC FOOTWEAR (Other Than Running)	
Own	88%
Purchased *	62
Plan To Purchase ***	59
ATHLETIC APPAREL (Other Than Running)	
Purchased *	
Swimsuit	58%
Bicycle Clothing	38
Ski Clothing	22
Golf Clothing	22

* Last 12 months   *** Next 12 months
(C) Based on circulation rate base of 430,000
Source: 1992 RUNNER'S WORLD Subscriber Study

EXHIBIT • 13–16

Many magazines conduct surveys to persuade advertisers they reach the best markets.

Summary

The printed page—in magazines and newspapers—provides a unique, flexible medium for advertising creativity.

Magazines offer distinct advantages. They are the most selective of all mass media and are flexible in both readership and advertising. They offer unsurpassed color, excellent reproduction quality, authority and believability, long shelf life, and prestige at an efficient cost. However, they often require long lead times, have problems offering reach and frequency, and are subject to heavy advertising competition. And the cost of advertising in some magazines is very high.

In selecting magazines for advertising, the media buyer must consider a publication's circulation, its readership, and its cost and mechanical requirements. A magazine's rates may be determined by several factors: its primary and secondary readership, the number of subscription and vendor sales, and the number of copies guaranteed versus those actually delivered.

Magazine rate cards follow a standard format so advertisers can readily determine advertising costs. They list black-and-white and color rates, discounts, issue and closing dates, and mechanical requirements.

The newspaper is a mass medium read by almost everybody. It offers great flexibility, which assists creativity, and its printed message lasts. However, newspapers also have disadvantages: lack of audience selectivity, short life span, poor production quality, heavy advertising competition, potentially poor ad placement, and overlapping circulation. Still, the newspaper is the major community-serving medium today for both news and advertising.

The newspaper's rate card lists prices, deadlines, mechanical requirements, and other pertinent information. The rates listed vary for local and national advertisers. Also listed are the newspaper's short-rate policy, combination rates, frequency discounts, run-of-paper rates, and other data.

Print is a worldwide medium—every country has newspapers and magazines. The international advertiser may have to choose between local and international media. The best educated consumers in these countries often read English-language publications. Political changes in Eastern Europe have spurred the introduction of many new trade and business publications edited and published in the local language. Advertisers must study the audience they wish to reach before buying any media—whether at home or abroad.

Questions for Review and Discussion

1. If you worked in the advertising department of a premium-priced furniture manufacturer, would you recommend magazine advertising? Why or why not?

2. If you were the advertising manager for a magazine aimed at senior citizens, what advantages would you cite to potential advertisers?

3. What is the advantage of magazine advertising to businesses that sell to other businesses?

4. If you were buying magazine space for a jeans manufacturer, what factors would you take into account in choosing the magazines?

5. What is the importance of the Audit Bureau of Circulation?

6. Why do retailers advertise so heavily in local newspapers?

7. In what ways can advertisers improve the selectivity of their newspaper ads?

8. What factors should advertisers consider in deciding among several local papers (including dailies and weeklies)?

9. Should national advertisers be charged a higher rate than local advertisers? Support your position.

10. Should agencies be liable for their clients' advertising bills? Why or why not?

Electronic Media

Objective: To present the factors advertisers weigh when considering electronic media—broadcast and cable television and radio. Each medium has its own characteristics, advantages, and drawbacks. Advertisers must be able to compare the merits of each and know the most cost-effective ways to buy advertising time.

After studying this chapter, you will be able to:

- Describe the advantages and drawbacks of broadcast television as an advertising medium.

- Describe different types of TV advertising and the process of audience measurement.

- Delineate the primary factors considered when buying television time.

- Outline the advantages and drawbacks of cable TV as an advertising medium.

- Compare the process of buying cable versus broadcast television time.

- Analyze the advantages and drawbacks of using radio in the creative mix.

- Explain the major factors to consider when buying radio time.

he competition in the alkaline segment of the battery market is highly charged. While Eveready is the perennial leader in the $3 billion battery business, in this particular segment it faces a stiff competitor—Duracell, with its copper-top battery.

A couple of years ago, Eveready started worrying. Duracell's foothold in the segment was gaining. Eveready had to get the consumer's attention on a grand scale in a short time. How would they do it? Their agency, Chiat/Day, was convinced that TV was the way to go. It could reach the target audience quickly with great impact if the message was right. But a funny thing happened. The message didn't turn out to be nearly as important as how well they optimized the medium itself.

In previous campaigns, Eveready used celebrities such as Robert Conrad and Australia's "Jack-O" to promote its Energizer brand. The ads had fizzled. Duracell's successful campaign featured rows of battery-powered toys that successively ran out of energy until only one was left—the one powered by Duracell.

In response, Chiat/Day created the "Energizer Bunny"—the toy with an attitude. Wearing a pair of shades and beating a big base drum, the fuzzy bunny exuded persona power. This might have been enough for some companies, but the little character known as E.B. had to do more.

When the ads hit the airwaves, they made advertising history. E. B. did it all with pure daring—first by marching through his own ads and then by defiantly interrupting what seemed to be other company's ads (see Exhibit 14–1).

Viewers who normally tuned out commercials were caught off guard. Something was different. So they watched. Then they began to realize it was a joke. The beginning of each spot was a carefully crafted spoof of a common type of ad or promotion for a fictitious program. One showed a fast-action scene of female SWAT officers wrestling thugs to the ground—as if a new action TV show were premiering. Then E.B. suddenly marches across the smoke-filled picture beating his drum while the actors stop in midstride to look on in amazement.

E X H I B I T • 14-1

Viewers remember the Energizer ad because of the unique way the bunny interrupts ads for unrelated products. Today, the unflappable bunny is a celebrity.

ANNCR: Don't be fooled by commercials where one battery company's toy outlasts the other's. Energizer was never invited to their playoffs. Because nothing outlasts the Energizer.

SUPER: ENERGIZER

ANNCR: They keep going and going and going . . .

(MUSIC: PIANO)

WOMAN 1: I love the sound of the rain.

WOMAN 2: And I love the taste of your fresh-brewed coffee.

WOMAN 1: Thanks, but it's not fresh-brewed. It's new Tres Caf . . .

(SFX: DRUMS)

ANNCR: . . . still going. Nothing outlasts the Energizer.

SUPER: ENERGIZER

ANNCR: They keep going and going and going . . .

Ad critics hailed the campaign as one of the best. But the real evidence of E.B.'s impact was an instant assimilation into popular culture, thanks to the help of real live celebrities like David Letterman on "Late Night," Jay Leno on the "Tonight" show, and the comedy cast of "Saturday Night Live." Eveready even started getting calls from customers desperately seeking E.B. dolls for their kids. During one eight-week period, the company sold 20,000 E.B. lookalikes, which no doubt helped cover the $90,000 it cost to build the two robot rabbits used in the spots.[1]

For the first time in its history, Energizer made *Advertising Age's* list of top 10 best-recalled ads.[2] Some advertisers tried to capitalize on E.B.'s success. Eveready even had to go to court—over a Coors Light ad that showed actor Leslie Nielsen wearing fuzzy rabbit ears and a cotton tail, marching across the screen beating a base drum.[3]

The Energizer campaign is an electrifying example of how an effective TV commercial can quickly reach a large portion of the population, get their attention, and establish product identity. This chapter explores the advantages of TV as well as its drawbacks. It also addresses the characteristics of other electronic media, including how cable television, videocassette rentals, and radio compete with broadcast TV and how they all add to an advertiser's creative mix. ◆

THE MEDIUM OF TELEVISION

In 1950, only 3 percent of total U.S. advertising volume, $171 million, was placed on television. By 1991, however, TV advertising grew to more than $27 *billion* and accounted for more than 21 percent of all ad spending.[4] Exhibit 14–2 lists the top network television advertisers in the United States and their annual expenditures.

Today, the medium of television is available to advertisers in two forms: broadcast TV and cable TV. **Broadcast television** reaches its audience by transmitting electromagnetic waves through the air across some geographic territory. **Cable TV** reaches its audience through wires, either strung from telephone poles or laid underground.

Broadcast TV

Broadcast television has grown faster than any other advertising medium in history. From its beginnings after World War II, TV emerged as the medium that attracts the largest volume of national advertising—more than $19 billion in 1991.[5]

The United States has over 1,100 commercial TV stations; Canada has another 127.[6] About half the U.S. stations are VHF (very high frequency—channels 2 through 13); the other half are UHF (ultrahigh frequency—channels 14 through 83). Stations in the U.S. operate as *independents* unless they are affiliated with one of the four national networks (ABC, NBC, CBS, Fox). In Canada, there are three national networks, 13 regional networks, and 12 speciality networks. Both network affiliates and independent stations may subscribe to nationally syndicated programs as well as originate their own programming. However, increasing competition from cable TV is causing the national network programs to lose viewers. To compensate, some of the networks are investing in cable TV systems or starting their own. NBC, for example, started CNBC, and ABC has an 80 percent interest in ESPN.

E X H I B I T • 14-2

Top 10 network TV advertisers in the United States.

Rank	Advertiser	TV ad expenditures, 1991*
1	General Motors Corp.	$527.8
2	Procter & Gamble Co.	515.7
3	Philip Morris Cos.	389.5
4	Johnson & Johnson	239.8
5	Kellogg Co.	236.6
6	Ford Motor Co.	217.5
7	PepsiCo	204.6
8	Sears, Roebuck & Co.	187.9
9	Chrysler Corp.	176.2
10	Toyota Motor Corp.	173.7

* Dollars are in millions.

Cable TV

For more than 30 years, broadcast TV, especially network TV, was the dominant entertainment medium for most Americans. Today, other electronic media are changing that dominance. Chief among the challengers is cable television.

Cable TV has been around since the late 1940s. It mainly carried TV signals by wire to areas with poor reception. But in the 1970s, cable suddenly became more attractive to viewers due to the advent of satellite TV signals, the proliferation of channels, and the introduction of uncut first-run movies via pay-cable channels such as Home Box Office and Showtime.

At first, many subscribers valued cable simply for the full array of regional channels and the access to premium services such as HBO. But once this novelty wore off, subscribers wanted more. A variety of advertiser-supported cable networks soon appeared, along with a variety of diversified pay services and many more local shows. All of this drew more and more subscribers.

In the last two decades, cable's growth has been extraordinary. In 1975, only 13 percent of TV households in the United States had cable. By 1994, cable is expected to be in 65 percent of all households. In Canada, 73 percent of homes are equipped with cable. Cable now reaches every county in the United States and Canada.[7]

Subscribers to cable TV pay a monthly fee to receive as many as 50 advertiser-supported stations, including local network affiliates and independents, cable networks, superstations, and local cable system channels. These fees represent about one-third of cable TV revenues; advertising makes up the remainder. Subscribers can also pay additional fees to receive premium services, such as HBO, the Disney Channel, and Cinemax, and to see special events such as first-run films, boxing matches, and baseball games (pay-per-view service).

There are now more than 25 national cable networks in the United States and a growing number of regional networks. Exhibit 14–3 lists the most widely carried networks. There are also a handful of **superstations**—local over-the-air TV stations whose signals are delivered via satellite to cable systems across the country and which carry some national advertising. (The term was coined by Ted Turner for his WTBS Atlanta, which is also the best known superstation.)

Television Audience Trends

While TV advertising is attacked regularly, no one denies its power and creative potential. Without TV advertising, Federal Express may never have gotten off the ground. As a means of reaching a mass audience, no other medium today has the unique creative abilities of television: the combination of sight, sound, and movement; the opportunity to demonstrate the product; the potential to use special effects; the empathy of the viewer; and the believability of seeing it happen right before your eyes. (See the Checklist: The Pros and Cons of Broadcast Television Advertising.) In fact, as Exhibit 14–4 shows, 57 percent of viewers surveyed said that TV is the most authoritative advertising source, compared to only 20 percent for newspapers, 11 percent for magazines, and 9 percent for radio.[8]

The heaviest viewers of broadcast TV are middle-income, high school-educated individuals and their families, so most programming is directed at this group. People with considerably higher incomes and education typically have a more diversified range of interests and entertainment options.

The average number of TV viewing hours ranges from a low of 23 hours per

EXHIBIT • 14–3

Major cable TV networks.

Network	Estimated home coverage (millions)	Cost range*	Program type
Arts & Entertainment	55.4	$4,500–7,000	Family/variety
Black Entertainment TV	34.0	350–1,000	Sports/family/entertainment/news/gossip/ethnic/music (video)/news/information
CNBC	47.1	500–2,000	Educational information/business/news/information/general
Cable News Network	64.2	5,000–11,000†	News/information
The Discovery Channel	58.0	550–4,000	Educational information/family/health/original/news/information/technology/science
ESPN, Inc.	60.4	N/A	Sports
The Family Channel	55.8	500–4,000	Family/general/original
Headline News	52.8	5,000–11,000†	News/information
Lifetime Television	56.0	450–12,650	Women's interest/family/general/health/news/information
Music Television	57.0	2,500–7,500	Music (video)
Nickelodeon	58.9	2,000–15,000	Youth interest
Nick at Night	58.9	1,700–3,000	Family/variety
TBS	63.0	1,000–12,000	Family/general/music (video)/sports/women's interest/youth interest
The Nashville Network	56.7	500–15,000	Family/sports/music (video)/news/information/variety general/women's interest
Turner Network Television	61.2	1,000–6,500	Family/general/sports/women's interest/youth interest
The Weather Channel	52.6	250–1,050	News/information
USA	59.2	550–2,500	Music (video)

* Refers to Average Prime Time costs only.
† CNN and Headline News sold in combination.

week to a high of 36. Children under 12, for example, view an average of 23 hours per week; middle-aged men, 24 hours; teens, 26 hours; and middle-aged women, 28 hours.[9] By age 18, the average child has spent more than two and a half years watching TV.

Around the world, older women watch TV the most (36 hours per week in both the United States and Canada). This makes the medium very popular with advertisers whose primary target is middle-aged and older women—like Weight-Watchers in the Netherlands (see Exhibit 14–5 on page 432).

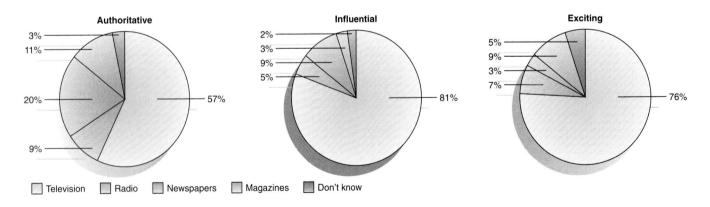

EXHIBIT • 14–4

Television is the most influential medium.

CHECKLIST   The Pros and Cons of Broadcast Television Advertising

The Pros

Contemporary broadcast television offers advertisers a variety of advantages over competing media.

◇ **Mass coverage.** A full 98 percent of all U.S. homes have a TV (most have more than one), and viewing time for the average household has increased from over five hours a day in 1960 to more than seven hours a day in 1991.*

◇ **Low cost.** Despite the often huge initial outlays for commercial production and advertising time, TV's equally huge audiences bring the cost per exposure to a comparatively low level—from $2 to $10 per thousand viewers.

◇ **Some selectivity.** Television audiences vary a great deal depending on the time of day, day of the week, and nature of the programming. Advertising messages can be presented when potential customers are watching, and advertisers can reach select geographic audiences by buying local and regional markets.

◇ **Impact.** Television offers an immediacy that other forms of advertising are unable to achieve, displaying and demonstrating the product with sound and full color right before the customer's eyes.

◇ **Creativity.** The various facets of the TV commercial—sight, sound, motion, and color—permit infinite original and imaginative appeals.

◇ **Prestige.** Since the public considers TV the most authoritative and influential medium, TV offers advertisers a prestigious image. Hallmark, Xerox, Mobil, Exxon, and IBM increased their prestige by regularly sponsoring cultural TV programs.

◇ **Social dominance.** In North America most people under age 35 grew up with TV as a window to their social environment. And they continue to be stirred by TV screenings of the Olympic Games, space travel, assassinations, wars, and political scandals.

The Cons

Sometimes broadcast TV just doesn't "fit" in the creative mix because of cost, lack of audience selectivity, inherent brevity, or the clutter of competitive messages.

◇ **High production cost.** One of broadcast TV's greatest handicaps is the high cost of producing quality commercials. Depending on the creative approach, the cost of filming a national commercial today may run from $200,000 to more than $1 million.†

◇ **High airtime cost.** The average cost of a prime-time, network commercial is about $125,000. A single 30-second commercial for a top-rated show in prime time may cost as much as $300,000 (see chart). Special attractions like

Network television advertising rates

	Average rating		Cost of 30-second commercial (000)	
	Low	High	Low	High
Daytime				
Early morning (7-9 A.M.)	2.3	4.5	$ 4.3	$ 17.6
Weekday (10 A.M.-4:30 P.M.)	1.8	8.0	3.4	27.9
Weekend (children)	1.5	5.5	3.4	20.5
Prime time	3.0	20.0	18.2	223.4
Late night	1.5	5.0	4.2	32.5

Advertising time on top-rated programs shown during the best viewing times carries a higher price tag because of the larger audience.

the Super Bowl cost much more ($800,000). The cost of large coverage, even at low rates, usually prices small and medium-sized advertisers out of the market.

◇ **Limited selectivity.** Broadcast TV is not cost-effective for advertisers seeking a very specific, small audience. And it is losing some of its selectivity because of changing audience trends. More women are working outside the home or watching cable TV, hurting advertisers who promote their products on network soap operas.

◇ **Brevity.** Studies show that most TV viewers can't remember the product or company in the most recent TV ad they watched—even if it was within the last five minutes.‡ Recall improves with the length of the commercial—people remember 60-second spots better than 30-second spots.

◇ **Clutter.** TV advertising is usually surrounded by station-break announcements, credits, and public-service announcements, as well as six or seven other spots. All these messages compete for attention, so viewers become annoyed and confused and often misidentify the product.

◇ **Zipping and zapping.** *Zipping* refers to VCR users who skip through commercials when replaying taped programs; *zapping* refers to remote-control users who change channels at the beginning of a commercial break.

* *TV Basics 1990–91* (New York: Television Bureau of Advertising, 1991), p. 5.
† David Kalish, "Putting the Touch on Media," *Marketing & Media Decisions*, July 1989, pp. 14–15.
‡ "Terminal Television," *American Demographics*, January 1987, p. 15.

EXHIBIT • 14-5

Around the globe, television is an ideal medium for Weight Watchers because older women—one of its target audiences—watch the most TV every week.

VIDEO: A young woman in a red dress.
AUDIO: Sounds as if someone was blowing up a balloon
VIDEO: The woman . . .
. . . keeps getting fatter . . .
. . . and fatter.

Horrified, she looks down at her disfigured body.
AUDIO: Then the type of noise you hear when air is let out of a balloon.
VIDEO: Slowly . . .
. . . she starts getting thinner . . .

. . . until she's got the kind of figure she wants.
Super: Weight Watchers. 06-83 60.
AUDIO: (MVO): "Go Weight-Watching too. Call 06-83 60 now."

Individual program audiences vary a great deal. Sports programs attract proportionately more men in the 18 to 34 age category than any other group. Look at the audience composition statistics in Exhibit 14–6. Who are the primary viewers of network feature films?

The presence of cable in U.S. and Canadian homes has significantly altered both TV viewing patterns and the use of other media. Households with cable spend less time watching broadcast TV. They also spend less time listening to the radio, reading, or going for drives or to the movies. These statistics indicate that, in many cases, cable reaches an audience difficult to get to in any other way. As a result of this *audience fragmentation*, advertising on the broadcast networks has become less cost-effective. However, the use of home video has also increased dramatically, drawing more viewers away from all advertiser-supported TV—both broadcast and cable—which is why ads on videos have now started appearing.

Cable households watch more television than noncable TV households— 56.2 hours per week for cable households versus 41.6 hours for noncable households. Cable households seem to watch cable programs at all times of the day, although more often in the late evening than in the early evening. In all, they watch about 22.8 hours of cable programming a week.[10]

National advertisers have been using cable since the late 1970s; and during the last decade, the top 50 nationally advertised brands could all be seen on cable. Since 1980, cable advertising revenues grew steadily, exceeding $2.5

EXHIBIT • 14-6

U.S. network TV audience composition
by program type.

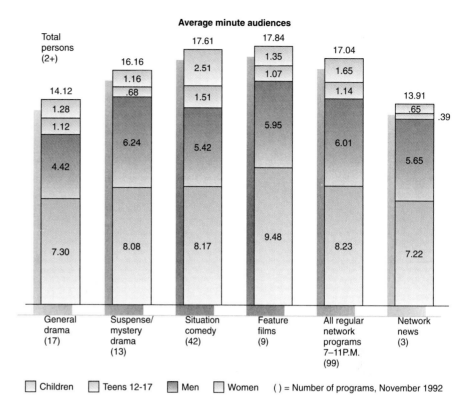

Average minute audiences

Children   Teens 12-17   Men   Women   ( ) = Number of programs, November 1992

billion in 1990.[11] Procter & Gamble traditionally spends the most, as shown in Exhibit 14–7.

Local retailers also find cable a good place to advertise. Fisher Big Wheel, a discount department store in Midvale, Ohio, became a cable devotee after its first cable promotion brought an extra 15,000 customers into the store. Even tiny businesses find cable advertising affordable and effective. A luncheonette on Main Street in Beacon, New York, placed a single spot on the cable newscast and was deluged with hungry customers the next day.[12]

Types of Television Advertising

Advertisers buy time on broadcast and cable TV using two different strategies. The major broadcast networks offer a variety of programs that appeal to different audiences. So the advertiser must buy ads based on the viewing audience of each program. An advertiser that wants to reach women ages 18 to 35 might choose "Murphy Brown." For the 16–21 age group, "TV's Funniest Home Videos" would be a good choice.

When buying cable TV, an advertiser can buy ads over the full schedule of a channel because cable networks typically aim their overall programming to relatively specific audiences. Programs on the LifeTime and Family channels are heavily weighted toward women and would probably be a good buy during any part of their daily schedule; MTV and VH-1 channels target the 16–25 age group. Because of this, cable companies sell their network channels in bundles at a discount price and offer discounts for *run of schedule positioning*—multiple ad purchases they can place throughout a channel's daily schedule. (See the Checklist: The Pros and Cons of Cable Television Advertising.)

There are various ways advertisers buy time on broadcast and cable TV. Some include: sponsoring an entire program, participating in a program, pur-

EXHIBIT • 14-7

Top 10 cable TV advertisers in the
United States.

Rank	Advertiser	Cable TV ad expenditures, 1991*
1	Procter & Gamble	$67.8
2	General Motors	32.4
3	General Mills	31.8
4	Anheuser-Busch	31.4
5	Time Warner	29.3
6	Philip Morris	24.1
7	Sears, Roebuck	20.3
8	AT&T	19.3
9	Eastman Kodak	19.1
10	American Home Products	19.1

* Dollars are in millions.

CHECKLIST   The Pros and Cons of Cable Television Advertising

The Pros

The primary advantages of cable TV are its selectivity, low cost, and great flexibility.

◇ **Selectivity.** Cable offers specialized programming aimed at particular types of viewers. *Narrowcasting* allows advertisers to choose programming with the viewer demographics that best match their target customers.

◇ **Audience demographics.** Cable subscribers are younger, better educated, more affluent, have higher-level jobs, live in larger households, and are more likely to try new products and buy more high-ticket items, such as cars, appliances, and high-tech equipment.*

◇ **Low cost.** Many small companies get TV's immediacy and impact without the enormous expenditures of broadcast TV. Cable advertising costs much less than broadcast television—sometimes about the same as radio. Many national advertisers find sponsorship particularly attractive, since an entire cable series can cost less to produce than a single broadcast TV commercial.†

◇ **Flexibility.** Broadcast TV commercials need to be short because of the high costs of production and airtime, but cable ads can run up to two minutes and, in the case of *infomercials*, much longer. They can also be tailored to fit the programming environment.

◇ **Testability.** Cable is a good place to experiment, testing both new products and various advertising approaches—ad frequency, copy impact, and different media mixes.‡

The Cons

Like every medium, cable TV has its drawbacks.

◇ **Limited reach.** About 40 percent of households don't have cable. This is cable's main weakness.

◇ **Fragmentation.** With more than 50 channels at their disposal, cable viewers do not watch any one show in enormous numbers. To reach the majority of the cable audience in a particular market, ads must run on a great many stations.

◇ **Quality.** Cable, particularly local cable, sometimes has poorer production quality and less desirable programming than broadcast TV.

◇ **Zipping and zapping.** Cable TV is also subject to some of the same drawbacks as broadcast TV, including zipping and zapping.

* "1991 Advertisers Guide to Cable," p. 21.
† David Samuel Barr, *Advertising on Cable: A Practical Guide for Users* (Englewood Cliffs, N.J.: Prentice Hall, 1985), p. 71.
‡ Judan Dagnoli, "Cable Test Hot-Wired to Consumer Preferences," *Advertising Age*, December 1, 1986, p. S10.

chasing spot announcements between programs, and purchasing spots from syndicators.

Broadcast Network Advertising

Major U.S. advertisers historically purchased airtime from one of the national broadcast **networks**: American Broadcasting Company (ABC), Columbia Broadcast Company (CBS), National Broadcasting Company (NBC), or the Fox Broadcasting Company (FBC). Networks offer large advertisers convenience and efficiency because their messages can be broadcast simultaneously via network affiliates throughout the country to masses of American consumers (see Exhibit 14–8).

An advertiser who underwrites the total cost of a program is engaging in **sponsorship.** The advertiser is responsible for both the program content and the cost of production. Sponsorship is so costly that single sponsorships are usually limited to specials. Companies that sponsor programs (AT&T, Xerox, and Hallmark, for example) gain two important advantages. First, the public more readily identifies with the product(s) due to the prestige attached to sponsoring first-rate entertainment. Second, the sponsor controls the placement and content of its commercials. The commercials can be fit to the program and run any length the sponsor desires so long as they remain within network or station regulations. Further, because networks are centralized, the advertiser gets only one bill. Moreover, while program sponsorship is very expensive, the

As cable television grows, the Network Television Association's role in promoting broadcast network advertising becomes more important.

advertiser can reach an incredibly large audience. This makes the cost per thousand viewers quite low—lower even than time purchased on a spot basis.

To save cost and reduce risk, many advertisers **cosponsor** programs. They may sponsor on alternate weeks or divide the program into segments. NFL games, for instance, are sold as multiple sponsorships.

Most network TV advertising is sold on the **participation basis,** with several advertisers buying 30- or 60-second segments within a program. Advertisers can participate in a program once or several times, regularly or irregularly. This enables them to spread out their budgets and avoid long-term commitments to any one program. It also lets smaller advertisers buy a limited amount of time and still get nationwide coverage.

However, network advertising has several disadvantages: lack of flexibility, long lead times, inconvenient restrictions, and forced adherence to network standards and practices.

Spot Announcements

National **spot announcements** run between programs in clusters. They are less expensive than participations and more flexible than network advertising because they can be concentrated in specific regions. An advertiser with a small budget or limited distribution may use spots to introduce a new product into one area at a time.

Spots may be sold nationally or locally in segments of 10, 15, 30, or 60 seconds. Spot advertising is more difficult to purchase then network advertising because it involves contacting each station directly. However, the *national rep system,* in which individuals act as sales and service representatives for a number of stations, is alleviating this problem.[13]

The late 1980s saw a significant shift toward greater regional advertising through national spots. Campbell Soup, for example, increased its local spot TV ad budget to address regional differences in eating habits. But spot advertising is available only at network station breaks and when network advertisers purchase less than a full lineup. So spot ads may get lost in the clutter—which is why they tend to have lower viewership.

Syndication

Syndicated programs are an increasingly popular alternative to network advertising. Television syndication comes in three forms: offnetwork, first-run, and barter. In **offnetwork syndication,** former popular network programs are sold to individual stations for rebroadcast. **First-run syndication** includes original shows produced specifically for the syndication market. One of the fastest-growing trends in television is **barter syndication**—first-run programs offered free or for a reduced rate, but with some of the ad space presold to national advertisers. "Wheel of Fortune," "Entertainment Tonight," and "The Oprah Winfrey Show" are popular examples. See Exhibit 14–9.

Program-Length Advertisements (PLAs)

In the fall of 1992, independent presidential candidate Ross Perot sat in front of a TV camera for 30 minutes with homemade flip charts and a down-home pitch for the White House and drew 20 million viewers. A month later, he pulled a respectable 19 percent of the vote.

Perot made advertising history by catapulting the **program length advertisement (PLA),** or "infomercial," into the limelight. He also proved what

---

ETHICAL DILEMMA   Children's Television Advertising: The Medium and the Message

Kids are a potent force in the U.S. economy. They spend over $6.2 billion of their own money every year and often influence their parents' purchasing decisions as well. According to James McNeal, author of *Children as Consumers,* kids influence their parents to the tune of $50 billion each year. It's no surprise that "adult" products are advertised to children.

Advertisers love kids because kids love to shop. Cy Schneider, author of *The Electronic Pied Piper: The Business and Art of Children's Television,* believes that "enlightened ads that really understand what's going on in the home, in terms of buying, are creating dialogues between parents and children about products and the pluses and minuses of buying one brand instead of another."

Consumers Union disagrees. CU charges that children's advertising is anything but enlightened and that naive youngsters are sitting ducks for sophisticated advertisers. CU accuses companies of "creating demand for products that are often unnecessary, shortlived, overpriced, or worthless."

Critics say that, as impressionable viewers who spend almost everything they earn, don't comparison shop, and don't make logical purchasing decisions, children are particularly vulnerable to TV advertising. In addition, peer pressure creates fads.

In the make-believe world of television, boundaries between fantasy and reality often blur. Which came first: the Teenage Mutant Turtles or their Saturday morning cartoon show? Kids couldn't care less. They're just mesmerized by the images and buy the products associated with those images.

Recently, advertisers turned the day after Thanksgiving into an annual event for toy-based television. Day-long programming of toy-related cartoons ran on Turner Broadcasting System, Fox Children's Network, and various syndication stations.*

Frank Orme, president of the National Association for Better Broadcasting, finds such programs "deceptive and cynical because the kids can't tell they're being pitched."

Or can they? Recent studies suggest that children are becoming increasingly savvy and display considerable skepticism about TV and commercials. Perhaps. But some Americans would prefer a system like Canada's where children are virtually off-limits to advertisers (see Chapter 2).

Some financially strapped school districts allow advertisers into the classroom in return for free teaching materials and equipment. The most controversial, Whittle Communications' *Channel One,* beams a 10-minute news broadcast to students and carries an additional 2 minutes of advertising.

How barter syndication works.

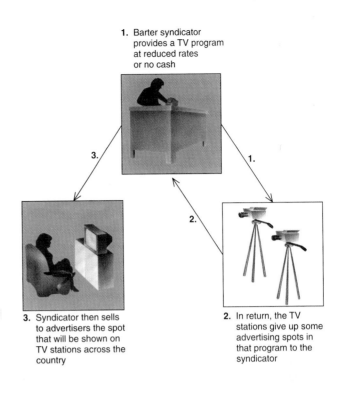

1. Barter syndicator provides a TV program at reduced rates or no cash

3. Syndicator then sells to advertisers the spot that will be shown on TV stations across the country

2. In return, the TV stations give up some advertising spots in that program to the syndicator

Whittle reports a reach of 8 million students and expects an additional 3,000 schools by the end of 1993. Schools that participate receive an average of $50,000 worth of free TV equipment in return for making the program required viewing.† Child psychologist Lee Salk opposes Channel One, stating that "kids are entitled to an education without having to be the object of commercial promotion." But he also concedes that "this is a free enterprise system, and selling to kids comes with the territory."

The free enterprise territory, of course, extends well beyond the classroom. Movies often contain quiet "product placements" for every conceivable item including tobacco and alcohol. Athletes and entertainers appear in commercials and print ads hawking products to their fans, many of whom are children.

Parents and schools can make a difference, though. The commercials on Channel One, for example, could be interesting topics for classroom discussion. Some parent groups criticized McDonald's *Batman* cross-promotion deal with Warner Brothers in the summer of 1992, saving the tie-in with McDonald's Happy Meal—a strictly kids product—was inappropriate with a PG-13 movie. Since that time, McDonald's has been more circumspect.‡ The best defense against irresponsible advertising is to teach children to be smart, responsible consumers who know how to save, as well as spend, money wisely.

Questions

1. Should the United States limit children-oriented commercials to late night TV?

2. Charlotte Baecher, director of educational services for Consumers Union, contends that "when a commercial message is delivered in school, it's an implicit endorsement." Do you agree? If so, should it ever be allowed? For what kinds of products and in what format?

3. "Advertisers have the responsibility to really get their messages across in a fair and reasonable way," says Nina Link, publisher of *Children's Television Workshop*. What does Link mean by "fair and reasonable"? How would you regulate the style and substance of children's advertising?

* Kate Fitzgerald and Marcy Magiera, "Hasbro, Mattel Serve Up 'Toons after Turkey Day," *Advertising Age*, November 23, 1992, p. 4.
† "Whittle Wrestles to Control His Four-Headed Hydra," *Advertising Age*, August 17, 1992, p. 32.
‡ "Kids, or Young Adult? Tie-ins Can Be PG-13," *Advertising Age*, February 3, 1993, p. S-14.

companies who produce and sell infomercials have been saying for years—long-form advertising can communicate a message in a way other forms can't.[14] As a result, *Advertising Age* named Perot its Adman of the Year.

Infomercials aren't new, but their respectability is. Prior to Perot, most PLA users were off-Madison Avenue marketers of hand mixers, juicers, and car waxes. Today major marketers like Avon, Redken, Corning, GTE, Braun, Saturn, and Volkswagen are readying forays into the infomercial arena. The reasons are simple:

1. Consumers pay attention and respond—and if the message is persuasive enough, they respond immediately.
2. Brand managers want the competitive edge of going where the competition isn't.
3. PLAs can fulfill some message objectives—product demonstration and brand differentiation—far better than 30-second commercials.
4. A well-conceived half-hour program offers results that are both measurable and accountable.
5. The ad campaign can pay for itself while supporting the retail trade.
6. PLAs combine the power of advertising, direct response, and sales promotion.[15]

Add to these factors the benefits of reasonable production costs and attractive, upscale audience demographics, and it's easy to see why national marketers are jumping on the infomercial bandwagon.

Local TV

Local businesses and retailers, often in cooperation with nationally known manufacturers, may buy time from local stations. Most local stations sell spot announcements. But some local advertisers develop and sponsor local programs or buy the rights to a syndicated series.

TELEVISION AUDIENCE MEASUREMENT

Audience measurement, an important, controversial subject, ensures that a specific commercial reaches the target market and that the price paid is proportional to the number of viewers.

Advertisers study the audiences of various programs and analyze their impact and cost-effectiveness against other media vehicles. To do so, they must understand audience measurement techniques and terminology.

Rating Services: *The Book*

A number of rating services measure the program audiences of TV and radio stations for advertisers and broadcasters. They pick a representative sample of the market and furnish data on the size and characteristics of the audiences that view or listen to the programs. Several research organizations gather the data at their own expense and publish it. Companies interested in their findings subscribe to the service and use it as a basis for planning media advertising.

The most commonly used TV services are A. C. Nielsen and Arbitron Ratings. For demographic studies of TV audiences, advertisers also use the Simmons Market Research Bureau and Mediamark Research. Research companies pub-

AD LAB 14–A   Where Do Those Infamous TV Ratings Come From?

For four decades, the life and death of network TV programs has been in the hands of the "Nielsen families"—randomly chosen households **A. C. Nielsen** uses to measure audience viewing patterns. Originally there were two types: those who kept diaries and those who simply had a "black box" attached to their TV sets. Someone in each of 2,400 diary homes kept a written record of which shows each member of the household watched during the week. In the 1,700 black-box households, an audimeter attached to the TV kept track of when the set was on and what channel it was tuned to. On the basis of data from these 4,100 households, Nielsen computed its Nielsen Television Index (NTI), the sole source of national TV ratings.

But that method of determining national ratings has been replaced by the **people meter** (see illustration), an electronic device that automatically records a household's TV viewing. The people meter records the channels watched, the number of minutes of viewing, and who in the household is watching. Each person must "punch in" and "punch out" on a keypad whenever beginning or ending a viewing session. The microwave-based people meter keeps track of second-by-second viewing choices of up to eight household members and relays the data to a central computer, which tabulates the data overnight.

The original people meter was developed by AGB Research, a British company. It appeared to eliminate a lot of the human problems that plagued the diary system and the technical drawbacks of the black boxes, which could not indicate *who* was watching.

AGB found clients in ad agencies, cable networks, and syndicators—all of whom felt that NTI overreported broadcast network shows and underreported other types. However, Nielsen developed its own people meter, and wasn't about to let AGB take over its market. AGB later abandoned the U.S. market.

Unfortunately, Nielsen's people meter had its share of problems. At one point, Nielsen's numbers showed millions of people suddenly stopped watching TV. The networks hit the roof, insisting something had to be wrong. Nielsen officials defended their system, and the networks gave advertisers $150 million worth of free time since rating guarantees weren't met. For the future, the networks decided to use eight-year trends for its ratings guarantees instead of just the current year's ratings. And critics are still convinced that people meter numbers are flawed.

Since that time, Nielsen developed a new "passive" peo-ple meter that will not require any special behavior and will actually record how many people watched the commercial, something advertisers have wanted to know since the beginning. The system, which should be introduced by 1995, uses digital scanning technology to record and remember images of participants' faces. Every two seconds, it scans the room to see who's there and who is actually watching the TV.

Nielsen conducts its survey "sweeps" four times a year in major market areas and publishes "sweeps books" that provide the basis for network and local station ad rates. With the advent of the passive people meter, advertisers may once again believe in the ratings they're paying for.

An interesting development in audience measurement is the **single source data** made available by supermarket scanners. Once information on families' viewing habits has been gathered, packaged goods purchases by the *same* family are measured. The implications are monumental for marketing and media planners. The leaders in single source measurement are Information Resources, Inc. (IRI), with its BehaviorScan service, and Nielsen, with its Home*Scan service.

Laboratory Applications

1. What are the advantages and disadvantages of the various measurement methods?

2. Which method do you consider best? Why?

lish their findings two or more times a year, depending on the size of the market, in a publication called *The Book. The Book* reports a wide array of statistics on how many people, what age groups, and which sex watch TV at various times of day in a specific market area. See Ad Lab 14–A.

Cable Ratings

Reliable information on cable programs is harder to gather. Traditional techniques often rely on too small a sample for findings to be statistically significant. So major cable programming services provide their own reports of varying timeliness, daypart division, and audience viewership by show.[16]

Interpreting cable ratings is a confusing process since the media planner has to integrate so many different sources of information.

Defining Television Markets

Television rating services define geographic television markets to minimize the confusion of overlapping TV signals. The two definitions typically used are: *areas of dominant influence* and *designated market areas.*

Areas of Dominant Influence (ADI)

Arbitron first referred to geographic TV markets as **areas of dominant influence (ADI).** An ADI is "an exclusive geographic area consisting of all counties in which the home market stations receive a preponderance of total viewing hours." For example, the ADI for Capital City–St. Pierre (see Exhibit 14–10) is all counties in which the Capital City or St. Pierre TV stations are the most watched.

Designated Market Areas

The Nielsen station index uses the similar **designated market areas (DMA)** for geographical areas in which local TV stations attract most viewing. Depending on which rating service the advertiser uses, the media planner will determine where to advertise—which ADIs or which DMAs.

Dayparts

Advertisers must decide *when* to air commercials and on *which programs.* Unlike radio listeners, TV viewers are loyal to programs not stations. Programs continue to run or are canceled depending on the size of their ratings (percentage of the population watching). Ratings also depend on the time of day a program runs.

Television time is divided into **dayparts** as follows:

Combine as early fringe	Daytime:	9 A.M.–4 P.M. (EST)
	Early fringe:	4–5:30 P.M. (EST)
	Early news:	5 or 5:30–7:30 P.M. (EST)
	Prime access:	7:30–8 P.M. (EST)
	Prime:	8–11 P.M. (EST)
Combine as late fringe	Late news:	11–11:30 P.M. (EST)
	Late fringe:	11:30 P.M.–1 A.M. (EST)

There are different levels of viewing during each daypart; the highest is **prime time** (8 to 11 P.M. EST). Late fringe ranks fairly high in most markets among adults, and daytime and early fringe tend to be viewed most heavily by women.

To reach the greatest percentage of the advertiser's target audience with maximum frequency, the media planner determines a **daypart mix** based on TV usage levels reported by the rating services.

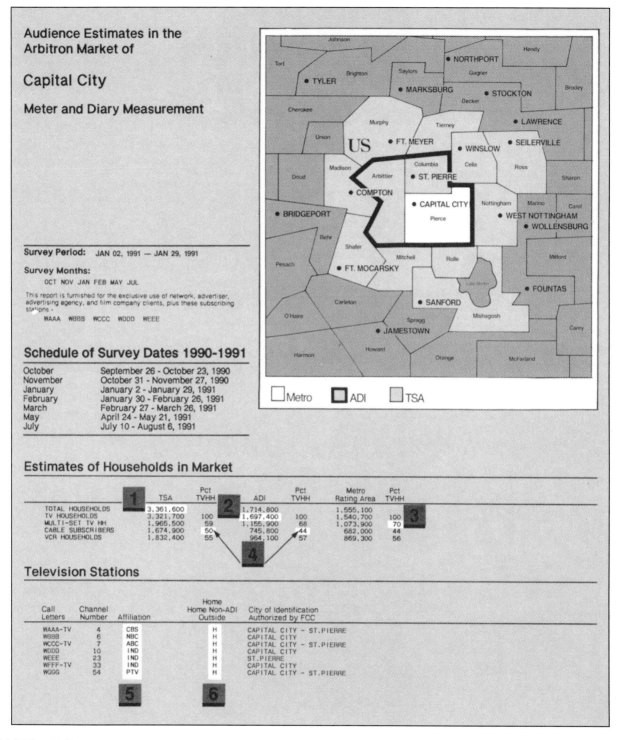

EXHIBIT • 14-10

A typical Arbitron ADI page.

Audience Measures

Rating services and media planners use many terms to define a station's audience, penetration, and efficiency. **TV households (TVHH)** refers to the number of households that own television sets. The number of TVHH in a particular market gives an advertiser a sense of the market's size. Likewise, the number of

TVHH tuned in to a particular program helps the advertiser estimate a program's popularity and how many people a commercial is likely to reach.

The percentage of homes in a given area that have one or more TV sets turned on at any particular time is expressed as **households using TV (HUT).** If there are 1,000 TV sets in the survey area and 500 are turned on, HUT is 50 percent.

Many TV shows are canceled because their ratings slipped. What does that really mean? The **program rating,** the percentage of TV households in an area (TVHH) tuned in to a specific program, is computed as follows:

$$\text{Rating} = \frac{\text{TVHH tuned to specific program}}{\text{Total TVHH in area}}$$

Networks are interested in high ratings because they measure a show's popularity. Advertisers don't want to advertise on unpopular shows, so a network's revenue can fall. Local stations often change their programming—buy different syndicated shows, for example—to increase their popularity and thereby their ratings.

The percentage of homes that have sets in use (HUT) tuned in to a specific program is called the program's **share of audience.** A program with only five viewers could have a 50 *share* if only 10 sets are turned on. So *rating* figures are important because they measure the audience as a percentage of all TVHH in the area, regardless of whether the TV sets are on or off.

The total number of homes reached by some portion of a program is referred to as **total audience.** This figure is normally broken down to determine **audience composition** (the distribution of audience into demographic categories).

Gross Rating Points

In television, **gross rating points (GRPs)** represent the total rating points achieved by a particular media schedule over a specific period, such as a week or a month. A weekly schedule of five commercials on programs with an average household rating of 20 would yield 100 GRPs.

BUYING TELEVISION TIME

The process of buying TV time can be rather lengthy and, depending on the number of stations in the buy, quite involved. Either the advertiser or the media buyer must:

- Determine which programs are available at what cost.
- Analyze the various programs for efficiency.
- Negotiate with station reps on price.
- Determine what reach and frequency they are achieving.
- Sign the broadcast contracts.
- Review the affidavits of performance to be sure the commercials ran as agreed.

These procedures are so complex that most large advertisers seek the assistance of ad agencies or media-buying services. Buying services are gaining in popularity because they charge less and can save advertisers money by negotiating for desirable time slots at reduced rates. Local advertisers rely on station reps to determine the best buys for the money.

Requesting Avails

To find out which programs are available, media buyers contact stations' sales reps—local station salespeople, national media rep organizations that sell for one station in each market, or network reps. The media buyer gives the rep information about the advertiser's media objectives and target audiences and asks the rep to supply a list of **avails** (available time slots) along with prices and estimated ratings.

The avails include all the data requested based on the most recent Nielsen or Arbitron book. Many media buyers ask for the information based on the last two or three books to see whether a show's ratings are consistent, rising, or falling.

Selecting Programs for Buys

The media buyer selects the most efficient programs in relation to the target audience using the **cost per rating (CPP) point** and the cost per thousand (CPM) for each program:

$$\text{CPP} = \frac{\text{Cost}}{\text{Rating}} \qquad \text{CPM} = \frac{\text{Cost}}{\text{Thousands of people}}$$

For example, assume "People's Court" has a rating of 25, reaches 200,000 people in the primary target audience, and costs $2,000 for a 30-second spot with a fixed guarantee on station WALB-TV in Albany, Georgia. Then,

$$\text{CPP} = \frac{\$2,000}{25} = \$80 \qquad \text{CPM} = \frac{\$2,000}{(200,000 \div 1,000)} = \$10$$

The lower the cost per thousand, the more efficient the show. The media buyer compares the packages of each station, substituting stronger programs for less efficient ones.

Negotiating Prices and Contracts

Television stations and cable companies publish rate cards to sell their airtime (see Exhibit 14–11). Because of their guaranteed circulation, print media adhere more closely to their rate cards; since TV audiences are, at best, estimated, television reps will negotiate prices.

The advertiser wants to get the best schedule possible within budget. The media buyer contacts the rep and explains what efficiency the advertiser needs in terms of delivery and CPM to make the buy. The buyer has numerous ways to negotiate lower rates: work out a package deal, accept run-of-schedule positioning (the station chooses when to run the commercials), or take advantage of **preemption rates.** A preemption rate is lower because the advertiser agrees to being "bumped" (preempted) if another advertiser pays the higher, non-preemption rate. Preemption rates save advertisers money if demand is down, and the station minimizes the risk of unsold airtime.

Each station's advertising contract is a legal document, so the media buyer must read it carefully before signing it. The contract indicates the dates, times, and programs on which the advertiser's commercials will run, the length of the spots, the rate per spot, and the total amount. The reverse side of the contract defines payment terms and various obligations and responsibilities of the advertiser, agency, and station.

WBRZ
(Airdate April 4, 1955)
BATON ROUGE

BLAIR TELEVISION

ABC Television Network

NAB   TVB

Location ID: 6 TLST LA   Mkt 007461-000
Louisiana Television Broadcasting Corp.
1650 Highland Rd., Baton Rouge, LA 70802. Phone 504-387-2222, Sales, 504-336-2226, Easylink, 62044844.
FAX: 504-336-2246.
Mailing Address: Box 2906, Baton Rouge, LA 70821.

1. PERSONNEL
Gen Mgr—Richard F. Manship.
Asst Gen Mgr—Patricia L. Cheramie.
Station Mgr—John M. Spain.
Dir of Sales—Jim Daboval III.

2. REPRESENTATIVES
Blair Television.

3. FACILITIES
Video 100,000 w., audio 15,000 w.: ch 2. Stereo.
Antenna ht.: 1,690 ft above average terrain.
Operating schedule: 24 hours day. (except Sun sign off 12:30 am, Mon sign on 5 am). CST.

4. AGENCY COMMISSION
15/0 to recognized agencies; 15 days.

5. GENERAL ADVERTISING REGULATIONS
General: 2a, 2b, 3a, 3b, 3c, 3d, 4a, 5, 6a, 7a, 8.
Rate Protection: 16b.
Contracts: 20c, 21, 22a, 25, 26, 28, 31b, 32a.
Basic Rates: 40b, 41b, 41c, 41d, 42, 43a, 45a, 47j, 51, 52a.
Cancellation: 70b, 70f, 71, 72, 73a, 73b, 73d.
Prod. Services: 80, 83, 84, 85, 86
Affiliated with ABC Television Network.

6. TIME RATES
No. 33 Effective January 1, 1990.
Rev. Received January 14, 1991.

7. SPOT ANNOUNCEMENTS

	30 sec
7-10 pm Mon thru Sat; 6-10 pm Sun,	
Prime Time	900-400
6:30-7 pm Mon thru Sat; 10:30-11:40 Mon thru Fri; 10:30-11:30 pm Sat & Sun,	
Prime Access	500-150
5-5:30 pm Mon thru Fri; 5:30-6 Sun; 6-6:30 pm Mon thru Sat; 10-10:35 pm Mon thru Sun,	
Eyewitness News	600-150
5 am-3 pm Mon thru Fri,	
Weekday Daytime	250-30
3-5 pm Mon thru Fri,	
Weekday Early Fringe	300-80
11:40 pm-approx 1:30 am Mon thru Fri; 11:30 pm-approx 2 am Sat & Sun,	
Late Fringe	300-30
Late Night	80-10
6 am-6 pm Sat & Sun,	
Family & Children's Programming	200-30

60 sec: double the 30 sec.
90 sec: 3 ti the 30 sec.
120 sec: 4 ti the 30 sec.
Spots ordered for all time periods & time blocks include adjacencies & may run as much as 120 seconds prior to the start of the segment due to station breaks preceding the clock hour.
10 sec & 15 sec spots are priced by daypart & program, & are subject to immediate preemptions by 30 or 60 sec spots on breaks which do not accommodate natural 10 sec or 15 sec spots.

11. SPECIAL FEATURES

COLOR
Schedules network color, film, slides, tape and live.
Equipped with 1" reel.

13. CLOSING TIME
48 hours prior on all commercial copy; 72 hours if station is to prepare video or audio tags.

EXHIBIT • 14-11

The SRDS *Spot Rate & Data* listing for TV station WBRZ provides background on the station and the rates for various dayparts.

After the spots run, the station returns a signed and notarized **affidavit of performance** to the advertiser or agency, indicating when the spots aired and what **makegoods** are available (free time an advertiser receives to compensate for spots the station missed or ran incorrectly). The affidavit of performance is the station's legal proof—based on the detailed airtime logs that all stations keep—that the advertiser got what was paid for.

Buying Cable Time

Cable can be bought at the national, regional, and local levels. As with broadcast TV, national advertising is divided into network and local spots. Cable network advertising operates much like broadcast network advertising—the media buyer can sponsor network shows or purchase spots on network shows. Because of lower rates, sponsorships are much more common on cable. Exhibit 14–12 shows the growth in cable TV revenue.

Buying national spot advertising on local cable systems is time consuming because media buyers must deal with over 1,000 cable systems. However, larger local systems are becoming more sophisticated in their ad sales and are receiving more assistance from networks in filling local spots on network shows.

To advertise regionally, sponsors use **interconnects**—groups of cable systems joined together for advertising purposes—to buy the same ad time on all the cable systems in a particular area. The largest, New York Interconnect, serves 3.1 million subscribers in the greater New York metropolitan area.

Ad spots and sponsorships on local cable stations are purchased almost the same way as ad time on local broadcast TV stations. Local advertisers like

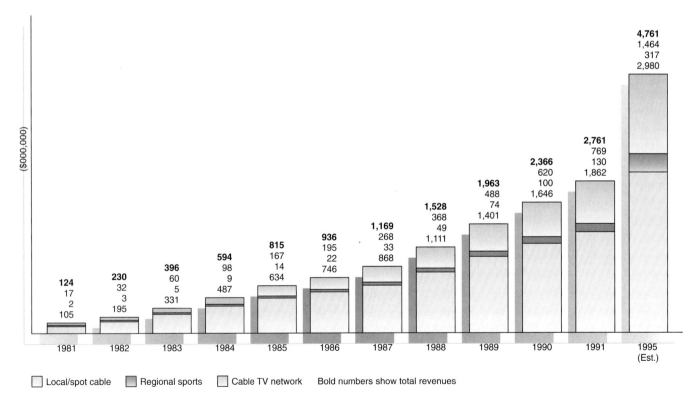

EXHIBIT • 14–12

Cable ad revenues continue to grow dramatically.

community-oriented local programs, such as newscasts and sports events, that reach customers in their immediate area. However, local cable stations often can't provide the same level of advertiser support that broadcast stations do. They need to invest more resources in quantifying audience demographics and tracking commercials to ensure they run as scheduled.

OTHER FORMS OF TELEVISION

Cable isn't the only electronic challenger to traditional broadcast TV. Cable has its own (minor) competitors: DBS, MDS, STV, and SMATV.

- **DBS (direct broadcast satellite)** beams programs from space via satellites to satellite dishes mounted in the home or yard. Up to now, DBS carried only four or five channels. However, DirecTv, a Hughes Communications subsidiary, recently announced agreements with the Disney Channel and Paramount Pictures for its proposed 150-channel service.[17]
- **MDS (multipoint distribution system),** a microwave delivery system that can carry up to a dozen channels, is usually offered in rural areas where cable isn't available.
- **STV (subscription television)** is over-the-air pay TV. Subscribers buy a descrambler that allows them to watch programs carried over a regular TV channel.
- **SMATV (satellite master antenna television)** uses a satellite dish to capture signals for TV sets in apartment buildings and other complexes, acting as a sort of minicable system.

Most are more expensive and carry fewer channels, so none has captured the public's imagination the way cable has.

ADVERTISING ON VIDEOCASSETTE RENTALS

Another challenger to both broadcast and cable TV is the rented videocassette. Ever since Pepsi sponsored the successful home-video release *Top Gun,* industry analysts have been expecting advertising on videocassette rentals to become a major new medium.[18]

A pilot study by Nielsen Media Research showed that home-video renters are older than expected (25 to 49) and 25 percent earn more than $50,000 a year.[19] And the majority of video renters watch the commercials that precede the movie—sometimes more than once. A Schweppes ad starring comedian John Cleese was viewed by an astounding 95 percent of households renting *A Fish Called Wanda*.[20]

The study also showed that households watch rented films an average of 1.3 times during the typical two-day rental period. When metered viewer data becomes regularly available, more advertisers are likely to consider placing commercials on videos.

THE MEDIUM OF RADIO

Radio is a personal, one-on-one medium—people listen alone. And radio is mobile. It can entertain people who are driving, walking, at home, or away from home. It's a particularly strong medium to reach people who commute by car.

Radio is also adaptable to moods. In the morning, people may want to hear the news, upbeat music, or interesting chatter; in the afternoon, they may want to unwind with classical or easy-listening music. Most people listen faithfully to two or three different radio stations with different types of programming.

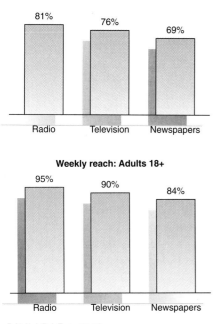

Daily reach: Adults 18+

81%   76%   69%

Radio   Television   Newspapers

Weekly reach: Adults 18+

95%   90%   84%

Radio   Television   Newspapers

EXHIBIT • 14–13

Daily and weekly reach of radio exceeds other media.

Who Uses Radio?

With its unique ability to relax, inform, and entertain, radio has become the daily companion of millions at work, at play, and on the highway. (See Ad Lab 14–B: The Eye versus the Ear.)

In an average week, 96.1 percent of the U.S. population listens to radio—in an average day, almost 80 percent. The average American spends about three hours a day listening to the radio.[21] As Exhibit 14–13 shows, radio leads all other media in both daily and weekly reach. As a result, radio's advertising revenues have grown steadily.

More national advertisers are discovering radio's reach and frequency potential. Schering Corporation tested radio's selling effectiveness on Tinactin, an antifungal product used for athlete's foot. For two months in four western cities, Schering aired a Tinactin commercial on radio. During that same period, Tinactin's chief competitors, Desenex and Micatin, advertised regularly on TV. With an 85 percent reach and a frequency of nine, Tinactin's market share jumped 12 points after the trial. Maria Boerlage, group brand director at Schering, said, "We do believe we have a good commercial, but we know the medium delivered those share points."[22]

Although many big-budget national companies spend a lot of money on radio advertising, smaller national companies are also using radio to gain on the competition. Dial Corporation, which makes Purex laundry products and has nowhere near the ad budget of goliath spenders like Procter & Gamble, calls radio its giant killer.

Local retailers also like the medium because they can tailor it to their needs. It offers defined audiences, and retailers can create an identity by doing their own ads. Many types of local businesses are spending more on radio ads. Grocery stores and supermarkets spent 335 percent more on radio advertising in 1990 than 1980; and major spending increases have also been posted by car dealers, home improvement stores, banks, and savings and loans.[23]

Radio Programming and Audiences

Radio stations plan their programming carefully to reach specific markets and to capture as many listeners as possible. The larger the audience, the more a station can charge for commercial time. Therefore, extensive planning and research go into radio programming and program changes.

Stations have a number of options. They can use tried-and-true formats, subscribe to network or syndicated programming, or devise unique approaches. One successful station in Santa Fe, New Mexico, for example, plays sets of classical, jazz, and light rock music back-to-back. However, programming choices are greatly influenced by whether a station is on the AM or FM band.

For years, AM dominated the airwaves. But in the 1960s, with the advent of stereo and the growth of underground programming on FM, things began to change. Today, FM has more than 70 percent of the radio audience, and AM stations are scrambling for listeners.[24] FM has much better sound fidelity (AM is more subject to interference), fewer commercial interruptions, and more varied programming.

To counteract FM's inroads, many AM stations switched to programs that don't rely on sound quality, such as news, talk, and sports. Some stations are experimenting with new formats, such as all-comedy, midday game shows with audience participation, children's programming, and formats geared to unique regions, such as KHJ's "car radio" in Los Angeles, which provides traffic reports

AD LAB 14–B   The Eye versus the Ear

Jack Trout and Al Ries, who pioneered the concepts of positioning, marketing warfare, and bottom-up marketing, here share their views on another controversial subject: the eye versus the ear.

What Is a Picture Worth?

We all know TV pictures are expensive. But what are they worth without the sound? Not much. In fact, without the words on the package or the graphics on the screen, pictures in a TV commercial have almost no communication value. If pictures alone make no sense, how about sound alone? Strange as it seems, sound alone can present an easily understood message. Most classic print ads illustrate the same principle. The visual alone usually makes no sense; it needs words.

Sound Alone Is Powerful

Laboratory studies show that when you present a list of words to people auditorily (say, on tape) or visually (say, on slides) they remember more of what they hear than what they see.

A Northwestern University study shows that if you try to convince people about a product with just a verbal message, they like it better and want to buy it more.

Two Kinds of Words

There are two kinds of words, printed and spoken, and there's a big difference between them.

The ear is faster than the eye. The mind can understand a spoken word in 140 milliseconds, compared to 180 milliseconds for a printed word. Psychologists speculate the brain translates visual information into aural sounds that the mind can comprehend, which accounts for this 40-millisecond delay.

In addition, a visual image—picture or words—fades in one second unless the mind files away the essence of the idea. Hearing lasts four or five times as long.

So listening to a message is much more effective than reading it. First, the mind holds spoken words in storage much longer, enabling people to follow the train of thought with greater clarity. Second, the tone of the human voice gives the words emotional impact that no picture can achieve.

But other things happen when people hear spoken words.

Auding and Reading

Children listen and eventually learn to comprehend spoken language. Only later do they learn to read.

In school, they learn to decode written words through phonics training. So there is a very intimate relationship between written and oral language. The mind apparently translates printed words into spoken equivalents before it can understand them. (Note how beginning readers often move their lips when reading.)

There is much evidence that the mind works by ear, that thinking is a process of manipulating sounds, not images—even when pictures or photographs are involved.

Implications for Advertising

Implications for the advertising industry are staggering. In many ways, they call for a complete reorientation from a visual to a verbal point of view.

Visuals do play an important role. But verbal messages should be the driver, and pictures should reinforce the words. All too often the opposite is true.

Laboratory Applications

1. What are some possible implications for the way advertising is created? For the ways copy is written? For the media advertisers use?

2. Do you agree with Trout and Ries's findings? What do you think most consumers prefer for communication and entertainment, the eye or the ear? What do most advertisers prefer for communicating their messages?

---

every 10 minutes, tips on driving, and features on cars and travel.[25] AM stations are also trying to win back music listeners by improving their sound quality and offering stereo broadcasting.

When buying radio time, advertisers usually buy the station's format, not its programs. The majority of stations, AM or FM, adopt one of the dozen or so standard programming formats: contemporary hit radio (CHR), adult contemporary, country, album-oriented rock, easy listening, news/talk, black/urban, middle of the road (MOR), nostalgia (big band), classical, religious, and so on. Each format tends to appeal to specific demographic groups, as shown in

EXHIBIT • 14-14

Profile of daily adult listeners of radio stations, by format, in the United States.

Format	Percent male	Percent female	Median age	Median household income	Percent with 1+ years college
Adult contemporary	40	60	39.0	$39,718	45
All news	59	41	48.7	44,403	48
Album-oriented rock	64	36	29.4	37,007	48
Black R&B	34	65	43.1	26,052	35
Classic rock	88	32	28.9	41,578	48
CHR Rock	43	67	30.3	38,490	40
Classical	50	50	45.8	49,713	68
Country	49	51	40.8	33,733	34
Beautiful	49	51	51.0	30,847	41
Golden oldies	51	49	40.3	41,685	44
MOR/nostalgia	51	49	57.3	37,708	38
News/talk	50	40	49.9	44,349	51
Religious	41	59	40.8	36,428	39
Urban contemporary	43	57	31.1	25,553	31
U.S. adult population	40	52	41.1	34,779	39.4

EXHIBIT • 14-15

Top 10 radio advertisers in the United States.

Rank	Advertiser	Radio ad expenditures, 1991*
1	Sears, Roebuck	$66.5
2	Gateway Educational Products	41.7
3	AT&T	30.1
4	Volkswagenwerk AG	22.0
5	General Motors	17.2
6	Accor SA (Motel 6, Sofitel)	15.7
7	Goodyear Tire & Rubber	15.4
8	Chrysler	14.6
9	Warner-Lambert	14.6
10	U.S. government	13.9

* Dollars are in millions.

Exhibit 14–14. The most popular format, contemporary hit radio (CHR), appeals primarily to teenagers and women under 30.

This format, always found on FM stations, emphasizes a constant flow of top 40 hits, usually with minimal intrusion by disk jockeys (although the talky, zany "zoo" approach to CHR caught on in several markets). Another popular format, adult contemporary (or "easy oldies"), is often advertised as "light rock, less talk." This format aims at the desirable target group of working women aged 25 to 44.[26] The news/talk, easy-listening, and nostalgia formats tend to have high listenership among men and women over 50.

Advertisers use listenership studies to determine which radio formats in a particular market deliver the greatest share of a product's target audience. For example, a manufacturer of acne cream would go for CHR stations.

A major trend in radio today has been a resurgence of radio networks. Unlike TV networks, which supply affiliates with the bulk of their programming, radio networks offer services and programs that complement a station's local programming. A single station might subscribe to ABC's hourly newscasts, CBS's weekly "Entertainment Coast-to-Coast," and Mutual Broadcasting System's nightly "Larry King Show."

There are now over 20 national radio networks, including the multiple "mini-networks" of ABC, NBC, and CBS. And numerous syndicators offer a variety of programs, from live rock concerts and sporting events to public-affairs programs and talk shows. To stand out in an increasingly competitive radio environment, more and more stations are opting for syndicated and network offerings.[27] And as more stations carry these programs and more listeners tune in, national advertisers are finding them increasingly attractive.

The largest national radio advertisers are major retailers, car companies, beer and wine producers, telecommunications companies, and the government. See Exhibit 14–15.

But radio's biggest source of revenue is local businesses. Of the almost $9 billion spent on radio ads in 1990, over $6.9 billion came from local advertisers.[28] Both national and local advertisers like radio's reach and frequency, selectivity, and cost-efficiency. (See the Checklist: The Pros and Cons of Radio Advertising.)

CHECKLIST   The Pros and Cons of Radio Advertising

The Pros

The principal advantages of radio are high reach and frequency, selectivity, and cost efficiency.

◇ **Reach and frequency**. Radio offers an excellent combination of reach and frequency. The average adult listens more than three hours a day, radio builds a large audience quickly, and a normal advertising schedule easily allows repeated impact on the listener.

◇ **Selectivity**. Specialized radio formats, with prescribed audiences and coverage areas, enable advertisers to select the market they want to reach—a specific sex, age group, ethnic or religious background, income group, employment category, educational level, or special interest.

◇ **Cost-efficiency**. Radio offers its reach, frequency, and selectivity at one of the lowest costs per thousand, and radio production is relatively inexpensive. National spots can be produced for about one-tenth the cost of a TV commercial. And local stations often produce local spots for free.

◇ **Other advantages**. Radio also offers timeliness, immediacy, local relevance, and creative flexibility.

The Cons

In spite of these advantages, radio has limitations: it's an aural medium only, its audience is highly segmented, the advertiser's commercials are short-lived and often only half heard, and each ad must compete with the clutter of other advertising.

◇ **Limitations of sound**. Radio is heard but not seen, a drawback if the product must be seen to be understood. Some agencies think radio restricts their creative options.

◇ **Segmented audiences**. If a large number of radio stations compete for the same audience, advertisers who want to blanket the market have to buy multiple stations, which may not be cost-effective.

◇ **Short-lived and half-heard commercials**. Radio commercials are brief and fleeting. They can't be kept like a newspaper or a magazine ad. Radio must compete with other activities for attention, and it doesn't always succeed.

◇ **Clutter**. Stations with the greatest appeal for advertisers have more commercials. Advertisers must produce a commercial that stands out from the rest.

BUYING RADIO TIME

As with television, advertisers need a basic knowledge of the medium to buy radio time effectively: the types of radio advertising available for commercial use, a basic understanding of radio terminology, and the steps involved in preparing a radio schedule.

Types of Radio Advertising

An advertiser may purchase network, spot, or local radio time. Local purchases account for 75 percent of all radio time sold; spot radio, another 20 percent; and networks, 5 percent.

Networks

Advertisers may use one of the national radio networks (ABC, CBS, NBC, Mutual, United Stations) to carry their messages to the entire national market simultaneously via stations that subscribe to the networks' programs. In addition, more than 100 regional radio networks in the United States operate as news, sports, and farm networks with information oriented toward specific geographic markets.

Networks provide national and regional advertisers with simple administration and low effective net cost per station. The advantage is less paperwork and lower costs per station. Typical costs per rating point of advertising on various national radio networks are listed in Exhibit 14–16. Disadvantages include lack of flexibility in choosing affiliated stations, the limited number of stations on a network's roster, and the long lead times required to book time.

Network radio advertising rates (cost of :30 commercial) by dayparts and demographic segments.

	Monday–Sunday 6 A.M.–midnight	Monday–Friday 6–10 A.M.	Monday–Friday 3–7 P.M.	Saturday/Sunday 6 A.M.–midnight
Adults 18+	$2,832	$3,051	$3,476	$2,819
Men 18+	2,787	3,212	3,593	2,758
Men 18–34	2,428	2,220	2,399	2,946
Men 25–54	2,937	2,979	3,292	2,905
Women 18+	2,609	2,830	3,179	2,585
Women 18–34	2,542	3,000	3,173	2,531
Women 25–54	2,937	2,970	3,460	3,132
Teens 12–17	2,054	2,211	1,740	1,977

Spot Radio

Spot radio affords national advertisers great flexibility in their choice of markets, stations, airtime, and copy. They can tailor commercials to the local market and put them on the air quickly—some stations will run a commercial with as little as 20 minutes' lead time. And advertisers can build local acceptance by using local personalities or by purchasing airtime on locally produced programs.

Local Radio

Local time denotes radio spots purchased by a local advertiser. It involves the same procedure as national spots.

Radio advertising is either live or taped. Most radio stations use recorded shows with live news in between. Likewise, nearly all radio commercials are prerecorded to reduce costs and maintain broadcast quality.

Radio Terminology

To buy radio time effectively, advertisers need to understand certain radio terminology. Much of the language is the same as that used for other media. But many terms are either peculiar to radio or have a special meaning when applied to radio. The most common are the concepts of *dayparts, average quarter-hour audiences,* and *cumes* (cumulative audiences).

Dayparts

The radio day is divided into five dayparts:

6 A.M.–10 A.M.	Morning drive
10 A.M.–3 P.M.	Daytime
3 P.M.–7 P.M.	Afternoon (or evening) drive
7 P.M.–12 A.M.	Nighttime
12 A.M.–6 A.M.	All night

The SRDS *Spot Rate & Data* listing for KWOD (FM) in Sacramento, California, provides data on the station and the rates for airtime based on volume and dayparts.

Rating services measure audiences for only the first four dayparts because all-night listening is very limited and not highly competitive. Ad Lab 14–C describes the three major audience rating services. Heaviest radio use occurs during drive times (6–10 A.M. and 3–7 P.M.) during the week (Monday–Friday).

This information is important to advertisers because usage and consumption vary for different products. For example, radio's morning drive time coincides

AD LAB 14–C   The Reports that Make or Break Radio Stations

Media buyers use the data from three major audience rating services to determine which programs and stations will deliver the greatest number of target listeners.

Arbitron

The Arbitron rating service chooses a group of representative listeners in each of 257 cities and gives them a diary for tracking the time they spend listening to radio. Listeners return the diaries to Arbitron at the end of each week for tabulation, and Arbitron compiles the results into a quarterly report.

The Arbitron *Book*, available by subscription, reports the number of listeners to particular stations and shows their age, sex, and preferred listening times. Major clients are radio stations, but some ad agencies and radio sales reps also subscribe.

Birch Research

Birch Research uses phone surveys rather than diaries to obtain listener data. Interviewers talk to representative listeners in 130 major radio markets. Results are published monthly and summarized quarterly. Birch also offers Birch-scan, a monthly computerized report.

RADAR

RADAR (Radio's All-Dimension Audience Research) rates network radio programs based on phone interviews with listeners. Each listener is called daily for a week and asked about listening habits from the day before until that moment. RADAR conducts research year-round and publishes results annually in *Radio Usage and Network Radio Audiences*. A number of specialized reports are also available.

Laboratory Applications

1. What are the advantages and disadvantages of these radio audience measurement methods?
2. Which audience measurement method, diary or phone interview, is best? Why?

---

with most people's desire for a steaming, fresh cup of coffee, so it's a great time for advertising coffee brands.

Radio stations base their rates on the time of day the advertiser wants commercials aired, but the rates are negotiable according to supply and demand at any given time. Exhibit 14–17 shows standard rates for airtime on KWOD-FM in Sacramento, California. For the lowest rate, an advertiser orders spots on a **run-of-station (ROS)** basis, similar to ROP in newspaper advertising. However, this leaves total control of spot placement up to the station. So most stations offer a **total audience plan (TAP)** package rate, which guarantees a certain percentage of spots in the better dayparts if the advertiser buys a total package of time.

Average Quarter-Hour Persons

Average quarter-hour persons identifies the average number of people who listen to a specific station for at least 5 minutes during a 15-minute period of any given daypart. For example, station KKDA in Dallas/Ft. Worth, Texas, has an average quarter-hour listenership of 33,800, meaning that any day, during any 15-minute period between 3 P.M. and 7 P.M., about 33,800 people over age 12 are tuned in (see Exhibit 14–18).

The same idea can be expressed in terms of **share**: the station's audience as a percentage of the total listening audience in the area. For example, the total average quarter-hour listening audience for all stations is 676,000, so the average quarter-hour share of radio station KKDA would be 5:

$$\frac{33,800}{676,000} = .05 \text{ or } 5 \text{ percent}$$

Specific Audience
MONDAY-FRIDAY   3PM-7PM

	Persons 12+	Persons 18+	Men 18+	Men 18-24	Men 25-34	Men 35-44	Men 45-54	Men 55-64	Women 18+	Women 18-24	Women 25-34	Women 35-44	Women 45-54	Women 55-64	Teens 12-17
KKDA-FM															
MET AQH PER (00)	338	260	107	20	54	15	8	9	153	52	42	31	1	4	78
MET AQH RATING	1.1	.9	.8	1.0	1.4	.4	.4	.7	1.0	2.5	1.1	.9		.3	2.5
MET AQH SHARE	5.0	4.2	3.6	4.0	6.3	2.1	1.7	3.2	4.8	9.4	4.9	4.1	.2	1.5	14.9
MET CUME PER(00)	1678	1282	626	93	314	117	45	35	656	224	202	141	8	17	396
MET CUME RATING	5.2	4.4	4.5	4.6	8.2	3.5	2.2	2.7	4.4	11.0	5.3	4.3	.4	1.2	12.7
TSA AQH PER(00)	368	283	123	29	58	15	8	12	160	53	45	31	3	4	85
TSA CUME PER(00)	2021	1547	800	208	328	117	45	69	747	246	227	141	39	17	474

EXHIBIT • 14-18

The Arbitron *Radio Market Report* for station KKDA-FM, Dallas/Fort Worth.

MET AQH PER (00) (Metropolitan Average Quarter Hour Persons) = Estimated number of persons who listened to a station for a minimum of five minutes within a quarter hour. TSA (Total Survey Area) may include counties surrounding the MET (metropolitan area).

MET AQH RATING (Rating Point) = Metropolitan Average Quarter Hour Persons estimate expressed as a percentage of the appropriate estimated population.

MET AQH SHARE = Metropolitan Average Quarter Hour Persons estimate for a given station expressed as a percentage of the total MET AQH estimate within a reported daypart.

MET CUME PER = Estimated number of *different* persons who listened to a station for a minimum of five minutes in a quarter-hour within a reported daypart. (Cume estimates may also be called *cumulative* or *unduplicated* estimates.)

MET CUME RATING = Estimated number of Cume Persons expressed as a percentage of the appropriate estimated Metropolitan population.

Average Quarter-Hour Rating Points

Rating points extend the computations a little further by showing the same audience as a percentage of the population. With radio station KKDA located in an area of 3,072,727 people, its average quarter-hour persons could be expressed as an **average quarter-hour rating** of 1:

$$\frac{33,800}{3,072,727} = .011 \text{ or } 1.1 \text{ percent}$$

To determine the **gross rating points** of a radio schedule, average quarter-hour rating is multiplied by the number of spots:

$$\text{Rating points} \times \text{Number of spots} = \text{GRPs}$$
$$1.1 \times 24 = 26.4$$

GRPs can also be determined by multiplying the average quarter-hour persons by the number of spots, dividing by the population, and multiplying by 100:

$$\text{Average quarter-hour audience} \times \text{Number of spots} = \text{Gross impressions}$$
$$33,800 \times 24 = 811,200$$

Therefore,

$$\frac{811,200}{3,072,727} \times 100 = 26.4 \text{ GRPs}$$

Cume Estimates

The **cume persons** is the total number of *different* people who listen to a radio station for a minimum of five minutes in a quarter-hour within a reported daypart.

In our example, we generated 811,200 gross impressions with our schedule on station KKDA. But that does *not* mean that 811,200 *different* people heard our commercials. Many people might have heard the commercials three, four, or five times.

By measuring the cumulative number of different people who listened to KKDA, rating services provide the *reach potential* of our radio schedule, which in this case is 167,800.

The **cume rating** is the estimated number of cume persons expressed as a percentage of the estimated population. For example,

$$\frac{167,800}{3,072,727} = .052 \text{ or } 5.2\%$$

Preparing a Radio Schedule

The procedure advertisers use to prepare radio schedules is similar to that used for TV schedules.

1. Identify stations with the greatest concentration (cume) of the advertiser's target audience by demographics (say, men aged 25 to 34).
2. Identify stations whose format typically offers the highest concentration of potential buyers. Many men and women between 35 and 49 listen to beautiful music stations, but the best format for potential tire purchasers in that age group is an all-news or sports format.
3. Determine which time periods (dayparts) on those stations offer the greatest number (average quarter-hour) of potential buyers. Prospective tire buyers are concentrated in drive time rather than midday.
4. Using the stations' rate cards for guidance, construct a schedule with a strong mix of the best time periods. An average weekly spot load per station may be anywhere from 12 to 30 announcements, depending on the advertiser's budget. At this point, it is often wise to contact the station reps, give them the advertiser's media objectives, suggest a possible budget for their station, and ask what they can provide for that budget. This gives the media buyer a starting point for analyzing costs and negotiating the buy.
5. Determine the cost for each 1,000 target people each station delivers. The operational word is *target:* the media buyer isn't interested in the station's total audience.
6. Negotiate and place the buy (see Exhibit 14–19).
7. Assess the buy (with the help of the agency's or radio station's computer) in terms of reach and frequency.

These steps are far from all-inclusive, but they demonstrate some of the complexity media planners and buyers deal with daily.

FCB

Foote, Cone & Belding
11601 Wilshire Boulevard
Los Angeles, CA 90025
(310) 312-7000

Spot Commercial Instructions

Station:_____   Commercial Material:_____

Air Dates:_____   Live Copy No(s):_____

Client/Product:_____   Estimate No.:_____

Rotation:_____

Commercials to run per media time order.
Call with questions.

Issued by:_____FCB/LA Forwarding

Phone:_____

Date:_____

FCB/LOS ANGELES   SPOT COMMERCIAL INSTRUCTIONS (RADIO)

11601 WILSHIRE BOULEVARD   Period JAN01/93 thru DEC31/93   Page   1
LOS ANGELES, CA 90025   Mon May 24, 1993
                                                                                    7:35 PM - 8JE
                                    Client   SP:TLETTER2
                                    Product EXP   EXPANSION

                                              Market   DOT AL DOTHAN, AL.
                                              Station WTVY-FM
                                              Phone   205-792-0047
                                              FAX   205-793-3947

```
-------------------------------------------     ------------------Commercial------------------
Prod                    Start
Code Product name       Length Date    End Date  Code No.  Title                    (Rot'n) Mat'ls
-------------------------------------------     ----------------------------------------------
EXP  EXPANSION                 MAR15/93 JUN13/93          Previously Trafficked

EXP  EXPANSION          :60    JUN14/93 UFN      FA2102A  GRADUATION :60            25.0%  On Hand

                                                 FA2104A  BABY :60                  25.0%  On Hand

****************************************** *      FA2106A  GUITAR :60                25.0%  On Hand
* YOU HAVE THESE SPOTS. CONTINUE RUNNING WITH TAGS AS  *
* PREVIOUSLY INSTRUCTED.                  *      FA8013   RECRUITING - INSURE SUCCESS 12.5% On Hand
*                                         *
* CALL JESSE BARNETT AT FCB (310) 312-7251 WITH QUESTIONS. *  FA8104  RECRUITING - LIKE WHAT YOU SEE  12.5% On Hand
******************************************
```

```
                                                 *** Billboards ***
                                                 :05  FA2020
                                                 BROUGHT TO YOU BY THE LOCAL AGENTS OF THE
                                                     ASK THEM ABOUT LIFE INSURANCE.
                                                 :10  FA2020A
                                                 BROUGHT TO YOU BY              YEAR AFTER YEAR,
                                                 MILLIONS OF FAMILIES ACROSS AMERICA DEPEND ON      FOR
                                                 HOME, AUTO, AND ESPECIALLY, LIFE INSURANCE.
                                                     ONE OF THE BIGGEST.  ONE OF THE BEST.
```

```
                                                 ** RADIO OPERATIONS DESK **
                                                 WTVY-FM
                                                 BOX 1089
                                                 DOTHAN, AL 36301
```

EXHIBIT • 14-19

Once the buy is completed, the agency's traffic department issues instructions to the station describing the rotation of commercials to be used. Shown here are the barebones instructions that a station would require, as well as a computerized set of instructions from Foote, Cone & Belding's internal buying/trafficking system.

Summary

As a means of reaching the masses, no other medium today has the unique creative ability of television. Broadcast television has grown faster than any other advertising medium in history because of the unique advantages it offers advertisers: mass coverage at low cost, audience selectivity, impact, prestige, and social dominance.

Television's power as a creative tool may be unmatched, but the medium still has many drawbacks, including high cost, limited selectivity, brevity, clutter, and susceptibility to zipping and zapping.

The five forms of TV advertising are network, spot, syndication, program length, and local.

To determine which shows to buy, the media buyer must select the most efficient ones against the target audience. He or she must compare the packages of each station, substitute stronger programs for less efficient ones, and negotiate prices to get the best buy.

Broadcast television's dominance is being challenged by new electronic media, particularly cable. Cable offers the visual and aural appeal of TV at a much lower cost and with greater flexibility. Cable audiences are highly fragmented, which helps advertisers target specific markets but is a drawback for those wanting to reach a mass audience. Cable advertising can be done at the national, regional, or local level and can take the form of program sponsorships, segment sponsorships, and spots of varying lengths, including the longer infomercials.

Like TV, radio is a highly creative medium. Its greatest attribute is its ability to offer excellent reach and frequency to selective audiences at a very efficient price. Its drawbacks are the limitations of sound, its segmented audiences, and its short-lived and half-heard commercials.

Radio stations are normally classified by the programming they offer and the audiences they serve. Radio stations may be AM or FM, may make use of network or syndicated programs, and may follow one of a dozen or more popular formats.

Advertisers purchase radio time in one of three forms: local, spot, or network.

Buying radio time requires a basic understanding of radio terminology. The most common terms are dayparts, average quarter-hour, and cumulative audiences.

Questions for Review and Discussion

1. What are the advantages of broadcast television advertising for a product such as Energizer batteries?
2. What are the advantages of 15-second TV commercials? The drawbacks?
3. What steps can advertisers take to overcome zipping and zapping?
4. Why is advertising on network TV less desirable in recent years?
5. How would you purchase time from a local TV station? Outline the procedure you would follow.
6. In what ways is cable TV's selectivity a strength? A drawback?
7. Why don't some advertisers believe in the effectiveness of radio advertising?
8. What is the format of the radio station you listen to most? How would you describe the demographics of its target audience?
9. What is the difference between average quarter-hour and cume audiences? Which is better?
10. What is the importance of dayparts to advertisers?

15

We could tell you **CATWALK** is a show
about love, **sex**, friendships, relationships
lust, trust, sexual harassment, **music**
AIDS, jealousy, infidelity,
success and failure.
Or we could just tell you
it's about **life**.

Direct Mail, Outdoor, Transit, and Supplementary Media

Objective: To present the media advertisers use to complement or replace print and broadcast; to evaluate the advantages and disadvantages of direct-mail, out-of-home, and supplementary media and explain how they're bought.

After studying this chapter, you will be able to:

- Differentiate between direct mail and other forms of direct advertising.

- Identify the three basic factors in the cost of direct mail.

- Cite the advantages and disadvantages of direct-mail advertising.

- Explain how advertisers measure exposure to outdoor media.

- Describe the types of standard outdoor advertising structures.

- Discuss the variables that influence the cost of transit and other out-of-home media.

- Identify common types of supplementary media.

Champion International, a major U.S. paper company, wanted to create enthusiasm among industrial purchasing decision makers for its new high-gloss paper stock.

With a tiny target audience (only 315 publishing executives), Champion decided to invest a major portion of its budget—several hundred thousand dollars—into a pinpointed direct-mail campaign. But with this kind of investment and such an important target market, Champion needed something extraordinary to get attention—to make the recipients sit up and take notice.

Working with an agency that specializes in *dimensional mailings,* Champion created a nine-part direct-mail campaign. (Dimensional mailings uses three-dimensional items instead of flat pieces.)

As shown in Exhibit 15–1, each of the nine mailings played off a common theme—billiards—to cleverly make a sales point about Champion and its new high-quality paper product. The first mailing was an attractive cardboard box with a headline printed on the outside: "We want to put something on the table." When executives opened the box, they discovered a miniature pool table along with supporting copy explaining that the company is "in position to pool our resources . . . and being in position is everything in our industry."

A later mailing included seven striped pool balls in a box headlined, "We've earned our stripes." The copy explained how Champion became an industry leader.

Other mailings included items such as a full-size cue stick, chalk, a pool bridge, and a ball rack. Says John H. Hildenbiddle, the company's vice president of creative services, the mailings were "a succinct way to get a key point across to our customers about our product and Champion." To prime the market, Champion launched the campaign a few months before the product was commercially available.

The mailings were a great success. They piqued recipients' curiosity and paved the way for later sales calls by Champion salespeople. In fact, the reps were able to complete a personal sales presentation with 95 percent of the executives who received the mailings. Hildenbiddle reports that virtually all the prospects reacted positively.[1] ◆

EXHIBIT • 15-1

Champion's "Influence" direct-mail campaign consisted of a series of nine packages. Each contained a billiards-related item and copy associating the item to Champion or its products.

DIRECT-MAIL ADVERTISING

Direct-mail advertising includes all forms of advertising sent directly to prospects through a government or private mail delivery service—in the United States, typically the U.S. Postal Service. In dollars spent, direct mail is the third-ranked advertising medium today, surpassed only by newspapers and TV.

Both large and small companies use direct mail. New firms usually use direct mail as their first advertising medium, and they continue to do so as they grow. The reason is clear: Of all media, direct-mail advertising offers the straightest line to the desired customer.

The Confusion Surrounding Direct-Mail Advertising

People frequently confuse direct-mail advertising with several similar terms: *direct advertising, direct marketing, direct-response advertising,* and *mail-order advertising.* How are these concepts similar, and how do they differ?

Direct Advertising

Direct advertising is any form of advertising issued directly to the prospect, whether through the mail, fax, on-line computer services, interactive electronic kiosks, salespeople, dealers, or other means rather than through the traditional mass media. Such advertising may be door-to-door circulars, telephone solicitations, handbills, computer diskettes, videocassettes, or direct-mail advertising.

Direct Marketing

Direct marketing (also called **database marketing**) uses a variety of communications media to build a database of customer information so a company can enhance its relationship with the customer. Direct marketing media may include any of the traditional advertising media—direct mail, newspapers, magazines, radio, or television—used alone or in combination. Or it may include other communication methods such as publicity, trade shows, and even personal salespeople. The goal of direct marketing is to get inquiries, to sell merchandise or services directly to customers, to provide support to salespeople and dealers, to encourage feedback, to get contributions, or to get people to visit stores.[2]

Direct marketing is such an important element of integrated marketing communications today that we deal with it extensively in the next chapter.

Direct-Response Advertising

Direct-response advertising (a kind of *action advertising*) asks the reader, listener, or viewer for an immediate response. A newspaper or magazine ad, like the one shown in Exhibit 15–2, may ask the reader to fill in and mail a coupon to obtain information or order the product. Direct-response advertisers use a variety of media—direct mail, magazines, radio, TV, or even matchbook covers or outdoor posters (billboards). TV ads (or infomercials) that urge viewers to "Call now! Operators are standing by!" are examples of direct-response advertising (see Exhibit 15–3).

Advertisers of both consumer goods and industrial products use direct-response advertising to stimulate sales. For business-to-business marketers, print and direct mail are the primary direct-response media. For high-ticket industrial products, direct-response advertising generates sales leads for followup by a sales rep.

EXHIBIT • 15-2

Apple's direct-response magazine ad does all it can to stimulate action: it promises a catalog full of useful computer products, provides a toll-free telephone number, displays Apple's mailing address prominently, and devotes 30 percent of its space to a coupon.

Mail-Order Advertising

Mail-order advertising is a form of direct-response advertising, but it's also a method of selling. Mail-order advertising promotes a product or service that the prospect can *purchase through the mail*—without a salesperson. Today marketers use three formats: mail-order catalogs (like Lands' End or Spiegel), mail-order ads in print and electronic media, or direct-mail advertising.

Growth of Direct Mail

Direct methods of advertising and selling grew astronomically in the last decade. During the 80s companies mailed 13.6 *billion* catalogs. And between 1983 and 1990, the number of adult Americans who shopped by mail or phone increased from 36 to 55 percent. By the beginning of the 90s, U.S. mail-order

EXHIBIT • 15-3

TV informercials, which may run for 30 minutes or more, are a rapidly growing form of direct-response advertising.

EXHIBIT • 15-4

Top 10 mail-order product categories.

Rank	Category	Sales ($ billions)
1	Insurance/financial	$13.3
2	Department stores	11.7
3	General merchandise	9.5
4	Apparel	8.6
5	Magazines	5.7
6	Sporting goods	3.6
7	Electronic goods	2.7
8	Collectibles	2.1
9	Books	2.0
10	Crafts	1.2

sales reached $211 billion, of which $108 billion were consumer purchases. Direct mail now accounts for 19 percent of all advertising spending.[3]

Direct mail is successful for two reasons. First, it meets the needs of today's changing lifestyles. With more and more women in the work force, families have less time to shop. Shopping at home by mail is much easier, and consumers often get more information about products from catalogs and sales brochures than they do from harried or unknowledgeable retail salespeople.

Second, marketers finally realized that next to personal selling, direct mail is the most effective medium for generating immediate results, whether inquiries or sales.

Marketers are expanding their profits by stuffing monthly credit card statements with tempting mail-order offers. Products that are innovative, can be shipped easily, and are not readily available through other distribution channels are the best candidates. Today's leading mail-order products include books, housewares, clothing, electronic gadgets, and the other products and services listed in Exhibit 15–4.

With more and more major companies entering the field, direct mail's image is improving daily. Consumers seem more comfortable ordering by mail, knowing that they can get quality merchandise from reputable companies, often at a reduced price. Many mail-order companies use sophisticated systems for ordering, fulfilling, and following up after the sale—all designed to make shopping easy and satisfying.

Among the biggest users of direct-mail advertising are insurance companies, financial institutions, and marketers of financial services. Dell Computers, started by a 19-year-old college dropout, became one of the largest computer manufacturers and marketers in the world thanks to direct mail and mail-order advertising.[4]

Of course, with such a high volume of direct mail, there has been some backlash. To protect and enhance direct mail's image, the Direct Marketing Association helps disgruntled recipients remove their names from mailing lists (see Exhibit 15–5).

Types of Direct-Mail Advertising

Direct-mail advertising comes in a variety of formats from sales letters and brochures to handwritten postcards. The message can be one sentence or dozens of pages. And within each format—from tiny coupon to thick catalog—the creative options are infinite.

Sales letters, the most common direct mail format, may be typewritten, typeset and printed, printed with a computer insert (such as the prospect's name), or fully computer-typed. They are often mailed with brochures, price lists, or reply cards and envelopes.

Postcards are used to announce sales, offer discounts, or generate customer traffic. National postal services regulate formats and dimensions. In the United States, first-class postcards may feature handwritten messages, but third-class postcards must be printed.

Some advertisers use a double postcard, enabling them to send both an advertising message and a perforated reply card. A recipient who wants the product or service tears off the reply card and mails it back to the advertiser. To encourage response, some advertisers use **business reply mail,** which enables the recipient to respond without paying postage. The advertiser needs a special first-class postal permit, available for a nominal fee from the local

E X H I B I T • 15-5

Direct mail is too expensive to waste on people who don't want it. For those who want to reduce the amount they receive, the Direct Marketing Association offers a unique service: removal of their names from many national lists. The DMA also offers consumers a chance to receive *more* direct mail if they want.

postmaster, and must print the number of the face of the return card or envelope. On receiving a response, the advertiser pays postage plus a handling fee of a few cents. "Postage-free" incentives usually increase the response rates.

Leaflets or **flyers** are generally single, standard-size (8½ by 11-inch) pages printed on one or both sides and folded one or more times. They usually accompany a sales letter and are used to supplement or expand the information it contains.

Folders, also called **brochures,** are usually larger than leaflets and printed on heavier paper stock so they reproduce printed images well. They often use full color with photos or other illustrations and can accommodate more detailed sales messages than most leaflets.

Broadsides are larger than folders and sometimes used as window displays or wall posters in stores. They fold to a compact size to fit in a mailbag.

Self-mailers are any form of direct mail (postcards, leaflets, folders, broadsides, brochures, catalogs, house organs, magazines) that can travel by mail without an envelope. Usually folded, and secured by a staple or seal, they have special blank spaces for the prospect's name and address to be written, stenciled, or labeled.

Reprints, direct-mail enclosures frequently sent by public relations agencies or departments, are duplicates of published articles or ads that show the company or its products in a favorable light.

Statement stuffers are ads enclosed in monthly customer statements from department stores, banks, or oil companies. To order, customers write in their credit card number and sign the reply card.

House organs are publications produced by associations or business organizations; for example, stockholder reports, newsletters, consumer magazines, and dealer publications.

Catalogs are reference books that list, describe, and often picture the products sold by a manufacturer, wholesaler, jobber, or retailer. See Exhibit 15–6. With more high-income families shopping at home, specialized catalogs are becoming big business. Some mail-order companies prosper with specialized approaches like outdoor clothing and equipment (L. L. Bean, Campmor), electronic gadgets (Sharper Image), gourmet foods (Balducci's), and children's items (Childcraft, Just for Kids).[5]

But with so many choices available, consumer response per catalog is dropping, while production and mailing costs are increasing. As a result, some companies, notably Sears and Montgomery Ward, pulled out of the mail-order business. And some strictly mail-order firms opened retail stores. Banana Republic was once just a mail-order firm, as was Sharper Image, which now gets 80 percent of its sales through its retail stores.[6]

Using Direct Mail in the Media Mix

Direct mail is an efficient, effective, and economical medium for sales and business promotion. (See the Checklist: The Pros and Cons of Direct-Mail Advertising.) That's why it's used by a wide variety of retail, commercial, and industrial companies; charity and service organizations; and individuals. In an integrated marketing communications program, direct mail can increase the effectiveness of ads in other media. Publishers Clearinghouse uses TV spots to alert viewers to the impending arrival of its direct-mail sweepstakes promotions.

EXHIBIT • 15-6

The popularity and variety of specialized direct-response catalogs have exploded as more and more people have opted to shop at home.

Buying Direct-Mail Advertising

Direct-mail advertising has three basic costs: list acquisition; creative production; and distribution.

Acquiring Direct-Mail Lists

Bob Stone, author of *Successful Direct Marketing Methods,* calls mailing lists the "heart" of every direct-mail operation. Each list actually defines a market segment. Direct-mail advertisers use three types of lists: house, mail-response, and compiled.[7]

House Lists A company's customers are its most important asset. A **house list** contains a company's current, recent, and long-past customers or future prospects. A store can build its own house list by:

- Offering a credit plan.
- Offering to send useful booklets or other service information.
- Exchanging names with other retailers with similar customer profiles.
- Capturing the names of customers who ask for home delivery.
- Offering warranties or service plans.
- Asking current customers for the names of their friends and neighbors.[8]

Consumer product companies like GE gather customer data by enclosing an owner registration form with their products. On the mail-in form, purchasers give their name, address, telephone number, birth date, occupation, income range, credit card preferences, home ownership status, and number of children. They also indicate their hobbies and interests, such as golf, foreign travel, photography, and bowling. Companies use this information for their own mailings and even sell the information to other direct-mail advertisers.

Mail-Response Lists After current customers, the advertiser's second most important prospects are people who respond to direct-mail pieces from other companies—especially those with complementary products or services. **Mail-response lists** are the house lists of other direct-mail advertisers, and they can be rented with a wide variety of demographic breakdowns. For example, a company that advertises sports-car caps might want the response list of a company that sells driving gloves.

Compiled Lists **Compiled lists,** the most readily available, are those that some source compiles for a particular reason—for example, lists of car owners, new-house purchasers, city business owners, Chamber of Commerce presidents, union members, and so on. They offer the lowest response rate. Compiled lists are often computer merged with mail-responses and house lists, then purged of duplicate names.

Direct-mail lists can be bought or rented. Purchased lists can be used without limit; rented lists must be used for a single mailing only. List owners plant decoy names in the list to be sure renters don't use the list more than once.[9] Most list owners require the prospective renter to submit sample mailers in advance to be sure the piece doesn't reflect poorly on them or compete with their own products or services.

Some list owners pay a **list broker** a commission (usually 20 percent) to handle the rental details. The advertiser, in turn, benefits from the broker's direct-mail expertise without having to pay more than the rental cost.

CHECKLIST   The Pros and Cons of Direct-Mail Advertising

The Pros

◇ **Selectivity.** Direct mail helps advertisers communicate directly with the people most likely to buy. Computerized mailing lists group people by occupation, region or state, income, and other characteristics.

◇ **Intensive coverage and extensive reach.** Everyone has a mailbox; with direct mail, an advertiser can reach 100 percent of the homes in a given area.

◇ **Flexibility.** Direct-mail advertising can be uniquely creative and novel, limited only by the advertiser's ingenuity and budget and postal regulations. Advertisers can produce direct-mail pieces fast and distribute them quickly.

◇ **Control.** Preprinted direct-mail pieces enable an advertiser to control circulation and reproduction quality.

◇ **Personal impact.** Advertisers can personalize direct mail to the needs, wants, and whims of specific audiences without offending other prospects or customers.

◇ **Exclusivity.** No distractions from competitive ads.

◇ **Response.** Direct mail achieves the highest response of any advertising medium. About 15 percent of the responses arrive within the first week, so the advertiser can quickly judge the campaign's success.

◇ **Testable.** Direct mail is good for testing prospect reactions to product acceptability, pricing, audiences, offers, copy approaches, sales literature, and so on.*

The Cons

◇ **High cost per exposure.** Direct mail has the highest cost per exposure of any major media—about 14 times as much as most magazines and newspaper advertising.

◇ **Delivery problems.** The mass media offer precise delivery times, but the Postal Service makes no delivery commitments on third-class mail. And up to 10 percent of mailings may be undeliverable because people move.†

◇ **Lack of content support.** Direct mail must capture and hold the reader's attention without editorial or entertainment content, and it must stand out from the other direct-mail pieces that arrive the same day.

◇ **Selectivity problems.** Effective direct mail depends on correctly identifying the target audience and obtaining a good list. Some groups of prospects—like physicians—are so saturated with direct mail they ignore it.

◇ **Negative attitudes.** Many consumers consider the pieces "junk mail" and automatically throw them away. And they may believe it's too difficult to return merchandise purchased by mail.

◇ **Environmental concerns.** Some consumers see direct mail as just more landfill fodder. Some direct marketers (Eddie Bauer and L. L. Bean) print parts of their catalogs on recycled paper, and new de-inking facilities will make more catalogs recyclable.‡

* Albert Haas, Jr., "How to Sell Almost Anything by Direct Mail," *Across the Board,* November 1986, p. 50.
† Karen Hochman, "15 Direct Mail Tips from the Pros: 8 Ways to Get Better Results," *Bank Marketing,* November 1988, pp. 28–30.
‡ John B. Hinge, "Catalog Houses That Once Boomed Find the Checks Are No Longer in the Mail," *The Wall Street Journal,* April 4, 1991, sec. b, pp. 1, 8.

Lists can be brokered or exchanged with list houses or other noncompetitive companies. And they can be tailored to reflect customer location (ZIP code); demographics such as age, income, and credit card ownership; or psychographic characteristics such as personality and lifestyle. The SRDS *Direct Mail List Rates and Data* comes in two volumes, *Consumer Lists* and *Business Lists,* and contains more than 50,000 list selections in hundreds of different classifications. See Exhibit 15–7.

The quality of mailing lists varies enormously. The owner of a wine store in San Francisco purchased a mailing list that turned out to include out-of-date addresses and names of people who lived too far away, didn't drink wine, and couldn't afford his expensive labels. He purchased a second list from a mailing list broker and got much better results. This list contained the names of people who lived near his shop, subscribed to an expensive wine journal, and owned moderately expensive homes.[10]

Doubleday Book Club

Doubleday List Marketing

Location ID: 10 DCLS 564   **Mid 019894-000**
Member: D.M.A.
Participant D.M.A. Mail Preference Service.
Doubleday Mailing Lists.
501 Franklin Ave., Garden City, NY 11530. Phone 516-
873-4477. Fax: 516-873-4774.
**Specific list selections are located in each
appropriate classification in their normal alphabetical
sequence.**

1. **PERSONNEL**
   Manager, List Marketing—Diane Silverman.
   Assistant Manager, List Mktg.—Liz Maletta.
   List Mktg. Coordinator—Linda Jackson.
   Broker and/or Authorized Agent
   All recognized brokers.
2. **DESCRIPTION**
   Doubleday Book Club members.
   ZIP Coded in numerical sequence 100%.
3. **LIST SOURCE**
   Direct mail and space ads.
4. **QUANTITY AND RENTAL RATES**
   Rec'd Mar. 8, 1990.

	Total Number	Price per/M
Members	900,000	75.00
Hotline	479,000	80.00
Completers (1989-90)	433,000	40.00
Age-coded names	2,130,000	80.00

   Selections: enrollment date, 5.00/M extra; dollar select,
   6.00/M extra; Mr./Mrs./Miss/Ms., sex, 3.00/M extra;
   state, SCF, ZIP tape, 4.00/M extra.
5. **COMMISSION, CREDIT POLICY**
   20% commission to all recognized brokers. Payments
   due 30 days after billing.
6. **METHOD OF ADDRESSING**
   4/5-up Cheshire labels.   4-up pressure sensitive labels,
   5.00/M extra. Magnetic tape (9T 1600/6250 BPI).
7. **DELIVERY SCHEDULE**
   Ten working days.
8. **RESTRICTIONS**
   Sample mailing piece required for approval.
9. **TEST ARRANGEMENT**
   Minimum 10,000.
11. **MAINTENANCE**
   Cleaned and updated quarterly.

EXHIBIT • 15-7

Typical listing from *Direct Mail List Rates and Data (Consumer Lists),* published by Standard Rate & Data Service.

Mailing list prices vary according to quality. Rental rates average about $50 per thousand names but can be as little as $15 per thousand or as much as $400 per thousand. The more stringent the advertiser's selection criteria, the more expensive the list. As the wine store owner discovered, an extra $10 per thousand is often well worth the savings in wasted mailers and postage.

The average mailing list changes more than 40 percent a year as people relocate, change jobs, get married, or die. So mailing lists must be continually updated or *cleaned* to be sure they're current and correct.

Today, computers enhance mailing lists by turning them into valuable databases. The process of **overlaying** combines information from several different sources to produce an in-depth profile of each customer or company on the list. Such detailed databases pave the way for the *maximarketing* techniques (introduced in Chapter 7), which advertisers use to pinpoint customers and narrowly target communications to those most likely to be interested. Some experts believe direct mail will eventually be so specific that "junk mail" will disappear—all mailers will be meaningful to the recipients.[11]

Advertisers can also test the validity and accuracy of a given list. They rent or buy every *n*th name and send a mailer to that person. If the results are favorable, they purchase additional names, usually in lots of 1,000.

Production and Handling

To create a direct-mail package, the advertiser may use in-house staff, an ad agency, or a freelance designer and writer. Some agencies specialize in direct mail.

The direct-mail piece normally goes through the same production process as any other print piece. The size and shape of the mailing package as well as the type, illustrations, and colors all affect printing costs. Special features such as simulated blue-ink signatures, cardboard pop-ups, and die cutting (the cutting of paper stock into an unusual shape) add to the cost. But the larger the printing volume, or "run," the lower the printing cost per unit.

Remaining production and handling tasks can be done by a local **letter shop** (or *mailing house*), or the advertiser can do them internally. On a cost-per-thousand basis, letter shops stuff and seal envelopes, affix labels, calculate postage, and sort, tie, and stack the mailers. Some shops also offer creative services. If the advertiser plans to use third-class bulk mail, the mailers must be separated by ZIP code and tied into bundles to qualify for low bulk rates. Then the letter shop delivers the mailers to the post office.

Distribution

Distribution costs are based chiefly on the weight of the mailer and the delivery method. U.S. advertisers can use the U.S. Postal Service, air freight, or private delivery services like United Parcel Service and Federal Express. The most common, the U.S. Postal Service, offers several types of delivery.

- *First-class mail.* Contrary to popular belief, a large amount of direct-mail advertising is sent first class. **First-class mail** ensures fast delivery, return of undeliverable mail, and forwarding (without additional charge) if the addressee moved and filed a forwarding address.
- *Third-class mail.* The four types of **third-class mail** are single piece, bulk, bound books or catalogs, and nonprofit organization mail. Most direct-mail advertising travels by third-class mail, which is much cheaper than first-class.

- ***Fourth-class mail.*** Only mail that weighs over 16 ounces qualifies for **fourth-class mail,** typically merchandise, books, printed matter, and all mailable matter not in first, second, or third class.

Direct mail is most effective when it arrives on Tuesdays, Wednesdays, and Thursdays.

OUTDOOR ADVERTISING

It was spring, and love was in the air. As people drove to work, they noticed a billboard that displayed a personal message: "Angel in Red: Saw You at Garcia's Irish Pub. Love to meet you. William."

Every Monday for nine weeks a new message went up, each more romantic—and more desperate—than the last (see Exhibit 15–8). People started going to Garcia's to see if they could spot her—or meet William. Soon a board appeared authored by Frankie warning William that *his* angel was out of bounds. William responded with a board saying "Angel in Red: Frankie be damned! I'd risk it all to meet you at Garcia's." Women started calling the local billboard company to see how they could get to meet romantic William.

The story became the talk of the town. And for nine weeks, nobody caught on—not even the employees at Garcia's.

Finally, the board everyone was waiting for appeared: "Dear William: I must be crazy. Garcia's, Friday, 8:30. Angel."

At the end of the nine-week run, the place was jammed. Garcia's had to hire two models to play William and Angel. Yes, William finally found his angel, and they danced to—what else—*The Lady in Red.*

The final board appeared the next week. "Angel: Thanks for Friday at Garcia's. I'm in heaven. Love, William."

The campaign was the brainchild of Crowley Webb & Associates—the ad agency next door to Garcia's. The owner of Garcia's was nervous about a new chain restaurant's plans to open a pub on the lakefront. So he hired Crowley Webb to come up with something really "way out." But he cautioned them that he couldn't spend more than $20,000.[12]

The agency demonstrated to Garcia's—and the world—that with a little imagination, outdoor advertising is an ideal medium for achieving local reach, frequency, and continuity on a very limited budget. (See the Portfolio of Outdoor Advertising: A 20th Century Art Form.)

As a national and global medium, outdoor has achieved great success. From Africa to Asia to Europe to South America, outdoor media are used by both local

EXHIBIT • 15–8

Over a nine-week period, a clever billboard campaign unveiled a charming story of romance that significantly increased business for Garcia's Irish Pub.

Continued on page 469

Portfolio of Outdoor Advertising:
A 20th-Century Art Form

A. The visual of the eye eliminates the need for a headline.

B. The wordplay on the old childrens' tale helps us remember the message.

C. The powerful visual of an ocean wave is an effective nonverbal device for cueing the reader to imagine waking up to the roar of pounding surf.

D. This award-winning billboard designed by Cossette Communications-Marketing in Montreal announces a new McDonald's product and reinforces the company's logo with immediacy.

E. The double entendre of "quiet cabin" promises a desirable automotive benefit while conjuring up an image of pastoral serenity.

EXHIBIT • 15-9

This huge 96-sheet billboard for Nike used participants in the 1993 London Marathon as the background for a succinct but challenging message.

and global marketers for the same reasons as Garcia's Irish Pub—to communicate a succinct message or image in the local language to a mass audience quickly and frequently at the lowest cost per thousand of any major medium (see Exhibit 15–9). In 1992, U.S. advertisers spent a total of $663 million in standardized outdoor advertising.[13]

Standardization of the Outdoor Advertising Business

Media that reach prospects outside their homes—like outdoor advertising, bus and taxicab advertising, subway posters, and terminal advertising—are called **out-of-home media.** The most common are *on-premise signs* that identify a place of business, but they don't provide market coverage, and they aren't an organized medium like the *standardized outdoor* business.

Standardized outdoor advertising uses scientifically located structures to deliver an advertiser's message to an entire market. This highly organized medium is available in thousands of communities across North America.

In the United States, outdoor ad structures are owned and maintained by about 600 local and regional companies known as *plants*. They are built on private land, which the plant operators own or lease, and are concentrated in commercial and business areas where they must conform to local building codes.

Plant operators find suitable locations, lease or buy the property, erect the structures, contract with advertisers for poster rentals, and post the panels or paint the bulletins. (Exhibit 15–10 shows how an outdoor ad is assembled.) Plant operators also maintain the outdoor structures and keep the surrounding areas clean and attractive.

The plant operator may have its own art staff to supply creative services for local advertisers; ad agencies usually do the creative work for national adver-

A.

B.

C.

EXHIBIT • 15-10

A. Printed poster sheets are collated, prepasted, and vacuum-sealed in plastic bags where they remain moist for weeks. Prepasting eliminates glue streaks from dark backgrounds. "Blanking paper" is posted on first to form a border. Next, beginning at the bottom, the prepasted

sheets are applied to the first section of the panel.

B. By starting at the bottom and working up, each sheet overlaps the previous section, forming a "rain-lap" that helps prevent flagging or tearing. A dry brush makes the paper adhere to the panel.

C. Sheet by sheet, the giant paper mosaic is assembled into a colorful 12' by 25' display. Since a poster is a series of sheets, sections can be varied for specific locations or to include a local dealer's name.

tisers. By far the biggest outdoor advertisers are retailers and tobacco companies, which together accounted for about 24 percent of all outdoor expenditures in 1990.[14] Usually the smaller the market, the larger the percentage of local advertisers.

Types of Outdoor Advertising

To buy outdoor advertising effectively, the media planner must understand its advantages and disadvantages and the types of structures available (See the Checklist: The Pros and Cons of Outdoor Advertising.) Standardized structures come in three basic forms: the poster panel, the bulletin, and the spectacular.

Poster Panels

Poster panels ("billboards") are the least costly per unit. A poster consists of blank panels with a standardized size and border. It is usually anchored in the ground but may be affixed to a wall or roof. Its message is first printed at a lithography or silk screen plant on large sheets of paper, then mounted by hand on the panel.

Poster sizes are referred to in terms of *sheets*. At one time, a structure 12' by 25' required 24 of the largest sheets a printing press could hold; "24-sheet" is still used even though press sizes and most poster sizes are now larger. The poster is still mounted on a board with a total surface of 12' by 25', but today there are two basic sizes of posters:

- 30-sheet poster—a 9'7" by 21'7" printed area surrounded by a margin of blank paper, it provides 25 percent more copy area than the old 24-sheet size of 8'8" by 19'6".
- Standard bleed poster—a 10'5" by 22'8" printed area extending to the frame, it is about 40 percent larger than the old 24-sheet poster.

Some local advertisers get high-quality outdoor advertising at lower-than-usual cost by using ready-made 30-sheet posters. These stock posters are

CHECKLIST   The Pros and Cons of Outdoor Advertising

The Pros

◇ **Reach**. For the same dollars, outdoor delivers a reach of 86.4% compared to spot TV (76.5%), radio (72.3%), and newspaper (72.2%) for the same target audience in the same city.* The audience is mostly young, educated, affluent, and mobile—an attractive target to many national advertisers.

◇ **Frequency**. Nine out of 10 people reached with a 100 GRP showing receive an average of 29 impressions *each* over a 30-day period.

◇ **Geographic flexibility**. Outdoor advertisers can place their advertising where they want it nationally, regionally, or locally—in more than 9,000 markets across North America.

◇ **Demographic flexibility**. Messages can be concentrated in areas frequented or traversed by young people, upper-income people, or people of specific ethnic backgrounds. With computerization, it's possible to characterize outdoor audiences by age, sex, income, and lifestyle down to the block level.†

◇ **Cost**. Outdoor offers the lowest cost per exposure of any major advertising medium. Rates vary depending on market size and intensity, but the GRP system makes cost comparison possible from market to market.

◇ **Impact**. Advertisers can build up GRPs very fast, ideal for those with a short, simple, dogmatic message.

◇ **Creative flexibility**. Outdoor offers large display and the spectacular features of lights, animation, and brilliant color. New fiber optics, giant video screens, and backlit display technologies offer more creative options.‡

◇ **Location**. Outdoor can target consumers by activity, reaching shoppers on their way to the store, businesspeople on their way to work, or travelers on their way to the airport, thereby influencing shoppers just before they make a purchase decision.

The Cons

◇ **Fleeting message**. Customers pass quickly, so outdoor advertising must intrude to be effective. The design and copy must tell a story briefly and crisply, and the words must sell.

◇ **Environmental influence**. Outdoor messages are influenced by their environment. Placement in a run-down area can detract from a product's image.

◇ **Audience measurement.** Outdoor has trouble reaching narrow demographic groups, and audience demographics are difficult to measure. Not every passerby sees or reads the ad, so some buyers distrust the space seller's reach estimates.

◇ **Control**. Unlike print and broadcast ads, it's hard to physically inspect each outdoor poster panel.

◇ **Planning and costs**. Outdoor messages usually require six to eight weeks of lead time for printing and posting. High initial preparation cost may discourage local use. And for national advertisers, buying outdoor is complex. As many as 30 different companies may be selling ad space in a single market.

◇ **Availability of locations**. Outdoor is so popular that demand now exceeds supply.

◇ **Visual pollution**. In the United States, outdoor advertising still suffers from complaints about visual pollution.

* *Guide to Out-of-Home*, Gannett Outdoor Network, U.S.A., 1992, p. 21.
† Robert Levy, "Breakout in Billboards," *Dun's Business Month*, May 1985, p. 44.
‡ *Guide to Out-of-Home* (New York: American Association of Advertising Agencies, 1988), p. 18.

available in any quantity and often feature the work of first-class artists and lithographers. Local advertisers simply have their name placed in the appropriate spot. Ready-made posters are particularly suitable for such local firms as florists, dairies, banks, and bakeries.

Advertisers of grocery products and many local advertisers use smaller poster sizes. Called "junior panels," these 8-sheet posters offer a 5′ by 11′ printing area on a panel surface 6′ wide by 12′ deep.

Painted Bulletins

Painted bulletins, or **displays,** are meant for long-term use and work best where traffic is heavy and visibility good. They are usually painted in sections in the plant's shop then brought to the site where they are assembled and hung on the billboard structure.

AD LAB 15–A   How to Use Color in Outdoor Advertising

Color Contrast and Value

In outdoor advertising, a full range of colors can be vividly and faithfully reproduced. A huge poster or bulletin alive with brilliant reds, greens, yellows, and blues produces an effect unmatched by any other medium.

In choosing colors for outdoor, the designer should seek high contrast in both hue (the identity of the color, such as red, green, yellow) and value (the color's lightness or darkness). Contrasting colors work well at outdoor-viewing distances; colors lacking contrast blend together and obscure the message.

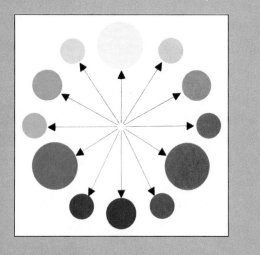

The color wheel illustrates the need for contrast in both hue and value. For example, green and red are opposite each other on the wheel and are therefore complementary colors. They represent a good contrast in *hues,* but having similar *values,* they create an annoying visual vibration. The same is true of blue and orange.

Blue and green, and orange and red, are especially poor combinations because they are similar in both hue *and* value.

Yellow and purple—*dissimilar* in both hue and value—provide a strong and effective contrast for outdoor. White goes well with any dark-value color, while black is good with colors of light value.

Color Impact

Among the color combinations shown below, legibility ranges from best in combination 1 (upper left) to poorest in combination 18 (lower right).

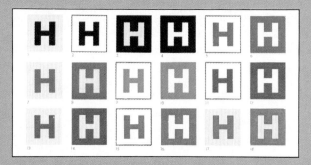

Laboratory Applications

1. Which outdoor ads in this chapter use color the most effectively?
2. What outdoor ads have you seen that don't use color effectively?

Although usually standardized in width and height, actual sizes depend on the available location, the advertiser's budget, and the character of the message. Bulletins are more often custom-made and generally larger and longer than posters. Typical bulletins are 14′ by 48′; some extend to 18′ by 62′10″.

Painted displays are normally lighted and repainted several times each year. (Color is very important to readability; see Ad Lab 15–A.) Some displays are three-dimensional or embellished by cutouts that extend beyond the frames as shown in Exhibit 15–11. Variations include cutout letters, plastic facing, backlighting, moving messages, clocks, thermometers, and electric time and temperature units called jump clocks.

Some advertisers overcome the higher expense of painted bulletins by using a **rotary plan.** They rotate the bulletins to different choice locations in the

EXHIBIT • 15-11

Some advertisers are willing to pay extra for the dramatic effect achieved by altering the billboard's standard dimensions.

EXHIBIT • 15-12

Spectaculars are expensive, elaborate animated signs found primarily in the heart of large cities such as New York and Osaka, Japan.

market every 30, 60, or 90 days, giving the impression of wide coverage over time.

Spectaculars

Spectaculars are giant electronic signs that incorporate movement, color, and flashy graphics to grab attention in high-traffic areas. Spectaculars are very expensive to produce and are found primarily in the world's largest cities. See Exhibit 15–12.

Buying Outdoor Advertising

When an advertiser needs to saturate a market to introduce a new product or announce a change in package design, outdoor advertising makes broad coverage possible overnight.

The basic unit of sale for billboards, or posters, is *100 gross rating points daily* or a **100 showing.** One rating point is equal to 1 percent of a particular market's population. Buying 100 gross rating points does not mean that the message will appear on 100 posters; it means the message will appear on as many panels as needed to provide a daily exposure theoretically equal to the total size of the market's population. Actually, a showing of 100 gross rating points achieves a *daily* reach of about 88.1 percent of the adults in a market over a 30-day period.[15]

Billboard locations throughout Los
Angeles and Orange counties that
achieve at least 100 GRPs each day for
four weeks. The cost of such a showing
is about $400,000.

For less saturation, units of sale can also be expressed as fractions of the
basic unit such as 75, 50, or 25 gross rating points (GRPs). If a showing provides
750,000 total impression opportunities daily in a market with a population of 1
million, it delivers 75 GRPs daily. Over a period of 30 days, the showing would
earn 2,250 GRPs (30 × 75).

Advertisers that want more saturation can increase the number of posters to
as high as 200 or 300 GRPs per day. The map in Exhibit 15–13 shows locations
in Southern California that provide 100 or more GRPs per day.

Local and national advertisers pay the same rates, which are quoted monthly
for various GRP levels. Rates vary considerably from market to market due to
variations in property rentals, labor costs, and market size. Larger markets with
high traffic volume have higher rates. See Exhibit 15–14.

Monthly rates for standard posters
(12′ by 25′) in selected metropolitan
markets.

Market	25 daily GRPs		50 daily GRPs		100 daily GRPs		Average/ poster for 100 daily GRPs
	Number	Cost	Number	Cost	Number	Cost	
Atlanta	30	$13,800	60	$ 27,000	120	$ 51,600	$430
Denver	21	11,700	39	21,000	78	41,000	526
Detroit Metro	45	31,275	90	62,550	180	125,550	698
Las Vegas	9	4,620	17	8,495	34	16,320	480
Los Angeles	120	82,700	240	164,000	480	324,000	675
Minneapolis/St. Paul	53	29,150	105	57,750	210	115,500	550
Baton Rouge	10	5,215	20	9,710	40	18,210	455
Tucson	10	5,500	20	10,500	40	19,750	494
Seattle/Tacoma	43	25,160	86	50,330	172	100,650	585
St. Louis	32	16,000	64	32,000	128	64,000	500

Note: Costs are for space only; they do not include production. Discounts are available.

Regulation of Outdoor Advertising

The Highway Beautification Act of 1965 controls outdoor advertising on U.S. interstates and other federally subsidized highways. It was enacted partially in response to consumer complaints that outdoor advertising was despoiling the environment. As a result of the act, 709,760 billboards were removed by 1991. Likewise, in 1991, Congress banned the construction of new billboards on all scenic highways.[16] Maine, Vermont, Hawaii, and Alaska prohibit outdoor advertising. Ironically, some of these states use outdoor advertising in other states to promote tourism!

TRANSIT ADVERTISING

Campbell Soup started advertising around 1910. The company spent its first $5,000 placing ads on one third of the buses in New York City for one year. After only six months, the ads were so successful, Campbell enlarged the contract to include all surface vehicles in the city. The campaign produced a 100 percent increase in business, and for 12 years transit advertising was Campbell's only medium. Today, Campbell is still a major user of transit advertising (see Exhibit 15–15).

Transit advertising is a category of out-of-home media that includes bus and taxicab advertising as well as posters on transit shelters, terminals, and subways. Today, standardization, better research, additional statistical data, and measured circulation make transit advertising more attractive to national advertisers. National marketers of tobacco, petroleum products, financial services, proprietary medicines, and foods and beverages are the principal users.

With larger and better transit systems, transit advertising now reaches mass audiences as well as ethnic and neighborhood groups. It's especially suitable for reaching middle- to lower-income urban consumers and for providing supplemental coverage of these groups. Researchers claim that 89 percent of all African-Americans and 90 percent of Hispanic adults in New York can be reached through subway ads.[17]

Transit advertising is equally popular with local advertisers. Theaters, restaurants, and retailers use it for reminders and special announcements (see the Checklist: The Pros and Cons of Transit Advertising).

Types of Transit Advertising

Transit advertising depends on the millions of people who use commercial transportation (buses, subways, elevated trains, commuter trains, trolleys, and airlines) plus pedestrians and auto passengers. And there are a variety of transit formats: inside cards; outside posters; and station, platform, and terminal posters.

Inside Cards

The standard size of the **inside card,** placed in a wall rack above the windows, is 11″ by 28″. Four other widths are available (11″ by 21″, 11″ by 42″, 11″ by 56″, and 11″ by 84″). Cost-conscious advertisers print both sides of the card so it can be reversed to change the message, thus saving on paper and shipping charges.

Inside car-end posters (in "bulkhead" positions) are usually larger, and sizes vary. A common size is 22″ by 21″; some top-end or over-door cards are 16″ by 39″ or 16″ by 44″. The end and side positions carry premium rates. See Exhibit 15–16.

EXHIBIT • 15-15

Campbell's Soup has been a transit advertiser since the turn of the century.

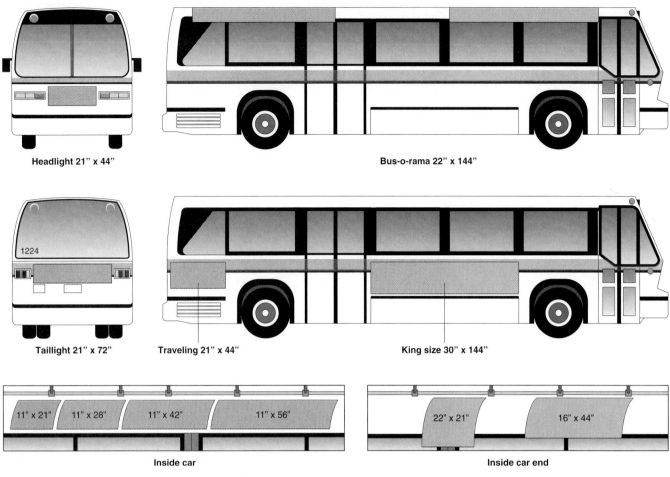

Headlight 21" x 44"

Bus-o-rama 22" x 144"

Taillight 21" x 72"

Traveling 21" x 44"

King size 30" x 144"

11" x 21"   11" x 28"   11" x 42"   11" x 56"

Inside car

22" x 21"   16" x 44"

Inside car end

EXHIBIT • 15–16

Common sizes for inside cards and outside posters.

Outside Posters

Printed on high-grade cardboard and often varnished to make them weather resistant, the most widely used **outside posters** are (1) side of bus—king size (30″ by 144″), queen size (30″ by 88″), and traveling display (21″ by 44″); (2) rear of bus—taillight spectacular (21″ by 72″); and (3) front of bus—headlight (17″ by 21″ and 21″ by 44″).

Terminal Posters

In many bus, subway, and commuter train stations, space is sold for one-, two-, and three-sheet **terminal posters.** Also, major train and airline terminals offer such special advertising forms as floor displays, island showcases, illuminated cards, dioramas (three-dimensional scenes), and clocks with special lighting and moving messages. In cities with major mass-transit systems, advertisers can also buy space on bus shelters and on the backs of bus-stop seats. See Exhibit 15–17.

Taxi Exteriors

Advertisers also buy space on taxi-cab roofs, generally for periods of 30 days, to display internally illuminated, two-sided posters.

CHECKLIST   The Pros and Cons of Transit Advertising

The Pros

◇ **Long exposure.** The average transit ride is 25 minutes.

◇ **Repetitive value.** Many people take the same routes day after day.

◇ **Eagerly read messages.** Riders get bored, so readership is high, and ad recall averages 55 percent.

◇ **Low cost.** Transit ads cost less than any other medium.

◇ **Creative flexibility.** Special constructions and color effects are available at relatively low cost.

◇ **Need satisfying.** Transit can target the needs of riders—with ads for cool drinks in summer, for example. Food ads do well as evening riders contemplate dinner.

◇ **Environmentally sensitive.** As social pressure to use public transportation increases, transit is well positioned as a medium of the future.

The Cons

◇ **Status.** Transit lacks the status of a major advertising medium.

◇ **Crowded environment.** Rush-hour crowding limits the opportunity and ease of reading, and the vehicle itself, which may be dirty, may tarnish the product's image.

◇ **Selectivity.** Transit reaches a nonselective audience, which may not meet the needs of some advertisers.

◇ **Clutter.** Cards are so numerous and look so similar they may be confusing or hard to remember.

◇ **Location.** With outlying shopping malls, fewer shoppers make trips downtown.

◇ **Creative restrictions.** Although transit cards may carry longer messages than billboards, copy is still somewhat limited.

Buying Transit Advertising

In transit advertising, just a few cents will buy 1,000 exposures.

The unit of purchase is a **showing,** also known as a *run* or *service.* A full showing (or No. 100 showing) means that one card will appear in each vehicle in the system. Space may also be purchased as a one-half (or No. 50) showing or a one-quarter (or No. 25) showing. Exterior displays like the Russian one in Exhibit 15–18 can be very effective.

EXHIBIT • 15-17

Modern bus shelters feature well-designed, colorful advertising posters.

Transit advertising can be purchased worldwide.

Rates are usually quoted for 30-day showings with discounts for 3-, 6-, 9-, and 12-month contracts. Advertisers supply the cards at their own expense, but the transit company can help with design and production.

Cost depends on the length and saturation of the showing and the size of the space. Rates vary extensively, depending primarily on the size of the transit system. Advertisers get rates for specific markets from local transit companies and the Transit Advertising Association's *TAA Rate Directory of Transit Advertising,* the industry's rate book.

Special Inside Buys

In some cities, advertisers gain complete dominantion by buying the **basic bus**—all the inside space on a group of buses. For an extra charge, pads of business reply cards or coupons (called **take-ones**) can be affixed to interior ads for passengers to request more detailed information, send in application blanks, or receive some other benefit.

Special Outside Buys

Some transit companies offer **bus-o-rama signs,** jumbo full-color transparencies backlighted by fluorescent tubes, running the length of the bus. A bus has two bus-o-rama positions on each side. A single advertiser may also buy a **total bus**—all the exterior space including the front, rear, sides, and top. This gives the message powerful exclusivity.

New advanced-design buses offer up to 20 feet of sign space along the street side. Such signs, made of pressure-sensitive vinyl, are affixed to the vehicle's smooth outer surface and can be die cut to any shape within the sign area.

The Transit Advertising Association, the national trade organization and promotion arm of the industry, performs research and supplies industry data on

EXHIBIT • 15–19

Mobile billboards—ads on the sides of tractor-trailers or on specially designed flatbed trucks—are starting to appear in some areas of the country, to mixed reaction.

the number of vehicles, trends, and rider demographics. TAA members represent 80 percent of the transit advertising volume in the United States and Canada.

The "mobile billboard," a cross between traditional billboards and transit advertising, was first conceived as advertising on the sides of tractor-trailer trucks.[18] (See Exhibit 15–19.) Today in some large cities, specially designed flatbed trucks carry long billboards up and down busy thoroughfares. Local routes for mobile ads are also available on delivery trucks in San Francisco, Los Angeles, and Seattle.

SUPPLEMENTARY MEDIA

Many promotional media are difficult to classify because they're tailored to individual needs. Such supplementary media include specialty advertising, trade shows and exhibits, directories and Yellow Pages, and a variety of emerging alternative media vehicles.

Specialty Advertising

The Speciality Advertising Association International (SAAI) defines **specialty advertising** as an advertising, sales promotion, and motivational communication medium that employs useful articles of merchandise imprinted with an advertiser's name, message, or logo.[19] Today, nearly every business uses advertising specialties (see Exhibit 15–20). As many as 15,000 different specialty items represent an annual volume of more than $3 billion.

An advertising specialty is different a premium. **Premiums** run the gamut from inexpensive trinkets to cars and often bear no advertising message. However, recipients must buy a product, send in a coupon, witness a demonstration, or perform some other action advantageous to the advertiser. An *advertising specialty,* on the other hand, is given free as a goodwill item. Some specialty items, particularly useful ones, may be kept for years and serve as continuous, friendly reminders of the advertiser's business. Companies often spend substantial sums for goodwill items, and must exercise care. Industry practice dictates that the advertiser pay for production overages up to an agreed-on limit. Since speciality items are produced according to each advertiser's specifications, overages are difficult or impossible to adapt and resell.

EXHIBIT • 15–20

Office and business items are popular specialty items because they serve as daily reminders where and when the customers do their ordering.

Consumer Specialties

Because consumers tend to associate the quality of a specialty item with the quality of the company providing it, companies are leaning toward more expensive gifts for consumers and business customers. Items costing $3 to $5 are becoming the norm, as opposed to cheap key rings and pencils.[20]

Specialties designed for consumers are particularly advantageous to small-business owners with a limited audience because they enable the company to reach a targeted market economically.

Business-to-Business Specialties

In the business-to-business arena, companies are using more structured promotions, in which target customers receive a series of specialties. Beckman Instruments sent clinical lab supervisors and purchasing agents in 250 hospitals and clinics a series of specialty gifts including coffee mugs, calendars, paper-clip dispensers, and a jigsaw puzzle.[21]

Does a specialty's dollar value play a significant role in influencing business buying or referral decisions? In one test, a group of realtors received a $1.49 ball point pen imprinted with a mortgage company's name, a second group received a $10 sports bag also imprinted, and a third group got nothing. In a follow-up questionnaire, realtors who received nothing were least inclined to recommend the product, but both the "sports bag" and "ball point" groups responded equally positively. Evidently, gift recipients felt obliged to reciprocate, but the value of the gift was not crucial. So the $1.49 pen was a much better investment.[22]

Inappropriate specialty items can backfire no matter what the cost. A recipient may perceive an overly expensive gift as a form of bribery; a cheap-looking trinket could make a quality-conscious business look chintzy. A specialty program's gifts should be small enough to activate reciprocal relations, but not large enough to backfire.

Trade Shows and Exhibitions

Every major industry sponsors annual **trade shows** and exhibitions where manufacturers, dealers, and buyers can get together for demonstrations and discussion. Exhibitors display their new products, literature, and samples to new customers and old. At the same time, they can meet potential new dealers for their products.

EXHIBIT • 15-21

Companies that promote their products at trade shows must carefully plan their booths, sales materials, and special trade-show promotions.

More than 9,000 industrial, scientific, and medical shows are held in the United States each year, and many companies exhibit at more than one show. And trade shows are very important as a global medium. They may be the only place an advertiser can meet the company's major international prospects at the same time. Moreover, some of the world's largest trade shows—the Paris Air Show, for example—are held overseas.

As a result, the construction of booths and **exhibits** has become a major factor in sales promotion plans. To stop traffic, booths must be simple and attractive, and have good lighting and a large visual. The exhibit should also provide a comfortable atmosphere to promote conversation between salespeople and prospects. Exhibit 15–21 shows a well-designed exhibit.

Many regular trade-show exhibitors use state-of-the-art technology, such as holograms, fiber optics, and interactive computer systems, to communicate product features quickly and dramatically. Pratt & Whitney uses holograms to present quarter-scale cutaway images of its aircraft engines because they're easier to transport, less expensive to make, and more dramatic than traditional engine models.[23]

In planning exhibits or trade-show booths, advertisers need to consider the following factors:

- Size and location of space.
- Desired image or impression of the exhibit.
- Complexities of shipping, installation, and dismantling.
- The number of products to be displayed.
- The need for storage and distribution of literature.
- The use of preshow advertising and promotion.
- The cost of all these factors.

Trade shows are expensive, and costs have increased substantially in the last decade. A large company may spend $1 million on a booth for one trade show. On average, it costs about $90 to reach each visitor at a trade show. With personnel, travel, living and salary expenses, and preshow promotion, the cost

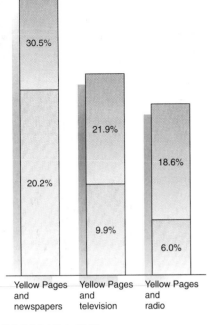

30.5%

21.9%

20.2%

18.6%

9.9%

6.0%

| Yellow Pages and newspapers | Yellow Pages and television | Yellow Pages and radio |

E X H I B I T • 15-22

Overall advertising reach from media combinations. When Yellow Pages advertising is used in conjunction with other media, reach increases significantly.

E X H I B I T • 15-23

Top 10 Yellow Pages operators, 1991.

Company	Revenues ($ millions)
BellSouth	$1,426.3
GTE	1,200.0
Bell Atlantic	994.6
Pacific Telesis Group	990.0
US West	853.7
Nynex	849.2
Southwestern Bell	847.7
Ameritech	515.4
Dun & Bradstreet	463.1
DonTech	459.6

per visitor reached rises to more than $141.[24] Despite the expense involved, trade shows are still a cost-effective way to reach sales prospects.

Directories and Yellow Pages

Thousands of **directories** are published each year by phone companies, trade associations, industrial groups, and others. They mainly serve as locators, buying guides, and mailing lists, but they also carry advertising aimed at specialized fields. When Yellow Pages advertising is combined with other media, reach increases significantly, as illustrated in Exhibit 15–22. In Yellow Pages advertising, ad content (not size) is most important.[25] The ad should tell people *how* to make the purchase, not why.

The United States has about 6,000 local telephone directories with a combined circulation of 286 million. Since deregulation of the phone industry and the 1984 breakup of AT&T, Yellow Pages business has been booming, with ad revenues reaching more than $9.1 billion in 1991.[26] The 10 largest operators, shown in Exhibit 15–23, account for more than 90 percent of the industry's advertising revenues.[27] In addition, 200 other publishers produce their own Yellow Pages (the Yellow Pages name and the walking-fingers logo are not trademarked, so anyone can use them).

Because of stiff competition, phone and directory companies try to make their Yellow Pages more distinctive. Some beef up the contents, offering emergency medical guides, color street maps, and other useful information. Others contain discount coupons. Highly specialized directories aim at particular audiences, such as the Chinese-language Yellow Pages in San Francisco and a directory for students at the University of Massachusetts.

Yellow Pages are often the sole advertising medium for local businesses, and nearly 90 percent of Yellow Pages revenue is derived from local advertisers.[28] However, Yellow Pages directories can be an important advertising medium for national advertisers too. U-Haul spends more than $10 million a year on Yellow Pages ads. To attract more national advertisers, Pacific Bell Directory is testing a phone-book version of national-brand advertising.[29] Brand ads are placed in related categories with an 800 number to "Call for the dealer nearest you."

For national advertisers with a smaller budget, a company called Yellow Spots sells filler space—a by-product of every directory's layout.[30] National advertisers can have their logo/image ads appear every 5, 10, or 15 pages.

Yellow Pages advertisers complain about the difficulty of verifying the amount of business the ads attract. Two directory companies (NYNEX and Donnelley) are testing special metered telephone lines that track customer responses.

Emerging Media

As traditional advertising media become more expensive and audiences become more fragmented, many advertisers are seeking new ways to reach their customers. Several types of alternative media are potentially viable options.

Movie Theaters

Advertising in movie theaters is a growing but controversial practice. Some audiences boo and hiss during commercials, but studies show that 87 percent of viewers recall theater ads the following day compared to 20 percent for TV ads.[31] Not all movie theater chains permit filmed advertising for fear of offending their audience. Walt Disney recently announced it will no longer allow U.S. theaters to run commercials before any of its movies. The cost of placing a commercial in about 5,700 of the nation's first-run theaters can run as high as $650,000.[32]

An alternative way to reach movie audiences is to pay a fee to have the product written into the movie. This practice (called **product placement**) is becoming more common—and more controversial.

Videotapes

People rent millions of videos every week. However, commercials on movie videos are as controversial as theater advertising. A less intrusive type of video advertising involves placing ads on the videocassette boxes. A third type of video advertising is the video brochure. Advertisers make their own videos, then mail them to customers and prospects.

Parking Meters and Public Phones

Thanks to a couple of enterprising companies, American Parking Meter Advertising and American Telephone Advertising (ATA), marketers can now advertise on parking meters and public phones. ATA offers 20 market segments, such as hotels and restaurants, airports, college campuses, and convenience stores.

Computer Software

More and more companies use **computer software** to reach both consumers and business buyers. Software ads include disks distributed by individual manufacturers and ad spots on computer information services such as Prodigy. Most disk ads feature games, animation, slick graphics, and other interactive features. MCI Communications uses software with sound effects and sophisticated graphics to sell its phone services to business managers. Advertisers spend about $10 million a year on software ads, but some companies get their customers to pay. More than 100,000 computer enthusiasts paid $6.95 each to view Ford's Simulator disk.[33]

Interactive Television

Some advertisers are helping to fund the development of **interactive television.** Using a hand-held device, viewers will be able to change camera angles or zero in on a particular scene. More important to advertisers, they will be able to respond to questions during a commercial, which will give advertisers a wealth of demographic information for future promotions.

Electronic Couponing

A growing number of supermarkets and retail chains are introducing electronic couponing. **Electronic couponing** refers to frequent-shopper cards or **"smart" cards** that automatically credit cardholders with coupon discounts when they check out. One such smart card is the Vision card, developed by Advanced Promotion Technologies. When combined with a touch-sensitive video screen, computer graphics, printer, and laser videodisc player, Vision cardholders can take advantage of a variety of retailer and manufacturer promotions by simply touching the video screens.[34] See Exhibit 15–24.

Electronic couponing eliminates the time-consuming chore of clipping and sorting printed coupons.

Grocery Cart Videos

Shopping carts are getting smarter too. Information Resources Inc. (IRI) introduced the VideOcart, which comes equipped with a video screen that shows spots from national advertisers as well as store specials. During a nine-week test, participating advertisers saw an average sales gain of 33 percent.[35] Grocers also saw their sales increase.

Electronic Signs

Electronic signs display text and graphic messages much like the big screens in sports stadiums. In Store Advertising offers an innovative electronic message board system. Advertisers pay In Store Advertising to program and transmit weekly commercial messages to hundreds of chain stores where shoppers see them on the electronic signs. The retail stores pay nothing for the signs and receive 25 percent of In Store's weekly gross revenues from its advertisers.[36] For 50 minutes each hour, the signs display the advertisers' commercials; individual stores use the other 10 minutes for their own promotions.

◆

Summary

Direct-mail advertising includes all forms of advertising sent directly to prospects through the mail. As an advertising medium, it ranks third in dollars spent, surpassed only by newspapers and television.

Next to the personal sales call, direct mail is the most effective way an advertiser can put a message in front of a prospect. It's also the most expensive on a cost-per-exposure basis. It offers several advantages: selectivity, intensive coverage, flexibility, control, personal impact, exclusivity, and response performance.

The drawbacks to direct mail include the high cost per exposure, delivery delays, lack of other content support, problems with selectivity, and some recipients' negative attitudes.

Direct-mail advertising comes in many forms: sales letters, brochures, and even handwritten postcards. The message can be one sentence or dozens of pages.

The direct-mail list defines a market segment. The three types of direct-mail lists include house lists, mail-response lists, and compiled lists. Their prices vary according to their quality.

Of the major advertising media, outdoor advertising offers the lowest cost per message delivered. In addition, the medium offers other attractive features: instant broad coverage (reach), very high frequency, great flexibility, and high impact. Drawbacks include the necessity for brief messages, limitations in reaching narrow demographic groups, the lead time required, the medium's past reputation, high initial preparation costs, and the difficulty of physically inspecting each billboard.

The standardized outdoor advertising industry consists of about 600 local and regional plant operators. National advertising makes up the bulk of outdoor business. The two most common forms of standard outdoor advertising structures are the poster panel and the painted bulletin. The poster panel, the basic form, is the least costly per unit and is available in a variety of sizes. Painted bulletins are meant for long use and are usually placed in the best locations where traffic is heavy and visibility good. Some advertisers overcome the relatively higher expense of painted bulletins by using a rotary plan. An additional form of outdoor available in some cities is the spectacular, an expensive electronic display.

Transit advertising offers the features of high reach, frequency, exposure, and attention values at very low cost. It gives long exposure to the advertiser's message and offers repetitive value and good geographic flexibility. In addition, advertisers have a wide choice in the size of space used.

But transit advertising does not cover some segments of society, it reaches a nonselective audience, it lacks prestige, and copy is still somewhat limited.

Supplementary media include speciality advertising, trade shows and exhibits, and Yellow Pages directories. Emerging media include movie theaters, videotapes, computer software, interactive television, electronic couponing, grocery cart videos, and electronic signs.

Questions for Review and Discussion

1. What advantage did direct mail offer Champion International that the mass media could not?
2. What is the difference between direct-mail and direct-response advertising?
3. Although direct mail offers the advantage of selectivity, what are the associated problems?
4. What are the three types of mailing lists? Which is the best? Why?
5. What costs are advertisers likely to incur in a direct-mail campaign?
6. Which advertising objectives are the outdoor media mostly suitable for?
7. Is outdoor an effective advertising medium for a politician? Why?
8. What's the difference between a poster panel and a painted bulletin?
9. Why is transit advertising considered three separate media forms?
10. Which characteristics of transit advertising benefit advertisers the most?

P · A · R · T

V

Integrated Marketing Communications

To create awareness for their products and services, and to reinforce the image of their brands, companies typically blend their advertising efforts with a variety of other communication techniques. These may include personal selling, direct marketing, sales promotion, public relations, and corporate advertising. The idea is to integrate and coordinate all these activities in such a way that the effect of the whole is greater than the sum of its parts.

Part V presents the concept of integrated marketing communications (IMC), explains the various communications methods marketers use in IMC programs, and discusses how national, local, and even noncommercial advertisers can use these programs to augment their marketing efforts.

Chapter 16, Integrated Marketing Communications: Direct Marketing and Sales Promotion, defines what an IMC program is and the various ways companies use it. The chapter then defines

and discusses direct marketing and sales promotion and presents the important roles they play in an IMC program. The trade-offs between advertising and sales promotion are detailed as are the differences between trade and consumer (push and pull) promotional strategies.

Chapter 17, Integrated Marketing Communications: Public Relations and Corporate Advertising, defines public relations, explains its role in integrated marketing communications, and discusses how companies use PR activities such as publicity, lobbying, special-events management, and fund raising to manage their relationships with various audiences. The tools of public relations are also discussed, including media kits, feature articles, and audiovisual materials. The chapter depicts how corporate advertising can be used in conjunction with other communication vehicles to build a company's reputation and enhance the image of the company's brands.

Chapter 18, Integrated Marketing Communications for Local and Non-commercial Advertisers, examines the benefits of IMC programs for businesses trying to reach customers within the same geographic area. Chapter topics include establishing local objectives, analyzing local markets, determining local strategies, establishing realistic budgets, and planning local media strategies. Other topics include analyzing seasonal patterns and developing local creative solutions with the help of ad agencies, consultants, manufacturers, or distributors.

Finally, the chapter discusses the interesting field of noncommercial advertising and shows how noncommercial advertisers can also benefit by integrating all their marketing communications.

McDonald's vous sert une pizza fraîche et cuite au four en moins de cinq minutes. Ça, c'est du sport!

L'automobile réinventée
de toutes pièces.

IMC: Direct Marketing
and Sales Promotion

Objective: To define integrated marketing communications (IMC), one of the most important trends in contemporary marketing and advertising. Direct marketing and sales promotion play different but important roles in IMC programs. They offer distinct opportunities but also have limitations advertisers should be aware of.

After studying this chapter, you will be able to:

- Explain the reasons for the new trends in marketing thinking.

- Discuss both the concept and the process of integrated marketing communications.

- Define direct marketing and discuss its role in IMC.

- Explain the importance of developing a database for direct marketing.

- Discuss the role of sales promotion in the marketing mix.

- Identify the benefits and drawbacks of sales promotion.

- Define push and pull strategies and describe the tactics they use.

Today, the company employs thousands and sells millions. But it wasn't always that way. Twenty years ago, nobody knew this high-tech computer company named after a fruit! In fact, nobody had heard of personal computers much less desktop publishing.

Apple Computer got its start in a garage. Two whiz-kids/computer hobbyists, Steve Jobs and Steve Wozniak, wanted to see if they could build a computer simple enough for anyone to operate. Wozniak finally hit on a design; Jobs came up with the idea of starting a company. Their device—the personal computer—revolutionized the world of information processing. They built computers for home use, students, and small businessowners—the little guy, not the Wall Street types (see Exhibit 16–1).

But the Steves did even more. They founded a company with an unusual corporate culture—young in age and spirit, technically creative, demanding of excellence, and guided by a progressive, innovative management philosophy. They invented and then refined the meaning of "user-friendly." And they listened to their customers so they could build better computers in the future.

Jobs also understood the importance of aesthetics in product design. At a time when corporate computers were big and blue, Apple introduced a cream-colored computer that could fit on a desk. The color was natural and warm—not the color of a cold, data-handling machine—and it soon became emblematic for the company's interest in working with everyday people rather than engineers and data processing specialists.

"Aesthetics," says Jobs, "communicate a company's sense of discipline in engineering." He carried that discipline to the extent of insisting that every line

EXHIBIT • 16-1

Apple Computer, the brainchild of two hobbyists working in their garage, emerged at a time when the only computers available to businesses were large and very expensive. Their little home computer spawned a whole new industry and a company with a corporate culture aimed at helping average consumers and small business people keep pace in today's high-tech environment.

of solder on the Apple circuit board had to be perfectly straight. He even wore a white glove in the factory to test for dust. "In an environment where excellence is expected, noticed, and respected, employees will do great work," he says.

Jobs believed in a new kind of marketing and advertising. He hired pre-eminent computer marketing consultant Regis McKenna. McKenna knew how to get attention for the upstart company; bypassing typical business and computer media, he ran Apple's first ads in *Playboy.* Over the years, Apple's creative shop, Chiat/Day, consistently created award-winning—and sales-winning—Apple advertising.

Apple also marketed accessories and software to its customers through the mail, using attractive mailers with images from its ads. It developed free mail-order videotapes and a host of other materials to make information readily available and easily accessible to as wide a range of potential customers as possible.

Early on, Apple involved itself in the community. Employees spoke at universities and computer seminars. Apple supported user groups and developed special cutting-edge training programs. In the early 80s, Apple even gave a free computer to every elementary school in California so that children could get the computer experience early in life.

To help listen, they established Apple Resource Coordinators—Apple users who worked for customer companies. These people became information centers, helping other employees understand and use the products and giving feedback to Apple.

Through a consistent program of integrated marketing communications (IMC)—advertising, direct marketing, sales promotion, personal selling, public relations, and any other way to make contact with customers—Apple conveyed its corporate culture to the world (see Exhibit 16–2). Founder Steve Jobs justly earned the title Entrepreneur of the Decade.[1] ◆

INTEGRATED MARKETING COMMUNICATIONS: THE CONCEPT AND THE PROCESS

The incredible explosion of technology during the last decade—helped along in no small way by Steve Jobs himself—has, for all practical purposes, shattered the mass market and thereby made obsolete many of the traditional techniques of mass marketing.[2] In so doing, though, technology has created astonishing diversity in the marketplace and society.[3]

At the same time, worldwide populations have grown to the point that even narrow markets can support the development of new product alternatives.

Today, consumers demand—and get—incredible variety and options in an ever-widening range of products. In the last decade, as technology spawned more and more products aimed at diverse, narrow market niches, the number of new products introduced annually has doubled. In 1992 alone, 15,886 new products were introduced into U.S. grocery stores, a 3.1% increase over 1991.[4] As Regis McKenna says, technology has transformed the consumer's selection alternatives creating the reality of almost unlimited choice—from designer jeans to designer genes.[5]

The effect of this diversity (i.e., competition) is a precipitous decline in the dominance of national brands—and national media—and an evolution in marketing thinking.

The Change in Marketing Thinking

Today, the Customer's role is so dominant that companies are shifting their focus from marketing oriented to *market driven.* They are using technology to

EXHIBIT • 16-2

When Apple Computer was in its infancy, co-founder Steve Jobs said that "aesthetics communicate a company's sense of discipline in engineering." The message and design of this commercial reflects that same philosophy today.

PROFESSOR: We are entering a whole new era . . . the decade of positive change. Around the world, organizations have realized . . . that you cannot intimidate human beings into productivity. The key is to let people do what they do best, whatever way works best for them. At the same time, fundamental principles of mass

production give ordinary people access to powerful technology. That which was affordable to the few becomes available to the many. Mass production becomes mass productivity. The Industrial Revolution meets the Age of Enlightenment. The walls have come down! Opportunity has gone up! And your only limits

will be the size of your ideas and the degree of your dedication! People, this is an exciting time to be alive.
SUPER: INTRODUCING THE MOST AFFORDABLE MACINTOSH COMPUTERS EVER.
SUPER: APPLE. THE POWER TO BE YOUR BEST.

adapt their products to fit customers' individual needs. This means flexible manufacturing—customizing products for customized markets. It means bundling more services with products to create a "unique product experience." It means companies and customers working together to find solutions.[6]

The counterpart to flexible manufacturing is flexible marketing—and integrated marketing communications to reach customers at different levels in new and better ways.

How the Customer Sees Marketing Communications

In one proprietary study conducted by ad agency Leo Burnett, consumers identified 102 different mediums as "advertising"—everything from TV to shopping bags to sponsored community events.[7] Customers also develop perceptions of the company or brand in many other ways—through such references as news reports, word-of-mouth, opinions of experts, financial reports, even the CEO's personality. All these communications or brand contacts—sponsored or not—create an "integrated product" in the consumer's mind.[8]

The Evolution of the IMC Concept

Along with technological change came a host of new, specialized media and the complete fragmentation of the mass market. Suddenly companies needed to coordinate the multiplicity of company and product messages being issued—many of which lacked consistency.

Companies initially took a narrow, inside-out view of IMC; they saw it as a way to coordinate and manage their marketing communications (advertising, sales promotion, public relations, personal selling, and direct marketing) to give the audience a consistent message about the company. Don Schultz of Northwestern University calls this the perspective of agencies and clients.[9]

In that same vein, Tom Duncan, the director of the IMC graduate program at the University of Colorado, remarks that the basic concept of integrated marketing communications is simply synergy—the whole is greater than the sum of its parts. The total effect of coordinating the various communication activities is greater than when they are executed independently—and in some cases in conflict with one another.[10]

Further study and research has led to a broader, more sophisticated, outside-in perspective of IMC as a concept—one that views customers as partners in an ongoing relationship, recognizes the references they use, acknowledges the importance of the whole communication system, and accepts the many ways they come in contact with the company or the brand.

Defined broadly, **integrated marketing communications** is the concept of building and reinforcing mutually profitable relationships with employees, customers, other stakeholders, and the general public by developing and coordinating a strategic communications program that enables them to make constructive contact with the company/brand through a variety of media.

The level of integration a company employs—the narrow view or the broad view—depends to a great extent on the organization's corporate culture. Some companies have enjoyed rapid growth and strong customer relationships because they intuitively integrated and focused all corporate, as well as marketing, activities—Apple, Honda, Nike, Banana Republic, to name just a few.

In the real world application of IMC programs, Duncan identifies four distinct levels of integration that companies use (see Exhibit 16–3). These levels demonstrate how IMC programs range from being narrowly focused corporate monologues to broad, interactive dialogues resulting in a corporate culture that permeates an organization and drives everything it does, internally and externally.[11]

The IMC Process

Using the outside-in process, Schultz points out that the integrated marketing communications approach starts with the customer. Marketers study the various media the customer uses, when the marketer's message is most *relevant* to the customer, and finally when customers and prospects are most *receptive* to the

EXHIBIT • 16–3

Levels of integration.

Level	Name	Description/focus	Examples
1	Unified image	One-look, one-voice; strong brand image focus	3M,
2	Consistent voice	Consistent tone and look; coordinated messages to various audiences (customers, trade, suppliers, etc.)	Hallmark, Coca-Cola
3	Good listener	Solicits two-way communication, enabling feedback through 800 numbers, surveys, trade shows, etc.; focus on long-term relationships	Andersen Windows, Saturn
4	World-class citizen	Social, environmental consciousness, strong company culture; focus on wider community	Ben & Jerry's, Apple, Honda

message. In short, in an IMC program, marketers begin with the customer and work back to the brand.[12]

One way to look at integrated marketing communications is by using the inverted pyramid model introduced in Chapter 7 (see Exhibit 16–4). At its simplest level, IMC starts with a single customer. By dealing with the customer one-on-one, the company discovers and serves the customer's needs and wants. If the experience is positive for both parties, a relationship develops, and the company has a very narrow specialty—serving *that* customer's needs. But that customer now becomes a reference for other potential customers.

Next, by coordinating database research, media advertising, sales promotion devices, direct-marketing tactics, personal selling, and public relations, the company locates other customers (and their references) with similar needs. As the company develops more knowledge and experience, soliciting constant feedback from its customers, it eventually becomes a specialist in that niche of customers. Finally, the company uses the same techniques to expand its specialty niche into a full market in which it also enjoys leadership. Most large markets evolve from niches.

The goal is market dominance—owning the market. And in marketing, leadership is ownership.[13]

That is precisely how Apple Computer became the leader in desktop publishing. It wasn't an application they thought of. It came from the niche of customers using their product. The customers discovered it. Apple listened and then developed the niche into market leadership.[14]

The IMC Approach to Marketing and Advertising Planning

What the inverted pyramid also suggests is a new approach to planning marketing and communications activities—one that differs substantially from the traditional process discussed in Chapter 7. As we shall see, it mixes marketing and communication planning together rather than separating them.

Thanks to the rapid diffusion of computer technology, marketers of mass merchandise today have a wealth of information at their fingertips. Wang and Schultz point out that with supermarket scanner data, for instance, marketers

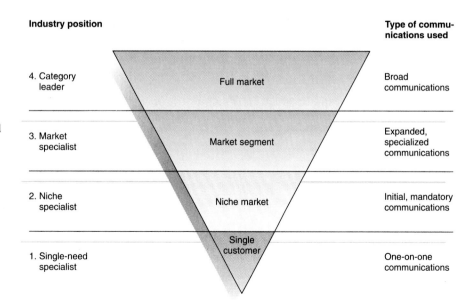

can (1) identify specific customers and users of products and services; (2) measure their actual purchase behavior and relate that to specific brand and product categories; (3) measure the impact of various advertising and marketing communications activities and relate them back to those consumers in terms of their value in influencing the actual purchase; and (4) capture and evaluate this information over time.[15]

This means that the ever-expanding database of information on actual customer behavior can become the basis for planning all future marketing and communications activities—especially if the database contains information by household of customer demographics, psychographics, purchase data, and brand or product category attitudes (see Exhibit 16–5).

Starting the whole planning process with the databse forces the company to

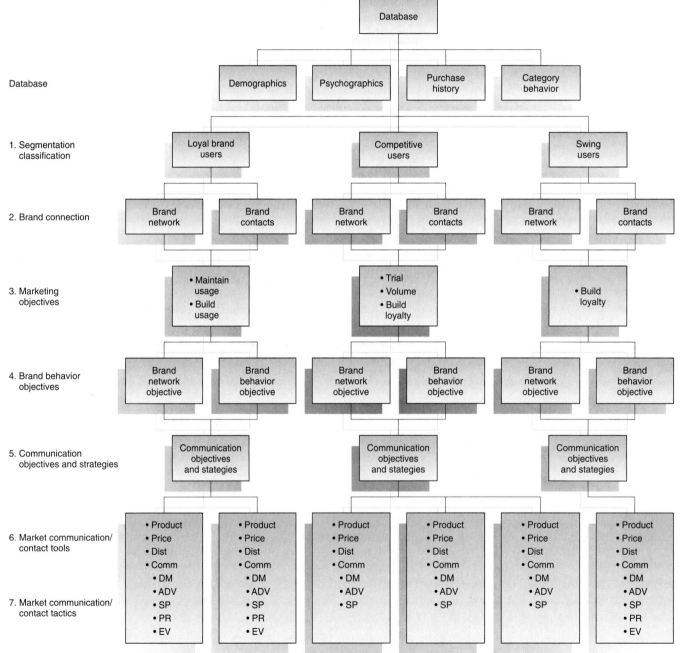

DM=Direct marketing   ADV=Advertising   SP=Sales promotion   PR=Public relations   EV= Event marketing

EXHIBIT • 16-5

Integrated marketing communication planning process.

focus on the consumer, customer, or prospect, not on the company's sales or profit goals. These marketing objectives are moved farther down in the planning process.[16]

The first step in Wang and Schultz's seven-step IMC Planning Model is to develop a scheme for segmenting the customers and prospects in the database. They may be segmented by brand loyalty, as illustrated, or by some other form of measurable purchase behavior—heavy usage, for instance.

The second step is to analyze the information on customers to understand their attitudes, history, and how they came (or come) in contact with the brand or product—in other words, determining the best time, place, and situation to communicate with them.

Next, based on this analysis, the planner sets marketing objectives. In the illustrated example, the marketing objectives relate to building and maintaining usage or nurturing brand loyalty.

Once these objectives have been set, the marketer identifies what brand contacts and what changes in attitude will be required to support the consumer's continuance or change of purchase behavior.

The fifth step, then, is to set communications objectives and strategies for making contact with the consumer and influencing his or her purchase behavior.

Then, the marketer decides what other elements of the marketing mix (product, price, place) can be used to further encourage the desired purchase behavior.

And finally, the planner determines what communications tactics to use—media advertising, direct marketing, public relations, sales promotion, special events, and so on—to make contact and influence the consumer's behavior.[17]

By following this model, Schultz points out, the marketer sets objectives based on an understanding of the customer or prospect and on what needs to be communicated. All forms of marketing are turned into communication, and all forms of communication into marketing.[18]

The Importance of IMC to the Study of Advertising

Since customers see all sponsored communications as advertising, advertising people—account managers, creatives, media planners—must grow beyond their specialty of "ads placed in the media." They must become enlightened generalists, familiar with and able to integrate all types of marketing communications.

In a recent survey of 100 company marketing executives, most respondents thought integration—of advertising, promotion, public relations, and other marketing communications—would have more influence on companies' marketing strategies in the next 3 to 5 years than economic trends, globalization, and even pricing (see Exhibit 16–6).[19]

Since direct marketing and sales promotion are so integral to the IMC concept and process, we discuss those topics in this chapter. Chapter 17 explores the importance of integrating public relations and corporate advertising in the communication mix. And finally, Chapter 18 discusses how local and noncommercial advertisers can integrate their marketing communications.

THE ROLE OF DIRECT MARKETING IN THE IMC PROCESS

The system of marketing in which the marketer builds and maintains its own database of customers and prospects and uses a variety of mediums (from personal contact to mass media) to communicate with them is called **direct marketing.** Consider the case of Andersen Windows.

Andersen knows that people don't buy new windows for their homes on

EXHIBIT • 16-6

Factors influencing marketing strategies.

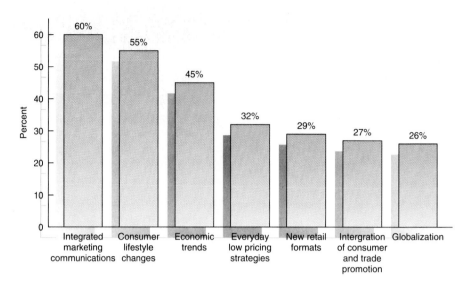

impulse. The number of details involved makes the purchase very complex. To establish a brand identity and educate consumers, Andersen Windows and Patio Doors uses an informative approach, teaching consumers about its products and helping them through the planning and buying process. It also uses a sophisticated blend of media advertising, direct marketing, sales promotion, retailing, and after-sale followup—all designed to learn about the customer and create a mutually beneficial relationship.

Working with Campbell-Mithun Esty, its agency for more than 60 years, Andersen uses innovative direct-response ads (both TV and print) to first find consumers interested in buying. The elegant ads feature eye-catching, four-color photographs of Andersen products in various household settings (see Exhibit 16–7). The copy is as inviting as the photography. Once engaged, the reader is invited to check the Yellow Pages for an Andersen dealer locally, call Andersen's toll-free 800 number, or send in the coupon in the ad.

All responses are fielded by a professional *fulfillment house,* Ruppman Marketing Services, which handles 12 million calls a year for its blue-chip roster of national clients. Both coupon and phone respondents provide their names and addresses as well as basic information about their plans to build, remodel, or replace windows. This is collected in Andersen's database of customer information.

Respondents are then sent a free copy of *The Andersen Window & Patio Door Factbook,* a colorful brochure of the company's handsome windows and doors, and a free copy of *Coming Home,* Andersen's proprietary magazine full of helpful articles on home remodeling, decorating, household products, and the like.

Andersen's manager of marketing communications, Joe Arndt, says *Coming Home* is "the ultimate followup." The magazine is regularly updated to keep it interesting, helpful, and contemporary, and each copy contains a Project Survey Card, which asks customers for more information about their project. For a nominal price, respondents can also request additional guidebook publications and even videos.

The magazine opens a dialogue with the customer and allows Andersen to start building trust. The magazine also draws the customers to the retail store—the ultimate objective of the direct marketing effort. Each issue contains a custom inkjet message on the address label inviting the customer to visit the local Andersen dealer and giving the dealer's address and phone number.

This magazine advertisement asks for immediate feedback from prospects and makes responding as simple as possible by picturing a goal—a catalog—and by providing both a toll-free phone number and a coupon.

All ancillary materials—publications, brochures, videos—use the same glamorous photos, reinforcing Andersen's high-quality image and building the company's relationship with consumers.

Andersen believes in relationships. The company is still located in Bayport, Minnesota, where it was founded by a Danish immigrant and his sons in 1903. Its 4,000 employees own 27 percent of the stock. And Andersen still buys from the same hardware supplier (since 1932) and works with the same ad agency (since 1933). In fact, Andersen was CME's first client.

Whether you call it relationship marketing or integrated marketing communications, one thing is certain: Andersen's program works.[20] Andersen has 15 percent of the window market with nearly $1 billion in annual sales—greater than its three largest competitors combined.

The Evolution of Direct Marketing

The key to Andersen's success is its database of customer information, and that's the basis of every successful *direct marketing* program today.

Andersen uses magazine and TV advertising to generate inquiries and build its database. Then it uses the database to communicate with prospects and encourage them to visit a retail store. Other companies purchase a mailing list and use that as the database for direct-mail advertising or telemarketing solicitations. In both cases, the marketer communicates *directly* with the prospect to effect some action.

Direct marketing is the oldest marketing method and the fastest growing, and social and technological changes are fueling the growth.

In the United States, about 57.5 percent of women now work outside the home; in Canada, the figure is 60 percent.[21] So while families have more income, they have less time to spend shopping—making credit cards and the telephone important factors in direct marketing.

The wide use of credit cards has revolutionized the way consumers buy goods and services. Electronic, cashless transactions make products—especially large, costly items—easier and faster to purchase. In 1991 alone, MasterCard holders bought $220.9 billion worth of goods and services.[22] Currently, card readers attached to cable TV services allow customers to "teleshop" from their homes.

Advances in telecommunications and computer technology make direct marketing a growing field worldwide. In the United Kingdom, direct-response commercials now represent 15 percent of all advertising minutes, and they're expected to increase to 33 percent by 1996. For example, Xerox Corporation's image-building TV commercials in England include a 10-second direct-response segment.[23]

Telephone companies worldwide now provide toll-free numbers so customers can call to place orders or request information. Toll-free numbers give companies immediate, direct responses and help them collect information to create and refine their databases.

Finally the computer, now affordable for even the smallest businesses, enables users to both compile and analyze information. When Bloomingdale's analyzed its database of customers, it discovered that 25 percent of them make 75 percent of the store's total purchases. So Bloomingdale's mails Christmas catalogs to a wide range of people, but sends postcards announcing clothing sales to only those customers who recently purchased clothing.[24]

The Importance of Direct Marketing

Perhaps the greatest reason for direct marketing's current growth is that marketers and agencies realize they can't do the job with one medium anymore. As the mass audience fragmented and companies began integrating their marketing communications, customer databases became key. And direct marketing is the best way to develop a valuable database. As Philip Kotler says:

> In the future marketing organization, marketing methods will be centered on the customer database, from which the different functional groups, including salespeople with laptop computers, will draw their information to compete in the global marketplace.[25]

The database enables the marketer to build a relationship by learning about customers in depth—their nuances, what and when they bought, what they're interested in, and what they need. It also allows the marketer to keep up with their changing tastes and to show genuine interest in them. Most important, marketers can select the customers they want to serve. "You don't want a relationship with every customer," says Kotler. "In fact there are some bad customers out there."[26] With a database, companies can pick the prospects they can serve most effectively and *profitably*—the purpose of all marketing.

People like to see themselves as unique, not as part of a 250-million member mass market. Through direct marketing, companies can send discrete messages to individual customers and prospects. By using varying types of sales promotion activities (discussed in the last part of this chapter), the company can encourage individuals, not masses, to respond and thus develop a relationship with each individual.[27]

Accountability is an important concept to cost-weary marketers today. Mass-media advertisers always wonder exactly what they're getting for their dollars.

EXHIBIT • 16-8

By using a database, Kay-Bee found 10 million homes with kids and sent them *GoodTimes*.

Direct marketing aims at getting a tangible response. Marketers can count the responses and determine the cost per response. They can also judge the effectiveness of the medium they're using and test different creative executions. They like that a lot.

For these reasons and many others, direct marketing is no longer limited to traditional direct marketers. As Exhibit 16–8 shows, retailers, packaged goods manufacturers, banks, resorts, and construction companies are building their own databases so they can learn more about how their customers actually behave—who they are, what they buy, and where they take it home to.[28]

Drawbacks to Direct Marketing

If direct marketing is so great, what took it so long to grow? Cost! It's very expensive to send a piece of mail to every possible customer. It seems much easier to spend a few million dollars for prime-time, network TV spots when everybody is home watching. (Unfortunately for the mass marketer, those days are over. Everybody's not home. And if they are, they're watching 40 different channels or a rented video.)

Further, to advertise on network TV is far more expensive today than it used to be. So the economics of direct marketing methods are becoming more competitive. Advertisers don't have to buy network, they can buy cable or local. They have the technology now to segment down to minuscule numbers. That has been possible only recently.

But direct marketing has other problems as well. In the past, direct marketers were sales oriented, not relationship oriented. Regulations—especially self-regulation—was lax, and scams tarnished direct marketing's image.

Finally, direct marketing suffers from clutter. People are deluged with mail, and cable channels are becoming filled with infomercials. Telemarketing pitches intrude on consumers at home and at work, some still from marketers with questionable ethics.

At a recent national forum of direct marketers, these issues were the focus of discussion. Marketers were told they must self-regulate, give consumers more control, and treat privacy like a customer service issue, or they would risk legislation restricting access to the information they desperately need. They were also warned that the result of neglecting restraint would be lower response rates.[29] Sophisticated marketers heed these warnings and develop methods and guidelines for responsible direct marketing. Using the outside-in approach, they integrate all their marketing communications and focus on building the *relationship value* of their brands—the bonds, actual and perceptual, created between the customer, the marketer, and the brand.[30] Andersen Windows illustrates this win-win partnership with customers.

DIRECT MARKETING STRATEGIES AND TACTICS

All direct marketers face two basic strategy decisions: the extent to which they will use *direct sales* and the extent to which they will use *direct-response advertising*. They can use one or the other or both.

Direct Sales

Marketers that use a **direct sales** strategy employ representatives who sell to customers directly, either at home or at work, rather than through a retail establishment or some other intermediary. Direct sales is done through *personal selling* or *telemarketing*.

Personal Selling

In **personal selling,** the representative introduces the product to the customer, convinces the customer of the product's value, and completes the sale. There are two main forms of personal selling: *person-to-person* and *group sales.* In person-to-person sales, the customer and salesperson conduct a dialogue, the salesperson presenting the benefits and the customer giving his or her objections. In group sales, an individual or group of individuals attempts to close a sale with a group of customers. This may occur in a seminar, at work, or at home (like a Tupperware party).

The type of product or service dictates the repetitiveness of the selling effort. The salesperson sells cosmetic items and insurance repeatedly to the same customer or group of customers; an encyclopedia salesperson may never see the buyer or group of buyers again.

Telemarketing

As a method of direct sales, telemarketing has been used for decades, but the term is relatively new. The old term, **telephone sales,** meant the selling of goods and services by using the telephone to contact prospects, persuade them, and complete the transaction. **Telemarketing** is a much broader term. It includes telephone sales, but it also refers to prospecting by phone (leads may be turned over to personal salespeople or retailers). It also refers to answering phone inquiries or providing sales-related services to callers. The resulting information updates the company's customer database. Telemarketing is the major source of income for some companies and organizations—charitable causes, political candidates and causes, and home-study courses.

Telemarketing—especially telephone sales—is demanding work. Good salespeople call hundreds of leads every day but only close a sale with 3 to 5 percent of the prospects they reach. Callers typically receive a base pay, usually just above minimum wage, and earn a commission on sales. They are continually monitored by supervisors and often given incentives (prizes) to make more sales.

Direct-Response Advertising

Advertising that asks the receiver (reader, viewer, or listener) to provide feedback straight to the sender is called **direct-response advertising.** Any medium can be used for direct response, but the most common are radio, TV, newspapers, magazines, and direct mail.

Direct Mail

Next to personal sales calls, direct mail is the most effective method for closing a sale or generating inquiries. It's the medium of choice for most direct marketers seeking an immediate response; along with the telephone, it's the medium of necessity for marketers responding to customer inquiries.

Direct mail has two main drawbacks: cost and the "junk mail" image—both of which are almost inescapable. No other medium, other than personal selling, has such a high cost per thousand. For this reason, many small advertisers participate in cooperative mailings with companies like ADVO that serve most major U.S. cities. ADVO mails an envelope containing a coupon for each company to the zip code areas that best serve all the participants. That certainly reduces their costs, but they still suffer the image problem.

Some large advertisers don't send unsolicited mail. They use other media for their direct-response advertising and use direct mail to respond to inquiries.

EXHIBIT • 16-9

To stimulate interest in Del Monte's new line of juice coolers, the company used a direct-mail approach. The campaign, called "The Renovation Project," featured a tool box filled with boxes of juice.

They save money by mailing only to qualified prospects and build their image by sending higher quality materials.

As we discussed in Chapter 15, the heart of any direct-mail program is the database. Assuming the product is desirable, the quality of the database has the largest effect on response rates because it determines the product's relevance to the customer (see Exhibit 16–9). The second most important factor is the creative quality of the direct-mail materials.

Direct-Response Print Advertising

As discussed in Chapter 13, newspaper and magazine ads and inserts featuring coupons or listing toll-free phone numbers can be very effective at stimulating customer responses (see Exhibit 16–10). Moreover, advertisers can devote most of the space to image-building, thus maximizing the medium's power.[31]

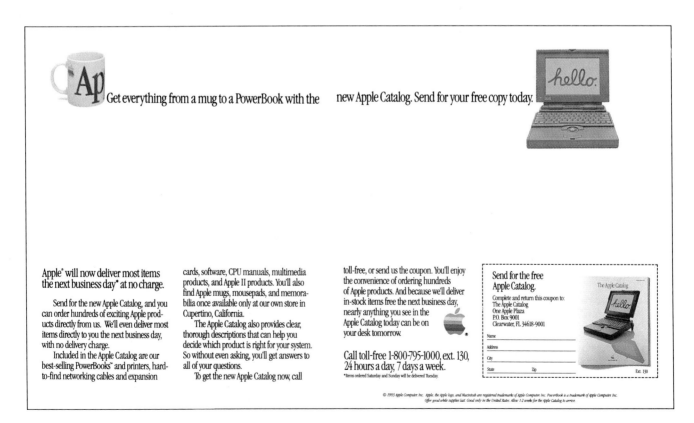

EXHIBIT • 16-10

Apple stimulates demand for its catalog through aggressive direct-response advertising that includes both a 24-hour toll-free phone number *and* a coupon, and that promises next-day delivery of most items at no extra charge.

Direct-Response Radio and TV Advertising

Direct marketers' use of radio and TV has increased dramatically in the last five years. As Rapp and Collins said in 1987, prospects

> may be weary of 50,000 commercials a year, but they're hungry for information, enjoyably presented. Infomercials, on over-the-air television as well as on cable, are a revolution waiting to happen.[32]

It happened. Avon, whose products are normally sold door-to-door, advertised its catalog and an 800 number in a 15-second network TV commercial and print ad. The campaign garnered 35,000 phone calls in four days. The response was so great that Avon developed a 30-minute *infomercial* featuring Linda Gray, star of the television show "Dallas."[33] Cher reportedly earned $1 million and a portion of the profits for appearing in an infomercial for Lori Davis Hair Products.[34] As Exhibit 16–11 shows, more people are watching infomercials and buying the advertised products.

Interactive Television

Although still in the development stage, interactive television will allow viewers to change camera angles or zoom in on a particular scene. More important to advertisers, viewers will be able to respond to questions during a commercial, giving advertisers a wealth of demographic information for future promotions.

EXHIBIT • 16-11

Who watches (and buys from) infomercials.*

	Seen an infomercial in the past year?	Ever purchased anything using 800-number at the end of an infomercial?	Ever purchased anything in a store based on information provided in an infomercial?
Sex			
Male	57%	8.0%	20.0%
Female	54	9.0	19.0
Age			
18–24	70	4.0	19.0
25–34	63	9.0	19.0
35–49	58	12.0	20.0
50–64	55	10.0	26.0
65+	33	3.0	13.0
Income			
Under $15,000	53	4.5	22.5
$15,000–$20,000	52	11.0	24.0
$20,000–$30,000	62	8.0	21.0
$30,000–$40,000	63	9.0	25.0
$40,000+	60	11.0	16.0
Region			
Northeast	56	7.0	24.0
North Central	52	9.0	14.0
South	57	8.0	21.0
West	55	10.0	17.0
Total	55%	8.5%	19.0%

* From a survey of 1,005 men and women ages 18 and older.

THE IMC PROCESS: SALES PROMOTION

The purpose of all marketing communications is to help the company achieve its marketing objectives (discussed in Chapter 7). Typical marketing objectives include:

- To introduce new products.
- To induce present customers to buy more.
- To attract new customers.
- To combat competition.
- To maintain sales in off-seasons.
- To increase retail inventories so more goods may be sold.
- To obtain greater shelf space.

The marketing strategy the company uses to achieve these objectives may include personal selling, advertising, public relations, and/or sales promotion.

Sales promotion is a direct inducement offering extra incentives all along the marketing route to enhance the product's movement from producer to consumer. There are three important elements to this definition. Sales promotion

- Is designed to speed up the selling process.
- Normally involves a direct inducement (such as money, prizes, extra products, gifts, or specialized information) that provides extra incentives to buy, visit the store, request literature, or take some other action.
- May be used anywhere along the marketing route: from manufacturer to dealer, dealer to customer, or manufacturer to customer.

Some consider sales promotion supplementary to advertising and personal selling because it binds the two together, making both more effective by increasing sales. In reality, however, sales promotion is far more than supplementary. In the mid-1970s, marketers began to shift marketing dollars from advertising to promotion. By the end of the 1980s, sales promotion averaged 13 percent annual growth while advertising averaged 10 percent.[35] Today, sales promotion expenditures consume 73 percent of the advertising/promotion budget compared to 27 percent for advertising.[36]

Sales promotion is expensive—very. But it's also effective. Unfortunately, it also has serious drawbacks, fostering a furious battle in marketing circles between proponents of sales promotion and proponents of advertising. There is an important role for both, but advertisers must understand their roles and get the balance right.

Benefits of Sales Promotion

Effective sales promotion maximizes sales volume. For that reason, advertising and sales promotion work well together. Advertising helps develop and reinforce a quality, differentiated brand reputation and build *market value*. Promotion helps build *market volume*. To become a market leader, a brand needs both advertising and promotion.[37]

Ideally, sales promotion generates sales that would not otherwise be achieved. However, for products whose sales are already rising, good promotion can establish a base sales level just a notch higher.[38]

Sales promotion can be more effective than advertising in motivating customers to select a specific brand—particularly when all brands appear to be equal. Promotion can also generate additional sales by motivating customers unmoved by other advertising efforts. And certain promotions generate a more immediate, measurable payoff than traditional advertising campaigns.

Drawbacks of Sales Promotion

Sales promotion is expensive, but it plays an important role in the marketing mix. It also has serious limitations. Extensive research on the advertising and sales promotion trade-off has yielded important data.

1. Excessive promotion at the expense of advertising hurts profits. A proper expenditure balance for consumer products should be approximately 60 percent for trade and consumer promotion, 40 advertising.
2. A higher level of advertising (relative to sales promotion) increases profits.
3. A high level of *trade* promotion relative to advertising and *consumer* promotion has a positive effect on short-term market share but a negative effect on brand attitudes and long-term market share.
4. Without an effective advertising effort to emphasize brand image and quality, customers become deal-prone rather than brand-loyal.
5. Overemphasis on price eventually destroys brand equity.[39]

Another drawback of promotion is high cost. One analysis showed that only 16 percent of promotions were profitable. In other words, the manufacturer spent more than $1 to generate an extra $1 of profits.[40]

Aggressive sales promotion can draw competitors into a promotion war with reduced sales and profits for everyone.

To get the most out of promotion dollars, a company's promotions should be creative and hard to imitate. The basic commandments for consumer promotion campaigns are outlined in Ad Lab 16–A.

In summary, if too much of the marketing mix is allocated to advertising, the brand may gain a high-quality, differentiated image but not enough volume to be a market leader. On the other hand, as Larry Light, the chairman of the AAAA's Coalition for Brand Equity says, "Too much promotion, and the brand will have high volume but low profitability. Market leadership can be bought through bribes," he says, "but enduring profitable market leadership must be earned through building both brand value as well as volume."[41]

SALES PROMOTION STRATEGIES AND TACTICS

Sales promotion employs two types of strategies—*push strategies* and *pull strategies.* Manufacturers who market through normal channels must secure the cooperation of retailers. So they use push strategies utilizing trade promotion tactics. Trade promotions are primarily defensive tactics designed to protect shelf space against competitors. Pull strategies use offensive consumer promotion tactics to attract customers and increase demand for the product. Although push and pull strategies are both important and can work successfully together, advertisers spend significantly more promotion dollars on trade promotions than on consumer promotions (see Exhibit 16–12). In recent years, this has been a source of great controversy in the marketing and advertising community.

Trade Promotion: Push Strategy

In supermarkets today, shelf space and floor space are hard to come by, and to maintain their own images, department stores set standards for manufacturers'

AD LAB 16–A   The 10 Commandments of Creative Promotion

Set Specific Objectives

Undisciplined, undirected creative work is a waste of time and resources.

Know How Basic Promotion Techniques Work

A sweepstakes shouldn't be used to encourage multiple purchases or a refund to get new customers. A price-off deal can't reverse a brand's downward sales trend.

Use Simple, Attention-Getting Copy

Most promotions are built around a simple idea: "save 75 cents." Emphasize the idea and don't try to be cute.

Use Contemporary, Easy-to-Track Graphics

Don't expect to fit 500 words and 20 illustrations into a quarter-page, free-standing insert.

Clearly Communicate the Concept

Words and graphics must work together to get the message across.

Reinforce the Brand's Advertising Message

Tie promotions to the brand's ad campaign.

Support the Brand's Positioning and Image

This is especially important for image-sensitive brands and categories—like family-oriented Kraft.

Coordinate Promotional Efforts with Other Marketing Plans

Be sure to coordinate schedules and plans. A consumer promotion should occur simultaneously with a trade promotion; a free sample promotion should be timed in conjunction with the introduction of a new line.

Know the Media You Work Through

Determine which media will work best. Should samples be distributed in-store, door-to-door, or through direct mail? Does the promotion need newspaper or magazine support?

Know When to Break the Other Nine Commandments

A confident creative person knows when breaking these rules is the smartest way to go.

Laboratory Application

Choose a currently running promotion for a product and determine whether the creators followed these commandments.

EXHIBIT • 16-12

Promotion versus advertising spending.

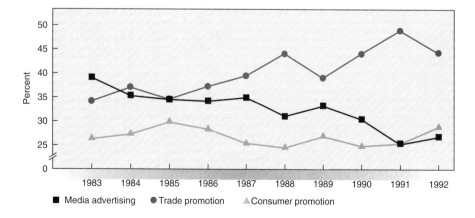

■ Media advertising   ● Trade promotion   ▲ Consumer promotion

displays. This means that retailers often can't use the special racks, sales aids, and promotional literature supplied by manufacturers. Many retailers are so pressed for time and personnel that promotional material remains in the stock room—unused and unassembled.

These are minor problems; major ones have to do with control of the marketplace. **Trade concentration**—more products going through fewer retailers—gives greater control to the retailer and less to the manufacturer. Increased competition for shelf space gives retailers even more power, enabling them to exact hefty deals and allowances. As a result, manufacturers of national brands often don't have enough money left to integrate consumer advertising or sales promotion.[42]

Despite these problems, many manufacturers still implement effective push strategies. And the smart ones safeguard enough money for consumer advertising. Trade tactics used today include: trade deals, slotting allowances, display allowances, buy-back allowances, advertising allowances, cooperative advertising and advertising materials, dealer premiums and contests, push money, collateral materials, and company conventions and dealer meetings.

Slotting Allowances

In response to the glut of new products, some retailers charge manufacturers **slotting allowances**—fees (ranging from $15,000 to $40,000) for the privilege of obtaining shelf or floor space for a new product. The practice is highly controversial because manufacturers think they're being forced to subsidize the retailer's cost of doing business. The Federal Trade Commission is looking into the legality of such allowances. Retailers say the allowances are justified because they have to spend more time redesigning shelves, finding warehouse space, entering information into computer systems, and relaying new product information to employees.

Campbell Soup found a way to get around the slotting allowance. It rewarded stores with free TV commercial time if they agreed to stock Swanson Great Starts frozen breakfast.[43] However, the supermarket ads, which aired immediately after a Great Starts commercial, had to mention the Swanson product at least once.

Trade Deals

Manufacturers make **trade deals** with their retailers by offering short-term discounts or other dollar inducements. To comply with the Robinson-Patman Act, trade deals must be offered on an equal basis to all dealers. Dealers usually pass the savings on to customers through short-term sale prices.

Reliance on trade deals to boost short-term sales is a controversial practice. Many marketers question whether trade deals create incremental profits through increased use, or whether the products would have sold eventually anyway.

Trade deals also threaten brand loyalty since they encourage customers to buy whatever brand is on sale. Furthermore, marketers who use trade discounts extensively find themselves in a trap—if they cut back on the promotions, they may lose shelf space and then market share.

In addition, many retailers abuse trade discounts by engaging in forward buying and diverting. With **forward buying,** a retailer stocks up on a product when it is on discount and buys smaller amounts when it sells at list price. **Diverting** means using the promotional discount to purchase large quantities of an item in one region then shipping portions of the buy to areas where the discount isn't offered. These practices cause large fluctuations in a manufacturer's sales and hence in work-force and other production needs.[44] Despite these problems, manufacturers persist in making trade deals—often to their own detriment.

Display Allowances

More stores are charging manufacturers **display allowances**—fees to make room for and set up displays. In-store displays include counter stands, floor stands, shelf signs, and special racks that give the retailer ready-made, professionally designed vehicles for selling more of the featured products (see Exhibit 16–13). Sometimes a well-designed dealer display induces dealers to stock more of the product than they normally would.

Surprisingly, retailers think the display allowance is the least important factor involved in accepting display materials. More important (in order of importance) are: increased profitability, display quality, service, graphics, ease of set-up, and size.[45]

Buy-Back Allowances

When introducing a new product, manufacturers sometimes offer retailers a **buy-back allowance** for the old product that hasn't sold. To convince retailers to take on their product line, some manufacturers even offer a buy-back allowance for a competitor's leftover stock. This practice is so common with certain types of merchandise that many retailers now expect prospective vendors to offer it.

Advertising Allowances

To encourage retailers to advertise their products, manufacturers often offer **advertising allowances** as either a percentage of gross purchases or a flat fee paid to the retailer. Advertising allowances are more common for consumer than industrial products and are offered primarily by large companies, but some smaller ones offer them to high-volume customers.

EXHIBIT • 16-13

Display allowances for in-store retail displays and shelf signs provide retailers like De Walt with promotional materials they would not produce on their own. Both the manufacturer and the retailer benefit from such trade promotions.

Cooperative Advertising and Advertising Materials

With **cooperative (co-op) advertising,** national manufacturers reimburse their dealers for advertising the manufacturer's products or logo in their trading area. The manufacturer usually pays 50 to 100 percent of the dealer's advertising costs based on the dealer's sales. Special co-op deals are used to introduce new products, advertise certain lines, or combat competitors.

Unlike advertising allowances, co-op programs typically require the dealer to submit proof of the advertising (tearsheets from the newspaper or affidavits of performance from radio or TV stations) along with invoices from the media.

In addition, many manufacturers provide their dealers with prepared advertising materials—ads, glossy photos, sample radio commercials, and so on. To control the image of their products, some insist that dealers use these materials to qualify for the co-op advertising money.

Dealer Premiums and Contests

To get retail dealers and salespeople to reach specific sales goals or to stock a certain product, manufacturers may offer special prizes and gifts. KLM Dutch Airlines, for instance, ran a *sweepstakes* for travel agency employees to help increase U.S. air travel to Amsterdam. Two grand prizes of dinner/dance parties were awarded in each of five U.S. regions (see Exhibit 16–14). However, ethics is an issue when companies award prizes and gifts to dealers and salespeople. Travel-related contests in particular receive scrutiny from some quarters.

Push Money

Retail salespeople are often encouraged to push the sale of particular products. One inducement is called **push money (PM)** or **spiffs.** In shoe stores, the salesperson may suggest shoe polish or some other high-profit extra; for each item sold, the salesperson receives a 25- to 50-cent spiff.

EXHIBIT • 16-14

To increase awareness, KLM Royal Dutch Airlines staged a sweepstakes for travel agents. Two grand prizes were awarded in each of five regions of the United States.

Collateral Sales Material

For industrial and high-ticket consumer products, buyers want a lot of information before they make a purchase decision. So dealers ask the manufacturer for **collateral sales material:** catalogs, manuals, technical specification sheets, brochures, presentation charts, films, audiovisual materials, or other sales aids. One savvy appliance manufacturer incorporated all necessary information into a compact monthly newsletter, which it sent to its dealers and distributors.

Company Conventions and Dealer Meetings

Most major manufacturers hold **company conventions** and **dealer meetings** to introduce new products, announce sales promotion programs, or show new advertising campaigns. They may also conduct sales and service training sessions. Meetings are good opportunities for sales reps to learn and to share experiences with other company salespeople and executives. They can be a dynamic sales promotion tool for the manufacturer.

Much advertising appears only in trade journals read by dealers or other businesspeople; it's virtually invisible to the consumer. Push strategies are equally invisible to consumers. Yet successful inducements mean the product gets more shelf space, a special display, or extra interest and enthusiasm from salespeople. And extra interest can spell the difference between failure and success.

Consumer Promotion: Pull Strategy

One reason for today's increased focus on consumer promotions is the change in TV viewing habits. With cable TV and VCRs, fewer people watch any one program. Advertising audiences are more fragmented, and major manufacturers must turn to new methods to reach these moving targets, such as coupons, sweepstakes, and in-store advertising.[46]

Some of the most common and successful **consumer promotions** include coupons, cents-off promotions, refunds/rebates, premiums, sampling, combination offers, sweepstakes and contests, and point-of-purchase advertising. Exhibit 16–15 shows the percentages of large and small firms that use various consumer promotions. A successful promotional campaign may integrate a combination of these techniques along with media advertising, product publicity, and direct marketing communications.

EXHIBIT • 16–15

Consumer promotion scorecard.

Types of promotion	Percent of respondents using	
	Larger firms*	Smaller firms†
Couponing consumer direct	93%	97%
Couponing in retailer's ad	71	46
Cents-off promotions	82	92
Money-back offers/cash refunds	75	71
Premium offers	79	49
Sampling new products	82	70
Sampling established products	68	57
Sweepstakes	75	62
Contests	43	22

* Annual sales = $1 billion or more.
† Annual sales = Less than $1 billion.

Coupons

A **coupon** is a certificate with a stated value presented to the retail store for a price reduction on a specified item (see Exhibit 16–16). A record 350 billion coupons were distributed in 1992, but only a small percentage (about 4 percent) were ever redeemed. Of all coupons distributed in 1992, the largest percentage were for health and beauty aids (22 percent), prepared foods (12 percent), and cereals (11 percent).[47]

Coupons may be distributed in newspapers or magazines, door-to-door, on packages, in stores, and by direct mail. But most (68 percent) reach consumers through colorful, pre-printed ads—called **free-standing inserts (FSIs)**—in newspapers.[48] FSIs have a higher redemption rate than regular newspaper and magazine coupons—4.2 percent compared to about 2.3 percent. Coupons in or on packages have the highest redemption levels (15.4 and 12.2 percent, respectively).[49]

After consumers redeem coupons, the retailer sorts the coupons, submits them to the manufacturer or a coupon clearinghouse, and is then reimbursed for the coupons' face value plus a handling charge.

Manufacturers lose about $250 million annually on fraudulent coupon submission. Some coupons are counterfeited, others are submitted for products that were never purchased. Quaker Oaks led manufacturers battling coupon fraud, or "misredemption." Unlike other companies, which generally check 5 percent of coupons, Quaker employees examined 100 percent and entered pertinent data about each into its computerized system. With this system, Quaker spotted fraud and also gathered useful data about how the coupons were used in various areas of the country. According to Quaker officials, the computerized process allowed the company to cut costs and increase efficiency as well as gather marketing data.[50]

EXHIBIT • 16-16

This coupon, which dominates a significant portion of the ad, is a public promise (in fact, a legal contract) from the manufacturer. It assures the retailer of reimbursement and promises the consumer that the coupon has exchange value.

Cents-Off Promotions and Refunds/Rebates

Cents-off promotions are short-term reductions in the price of a product in the form of cents-off packages, one-cent sales, free offers, and box-top refunds. Some packages bear a special cents-off sticker which the clerk removes at the check-out counter.

Some companies offer a refund in the form of cash or coupons that can be applied to future purchases of the product. To obtain the refund, the consumer must supply proof of purchase of the product, such as three box tops. Ninety percent of the coupons sent to consumers as refunds are redeemed. Manufacturers have no way of knowing whether a consumer spends a cash refund to buy more of their product.

Rebates are larger cash refunds on items such as cars or household appliances. Large rebates (like those given on cars) are handled by the seller. For small rebates (like those given for coffee makers), the consumer must send in a coupon.

Cents-off and refund promotions are often combined with sweepstakes and contests. In the late 1980s, Peter Paul sponsored a contest offering a $6,000 island vacation. Accompanying the contest was an offer of a $1 refund for six Peter Paul Almond Joy and Mounds candy wrappers. Sales of the candy bars increased 50 percent during the promotion, and more than 400,000 consumers sent in the proofs of purchase for the $1 refund.[51]

Premiums

A **premium** is an item offered free or at a bargain price to encourage the consumer to buy an advertised product. A recent survey shows that premiums affect purchase behavior the same way as rebates but tend to be more effective at getting consumers to buy a product they didn't really need.[52] See Exhibit 16–17. Premiums are intended to improve the product's image, gain goodwill, broaden the customer base, and produce quick sales.

A growing trend in recent years is joint sponsorship of premium offers. Coca-Cola and Sony teamed up to sponsor a multimillion-dollar campaign in which Coke gave away 5.6 million miniature compact discs.[53]

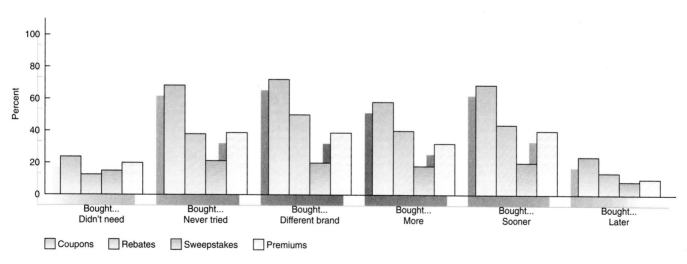

E X H I B I T • 16–17

Next to coupons, premiums are one of the most effective promotion techniques for changing consumer behavior.

A good premium should have strong appeal and value and should be useful or unusual. It may be included in the product's package, or mailed free or for a certain amount of money, on receipt of proof of purchase (box top or label). Or the premium may be given with the product at the time of purchase. Cosmetics companies often hold department store promotions in which scarves, purses, and cosmetic samplers are given free or for a low price with a cosmetics purchase.

The purchased cosmetics sampler is an example of a **self-liquidating premium**—the consumer pays enough for the premium so that the seller breaks even but doesn't make a profit. A variation is the *continuity premium,* a type of premium given weekly to customers who frequent the same store. With a minimum dollar purchase of other items, the customer gets a dish or book to complete a set of dinnerware or encyclopedias.

In-pack premiums, such as the prizes in Cracker Jack, are particularly popular in the food field, especially with cereals. **On-pack premiums** (those attached to the outside of the package) have good impulse value, but they may encourage theft. Another drawback to on-pack premiums is that they sometimes make the package difficult to stack.

Coupon premiums, which require customers to save and collect in-pack coupons for later redemption of valuable premiums, can create great consumer loyalty. General Mills includes on its breakfast cereal boxes coupons that can be collected and redeemed for savings on hundreds of kitchen, home, gift, and children's items.

Sampling

Sampling is the most costly of all sales promotions. However, it is one of the most effective for new products because it offers consumers a free trial in hopes of converting them to habitual use. To be successful, sampling should be supported by advertising and must deal with a product available in small sizes and purchased frequently. Successful sampling depends heavily on the product's merits.

Samples may be distributed by mail, door-to-door, via coupon advertising, or by a person in the store and may be given free or for a small charge. Cold remedies, candy, teabags, shampoos, disposable shavers, laundry products, and even computer software are some of the many products sampled through direct mail.[54] Sometimes, samples are distributed with related items, but this limits their distribution to those who buy the other product.

In-store sampling is becoming very popular. Campbell Soup used men in tuxedos to dish out samples of its new entrees in Washington, D.C., supermarkets. Most in-store sampling programs are tied to a coupon campaign.

Samples are often distributed to target markets, such as cosmetics to college women (pull strategy), new drugs to physicians (push strategy), or shampoo to beauticians (push strategy). Several firms provide specialized sample distribution services, including Welcome Wagon and Gift Pax.

Combination Offers

Food and drug marketers use **combination offers,** such as a razor and a package of blades or a toothbrush with a tube of toothpaste, at a reduced price for the two. For best results, the items should be related. Sometimes, a combination offer may be used to introduce a new product by tying its purchase to an established product at a special price.

EXHIBIT • 16-18

Publishers Clearing House conducts one of the best-known national sweepstakes. It is promoted through TV commercials and direct mail (shown here).

Contests and Sweepstakes

A **contest** offers prizes based on the skill of the entrants. A **sweepstakes** offers prizes based on a chance drawing of entrants' names (see Exhibit 16–18). A **game** has the chance element of a sweepstakes but is conducted over a longer time (like local bingo-type games designed to build store traffic). A game's big marketing advantage is that customers must make repeat visits to the dealer to continue playing.

Both contests and sweepstakes encourage consumption of the product by creating consumer involvement. Highly popular, these devices pull millions of entries. Usually, contest entrants must send in some proof of purchase, such as a box top or label. For more expensive products, consumers may only have to visit the dealer to pick up an entry blank.

Sweepstakes and games are now more popular than contests because they are much easier to enter and take less time. Exhibit 16–19 shows participation in sweepstakes by age, income, and education level. Sweepstakes require careful planning. Companies cannot require a purchase as a condition for entry or the sweepstakes becomes a lottery and therefore illegal. Importantly, marketers must obey all postal laws; and if they plan to run it in Canada, they may have to pay a percentage of the prizes to the Quebec government.

EXHIBIT • 16-19

Sweepstakes participation: More affluent, better-educated, older consumers are more likely to participate.

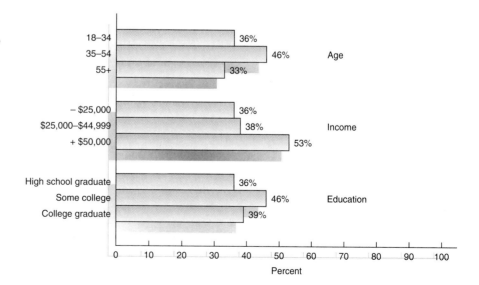

AD LAB 16–B   Smell: Powerful Armament in the Retailer's Arsenal

Strolling past the bakery in your local shopping mall, you smell the irresistible aroma of fresh-baked chocolate chip cookies. Is someone baking?

Maybe not.

International Flavors & Fragrances synthesizes the mouth-watering aroma of not only chocolate chip cookies but also hot apple pie, fresh pizza, baking ham, and even nongreasy french fries.

IF&F packages the artificial odors in aerosol cans and markets them with time-released devices that periodically fire a burst of scent into the shopping mall to tempt customers. The sprays are selling briskly and cost retailers just pennies a day.

Ledan, Inc., a New York promotion firm, is developing scented materials that stick to in-store displays. The company is already marketing chocolate scents for candy racks and pina colada aromas for the liquor department, and it hopes to have the smell of bacon available before long.

These smells, of course, are intended to make people feel hungry or thirsty. But in a store full of competing odors, the idea of using smells as a promotional gimmick could be a real stinker.

Laboratory Application

Do you think using artificial odors is a legitimate sales promotion technique?

To encourage a large number of entries, sponsors try to keep their contests as simple as possible. The prize structure must be clearly stated and rules clearly defined. National contests and sweepstakes are handled and judged by independent, professional contest firms.

Contests and sweepstakes must be promoted and advertised to be successful, and this can be expensive. And promotions need dealer support. To ensure dealer cooperation, many contests and sweepstakes require the entrant to name the product's local dealer. Prizes may also be awarded to the dealer who made the sale.

Point-of-Purchase Advertising

As a *push* technique, good dealer displays may induce a retailer to carry a line or promote a product. However, **point-of-purchase (P-O-P) advertising** is primarily a *pull* technique. Advertising or display materials at the retail location build traffic, advertise the product, and promote impulse buying. Ad Lab 16–B discusses the use of artificial aromas in point-of-purchase advertising.

Point-of-purchase programs are becoming increasingly important because more than 80 percent of purchase decisions aren't made until the customer is in the store.[55]

P-O-P materials may include window displays, counter displays, floor and wall racks to hold the merchandise, streamers, and posters. Often, the product's shipping cartons are designed to double as display units. At times, a complete "information center" provides literature, samples, and product photos. See Exhibit 16–20.

With the trend toward self-service retailing, in-store materials are becoming more and more important. Fewer and less knowledgeable salespeople are available to help, so customers are on their own. Eye-catching and informative displays give them the push they need to make a choice. Even in well-staffed stores, display material offers extra selling information and makes the product stand out.

EXHIBIT • 16-20

Point-of-purchase advertising reminds consumers of the product's benefits at the most convenient location for buying. In this Lee jeans in-store section, the consumer is literally surrounded by the advertising—which makes a powerful suggestion to buy.

There are so many P-O-P displays now that retailers are becoming quite selective. Most insist on well-designed, attractive materials that will blend with their store atmosphere. Some retailers work with manufacturers to develop P-O-P displays; a few even design their own.

Marketers are developing new approaches to P-O-P including ads on shopping carts, "talking" antacid boxes, beverage jingles activated by opening in-store refrigerator doors, and interactive computer systems for selecting everything from shoe styles to floor coverings. One technique is the **product information center (PIC).** A video-display terminal located primarily in supermarkets, the PIC carries a series of 15-second commercials in a five-minute rotation interspersed with community-interest items. Some companies use PIC spots in conjunction with an overall promotional campaign. In a promotion for Band-Aid Medicated 20's, Johnson & Johnson achieved a 75 percent sales increase in Ft. Worth, Texas, where PIC spots were used and only 24 to 38 percent in other cities.[56]

Summary

The technological explosion of the last decade fragmented the mass market, created new diversity in product choices, and greatly altered the social environment. With the resulting decline in national brand dominance, marketing thinking evolved from a marketing orientation to a market-driven orientation.

Flexible manufacturing—customizing products for customized markets—led to flexible marketing where the customer is dominant. But the customer is no longer a captive of prime time network TV. Companies searched for other ways to reach the customer, fostering the trend to integrated marketing communications (IMC).

Integrated marketing communications may be defined from two perspectives: inside-out or outside-in. The outside-in perspective defines IMC as the concept of building and reinforcing mutually profitable relationships with customers, other stakeholders, and the general public by developing communications programs that enable them to make contact with the company/brand through a variety of mediums.

To implement the IMC process, the marketer starts with the customer and works back to the brand. The inverted pyramid shows how an IMC program helps a company become a specialist in a niche category and then grow to become a market leader.

Direct marketing and sales promotion are integral elements in most IMC programs. In direct marketing, the marketer builds and maintains a database of customers and prospects and uses a variety of mediums (from personal contact to mass media) for communicating with them directly to generate a response or a transaction.

Advertisers and agencies now realize they can't do the job with one medium. Further, databases are accessible and affordable to every size business, and they let companies choose the prospects they can serve most effectively and profitably. Direct marketing is a rapid-growth industry, but it still suffers from problems of cost and image.

Direct marketers can use direct sales (personal selling and telemarketing) and/or direct-response advertising.

Direct-response advertising uses a variety of media to generate immediate inquiries or some other action on the part of the target audience. Direct mail is the medium of choice for most direct marketers, but more are beginning to use other media, especially infomercials on broadcast and cable television. Interactive television may be the direct marketing medium of the future.

Sales promotion complements advertising and personal selling by stimulating or accelerating sales. Marketers are shifting more marketing dollars from advertising to the promotion side of the mix. Sales promotion includes promotional activities aimed at salespeople, distributors, retailers, consumers, and industrial buyers. By offering direct inducements, such as money, prizes, gifts, or other opportunities, sales promotion provides extra incentives to buy a product, visit a store, request literature, or take other action.

Marketers must balance sales promotion with advertising. Advertising creates market value for a brand; promotion creates market volume. Advertising has a positive effect on profits, promotion a negative effect.

Sales promotion techniques are used in the trade to push products through the distribution channels or, with the consumer, to pull them through.

Manufacturers use a variety of sales promotion techniques with dealers: slotting allowances, trade deals, buy-back allowances, display allowances, advertising allowances, cooperative advertising and advertising materials, dealer premiums and contests, push money, collateral material, and company conventions and dealer meetings.

Sales promotions aimed at the ultimate purchaser of the product include coupons, cents-off promotions and refunds/rebates, premiums, sampling, combination offers, contests and sweepstakes, and point-of-purchase advertising.

Questions for Review and Discussion

1. What's the difference between marketing oriented and market-driven?

2. How should a large insurance company view integrated marketing communications?

3. How important is direct marketing to an integrated marketing communications program?

4. What are the basic strategic and tactical decisions direct marketers face?

5. How can an advertiser use the newspaper for direct-response advertising?

6. What are the main purposes of sales promotion?

7. Which is more important, advertising or sales promotion?

8. Why is trade promotion controversial?

9. What are the most common pull strategies? Which would you use to launch a new soft drink?

10. Why is there a trend away from push strategies and toward pull strategies?

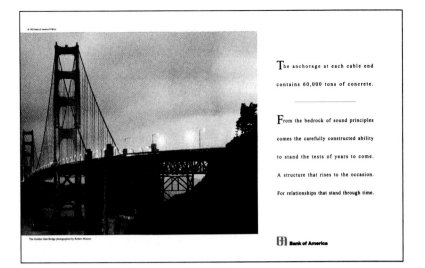

The anchorage at each cable end contains 60,000 tons of concrete.

From the bedrock of sound principles comes the carefully constructed ability to stand the tests of years to come. A structure that rises to the occasion. For relationships that stand through time.

The Golden Gate Bridge photographed by Robert Mizono

Bank of America

IMC: Public Relations and Corporate Advertising

Objective: To explain the role of public relations and corporate advertising in integrated marketing communications. By enhancing the advertiser's image, public relations and institutional advertising improve the effectiveness of a company's marketing efforts.

After studying this chapter, you will be able to:

- Distinguish between advertising and public relations.

- Discuss key elements of crisis communications.

- Describe the difference between press agentry and publicity.

- Identify the tools used by public relations practitioners.

- Define advocacy advertising and debate its role in a free society.

- Explain the role of corporate identity advertising.

T
he name *Exxon Valdez* conjures up a number of images: oil-soaked sea birds and otters, a four-mile-long slick oozing over formerly pristine Alaskan waters, and workers struggling to save suffocating animals, mop up oil, and restore a violated shoreline. But another image, one equally troubling, lingers in the minds of advertising and public relations professionals—the televised picture of Lawrence G. Rawl, chairman of Exxon Corp., tersely fielding reporters' questions.

On March 24, 1989, when the tanker *Exxon Valdez* ran aground on Bligh Reef in Prince William Sound, it precipitated the worst oil spill in U.S. history (see Exhibit 17–1). For Exxon, it also signaled an unprecedented public relations challenge, one the petroleum giant fumbled badly with its tardy, defensive media response.

Exxon was not prepared for such a crisis. The company first erred by disseminating false information—perhaps unintentionally. While the tanker was still leaking, an Exxon spokesperson estimated "minimal environmental damage." Even after tens of thousands of dead animals were counted and the public watched horrifying TV reports, Exxon stuck to its count: 300 dead birds and 70 dead otters.

Exxon further erred in failing to make Chairman Rawl available to the media. When Rawl finally did comment, he tried to shift the blame for cleanup delays to Alaskan officials and the Coast Guard. Exxon blundered again by setting up media headquarters in Valdez, Alaska, the site of the accident, rather than in a communication center such as New York, where it would have been easier to handle the deluge of press inquiries.

Thanks to its multiple PR fumbles, Exxon rapidly lost credibility with the public. A month after the spill, an NBC News/*Wall Street Journal* poll showed that 77 percent of those surveyed thought the company "could have done more" to clean up the spill, and 41 percent said they would seriously consider boycotting Exxon. In a separate poll, conducted two months after the spill, 11 percent of adult respondents said they refused to buy Exxon gasoline.[1] The company suffered a boycott of its products, and thousands of people returned their credit cards. Four years later, after spending $3 billion to clean up the spill and another $1 billion to settle federal and state lawsuits, Exxon employees

EXHIBIT • 17–1

When 11 million gallons of crude oil spilled from the *Exxon Valdez* off the coast of Alaska, Exxon's poorly handled public relations severely damaged the company's reputation.

were still suffering from poor morale and frustration over the company's flagging reputation.[2]

Exxon was unprepared to speak to the public, unskilled at relating to the public, and unwilling to deal openly with the crisis. Result: Exxon failed to achieve the most basic objective of good public relations—credibility—and the company paid dearly for it. ◆

THE ROLE OF PUBLIC RELATIONS

The term *public relations* is widely misunderstood and misused. Part of the confusion is due to the fact that public relations is a very broad term. It can be a concept, a profession, a management function, and a practice. We define **public relations** (PR) as the management function that focuses on the relationships and communications that individuals and organizations have with other groups for the purpose of creating mutual goodwill.

Every company, organization, or government body has relationships with groups of people who are affected by what it does or says. They might be employees, customers, stockholders, competitors, suppliers, or just the general population of consumers. Each group is considered one of the organization's *publics*; and each organization must develop and maintain goodwill with most, if not all, of its publics. If it fails to do so, consequences can be severe—loss of customers and revenues, time lost dealing with complaints or lawsuits, and loss of esteem (which weakens the organization's ability to secure financing, make sales, and expand).

With the ebb and flow of time and events, a company's publics change constantly. As soon as word of the *Valdez* spill got out, Exxon's publics multiplied rapidly. The PR staff at Exxon was barraged with inquiries from the press and the public. Simultaneously, other company departments had to deal with local, state, and federal government agencies and with the community at large—not just in Valdez, Alaska, but everywhere in the world. And myriad other publics suddenly popped up: Alaskan fishermen, both houses of Congress, local politicians, the financial community, stockholders, employees, the local press, national networks, Exxon dealers, environmental groups, and others.

Because of the powerful effect of public opinion, companies and organizations must consider the public impact of their actions and decisions. This is especially true in times of crisis, emergency, or disaster. But it also holds true for major policy decisions—changes in management or pricing, labor negotiations, introduction of new products, or changes in distribution methods. Each decision affects different groups in different ways. Through effective public relations, managers can channel groups' opinions toward mutual understanding and positive outcomes.

In short, the purpose of *public relations* is to favorably influence public opinion, build goodwill, and establish and maintain a satisfactory reputation for the organization. PR efforts might rally public support, obtain public understanding or neutrality, or simply respond to inquiries. Well-executed public relations is an on-going process that molds good, long-term relationships.

The Difference between Advertising and Public Relations

Since they both use the media to create awareness or to influence markets (publics), advertising and public relations share some similarities—but they're not the same. Advertising reaches its audience through media the advertiser pays for. Also, advertising appears just as the advertiser designed it, with the advertiser's bias built in. Knowing this, the public views ads with some skepticism—or ignores them outright. So in an integrated marketing communications program, advertising may *not* be the best vehicle for building credibility.

Certain public relations communications—like publicity—are not openly sponsored or paid for. People receive these communications in the form of news articles, editorial interviews, or feature stories after the messages have been reviewed and edited—filtered—by the media. Since the public thinks such messages are coming from the medium rather than a company, it accepts and trusts them more readily. For building credibility, public relations is usually the best choice.

However, public relations expert Amelia Lobsenz points out that PR is less precise than advertising. Advertising can be strictly controlled to ensure its reach and impact, but public relations communications are not so easily quantifiable: "PR's results depend more on the experience, ingenuity, and tenacity of the people engaged in its day-to-day execution."[3] So while PR offers greater credibility, companies have much less control over the message. For this reason, many companies relay their public relations messages through *corporate advertising*, a topic discussed later in this chapter.

Advertising and PR in the Eyes of Practitioners

Another difference between public relations and advertising is the orientation of professional practitioners. Advertising professionals see marketing as the umbrella process companies use to determine what products and services the market needs and how to distribute and sell them. To advertising professionals, advertising and public relations are "good news" marketing tools used to promote sales.

Public relations professionals, with their background in journalism rather than marketing, believe public relations should be the umbrella process. They think companies should use PR to maintain relationships with *all* publics—including consumers. As *INSIDE PR* magazine says, "Public relations is a management discipline that encompasses a wide range of activities, from marketing and advertising to investor relations and government affairs."[4] To PR professionals, public relations is *integrated corporate communications*—broader than integrated *marketing* communications.

Very few companies are structured with a public relations orientation; they prefer a marketing-oriented structure. But in times of crisis or emergency, PR is the better perspective to adopt.

In an integrated marketing communications program—where PR activities are used as a marketing tool—advertising and PR should be closely coordinated. Many advertising agencies now have a PR department. And many companies now have *marketing communications departments* to manage both advertising and PR.

THE PUBLIC RELATIONS JOB

The public relations job comprises a variety of activities—from crisis communications to fund raising. And the practitioner uses many tools besides press conferences and news releases.

Crisis Communications

As the *Exxon Valdez* episode illustrates, one of the most important public relations tasks for any corporation is **crisis management.** Even companies that earn the public's trust and goodwill over decades can lose their status fast if they mismanage their response to a crisis.

Johnson & Johnson did exemplary crisis communications in a 1982 product tampering case. Several people died when a criminal laced bottles of J&J's

Extra-Strength Tylenol with cyanide and put them back on retail shelves.[5] The moment they received the news, management strategists at J&J and McNeil Products Company (the J&J subsidiary that markets Tylenol) quickly formulated three stages of action:

1. Identify the problem and take immediate corrective action. J&J strategists got information from the press, police, FDA, and FBI, identified the geographic area affected, corrected rumors, and immediately withdrew product from the marketplace.

2. Actively cooperate with authorities in the investigation. Johnson & Johnson was pro-active—the company helped the FBI and other law enforcement agencies generate leads and investigate security at the plants, and it offered a $100,000 reward.

3. Quickly rebuild the Tylenol name and capsule line, including Regular Strength capsules, which were recalled too. Although J&J believed the poisoning took place at the retail end of the chain, it first had to be sure that the tampering didn't occur at McNeil. The company's two capsule production lines were shut down, and dog teams were brought in to search for evidence of cyanide.

The insatiable appetite of the news media plus a flood of inquiries from anxious consumers put J&J's PR people under enormous pressure. All communications between the media and the company were channeled through the corporate communications department. In addition, all customer, trade, and government communications were coordinated within the company. This way, J&J maintained open, clear, consistent, legal, and credible communications and avoided rumors, political backbiting, and corporate defensiveness.

In the first 48 hours after the news broke, phone calls to Johnson & Johnson and McNeil were incessant. In the basement at McNeil, a bank of phones usually used for sales was pressed into service and staffed by employees who were briefed as to what to say, what not to say, and where to refer hard-to-answer questions.

At the same time, management and employees had to be informed, authorities contacted, and many others notified. J&J and McNeil public relations managers and staff had to plan, coordinate, and supervise this enormous task.

As infrequent as disasters are, there is no more important activity for PR professionals and public information officers—especially those in highly sensitive industries like the airlines, law enforcement agencies, the military, chemical and oil companies, and public utilities.

And since the Tylenol incident, many companies in normally nonsensitive industries have crisis-management plans ready. PR expert Art Stevens notes, "How a corporation handles news during crises determines in large measure the impact that news has on the public. When corporations have no plans for coping with crisis news, the resulting press coverage can be disastrous."[6] Experts on crisis management encourage all companies to follow J&J's example by being open and candid. Says Stevens, "Withholding information or evading questions is almost certain to backfire."[7] Exhibit 17–2 is a classic example of an advertiser coming clean.

Other Public Relations Activities

Fortunately, public relations professionals spend most of their time *generating* news from basically low-news-demand organizations. Their activities range

TOSHIBA CORPORATION EXTENDS ITS DEEPEST REGRETS TO THE AMERICAN PEOPLE.

Toshiba Corporation shares the shock and anger of the American people, the Administration and Congress at the recent conduct of one of our 50 major subsidiaries, Toshiba Machine Company. We are equally concerned about the serious impact of TMC's diversion on the security of the United States, Japan, and other countries of the Free World.

Toshiba Corporation had no knowledge of this unauthorized action by TMC. And the United States and Japanese Governments have not claimed that Toshiba Corporation itself had any knowledge or involvement.

Nevertheless, Toshiba Corporation, as a majority shareholder of TMC, profoundly apologizes for these past actions by a subsidiary of Toshiba.
- As a measure of *personal* recognition of the grievous nature of TMC's action, both the Chairman and the President of Toshiba Corporation have resigned. *For the Japanese business world, this is the highest form of apology.*
- In TMC, the subsidiary where the diversion occurred, wrongdoers are now being prosecuted.

For the future, Toshiba Corporation takes full responsibility to insure that never again will such activity take place within the Toshiba Group of companies.
- We are working with the Governments of the United States and Japan in this endeavor.

The relationship of Toshiba Corporation, its subsidiaries and their American employees with the American people, one marked by mutual trust and cooperation, has developed over many years of doing business together. We pledge to do whatever it takes to repair, preserve, and enhance this relationship.

Toshiba Corporation already has begun to take corrective measures throughout its hundreds of subsidiaries and affiliate companies:
- We immediately directed all our companies to institute stringent measures guarding more securely against this kind of misconduct.
- We obtained the resignation of the President of TMC and the three other Board members who had corporate responsibility for the conduct of those TMC employees actually involved.

- We also obtained TMC's commitment to stop exports to the Soviet Bloc countries for an unlimited time.
- We have authorized an extensive investigation to find all the facts concerning TMC's actions and to design safeguards to prevent repetition of such conduct. This investigation is being directed by American counsel, assisted by a major independent accounting firm.
- We will discharge all officers and employees found to have knowingly participated in this wrongful export sale.
- We have appointed the former senior auditing official of Toshiba Corporation to TMC's Board with direct responsibility for Toshiba's policy of full observance of the law and of Japan's security arrangements with its allies.
- We are going to develop a rigid compliance program in cooperation with the Governments of Japan and the United States.
- We intend to establish Toshiba's new compliance program as a model for all future export controls throughout Japanese industry.

In its 22 years of doing business with the United States, Toshiba Corporation has been a leader in introducing American products to the Japanese market, and also has significantly shifted the manufacture of Toshiba products to the United States. At a time when many of the U.S.-based corporations competing with Toshiba are moving production facilities and jobs abroad, Toshiba's American companies are steadily expanding the extent to which their products are manufactured in the United States. Today, Toshiba employs thousands of Americans in 21 states from New York to Texas to California. It is these Americans who have played a large and crucial part in earning Toshiba its reputation for producing top quality products, reliable service, and ongoing innovation that millions of American consumers and industrial customers know they can trust.

These bonds of cooperation are signs of our commitment to America. We earnestly wish to continue our efforts to develop our relationship with America.

We ask our American friends to work with us and help us to do so.

Joichi Aoi

Joichi Aoi
President/CEO
Toshiba Corporation

EXHIBIT • 17–2

The President of Toshiba Corporation ran this apology in 60 U.S. publications after the discovery that one of its subsidiaries exported a restricted submarine propeller-milling machine to the Soviet Union. Note that the illegal diversion is not precisely described. But the extensive list of corrective actions following the apology helps reassure readers that the misconduct will never happen again. Facing congressional threats to end all its U.S. business, Toshiba uses the last paragraph to point out that it employs thousands of workers in 21 states—the company's loss might be our loss, too.

from product publicity and press agentry to special-events management and speech writing.

Planning

The first function of a PR practitioner is to plan and execute the public relations program. Part of this task might be integrated with the company's marketing efforts (for instance, product publicity), but the PR person typically takes a broader view. He or she must prepare an overall public relations program for the whole organization.

The practitioner analyzes the relationships between the organization and its publics; evaluates people's attitudes and opinions toward the organization; assesses how the organization's policies and actions relate to its publics; determines PR objectives and strategies; develops and implements a mix of PR activities, integrating them whenever possible with the company's other marketing communications; and finally, solicits feedback to review and evaluate the program's effectiveness.

Publicity and Press Agentry

A subset of public relations, **publicity** refers to the generation of news about a person, product, or service that appears in broadcast or print media.[8]

Publicity is thought of as "free" because firms don't pay the media to run it, and the media don't charge. (They also don't guarantee they'll use it.) As a marketing communications vehicle, publicity offers a greater return on money invested than other communications activities. A large ad campaign might require an investment of 5 to 20 percent of sales; a major publicity program, only 1 to 2 percent.[9]

To be effective, publicity must be newsworthy. Typical publicity opportunities include new product introductions, awards, company sales and earnings, mergers, retirements, parades, and speeches by company executives. Sometimes publicity accrues unintentionally, as in the case of Exxon. And since publicity can originate from any source, it may be difficult—or impossible—to control.

ETHICAL DILEMMA   When Is Advertising Not Really Advertising?

The **advertorial** is a strange creature—half advertising, half editorial, and totally controversial. Advertorials are the primary form of *advocacy advertising*, and their aim is to sway public opinion rather than sell products. Although advertorials account for only 5 percent of all corporate advertising, they can move mountains.

In 1908, AT&T used advertorials to extol the virtues of private monopoly and lay the foundation for its telecommunications empire. The AT&T campaign was a prototype. It defined the issue, presented facts selectively, and argued for the conclusion that best served its interests.

Since AT&T's pioneering effort, a few outspoken corporations like Mobil Oil routinely use advertorials as an integral part of their corporate advertising effort. But most companies avoid controversial issues for fear of making enemies.

In the 1970s, activist groups began to demand greater social responsibility from corporations, and embattled companies and business associations rose to their industries' defense. Many used advertorials to educate people about the role and responsibilities of business in a free society.

The political climate changed in the 1980s, and advocacy advertising decreased significantly. During the Reagan years, corporations turned to lobbying, believing they now had supporters in Washington.

Well done advertorials do influence public opinion. One classic study revealed that advocacy advertising was most successful when it presented facts that convinced people they weren't as well-informed as they thought. Another study showed that advocacy advertising "may be perceived as more interesting and more informative and, hence, be more

Press agentry is the planning and staging of events to attract attention and generate publicity. Most PR people engage in press agentry to bring attention to new products or services or to portray their organization favorably. For print media, the publicity person deals with editors and feature writers. For broadcast media, he or she deals with a program director, assignment editor, or news editor. Successful PR practitioners develop and maintain close, cordial relations with their editorial contacts.

Public Affairs and Lobbying

Organizations often need to deal with elected officials, regulatory and legislative bodies, and various community groups—the realm of **public affairs.** Public affairs usually requires a specialist. Many think PR and public affairs should become more integrated to combine the skills and policy expertise of the specialist with the PR person's media and community relations savvy.[10]

Lobbying refers to informing and persuading government officials to support or thwart administrative action or legislation in the interests of some client. Every organization is affected by the government, so lobbying is big business.

Community Involvement

The goal of *community involvement* is "to have the company officers, management, and employees contribute to the community's social and economic development."[11] Every community offers opportunities: civic and youth groups, charitable fund-raising drives, cultural or recreational activities, and so on. A company's public relations department may help set up such programs and then publicize them to the community.

Promotion and Special-Events Management

In profit-making organizations, **promotion** means using advertising and public relations techniques to sell a product or service and to enhance the organization's reputation. Typical promotional activities include press parties, open houses, celebrations, contests, and others discussed in Chapter 16.

persuasive than a message presented in a news format." That leads to a key distinction that corporations and the FTC can't seem to agree on: Is an advertorial news in an advertising format, or vice versa?

If advertorials are treated like all other advertising, the FTC can review their content for truth and accuracy. Corporations contend that advertorials are editorial rather than commercial and shouldn't fall under the purview of the FTC.

Television balks at running advocacy advertising. George Schweitzer, VP/communications of CBS television news, says, "We haven't accepted advocacy advertising for the simple reason that we feel it would allow those with the biggest wallets to have the loudest voices." In 1987, Drexel Burnham Lambert spent $600,000 running 11 ads to sell the idea that high-yield junk bonds were important to the econ-

omy. The ads were persuasive, but Drexel—and some of its customers—eventually went broke.

Corporations have the same right as anyone else to express their views. The government should not be allowed to regulate corporate advertisers while allowing their adversaries unfettered First Amendment freedom. Perhaps the guiding principle should be: If it looks like an ad and talks like an ad, then it is an ad, and it should be closely scrutinized by the FTC and the public.

Questions

1   Should corporations use persuasive advertising techniques to influence key decision makers?

2. How can you determine if an advocacy ad is deceptive? If deception is established, what should the penalty be?

Sports-event sponsorship is a frequent
strategy for corporations.

PR people use two kinds of **special events:** those designed to create publicity and those designed to improve public relations through personal contact. Often the two purposes overlap.

An increasingly popular promotion is the company-sponsored cultural or sports event. See Exhibit 17–3. Corporate sponsorship of events is growing rapidly, reaching $2.94 billion in 1991.[12]

Corporations spend hundreds of millions of dollars a year solely on sports marketing. 3M spent about $12 million to become an official sponsor of the 1988 Olympic Games.[13] The return on that investment was so good that 3M became a corporate sponsor of the 1992 Games. Firms with more modest event-marketing budgets use other options, ranging from local golf tournaments and dance concerts to surfing contests.

Some companies associate their names with existing events. Mercedes-Benz, Perrier, and Seiko sponsor the New York Marathon; and Visa sponsored Paul McCartney's 1990 concert tour.[14] Sponsorship of charity events is another tried-and-true PR activity. A number of large corporations, including Chevrolet, AT&T, American Airlines, Pepsi, and Kodak, cosponsored the Live Aid concert in 1985. "Helping the less fortunate is good business," said one Live Aid organizer.[15]

Publications

Public relations people prepare many of a company's communication materials: news releases and media kits; booklets, leaflets, pamphlets, brochures, manuals, and books; letters, inserts, and enclosures; annual reports; posters, bulletin boards, and exhibits; audiovisual materials; and speeches and position papers.

Research

Since public opinion is so important, the PR person must constantly monitor, measure, and analyze changes in public attitudes. In 1990, Perrier used research to monitor its standing with the public after traces of benzene, a carcinogen, were found in bottles of Perrier water. Perrier found that 82 percent of its customers knew about the contamination, but 80 percent planned to buy the water when it became available again.[16]

A common form of public relations research is **opinion sampling** using many of the techniques discussed in Chapter 6—shopping center or phone interviews, focus groups, analysis of incoming mail, and field reports. Some advertisers set up toll-free phone lines and invite consumer feedback.

Fund Raising and Membership Drives

A public relations person may be responsible for soliciting money for a non-profit organization or for a cause the company deems worthwhile, such as the United Way or a political action committee (PAC).

Charitable organizations, labor unions, professional societies, trade associations, and other groups rely on membership fees or contributions. The PR specialist must communicate to potential contributors or members the purposes and goals of the organization and may integrate promotional tie-ins to help publicize the drive or encourage participation.

Public Speaking

PR practitioners often represent their employers at special events, press conferences, and interviews, so they must be articulate public speakers. They may also prepare speeches for company officials to give at stockholder meetings, conferences, or conventions. And they arrange for speaking opportunities and develop answers for common questions company representatives might be asked.

Public Relations Tools

The communication tools at the PR person's disposal vary widely—from news releases and photos to audiovisual materials and even advertising.

News Releases and Media Kits

A **news release** (or **press release**), the most widely used PR tool, consists of one or more typewritten sheets of information (usually 8½ by 11 inches) issued to generate publicity or shed light on a subject of interest. News releases cover *hard news*—news important at the time of release. Topics may include the announcement of a new product, promotion of an executive, an unusual contest, landing of a major contract, or establishment of a scholarship fund, to name a few. Exhibit 17–4 shows a standard news release format. For pointers in preparing releases, see the Checklist for Writing News Releases.

A **press kit** (or **media kit**) supports the publicity gained at staged events such as press conferences or open houses. Such a kit includes a basic fact sheet of information about the event, a program or schedule of activities, and a list of the participants and their biographical data. In addition, the kit contains a news story about the event for the broadcast media, and news and feature stories for the print media along with photos and brochures.

Photography

Photos of events, products in use, new equipment, or newly promoted executives can lend credence or interest to a dull news story. In fact, a photo tells the

This typical news release shows the company logo, a release date, contact person, headline, and the story in double-spaced type.

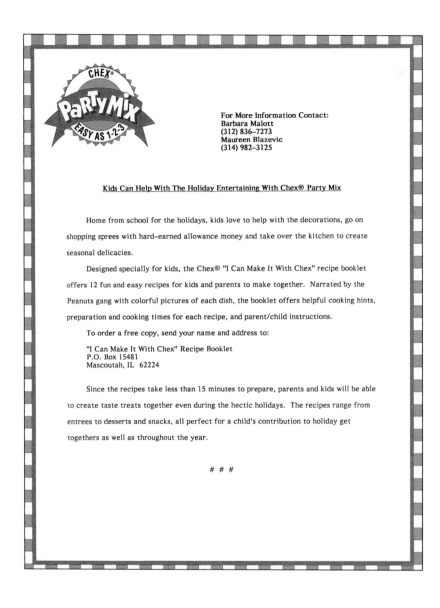

For More Information Contact:
Barbara Malott
(312) 836–7273
Maureen Blazevic
(314) 982–3125

Kids Can Help With The Holiday Entertaining With Chex® Party Mix

Home from school for the holidays, kids love to help with the decorations, go on shopping sprees with hard–earned allowance money and take over the kitchen to create seasonal delicacies.

Designed specially for kids, the Chex® "I Can Make It With Chex" recipe booklet offers 12 fun and easy recipes for kids and parents to make together. Narrated by the Peanuts gang with colorful pictures of each dish, the booklet offers helpful cooking hints, preparation and cooking times for each recipe, and parent/child instructions.

To order a free copy, send your name and address to:

"I Can Make It With Chex" Recipe Booklet
P.O. Box 15481
Mascoutah, IL 62224

Since the recipes take less than 15 minutes to prepare, parents and kids will be able to create taste treats together even during the hectic holidays. The recipes range from entrees to desserts and snacks, all perfect for a child's contribution to holiday get togethers as well as throughout the year.

\# \# \#

story faster. Photos should be good quality and need little or no explanation. Typed captions should describe the subject of the photo and accurately identify the people shown.

Feature Articles

Many publications, particularly trade publications, run feature articles—or *soft news*—about companies, products, or services. Such articles may be written by a PR person, the publication's staff, or a third party (such as a free-lance business writer). Feature articles give the company or product credibility. Editors like them because they have no immediate deadline and can be published whenever the editor chooses.

Features may include case histories, illustrate how-to's (such as how to use the company's product), problem-solving scenarios (how one customer uses the company's product to increase production), and state-of-the-art technology updates. Other formats include roundups of what's happening in a specific industry and editorials (such as a speech or essay by a company executive on a current issue).[17]

CHECKLIST   Writing News Releases

◇ **Identify yourself.** Include the name and address of the company (preferably on a letterhead) and the name and number to contact for further information.

◇ **Provide a release date**—even if the item is marked "for immediate release."

◇ **Use wide margins.** Copy should be double-spaced for print media and triple-spaced for broadcast media.

◇ **Keep it short.** One page is preferred. If the release is longer, don't break in the middle of a paragraph.

◇ **Proof the copy.** Typos, grammatical errors, and other mistakes detract from the message.

◇ **Update your mailing list.** Editors change, offices move.

◇ **Don't call to see whether the editor received your release.** Editors don't like to be pressured.

◇ **Don't ask for tearsheets.** Don't expect the editor to send you a copy.

◇ **Don't promise you'll advertise if the item is published.** You'll offend the editor.

◇ If an article runs, **send a thank you** to the editor.

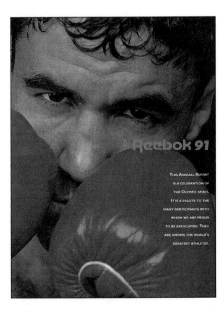

EXHIBIT • 17–5

Because annual reports help sell the company to investors and are a key element in establishing a company's image, many corporations produce elaborate, full-color annual reports like this one for Reebok.

Printed Materials

Printed materials are used extensively in public relations and advertising. They may be brochures or pamphlets about the company or its products, letters to customers, inserts or enclosures that accompany monthly statements, the **annual report** to stockholders, other reports, or house organs. Exhibit 17–5 illustrates their potential for creative design.

A **house organ** is a publication about happenings and policies at the company. An internal house organ is for employees only. External house publications go to company-connected people (customers, stockholders, suppliers, and dealers) or to the public. They may take the form of a newsletter, tabloid newspaper, or magazine. The purpose of house organs is to promote goodwill, increase sales, or mold public opinion. A well-produced house organ can do a great deal to motivate employees and appeal to customers. However, writing, printing, and distributing can be expensive—and very time consuming.

Posters, Exhibits, and Bulletin Boards

Posters can be used internally to stress safety, security, reduction of waste, and courtesy. Externally, they can impart production information or other news of interest to the consumer.

Companies use exhibits to describe the organization's history, present new products, show how products are made, or explain future plans. Exhibits are often prepared for local fairs, colleges and universities, and trade shows.

Internally, the public relations staff often uses **bulletin boards** to announce new equipment, meetings, promotions, new products, construction plans, and recreation news to employees.

Audiovisual Materials

Audiovisual materials can take many forms, including slides, films, filmstrips, and videocassettes used for training, sales, or public relations. Considered a form of corporate advertising, "nontheatrical" or "sponsored" films (developed for public relations reasons) are furnished without charge to movie theaters, organizations, and special groups, particularly schools and colleges. Classic examples include *Why Man Creates,* produced for Kaiser Aluminum, and Mobil Oil Corporation's *A Fable,* starring the famous French mime Marcel Marceau.

Many public relations departments provide **video press releases**—news or feature stories prepared by a company and offered free to TV stations. The TV stations can use the whole video or just segments. Video press releases are somewhat controversial. Critics see them as subtle commercials or even propaganda, and take issue when stations run the stories without disclosing that they came from a public relations firm, not the station's news staff.[18]

CORPORATE ADVERTISING

PR people use corporate advertising when they want to control the message. In an integrated marketing communications program, corporate advertising can set the tone for all of a company's public communications. **Corporate advertising** covers the broad area of nonproduct advertising including public relations advertising, institutional advertising, corporate identity advertising, and recruitment advertising.

Public Relations Advertising

When a company wants to direct a controlled public relations message to one of its important publics, it uses **public relations advertising.** The ad in Exhibit 17–6 targets customers, investors, and stock analysts. Public relations ads try to improve the company's relations with labor, government, customers, suppliers, and even voters.

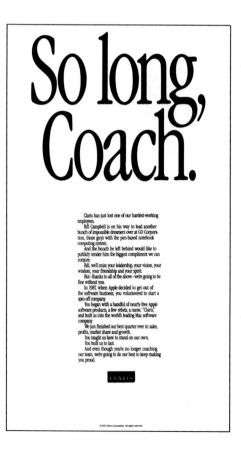

EXHIBIT • 17-7

Many corporations support funding for cultural events and other humanistic endeavors like the arts.

When companies sponsor art events, programs on public television, or charitable activities, they frequently place public relations ads in other media to promote the programs and their sponsorship, enhance their community citizenship, and create public goodwill. The ad in Exhibit 17–7 promotes an art exhibit and Southwestern Bell's sponsorship role.

Corporate/Institutional Advertising

In recent years, the term **corporate advertising** has come to denote the type of nonproduct advertising used to enhance a company's image and increase awareness. The traditional term for this is *institutional advertising*.

Institutional or corporate ad campaigns serve a variety of purposes—to report the company's accomplishments, position the company competitively in the market, reflect a change in corporate personality, shore up stock prices, improve employee morale, or avoid communications problems with agents, dealers, suppliers, or customers. (For some excellent examples, see the Portfolio of Corporate Advertising on pages 532–535.)

Companies and professional advertising people historically questioned, or simply misunderstood, the effectiveness of corporate advertising. Retailers, in particular, cling to the idea that institutional advertising, although attractive and nice, "doesn't make the cash register ring." However, a series of marketing research studies offered dramatic evidence to the contrary.

Continued on page 536

Portfolio of Corporate Advertising

A. This corporate ad for American Honda points out how the company supports education programs for minorities. The company also participates in community-oriented social programs.

B. Event sponsorship reflects favorably on the corporation—especially when it helps make the event possible. The event's participants and audiences may tell others and return the favor of goodwill. (© Copyright Mercedes-Benz of North America, Inc.)

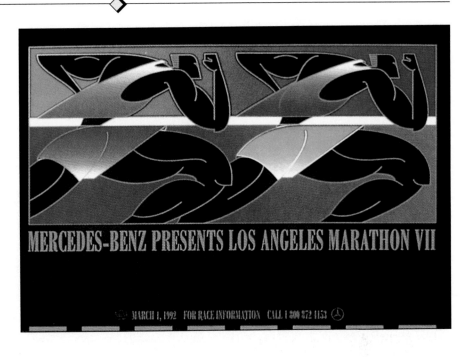

C. The understated, artistic use of common, everyday items like a toothbrush and an onion helps differentiate Kaneka's corporate image from other chemical companies.

D. The visual of Hitachi's name in lights across these city buildings stimulates the image of the corporation's omnipresence.

E. The fact that all these popular products appear in a single corporate ad for Nabisco educates the consumer about the singularity of their relationship. This enlarges the consumer's perception of the company's overall business strength which, in turn, creates added market value for each product and the company's stock.

EXHIBIT • 17-8

This poster by a college fraternity, Pi Kappa Phi, publicly advocates a socially correct point of view for all its publics to see—including its own members.

Researchers found that companies using corporate advertising registered significantly better awareness, familiarity, and overall impression than companies using only product advertising. Five corporate advertisers in the study drew higher ratings in every one of 16 characteristics measured, including being known for quality products, having competent management, and paying higher dividends.[19] Perhaps the most interesting aspect of the research was that the companies that did no corporate advertising spent far more in total advertising their products.

David Ogilvy, founder and creative head of Ogilvy & Mather, is an outspoken advocate of corporate advertising, but he is appalled by some corporate ads. (For more on Ogilvy's views, see Ad Lab 17–A.)

Responding to such criticisms and to marketplace forces, corporations now design their corporate advertising to achieve specific objectives: develop awareness of the company and its activities, attract investors, improve a tarnished image, attract quality employees, tie a diverse product line together, and take a stand on important public issues. Expenditures for this type of advertising are increasing dramatically.[20] The primary medium used is consumer business magazines followed by network television.[21]

A company uses **advocacy advertising** to communicate its views on issues that affect its business (to protect its position in the marketplace) or to promote its philosophy or make a political or social statement (see Exhibit 17–8).[22]

Corporate advertising can also build a foundation for future sales, traditionally the realm of product advertising. Many advertisers use "umbrella" campaigns, called **market prep corporate advertising,** to simultaneously communicate messages about the products and the company.

Of course, no amount of image advertising can accomplish desired goals if the image doesn't fit. As one noted image consultant put it, "You can't get away with a dissonance between the image and the reality—at least not for long."[23] If a high-tech corporation like GE tried to project a homey, small-town image, it would lose credibility.

Corporate Identity Advertising

Companies take pride in their logos and corporate signatures. The graphic designs that identify corporate names and products are valuable assets, and companies take great pains to protect their individuality and ownership. See Exhibit 17–9. What does a company do when it changes its name, logos, trademarks, or corporate signatures, as when it merges with another company? This is the job of **corporate identity advertising.**

When software publisher Productivity Products International changed its name to Stepstone, Inc., it faced an interesting dilemma. It needed to advertise the change. But in Europe, one of its key markets, a corporate name change implies that a bankrupt business is starting over with a new identity. So rather than announcing its new name in the print media, Stepstone used a direct-mail campaign. It mailed an announcement to customers, prospects, investors, and the press. The campaign was a success.[24]

More familiar corporate name changes include the switch from American Harvester to Navistar International and Consolidated Foods to Sara Lee Corporation, and the creation of Unisys to replace the premerger identities of Burroughs and Sperry.

AD LAB 17-A David Ogilvy Talks about Corporate Advertising

I have had some experience with corporate advertising—for Shell, Sears, IBM, International Paper, Merrill Lynch, General Dynamics, Standard Oil of New Jersey, and other great corporations.

Big corporations are increasingly under attack—from consumer groups, from environmentalists, from governments, from antitrust prosecutors who try their cases in the newspapers. If a big corporation does not take the initiative in cultivating its reputation, its case goes by default.

If it were possible, it would be better for corporations to rely on public relations (i.e., favorable news stories and editorials) rather than paid advertising. But the media are too niggardly about disseminating favorable information about corporations. That is why an increasing number of public relations directors have come to use paid advertising as their main channel of communication. It is the only one they can control with respect to *content,* with respect to *timing,* and with respect to *noise level.* And it is the only one which enables them to *select their own battleground.*

So I guess that corporate advertising is here to stay. Why is most of it a *flop?*

First, because corporations fail to define the *purpose* of their corporate campaigns.

Second, because they don't *measure the results.* In a recent survey conducted by *The Gallagher Report,* only one in four U.S. corporate advertisers said that it measured changes in attitude brought about by its corporate campaigns. The majority fly blind.

Third, because so little is known about what works and what doesn't work in corporate advertising. The marketing departments and their agencies know a good deal about what works in *brand* advertising, but when it comes to *corporate* advertising they are amateurs. It isn't their bag.

Fourth, very few advertising agencies know much about corporate advertising. It is only a marginal part of their business. Their creative people know how to talk to housewives about toilet paper, and how to write chewing-gum jingles for kids, and how to sell beer to blue-collar workers. But corporate advertising requires copywriters who are at home in the world of big business. There aren't many of them.

I am appalled by the *humbug* in corporate advertising. The *pomposity.* The *vague generalities* and the *fatuous platitudes.*

Corporate advertising should not insult the intelligence of the public.

Unlike product advertising, a corporate campaign is the voice of the chief executive and his board of directors. It should not be delegated.

What can good corporate advertising hope to achieve? In my experience, one or more of four objectives:

1. It can build *awareness* of the company. Opinion Research Corporation states, "The invisibility and remoteness of most companies is the main handicap. People who feel they know a company well are five times more likely to have a highly favorable opinion of the company than those who have little familiarity."

2. Corporate advertising can make a good impression on the financial community, thus enabling you to raise capital at lower cost—and make more acquisitions.

3. It can motivate your present employees and attract better recruits. Good public relations begins at home. If your employees understand your policies and feel proud of your company, they will be your best ambassadors.

4. Corporate advertising can influence public opinion on specific issues.

Abraham Lincoln said, "With public opinion against it, nothing can succeed. With public opinion on its side, nothing can fail."

Stop and Go—that is the typical pattern of corporate advertising. What a waste of money. It takes time, it takes *years,* for corporate advertising to do a job. It doesn't work overnight—even if you use television.

A few companies—a *very* few—have kept it going long enough to achieve measurable results.

Laboratory Application

Find and discuss a corporate ad that demonstrates what Ogilvy refers to as the humbug in corporate advertising, the pomposity, vague generalities, and fatuous platitudes.

EXHIBIT • 17-9

A unique logo puts a face on a corporation. A memorable visual symbol gives a corporation personality.

Recruitment Advertising

Companies use **recruitment advertising** to attract employment applications. Most recruitment advertising appears in the classified sections of daily newspapers and is placed by the personnel rather than the advertising department. Many ad agencies now employ recruitment specialists, and some agencies specialize in recruitment advertising.

Summary

Public relations is a process used to manage an organization's relationships with its various publics including employees, customers, stockholders, competitors, and the general populace. Many public relations activities involve media communications. However, unlike product advertising, these communications are not normally sponsored or paid for.

Public relations activities include planning, publicity and press agentry, public affairs and lobbying, promotion and special-events management, publication preparation, research, fund-raising and membership drives, and public speaking.

The tools used in public relations include: news releases and media kits, photography, feature articles, all sorts of printed materials, posters and exhibits, and audiovisual materials. To help create a favorable reputation in the marketplace, companies use various types of corporate advertising, including public relations advertising, corporate (or institutional) advertising, corporate identity advertising, and recruitment advertising.

Questions for Review and Discussion

1. How does the definition of public relations differ from the definition of advertising?

2. How is the perspective of advertising practitioners different from that of PR professionals?

3. What is the role of public relations in an integrated marketing communications program?

4. Why is it important to establish a crisis-management plan? What types of companies are most likely to need one?

5. If you handled the public relations for a utility company, what activities would be the most useful?

6. What are the most important public relations tools for a major corporation? Why?

7. What are the various types of corporate advertising? Describe them.

8. How is the line between product and corporate advertising beginning to blur?

9. What is the purpose of corporate identity advertising?

10. What is the purpose of recruitment advertising? Why is it under the domain of corporate advertising and public relations?

If You Smoke, You Might As Well Start The Day With A Mouthful Of This.

Minnesota Department of Health

Integrated Marketing Communications for Local and Noncommercial Advertisers

Objective: To define local and noncommercial advertising and describe how the principles of IMC are applied in these areas. The advertising person who works on the local or noncommercial level deals with the unique circumstances and special problems of small businesses and non-profit organizations.

After studying this chapter, you will be able to:

- Define local advertising and describe the four main categories of local advertisers.

- Explain how local advertisers differ from national advertisers.

- Discuss the importance of the advertiser's local trading area.

- List the steps involved in planning local advertising.

- Describe the types of market research local advertisers should conduct.

- Discuss the factors that affect the local advertiser's budget and media choices.

- Identify the common sources of creative assistance.

- Evaluate the importance of public service announcements.

Ralph Rubio worked his way through college as a waiter. After graduation he managed several restaurants in the San Diego area. In the process, he saw a need for better Mexican food; so he decided to start his own restaurant, gearing the menu to his own palate.

Rubio opened his Mexican restaurant in 1983 with an unusual specialty—*fish tacos*—lightly battered and fried whitefish served in soft-shelled corn tortillas with white sauce, salsa, cabbage, and a wedge of lime. At the time, very few other Mexican eateries offered fish tacos, and none featured them. So Rubio found fish tacos hard to sell—even with his secret batter recipe (given to him by a street vendor in San Felipe, Mexico). The first month's sales at the restaurant averaged only $163 a day.

Using small newspaper ads with coupons to lure courageous customers, Rubio started advertising. It worked. As business picked up, he expanded his advertising to radio and TV, targeting his market further with ads on Hispanic stations (listeners knew what fish tacos were). And he went after younger, venturesome customers in the 18-to-34 range by advertising at local movie theaters. Business picked up some more. Rubio soon opened another restaurant . . . and another.

With each new opening, Rubio distributed direct-mail flyers in the surrounding area and visited nearby stores with free samples. Working with an artist, he created a cartoon character out of the fish taco named Pesky Pescado (see Exhibit 18–1). He also purchased a 15-foot inflatable Pesky to appear at his restaurants. Employees wore T-shirts sporting Pesky's picture, and Rubio sold Pesky T-shirts and sweatshirts to enthusiastic patrons. He also ordered bumper stickers and antenna balls to promote his growing restaurant chain. Finally, to further integrate his activities, Rubio took an active part in community affairs including tie-ins with a blood bank, a literacy program, and fund-raising activities for both a Tijuana medical clinic and a local university's athletic program.

As the popularity of the fish taco grew, so did Rubio's revenues, doubling every year for the first five years. After eight years, Rubio had 10 restaurants serving over 16,000 fish tacos a day. He trademarked the phrase "Rubio's, Home of the Fish Taco"; and a local restaurant critic called it "the food San

EXHIBIT • 18–1

Rubio's made fish tacos world famous with the help of integrated local advertising and a character named Pesky Pescado.

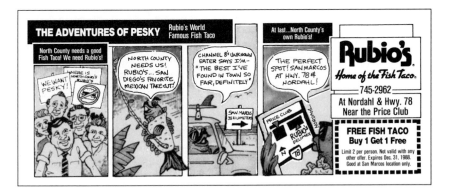

Diegans would miss the most." Rubio plans to expand his restaurants throughout Southern California and eventually statewide. Thanks to integrated marketing communications, the fish taco has become a local staple.[1] ◆

LOCAL ADVERTISING: WHERE THE ACTION IS

Of the billions of dollars spent every year on advertising in the United States, almost half is spent by local businesses on **local advertising**—businesses in a particular city or county targeting customers in the same geographic area.

Local advertising is sometimes called *retail advertising* because so much is placed by retail stores. But retail advertising isn't *necessarily* local—Sears and J. C. Penney advertise nationally. Many businesses besides retail stores use local advertising—banks, real estate brokers, movie theaters, auto mechanics, plumbers, radio and TV stations, restaurants, funeral homes, museums, and arts organizations (see Exhibit 18–2).

Local advertising is critically important because most consumer sales are made—or lost—locally. An auto manufacturer may spend millions advertising new cars nationwide, but if its dealers don't make a strong effort locally, the dollars will be wasted. When it comes to making the sale and dealing with customers, local advertising is where the action is.

Types of Local Advertisers

There are four main types of local advertisers.

- Dealerships or local franchises of regional and national companies that specialize in one main product line or service (Toyota, Wendy's, Mailboxes Etc., or H&R Block).
- Stores that sell a variety of branded merchandise usually on a nonexclusive basis (convenience, grocery, and department stores).

EXHIBIT • 18-2

Many nonretail businesses, including arts organizations, use local advertising.

- Specialty businesses and services (banks, insurance brokers, restaurants, music stores, shoe repair shops, remodeling contractors, florists, hair salons, travel agencies, attorneys, and accountants).
- Governmental, quasi-governmental, and nonprofit organizations (municipalities, utility companies, charities, arts organizations, political candidates).

The Difference between National and Local Advertising

The basic principles used in national advertising also apply to local advertising. But local advertisers have special problems stemming from the practical, day-to-day realities of running a small business. As a result, local and national advertisers differ in terms of *focus, time orientation,* and *resources* (see Exhibit 18–3).

Focus

National companies are concerned about building their brands, so their advertising focuses on the competitive features of one brand over another, especially in conquest sales situations. Local merchants or dealers often carry hundreds of different brands or numerous models of an exclusive brand, so they focus on attracting customers to a particular **point**—their place of business. That's why local car dealers typically advertise their dealerships rather than the make of car. And local grocers promote brands for which they receive co-op advertising and trade allowances from the national manufacturer.

In every product category, big companies wage an incessant battle for share of market against a small number of competitors, and every share point is worth millions of dollars. Local advertisers, faced with many companies competing for consumer dollars, focus on gross sales or volume—60 cars a month, 5 new insurance policies a week, 55 oil changes a day.

National advertisers plan *strategically* to launch, build, and sustain brands. Local advertisers think *tactically.* Will a new $15,000 sign bring more people in the store? Should we stay open Labor Day? Can we attract more lunchtime customers by offering free refills on soft drinks?

The relationship with the customer may be the greatest difference between national and local advertisers. National advertisers' marketing executives rarely see customers; instead they traditionally think in terms of large groups of people—segments, niches, target markets—with various geographic, demographic, or psychographic descriptions. Their strategies and campaigns are designed to appeal to these large groups.

But local advertisers deal with customers every day. And local advertisers (and their families) interact with their customers in nonbusiness ways—they may be neighbors, friends, or schoolmates. The local advertiser gets feedback

EXHIBIT • 18-3

Differences between local and national advertisers.

	National	Local
Focus	Brand Share of market Strategies Markets	Point Volume, gross sales Tactics Customers
Time	Long-term campaigns	Short-term ads
Resources	$5–$10 million+ Many specialists	Less than $1 million A few generalists

every day—on the company's advertising, prices, product performance, employee service, store decor, and the new sign out front.

Time Orientation

Due to differences in their focus and perspective, national and local advertisers also have a different time orientation. National companies think long-term. They develop five-year strategic plans and budget for annual advertising campaigns. Local advertisers worry that this week's ad in the *Pennysaver* didn't *pull* as well as last week's—a term rarely used by national marketers. A New York ad agency may have months to develop a network TV campaign; the little agency on Main Street may have to churn out a new newspaper ad every week for each of its local clients.

Resources

Finally, national advertisers have more resources available—both money and people. Local advertisers who spend $100,000 a year have a very large budget. National advertisers need *at least* $5 million to $10 million a year (Chrysler spends $400 million) just to get started.

The national advertiser has an army of specialists dedicated to the successful marketing of its brands. The local advertiser may have a small staff or just one person—the owner—to market the business. The local entrepreneur has to know as much as possible about every facet of marketing communications.

LOCAL ADVERTISERS: THE ORIGINAL INTEGRATORS

At the 1993 meeting of the American Association of Advertising Agencies, its president John O'Toole said that larger agencies must learn from their smaller brethren whose top account managers (often the agency owners) have become expert in the other, increasingly popular avenues to the consumer's consciousness—sales promotion, direct marketing, product PR, and Yellow Pages, for example—because that's what the client needed.[2]

O'Toole was referring to the simple fact that local advertisers—and their agencies—are not stuck with the traditional national view that advertising means "ads placed in the media." By necessity, local advertisers wear many hats every day—tending the cash register, dealing with customers, preparing mailers, writing and placing ads, evaluating suppliers' trade promotions, answering phone inquiries, sprucing up the office, talking to newspaper editors, or coordinating the graphics on premiums for a seasonal promotion (see Exhibit 18–4). By successfully combining personal selling with media advertising, direct marketing, sales promotion, and public relations, the local advertiser is the consummate integrator of marketing communications.

PLANNING THE ADVERTISING EFFORT

The key to success in advertising is adequate and continuous planning, and this is just as true on the local level as on the national. Ralph Rubio made planning a continuous, flexible process that allowed for change, improvement, new facts, and new ideas. Successful local advertisers follow the same steps as national advertisers: analyzing the market and the competitive situation, conducting research, determining objectives and strategy, establishing a realistic budget, and planning media and creative strategy (see Appendixes A and B for practical marketing and advertising plan outlines).

A local company has several planning alternatives, depending on the nature of the business and the market. It can use the traditional planning process or a bottom-up marketing approach, both of which we discussed in Chapter 7. Or,

EXHIBIT • 18-4

A business that sells locally promotes its company's identity in a variety of ways—such as designing a logo and putting it everywhere a customer might see it.

once it has developed a viable database of customers and prospects, it can use the seven-step IMC Planning Model discussed in Chapter 16. The latter can even be used to project the return on investment that would be produced by using different strategies.[3]

Analyzing the Local Market and Competitive Situation

The needs of the local market and the purchase behavior of potential customers influence the goods and services a local business offers, the prices it sets, and the design, style, and placement of its advertising and other marketing communications. An area may be rural or urban, conservative or progressive, high- or low-income, white-collar or blue-collar. Local advertisers must understand the needs of their marketplace to prevent advertising misfires (see Exhibit 18–5).

Within a five-mile radius of a business may be many different areas where people work and live. Competing for customers within the same radius may be shopping centers, malls, and a central business district. Advertisers have to decide on the type of customers they want to attract and then determine the boundaries of their **local trading area**—the primary geographic area from which most customers come. Advertising outside the local trading area is a waste. Depending on the type of business, customers may come from the immediate neighborhood or miles away. Arby's identifies its local trading area and segments markets within it by drive time; 75 percent of Arby's customers travel 11 minutes or less from their home or workplace to the restaurant (see Exhibit 18–6).[4]

Advertisers need to study their local competitors. What merchandise and

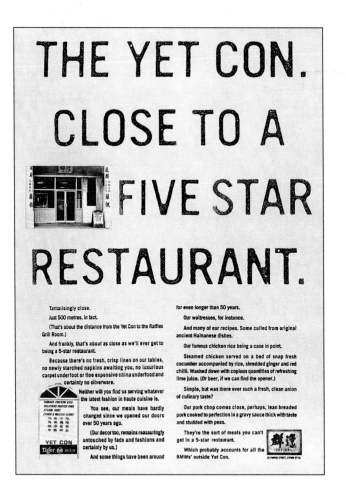

services do they offer? What is the pricing strategy? Where are they located?
How large are they? What is their advertising strategy? What media do they use?
How much do they spend on advertising? Do their places of business invite or
repel customers? By constantly studying the competition, local advertisers discover new ideas, comparative advantages and disadvantages, new merchandising techniques, and new material for ad campaigns.

Conducting Adequate Research

To analyze their situation correctly, local advertisers must answer many important questions. Who are our present customers and our potential customers?
How many are there? Where are they located? Where do they now buy the
merchandise or services we want to sell to them? Can we offer customers
anything they are not getting at the present time? If so, what? How can our
company best appeal to them? What are the best ways to make contact with
them?

Frequently, local advertisers can't afford to use market research firms so they
conduct their research informally. And local ad agencies can often help.

Chapter 6 discusses the two types of research data: *secondary data,* information collected by others that can be adapted to the needs of the advertiser, and
primary data, collected directly from the marketplace about the problem at
hand. How does the local advertiser get access to this information?

Arby's can segment markets by how long it takes customers to drive to the restaurant. The advertising appeal to people closer to the restaurant is convenience; for those farther away, it might be special menu selections.

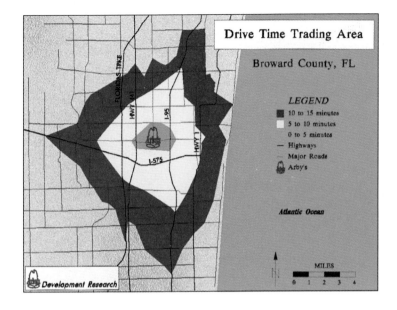

Sources of Secondary Data

Local advertisers get secondary data from their own customer and sales records and from manufacturers and suppliers, trade publications and associations, local advertising media, and various government organizations.

Customer and Sales Analysis Smart local advertisers build a database of charge and cash customers—using sales slips, coupons, customer complaint cards, etc. By correlating their customers' addresses with census information, they can develop other useful information, including average age and income, family size, education, and vehicle and home ownership.

Retail stores should tabulate sales by merchandise classification to identify changes in consumer buying patterns. Some retailers also compare their sales to those of others in the area. (Information about other companies' sales can be obtained from some of the sources mentioned below.)

Manufacturers and Suppliers Many manufacturers and suppliers supply data on the consumers of their products, and some conduct dealer seminars to explain their research findings. They want their dealers to succeed.

Retail Trade Publications and Associations Hundreds of trade publications (like *Stores, Progressive Grocer, Automotive News, Farm Supplier, Hotel & Motel Management*) contain news of important trends, new technologies, and relevant research studies. A complete list of publications is available at any library in *The Standard Periodical Directory* or *Ulrich's International Periodicals Directory*.

Many trade associations (like the Menswear Retailers of America, National Association of Drug Stores, and American Society of Travel Agents) also publish research findings for their members.

Advertising Media and Media Associations In large cities, major newspapers and broadcast stations provide in-depth market data about the communities they serve. Local newspapers and broadcasters also usually belong to national associations whose research findings can be passed on to advertisers.

CHECKLIST   Local Advertising Objectives

◇ **To introduce new customers.** Every year, many customers are lost due to relocation, death, inconvenience, or dissatisfaction. To thrive, a business must continually seek new customers, primarily through advertising.

◇ **To build awareness and image.** Many local businesses provide the same services, so stores use advertising to distinguish themselves.

◇ **To help retain local customers and increase their frequency of visits.** A steady, consistent advertising program keeps present customers informed and reinforces their desire to visit more often.

◇ **To reduce sales expense.** By building traffic and preselling many customers, advertising lightens the load on sales personnel and allows them to make more sales in a shorter time.

◇ **To curtail seasonal peaks.** Consistent advertising helps level sales peaks and valleys.

◇ **To accelerate inventory turnover.** Advertising can increase retail sales. The more times inventory turns, the more profit can be made.

Government Organizations Various government bureaus provide information to local advertisers—data on population projections, births and deaths, marriages, and so on. The Small Business Administration (SBA) publishes a wealth of information on a wide variety of topics, most of it free or available for a nominal charge.

And the U.S. Department of Commerce also offers publications including *Retail Data Sources for Market Analysis, Census Tract Studies,* the *U.S. Industrial Outlook, Current Retail Trade, Survey of Current Business, Monthly Department Store Sales, County and City Data Book,* and more.

Acquiring Primary Data

Local advertisers sometimes perform their own research to study customer attitudes and satisfaction or advertising effectiveness.

Customer Attitudes and Satisfaction Salespeople often provide valuable information about customers and their likes and complaints. Customers think a store cares if it actively seeks such information from them. Some businesses provide customer comment forms for suggestions, improvement ideas, and merchandise recommendations.

Advertising Testing Local advertisers run so many ads that pretesting is unusual. But posttesting does help determine an ad's impact. Some advertisers provide a discount coupon in an ad—or offer a premium to the first 50 callers—and tabulate the number of responses. And employees can ask customers where they heard about the business or promotion.

Determining Objectives and Strategy

Determining the objectives and strategies of any business—local, regional, or national—is the most important policy decision management ever makes. Objectives and strategies give direction to the enterprise and continuity to its promotional efforts. They should be highly specific, written, reviewed frequently, and updated or revised regularly.

The objectives of local advertisers frequently differ from those of national advertisers. National manufacturers typically emphasize long-term objectives (share of market, image, and brand loyalty); local advertisers want to keep the cash register ringing by increasing traffic, turning over inventory, and bringing in new customers (see the Checklist of Local Advertising Objectives). So local advertisers stage constant promotions, sales, and clearances to create immediate activity. The trade-off, of course, is that after a promotion or sale the traffic may stop.

While John O'Toole correctly suggests that large companies can learn a lot from their smaller brethren, the reverse is also true. Local advertisers need to think of longer-term objectives first and then develop short-term goals to achieve them. This tends to reduce their reliance on constant promotions and helps them develop a more stable image.

A local advertiser has the same options as a national advertiser for developing its marketing strategy: product, price, place, and promotion.

Product

A local company's advertising creates awareness of the type and range of merchandise and services it offers. But local advertisers must also find ways to differentiate their businesses and position them competitively. An unusual tactic (like phone orders, free home delivery, or a fish taco) might give the business a competitive angle—if it's different enough. (Review the discussion of bottom-up marketing in Chapter 7.) Exhibit 18–7 shows how one advertiser differentiates itself.

For the new or expanding business, research can help determine if a product concept is viable and the best merchandise and services to offer—at what price.

Price

For the local advertiser, pricing strategy is critical; it's a competitive decision, a major element of the overall product concept, and an important influence on the advertising used. What prices will the local market support? What should be included in the price? What about terms, warranties, and refunds? What about the use of charge cards? Do pricing policies support the business's desired image?

In spite of the tendency to cut prices in competitive situations, local advertisers can succeed without competing on price. But they must offer substantial added value—and all their marketing communications must reflect that value.

EXHIBIT • 18-7

This ad differentiates the advertiser from other professional services.

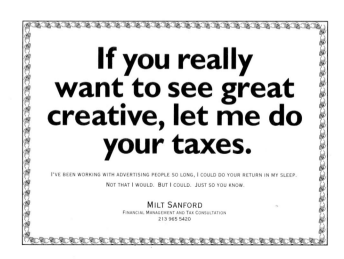

If you really want to see great creative, let me do your taxes.

I'VE BEEN WORKING WITH ADVERTISING PEOPLE SO LONG, I COULD DO YOUR RETURN IN MY SLEEP. NOT THAT I WOULD. BUT I COULD. JUST SO YOU KNOW.

MILT SANFORD
FINANCIAL MANAGEMENT AND TAX CONSULTATION
213 965 5420

AD LAB 18-A   Mistakes Commonly Made by Local Advertisers

Inattention to the Advertising Effort Advertising may get too little attention because of distractions, lack of time, or lack of skill or interest.

Ego Involvement Some advertisers appear in their own ads. This practice is dangerous: most are not effective spokespersons.

Inadequate Supply of Merchandise If advertised merchandise isn't available, advertising dollars are wasted, and customer goodwill suffers.

Unqualified Individuals Handling the Advertising Successful advertising requires competent people to plan, produce, and implement it.

Using Advertising to Compensate for Mistakes Good advertising can't compensate for a bad location, poor selection, untrained personnel, unreasonably high prices, or bad service.

Lack of Knowledge about What to Advertise To succeed, an ad

must tout merchandise or services people want. Advertise items that already sell well. Promote nationally advertised brands. They're known, they take less explanation, and they build the local advertiser's reputation by association with a well-known product.

Overspending on Noncommercial Advertising Ads in charity publications rarely prove cost-effective.

Lack of Coordination Employees must know about the ads so they can answer customer questions, merchandise must be priced and marked as advertised, and local advertising should be coordinated with manufacturers' national advertising to strengthen the campaign.

Laboratory Applications

1. As a consumer of local advertising, identify and describe mistakes you've noticed in addition to those given above.
2. What should local advertisers do to correct their mistakes?

Place

It has been said that the three most important things in retail are location, location, and location. Certainly, a good, high-visibility location can reduce the amount of money needed for advertising, but the savings may be more than offset by high rent. The location decision is a difficult one that requires extensive research and analysis.

Three principal factors influence where a business should be located: the intended product concept, the size and proximity of the trading area needed for the business to prosper, and the rent the business can afford. Some advertisers use low rent as a tactic and promote the fact that their location is hard to find but worth the search. They claim they pass the savings on to their customers.

Promotion

A local business's strategic plan should spell out the role of personal selling, media advertising, product or store publicity, sales promotion, direct mail, collateral materials, and local event sponsorship.

Businesses can be highly promotional, semipromotional, or nonpromotional. A business that has few regular customers and relies on discount prices, sales, and other promotions (such as auto dealers) has to do a great deal of advertising (**highly promotional strategy**). A business that has regular customers but uses periodic sales and promotions to increase store traffic (such as a men's clothing store) needs a **semipromotional strategy.** A business with a loyal, regular clientele (a hair salon, for example) may need only minimal advertising or promotion—a **nonpromotional strategy.**

The promotional strategy dictates the style of advertising and the type of media employed. Unfortunately, many local advertisers give too little thought to integrating their advertising with their overall business objectives. See Ad Lab 18-A.

Establishing the Budget

Most businesses find it difficult to determine an appropriate advertising budget. The most important influence is the policies established when the business sets its objectives and strategies. Other influences include:

- Location. A business that depends on walk-in traffic probably needs to do more advertising if it is located in an isolated, hard-to-find area.
- Age and character of the firm. New businesses need to advertise more.
- Size of the business. A small business doesn't have the revenues to spend on extensive advertising.
- Type of product or service offered. A well-known, highly regarded business may need only a minimal ad budget because of good word of mouth.
- Size of the trading area. Small trading areas justify small ad budgets.
- Competitive activity. Businesses often need to match the ad budgets of their competitors.
- Media availability, coverage, and cost. Although local media cost less, advertisers must be careful not to waste money on unnecessary coverage.
- Previous advertising results. Positive results from previous campaigns usually justify a similar or larger budget. If results were disappointing, the budget is likely to be reduced—although that may be the wrong conclusion.

Local advertisers should set a budget that optimizes the amount of advertising money spent. It's actually easier to waste money by spending too little than by spending too much. (Local retailers typically spend about 1 to 3 percent of total sales on advertising, although furniture stores, hotels, theaters, and jewelry stores may spend 4 to 7 percent.)

Budgeting Strategy

Advertising programs must have continuity, and be timed when prospects are most receptive to buying. Many businesses' sales fluctuate month to month (as shown in Exhibit 18–8); advertising dollars should be timed to correlate with their potential sales volume.

Local advertisers use several methods to budget their advertising expenditures (some were discussed in Chapter 7). However, most use the percentage-of-sales method since it is the simplest to calculate and the easiest to defend with bookkeepers and accountants.

Advertising has become such a large and complicated activity that many

EXHIBIT • 18-8

Total retail sales by types of stores. Note that different types have different peak seasons.

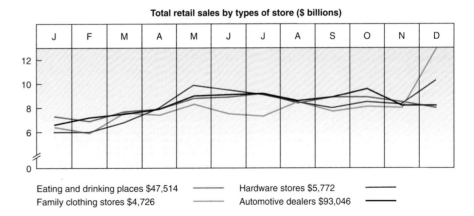

Total retail sales by types of store ($ billions)

Eating and drinking places $47,514 ———   Hardware stores $5,772 ———
Family clothing stores $4,726 ———   Automotive dealers $93,046 ———

local advertisers use computers to determine their advertising budgets. Software programs can analyze the previous year's sales along with various influencing factors to determine a budget based on anticipated sales for the current year.

Developing the Annual Sales and Advertising Calendar

Not all local advertisers have the computer software to forecast sales, but by doing some basic research, most can do an adequate job on their own. Questions to answer include: What is the anticipated increase in population for the local area during the next year? What is the anticipated increase or decrease in overall retail sales? What is the outlook for local employment? How are similar businesses doing? Local accountants, bankers, trade associations, media representatives, and the local Chamber of Commerce can help answer these questions.

Advertisers need to develop a realistic sales plan for the year, month by month and even week by week. Then they can formulate an advertising expense plan. (See the Checklist for Setting Local Advertising Budgets.)

Advertising should precede sales—i.e., the money should be spent just before customers are most likely to buy. Experienced advertisers first compute the percentage of yearly sales anticipated for each month (or, better yet, each week) and plot this information on a graph. Next, they plot an advertising curve that slightly precedes the sales curve, as shown by the dashed lines in Exhibit 18–9. (Note that advertising peaks are slightly lower than sales peaks but valleys are slightly higher, indicating that the unit cost of advertising is typically a little higher when sales are low.) The advertising curve indicates what percentage of the annual advertising expenditure the business should spend each month.

Finally, by plotting sales as the year progresses, advertisers can compare actual figures to their weekly and monthly projections.

Many local advertisers also use a **monthly promotional calendar** to track media schedules, costs, in-house promotions, sales, and special events.

Selecting Local Advertising Media

Choosing the right media vehicles for local advertising is important for two reasons. First, most local advertisers' budgets are limited. Second, certain media are more effective than others for certain types of businesses.

In developing their communication strategy, local advertisers should consider all avenues available and integrate them creatively. This includes mass media as well as direct mail, sales promotion, publicity, community events, and

EXHIBIT • 18-9

A budget from a properly funded advertising program should look like this —— not like this ——.

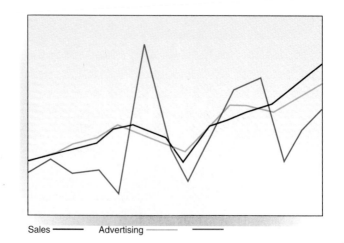

Sales ————   Advertising ————   ————

CHECKLIST   Setting Local Advertising Budgets

Set a Sales Goal

◇ Write the sales figures for each month last year—for the whole store and each department. Review this performance, your own knowledge of this year's picture, and estimate sales goals for next year. Use these profit pointers:

- Last year's sales by month.
- Population, income, employment levels.
- New and expanded departments.
- Tie-ins with merchandising events.
- What competitors are doing, getting.
- New selling and advertising alternatives.

Decide How Much Advertising

◇ Write the advertising dollars spent each month last year. Then, considering the planned sales goal and what the competition is likely to do, write the planned advertising budget for the coming year. Check the budget (as a percent of sales) against the expenditures of other stores in the same classification using the following profit pointers:

- Stores in less favorable locations advertise more.
- So do stores that are new and expanding.
- Strong competition raises the size of the budget needed.
- Stores emphasizing price usually promote more.
- Special dates and events offer additional sales opportunities.

- Added sales produced by increased expenditure are more profitable—more money can be spent to get them.
- Co-op support can stretch ad dollars and increase ad frequency.

Decide What to Promote

◇ Let experience guide what advertising weight to give each department each month.

- Check the month's heavy traffic pullers.
- Look for departments whose seasonal curve is about to drop.
- Look for "sleepers"—hot-selling items that didn't show up in last year's figures.
- Promote newly expanded departments harder.
- Calculate co-op support.

Make a Schedule

◇ For each month, fill in a day-by-day schedule to take full advantage of:

- Paydays of important local employers.
- Days of the week traffic is heaviest.
- National and local merchandising events.
- New or expanded departments.
- Current prices and stock on hand—jot down items, prices, and ad sizes for each day.

---

even decor, packaging, and signage. The objective must always be clear, consistent communications to all stakeholders—employees, customers, prospects, and the references that influence them.

Local Mass Media

Every community has some form of mass media available to local advertisers: a daily or weekly paper, free distribution shoppers, local consumer or business magazines, outdoor advertising, and local radio or TV.

Newspapers Local advertisers use newspapers more than any other medium. The local newspaper is the shopper's most trusted source of local information.[5] (See Exhibit 18–10.) Newspapers offer other advantages as well:

- Most newspapers are oriented to the local community.
- The cost is low for the number of prospects reached.
- Advertising can be placed on very short notice.
- Some selectivity is possible by advertising in special-interest sections.
- Consumers take their time to read the newspaper so ads have a longer life.

Drawbacks to newspapers include limited selectivity, inconsistent reproduction quality, and potential ad clutter. Nevertheless, more than 50 percent of local advertising expenditures go to newspapers, with television and radio far behind

Some of the benefits local newspapers offer are shown in this ad for the *Oregonian*.

Run your ads in The Oregonian instead of on TV, and eliminate the competition.

The Oregonian has some bad news to report: Studies indicate that over 50% of today's television viewers don't pay attention to commercials.

They're busy doing more interesting things. Like sprinting for the bathroom. Raiding the fridge. Exercising their thumbs on the remote control.

Problems, we'd like to remind you, you'll never encounter when running a newspaper ad. Because newspaper is the one, and probably only, medium where people actually look forward to seeing your advertising.

In study after study, consumers call the newspaper the most helpful, believable and influential source of advertising information available.

And The Oregonian delivers over 555,000 of those consumers every day—a whopping 91% of the Portland metro population after just one week.

To find out more, call Brian Bounous here at The Oregonian: 221-8279. Because not even the best TV spot can grab the consumer's mind if it's in the bathroom at the moment. **The Oregonian**

at 13 and 11 percent, respectively. The rest of the local advertising pie is split between direct mail, outdoor, magazines, and miscellaneous forms of advertising.

Many daily newspapers offer a service called **total market coverage (TMC)** to compete with such increasingly popular ad media as free papers, direct mail, and "shoppers" (to be discussed shortly). A TMC is a free advertising vehicle sent weekly to 100 percent of the residents in the newspaper's market area. It may be in tabloid or similar format and may contain varying amounts of editorial matter as well as ads. Some newspapers prefer to call the TMC "alternative distribution" since the publication may be sent through the mail or hand delivered by newspaper employees.

Since the ads in TMCs are the same as those run in the paper, no ad production costs are incurred. The biggest drawback is uncertainty of readership. Just because people receive something doesn't mean they read it.

Newspapers have both display and classified advertising departments; both are usually equipped to handle copy, art, typesetting, and layout/design. Often the service is free. Large papers even have personnel who visit an advertiser's place of business to do artwork for ads.

For more details on newspaper advertising, review Chapter 13.

Shoppers and Free Papers A growing number of cities have all-ad publications called **shoppers** (or *Pennysavers*) published as a forum for local advertisers. Some shoppers distribute their publications through the mail and offer total circulation in a given area; others print separate editions for ZIP code groupings.

Some shopper publications respond to competition from TMCs by adding editorial content. The Long Island *Center Island Pennysavers* used to be 100 percent ads. But with competition from *Newsday Extra*, a weekly TMC of the giant New York daily, the shopper switched to 70 percent ads and 30 percent local news. Said the shopper's publisher: "We went to local news because our

EXHIBIT • 18-11

Magazines use glossy paper, colored inks, and fine image and text resolution—all elements that make them an ideal medium for upscale ads.

advertisers wanted it and because *Newsday* couldn't really cover the local news."[6]

In addition to shoppers, many cities have free newspapers, usually geared toward entertainment information and distributed in establishments that advertise in them and at other key locations. People tend to like them and read them, often because the papers provide information they can't get elsewhere. But distribution can be erratic.

Magazines Slick, special-interest city magazines give local advertisers the opportunity to reach upper-income prospects through a prestigious medium. See Exhibit 18–11. Publications like *Palm Springs, Life, Dallas Home and Garden,* and *Los Angeles Magazine* offer excellent photographic reproduction as well. Local advertisers who seek even greater prestige and selectivity can use special city or regional editions of major national publications such as *Time, Newsweek,* and *Sports Illustrated.* However, magazine advertising is costly, it may reach people outside the advertiser's trading area, and it requires two or three months' lead time.

Review Chapter 13 for further information about magazine advertising.

Electronic Media Local advertisers buy time on radio and TV because these media usually reach a strictly local audience, offer high impact, and have a relatively low cost per thousand. Because effective broadcast advertising requires multiple exposures, however, some advertisers consider it too costly.

Radio and TV advertising offers good selectivity, immediacy, believability, and prestige. Top-40 radio stations, for example, are ideal advertising media for stereo stores. Local personalities, or the advertisers themselves, can present the commercial message personally. Even Hollywood celebrities will pitch local business; former sitcom stars often work for scale—$366 a day for local TV ads, less for radio commercials.[7]

Most radio and TV stations help local advertisers write and produce commercials for a nominal charge.

For additional information on broadcast advertising, review Chapters 11 and 14.

EXHIBIT • 18-12

Carlos Murphy's restaurant uses the stopping power of outdoor advertising to put across a witty wordplay on the restaurant's sea-food selections and create the perception of a fun place to go—which it is.

Local Outdoor and Sign Advertising The most direct way for local businesses to reach customers is with signs. Local advertisers use in-store and on-store signs, outdoor advertising, and transit advertising. See Exhibit 18–12. Signs offer mass exposure with color, size, and very low cost per viewer. Signs used to promote specific products usually tout items with continuous appeal such as cars or fast-food restaurants.

One disadvantage of signs is the advertiser's inability to make frequent changes. Also most local governments have strict sign ordinances. An upscale Beverly Hills supermarket was allowed only one sign—the name of the store minus the logo.[8]

Most sign companies offer free copy and art services, but sign production is usually quite expensive.

Chapter 15 gives more complete information on the use of outdoor and transit advertising.

Local Direct Mail

Direct-mail advertising can reach specific market segments and neighborhoods. One popular type of local direct mail is **shared mail** in which ads of two or more advertisers are included in a single mail package targeted by ZIP code. The method was introduced in 1980 by ADVO-System of Windsor, Connecticut; in 1990 alone the company mailed more than 18 billion ad pieces.[9] Two-thirds of ADVO-System's 25,000 clients are small, local businesses—mostly retail stores, food stores, do-it-yourself stores, and chain drugstores. Shared mail can be sent to selected ZIP codes to reach only those households in the advertiser's targeted area.

Direct mail has no competition from other advertisers at the same time. And local advertisers with limited budgets use direct mail to great advantage. Most local direct-mail houses offer copy, art, and printing as well as mailing services.

For more on direct-mail advertising, review Chapter 15.

Specialized Media for Local Advertisers

In addition to mass media and direct mail, local advertisers have a wide selection of alternative communication vehicles at their disposal: classified directories, handbills and flyers, various sales promotion techniques, free publicity in the news media, and community involvement.

EXHIBIT • 18-13

Newspaper advertising, a favorite medium for local advertisers, allows use of coupons.

Classified Directories Yellow Pages directories, published by both telephone and private companies, are a vital advertising medium for local businesses because Yellow Pages stay in the home or office as a ready source of information. In fact, the Yellow Pages are the sole means of advertising for many local businesses. Every business with a telephone gets a one-line listing free; additional advertising must be paid for (depending on the community, it can be quite expensive).

Local communities in large urban areas and on military bases usually have privately published classified telephone directories, which are less expensive than the large telephone company directories. These directories cater to the special interests of the immediate locale and therefore offer excellent support to the small retail merchant or professional service.

The current proliferation of directories makes it difficult for advertisers to choose. If advertisers appear in every directory, their ad budget will be shot; but staying out of key directories might be a mistake as well.

Chapter 15 provides additional information on the use of Yellow Pages advertising.

Handbills **Handbills** may be single sheets **(flyers)** or multipage ads **(circulars)** and can be distributed on the street, in parking lots, or door-to-door. The main advantages of handbills are low cost, fast production, flexibility, and direct distribution to the target audience. Disadvantages include a high level of throwaways, poor production quality, and clutter.[10] Handbills are especially useful for announcing a grand opening or sale, or for informing people of a special service (like car detailing). Handbills should be carefully planned for a good appearance. A good printer can provide advice about the quality of paper, colors, size, cost, and general appearance. The copy is the advertiser's responsibility.

Sales Promotion Vehicles Many sales promotion methods discussed in Chapter 16—including coupons, sampling, specialty advertising, and contests and special events—are particularly effective for local advertisers.

Coupons provide a special inducement to make a purchase. They can be used to build store traffic, to encourage first use, and to test the effectiveness of a particular ad. See Exhibit 18–13. Some local advertisers leave space in the coupon for the name, address, and phone number of the respondent—a great way to build a database for an IMC or bottom-up marketing program.

Debbie Fields—of Mrs. Fields' Cookies—discovered that giving the customer a small **sample** is highly effective. Other businesses that use sampling are ice cream stores, delicatessens, bakeries, and fabric stores.

Specialty items, including calendars, rulers, coffee mugs, shoehorns, and pens, are inexpensive for the retailer but can be valuable to the customer. These items generally contain the store name, and often a brief sales message. Some specialty items are so popular, customers will buy them. T-shirts, caps, and clever bumper stickers help advertise the business all over town.

Local advertisers often schedule **contests and special events,** ranging from grand opening contests to product demonstrations to lectures and films, to get customers in the door. The First Wisconsin Bank of Appleton designed several grand opening contests as part of a promotional extravaganza that cost about $100,000 and brought in a remarkable $8 million in deposits within three months.[11]

Many retailers develop their own demonstrations tailored to their product line and market. Bridal shops give sessions on how to plan for a wedding, and sporting goods stores hire a golf pro to give lessons. Other retailers rely on manufacturers to present demonstrations.

Another type of special event is a show. Clothing stores sponsor fashion shows, hardware stores stage building and home shows, and local car dealers stage new-car shows.

Publicity Local firms find that **publicity** is often more cost-effective than advertising and offers greater credibility. The media are always on the lookout for unusual items that may interest their audiences. However, the advertiser must take the initiative to call the media or send a well-written press release— and then hope the media follows through.

Examples of newsworthy events might include major grand openings, unusual merchandise, important personnel changes, an autograph signing by a celebrity, an unusual display, or a tie-in with a local sports event (giving away free baseball caps to everyone who attends a game).

When *Les Misérables* played in Montreal, the production company did something unusual. They presented the whole musical in both English and French—on alternate nights. This created intense interest from local media editors, and the show was sold out every night (see Exhibit 18–14).

Community involvement can effectively enhance a business's image. It can involve sponsoring a local activity such as a baseball team, a summer camp for needy youngsters, or a scholarship. Some businesses allow store facilities to be used for social or civic organizations for fund-raisers or meetings. Many businesses such as banks and savings associations have rooms designed for community use.

The Local Media Mix: Integrating All the Elements

A local advertising plan usually involves a mix of media. Younkers department stores in Des Moines, Iowa, advertises primarily in the Des Moines *Register.* But the company also uses smaller newspapers, radio, TV, telemarketing, and direct mail. In the *Register,* Younkers runs hard-sell ads every Thursday, Friday, and Saturday and an idea ad on Sundays. Radio stations are carefully selected for specific commercials aimed at particular markets. TV commercials are used for major promotions, such as spring and fall sales. But Younkers management considers direct mail the most dollar-effective. The store mails primarily to its own list of charge customers, but the direct-mail program has been so success-

When *Les Misérables* ran in Montreal, the ads and the show ran in English and French.

ful that many former and random-purchase customers return as steady buyers.[12] The majority of Younkers' direct-mail pieces are tabloids or catalogs. Customers can order through the mail or by phone in addition to purchasing the items in the store. Younkers also transforms its direct-mail pieces into inserts for the *Register* and other papers.

Although this media mix works well for a department store in the Midwest, choosing the best mix for a particular business in a specific location is an art in itself.

CREATING LOCAL ADVERTISING

Cal Worthington first pitched his car dealership on Los Angeles TV stations in 1951. He sponsors third-rate movies on late-night and Saturday afternoon TV, and 42 years later, he's still at it. In his zany ads, he often appears in cowboy garb with a variety of domesticated wild animals (all introduced as "my dog Spot"). Some low-budget, do-it-yourself advertisers like Worthington are so successful they engender a near-cult following. Others who try the same approach fail miserably.

In print advertising, many local advertisers achieve remarkable success with what professionals would call a "schlock" approach—heavy bold type, items crowded into advertising space, loud headlines, and unsophisticated graphic design.

If the message is honest, consistent, effective, and meets the advertiser's objectives, that may be all that matters. To direct and control the creative aspects of their ads and commercials—and ensure consistency—local advertisers should develop a checklist of creative dos and don'ts. (See the Checklist for Creating Local Advertising.)

Types of Local Advertising

Most local media ads are either *product* or *institutional* advertising. **Product advertising** promotes a specific product or service and stimulates short-term

---

CHECKLIST   Creating Local Advertising

◇ **Make your ads easily recognizable.** Ads with unique art, layout, and typefaces have higher readership. Make the ads distinctively different but keep the appearance consistent.

◇ **Use a simple layout.** The layout should carry the reader's eye through the message easily and in proper sequence from headline to illustration to explanatory copy to price to store name. Avoid using too many typefaces.

◇ **Use a dominant element—a large picture or headline—to ensure quick visibility.** Photos of real people and action pictures win more readership as do photos of local people or places. Color attracts more readers.

◇ **Use a prominent benefit headline.** Feature the main benefit of the merchandise in a compelling headline.

◇ **Let white space work for you.** White space focuses the reader's attention on the ad and makes the headline and illustration stand out.

◇ **Make the copy complete.** Emphasize the benefits most appealing to customers.

◇ **State price or range of prices.** Dollar figures have good attention value, and readers often overestimate omitted prices. Spell out credit and layaway plans.

◇ **Specify branded merchandise.** If the item is a known brand, say so.

◇ **Include related items.** Make two sales instead of one by offering related items along with a featured one.

◇ **Urge readers to buy now.** Ask for the sale. Stimulate prompt action by using "limited supply" or "this week only."

◇ **Don't forget the store name and address.** Check every ad to be certain the store name, address, phone number, and store hours are included.

◇ **Don't be too clever.** Many people distrust or misunderstand cleverness.

◇ **Don't use unusual or difficult words.** Everyone understands simple language. Use it.

◇ **Don't generalize.** Be specific. Shoppers want all the facts before they buy.

◇ **Don't make excessive claims.** Advertisers lose customers by making claims they can't back up.

◇ **Plan ad size carefully.** Attention increases with size.

◇ **Consider your target customers.** People notice ads more if they are directed at their own sex.

◇ **Use tie-ins with local or special news events.**

---

action. **Institutional advertising** attempts to create a specific, favorable, long-term perception of the business as a whole, rather than for a particular product or service.

Product Advertising

Most local product advertising falls into one of three major types: *regular price-line, sale,* and *clearance.*

Regular Price-Line Advertising   These ads inform consumers about services or merchandise offered at regular prices (see Exhibit 18–15). An accounting firm may use regular price-line advertising to promote its accounting and tax services for small businesses. Cal Worthington's commercials fall in this category.

Sale Advertising   To stimulate sales of particular merchandise or increase store traffic, local merchants occasionally place items on sale and advertise special offers—two-for-one specials or reduced prices. Service businesses also run sale ads. A travel agency may advertise a special reduced-fare cruise or a hair salon reduced-price perms.

Clearance Advertising   Local advertisers use **clearance advertising** (a special form of sale advertising) to make room for new product lines or new models and to get rid of slow-moving lines, floor samples, broken or distressed merchandise, or out-of-season items. Companies going out of business also use clearance advertising (see Exhibit 18–16).

Although it doesn't mention price, this ad is regular price-line advertising.

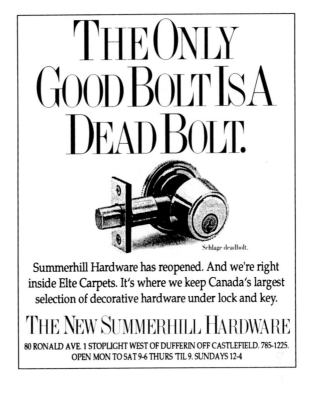

Institutional Advertising

To promote an *idea* about the company and build long-term goodwill, many types of businesses (stores, restaurants, banks, professional firms, and hospitals) use institutional advertising. It makes the public aware of what the business stands for and attempts to build reputation and image. An institutional ad might focus on convenient hours, a new credit policy, store expansion, or company philosophy.

An example of clearance advertising.

This institutional ad educates citizens about the danger of downed power lines and PGE's ability to handle the problem.

(MUSIC MOODY WIND INSTRUMENTS)

ANNCR: The frightening thing about downed pow-erlines is that it's impossible to tell if they're

dangerous or not. Just like it is hard to tell a harless but snake from a deadly cottonmouth. Now, would you pick one up . . . hoping it's the

harmless snake? If you see a downed powerline, don't touch it. Call PGE. We'll handle it.

SUPER: *PORTLAND GENERAL ELECTRIC.*

Although readership is often lower, effective institutional ads can build a favorable image for a business, attract new customers, and encourage customer loyalty. See Exhibit 18–17.

Creating the Message

Coming up with ideas for local ad campaigns can be extremely difficult. When the editors of *Ad/Pro* magazine asked various people "Where do your ideas come from?" the answers were wide ranging. Some looked to the merchandise for ideas; others looked to the customer. Respondents also mentioned magazines, scrapbooks, photography exhibits, and recent movies.[13] Current economic or political events also provide inspiration as shown in Exhibit 18–18.

An important goal of local advertisers is to achieve a consistent, distinctive look that makes the ads both appealing and identifiable. Since 1985 Bullock's department store has placed an ad on the back page of every Sunday edition of the *Los Angeles Times*. And the layout is always the same. Judy Farris, vice president for sales and promotion, noted, "The ad's position is important. It is a consistent statement. Repetition in advertising is important. You can establish an image over time. It has a cumulative effect."[14]

Seeking Creative Assistance

Local advertisers have a number of sources they can turn to for creative help including advertising agencies, the local media, free-lancers and consultants, creative boutiques, syndicated art services, and the co-op advertising programs of wholesalers, manufacturers, and trade associations.

Advertising Agencies

Local advertisers use advertising agencies less extensively than national advertisers. A major reason is that most media, including newspapers, have two sets of advertising rates—one for national advertisers and another for retail or local advertisers. The local rate is lower and not commissionable. Frequency and quantity discounts give local advertisers additional savings.

Many advertisers simply don't spend enough money on advertising to warrant hiring of an agency. And some large agencies don't accept local advertisers because their budgets are too low to support the agency's overhead.

The best ideas for ads come from product features and the market environment. Properly combined, a powerful message can evoke awareness, sentiment, and action.

But every community of any size has reputable small agencies that offer expert assistance to local advertisers. Exhibit 18–19 shows one of a series of inexpensive, local newspaper ads developed by Bos Advertising for a two-store pizza chain in Montreal. The campaign's campy, tongue-in-cheek humor, created in two languages, garnered the Coq D'Or (Golden Rooster) award for best black-and-white campaign of the year—against a lot of high-budget national competition.

A competent agency can help:

Bos Advertising makes fun of advertising in general with turn-of-the century engravings and fictional scenes of people discussing the virtues of Pizzaiolle.

- Analyze the local advertiser's business and the product or service being sold; evaluate the markets for the business including channels of distribution;
- Evaluate the advertiser's competitive position in the marketplace and offer strategic solutions;
- Determine the best communications media and provide advice on the costs and effectiveness of each;
- Devise an integrated communications plan and, once approved, implement it with consistency and creativity.
- Save the advertiser valuable time by taking over media interviewing, analysis, checking, billing, and bookkeeping; and
- Assist in other aspects of the advertising and promotion effort by implementing sales contests, publicity, grand openings, and other activities.

For a complete discussion of advertising agencies, review Chapter 3.

Local Media

Advertising media also offer services to local advertisers from planning campaigns to preparing the ad—often at no charge.

Free-Lancers and Consultants

Free-lance advertising specialists work out of home offices preparing copy, art and layout, photography, or other services at lower rates than an agency. Exhibit 18–20 is a free-lancer's clever ad for his services. Free-lancers often

EXHIBIT • 18–20

In this ad, a local layout artist who also draws displays his work alongside the drawings of well-known advertising agency principals.

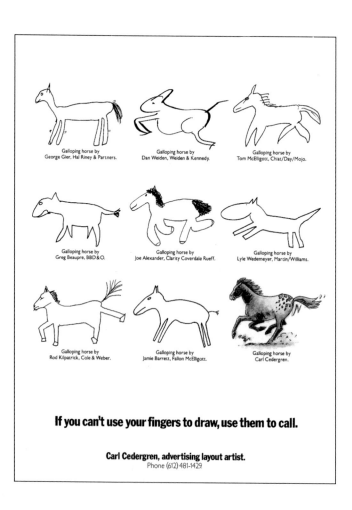

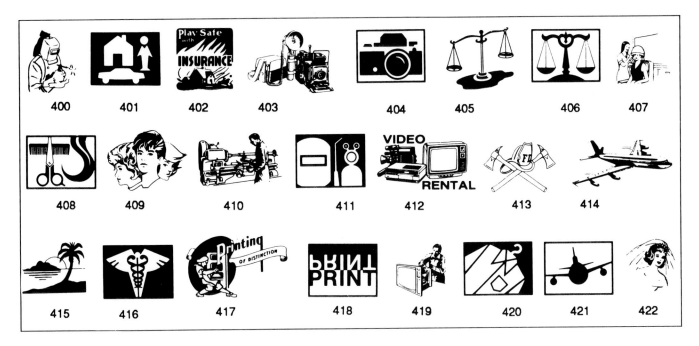

It takes longer to create an original illustration than to research, select, and position a piece of clip art. When local advertisers must do a print ad themselves, clip art is fast and inexpensive. Unfortunately, it tends to be low quality.

specialize by type of work and type of client such as car dealerships, clothing or furniture stores, or travel agencies.

Creative Boutiques

A boutique performs only the creative work; employees specialize as copywriters, graphic designers, and illustrators. Boutiques charge a negotiated fee or a percentage of the media expenditure. Local advertisers who want the best creative work but aren't interested in other services frequently turn to boutiques for help in designing ads and brochures, packaging and signage.

Syndicated Art Services and Desktop Publishing Programs

The importance of co-op advertising dollars.

Store	Co-op dollars as a percentage of total ad budget
Appliance dealers	80%
Clothing stores	35
Department stores	50
Discount stores	20
Drugstores	70
Food stores	75
Furniture stores	30
Household goods	30
Jewelers	30
Shoe stores	50

Syndicated art services offer basic illustrations and graphic elements, called **clip art,** that can be clipped and used in ads. Clip art is available for various types of businesses and is often tied to seasons, holidays, and other promotional angles. Clip art is available by direct subscription, through the advertising department of a local newspaper, and through desktop computer software programs. Exhibit 18–21 shows typical examples from a clip art book.

Cooperative Advertising Programs

Finally, local advertisers can turn to their suppliers and even to their competitors for help. As a service to their distributors and dealers, and to assure proper reproduction of their products, wholesalers and manufacturers as well as trade associations often provide local advertisers with ready-made advertising materials.

In **vertical cooperative advertising,** the manufacturer provides the complete ad and shares the cost of the advertising time or space. The local newspaper sets the name and address of the local advertiser, or the radio station adds a tag line with the advertiser's name, address, and phone number. Exhibit 18–22

AD LAB 18–B   The Co-Op Battleground

On the surface, co-op advertising seems like a great arrangement for retailers. A manufacturer supplies advertising materials (saving the retailer production costs) and pays a percentage of the media cost. The retailer drops in the store's logo, arranges for the ad to run, and collects the co-op dollars from the manufacturer.

Through co-op advertising, the retailer can stretch its ad budget and associate its business with a nationally advertised product. The retailer receives professionally prepared ads and acquires greater leverage with the local media that carry the co-op ads.

But there are some significant drawbacks to the co-op system. A retailer may have to sell a lot of merchandise to qualify for significant co-op funds. More often, the retailer and manufacturer have different advertising objectives and different ideas about how the ads should be executed.

The manufacturer often wants total control, specifying when, where, and in what form the ad runs. The manufacturer expects co-op ads to tie in with its national advertising promotions. It wants the right product advertised at the right time. Retailers have their own ideas about which products to advertise when. They're more concerned with daily volume and with projecting an image of value and variety. An appliance store might prefer to advertise inexpensive TVs even though the manufacturer wants to emphasize its top-of-the-line models.

Manufacturers worry that retailers will place the product in a cluttered, ugly ad or next to inferior products, that the ad will run in inappropriate publications, and that it will not run at the best time. Retailers counter that they know the local market better. In short, manufacturers think they don't have enough control; retailers think they have too much.

A retailer contemplating co-op funds should consider the following questions:

◇ What advertising qualifies in terms of products and special requirements?
◇ What percentage is paid by each party?
◇ When can ads be run?
◇ What media can be used?
◇ Are there special provisions for message content?
◇ What documentation is required for reimbursement?
◇ How does each party benefit?
◇ Do cooperative ads obscure the retailer's image?

Laboratory Application

Look through today's edition of a daily paper in your city. Try to determine which ads qualify as co-op. Do the ads fit the store's image? How do the ads affect the images of the products being featured?

---

lists typical co-op advertising allowances. (See Ad Lab 18–B for the advantages and disadvantages for co-op advertising.)

With **horizontal cooperative advertising,** firms in the same business (real estate agents, insurance agents, pharmacies, car dealers, or travel agents, for example) or in the same part of town advertise jointly. Competing auto dealers pool their dollars to advertise their common retail area as the "Mile of Cars."

NONCOMMERCIAL ADVERTISING

Nonprofit organizations—the government, charities, trade associations, and religious groups—use the same kinds of creative and media strategies as their for-profit counterparts to convey messages to the public. But while commercial advertising is used to stimulate sales, **noncommercial advertising** is used to affect opinions, perceptions, or behavior (see Exhibit 18–23). The objective for an energy conservation program might be to modify behavior, such as turning off the lights. This is an example of *demarketing*; the advertiser is trying to get consumers to buy *less* of a product or service. Exhibit 18–24 compares objectives of commercial and noncommercial advertisers.

Examples of Noncommercial Advertising

In its Partnership for a Drug-Free America a coalition of more than 200 ad agencies, the media, and many other companies in the communications business launched an all-out attack on drug abuse. The coalition stated its goal as

EXHIBIT • 18-23

Urgent Need of Money is the headline in this Canadian Red Cross ad for its annual fund-raising campaign.

the "fundamental reshaping of social attitudes about illegal drug usage." The $1.5 billion antidrug campaign, created at the agencies' own expense, includes hundreds of newspaper and magazine ads as well as 200 different commercials and print ads. The ads' space and time, donated by the media, are worth an estimated $310 million a year.[15] Most of the creative and production suppliers also donate their services.

The ads aim at various target groups: cocaine users, marijuana smokers, parents, and children. Most present hard-hitting messages about the dangers of drug abuse. See Exhibit 18–25.

The effort is billed as the "largest and most ambitious private-sector, voluntary peacetime effort ever undertaken." Participants believe that the United States cannot succeed as a drug culture and that advertising can "de-moralize" drug use.

Not all public service advertising is done on such a massive scale. Many ads tout humanitarian social causes (Cancer Society), political ideas or issues (political candidates), philosophical or religious positions (Church of Jesus Christ of Latter Day Saints), or attitudes and viewpoints (labor unions). In most cases, these ads are created for and placed by nonprofit organizations, and the product they advertise is the organization's particular mission—politics, welfare, religion, conservation, health, art, happiness, or love.

Research conducted by the Partnership for a Drug-Free America proves that noncommercial advertising does change attitudes. The L.A. Fire Department campaign (see Exhibit 18–26) saved innumerable lives and hundreds of thousands of dollars in property damage. By providing information to the public on issues such as health, safety, education, and the environment, noncommercial advertising helps build a better society.

Types of Noncommercial Advertising

One way to categorize noncommercial advertising is by the organizations that use it. Advertising is used by churches, schools, universities, charitable organizations, political groups, and many other *nonbusiness institutions,* and by *associations,* such as labor groups, professional organizations, and trade and civic associations. *Government organizations* also place ads: the U.S. military branches and the Postal Service, the Canadian Ministry of Health, the Social Security Administration, the Internal Revenue Service, and various state and provincial governments (see Exhibit 18–27).

Advertising by Nonbusiness Institutions

Every year, the American Lung Association ("It's a matter of life and breath") places an estimated $10 million worth of ads on TV, radio, newspapers, maga-

EXHIBIT • 18-24

Comparison of advertising objectives.

Product advertising	Noncommercial advertising
Create store traffic.	Stimulate inquiries for information.
Stimulate brand loyalty.	Popularize social cause.
Change buying habits.	Change activity habits.
Increase product use.	Decrease waste of resources.
Communicate product features.	Communicate political viewpoint.
Improve product image.	Improve public attitude.
Inform public of new product.	Inform public of new cure.
Remind people to buy again.	Remind people to give again.

EXHIBIT • 18–25

The Partnership for a Drug Free America is instrumental in focusing attention on the U.S. drug problem. A volunteer effort by the advertising community, the partnership created many award-winning ads like this one urging parents to talk to their kids about drugs.

EXHIBIT • 18–26

This *pro bono* campaign appeared on 120 billboards—English and Spanish versions—as well as numerous magazines and newspapers in the Log Angeles area.

E X H I B I T • 18–27

State governments use advertising to promote and advocate public interest causes.

zines, and outdoor and transit media. The media donate this space and time as a public service. Such donated ads are termed *public service announcements (PSAs)*. The Foster Parents Plan uses advertising to ask readers to adopt children from other countries. The Church of the Nazarene advertises, "Our church can be your home." The National Council on Alcoholism wants children and teenagers to say *no* to drinking, "And say yes to life."

Since newspaper, radio, and TV advertising sales departments are besieged with requests from local churches, charity groups, hospital guilds, and other social organizations, they must charge for most local nonbusiness institution advertising. But every year, each of the three major U.S. networks, ABC, NBC, and CBS, receives ads from about 300 organizations and runs about 8,000 spots—for free.[16]

Advertising by Nonprofit Business Associations

Business, professional, trade, labor, farm, and civic associations use advertising to achieve their objectives. Labor unions advertise to inform the public how important union workers are to the nation's economy.

Other business association ads promote the product their members produce: dairy products, California raisins, Florida grapefruit, and so on.

Finally, some business association ads champion causes linked to their business. The Canadian Pharmaceutical Manufacturers Association campaigned hard for better patent protection on drugs (see Exhibit 18–28).

Advertising by Government Organizations

In an effort to communicate with voters, many government departments employ ad agencies and public relations firms and maintain well-staffed in-house graphics, communications, and press-relations departments. In Canada, the government is the largest advertiser—both nationally and on the provincial

The Pharmaceutical Manufacturers
Association of Canada promises more
research, more jobs, and fair prices
with better patent protection of new
medicines.

level. Much government advertising explains how to use government services
such as consumer assistance, welfare, or career guidance.

In the 1970s, the military draft ended, and the U.S. government had to recruit
an all-volunteer force. Each branch of the military waged an aggressive, paid
advertising campaign supplemented by the Defense Department's joint military
ad program.[17]

On the international level, many governments use advertising to attract new
businesses, tourists, or workers. See Exhibit 18–29.

Political Advertising

Politicians use advertising to make voters aware of their record, their stand on
issues, and their political vision. Early in a campaign, political candidates often
run ads with a positive message to build credibility with voters. Then—in an
effort to differentiate themselves—they often follow up with ads that attack
their opponent's record.[18]

Political advertising has grown significantly with the expansion of broadcast
media. TV advertising by gubernatorial and congressional candidates in the
six nonpresidential election years between 1970 and 1990 ballooned from
$12 million to $230.5 million.[19]

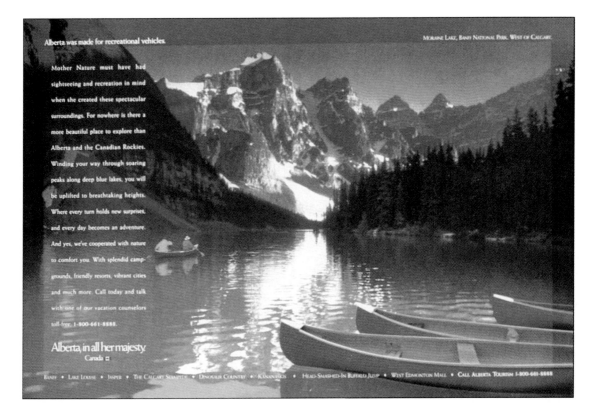

EXHIBIT • 18-29

To encourage business relationships and tourism, national governments hire agencies to prepare ads for use in other countries.

The Advertising Council

Most of the national PSAs on television are placed by the **Advertising Council,** a private, nonprofit organization that links noncommercial campaign sponsors with ad agencies. The sponsors pay for production costs, and the agencies donate their creative services.

The Ad Council's policy remains basically the same since the Council's creation during World War II:

> Accept no subsidy from government and remain independent of it. Conduct campaigns of service to the nation at large, avoiding regional, sectarian, or special-interest drives of all kinds. Remain nonpartisan and nonpolitical. Conduct the Council on a voluntary basis. Accept no project that does not lend itself to the advertising method. Accept no campaign with a commercial interest unless the public interest is obviously overriding.

The Ad Council created campaigns for the United Negro College Fund ("A mind is a terrible thing to waste"), the United Way ("It works for all of us"), and crime prevention ("Take a bite out of crime"). Exhibit 18–30 shows an Ad Council print ad that links drugs to AIDS. The Ad Council's two longest-running campaigns are for the American Red Cross and forest fire prevention. According to Ad Council research, the number of forest fires has been cut in half over the life of the Smokey Bear campaign.[20]

The Ad Council brings together the best talent in the advertising industry to create public service advertising.

Summary

Local advertising is placed by businesses in a particular city or county and aimed at customers in the same geographic area. Local advertising is important because sales are made or lost in the local arena. While the basic principles used by national advertisers are applicable to local advertisers, local advertisers have special problems resulting from the day-to-day operation of a small business.

Local and national advertisers differ in focus, time orientation, and resources. National advertisers focus on brand-building, share of market, grand strategies, and market groups. Local advertisers focus on daily traffic, gross sales or volume, tactical solutions, and the individual customers they see every day. National advertisers have a long-term perspective, local advertisers a short-term one. National advertisers also have more money and people.

Successful local advertisers are adept at integrating marketing communications. They wear many hats every day, and many of their daily activities help "advertise" the business.

Local advertisers should conduct marketing and advertising planning—analyze the local market and competitive situation, conduct adequate research, determine objectives and strategy, establish a realistic budget, and plan media strategy.

The objectives of local advertising differ from those of national advertising. Local advertising is intended to increase traffic, turn over inventory, or bring in new customers right away. Local advertisers have the same strategic options as national marketers—product, price, place, and promotion. The place element—the local trading area—is often the most critical.

Local businesses are often seasonal. By plotting anticipated sales patterns throughout the year, business owners can allot a percentage of their total yearly advertising budget to each month. Most advertising dollars should be spent just before customers are most likely to buy.

There are many media available to local advertisers: newspapers, individual shopping guides, local magazines, local radio and TV, and outdoor advertising. In addition, many advertisers use direct mail, classified directories, sales promotion, free publicity, and community events.

Local advertising is either product advertising or institutional advertising. Product advertising can be further divided into regular price-line advertising, sale advertising, and clearance advertising.

Local advertisers can get creative assistance from local ad agencies, local media, free-lancers and consultants, creative boutiques, syndicated art services, and wholesalers, manufacturers, and trade associations.

Noncommercial advertising includes advertising by nonbusiness institutions (churches, schools, charitable organizations), associations (labor groups, business and professional organizations), political candidates, and governments.

To assist with important causes, members of the advertising profession formed the Advertising Council during World War II. During its more than four decades of operation, the Ad Council has conducted memorable campaigns for such projects as child abuse prevention and the United Way.

Questions for Review and Discussion

1. How is local advertising different from national advertising?

2. What does a local advertiser learn by analyzing the local market and the competition?

3. What is the importance of an advertiser's local trading area?

4. What sources of primary and secondary research data might inform local advertisers about future retail trends?

5. What questions would a local merchant need to answer to formulate an annual advertising plan and budget?

6. Which media do local advertisers use most? Why?

7. Which sales promotional tools are useful for local advertisers? Why?

8. If you were a local advertiser, where would you turn for creative assistance? Why?

9. What is the difference between commercial and noncommercial advertising?

10. Which types of noncommercial advertising are more likely to receive free media space?

Marketing Plan Outline

DATE:

COMPANY NAME:

TITLE OR PRODUCT:

Encapsulation, for executive review, of entire marketing plan in no more than two or three pages.

I. Executive Summary

    A. Summary of situation analysis
    B. Summary of marketing objectives
    C. Summary of marketing strategies
    D. Budget summary

Complete statement of where the organization is today and how it got there.

What business the organization is in and characteristics of the industry as a whole. Information available from industry trade publications, trade association newsletters, consumer business press, Department of Commerce publications.

II. Situation Analysis

    A. The industry
      1. Definition of industry and company business
      2. History of industry
        a. Technological advances
        b. Trends
      3. Growth patterns within industry
        a. Demand curve
        b. Per capita consumption
        c. Growth potential
      4. Characteristics of industry
        a. Distribution patterns and traditional channels
        b. Regulation and control within industry
        c. Typical promotional activity
        d. Geographical characteristics
        e. Profit patterns

All relevant information on the company and its capabilities, opportunities, and/or problems. Information may be found in annual reports, sales records, warranty card records, customer correspondence, sales staff reports.

Complete description and all relevant information on the product/service mix, sales, and the strengths and weaknesses therein. See sales literature, sales reports, dealer correspondence, and so on.

B. The company
  1. Brief history
  2. Scope of business
  3. Current size, growth, profitability
  4. Reputation
  5. Competence in various areas
    a. Strengths
    b. Weaknesses

C. The product/service
  1. The product story
    a. Development and history
    b. Stage of product life cycle
      (1) Introduction
      (2) Growth
      (3) Maturity
      (4) Decline
    c. Quality factors
    d. Design considerations
    e. Goods classification
      (1) Consumer or industrial good
      (2) Durable or nondurable good or service
      (3) Convenience, shopping, or specialty good
      (4) Package good, hard good, soft good, service
    f. Packaging
    g. Price structure
    h. Uses
      (1) Primary
      (2) Secondary
      (3) Potential
    i. Image and reputation
    j. Product/service strengths
    k. Product/service weaknesses
  2. Product sales features
    a. Differentiating factors
      (1) Perceptible, imperceptible, or induced
      (2) Exclusive or nonexclusive
    b. Position in mind of customer
    c. Advantages and disadvantages (customer perception)
  3. Product research and development
    a. Technological breakthroughs
    b. Improvements planned
    c. Technical or service problems
  4. Sales history
    a. Sales and cost of sales
      (1) By product/service
      (2) By model
      (3) By territory
      (4) By market
    b. Profit history for same factors
  5. Share of market
    a. Industry sales by market
    b. Market share in dollars and units
    c. Market potential and trends

All relevant information about the people or organizations that comprise the current and prospective market for the firm's offerings. See market research reports, consumer/business press, trade publications, Census of Manufacturers, trade association reports.

D. The market
1. Definition and location of market
   a. Identified market segments
      (1) Past
      (2) Potential
   b. Market needs, desires
   c. Characteristics of market
      (1) Geographic
      (2) Demographic
      (3) Psychographic
      (4) Behavioral
   d. Typical buying patterns
      (1) Purchase patterns
      (2) Heavy users/light users
      (3) Frequency of purchase
   e. Buying influences on market
2. Definition of our customers
   a. Present, past, and future
   b. Characteristics
      (1) Shared characteristics with rest of market
      (2) Characteristics unique to our customers
   c. What they like about us or our product
   d. What they don't like
3. Consumer appeals
   a. Past advertising appeals
      (1) What has worked
      (2) What has not worked and why
   b. Possible future appeals
4. Results of research studies about market and customers

Complete information about the competition, the competitive environment, and the opportunities or challenges presented by current or prospective competitors. See SEC Form 10-Ks, consumer/business press articles, *Moody's Industrial Manual*, Standard & Poor's reports, Dun & Bradstreet report, *Thomas Register of American Corporations*.

E. The competition
1. Identification of competitors
   a. Primary competitors
   b. Secondary competitors
   c. Product/service descriptions
   d. Growth and size of competitors
   e. Share of market held by competitors
2. Strengths of competition
   a. Product quality
   b. Sales features
   c. Price, distribution, promotion
3. Weaknesses of competition
   a. Product features
   b. Consumer attitude
   c. Price, distribution, promotion
4. Marketing activities of competition
   a. Product positioning
   b. Pricing strategies
   c. Distribution
   d. Sales force
   e. Advertising, publicity
   f. Estimated budgets

Complete discussion of how the firm's products/services are distributed and sold, what channels are available, and characteristics of channel members. See dealer and distributor correspondence, sales staff reports, advertising reports, trade publication articles.

Background and rationale for firm's pricing policies and strategies, discussion of alternative options. Study sales reports, channel-member correspondence, customer correspondence, competitive information.

All relevant data concerning the firm's personal sales efforts and effectiveness as well as complete discussion of the firm's use of advertising public relations, and sales promotion programs. Examine sales reports, advertising reports, articles in *Advertising Age, Marketing Communications*, and so on, in-house data on advertising, sales, and training.

Enumeration of environmental factors that may be beyond the firm's immediate control but affect the firm's business efforts. See government reports and announcements, consumer/business press, trade association articles.

Recitation of relevant attitudes and directives of management as they pertain to the firm's marketing and advertising efforts. Information available from corporate business plan, management interviews, internal memos and directives.

F. Distribution strategies
   1. Type of distribution network used
      a. History of development
      b. Trends
   2. Evaluation of how distribution is accomplished
   3. Description and evaluation with channel members
   4. Promotional relationship with channel members
      a. Trade advertising and allowances
      b. Co-op advertising
      c. Use of promotion by dealer or middlemen
      d. Point-of-purchase displays, literature
      e. Dealer incentive programs

G. Pricing policies
   1. Price history
      a. Trends
      b. Affordability
      c. Competition
   2. Price objectives and strategies in past
      a. Management attitudes
      b. Buyer attitudes
      c. Channel attitudes

H. Promotion strategies
   1. Past promotion policy
      a. Personal versus nonpersonal selling
         (1) Use of sales force
         (2) Use of advertising, public relations, sales promotion
      b. Successes and failure of past policy
   2. Sales Force
      a. Size
      b. Scope
      c. Ability/training
      d. Cost per sale
   3. Advertising programs
      a. Successes and failure
      b. Strategies, themes, campaigns
      c. Appeals, positionings, and so on
      d. Expenditures
         (1) Past budgets
         (2) Method of allocation
         (3) Competitor budgets
         (4) Trend

I. Environmental factors
   1. Economy
      a. Current economic status
      b. Business outlook and economic forecasts
   2. Political situation
   3. Societal concerns
   4. Technological influences

J. Corporate objectives and strategies
   1. Profitability
      a. Sales revenue
      b. Cost reductions
   2. Return on investment
   3. Stock price
   4. Shareholder equity

5. Community image
6. New product development
7. Technological leadership
8. Mergers and/or acquisitions

K. Potential marketing problems

Enumeration or summary of problems considered most serious to the firm's marketing success.

Summary of those opportunities which offer the greatest potential for the firm's success.

L. Potential marketing opportunities

What general and specific needs the firm seeks to satisfy. Determine through study of situation analysis factors and management discussions and interviews.

Organization sales goals defined for whole company or for individual products by target market, by geographic territory, by department, or by some other category. Must be specific and realistic based on study of company capabilities, funding, and objectives.

III. Marketing Objectives

A. Market need objectives
   1. Market need-satisfying objectives
   2. Community need-satisfying objectives
   3. Corporate need-satisfying objectives
B. Sales target objectives
   1. Sales volume
      a. Dollars
      b. Units
      c. Territories
      d. Markets
   2. Share of market
   3. Distribution expansion
   4. Other

IV. Marketing Strategy

The method(s) by which the organization plans to achieve the objectives enumerated above.

A. General marketing strategy
   1. Positioning strategy
   2. Product differentiation strategy
   3. Price/quality differentiation strategy

A general description of the type of marketing strategy the organization intends to employ.

B. Specific market strategies
   1. Target market A
      a. Product
      b. Price
      c. Place
      d. Promotion
         (1) Personal selling
         (2) Advertising
         (3) Direct marketing
         (4) Sales promotion
         (5) Public relations

A detailed description of the marketing mix(es) the firm intends to use to achieve its objectives.

   2. Target market B
      a. Product
      b. Price
      c. Place
      d. Promotion
         (1) Personal selling
         (2) Advertising
         (3) Direct marketing
         (4) Sales promotion
         (5) Public relations

The detailed tactical plans for implementing each of the elements of the firm's marketing mix.

V. Action Programs (Tactics)

   A. Product plans
   B. Pricing plans
   C. Distribution plans
   D. Promotional plans
      1. Sales plan
      2. Advertising plan
      3. Direct marketing plan
      4. Sales promotion plan
      5. Public relations plan

Description of the methods the firm will use to review, evaluate, and control its progress toward the achievement of its marketing objectives.

VI. Measurement, Review, and Control

   A. Organizational structure
   B. Methodology for review and evaluation

Determination of the amount of money needed to conduct the marketing effort, the rationale for that budget, and the allocation to various functions.

VII. Marketing Budget

   A. Method of allocation
   B. Enumeration of marketing costs by division
      1. New product research
      2. Marketing research
      3. Sales expenses
      4. Advertising, direct marketing, sales promotion, public relations

Details of information, secondary data, or research conducted to develop information discussed in the marketing plan.

VIII. Appendixes

   A. Sales reports
   B. Reports of market research studies
   C. Reprints of journal or magazine articles
   D. Other supporting documents

Advertising Plan Outline

DATE:

COMPANY (PRODUCT) NAME:

Brief encapsulation, for executive review, of entire advertising plan in no more than two or three pages.

I. Executive Summary

    A. Premises—summary of information presented in marketing plan

    B. Summary of advertising objectives

    C. Summary of advertising strategy

    D. Budget summary

Condensed review of pertinent elements presented in the marketing plan.

II. Situation Analysis

    A. Company's (or product's) current marketing situation

        1. Business or industry information

        2. Description of company, product, or service

            a. Stage of product life cycle

            b. Goods classification

            c. Competitive or market positioning

        3. General description of market(s) served

        4. Sales history and share of market

        5. Description of consumer purchase process

        6. Methods of distribution

        7. Pricing strategies employed

        8. Implications of any marketing research

        9. Promotional history

    B. Target market description

        1. Market segments identified

        2. Primary market

        3. Secondary markets

        4. Market characteristics

        a. Geographic
        b. Demographic
        c. Psychographic
        d. Behavioral

C. Marketing objectives
  1. Generic market objectives
  2. Long- and short-term sales target objectives

D. Marketing mix for each target market—summarized from marketing plan
  1. Product
  2. Price
  3. Place
  4. Promotion

E. Intended role of advertising in the promotional mix

F. Miscellaneous information not included above

Analysis and statement of what the advertising is expected to accomplish—see Checklist for Developing Advertising Objectives (Chapter 7).

III. Advertising Objectives

A. Primary or selective demand

B. Direct action or indirect action

C. Objectives stated in terms of advertising pyramid
  1. Awareness
  2. Comprehension
  3. Conviction
  4. Desire
  5. Action
  6. Repurchase reinforcement

D. Quantified expression of objectives
  1. Specific quantities or percentages
  2. Length of time for achievement of objectives
  3. Other possible measurements
    a. Inquiries
    b. Increased order size
    c. Morale building
    d. Other

Intended blend of the creative mix for the company as a whole, for each product, or for each target market.

IV. Advertising (Creative) Strategy

A. Product concept—how the advertising will present the product in terms of:
  1. Product or market positioning
  2. Product differentiation
  3. Life cycle
  4. Classification, packaging, branding
  5. FCB Grid purchase-decision position
    a. High/low involvement
    b. Rational/emotional involvement

B. Target audience—the specific people the advertising will address
  1. Detailed description of target audiences
    a. Relationship of target audience to target market
    b. Prospective buying influences
    c. Benefits sought/advertising appeals
    d. Demographics
    e. Psychographics
    f. Behavioristics

The strategy for selecting the various media vehicles that will communicate the advertising message to the target audience—see Chapters 12–16.

What the company wants to say and how it wants to say it, verbally and nonverbally—see Chapters 8–11.

    2. Prioritization of target audiences
       a. Primary
       b. Secondary
       c. Supplementary
 C. Communications media
    1. Definition of media objectives
       a. Reach
       b. Frequency
       c. Gross rating points
       d. Continuity/fighting/pulsing
    2. Determination of which media reach the target audience best
       a. Traditional mass media
          (1) Radio
          (2) Television
          (3) Newspapers
          (4) Magazines
          (5) Outdoor
       b. Other media
          (1) Direct mail
          (2) Publicity
       c. Supplemental media
          (1) Trade shows
          (2) Sales promotion devices
          (3) Other media
          (4) Off-the-wall media
    3. Availability of media relative to purchase patterns
    4. Potential for communication effectiveness
    5. Cost considerations
       a. Size/mechanical considerations of message units
       b. Cost efficiency of media plan against target audiences
       c. Production costs
    6. Relevance to other elements of creative mix
    7. Scope of media plan
    8. Exposure/attention/motivation values of intended media vehicles
 D. Advertising message
    1. Copy elements
       a. Advertising appeals
       b. Copy platform
       c. Key consumer benefits
       d. Benefit supports or reinforcements
       e. Product personality or image
    2. Art elements
       a. Visual appeals
          (1) In ads and commercials
          (2) In packaging
          (3) In point-of-purchase and sales materials
       b. Art platform
          (1) Layout
          (2) Design
          (3) Illustration style
    3. Production elements
       a. Mechanical considerations in producing ads
          (1) Color
          (2) Size
          (3) Style

    b. Production values sought
       (1) Typography
       (2) Printing
       (3) Color reproduction
       (4) Photography/illustration
       (5) Paper
       (6) Electronic effects
       (7) Animation
       (8) Film or videotape
       (9) Sound effects
     (10) Music

V. The Advertising Budget

The amount of money to be allocated to advertising and the intended method of allocation.

  A. Impact of marketing situation on method of allocation
    1. New or old product
    2. Primary demand curve for product class
    3. Competitive situation
    4. Marketing objectives and strategy
    5. Profit or growth considerations
    6. Relationship of advertising to sales and profits
    7. Empirical experience
  B. Method of allocation
    1. Percentage of sales or profit
    2. Share of market
    3. Task method
    4. Unit of sale
    5. Competitive parity

VI. Testing and Evaluation

The research techniques that will be used to create the advertising and evaluate its effectiveness—see Chapter 6.

  A. Advertising research conducted
    1. Strategy determination
    2. Concept development
  B. Pretesting and posttesting
    1. Elements tested
      a. Markets
      b. Motives
      c. Messages
      d. Media
      e. Budgeting
      f. Scheduling
    2. Methodology
      a. Central location tests
      b. Sales experiments
      c. Physiological testing
      d. Aided recall tests
      e. Unaided recall tests
      f. Attitude tests
      g. Inquiry tests
      h. Sales tests
      i. Other
    3. Cost of testing

Career Planning in Advertising

The cliché is old but true: Looking for a job is a full-time job in itself. Careful research and planning (and lots of patience) are the way to a job in advertising—one that fits your abilities, interests, and career goals.

The job-hunting process, in advertising or any other field, can be broken down into five main steps:

1. Self-assessment and goal setting.
2. Conducting the job search.
3. Preparing a résumé, cover letter, and portfolio.
4. Interviewing.
5. Following up.

Self-Assessment and Goal Setting

The first (and some would argue the most important) step is to determine exactly what you have to offer potential employers and what you really want out of your career. First, you must assess your interests, marketable skills, strengths and weaknesses, and any other elements you believe are essential to finding and keeping the kind of job you want. The goal: determine the kind of job you will do best in.

Many books on career planning provide inventories and questionnaires to help you in such a self-assessment. Some are listed at the end of this appendix.

Self-evaluation can help you determine your career goals and objectives. What type of work would you like to do? What do you expect to get out of your work? Money? Power? Recognition? What work environment do you prefer? This is often called career planning. Make a list of musts and preferences regarding size of company, location, salary, benefits, training programs, and other employer characteristics.

After completing your self-assessment, you may find you are simply unprepared to enter the career area of your choice or that your qualifications are not sufficient to get you the kind of job you really want.

At this point, you may undertake additional learning—either with more school or by getting experience. Schooling is certainly helpful, but job experience is mandatory. Consider taking a summer or part-time job in a related field or serving as an *intern* (unpaid worker) at an advertising agency, in a company advertising department, with the media, or with a supplier. Your objective should be to build your base of job experience so you can prove to an employer that you understand what needs doing and that you know how to do it.

Conducting the Job Search

Before looking into specific jobs, investigate the overall advertising field to determine what types of jobs best fit your career goals. Advertising includes six main areas: creative (art direction, copywriting), account services (coordination, management, sales), media (planning, scheduling, buying), production (print, broadcast), research, and public relations. (See Exhibit C–1 for specific jobs and salaries.) Although many advertising jobs are found in agencies, there are many others in the advertising departments of both large and small companies, in the media, and in allied services (such as media-buying firms or production companies). Read books about the field, write to organizations that have career information, and keep up with the most popular periodicals—especially *Advertising Age* and *Adweek* in the United States and *Marketing* or *Info-Press* in Canada.

To explore what the advertising industry is really like, find out the names of advertising people who are highly regarded in your community and ask for a brief, informative interview. Many will be flattered to be sought out as experts in their field. Be prepared to ask specific questions; don't take up too much of the person's time; and always follow-up with a brief thank-you note.

When ready to conduct your actual job search, you can access many sources. The most obvious source is the want ads in your local paper or in the city where you would like to work. However, about 80 percent of jobs are filled before an ad ever appears. How do you hear about these job openings? Cracking this hidden job market requires time and effort—you need to create a network of people who are aware of and can help you find these unadvertised jobs. This entails letting everyone know that you are looking for a job—family, friends, distant relatives, teachers, and their associates. Join the local ad or PR club, attend their meetings, and participate in their activities. Follow up every lead and ask each new person for additional leads. Over time, networking should land you some interviews.

While building your network, prepare a list of target employers—the companies you most want to work for. This requires research, such as checking the *Standard Directory of Advertisers*, the *Standard Directory of Advertising Agencies*, and the *Advertising Career Directory*. Make a file card for each company, including who is in charge of the specific department where you would like to work. Other leads include college placement offices, employment sections of industry trade papers, and employment agencies (some specialize in jobs in the advertising field).

Preparing a Résumé, a Cover Letter, and a Portfolio

Armed with your list of potential employers, you are ready to contact them for a job. In most cases, a résumé and cover letter will be your initial tools of contact. Because they are such important tools for marketing your product—*you*—they must be carefully prepared to create a good first impression.

EXHIBIT • C-1

Careers in advertising.

Job title	Job description	Requirements	Salary range	Entry level
Art director	Responsible for visual elements in print and broadcast ads; supervises or creates layouts; hires photographers, illustrators.	B.A. desirable but not required; art school degree helpful; portfolio a must.	$27,600–$70,150 (senior art director)	Assistant art director ($20,700)
Copywriter	Writes copy for print and broadcast advertisements; works with art director to develop ad concept; can work for ad agency or advertiser.	B.A. with courses in advertising, marketing, liberal arts, social sciences; portfolio a must.	$28,750–$70,150 (senior copywriter)	Junior copywriter ($20,700)
Account executive	Serves as link between client and ad agency; acts as business manager for account; does market planning; coordinates advertising planning process; assists in new business acquisition.	B.A. in business; M.B.A. often preferred; marketing background desirable.	$39,100–$94,300	Junior account executive (B.A.: $20,700–$26,450; M.B.A.: $29,900–$39,100)
Media planner	Selects media to advertise in and plans media mix; chooses media vehicles; conducts media tests.	B.A. with emphasis in marketing, merchandising, or psychology.	$29,900–$172,500 (media director)	Trainee ($13,500–$16,100)
Media buyer	Buys space in print media and time in electronic media; negotiates price and position of ads; may work for ad agency or media-buying firm.	B.A. with emphasis in marketing, economics, mathematics, or statistics; M.B.A. preferred.	$29,900–$172,500 (media director)	Trainee ($13,000–$16,100)
Traffic manager	Schedules, supervises, and controls an ad agency's work flow.	B.A. not required but highly desirable; good general education helpful.	$23,000–$43,700	Traffic assistant ($15,525)
Print production manager	Prepares ads for printing; works with typesetters, color separators, printers, and other suppliers.	B.A. helpful but not essential; background in graphic arts, printing useful.	$25,300–$64,400	Production assistant ($14,950–$17,250)
Broadcast producer	Supervises all aspects of production for radio and TV commercials, including hiring the director and production company and controlling budget.	B.A. preferred; background in some area of broadcasting helpful.	$31,500–$102,350	Production assistant ($14,950–$17,250)
Market researcher	Conducts studies of consumers and their buying habits; conducts tests of consumer reactions to products and ads; may work in ad agency or with research firm.	Degree a must; M.B.A. or Ph.D. desirable; background in statistics useful; computer literacy an advantage.	$42,550–$105,800 (market research manager)	Trainee ($15,525)
Public relations manager	Obtains publicity for clients; serves as intermediary between client and public; handles contacts with press; may work for ad agency, client company, or public relations firm.	College degree with emphasis on liberal arts; journalism or marketing background helpful.	$29,900–$96,600	PR assistant or trainee ($17,250–$19,550)
Advertising director/manager	Runs advertising department at company, managing all advertising and coordinating with any outside agencies used.	B.A. or M.B.A. in marketing	$36,800–$52,900	Advertising assistant ($19,550–$23,000)
Brand/product manager	Is responsible for the marketing of a specific product or brand at a company, including sales and advertising.	B.A. in marketing or M.B.A.	$40,250–$52,900	Advertising assistant ($19,550–$23,000)
Copywriter for retail ad department	Writes copy for newspaper ads, catalogs, direct-mail pieces for retail business.	B.A. preferred, with courses in advertising, English, sociology, psychology; portfolio helpful.	$31,050–$36,800	($17,250–$25,300)
Artist for retail ad department	Illustrates print ads, catalogs, and direct-mail pieces for retail business.	B.A. desirable; commercial art courses useful; portfolio a must.	$32,200–$36,800	($22,500–$26,450)
Photographer	Photographs products, other setup shots for ad agency or in-house ad department.	B.A. from professional art school; portfolio a must.	$25,300–$37,950	Usually free-lance
Sales representative	Handles advertising sales for a particular newspaper, magazine, radio or TV station, or other medium.	B.A. preferred, with emphasis on business courses; sales experience valuable.	Commission ($25,000–$100,000+)	Sales trainee ($15,000–$20,000)
Jingle creator	Writes the music and lyrics for jingles used in radio and TV commercials, usually on a contract or free-lance basis.	B.A. preferred (but not required), with emphasis on music and business.	$40,250–$690.000	$28,750

Your résumé should be attractive, well written, and professional in appearance and wording. Always proofread it carefully (better to have a more qualified person proof it) to be sure there are no grammatical, punctuation, or spelling errors. For an impressive looking résumé stick with clean black type on white bond paper. Leave generous margins to enhance readability. And keep it short—two pages maximum. Employers are busy—they usually go directly to the résumé's content and ignore colored paper, professional typesetting, and slick design. The exception may be when you apply for a creative art position—but, again, limit your creativity (do not use decorative type faces and keep the design simple and clean).

A sample résumé is shown in Exhibit C–2. Use the following tips for preparing your résumé.

Heading

The heading should include a title (such as "Résumé") and basic information about you (name, address, phone number). It should also include your career

EXHIBIT • C-2

An example of a résumé.

RÉSUMÉ

SHARON LEE ANDERSON

4150 Prairie Avenue   Elgin, Illinois 60120   Phone (708) 888-7043

Career Objective: Copywriter in a medium-sized Chicago agency.
Advancement to creative supervisor within five years.

Education for Advertising

Bachelor of Arts (1989), University of Illinois, Chicago, Illinois.
Major: Advertising and Journalism. Minor: Marketing.

Honors: Dean's list, six semesters. Graduated in upper 10 percent of class.

Advertising Experience

Junior Copywriter (part-time)	Advertising Salesperson
Goldblatt's Department Store	Campus newspaper
Skokie, Illinois	University of Illinois
(May 1989-September 1990)	(October 1988-March 1989)
Responsible for creative copy for direct-mail brochures	Serviced existing accounts and contracted with 22 new accounts

Awards, Activities, Affiliations

First-place winner. Copywriting category. National Student Advertising Campaign Competition, 1991. Sponsored by the Federation of Advertising Agencies.

Program Chairman, 1990–91. University of Illinois Advertising Club.

Recipient. Summer 1990 scholarship from Advertising Institute.

Other Relevant Information

Write and speak Spanish. Type 70 wpm. Proficient with WordPerfect and Microsoft Word programs for IBM PC and PageMaker for Macintosh.

Personal Data

Hobbies include reading (science fiction, history, behavioral sciences), flute playing, dancing, racquetball.

References

Dr. Harold O. Simpson, Professor of Advertising, School of Journalism, University of Illinois, Chicago, Illinois 60680

Dr. Barbara Wasserman, Professor of Marketing, School of Business, University of Illinois, Chicago, Illinois 60680

Linda Dolan, Director of Advertising, Goldblatt's Department Store, Skokie, Illinois 60076

objective stated as specifically as possible ("an entry-level position in the media department of a large ad agency with a long-term goal of media planning for major accounts"). Avoid being vague ("a challenging position in the advertising industry" or "a job where I can put my enthusiasm and interpersonal skills to good use").

Education

Include any degrees you have already earned and any outstanding honors or scholarships. If you have little work experience, emphasize all applicable study programs, courses, and projects you have completed.

Work Experience

Emphasize jobs that are relevant to your target field. Include any part-time or volunteer work that reflects an interest in the type of job you are seeking. For all relevant work experience, be sure to include a brief description of your duties and any worthy accomplishments. Briefly list other jobs held to prove you can get and hold a job and have at least contributed to your own support.

Activities and Achievements

Include any other information that might be of interest to an employer, such as language skills, relevant hobbies, and community activities.

References

If you wish to list past employers who can be contacted about your skills and experience, be sure to get their permission first. If you have good references, it's best to list them. It's also acceptable to state "References available upon request."

The Cover Letter

Accompanying the résumé should be a cover letter that catches the reader's attention, provides evidence of your qualifications, and requests an interview (see Exhibit C–3). Like the résumé, the letter should be professionally presented (not handwritten, for instance) and businesslike. It should answer the employer's question, "What's in it for me?" A number of books that can provide help with writing good résumés and cover letters are listed at the end of this appendix.

Portfolio

If you are looking for an art director or a copywriter position, you will also need to prepare a portfolio, or "book," that shows potential employers your published works, pieces done for school courses, or self-projects. Remember: the fact that something you did was published does not automatically qualify it for your portfolio, especially if it is *not* among your best work. A portfolio should be carefully thought out and prepared, as it may be the sole basis on which some employers do their hiring. It should contain a small number of items that represent the kinds and quality of work you can do.

Artists and writers are often asked to mail or drop off their portfolios and then pick them up a week or two later. Therefore it's wise to prepare two or more portfolios.

EXHIBIT · C-3

An example of a letter of application.

4150 Prairie Avenue
Elgin, IL 60120
June 10, 1991

Mr. Harold Lessler
Henley, Schmidt and Kaiser Advertising
5948 Lakeshore Drive
Chicago, IL 60034

Dear Mr. Lessler:

If a woman were seeking a copywriting position in your agency, would you
be interested if you discovered she'd had experience as a department store
copywriter? Would you become even more interested to find she'd had practical
selling experience with a campus newspaper and had graduated in the top 10
percent of her class from a major university? I'm just such a woman, Mr.
Lessler.

Writing brochure copy aimed at women with young children and at working women
age 25-40 taught me the importance of adapting advertising to a specific
target audience. My year and a half of experience at Goldblatt's Department
Store in Skokie, Illinois, gave me training in copywriting that can be put
to work for your agency.

As helpful as this experience was, a fledgling copywriter also needs to know
what real selling is all about. That is why I believe you'll find my newspaper
ad-selling experience valuable. It helped me immeasurably in learning to
turn out copy that sells.

I majored in advertising at the University of Illinois. To make sure I understood the world in which advertising works, I minored in marketing. My courses
paid off: I was the first-place winner, copywriting category, in the 1989
National Student Advertising Campaign Competition. I like to win awards.
And I'd try to win many for your agency!

My research shows that you have several accounts needing copywriting in
Spanish. I speak and write Spanish fluently. In addition, my 70 wpm typing
ability, my proficiency in using word processing programs, and my ability
to work constructively with others (as evidenced by my tour of duty as Program
Chairman of the campus Advertising Club) make up a background that will enable
me to serve your agency well.

After you've had an opportunity to review the enclosed resume, please call
me at (312) 698-5894. I'd be grateful for an interview to discuss my qualifications with you.

Cordially yours,

Sharon Lee Anderson

Sharon Lee Anderson

Enclosure

One enterprising graduate of Glasboro State College skipped the standard resume and portfolio process altogether. He used his education in direct marketing to prepare a direct-mail campaign that clearly demonstrated the skills he had to offer (see Exhibit C–4).

Interviewing

The purpose of the résumé and cover letter is to land a job interview. Employers hire on the basis of the interview (and your portfolio) so perfect your interviewing skills. Learn the most commonly asked interview questions and rehearse your answers. Read about preparing for an interview and follow suggestions for scheduling, attire, and appropriate interview behavior.

Before scheduling an interview, find out about the company. If it is an advertising agency, how large is it? How is it structured? What are its major accounts? Who are the major figures? Who will you be talking to, and what is the correct pronunciation of his or her name?

At the close of the interview, be sure to thank the interviewer and to politely inquire about what will happen next. Should you expect additional interviews? Will someone from the company be in touch? Show that you are interested— but not desperate.

EXHIBIT • C-4

Karl Dentino created this direct-mail ad to secure his first job out of college. After testing it in the Philadelphia area, he made some revisions and then mailed it to 24 chief executive officers of direct-response marketing agencies in New York. The approach secured nine interviews and landed him two job offers.

Following Up

Record-keeping is a must when conducting a job search. Keep files or cards for recording letters and résumés sent, dates of interviews, and so forth. If you do not receive responses to your letters to certain target employers within a reasonable time, write follow-up letters. After an interview, write a brief, typewritten, thank-you note. Reiterate your interest in the job.

Eventually, these techniques and your persistent effort will lead to job offers. Accept the job that best fits your objectives, and you will be on your way to a career in advertising.

CAREER PLANNING PUBLICATIONS

Books

Advertising Career Directory. 2nd ed. Hawthorne, N.J.: The Career Press, 1987.

Asher, Donald. *The Overnight Resume.* Berkeley, Calif.: Ten Speed Press, 1991.

Birch, David. *Job Creation in America.* New York: Free Press, 1987.

Bolles, Richard J. N. *What Color Is Your Parachute? A Practical Manual for Job Hunters and Career Changes.* Berkeley, Calif.: Ten Speed Press (updated annually).

Bolt, Laurence G. *Zen and the Art of Making a Living in the Post-Modern World.* Santa Barbara, Calif.: Lightning Press, 1991.

Caples, John. *The Ultimate Interview.* New York: Doubleday, 1991.

Deckinger, E. L., and Jules B. Singer. *Exploring Careers in Advertising.* New York: Rosen Publishing Group, 1985.

Frank, William S. *200 Letters for Job Hunters.* Berkeley, Calif.: Ten Speed Press, 1990.

Greenberg, Jan. *How Advertising Works and the People Who Make It Happen.* New York: Henry Holt, 1987.

Holland, John, and Gary Gottfredson. *Dictionary of Holland Occupational Codes.* Lutz, Fla.: Psychological Assessment Resources, 1989.

Jackson, Tom. *Guerilla Tactics in the New Job Market.* New York: Bantam, 1991.

Jackson, Tom, and Bill Buckingham. *The Perfect Resume Kit.* Madison, Wis.: Permex Systems, 1991.

Jackson, Tom, and Ellen Jackson. *Perfect Resume Strategies.* New York: Doubleday, 1992.

Jackson, Tom. *Not Just Another Job.* New York: Random House, 1992.

Jackson, Tom. *The Perfect Resume.* New York: Doubleday, 1990.

Lareau, William. *The Inside Track: A Successful Job Search Method.* New York: New Century Publishers, 1986.

Laskin, David. *Getting into Advertising: A Career Guide.* New York: Ballantine Books, 1986.

Lathrop, Richard. *Who's Hiring Who?* Berkeley, Calif.: Ten Speed Press, 1991.

Lipnack, Jessica, and Jeffrey Stamps. *The Network Book: People Connecting with People.* Portsmouth, N.H.: Metheun, 1986.

Lock, Robert. *Taking Charge of Your Career Direction.* Pacific Grove, Calif.: Brooks/Cole, 1988.

Mogel, Leonard. *Making It in the Media Professions: A Realistic Guide to Career Opportunities in Newspapers, Magazines, Books, Television, Radio, the Movies, and Advertising.* Chester, Conn.: Globe Pequot, 1987.

Parker, Yana. *The Damn Good Resume Guide.* Berkeley, Calif.: Ten Speed Press, 1989.

Parker, Yana. *The Resume Catalog: 200 Damn Good Examples.* Berkeley, Calif.: Ten Speed Press, 1988.

Public Relations Career Directory. 2nd ed. Hawthorne, N.J.: The Career Press, 1987.

Schmidt, Peggy J. *Making It on Your First Job: When You're Young, Inexperienced, and Ambitious.* New York: Avon Books, 1981.

Snelling, Robert. *Jobs! What Are They? Where They Are . . . What They Pay!* New York: Simon & Schuster, 1986.

Sturman, Gerald M. *The Career Discovery Project.* New York: Doubleday, 1993. (Previously: Sturman, Gerald M. *If You Knew Who You Were . . . You Could Be Who You Are.* Woodstock, N.Y.: Bierman House, 1990.)

Swanson, David. *The Resume Solution.* Indianapolis: JIST Works, 1991.

Truitt, John. *Telesearch: Direct Dial the Best Job of Your Life.* New York: Macmillan, 1985.

Wasserman, Dick. *How to Get Your First Copywriting Job.* New York: Center for Advancement of Advertising, 1985.

Wegmann, Robert, Robert Chapman, and Miriam Johnson. *Work in the New Economy: Careers and Job Seeking into the 21st Century.* Indianapolis: JIST Works, 1989.

Wright, John. *The American Almanac of Jobs and Salaries.* New York: Avon Books, 1988.

Yate, Martin. *Knock 'em Dead—with Great Answers to Tough Interview Questions.* Boston: Bob Adams, Inc., 1991.

Periodicals

Business Week's Guide to Careers, 1221 Avenue of the Americas, New York, NY 10010.

Career Opportunity News, Garrett Park Press, Garrett Park, MD 20896.

Journal of Career Planning and Employment, College Placement Council, 62 Highland Avenue, Bethlehem, PA 18017.

Occupational Outlook Quarterly, Superintendent of Documents, U.S. Government Printing Office, Washington, DC 20402.

Pamphlets

Advertising: A Guide to Careers in Advertising, American Association of Advertising Agencies, 200 Park Avenue, New York, NY 10017.

Where Shall I Go to Study Advertising? Advertising Educational Publications, 3429 Fifty-fifth Street, Lubbock, TX 79413.

SELECTED PERIODICALS

Advertising Age, 740 North Rush Street, Chicago, IL 60611.

Advertising Techniques, 10 East 39th Street, New York, NY 10016.

Adweek, 49 East 21st Street, New York, NY 10010.

Adweek's Marketing Week, 49 East 21st Street, New York, NY 10010.

Applied Arts Quarterly, 20 Holy Street, Suite 208, Toronto, Ontario, Canada M4S 3BI.

Archive, P.O. Box 6338, Syracuse, NY 13217.

Art Direction, 10 East 39th Street, New York, NY 10016.

Broadcasting, 1735 DeSales Street N.W., Washington, DC 20036.

Business Marketing, 740 Rush Street, Chicago, IL 60611.

Canadian Business, 70 The Esplanade, 2nd Floor, Toronto, Canada M5E 1R2.

Canadian Journal of Communication, St. Thomas More College, 1437 College Drive, Saskatoon, Saskatchewan, Canada S7N OW6.

Communication Arts, P.O. Box 10300, Palo Alto, CA 94303.

Direct Marketing, 224 Seventh Street, Garden City, NY 11530.

Editor & Publisher, 575 Lexington Avenue, New York, NY 10022.

Incentive Marketing, 633 Third Avenue, New York, NY 10017.

Info-Presse Communications, 4316 Rue St-Laurent, Suite 400, Montreal, Quebec, Canada H2W 1Z3.

Journal of Advertising, American Academy of Advertising, c/o Ron Lane, School of Journalism, The University of Georgia, Athens, GA 30602.

Journal of Advertising Research, Advertising Research Foundation, 3 East 54th Street, New York, NY 10022.

Journal of Broadcasting, Broadcast Education Association, 1771 N Street N.W., Washington, DC 20036.

Journal of Marketing, American Marketing Association, 250 South Wacker Drive, Suite 200, Chicago, IL 60606.

Marketing, Maclean-Hunter Ltd., 777 Bay Street, Toronto, Ontario, Canada M5W 1A7.

Marketing News, American Marketing Association, 250 South Wacker Drive, Suite 200, Chicago, IL 60606.

Mediaweek, 1515 Broadway, New York, NY 10036.

MIN/Media Industry Newsletter, 145 East 49th Street, New York, NY 10017.

Modern Packaging, 205 East 42nd Street, New York, NY 10017.

Print, 355 Lexington Avenue, New York, NY 10017.

Public Relations Journal, 845 Third Avenue, New York, NY 10020.

Sales & Marketing Management, 633 Third Avenue, New York, NY 10164.

Sales & Marketing Management in Canada, 1077 St. James Street, Winnipeg, Manitoba, Canada R3C 3B1.

Stores, National Retail Merchants Association, 100 West 31st Street, New York, NY 10001.

Television/Radio Age, 1270 Avenue of the Americas, New York, NY 10020.

Zip, 401 North Broad Street, Philadelphia, PA 19108.

REFERENCE BOOKS AND DIRECTORIES

Occupational Outlook Handbook. U.S. Department of Labor, Bureau of Labor Statistics, Washington, D.C.

Standard Directory of Advertisers. Wilmette, Ill.: National Register Publishing Company, 1989.

Standard Directory of Advertising Agencies. Wilmette, Ill.: National Register Publishing Company, 1989.

The Corporate 1000 or *The Financial 1000.* Monitor Publishing, 104 Fifth Street, New York, NY 10011. (212) 627-4140.

RESEARCH AND INFORMATION SERVICES

A. C. Nielsen Company, Nielsen Plaza, Northbrook, IL 60062.

Advertising Checking Bureau, 165 North Canal Street, Chicago, IL 60606.

Audit Bureau of Circulations, 900 North Meacham Road, Schaumburg, IL 60195.

Broadcast Advertisers Report (BAR), 500 Fifth Avenue, New York, NY 10036.

Gallup & Robinson, Research Park, Princeton, NJ 08540.

Leading National Advertisers (LNA), 515 Madison Avenue, New York, NY 10022.

Mediamark Research, 341 Madison Avenue, New York, NY 10017.

Simmons Marketing Research Bureau, 219 East 42nd Street, New York, NY 10019.

Starch INRA Hooper, 566 East Boston Post Road, Mamaroneck, NY 10543.

The Arbitron Company, 1350 Avenue of the Americas, New York, NY 10019.

PROFESSIONAL AND TRADE ASSOCIATIONS

The Advertising Council, 825 Third Avenue, New York, NY 10022.

Advertising Research Foundation (ARF), 3 East 54th Street, New York, NY 10022.

American Advertising Federation, 1400 K Street N.W., Suite 1000, Washington, DC 20005.

American Association of Advertising Agencies, 666 Third Avenue, 13th Floor, New York, NY 10017.

American Business Press, 205 East 42nd Street, New York, NY 10017.

American Marketing Association, 250 South Wacker Drive, Chicago, IL 60606.

Association of National Advertisers, 155 East 44th Street, New York, NY 10017.

Business/Professional Advertising Association, 205 East 42nd Street, New York, NY 10017.

Council of Better Business Bureaus, 1515 Wilson Boulevard, Arlington, VA 22209.

Direct Marketing Association, 6 East 43rd Street, New York, NY 10017.

International Advertising Association, 475 Fifth Avenue, New York, NY 10017.

Magazine Publishers Association, 575 Lexington Avenue, New York, NY 10022.

Marketing Communications Executives International, 2602 McKinney Avenue, Dallas, TX 75204.

Marketing Research Association, 111 East Wacker Drive, Suite 600, Chicago, IL 60601.

National Advertising Review Board (NARB), 845 Third Avenue, New York, NY 10022.

National Association of Broadcasters, 1771 N Street, N.W., Washington, DC 20036.

National Council of Affiliated Advertising Agencies, 6 East 45th Street, New York, NY 10017.

National Retail Merchants Association, 100 West 31st Street, New York, NY 10001.

National Yellow Pages Service, 999 West Big Beaver Road, Troy, MI 48084.

Newspaper Advertising Bureau, 1180 Avenue of the Americas, New York, NY 10036.

Outdoor Advertising Association of America, 1899 L Street N.W., Suite 403, Washington, DC 20036.

Point-of-Purchase Advertising Institute, 2 Executive Drive, Ft. Lee, NJ 07024.

Public Relations Society of America, 845 Third Avenue, New York, NY 10022.

Radio Advertising Bureau, 304 Park Avenue South, New York, NY 10010.

Sales and Marketing Executives International, 6151 Wilson Mills Road, Suite 200, Cleveland, OH 44143.

Specialty Advertising Association International, 1404 Walnut Hill Lane, Irving, TX 75062.

Television Bureau of Advertising, 477 Madison Avenue, New York, NY 10022.

Transit Advertising Association, 1025 Thomas Jefferson Avenue, Suite 502E, Washington, DC 20007.

Glossary*

AAAA (2) See *American Association of Advertising Agencies*.

AAF (2) See *American Advertising Federation*.

ABC (13) See *Audit Bureau of Circulations*.

abundance principle (1) The idea that in an economy that produces more goods and services than can be consumed, advertising serves two purposes: keeping consumers informed of selection alternatives and allowing companies to compete more effectively for consumer dollars.

account executive (3) The liaison between the agency and the client. The account executive is responsible both for managing all the agency's services for the benefit of the client and for representing the agency's point of view to the client.

account planning (3) A hybrid discipline that bridges the gap between traditional research, account management, and creative direction whereby agency people represent the view of the consumer in order to better define and plan the client's advertising program.

account planner (3) Individual in an agency who acts as a surrogate for a consumer. See *account planning*.

account supervisor (3) See *management supervisor*.

A. C. Nielsen (14) The largest market research company in the world. See *Nielsen Station Index*.

action advertising (1) Advertising intended to bring about immediate action on the part of the reader or viewer.

action block (7) The top step in the advertising pyramid, in which people actually go out and test the product or even purchase it.

action programs (7) See *tactics*.

ADI (14) See *area of dominant influence*.

advertisers (3) See *clients*.

advertising (1) The nonpersonal communication of information, usually paid for and usually persuasive in nature, about products (goods and services) or ideas by identified sponsors through various media.

advertising agency (3) An independent organization of creative people and businesspeople who specialize in developing and preparing advertising plans, advertisements, and other promotional tools for advertisers. The agency also arranges for or contracts for purchase of space and time in various media.

advertising allowance (16) Either a percentage of gross purchases or a flat fee paid to the retailer for advertising the manufacturer's product.

Advertising Council (17) A nonpartisan, nonpolitical, volunteer organization supported by the American Association of Advertising Agencies. It conducts public service ad campaigns to the nation at large, avoiding regional, sectarian, or special-interest drives of all kinds.

advertising manager (3) The advertiser's person who is in charge of planning, coordinating, budgeting, and directing the company's advertising program.

advertising medium (1) Any vehicle of communication that an advertiser may use; see *media*.

advertising message (7) An element of the creative mix comprising what the company plans to say in its advertisements and how it plans to say it—verbally or nonverbally.

advertising objectives (7) What the advertiser hopes to achieve through advertising, usually with respect to customer awareness, attitude, and preference.

advertising plan (7) The plan that directs the company's advertising effort. A natural outgrowth of the marketing plan, it analyzes the situation, sets advertising objectives, and lays out a specific strategy from which ads and campaigns are created.

advertising pyramid (7) A simple five-step model for understanding some of the tasks advertising can perform and for setting advertising objectives. The five steps include awareness, comprehension, conviction, desire, and action.

advertising research (6) The systematic gathering and analysis of information specifically to facilitate the development or evaluation of advertising strategies, ads and commercials, and media campaigns.

Advertising Standards Council (2) Investigative and arbitrating branch of the Canadian Advertising Foundation. Its French-Canadian counterpart is called the Conseil des normes.

advertising strategy (7) The methodology advertisers use to achieve their advertising objectives. The strategy is determined by the particular creative mix of advertising elements the advertiser selects, namely: target audience; product concept; communications media; and advertising message. (Also called the *creative mix*.)

advertorial (17) An ad that is half advertising, half editorial, aimed at swaying public opinion rather than selling products.

advocacy advertising (17) Advertising used to communicate an organization's views on issues that affect society or business.

affidavit of performance (14) A signed and notarized form sent by a television station to an advertiser or agency indicating what spots ran and when. It is the station's legal proof that the advertiser got what was paid for.

agency commission (3) Compensation paid by a medium to recognized advertising agencies, usually 15 percent (16 2/3 percent for outdoor), for advertising placed with it.

---

* Numbers in parentheses after term indicate chapter(s) where term is discussed.

agency network (3) An international affiliation of advertising agencies organized to give and receive media counsel, translation services, production assistance, or other specialized services in unfamiliar markets.

agricultural advertising (1) See *farm advertising.*

American Advertising Federation (AAF) (2) A nationwide association of advertising people. The AAF helped to establish the Federal Trade Commission, and its early "vigilance" committees were the forerunners of the Better Business Bureaus.

American Association of Advertising Agencies (AAAA) (2) The national organization of the advertising business. It has members throughout the United States and controls agency practices by denying membership to any agency judged unethical.

ANA (2) See *Association of National Advertisers.*

animatic (9) A rough television commercial produced by photographing storyboard sketches on a film strip or video with the audio portion synchronized on tape. It is used primarily for testing purposes.

animation (11) The use of cartoons, puppet characters, or demonstrations of inanimate characters come to life in television commercials; often used for communicating difficult messages or for reaching specialized markets, such as children.

annual report (17) A formal document issued yearly by a corporation to its stockholders to reflect the corporation's condition at the close of the business year.

answer print (11) The final print of a filmed commercial, along with all the required optical effects and titles, used for review and approval before duplicating.

aperture (11) The opening in a camera that determines the amount of light that reaches the film or videotape.

appeal (8) The specific approach advertisers use to communicate how their products will satisfy customer needs. The two broad types of appeals advertisers use are rational and emotional appeals.

Arbitron (14) A commonly used rating service that regularly publishes statistics on how many people, in what age groups, and of what sex, are watching TV or listening to radio at various times of the day within a specific market area.

area of dominant influence (ADI) (14) Arbitron's term for a television market—defined as "an exclusive geographic area consisting of all counties in which the home market stations receive a preponderance of total viewing hours."

art (8) (9) The whole visual presentation of a commercial or advertisement—the body language of an ad. Art also refers to the style of photography or illustration employed, the way color is used, and the arrangement of elements in an ad so that they relate to one another in size and proportion.

art direction (9) The act or process of managing the visual presentation of an ad or commercial.

ascender (10) In typography, the stroke of any letter that rises above the x-height; for example, d, t, l.

Association des agences de publicite du Quebec (2) An association of the largest advertisng agencies in Quebec.

Association of Canadian Advertisers (2) An association of the largest national advertisers in Canada which promotes freedom of commercial speech, deals with government agencies, and negotiates radio and TV contracts with Canadian talent unions.

Association of National Advertisers (ANA) (2) An organization composed of 400 major manufacturing and service companies that are clients of member agencies of the AAAA. These companies, which are pledged to uphold the ANA code of advertising ethics, work with the ANA through a joint Committee for Improvement of Advertising Content.

attention value (12) A consideration in selecting media based on the degree of attention paid to ads in particular media by those exposed to them. Attention value relates to the advertising message and copy just as much as to the medium.

attitude (4) The acquired mental position—positive or negative—that we hold in regard to some idea or object.

attitude test (6) A type of posttest that usually seeks to measure the effectiveness of an advertising campaign in creating a favorable image for a company, its brand, or its products.

audience (12) The total number of people exposed to a particular medium.

audience composition (14) The distribution of an audience into demographic or other categories.

audience objectives (12) Definitions of the specific types of people the advertiser wants to reach.

audio (8) The sound portion of a commercial. Also, the right side of a script for a television commercial, indicating spoken copy, sound effects, and music.

audio console (11) In a sound studio control room, the board that channels sound to the appropriate recording devices and that blends both live and prerecorded sounds for immediate or delayed broadcast.

Audit Bureau of Circulations (ABC) (13) An organization supported by advertising agencies, advertisers, and publishers that verifies circulation and other marketing data on newspapers and magazines for the benefit of its members.

avails (14) An abbreviated term referring to the TV time slots that are *available* to an advertiser.

average frequency (12) Total exposures divided by audience reach.

average quarter-hour persons (14) A radio term referring to the average number of people who are listening to a specific station for at least 5 minutes during a 15-minute period of any given daypart.

average quarter-hour rating (14) The average quarter-hour persons estimate expressed as a percentage of the estimated population.

awareness advertising (1) Advertising that attempts to build the image of a product or familiarity with the name and package.

awareness block (7) The foundation block of the advertising pyramid, in which people are acquainted with the company, good, service, or brand.

back light (11) A light that is either directly behind or behind and above a subject, aimed toward the camera to outline the subject and set the subject apart from the background.

barter syndication (14) Marketing of first-run television programs to local stations free or for a reduced rate because some of the ad space has been presold to national advertisers.

base art (10) The first image on an artboard on which an overlay may be placed.

basic bus (15) In transit advertising, all the inside space on a group of buses, which thereby gives the advertiser complete domination.

behavioral sciences (4) The social sciences: anthropology, sociology, psychology, and so on.

behavioristic segmentation (5) Method of determining market segments by aggregating consumers into product-related groups based on their knowledge, attitude, use, or response to actual products or product attributes.

benefit headline (8) Type of headline that makes a direct promise to the reader.

benefits (5) The particular product attributes offered to customers, such as high quality, low price, status, speed, sex appeal, good taste, and so on.

benefit segmentation (5) Method of segmenting markets by determining the major benefits consumers seek in a product (high quality, low price, status, speed, sex appeal, good taste, etc.).

Better Business Bureau (BBB) (2) A business-monitoring organization funded by dues from over 100,000 member companies. It operates primarily at the local level to protect consumers against fraudulent and deceptive advertising.

bidirectional microphone (11) A microphone designed to capture sounds from two opposing directions simultaneously.

big idea (8) The flash of creative insight—the bold advertising initiative—that captures the essence of the strategy in an imaginative, involving way and brings the subject to life to make the reader stop, look, and listen.

billboards (15) See *poster panel*.

Birch Research (14) A radio research service that relies on telephone surveys to obtain listener data.

Birchscan (14) A monthly computerized report of radio data, published by Birch Research.

blanket (10) In offset printing, the intermediate rubber surface that comes into contact with the paper.

bleed pages (13) Magazine advertisements in which the dark or colored background of the ad extends to the edge of the page. Most magazines offer bleed pages, but they normally charge advertisers a 10 to 15 percent premium for them.

bleeds (10) The colors, type, or visuals that run off the edge of the page.

blinking (12) A type of media schedule in which ads are run only on specific days when the target audience is most likely to be reading or watching.

block type (10) See *sans serif type*.

board (11) See *audio console*.

body copy (8) The text of an advertisement that tells the complete story and attempts to close the sale. It is a logical continuation of the headline and subheads and is usually set in a smaller type size than headlines or subheads.

boldface (8) Heavier type.

bottom-up marketing (7) The opposite of standard, top-down marketing planning, bottom-up marketing focuses on one specific tactic and develops it into an overall strategy.

boxes and panels (8) A *box* is copy around which a line has been drawn, while a *panel* is an elongated box that usually runs the whole length or width of an ad. Boxes and panels are generally used in advertisements to set apart coupons, special offers, contest rules, and order blanks.

brand (5) The combination of name, word, symbols, or design that identifies one particular product and differentiates it from competing products.

brand development index (BDI) (12) The percentage of a brand's total sales in an area divided by the total population in the area; it indicates the sales potential of the particular brand in the specific market area.

brand equity (5) The totality of what consumers, distributors, dealers, and competitors feel and think about a brand over an extended period of time; in short, it is the value of the brand's capital.

brand loyalty (4) The consumer's conscious or unconscious decision—expressed through intention or behavior—to repurchase a brand continually. This occurs because the consumer perceives that the brand has the right product features, image, quality, or relationship at the right price.

brand manager (3) The individual within the advertiser's company who is assigned the authority and responsibility for the successful marketing of a particular brand.

broadcast television (14) Television sent over airwaves as opposed to over cables.

broadside (15) A form of direct-mail advertisement, larger than a folder and sometimes used as a window display or wall poster in stores. It can be folded to a compact size and fitted into a mailer.

brochure (15) Sales materials printed on heavier paper and featuring color photographs, illustrations, typography. See also *folders*.

budget buildup method (7) See *objective/task method*.

bulletin boards (17) An internal public relations means for announcing new equipment, meetings, promotions, new products, construction plans, and recreation news.

burn (10) The process of exposing a photosensitive plate to light.

bursting (12) A media scheduling method for promoting high-ticket items that require careful consideration, such as running the same commercial every half-hour on the same network in prime time.

business advertising (1) Advertising directed at people who buy or specify goods and services for business use.

business magazines (13) Periodicals that target business readers; they may be trade, industrial, or professional magazines.

business markets (4) Organizations that buy natural resources, component products, and services that they either resell or use in making another product or running their business.

business reply mail (15) A type of mail that enables the recipient of direct-mail advertising to respond without paying postage.

business-to-business (3) See *industrial advertising*.

bus-o-rama (15) In transit advertising, a jumbo roof sign, which is actually a full-color transparency backlighted by fluorescent tubes, running the length of the bus.

buy-back allowance (16) A manufacturer's offer to pay for an old product so that it will be taken off the shelf to make room for a new product.

cable television (14) Television signals carried to households by cable and paid by subscription.

camera-ready (10) A finished ad that is ready for the printer's camera to shoot—to make negatives or plates—according to the publication's specifications.

Canadian Advertising Foundation (CAF) (2) The primary self-regulatory mechanism in Canada, the CAF administers the Canadian Code of Advertising Standards.

Canadian Broadcasting Corporation (CBC) (2) A government subsidized radio and television network and, with its French-Canadian branch (Radio Canada), the dominant force in Canadian broadcasting.

Canadian Radio-Television and Telecommunications Commission (CRTC) (2) A federal regulator in Canada, the CRTC plays an active role in regulating all broadcast advertising by limiting licenses and by requiring preapproval for commercials dealing with food, drugs, and cosmetics.

cartoon (11) Animation technique achieved by drawing loose, childlike illustrations of each step in the action and photographing them one frame at a time such that when the film is projected, it gives the illusion of movement.

catalogs (15) Reference books mailed to prospective customers that list, describe, and often picture the products sold by a manufacturer, wholesaler, jobber, or retailer.

category development index (CDI) (12) The percent of a product category's total U.S. sales in an area divided by the percent of total U.S. population in the area.

CCAC (2) See *Ministry of Corporate Affairs Canada.*

centers of influence (4) Customers, prospective customers, or opinion leaders whose actions are respected and may be emulated by others.

centralized advertising department (1) A staff of employees, usually located at corporate headquarters, responsible for all the organization's advertising. The department is often structured by product, advertising subfunction, end user, media, or geography.

centralized organization (3) Corporate structure in which all the major decisions of a company's field offices and divisions are coordinated and finalized by a staff of officers usually located at corporate headquarters.

central location test (6) A type of pretest in which videotapes of test commercials are shown to respondents on a one-to-one basis, usually in shopping center locations.

cents-off promotion (16) A short-term reduction in the price of a product designed to induce trial and usage. Cents-off promotions take various forms, including basic cents-off packages, one-cent sales, free offers, and box-top refunds.

channels of distribution (5) See *distribution channels.*

character-count method (10) A method of copy casting in which an actual count is made of the number of characters in the copy.

cinematographer (11) A motion picture photographer.

circulars (17) Multipage handbills.

circulation audit (13) Thorough analysis of circulation procedures, distribution outlets, and other distribution factors by a company such as the Audit Bureau of Circulation (ABC).

classified advertising (13) Newspaper and magazine advertisements usually arranged under subheads that describe the class of goods or the need the ads seek to satisfy. Rates are based on the number of lines the ad occupies. Most employment, housing, and automotive advertising is in the form of classified advertising.

classified display advertising (13) Ads that run in the classified section of the newspaper but have larger-size type, photos, art borders, abundant white space, and sometimes color.

clearance advertising (18) A type of local advertising designed to make room for new product lines or new models or to get rid of slow-moving product lines, floor samples, broken or distressed merchandise, or items that are no longer in season.

clients (3) The various businesses that advertise themselves or their products and for whom advertising agencies work in an effort to find customers for their goods and services.

clip art (18) Syndicated source for preprinted images that can be purchased and used by advertisers to illustrate ads.

close (8) That part of an advertisement that asks customers to do something and tells them how to do it—the action step in the ad's copy.

closing date (10) (13) A publication's final deadline for supplying printing material for an advertisement.

clutter tests (6) Method of pretesting in which commercials are grouped with noncompetitive control commercials and shown to prospective customers to measure their effectiveness in gaining attention, increasing brand awareness and comprehension, and causing attitude shifts.

cognition (4) The point of awareness and comprehension of a stimulus.

cognitive dissonance (4) See *theory of cognitive dissonance.*

cognitive theory (4) An approach that views learning as a mental process of memory, thinking, and the rational application of knowledge to practical problem solving.

collateral sales material (5) (16) All the accessory nonmedia advertising materials prepared by manufacturers to help dealers sell a product—booklets, catalogs, brochures, films, trade-show exhibits, sales kits, and so on.

color light meter (11) A type of light meter that indicates the overall degrees on the Kelvin scale for the light reflected from an area within the light meter's view. Thus, it indicates whether a scene is generally too blue, green, or red in relation to daylight or tungsten film.

color separation negatives (10) Four separate continuous-tone negatives produced by photographing artwork through color filters that eliminate all the colors but one. The negatives are used to make four printing plates—one each for yellow, magenta, cyan, and black—for reproducing the color artwork.

color strip (13) A sample of eye shadow, blusher, lipstick, or makeup provided in a magazine advertisement.

column inch (13) In newspaper advertising, a measurement of depth one inch deep by one column wide. Most newspapers now sell advertising space by the column inch.

combination offers (16) A sales promotion device in which two related products are packaged together at a special price, such as a razor and a package of blades. Sometimes a combination offer may be used to introduce a new product by tying its purchase to an established product at a special price.

combination rates (13) Special newspaper advertising rates offered for placing a given ad in (1) morning and evening editions of the same newspaper; (2) two or more newspapers owned by the same publisher; or (3) two or more newspapers affiliated in a syndicate or newspaper group.

command headline (8) A type of headline that orders the reader to do something.

commercial advertising (1) Advertising that promotes goods, services, or ideas for a business with the expectation of making a profit.

commission (3) See *agency commission.*

commoncase (10) Typeset material that appears in capital letters and small caps.

communicating arts (4) Writing and printing, drama and theatrical production, graphic design, photography, and so on.

communications media (7) An element of the creative mix, comprising the various methods or vehicles that will be used to transmit the advertiser's message.

communication vehicle (1) See *medium.*

community involvement (18) A local public relations activity in which companies sponsor or participate in a local activity or supply a location for an event.

company conventions and dealer meetings (16) Events held by manufacturers to introduce new products, sales promotion programs, or advertising campaigns.

comparative advertising (2) Advertising that claims superiority to competitors in some aspect.

compiled list (15) A type of direct-mail list that has been compiled by another source, such as lists of automobile owners, newhouse purchasers, business owners, union members, and so forth. It is the most readily available type of list but offers the lowest response expectation.

comprehension block (7) In the advertising pyramid, the stage at which target consumers are not only aware of the product but also recognize its purpose and perhaps some of its features.

comprehensive layout (9) A facsimile of a finished ad with copy set in type and pasted into position along with proposed illustrations. The "comp" is prepared so the advertiser can gauge the effect of the final ad.

computer software (15) Used as an advertising medium, disks distributed by individual manufacturers with ads on computer information services.

conceptualization (8) See *visualization.*

conditioning theory (4) Also called stimulus-response theory, the idea that learning is a trial-and-error process.

consumer advertising (1) Advertising directed at the ultimate consumer of the product, or at the person who will buy the product for someone else's personal use.

consumer behavior (4) The activities, actions, and influencers of people who purchase and use goods and services to satisfy their personal or household needs and wants.

consumer decision-making process (4) The series of steps a consumer goes through in deciding to make a purchase.

consumerism (2) Social action designed to dramatize the rights of the buying public.

consumer magazines (13) Information- or entertainment-oriented periodicals directed toward people who buy products for their own consumption.

consumer promotions (16) Marketing, advertising, and sales promotion activities aimed at inducing trial, purchase, and repurchase by the consumer. (Also called *pull strategy.*)

consumers, consumer market (1) (4) People who buy products and services for their own, or someone else's, personal use.

contest (16) (18) A sales promotion device for creating consumer involvement in which prizes are offered based on the skill of the entrants.

continuity (12) The length of an advertising campaign and the manner in which it is scheduled and sustained over an extended period of time.

continuous schedule (12) A method of scheduling media in which advertising runs steadily with little variation.

contract rate (13) A special rate for newspaper advertising usually offered to local advertisers who sign an annual contract for frequent or bulk space purchases. As the number of inches contracted for increases, the rate decreases.

controlled circulation (13) A free publication mailed to a select list of individuals the publisher feels are in a unique position to influence the purchase of advertised products.

control room (11) In a recording studio, the place where the producer, director, and sound engineer sit, monitoring and controlling all the sounds generated in the sound studio.

conviction block (7) In the advertising pyramid, the stage at which a certain number of people believe in the value of the product.

cooperative advertising (5) (13) (16) (18) The sharing of advertising costs by the manufacturer and the distributor or retailer. The manufacturer may repay 50 or 100 percent of the dealer's advertising costs or some other amount based on sales. See also *horizontal cooperative advertising; vertical cooperative advertising.*

copy (3) (8) The words that make up the headline and message of an advertisement or commercial.

copy casting (10) The process of determining how much type will fit into an advertisement. The two methods of copy casting include the word-count and the character-count methods.

copy platform (8) A document that serves as a guide for writing an ad. It describes the most important issues that should be considered in writing the copy, including a definition and description of the target audience; the rational and emotional appeals to be used; the product features that will satisfy the customer's needs; the style, approach, or tone that will be used in the copy; and, generally, what the copy will say.

copy points (5) Copywriting themes.

copyright (2) An exclusive right granted by the Copyright Act to authors and artists to protect their original work from being plagiarized, sold, or used by another without their express consent.

copywriters (3) People who create the words and concepts for ads and commercials.

copywriter's pyramid (8) A simple, five-step model for setting copy objectives in writing ads and commercials.

copywriting (8) Creating the verbal element of the advertising message.

corporate advertising (1) (17) The broad area of nonproduct advertising aimed specifically at enhancing a company's image and increasing lagging awareness.

corporate objectives (7) Goals of the company stated in terms of profit or return on investment. Objectives may also be stated in terms of net worth, earnings ratios, growth, or corporate reputation.

cosponsor (14) One of multiple sponsors of a television program or series.

cost efficiency (12) The cost of reaching the target audience through a particular medium as opposed to the cost of reaching the medium's total circulation.

cost per rating point (CPP) (14) A simple computation used by media buyers to determine which broadcast programs are the most efficient in relation to the target audience. The CPP is determined by dividing the cost of the show by the show's expected rating against the target audience.

cost per thousand (CPM) (12) A common term describing the cost of reaching 1,000 people in a medium's audience. It is used by media planners to compare the cost of various media vehicles.

coupon (16) (18) A certificate with a stated value that is presented to a retail store for a price reduction on a specified item.

coupon premiums (16) Premiums for which consumers must collect in-pack coupons.

cover date (13) The date printed on the cover of a publication.

cover paper (10) A thick, durable paper stock used for softcover book covers and direct mail advertising pieces.

cover position (13) Advertising space on the front inside, back inside, and back cover pages of a publication which is usually sold at a premium price.

CPM (12) See *cost per thousand.*

creative boutique (3) An organization of creative specialists (such as art directors, designers, and copywriters) who work for advertisers and occasionally advertising agencies to develop creative concepts, advertising messages, and specialized art. A boutique performs only the creative work.

creative department (3) That department in an advertising agency that is responsible for conceiving, writing, laying out, and producing ads and commercials.

creative mix (7) Those advertising elements the company controls to achieve its advertising objectives, including the target audience, the product concept, the communications media, and the advertising message. (See also *advertising strategy.*)

crisis management (17) A company's plan for handling news and public relations during crises.

CRTC (2) See *Canadian Radio-Television and Telecommunications Commission.*

cume persons (14) The total number of different people listening to a radio station for at least one 15-minute segment over the course of a given week, day, or daypart.

cume rating (14) The estimated number of cume persons expressed as a percentage of the estimated population.

current customers (4) People who have already purchased something from a business and who may purchase on a regular basis.

cursive type (10) A type style that resembles handwriting. Also called *script.*

customers (4) The people or organizations who consume goods and services. See also *centers of influence, current customers,* and *prospective customers.*

cycle (11) One compressed section of air plus one decompressed section which, in concert with other cycles, produces sound. Cycles are measured on the hertz scale, and the more cycles per second, the higher the sound's pitch.

daily newspapers (13) Often called dailies, these newspapers are published at least five times a week, in either morning or evening editions.

database marketing (15) (16) Tracking and analyzing the purchasing patterns of specific customers in a computer database and then targeting advertising to their needs.

daypart (12) A part of the broadcast day. See also *radio dayparts; television dayparts.*

daypart mix (14) A media scheduling strategy based on the TV usage levels reported by the rating services.

dealer meeting (16) See *company conventions.*

decentralized organization (3) The establishment of advertising departments by products or brands or in various divisions, subsidiaries, countries, regions, or whatever other categories most suit the firm's needs, which operate with a major degree of independence.

deceptive advertising (2) According to the FTC, any ad in which "there is a misrepresentation, omission, or other practice that is likely to mislead the consumer acting reasonably in the circumstances, to the consumer's detriment."

decibel (11) Unit of measure for the loudness of sound determined by measuring the *volume* of air compressed in each cycle.

decline stage (5) The last phase of the product life cycle when the product has become obsolete due to changing consumer taste or new technology.

decoding (4) The interpretation of a message by the receiver.

defamation (8) Making a false statement or allegation about a person or holding a person up to contempt.

defensive strategy (1) In marketing warfare, the strategy used by the dominant company in a given market, which must defend itself against the onslaught of competitors.

demarketing (1) The marketing and advertising techniques used by some companies and organizations to discourage the purchase or use of certain products.

demographics (5) The study of the numerical characteristics of the population.

demonstration (9) A type of TV commercial in which the product is shown in use.

departmental system (3) The organization of an ad agency into departments based on function: account services, creative services, marketing services, and administration.

descender (10) In typography, the stroke of a letter that drops below the base line; for example, p, g, y.

design (9) Visual pattern or composition of artistic elements created by the graphic artist.

designated market areas (DMA) (14) The geographical areas in which TV stations attract most of their viewers, according to the Nielsen station index.

desire block (7) In the advertising pyramid, the group of people who actually desire the product.

desktop publishing (10) The process that enables individuals, through the use of desktop computers, to personally prepare, and occasionally even print, moderate-quality ads, documents, and publications.

development stage (3) In the agency-client relationship, the honeymoon period when both agency and client are at the peak of their optimism and are most eager to quickly develop a mutually profitable mechanism for working together.

device copy (8) Advertising copy that relies on wordplay, humor, poetry, rhymes, great exaggeration, gags, and other tricks or gimmicks.

dialogue/monologue copy (8) A type of body copy in which the characters illustrated in the advertisement do the selling in their own words either through a quasi-testimonial technique or through a comic strip panel.

digital video effects (DVE) unit (11) In video, special-effects equipment for manipulating graphics on the screen to produce fades, wipes, zooms, rotations, and so on.

direct advertising (15) Any form of advertising issued directly to the prospect through the use of mails, fax machines, on-line computer services, interactive electronic kiosks, salespeople, dealers, or other means rather than through the traditional mass media.

direct broadcast satellite (DBS) (14) A television delivery system that involves beaming programs from satellites to special satellite dishes mounted in the home or yard.

direct distribution (5) The method of marketing in which the manufacturer sells directly to customers without the use of retailers.

direct-mail advertising (15) All forms of advertising sent directly to prospects through U.S. or private postal services.

direct marketing (15) (16) A marketing system in which the seller builds and maintains its own database of customers and uses a variety of media to communicate directly with those customers.

directories (15) Listings, often in booklet form, that serve as locators, buying guides, and mailing lists.

direct questioning (6) A method of pretesting designed to elicit a full range of responses to the advertising. Direct questioning is especially effective for testing alternative advertisements in the early stages of development.

direct-response advertising (15) (16) An advertising message that asks the reader, listener, or viewer to provide feedback straight to the sender. Direct-response advertising can take the form of direct mail, or it can use a wide range of other media, from matchbook covers or magazines to radio, TV, or billboards.

direct sales (16) Strategy where representatives sell to customers directly at home or work rather than through a retail outlet or other intermediary.

display advertising (13) Newspaper and magazine ads that normally use not only copy but also illustrations or photos, headlines, and other visual components.

display allowances (16) Fees paid to retailers to make room for and set up manufacturers' displays.

displays (15) See *painted bulletins.*

display type (10) Large, bold type, heavier than text type, used in headlines, subheads, logos, addresses, or wherever there is a need for emphasis in an advertisement.

distribution channel (5) The network of all the firms and individuals that take title, or assist in taking title, to the product as it moves from the producer to the consumer.

distribution objectives (12) Where, when, and how advertising should appear.

diverting (16) Purchasing large quantities of an item at a regional promotional discount and shipping portions to areas of the country where the discount isn't being offered.

DMA (14) See *designated market areas.*

dubs (11) Duplicates of radio commercials made from the master tape and sent to stations for broadcast.

dummy (9) A three-dimensional, hand-made layout of a brochure or other multipage advertising piece put together, page for page, just like the finished product will eventually appear.

dupes (11) Copies of a finished television commercial that are delivered to the networks or TV stations for airing.

earned rate (13) See *contract rate.*

effective frequency (12) The range of exposures between the minimum number of times a person must see or hear a message before becoming aware of it and the maximum level that starts to become overexposure.

effective reach (12) The size of the audience that has been exposed to a message enough times to be aware of it.

electronic couponing (16) In supermarkets, the use of frequent-shopper cards that automatically credit cardholders with coupon discounts when they check out.

electronic signs (15) Signs in supermarkets that electronically display text and graphic messages, including advertisements.

em space (10) Spacing in typography with the width and proportions of the letter M.

emotional appeal (8) Advertising appeal which relates to the consumer's psychological, social, or symbolic needs or wants.

empirical research method (7) A method of allocating funds for advertising that uses experimentation to determine the best level of advertising expenditure. By running a series of tests in different markets with different budgets, companies determine the most efficient level of expenditure.

encoding (4) Translating an idea or message into words, symbols, and illustrations.

en space (10) Spacing in typography with the width and proportions of the letter N.

entrepreneurial agency (3) Any of the thousands of small advertising agencies that inhabit every major city in the country.

environments (4) Surroundings that can affect the purchase decision.

equipment-based service (5) A service business that relies mainly on the use of specialized equipment.

ethical dilemma (2) A situation in which there are two conflicting but valid sides to an issue.

ethical lapse (2) A situation in which an advertiser makes a clearly unethical and sometimes illegal decision.

euphemism (8) The substitution of an inoffensive, mild word for a word that is offensive, harsh, or blunt.

evaluation of selection alternatives (4) Choosing among brands, sizes, styles, and colors.

evaluative criteria (4) The standards a consumer uses for judging the features and benefits of alternative products.

evoked set (4) The particular group of alternative goods or services a consumer considers when making a buying decision.

exchange (4) The trading of one thing of value for another thing of value.

exclusive distribution (5) The strategy of limiting the number of wholesalers or retailers who can sell a product in order to gain a prestige image, maintain premium prices, or protect other dealers in a geographic region.

exhibits (15) (17) A marketing or public relations approach that involves preparing displays that tell about an organization or its products; exhibits may be used at fairs, colleges and universities, or trade shows.

experimental method (6) A method of scientific investigation in which a researcher alters the stimulus received by a test group or groups and compares the results with that of a control group that did not receive the altered stimulus.

exploratory research (6) See *informal research*.

export agency (3) An agency that specializes in creating ads for American companies engaged in international advertising.

exposure (12) A consideration in selecting media based on the number of people who actually see an advertisement in a given medium as opposed to the total audience of that medium. (Or, from another perspective, how many people an ad sees in a given medium.)

family brand (5) The marketing of various products under the same umbrella name.

farm advertising (1) Advertising directed to farmers as businesspeople and to others in the agricultural business.

farm publications (13) Magazines directed to farmers and their families or to companies that manufacture or sell agricultural equipment, supplies, and services.

FCB grid (7) A conceptual model developed by the Foote, Cone & Belding advertising agency to illustrate the nature of product purchases from the consumer's point of view. The grid has two dimensions: one to illustrate the degree of personal involvement (high or low) required to make a purchase, and the other to demonstrate the kind of involvement (think or feel) required.

FCC (2) See *Federal Communications Commission.*

FDA (2) See *Food and Drug Administration.*

Federal Communications Commission (FCC) (2) Federal regulatory body with jurisdiction over radio, television, telephone, and telegraph industries. Through its licensing authority, the FCC has indirect control over broadcast advertising.

Federal Trade Commission (FTC) (2) The major federal regulator of advertising used to promote products sold in interstate commerce.

fee-commission method (3) Compensation method whereby an ad agency establishes a fixed monthly fee for all its services to the client and retains any commissions earned for space or time purchased on behalf of the client.

feedback (4) A message that acknowledges or responds to an initial message indicating that the first message was received.

fill light (11) A light used to slightly brighten up a shadow area to reveal details without losing the overall effect of the shadow.

film negatives (10) Photographic negatives of camera-ready ads, from which printing plates are made.

first-class mail (15) A U.S. Postal Service classification of mail delivery used by direct-mail advertisers to ensure fast delivery, mail forwarding (at no additional charge), and return of undeliverable mail.

first-run syndication (14) Programs produced specifically for the syndication market.

flanking strategy (1) (7) In marketing warfare, the strategy adopted by middle companies in the hierarchy, who must point out the qualities that make them different from the top three companies.

flash (10) A technique for lightening the dark areas of a halftone in order to keep the areas from plugging up with ink and looking blotchy.

flat rate (13) A standard newspaper advertising rate with no discount allowance for large or repeated space buys.

flighting (12) An intermittent media scheduling pattern in which periods of advertising are alternated with periods of no advertising at all.

flyer (15) (18) A form of direct-mail advertising that is usually a single, standard-size (8½ by 11 inches) page printed on one or both sides and folded one or more times. It often accompanies a sales letter to supplement or expand on the information it contains.

focus group (6) A qualitative method of research in which 8 to 10 people, "typical" of the target market, are invited to a group session to discuss the product, the service, or the marketing situation for an hour or more.

folders (15) Large, heavy-stock flyers, often folded and sent out as self-mailers.

font (10) For a particular typeface and size of type, the complete assortment of capitals, small caps, lowercase letters, numerals, and punctuation marks.

Food and Drug Administration (FDA) (2) Federal agency that has authority over the labeling, packaging, and branding of packaged foods and therapeutic devices.

formal research (6) Collecting primary data directly from the marketplace using qualitative or quantitative methods.

formula model (12) A type of computer program used to calculate the reach, frequency, and other statistics for various media vehicles and to rank the vehicles according to selected parameters.

forward buying (16) A retailers' stocking up on a product when it is discounted and buying smaller amounts when it is at list price.

four-color process (10) The method for printing color advertisements with tonal values, such as photographs and paintings. This process is based on the principle that all colors can be printed by combining the three primary colors—yellow, magenta (red), and cyan (blue)—plus black (which provides greater detail and density as well as shades of gray).

four Ms (12) See *media mix.*

four Ps (5) See *marketing mix*.

fourth-class mail (15) Mail that weighs over 16 ounces and all remaining mailables not in first, second, or third class categories.

fragrance strips (13) Perfume samples included in sealed inserts in magazines.

franchising (5) A type of vertical marketing system in which dealers pay a fee to operate under the guidelines and direction of the manufacturer.

free-standing inserts (FSIs) (16) Coupons distributed through inserts in newspapers.

frequency (12) The number of times the same person or household is exposed to a vehicle in a specified time span. Across a total audience, frequency is calculated as the average number of times individuals or homes are exposed to the vehicle.

FTC (2) See *Federal Trade Commission*.

full position (13) In newspaper advertising, the preferred position near the top of a page or on the top of a column next to reading matter. It is usually surrounded by editorial text and may cost the advertiser 25 to 50 percent more than ROP rates.

full-service advertising agency (3) An agency equipped to serve its clients in all areas of communication and promotion. Its advertising services include planning, creating, and producing advertisements as well as performing research and media selection services. Nonadvertising functions include producing sales promotion materials, publicity articles, annual reports, trade show exhibits, and sales training materials.

gain (11) On an audio console, the dial used to control the overall master volume.

game (16) A sales promotion activity in which prizes are offered based on chance. The big marketing advantage of games is that customers must make repeat visits to the dealer to continue playing.

gatefold (13) A magazine cover or page extended and folded over to fit into the magazine. The gatefold may be a fraction of a page or two or more pages, and it is always sold at a premium.

general agency (3) An agency that is willing to represent the widest variety of accounts but that concentrates on companies that make goods purchased chiefly by consumers.

geographic segmentation (5) A method of segmenting markets by geographic regions based on the shared characteristics, needs, or wants of people within the region.

global advertising (1) (3) Using the identical ad, with translation, in all international markets.

global brand (3) A brand for which the same marketing and advertising is used throughout the world.

global corporations (3) Multinational corporations that market global brands and use the same marketing and advertising in all countries.

global marketing (3) The theory that, thanks to cheap air travel and modern telecommunications technology, the world is becoming a common marketplace in which people have the same tastes and desires and want the same products and lifestyles no matter where they live—thus allowing for world-standardized products at low prices sold the same way around the world.

goods (1) Tangible products such as suits, soap, and soft drinks.

gothic type (10) See *sans serif type*.

government markets (4) Governmental bodies that buy products for the successful coordination of municipal, state, federal, or other government activities.

gross impressions (12) The total of all the audiences delivered by a media plan.

gross rating points (GRPs) (12) (14) The total audience delivery or weight of a specific media schedule. It is computed by dividing the total number of impressions by the size of the target population and multiplying by 100, or by multiplying the reach, expressed as a percentage of the population, by the average frequency. In television, gross rating points are the total rating points achieved by a particular media schedule over a specific period. For example, a weekly schedule of five commercials with an average household rating of 20 would yield 100 GRPs. In outdoor advertising, a 100 gross rating point showing (also called a number 100 showing) covers a market fully by reaching 9 out of 10 adults daily over a 30-day period.

group system (3) System in which an ad agency is divided into a number of little agencies or groups, each composed of an account supervisor, account executives, copywriters, art directors, a media director, and any other specialists required to meet the needs of the particular clients being served by the group.

growth stage (5) The period in a product life cycle that is marked by market expansion as more and more customers make their first purchases while others are already making their second and third purchases.

GRPs (12) (14) (15) See *gross rating points*.

guaranteed circulation (13) The number of copies of a magazine that the publisher expects to sell. If this figure is not reached, the publisher must give a refund to advertisers.

guerrilla strategy (1) (7) In marketing warfare, carving out a small niche that one can defend successfully in the larger marketplace.

habit (4) An acquired or developed behavior pattern that has become nearly or completely involuntary.

halftone screen (10) A glass or plastic screen, crisscrossed with fine black lines at right angles like a window screen, which breaks continuous-tone artwork into dots so that it can be reproduced.

halo effect (6) In ad pretesting, the fact that consumers are likely to rate the one or two ads that make the best first impression as the highest in all categories.

handbills (18) Low-cost flyers or other simple brochures distributed by hand on the street, in parking lots, or door-to-door.

headline (8) The words in the leading position of an advertisement—the words that will be read first or that are positioned to draw the most attention.

Health Protection Branch of the Ministry of Health and Welfare Canada (HPB) One of the principal federal regulators of advertising in Canada, the HPB must preapprove all advertising for nonprescription drugs and cosmetics and enforces Canada's strict ban on all tobacco advertising.

hidden differences (5) Imperceptible but existing differences that may greatly affect the desirability of a product.

hierarchy of needs (4) Maslow's theory that the lower biologic or survival needs are dominant in human behavior and must be satisfied before higher, socially acquired needs become meaningful.

highly promotional strategy (18) In retailing, doing a great deal of advertising in order to keep bringing customers in.

horizontal cooperative advertising (18) Joint advertising effort of related businesses (car dealers, realtors, etc.) to create traffic for their type of business.

horizontal publications (13) Business publications targeted at people with particular job functions that cut across industry lines, such as *Purchasing* magazine.

Households using TV (HUT) (14) The percentage of homes in a given area that have one or more TV sets turned on at any particular time. If 1,000 TV sets are in the survey area and 500 are turned on, the HUT figure is 50 percent.

house list (15) A company's most important and valuable direct-mail list, which may contain current, recent, and long-past customers or future prospects.

house organs (15) (17) Internal and external publications produced by business organizations, including stockholder reports, newsletters, consumer magazines, and dealer publications. Most are produced by a company's advertising or public relations department or by its agency.

house publications (15) (17) See *house organs.*

HPB (2) See *Health Protection Branch.*

icon (9) A pictorial image that represents an idea or thing.

ideas (1) Economic, political, religious, or social viewpoints that advertising may attempt to sell.

illustrators (9) The artists who paint, sketch, or draw the pictures we see in advertising.

imperceptible differences (4) Distinguishing characteristics of products that are not readily apparent without close inspection or use.

imposition (10) The positioning of images on a sheet of paper for the purposes of printing.

incentive system (3) A form of compensation in which the agency shares in the client's success when a campaign attains specific, agreed-upon goals.

incident light meter (11) A light meter that indicates the intensity, or volume, of a light source. The meter displays the amount of light measured and indicates the correct aperture setting for the type of film being used.

independent shopping guide (13) Weekly local ad vehicles that may or may not contain editorial matter. They can be segmented into highly select market areas.

in-depth interview (6) An intensive interview technique that uses carefully planned but loosely structured questions to probe respondents' deeper feelings.

individual brand (5) Assigning a unique name to each product a manufacturer produces.

induced differences (5) Distinguishing characteristics of products effected through unique branding, packaging, distribution, merchandising, and advertising.

industrial advertising (1) (3) Advertising aimed at individuals in business who buy or influence the purchase of industrial products.

industrial agency (3) An advertising agency representing client companies that make goods to be sold to other businesses.

industrial buyers (4) The people who purchase industrial goods and services for use in their business.

industrial markets (4) Individuals or companies that buy products needed for the production of other goods or services such as plant equipment and telephone systems.

industrial products (1) Goods and services that are used in the manufacture of other goods or that become a physical part of another product. Industrial goods also include products that are used to conduct business and that do not become part of another product, such as capital goods (office machines, desks, operating supplies) and business services for which the user contracts.

infomercial (14) A long (three to sixty minutes) TV commercial that gives consumers detailed information about a product or service; see also *program length advertisement.*

informal research (6) The second step in the research process, designed to explore a problem by reviewing secondary data and interviewing a few key people with the most information to share. Also called *exploratory research.*

in-house agency (3) Agency wholly owned by an advertiser and set up and staffed to do all the work of an independent full-service agency.

in-pack premiums (16) Sales promotion device, popular in the food field, in which inexpensive gifts are placed inside the package for the buyer.

inquiry test (6) A form of test in which consumer responses to an ad for information or free samples are tabulated.

insert (13) An ad or brochure which the advertiser prints and ships to the publisher for insertion into a magazine or newspaper.

insertion order (13) A form submitted to a newspaper or magazine when an advertiser wants to run an advertisement. This form states the date(s) on which the ad is to run, its size, the requested position, and the rate.

inside card (15) A transit advertisement, normally 11 by 28 inches, placed in a wall rack above the windows of a bus.

Institute of Canadian Advertising (2) An association of the largest advertising agencies in English Canada.

institutional advertising (1) (17) (18) A type of advertising that attempts to obtain favorable attention for the business as a whole, not for a specific product or service the store or business sells. The effects of institutional advertising are intended to be long term rather than short range.

institutional copy (8) A type of body copy in which the advertiser tries to sell an idea or the merits of the organization or service rather than the sales features of a particular product.

in-store sampling (16) The handing out of free product samples to passing shoppers.

integrated commercial (9) A straight radio announcement, usually delivered by one person, woven into a show or tailored to a given program to avoid any perceptible interruption.

integrated marketing communications (16) The concept of building and reinforcing mutual profitable relationships with employees, customers, other stakeholders, and the general public by developing and coordinating a strategic communications program that enables them to make constructive contact with the company/brand through a variety of media.

intensive distribution (5) A distribution strategy based on making the product available to consumers at every possible location so that consumers can buy with a minimum of effort.

intensive techniques (6) Qualitative research aimed at probing the deepest feelings, attitudes, and beliefs of respondents through direct questioning. Typical methods include in-depth interviews and focus groups.·

interactive television (15) Television in which the viewer is able to alter the images on the screen, respond to questions, and so on.

interconnects (14) Groups of cable systems joined together for advertising purposes.

interior paragraphs (8) Text within the body copy of an ad where the credibility and desire steps of the message are presented.

interlock (11) See *work print*.

internal data (6) Company records, such as product shipment figures, billings to customers, advertising expenditures, and so on.

international advertising (1) Advertising directed at foreign markets.

international marketing (3) The distribution and sale of products to foreign markets.

international marketing structure (3) Organization of companies with foreign marketing divisions, typically decentralized with autonomous units in various foreign countries.

international markets (4) Consumer, business, or government markets located in foreign countries. Also called *global markets*.

interpersonal influences (4) Social influences on the consumer decision-making process, including family, society, and cultural environment.

interview (6) See *in-depth interview*.

introductory phase (5) The initial phase of the product life cycle (also called the *pioneering phase*) when a new product is introduced, costs are highest, and profits the lowest.

inverted pyramid (7) A simple model shaped like an upside-down pyramid, which represents the growing number of people who have joined the action block of the advertising pyramid and developed the repurchasing habit.

island half (13) A half-page of magazine space that is surrounded on two or more sides by editorial matter. This type of ad is designed to dominate a page and is therefore sold at a premium price.

issue advertising (17) A type of corporate advertising that advocates a particular point of view on a public issue. See *advocacy advertising*.

jingle (9) (11) A musical commercial, usually sung with the sales message in the verse.

junior unit (13) A large magazine advertisement (60 percent of the page) placed in the middle of a page and surrounded by editorial matter.

key light (11) The primary light to fall upon a subject.

keys (11) On an audio console, the toggle switches that send sounds either to the active program line or to an audition line.

kerning (10) Spreading or narrowing the spaces between letters of type.

kicker (8) A subhead that appears above the headline.

lavaliere microphone (11) A small, unobtrusive microphone that can hook onto a person's lapel, shirt, or tie.

layout (9) An orderly formation of all the parts of an advertisement. In print, it refers to the arrangement of the headline, subheads, visuals, copy, picture captions, trademarks, slogans, and signature. In television, it refers to the placement of characters, props, scenery, and product elements, the location and angle of the camera, and the use of lighting. See also *design*.

leading (10) Pronounced *ledding*, the space between lines of type. Art directors may vary this space to give a slightly more airy or condensed feeling.

lead-in paragraph (8) In print ads, a bridge between the headlines, the subheads, and the sales ideas presented in the text. It transfers reader interest to product interest.

lead time (13) The length of time between the closing date for the purchase of advertising space or time and the publication or broadcast of the ad. Advertising in magazines requires a long lead time—sometimes as long as three months. And once the closing date has been reached, no changes in copy of art can be allowed.

leaflet (15) See *flyer*.

learning (4) A relatively permanent change in thought processes or behavior that occurs as a result of reinforced experience.

letterpress (10) The forerunner of today's printing processes, but now rarely used. In letterpress, the process is similar to the way a rubber stamp works. Like a stamp, the image to be transferred is backward (wrong reading) on the plate. The ink is applied to a raised (relief) surface on the plate and then transferred to the paper.

letter shop (15) A firm that stuffs envelopes, affixes labels, calculates postage, sorts pieces into stacks or bundles, and otherwise prepares items for mailing.

libel (8) Defaming a person in print.

Library of Congress (2) The federal body that registers and protects all copyrighted material, including advertising.

licensed brands (5) Brand names that other companies can buy the right to use.

lifestyle (9) Type of commercial in which the user is presented rather than the product. Typically used by clothing and soft drink advertisers to affiliate their brands with the trendy lifestyles of their consumers.

linear programming model (12) A type of computer program designed to create a complete media schedule that maximizes exposure within a given budget.

line film (10) Film made from typeset copy and solid black and white (no tonal values) illustrations. From the line film, a line plate is produced for printing.

line plates (10) The plates used to print solid black-and-white images (not tonal values) such as typeset copy, pen-and-ink drawings, or charcoal illustrations.

lines (13) A unit of measuring space in newspapers and magazines: 14 lines to a column inch. Also called *agate lines*.

list broker (15) An intermediary who handles rental of mailing lists for list owners on a commission basis.

live action (11) The basic production technique in television that portrays people and things in lifelike, everyday situations.

local advertising (1) (18) Advertising by businesses within a city or county directed toward customers within the same geographical area.

local time (14) Radio spots purchased by a local advertiser.

local trading area (18) Primary geographic area from which most of a company's customers come.

logotype (8) Special design of the advertiser's name (or product name) that appears in all advertisements. Also called a *signature block*, it is like a trademark because it gives the advertiser individuality and provides quick recognition at the point of purchase.

lot (11) Acreage outside a studio that is shielded from stray, off-site sounds.

lowercase (10) Small letters, as opposed to capital letters.

Magazine Publishers Association (MPA) (13) A trade group made up of more than 230 publishers who represent 1,200 magazines. It compiles circulation figures on ABC member magazines and promotes greater and more effective use of magazine advertising.

mail-order advertising (15) A form of direct-response advertising and a method of selling in which the product or service is promoted through advertising and the prospect orders it. Mail-order advertising is usually received in three distinct forms: catalogs, advertisements in magazines and newspapers, and direct-mail advertising.

mail-response list (15) A type of direct-mail list, composed of people who have responded to the direct-mail solicitations of other companies, especially those whose efforts are complementary to the advertiser's.

maintenance stage (3) In the client-agency relationship, the day-to-day interaction that, when successful, may go on for years.

majority fallacy (5) A common marketing misconception that, to be successful, a product or service must appeal to the majority of people.

makegoods (14) TV spots that are aired to compensate for spots that were missed or run incorrectly.

management supervisors (3) Managers who supervise account executives and who report to the agency's director of account services.

market (4) (12) A group of potential customers who share a common interest, need, or desire, who can use the offered good or service to some advantage, and who can afford or are willing to pay the purchase price. Also, an element of the media mix referring to the targets of a media plan.

marketer (4) Any person or organization that has a good, service, or idea to sell.

marketing (4) The process of planning and executing the conception, pricing, promotion, and distribution of ideas, goods, and services to create exchanges that satisfy the perceived needs, wants, and objectives of individuals and organizations.

marketing exchange cycle (4) A cycle that consists of (1) discovering, locating, and measuring the needs, attitudes, and desires of prospective customers; (2) interpreting this information for management so that goods and services may be improved and new ones developed; and (3) devising and implementing a system to make the good or service available, to inform prospective customers about the product's need-satisfying capabilities, and to execute the exchange.

marketing information system (MIS) (6) A set of procedures and methods for generating an orderly flow of pertinent information for use in making marketing decisions.

marketing mix (5) (7) Four elements, called the four Ps (product, price, place, and promotion), that every company has the option of adding, subtracting, or modifying in order to create a desired marketing strategy.

marketing objectives (7) Goals of the marketing effort that may be expressed in terms of the needs of specific target markets and specific sales objectives.

marketing-oriented period (4) The modern marketing era in which companies determine in advance what customers want and then develop goods and services that will satisfy those needs or desires.

marketing plan (7) The plan that directs the company's marketing effort. First, it assembles all the pertinent facts about the organization, the markets it serves, and its products, services, customers, and competition. Second, it forces the functional managers within the company to work together—product development, production, selling, advertising, credit, transportation—to focus efficiently on the customer. Third, it sets goals and objectives to be attained within specified periods of time and lays out the precise strategies that will be used to achieve them.

marketing research (6) The systematic gathering, recording, and analysis of information to help managers make marketing decisions.

marketing strategy (7) The statement of how the company is going to accomplish its marketing objectives. The strategy is the total directional thrust of the company, that is, the "how-to" of the marketing plan, and is determined by the particular blend of the marketing mix elements (the 4 Ps) which the company can control.

market-need objectives (7) Marketing objectives that orient the company as a satisfier of target market needs rather than as a producer of goods or services.

market prep corporate advertising (17) Corporate advertising that is used to set the company up for future sales; it simultaneously communicates messages about the products and the company.

market research (6) The systematic gathering of information about a specific market or market segment, including its size, composition, structure, and so forth.

markets (12) An element of the media mix. See *market*.

market segmentation (5) The strategic process of (1) identifying groups of people with certain shared characteristics within the broader product market and (2) aggregating these groups into larger market segments according to their mutual interest in the product's utility.

markup (3) A source of agency income gained by adding some amount to a supplier's bill, usually 17.65 percent.

master tape (11) The final recording of a radio commercial, with all the music, sound, and vocals mixed, from which dubs (duplicates) are recorded and sent to radio stations for broadcast.

maturity stage (5) That point in the product life cycle when the market has become saturated with products, the number of new customers has dwindled, and competition is most intense.

mechanical (9) (10) The set type and illustrations or photographs pasted into the exact position in which they will appear in the final ad. Also called a *pasteup*, this is then used as the basis for the next step in the reproduction process.

media (1) (3) (12) A plural form of *medium*, referring to communications vehicles paid to present an advertisement to its target audience. Most often used to refer to radio and television networks, stations that have news reporters, and publications that carry news and advertising.

media-buying service (3) An organization that specializes in purchasing and packaging radio and television time.

media classes (6) The broad media categories: print, electronic, outdoor, and direct mail.

media commission (3) See *agency commission*.

media kit (17) A package of publicity materials used to give information to the press at staged events such as press conferences or open houses. Also, a package of sales material promoting a specific media vehicle.

media mix (12) Four elements called the *four Ms* (markets, money, media, and methodology) which advertisers combine to develop a media strategy.

media planning (12) The process that directs the advertising message to the right people at the right time.

media research (6) The systematic gathering and analysis of information on the reach and effectiveness of media vehicles.

media strategy (12) A description of how the advertiser will achieve stated media objectives: which media will be used, how often, and when. See also *media mix*.

media subclasses (6) Smaller divisions of media classes, such as radio, TV, magazines, newspapers, and so on.

media units (6) Specific units of advertising in each type of medium, such as half-page magazine ads, 30-second spots, and so on.

media vehicles (6) See *vehicles*.

medium (1) (4) An instrument or communications vehicle that carries or helps transfer a message from the sender to the receiver. Plurals are mediums and media. See also *media*.

mental files (4) Stored memories in the consumer's mind.

merge and purge (15) In compiling mailing lists, the process of merging mail response and house lists and purging all duplicates.

message strategy (8) The specific determination of what an ad or campaign will say and how it will say it. The elements of the message strategy include the copy platform, art direction, and production values.

message weight (12) The size of the audience for several commercials or ads combined or for an entire media plan.

methodology (12) A systematic way of conducting a procedure such as buying and scheduling advertising space in the media.

microphone (11) An instrument used to capture sound for radio or television commercials.

middleman (5) A business firm that operates between the producer and the consumer or industrial purchaser—someone who deals in trade rather than in production.

Ministry of Corporate Affairs Canada (CCAC) (2) One of the principal federal regulators of advertising in Canada, the CCAC regulates false and misleading advertising and oversees packaging, labeling, and advertising of all foods in Canada.

mixed interlock (11) The edited version of a filmed television commercial mixed with the finished sound track. Used for initial review and approval prior to being duplicated for airing.

mixed media approach (12) Using a combination of advertising media vehicles in a single advertising campaign.

mnemonic device (9) A gimmick used to dramatize the product benefit and make it memorable, such as the Imperial Margarine crown or the Avon doorbell.

monthly promotional calendar (18) A local advertiser's monthly schedule of sales, special events, in-house promotions, ad placements, and so on.

motivation (4) The underlying drives that stem from the conscious or unconscious needs of the consumer and contribute to the individual consumer's purchasing actions.

motivation research (6) Qualitative research used to give advertisers a general impression of the market, the consumer, or the product.

motivation value (12) A consideration in selecting media based on the medium's ability to motivate people to act. Positive factors include prestige, good quality reproduction, timeliness, and editorial relevance.

MPA (13) See *Magazine Publishers Association*.

multinational corporations (3) Corporations operating and investing throughout many countries and making decisions based on availabilities worldwide.

multinational marketing structure (3) An approach to international marketing in which a corporation has full and integrated participation in world markets and a view toward business based on choices available anywhere in the world. The multinational's marketing activities are typically characterized by strong centralized control and coordination. See also *international marketing structure*.

multipoint distribution system (MDS) (14) A microwave TV delivery system that can carry up to a dozen channels.

musical commercial (11) See *jingle*.

musical logotype (9) (11) A jingle that becomes associated with a product or company through consistent use.

NAB (13) See *Newspaper Advertising Bureau*.

NAD (2) See *National Advertising Division*.

NARB (2) See *National Advertising Review Board*.

NARC (2) See *National Advertising Review Council*.

narrative copy (8) A type of body copy that tells a story. It sets up a problem and then creates a solution using the particular sales features of the product or service as the key to the solution.

narrowcasting (14) The ability of cable networks to offer specialized programming aimed at particular types of viewers.

national advertisers (1) Companies that place advertising in more than one region of the country.

national advertising (1) Advertising aimed at customers in several regions of the country.

National Advertising Division (NAD) (2) The National Advertising Division of the Council of Better Business Bureaus. It investigates and monitors advertising industry practices.

National Advertising Review Board (NARB) (2) A five-member panel, composed of three advertisers, one agency representative, and one layperson, selected to review decisions of the NAD.

National Advertising Review Council (NARC) (2) An organization founded by the Council of Better Business Bureaus and various advertising industry groups to promote and enforce standards of truth, accuracy, taste, morality, and social responsibility in advertising.

national brands (5) Product brands that are marketed in several regions of the country.

NCN (13) See *Newspaper Co-op Network.*

needs (4) The basic, often instinctive, human forces that motivate a person to do something.

networks (14) Any of the national television or radio broadcasting chains or companies such as Columbia Broadcasting System (CBS), National Broadcasting Company (NBC), American Broadcasting Company (ABC), or Canadian Broadcasting Corporation (CBC). Networks offer the large advertiser convenience and efficiency because the message can be broadcast simultaneously throughout the country.

news/information headline (8) A type of headline that includes many of the "how-to" headlines as well as headlines that seek to gain identification for their sponsors by announcing some news or providing some promise of information.

Newspaper Advertising Bureau (NAB) (13) A bureau of the American Newspaper Publishers Association. It provides newspapers with market information by conducting field research and offers national advertisers help with obtaining better newspaper ad rates and with timely placement of ads in multiple markets.

Newspaper Co-op Network (NCN) (13) The NAB's system by which advertisers are able to line up local dealers for ads through a central clearinghouse.

news release (17) A typewritten sheet of information (usually 8½ by 11 inches) issued to print and broadcast outlets to generate publicity or shed light on a subject of interest.

Nielsen Station Index (14) Data that provide a wide array of statistics on how many people, in what age groups, and of what sex are watching TV at various times of the day within a specific market area. Prepared by the A. C. Nielsen organization.

nonbusiness institutions (18) Nonprofit organizations whose primary objective is noncommercial: churches, schools, universities, charitable organizations, and so forth.

noncommercial advertising (1) (18) Advertising sponsored by or for a charitable institution, civic group, religious order, political organization, or some other nonprofit group to stimulate donations, persuade people to vote one way or another, or bring attention to social causes.

nonpersonal influences (4) Factors influencing the consumer decision-making process that are often out of the consumer's control, such as time, place, and environment.

nonpersonal selling (5) All selling activities that use some medium as an intermediary for communication, including advertising, public relations, sales promotion, and collateral materials.

nonprobability samples (6) Research samples that do not provide every unit in the population with an equal chance of being included. As a result, there is no guarantee that the sample will be representative.

nonproduct advertising (1) Advertising designed to sell ideas or a philosophy rather than products or services.

nonpromotional strategy (18) For local businesses, reliance on word-of-mouth and return customers as opposed to advertising and related types of promotion.

nonverbal (8) Communication other than through the use of words, normally visual.

objectives (7) See *marketing objectives* and *advertising objectives.*

objective/task method (7) A method of determining advertising allocations, also referred to as the *budget-buildup method*, that defines objectives and how advertising is to be used to accomplish them. It has three steps: defining the objectives, determining strategy, and estimating the cost.

observation method (6) A method of research used when researchers actually monitor the overt actions of the person being studied.

offensive strategy (1) In marketing warfare, the strategy used by the second- and third-place companies to capture portions of the number-one company's market.

Office of Consumer Affairs (2) The chief consumer protection agency of the U.S. federal government.

off-network syndication (14) The availability of programs that originally appeared on networks to individual stations for rebroadcast.

offset lithography (10) The most popular printing process in the United States and Canada today. Unlike letterpress and rotogravure, the image on the offset plate is right reading. As the plate is covered with an oily ink, the moist, blank portions of the plate repel the ink. The greasy-coated image retains the ink for transfer to an intermediate rubber surface called a blanket, which comes in contact with the paper and enables the image to be printed.

omni-directional microphone (11) A microphone that captures sound from all directions.

on-camera (8) Actually seen by the camera, as an announcer, a spokesperson, or actor playing out a scene.

on-pack premium (16) A premium designed to have a good impulse value attached to the outside of a package.

on-sale date (13) The date a magazine is actually issued.

open rate (13) The highest newspaper advertising rate for one-time insertions.

opinion leader (4) Someone whose beliefs or attitudes are respected by people who share an interest in some specific activity.

opinion sampling (17) A form of public relations research in which consumers provide feedback via interviews, toll-free phone lines, focus groups, and similar methods.

ornamental type (10) A group of typefaces comprising designs that provide novelty and are decorative or highly embellished.

orthographic film (10) A high-contrast photographic film yielding only black-and-white images, no gray tones.

out-of-home media (15) Media such as outdoor advertising (billboards) and transit advertising (bus and car cards) that reach prospects outside their homes.

outside posters (15) The variety of transit advertisements appearing on the outside of buses, including king size, queen size, traveling display, rear of bus, and front of bus.

overlay (10) A piece of clear plastic containing a second image from which a second printing plate can be made for color printing.

overlaying (15) In developing mailing lists, the process of combining information from several sources to produce an in-depth profile of each customer or company.

overprint (10) The printing of black ink on top of another color of ink.

packaging (5) (9) The container for a product—encompassing the physical appearance of the container and including the design, color, shape, labeling, and materials used.

packaging specialists (9) Firms, departments, or container manufacturers who design packages.

paid circulation (13) The total number of copies of an average issue of a newspaper or magazine that are distributed through subscriptions and newsstand sales.

painted bulletins (15) Large outdoor painted displays and walls, normally 14′ by 48′ or larger, meant for long use and usually placed in only the best locations where traffic is heavy and visibility is good.

panels (8) See *boxes and panels.*

PANTONE MATCHING SYSTEM (PMS) (10) A set of solid colors for printing created by blending inks according to formulations specified by the Pantone company.

participation basis (14) The basis on which most network television advertising is sold. Advertisers can participate in a program once or several times on a regular or irregular basis by buying 30- or 60-second segments within the program. This allows the advertiser to spread out the budget and makes it easier to get in and out of a program without a long-term commitment.

pass-along readership (13) Readers of a publication in addition to the purchaser or subscriber.

pasteup (10) See *mechanical.*

people-based service (5) A service that relies on the talents and skills of individuals rather than on highly technical or specialized equipment.

people meter (14) An electronic device that automatically records a household's TV viewing, including channels watched, number of minutes of viewing, and who is watching.

perceived value (5) The value of a product in the customer's eyes, which may be created through actual differentiation or through unique branding, distribution, dealer service, and advertising.

percentage-of-sales method (7) A method of advertising budget allocation based on a percentage of the previous year's sales, the anticipated sales for the next year, or a combination of the two.

perceptible differences (5) Differences between products that are visibly apparent to the consumer.

perception (4) Our personalized way of sensing and comprehending the stimuli to which we are exposed.

perceptual screens (4) The physiological or psychological perceptual filters that messages must pass through.

personal processes (4) The three internal, human operations—

perception, learning, and motivation—which govern the way consumers discern raw data (stimuli) and translate them into feelings, thoughts, beliefs, and actions.

personal selling (5) (16) A sales method based on person-to-person contact, such as by a salesperson at a retail establishment or by a telephone solicitor.

photo animation (11) An animation technique that uses still photography instead of illustrations or puppets. By making slight movements of the photos from one frame to the next, the animated illusion is created.

photocomposition (10) A method of typesetting that combines computer technology, electronics, and photography. It offers an almost unlimited number of typefaces and sizes, fast reproduction at relatively low cost, and clear, sharp images.

photographers (9) The artists who use cameras to create visuals for advertisements.

photoplatemaking (10) A process for making printing plates, similar to taking a picture, in which an image is photographed and the negative is printed in reverse on a sensitized metal plate rather than on paper. This plate is then used for printing.

photoprints (10) Screened prints or Veloxes which publications can use for making their own printing plates.

physiological screens (4) The perceptual screens which use the five senses—sight, hearing, touch, taste, and smell—to detect incoming data and measure the dimension and intensity of the physical stimulus.

pica (10) The unit of measurement for the horizontal width of lines of type. There are six picas to the inch and 12 points to the pica.

picture-caption copy (8) A type of body copy in which the story is told through a series of illustrations and captions rather than through the use of a copy block alone.

pitch (11) The perception of the highness or lowness of a sound depending on the number of cycles per second of sound waves hitting the eardrum—as measured on the hertz scale.

PLA (14) See *program length advertisement.*

place element (5) In the marketing mix, how and where customers purchase a good or service; distribution.

PM (16) See *push money.*

PMS (10) See *PANTONE MATCHING SYSTEM.*

point (10) (18) The unit of measurement for the depth (or height) of type. There are 72 points to the inch, so 1 point equals 1⁄72 of an inch. Also, a retail place of business.

point-of-purchase (P-O-P) advertising (16) Materials set up at a retail location to build traffic, advertise the product, and promote impulse buying. Materials may include window displays, counter displays, floor and wall displays, streamers, and posters.

pop-up ad (13) A three-dimensional magazine ad.

positioning (1) (4) (5) The way in which a product is ranked in the consumer's mind by the benefits it offers, by the way it is classified or differentiated from the competition, or by its relationship to certain target markets.

positioning era (1) The 1970s, when marketers focused on how their product ranked against the competition in the consumer's mind.

postcards (15) Cards sent by advertisers to announce sales, offer discounts, or otherwise generate consumer traffic.

poster panel (15) The basic form of outdoor advertising and the least costly per unit. It is a structure of a blank panel with a standardized size and border, usually anchored in the ground, with its advertising message printed by lithography or silkscreen and mounted by hand on the panel.

posters (17) For public relations purposes, signs that impart product information or other news of interest to consumers, or that are aimed at employee behavior, such as safety, courtesy, or waste reduction.

postproduction (11) The finishing phase in commercial production—the period after recording and shooting when a radio or TV commercial is edited and sweetened with music and sound effects.

postpurchase dissonance (4) See *theory of cognitive dissonance.*

postpurchase evaluation (4) Determining whether a purchase has been a satisfactory or unsatisfactory one.

posttesting (6) The fourth stage of advertising research, designed to determine the effectiveness of an advertisement or campaign *after* it runs.

potentiometer (11) On an audio console, the dial or sliding linear button for controlling volume; also called a *pot.*

preemption rates (14) Lower TV advertising rates that stations charge when the advertiser agrees to allow the station to sell its time to another advertiser willing to pay a higher rate.

preferred position (13) A choice position for a newspaper or magazine ad for which a higher rate is charged.

premium (16) An item offered free or at a bargain price to encourage the consumer to buy an advertised product.

prepress production (10) The process of converting page art and visuals into materials (generally film negatives and color separation) needed for printing.

preprinted inserts (13) Newspaper advertisements printed in advance by the advertiser and then delivered to the newspaper plant to be inserted into a specific edition. Preprints are inserted into the fold of the newspaper and look like a separate, smaller section of the paper.

preproduction (11) The period of time before the actual recording or shooting of a commercial—the planning phase in commercial production.

prerelationship stage (3) All the time before an agency and client officially get together to do business.

presenter commercial (9) A commercial format in which one person or character presents the product and sales message.

press agentry (17) The planning of activities and the staging of events to attract attention to new products or services and to generate publicity about the company or organization that will be of interest to the media.

press kit (17) See *media kit.*

press release (17) See *news release.*

pretesting (6) The third stage of advertising research, used to increase the likelihood of preparing the most effective advertising messages.

price element (5) In the marketing mix, the amount charged for the good or service—including deals, discounts, terms, warran-

ties, and so on. The factors affecting price are market demand, cost of production and distribution, competition, and corporate objectives.

primary circulation (13) The number of people who receive a publication, whether through direct purchase or subscription.

primary data (6) Research information gained directly from the marketplace.

primary demand (5) Consumer demand for a whole product category.

primary demand trend (5) The projection of future consumer demand for a whole product category based on past demand and other market influences.

prime time (14) Highest level of TV viewing (8 P.M. to 11 P.M., EST).

print production (10) The systematic process a layout for an ad or a brochure goes through from concept to final printing.

private brands (5) Personalized brands applied by distributors or dealers to products supplied by manufacturers. Private brands are typically sold at lower prices in large retail chain stores.

process (4) A series of actions or methods that take place sequentially.

process blue, red, and yellow (10) The three primary colors (plus black) that are combined in four-color printing.

product (1) (6) (7) The particular good or service a company sells. See also *product concept.*

product advertising (1) (18) Advertising intended to promote goods and services; also a functional classification of advertising.

product concept (5) (7) The consumer's perception of a product as a "bundle" of utilitarian and symbolic values that satisfy functional, social, psychological, economic, and other wants and needs. Also, as an element of the creative mix used by advertisers to develop advertising strategy, it is the bundle of product values the advertiser presents to the consumer.

product differentiation (5) The competitive strategy of creating a difference in a product to appeal to the preferences of a distinct market segment.

product element (5) The most important element of the marketing mix: the good or service being offered and the values associated with it—including the way the product is designed and classified, positioned, branded, and packaged.

product information center (16) A video-display terminal in stores such as supermarkets that carries a series of 15-second "commercials" in a five-minute rotation, interspersed with community-interest items.

production (8) (10) (11) An element of creative strategy. The whole physical process of producing ads and commercials; also the particular phase in the process when the recording and shooting of commercials is done.

production-oriented period (4) An era when there were few products and many consumers, and companies had only to worry about creating and producing enough products to satisfy the huge demand.

production values (8) One of the elements of message strategy. Production values determine what is to be created mechanically and how it is to be created.

product life cycle (5) Progressive stages in the life of a product—

including introduction, growth, maturity, and decline—that affect the way a product is marketed and advertised.

product marketing process (5) The sequence of activities marketers perform to select markets and develop marketing mixes that eventually lead to exchanges.

product placement (15) Paying a fee to have a product included in a movie.

product shaping (4) Designing and building products to solve the customer's problems.

professional advertising (1) Advertising directed at individuals who are normally licensed to operate under a code of ethics or set of professional standards.

program length advertisement (14) A long-form television commercial that may run as long as an hour; also called an *infomercial.*

program rating (14) The percentage of TV households in an area that are tuned in to a specific program.

projective techniques (6) In marketing research, asking indirect questions or otherwise involving consumers in a situation where they can express feelings about the problem or product. The purpose is to get an understanding of people's underlying or subconscious feelings, attitudes, opinions, needs, and motives.

promotion (17) (18) The marketing-related communication between the seller and the buyer. For profit-making organizations, promotion means using advertising and public relations techniques to sell a good or service and to enhance the reputation of an organization. See also *promotion element.*

promotional mix (7) The combination of personal selling, advertising, public relations, direct marketing, sales promotion, and collateral that an advertiser uses to develop a promotional strategy. See also *promotion element.*

promotion element (5) (7) The aspect of the marketing mix that consists of marketing communications between seller and buyer.

proof copy (13) A copy of a newspaper-created ad provided to the advertiser for checking purposes before the ad runs.

prospective customers (4) People who are about to make an exchange, are considering it, or may consider it.

provocative headline (8) A type of headline written to provoke the reader's curiosity so that, to learn more, the reader will read the body copy.

psychographics (5) The grouping of consumers into market segments on the basis of psychological makeup—values, attitudes, personality, and lifestyle.

psychological screens (4) The perceptual screens consumers use to evaluate, filter, and personalize information according to subjective standards, primarily emotions and personality.

public affairs (17) All activities related to the community citizenship of an organization, including dealing with community officials and working with regulatory bodies and legislative groups.

publicity (17) (18) The generation of news about a person, product, or service that appears in broadcast or print media.

public relations (5) (17) Communications activities, usually not overtly sponsored, that act as supplements to advertising to inform various publics about the company and its products and to help build corporate credibility and image.

public relations advertising (17) Advertising that attempts to improve a company's relationship with its publics (labor, government, customers, suppliers, etc.).

pull strategy (5) (16) Marketing, advertising, and sales promotion activities aimed at inducing trial, purchase, and repurchase by consumers.

pulse (12) An increased schedule of advertising above normal levels, usually during peak selling periods.

pulsing (12) Mixing continuity and flighting strategies in media scheduling.

purchase occasion (5) A method of segmenting markets on the basis of *when* consumers buy and use a good or service.

push money (16) A monetary inducement for retail salespeople to push the sale of particular products. Also called *spiffs.*

push strategy (5) (16) Marketing, advertising, and sales promotion activities aimed at getting products into the dealer pipeline and accelerating sales by offering inducements to dealers, retailers, and salespeople. Inducements might include introductory price allowances, distribution allowances, and advertising dollar allowances to stock the product and set up displays.

qualitative research (6) The use of in-depth, open-ended questions to get people to share their thoughts and feelings on a subject in order to gain impressions rather than definitions.

quantitative mathematical models (7) Specialized computer-based techniques for budgeting and allocating advertising dollars.

quantitative research (6) A data collection method used by market researchers to develop hard numbers so they can completely and accurately measure a particular market situation.

question headline (8) A type of headline that asks the reader a question.

RADAR Report (14) Radio's All-Dimensional Audience Research audience estimates (ratings), based on daily telephone interviews that cover seven days of radio listening behavior.

radio dayparts (14) The five basic parts into which the radio day is divided: morning drive, daytime, afternoon drive, nighttime, all night. The rating services measure the audiences for only the first four of these dayparts, as all-night listening is very limited and not highly competitive.

radio personality (9) (11) A disc jockey or talk show host.

random probability samples (6) A sampling method in which every unit in the population universe is given an equal chance of being selected for the research.

rate card (13) A printed information form listing a publication's advertising rates, mechanical and copy requirements, advertising deadlines, and other information the advertiser needs to know before placing an order.

rating points (14) The average quarter-hour persons rating of a station as a percentage of population.

ratings (14) See *program rating.*

rational appeal (8) Advertising appeal based on the consumer's practical, functional need for the product or service.

reach (12) The total number of *different* people or households exposed to an advertising schedule during a given time, usually four weeks. Reach measures the *unduplicated* extent of audience exposure to a media vehicle and may be expressed either as a percentage of the total market or as a raw number.

reading notice (13) A variation of a display ad designed to look like editorial matter. It is sometimes charged at a higher space rate than normal display advertising, and the law requires that the word *advertisement* appear at the top.

recall tests (6) Posttesting methods used to determine the extent to which an advertisement and its message have been noticed, read, or watched.

recruitment advertising (17) A special type of advertising, most frequently found in the classified sections of daily newspapers and typically the responsibility of a personnel department, aimed at attracting employment applications.

reference groups (4) People we try to emulate or whose approval concerns us.

reflected light meter (11) Light meter that measures the volume of light reflected off a subject.

regional advertising (1) Advertising for products sold in only one area or region of the country. The region might cover several states but not the entire nation.

regular price-line advertising (18) A type of retail advertising designed to inform consumers about the services available or the wide selection and quality of merchandise offered at regular prices.

reinforcement advertising (7) Advertising designed to remind people of their successful experience with a product and to suggest using it again.

reliability (6) An important characteristic of research test results. For a test to be reliable, it must be repeatable, producing the same result each time it is administered.

reprints (15) Duplications of published articles that show the company or its products in a favorable light, used as direct-mail enclosures and frequently sent by public relations agencies or departments.

reseller markets (4) Individuals or companies that buy products for the purpose of reselling them.

resolution (10) Fineness of edge in creating art and typesetting, particularly when using computers.

retail advertising (18) Advertising by retail stores, primarily at the local level (although it can also be regional or national).

retainer (3) See *straight-fee method.*

reverse knockout (10) Area within a field of printed color on a page that is free of ink and allows the paper's surface to show.

roadblocking (12) Buying simultaneous airtime on all three television networks.

roman type (10) The most popular type group, considered to be the most readable and offering the greatest number of designs. It is characterized by the serifs (or tails) that cross the ends of the main strokes and by variations in the thickness of the strokes.

ROP (13) Run of paper. A term referring to a newspaper's normal discretionary right to place a given ad on any page or in any position it desires—in other words, where space permits. Most newspapers make an effort to place an ad in the position requested by the advertiser.

ROS (14) Run of station. Refers to a broadcast station's discretionary right to place a given ad in the time slot, usually randomly placed as time permits.

rotary plan (15) In outdoor advertising, the rotation of painted bulletins to different choice locations in the market every 30, 60, or 90 days, giving the impression of wide coverage over time.

rotogravure (10) A printing process that works in the reverse of letterpress. Instead of the printing design being raised above the printing plate as in letterpress, the rotogravure process prints from a depressed surface. Ink in the tiny depressions is transferred to the paper by pressure and suction.

rough (9) Penciled sketch of a proposed design or layout.

rough cut (11) See *work print.*

run of paper (13) See *ROP.*

run of station (ROS) (14) Leaving placement of radio spots up to the station in order to achieve a lower ad rate.

sale advertising (18) A type of retail advertising designed to stimulate the movement of particular merchandise or generally increase store traffic by placing the emphasis on special reduced prices.

sales letters (15) The most common form of direct mail. Sales letters may be typewritten, typeset and printed, printed with a computer insert (such as your name), or fully computer typed.

sales-oriented period (4) An era when the marketplace was glutted with products and the selling function was characterized by business's use of extravagant advertising claims and an attitude of *caveat emptor* (let the buyer beware).

sales promotion (5) (16) A direct inducement offering extra incentives all along the marketing route—from manufacturers through distribution channels to customers—to accelerate the movement of the product from the producer to the consumer.

sales-target objectives (7) Marketing objectives that relate to a company's sales. They should be specific as to product and market, quantified as to time and amount, and realistic. They may be expressed in terms of total sales volume; sales by product, market segment, or customer type; market share; growth rate of sales volume; or gross profit.

sales tests (6) Methods used to obtain information on the sales-producing value of specific ads or whole campaigns.

sample (6) (18) A portion of the population selected by market researchers to represent the appropriate targeted population. Also, a free trial of a product.

sample unit (6) The actual individuals chosen to be surveyed or studied.

sampling (16) (18) Offering consumers a free trial of the product, hoping to convert them to habitual use.

sans serif type (10) A large group of typefaces characterized by the lack of serifs (thus the name, sans serif) and by a relatively uniform thickness of the strokes. Also referred to as *block, contemporary,* or *gothic.*

satellite master antenna television (SMATV) (14) A method for TV signal delivery that makes use of a satellite dish to capture signals for TV sets in apartment buildings and other complexes.

SAU system (13) See *standard advertising unit system.*

screen printing (10) An old printing process that requires no plates and is based on the stencil principle. As ink is squeezed through a special stencil screen stretched tightly on a frame, the desired image is reproduced. For printing in color, a separate stencil is made for each color. Also called *serigraphy.*

script (8) Format for radio and television copywriting resembling a two-column list showing dialogue and/or visuals.

script type (10) See *cursive type.*

seal (8) A type of certification mark offered by such organizations as the Good Housekeeping Institute and Underwriters' Laboratories when a product meets standards established by these institutions. Seals provide an independent, valued endorsement for the advertised product.

secondary data (6) Information that has previously been collected or published.

secondary readership (13) The number of people who read a publication in addition to the primary purchasers.

selective demand (5) Consumer demand for the particular advantages of one brand over another.

selective distribution (5) (7) Strategy of limiting the distribution of a product to select outlets in order to reduce distribution and promotion costs.

selective perception (4) The ability of humans to select from the many sensations bombarding their central processing unit those sensations that fit well with their current or previous experiences, needs, desires, attitudes, and beliefs, focusing attention on some things and ignoring others.

self-concept (4) The images we carry in our minds of the type of person we are and who we desire to be.

self-liquidating premium (16) A special offer in which the consumer pays the cost of the premium. The seller does not attempt to make a profit on such a premium but only tries to break even.

self-mailer (15) Any type of direct-mail piece that can travel by mail without an envelope. Usually folded and secured by a staple or a seal, self-mailers have a special blank space for the prospect's name and address.

semipromotional strategy (18) An approach to local advertising that entails using periodic sales and promotions to increase store traffic for a business that otherwise has regular customers.

serifs (10) Delicate curved tails that cross the end of each letter stroke of roman type.

service (1) (5) A bundle of benefits that may or may not be physical, that are temporary in nature, and that come from the completion of a task.

session (11) The time when the recording and mixing of a radio commercial takes place.

set width (10) Width of a letter of type. See *em space.*

share (14) See *share of audience*; also *share of market.*

shared mail (18) A direct-mail vehicle in which ads from two or more advertisers are included in a single mail package targeted by ZIP code.

share of audience (14) The percentage of homes that have sets in use (HUT) tuned in to a specific program. A program with only five viewers could have a 50 share if only 10 sets are turned on.

share-of-market/share-of-voice method (7) A method of allocating advertising funds based on determining the firm's goals for a certain share of the market and then applying a slightly higher percentage of industry advertising dollars to the firm's budget.

sheetwise imposition (10) An arrangement for printing in which half the pages are printed on one side of the sheet and the other half on the reverse.

shoppers (18) Weekly local ad vehicles that may or may not contain editorial matter. They can be segmented into highly selected market areas.

short rate (13) The rate charged to advertisers who, during the year, fail to fulfill the amount of space for which they have contracted. This is computed by determining the difference between the standard rate for the lines run and the discount rate contracted.

shotgun microphone (11) A unidirectional microphone engineered to capture sounds from long distances.

showing (15) A traditional term referring to the relative number of outdoor posters used during a contract period, indicating the intensity of market coverage. For example, a 100 showing provides an even and thorough coverage of the entire market.

SIC codes (5) See *Standard Industrial Classification codes.*

signature cuts (8) See *logotypes.*

silk screen (10) See *screen printing.*

simulation model (12) A type of computer program used to estimate the ability of specific media vehicles to reach target individuals.

situation analysis (7) A statement in the marketing plan telling where the organization is and how it got there. It includes relevant facts about the company's history, growth, goods and services, sales volume, share of market, competitive status, market served, distribution system, past advertising programs, results of market research studies, company capabilities, and strengths and weaknesses.

single source data (14) Information on consumer buying habits made available by supermarket scanners.

size of type (10) Height of a character of type measured in points (72 per inch) from its ascender to its descender.

slander (8) Defamation of a person in broadcast advertising or verbal statements.

slice-of-life commercial (9) A type of commercial consisting of a short play that portrays a real-life situation in which the product is tried and becomes the solution to a problem.

slogan (8) A standard company statement (also called a *tag line* or a *theme line*) for advertisements, salespeople, and company employees. Slogans have two basic purposes: to provide continuity for a campaign and to reduce a key theme or idea to a brief, memorable positioning statement.

slotting allowances (16) Fees that manufacturers pay to retailers for the privilege of obtaining shelf or floor space for a new product.

smart cards (15) (16) Frequent-shopper cards, issued by supermarkets and retail chains, that are used for electronic couponing and other purposes.

social sciences (4) See *behavioral sciences.*

sound booth (11) A small windowed room or practice area in a sound studio.

special effects (11) Unusual visual effects created for commercials.

special-effects lighting (11) Lighting used to create enhancements or distortions to add visual excitement to a scene.

special events (17) (18) Scheduled meetings, parties, and demonstrations aimed at creating awareness and understanding for a product or company.

specialty advertising (15) (18) An advertising, sales promotion, and motivational communication medium that employs useful articles of merchandise imprinted with the advertiser's name, message, or logo.

specialty items (18) See *specialty advertising.*

specify type (10) Writing instructions for typesetters describing the size, weight, style, and positioning of type.

spectaculars (15) Giant electronic signs that usually incorporate movement, color, and flashy graphics to grab the attention of viewers in high-traffic areas.

speculative presentation (3) An agency's presentation of the advertisement it proposes using in the event it is hired. It is usually made at the request of a prospective client and is often not paid for by the client.

spiff (16) See *push money.*

spillover media (12) Foreign media aimed at a national population that is inadvertently received by a substantial number of the consumers in a neighboring country.

split run (13) A feature of many newspapers (as well as magazines) that allows advertisers to test the comparative effectiveness of two different advertising approaches by running two different ads of identical size, but different content, in the same or different press runs on the same day.

split-30s (14) 30-second TV spots in which the advertiser promotes two separate products with separate messages.

sponsorship (14) The presentation of a radio or TV program by a sole advertiser. The advertiser is responsible for the program content and the cost of production as well as the advertising. This is generally so costly that single sponsorships are usually limited to specials.

spot announcement (14) An individual commercial message run between programs but having no relationship to either. Spots may be sold nationally or locally. They must be purchased by contacting individual stations directly.

spot radio (14) National advertisers' purchase of airtime on individual stations. Buying spot radio affords advertisers great flexibility in their choice of markets, stations, airtime, and copy. In addition, spot advertising enables the message to be tailored to the local market and presented to listeners at the most favorable times.

square serif type (10) A kind of typeface that combines sans serif and roman. The serifs have the same weight and thickness as the main strokes of the letters.

SRDS (13) See *Standard Rate and Data Service.*

standard advertising unit (SAU) system (13) A system of standardized newspaper advertisement sizes that can be accepted by all standard-sized newspapers without consideration of their precise format or page size. This system allows advertisers to prepare one advertisement in a particular size or SAU and place it in various newspapers regardless of the format.

Standard Industrial Classification (SIC) codes (5) Method used by the U.S. Department of Commerce to classify all businesses. The SIC codes are based on broad industry groups, which are then subdivided into major groups, subgroups, and detailed groups of firms in similar lines of business.

standardized outdoor advertising (15) Specialized system of outdoor advertising structures located scientifically to deliver an advertiser's message to an entire market.

Standard Rate and Data Service (SRDS) (13) A publisher of media information directories that eliminate the necessity for advertisers and their agencies to obtain rate cards for every publication.

standard size (13) A newspaper size generally 22 inches deep and 13 inches wide, divided into six columns.

statement stuffers (15) Advertisements enclosed in the monthly customer statements mailed by department stores, banks, utilities, or oil companies.

stimulus (4) Physical data that can be sensed.

stock photos (10) Existing photos that can be purchased for advertising purposes, usually from stock photo companies.

stop-motion photography (11) An animation technique whereby objects and animals come to life—walk, run, dance, and do tricks. Each frame of film is shot individually. An arm may be moved only $\frac{1}{32}$ of an inch on each frame, but when the frames are assembled, the effect is smooth and natural.

storyboard (8) (9) Drawings of a series of sequential frames to indicate the conception of a television commercial.

storyboard roughs (9) A rough layout of a television commercial in storyboard form.

straight announcement (9) The oldest type of radio or television commercial, in which an announcer delivers a sales message directly into the microphone or on-camera or does so off-screen while a slide or film is shown on-screen.

straight-fee method (3) A method of compensation for ad agency services in which a straight fee, or *retainer,* is based on a cost-plus-fixed-fees formula. Under this system, the agency estimates the amount of personnel time required by the client, determines the cost of that personnel, and multiplies by some factor.

straight-sell copy (8) A type of body copy in which the text immediately explains or develops the headline and visual in a straightforward attempt to sell the product.

strategy (7) The methodology a company uses to achieve its objectives—the "how to" of a plan. See *marketing strategy.*

stripping (10) Assembling line and halftone negatives into one single negative, which is then used to produce a combination plate.

studio (11) The place where commercials are recorded.

subhead (8) Secondary headline in advertisements that may appear above or below the headline or in the text of the ad. Subheads are usually set in a type size smaller than the headline but larger than the body copy or text type size. They may also appear in boldface type or in a different ink color.

subscription television (STV) (14) Over-the-air pay TV. Subscribers pay for a descrambler that allows them to watch programs carried over a regular television channel.

Sunday supplement (13) A newspaper-distributed Sunday magazine. Sunday supplements are distinct from other sections of the newspaper since they are printed by rotogravure on smoother paper stock.

supers (11) Words superimposed on the picture in a television commercial.

superstations (14) Local TV stations that broadcast to the rest of the country via satellite and carry national advertising. The best-known superstation is Ted Turner's WTBS out of Atlanta, for which the term was coined.

suppliers (3) People and organizations that assist both advertisers and agencies in the preparation of advertising materials, such as photography, illustration, printing, and production.

survey (6) The most common way to gather primary research data. By asking questions of current or prospective customers, the researcher hopes to obtain information on attitudes, opinions, or motivations.

sweepstakes (16) A sales promotion activity in which prizes are offered based on a chance drawing of entrants' names. The purpose is to encourage consumption of the product by creating consumer involvement.

syndicated research services (6) Companies that continuously monitor and publish information on subjects of interest to marketers, such as the reach and effectiveness of media vehicles.

syndication (14) See *barter syndication, first-run syndication, off-network syndication.*

synergy (12) (16) An effect achieved when the sum of the parts is greater than that expected from simply adding together the individual components.

syntax (8) The harmonious sequencing of symbols to express meaning.

tabloid (13) A newspaper size generally about half as deep as a standard-sized newspaper; it is usually about 14 inches deep and 11 inches wide.

tactics (7) The precise details of a company's marketing strategy that spell out the specific details of the methods that will be used to achieve its marketing objectives.

tag line (8) See *slogan.*

take ones (15) In transit advertising, pads of business reply cards or coupons, affixed to interior advertisements for an extra charge, that allow passengers to request more detailed information, send in application blanks, or receive some other product benefit.

talent (11) The actors in commercials.

target audience (1) (7) The specific group of individuals to whom the advertising message is directed.

target market (5) (6) (7) The market segment or group within the market segment toward which all marketing activities will be directed.

target marketing process (5) The sequence of activities aimed at assessing various market segments, designating certain ones as the focus of marketing activities, and designing marketing mixes to communicate with and make sales to these targets.

tear sheets (13) The printed ad cut out and sent by the publisher to the advertiser as a proof of the ad's print quality and that it was published.

telemarketing (5) (16) Selling products and services by using the telephone to contact prospective customers.

telephone sales (16) See *telemarketing.*

teleprompter (11) A two-way mirror mounted on the front of a studio video camera that reflects moving text to be read by the speaker being taped.

television dayparts (14) The various parts of the day into which TV programming and viewing is divided. These include daytime, early fringe, early news, prime access, prime time, late news, and late fringe.

terminal posters (15) One-sheet, two-sheet, and three-sheet posters in many bus, subway, and commuter train stations as well as in major train and airline terminals. They are usually custom designed and include such attention getters as floor displays, island showcases, illuminated signs, dioramas (three-dimensional scenes), and clocks with special lighting and moving messages.

termination stage (3) The ending of a client-agency relationship.

testimonial (9) The use of satisfied customers and celebrities to endorse a product in advertising.

testing (6) See *posttesting; pretesting.*

text (8) See *body copy.*

text paper (10) Range of less expensive papers that are light-weight. More porous versions are used in printing newspapers and finer, glossier versions are used for quality printed materials like magazines and brochures.

text type (10) The smaller type used in the body copy of an advertisement.

theme line (8) See *slogan.*

theory of cognitive dissonance (4) The theory that people try to justify their behavior by reducing the degree to which their impressions or beliefs are inconsistent with reality.

third-class mail (15) The inexpensive type of U.S. mail delivery usually used for direct-mail advertising. The four types of third-class mail are single piece, bulk, bound books or catalogs, and nonprofit organization mail.

3-D ads (13) Magazine ads requiring the use of 3-D glasses.

thumbnail sketch (9) A rough, rapidly produced pencil sketch, approximately one-fourth to one-eighth the size of the finished ad, that is used for trying out ideas.

top-down planning (7) The traditional planning process of analyzing a situation, establishing objectives, setting strategy, and determining tactics, in that order.

total audience (14) The total number of homes reached by some portion of a TV program. This figure is normally broken down to determine the distribution of audience into demographic categories.

total audience plan (TAP) (14) A radio advertising package rate that guarantees a certain percentage of spots in the better dayparts.

total bus (15) In transit advertising, all the exterior space on a bus, including the front, rear, sides, and top, giving the product message powerful exclusivity.

total market coverage (TMC) (18) A free advertising vehicle delivered weekly to 100 percent of residents in a newspaper's market area.

trade advertising (1) The advertising of goods and services to middlemen to stimulate wholesalers and retailers to buy goods for resale to their customers or for use in their own businesses.

trade concentration (16) More products being sold by fewer retailers.

trade deals (16) Short-term dealer discounts on the cost of a product or other dollar inducements to sell a product.

trademark (2) Any word, name, symbol, device, or any combination thereof adopted and used by manufacturers or merchants to identify their goods and distinguish them from those manufactured or sold by others.

trade promotions (16) See *push strategy*.

trade shows (15) Exhibitions where manufacturers, dealers, and buyers of an industry's products can get together for demonstrations and discussion; expose new products, literature, and samples to customers; and meet potential new dealers for their products.

transit advertising (15) An out-of-home medium that actually includes three separate media forms: inside cards; outside posters; and station, platform, and terminal posters.

trap (10) Where, in the printing process, one color overlays the edge of another to keep the paper from showing through.

trial close (8) In ad copy, requests for the order that are made before the close in the ad.

TVHH (TV households) (14) The number of households in a market area that own television sets.

type families (10) Related typefaces in which the basic design remains the same but in which variations occur in the proportion, weight, and slant of the characters. Variations commonly include light, medium, bold, extra bold, condensed, extended, and italic.

typography (10) The art of selecting, setting, and arranging type.

unfair advertising (2) According to the FTC, advertising that causes a consumer to be "unjustifiably injured" or that violates public policy.

unidirectional microphone (11) A microphone that captures sound from one direction only.

Universal Product Code (UPC) (6) A series of linear bars and a 10-digit number that identify a product and its price.

universe (6) The entire target population of a research study.

uppercase (10) Capital letters.

usage rates (5) The extent to which consumers use a product: light, medium, or heavy.

user-status (5) A method of segmenting markets by types of product users, such as nonusers, ex-users, potential users, new users, and regular users.

USP (1) The *unique selling proposition*, or the differentiating features, of every product advertised; a concept developed by Rosser Reeves of the Ted Bates advertising agency.

utility (4) A product's ability to provide both symbolic or psychological want satisfaction and functional satisfaction. A product's problem-solving potential may include form, time, place, or possession utility.

validity (6) An important characteristic of a research test. For a test to be valid, it must reflect the true status of the market.

values and lifestyles (VALS) (5) A psychographic typology for segmenting U.S. consumers and predicting their purchase behavior.

vehicles (6) (12) Particular media programs or publications.

verbal (8) Words, written or spoken.

vertical cooperative advertising (18) Co-op advertising in which the manufacturer provides the ad and pays a percentage of the cost of placement.

vertical marketing system (VMS) (5) A centrally programmed and managed system that supplies or otherwise serves a group of stores or other businesses.

vertical publications (13) Business publications aimed at people within a specific industry; for example, *Restaurants & Institutions*.

video (8) (9) The visual part of a television commercial. Also, the left side of a television script, indicating camera action, scenes, and stage directions.

VideOcart (15) A shopping cart equipped with a video screen that shows spots from national advertisers as well as store specials.

video press release (17) A news or feature story prepared in video form and offered free to TV stations.

visual (9) The picture or illustration in an advertisement.

visualization (8) The creative point in advertising where the search for the "big idea" takes place. It includes the task of analyzing the problem, assembling any and all pertinent information, and developing some verbal or visual concept of how to communicate what needs to be said.

voice-over (8) In television advertising, the spoken copy or dialogue delivered by an announcer who is not seen but whose voice is heard.

volume discounts (13) Reduced newspaper ad rates earned by purchasing large or repeated amounts of space.

volume segmentation (5) Defining consumers as light, medium, or heavy users of products.

volume unit (VU) meter (11) On an audio console, a needle indicating the loudness of sounds.

wants (4) Needs learned during a person's lifetime.

weeklies (13) Newspapers that are published once a week and characteristically serve readers in small urban or suburban areas or farm communities with exclusive emphasis on local news and advertising.

word-count method (10) A method of copy casting in which all the words in the copy are counted and then divided by the number of words per square inch that can be set in a particular type style and size, as given in a standard table.

work & turn imposition (10) A method of printing in which both sides of the art are printed on one side of the sheet. After the first side has been run, the sheets are then turned over to the blank side, and the same plate is used to run the second side. The images are registered so that the front and the back of the piece are printed on opposite sides of the paper and can be cut and folded down to make a complete set of pages in sequence.

work print (11) The first visual portion of a filmed commercial assembled without the extra effects or dissolves, titles, or supers. At this time, scenes may be substituted, music and sound effects added, or other changes made.

writing paper (10) Form of plain, lightweight paper commonly used for printing of flyers and for letterhead.

yellow pages advertising (15) See *directories*.

zapping (14) The tendency of remote-control users to change TV channels during commercials.

zipping (14) The ability of VCR users to skip through commercials when replaying taped programs.

Notes

Chapter 1

1. "A New Look for Coca-Cola: A Synopsis of the 70s," Coca-Cola Company, 1970.

2. Stan Rapp and Tom Collins, *MaxiMarketing: The New Direction in Advertising, Promotion and Marketing Strategy* (New York: McGraw-Hill, 1987), pp. 17–30.

3. Marshall McLuhan, *Understanding Media: The Extensions of Man* (New York: McGraw-Hill, 1965), pp. 45–58; Desmond Smith, "Tomorrow's Media Are in Place Today," *Advertising Age*, December 19, 1983, pp. M14, M16; Walter A. Kleinschrod, "The Management Message in Electronic Messaging Media," *Administrative Management*, October 1987, p. 13; H. T. Eckhardt, "Electronics and Print Co-Exist in the Wired City," *American Printer*, July 1988, pp. 94, 96; Deborah Pfeiffer and Czatdana Inan, "The Times They Are a Changin'," *Telephony*, January 7, 1991, pp. 22–30.

4. James Burke, *The Day the Universe Changed* (Boston: Little, Brown, 1985) pp. 91–92.

5. Marcel Bleustein-Blanchet, *La Rage de Convaincre* (Paris, Editions Robert Laffont, 1970), p. 68.

6. Al Ries and Jack Trout, *Positioning: The Battle for Your Mind,* rev. ed. (New York: McGraw-Hill, 1986), pp. 23–27, 39, 101.

7. Daniel Thomas Seymour, "Demarketing: New Segmenting Tool," *United States Banker,* August 1983, pp. 71–72, 74; Lawrence R. Lepisto, "Demarketing Strategies: Assessment and Implementation," *Mid-Atlantic Journal of Business,* Winter 1983/1984, pp. 31–41; Linda Hersch, "The Demarketing Zone," *ZIP/Target Marketing,* October 1984, pp. TM38–TM39; Kathleen A. Krentler, "Maintaining Quality Control during the 'Crunch' in Service Firms," *Journal of Services Marketing,* Winter 1988, pp. 71–74; Allan C. Reddy, "Reducing Health Care Cost by Demarketing Benefits," *Health Marketing Quarterly,* 1989, pp. 137–45.

8. Raymond Serafin and Cleveland Horton, "Chrysler Rides Pro-U.S. Tide," *Advertising Age,* March 5, 1990, pp. 1, 42, 2.

9. Debra Goldman, "Study: Advertisers Aren't Talking to Consumers," *Adweek,* August 27, 1990, p. 25.

10. Hank Seiden, *Advertising Pure and Simple, The New Edition* (New York: AMACOM, 1990), pp. 23, 47, 57.

11. John McManus, "Cable Proves It's Media's Live Wire," *Advertising Age,* November 26, 1990, p. S6; see also, "Media & Measurement Technologies (Part 1)," *Direct Marketing,* March 1991, pp. 25–27, 79.

12. "Total National Ad Spending by Media," *Advertising Age,* September 26, 1990, p. 8; Gary Levin and Jon Lafayette, "Ad Spending Hikes May Lag Inflation," *Advertising Age,* December 17, 1990, pp. 3, 34.

13. Ibid.

14. David Lanchner, "The Rush to Russia," *Adweek's Marketing Week,* February 20, 1989, pp. 24–32.

15. McGraw-Hill Laboratory/Laboratory of Advertising Performance, 1985 study.

16. "Total National Ad Spending by Media," *Advertising Age,* September 26, 1990, p. 8; George Garneau, "Slight Ad Growth Expected for Newspapers," *Editor & Publisher,* January 5, 1991, pp. 14, 73.

17. Marcel Bleustein-Blanchet, *La Rage de Convaincre,* p. 25.

18. Ernest Dichter, *Handbook of Consumer Motivations* (New York: McGraw-Hill, 1964), pp. 6, 422–31.

19. Richard E. Kihlstrom and Michael H. Riordan, "Advertising as a Signal," *Journal of Political Economy,* June 1984, pp. 427–50.

20. John Kenneth Galbraith, "Economics and Advertising: Exercise in Denial," *Advertising Age,* November 9, 1988, pp. 80–84.

21. Rebecca Colwell Quarles, "Marketing Research Turns Recession into a Business Opportunity," *Marketing News,* January 7, 1991, pp. 27, 29.

Chapter 2

1. John O'Toole, "Afterword," *Madison Avenue,* May 1980, p. 98.

2. Jack Haberstroh, "Can't Ignore Subliminal Ad Charges," *Advertising Age,* September 17, 1984, p. 42; Martha Rogers and Kirk H. Smith, "Public Perceptions of Subliminal Advertising," *Journal of Advertising Research*, March/April 1993, p. 10.

3. Michael Shudson, *Advertising, the Uneasy Persuasion* (New York: Basic Books, 1985), p. 24.

4. "Importance of Image," *The Wall Street Journal*, August 12, 1985, p. 19.

5. Robert J. Samuelson, "The Sovereign Consumer," *Newsweek,* July 29, 1985, p. 54.

6. "Ads That Shatter an Old Taboo," *Time,* February 2, 1987, p. 63.

7. Jeffrey A. Trachtenberg, "It's Become Part of Our Culture," *Forbes,* May 5, 1986, p. 134.

8. Adrienne Ward, "What Role Do Ads Play in Racial Tension," *Advertising Age,* August 10, 1992, pp. 1, 35.

9. Federal Trade Commission, 1991.

10. Bill Shaw, "Foreign Corrupt Practices Act: A Legal and Ethical Analysis," *Journal of Business Ethics*, October 1988, pp. 789–95.

11. Joanne Lipman, "Brand-Name Products Are Popping Up in TV Shows," *The Wall Street Journal,* February 19, 1991, p. B1.

12. Ibid.

13. "Volvo Admits That Its 'Car-Crusher' Ads Were Fakes," *San Diego Union,* November 6, 1990, p. A9.

14. Joanne Lipman, "Ad Industry Debates about Line between Patriotism, Opportunism," *The Wall Street Journal,* January 30, 1991, p. B6.

15. Brian Bremner, "A New Sales Pitch: The Environment," *Business Week,* July 24, 1989, p. 50.

16. Judith D. Schwartz, "Wal-Mart's 'Green' Campaign to Emphasize Recycling Next," *Adweek's Marketing Week,* February 12, 1990, p. 61.

17. Ronald E. Dimock, *Canadian Marketing Law Handbook* (Scarborough, Ontario, Can.: Thomson Professional Publishing Canada, 1991), pp. 97–120.

18. Eric Gross and Susan Vogt, "Canada," in James Maxeiner and Peter Schotthoffer, eds., *Advertising Law in Europe and North America* (Deventer, The Netherlands: Kluwer Law and Taxation Publishers, 1992), pp. 39, 41.

19. Jane Bryant Quinn, "New Handcuffs on the Cops," *Newsweek,* September 3, 1984, p. 62.

20. Richard W. Anderson, "Wanna Watch Miami Vice or a Half-Hour Ad?" *Business Week*, November 28, 1988, p. 114.

21. David Riggle, "Say What You Mean, Mean What You Say," *In Business*, May/June 1990, pp. 50–51.

22. Dean Keith Fueroghne, "But the People in Legal Said . . . ," (Homewood, Ill.: Dow Jones-Irwin, 1989), p. 14.

23. Robert J. Watkins, "Government Controls of Advertising," in *Legal and Business Aspects of the Advertising Industry*, ed. Felix H. Kent and Elhanan C. Stone (New York: Practising Law Institute, 1986), p. 83.

24. Robert Garfield, "Advertisers: All's Fair in Commercials," *USA Today*, April 19, 1985, p. 83.

25. Watkins, "Government Controls of Advertising," p. 88.

26. Steven A. Meyerowitz, "Endorsements: What You Can and Cannot Do," *Business Marketing*, March 1986, p. 8.

27. Gross and Vogt, "Canada," pp. 50, 67.

28. "The Growing Brouhaha over Drug Advertisements," *New York Times*, May 14, 1989, p. F8.

29. Ibid.

30. William Mueller, "Who Reads the Label?" *American Demographics*, January 1991, pp. 36, 39.

31. Thomas R. King, "For Perrier, New Woes Spring up," *The Wall Street Journal*, April 26, 1990, p. B1.

32. Brian Fraser (Hooey & Remus), personal interview, Toronto, Ontario, June 1993.

33. Gross and Vogt, "Canada," p. 55.

34. Joe Mandese, "Reregulation," *Advertising Age*, November 30, 1992, p. 23.

35. "The Experts Speak out," *TV Guide*, August 22, 1992, p. 19.

36. Douglas T. Brownlie, "Protecting Marketing Intelligence: The Role of Trademarks," *Marketing Intelligence and Planning*, 6, no. 4 (1988), pp. 2126; Steven A. Meyerowitz, "Don't 'Xerox' This Article! How to Defend Your Trademarks," *Business Marketing*, December 1984, p. 64.

37. Dimock, *Canadian Marketing Law Handbook*, pp. 14–15.

38. Gross and Vogt, "Canada," pp. 55–56; Eric Gross (Gowling & Henderson), personal interview, Toronto, Ontario, June 1993.

39. Wayne E. Green, "Lawyers Give Deceptive-Trade Statutes New Day in Court, Wider Interpretations," *The Wall Street Journal*, January 24, 1990, p. B1.

40. Steven A. Meyerowitz, "The Marketing Downside to States' Rights," *Business Marketing*, November 1986, p. 64.

41. Gross and Vogt, "Canada," p. 55; Robert Legault (Legault & Joly), personal interview, Montreal, Quebec, May 1993.

42. "Volvo Admits That Its 'Car-Crusher' Ads Were Fakes," p. A-1.

43. Robert Johnson and John Koten, "Sears Has Everything, Including Messy Fight over Ads in New York," *The Wall Street Journal*, June 28, 1988, p. A1.

44. Gross and Vogt, "Canada," p. 40.

45. Steven A. Meyerowitz, "The New Threat to Advertising Freedom," *Business Marketing*, October 1986, p. 20.

46. Ellen Joan Pollock, "'I love My Lawyer' Ads May Spread to More States," *The Wall Street Journal*, December 7, 1990, p. B1.

47. Ibid.

48. Steven W. Colford, "Big Win for Commercial Speech," *Advertising Age*, March 29, 1993, pp. 1, 47.

49. Steven Meyerowitz, "When Privacy Goes Public in Advertising," *Business Marketing*, March 1987, p. 104.

50. Michele Galen, "A Comeback May Be Ahead for Brand X," *Business Week*, December 4, 1989, p. 35.

51. Ibid.

52. Bruce Buchanan and Doron Goldman, "US vs. Them: The Minefield of Comparative Ads," *Harvard Business Review*, May/June 1989, p. 38.

53. Steven A. Meyerowitz, "The Developing Law of Comparative Advertising," Business Marketing, August 1985, p. 81; *Consumer Reports*, November 1992, p. 687.

54. Maria Katz, "No Women, No Alcohol; Learn Saudis Taboos Before Placing Ads," *International Advertiser*, February 1986, p. 11.

55. Felix H. Kent, "Control of Ads by Private Sector," *New York Law Journal*, December 27, 1985; reprinted in Kent and Stone, eds., *Legal and Business Aspects of the Advertising Industry*, 1986, pp. 20–79.

56. *NAD Case Report*, National Advertising Division, Council of Better Business Bureaus 20, no. 10 (January 21, 1991).

57. Dimock, *Canadian Marketing Law Handbook*, p. 97.

58. Gross and Vogt, "Canada," pp. 41–42.

59. Thomas R. King, "In More TV Ads, the Fine Print Gets Evil Eye," *The Wall Street Journal*, July 12, 1990, p. B1.

60. Gross and Vogt, "Canada," pp. 41–42.

61. Public Relations Department, KLBJ, Austin, Texas, 1991.

62. Public Relations Department, KDWB, Minneapolis/St. Paul, Minnesota, 1991.

63. Public Relations Department, KSDO, San Diego, California, 1991.

64. David Shaw, "Newspapers Draw Foggy Lines on Ads," *Los Angeles Times*, February 15, 1987, p. 1.

65. Ibid.

66. Dimock, *Canadian Marketing Law Handbook*, pp. 105–106.

Chapter 3

1. Frederick R. Gamble, *What Advertising Agencies Are—What They Do and How They Do It*, 7th ed. (New York: American Association of Advertising Agencies, 1970), p. 4; see also Ralph S. Blois, "Do You Really Need an Agency," *Sales & Marketing Management*, October 1988, pp. 120–23.

2. "Brands on Trial," *Ad Week*, May 24, 1993, pp. 24–31.

3. John K. Smalley, "Creative Ad Ventures/Automatic Returns/Great Moments in Advertising/Zapping Viewer Apathy," *World*, January/February 1986, pp. 820

4. "The Mice That Roar," *Venture*, June 1985, pp. 110–14.

5. Dianne Lynne Kastiel, "Are You Using Your Agency Enough?" *Business Marketing*, January 1987, pp. 85–89.

6. Bob Garfield, "Coke Ads Great but Not Always," *Advertising Age*, February 15, 1993, pp. 1, 60.

7. John H. Taylor, "Western International Media: Running Scared," *Forbes*, May 28, 1990, pp. 146–48.

8. *Inside the AAAA*, American Association of Advertising Agencies, 1990, p. 5.

9. Ibid., pp. 40–41.

10. George A. Hathaway III, "Account Execs—Choosing the Right Path," *Advertising Age*, September 2, 1985, p. 30.

11. Daniel S. Levine, "For Goodby, Waiting Was the Hardest Part," *Adweek*, Western Edition, March 22, 1993, p. 4.

12. William Sharfman, "Account Planners Have Arrived," *Advertising Age*, April 7, 1986, pp. 18, 22; Tom Lester, "Choosing Your Advertising Agency: The Data Chasers," *Marketing* (UK), January 7, 1988, pp. 35–36; Jon Lafayette, "Shops Embrace 'Account Planning,' " *Advertising Age*, December 11, 1989, p. 28; Pat Sloan, "DDB Boosts Planning by Hiring Brit Expert," *Advertising Age*, September 21, 1992, pp. 3, 53.

13. Thomas E. Barry, Ron L. Peterson, W. Bradford Todd, "The Role of Account Planning in the Future of Advertising Agency Research,"

Journal of Advertising Research, February/March, 1987, pp. 15–21; Paul C. N. Michell, "A Structured Approach to Planning Creative Strategy," *Quarterly Review of Marketing,* Summer 1990, pp. 12–15.

14. William F. Arens and Jack J. Whidden, "La Publicité aux Éstats-Unis: Les symptômes et les stratégies d'une industrie surpleuplée," *"L-Industric de la Publicité au Quebec* (Montreal: Le Publicité-Club de Montreal, 1992), pp. 383–84.

15. Ibid., pp. 365–71.

16. "15% System: Fair or Faulty," *Advertising Age,* May 1, 1989, pp. 20, 76.

17. Jon Lafayette and Cleveland Horton, "Shops to Clients: Pay Up—4A's Members Call for an End to Free Services," *Advertising Age,* March 19, 1990, pp. 1, 66.

18. Edward Tashjian, "Marketing Services Has Big Role in Biz-to-Biz Advertising and PR," *Marketing News,* March 4, 1991, pp. 11, 30.

19. John Micklethwait, "Cut the Ribbon," *The Economist,* June 9, 1990, pp. S16–S17; Tom Eisenhart, "Guaranteed Results' Plan May Suit Business Marketers," *Business Marketing,* July 1990, p. 32.

20. Bowen-Jones, "Knowingly Undersold,"; Nancy Zeldix, "A Bit of Sweden in Connecticut," *Management Review,* October 1987, pp. 12–14.

21. "100 Leading National Advertisers," *Advertising Age,* September 26, 1990, pp. 64–73; Stephanie Overman, "A Company of Champions," *HR Magazine,* October 1990, pp. 58–60.

22. *D&B—Dun's Market Identifiers,* April 1991; R. Craig Endicott, "100 Leading National Advertisers," *Advertising Age,* September 23, 1992, p. 53.

23. Laurie Freeman, "The House That Ivory Build," *Advertising Age,* August 20, 1987, pp. 414, 162–200; "100 Leading National Advertisers," *Advertising Age,* September 23, 1992, p. 53.

24. Jolie Solomon and Carol Hymowitz, "Team Strategy: P&G Makes Changes in the Way It Develops Its Products," *The Wall Street Journal,* August 11, 1987, pp. 1, 10.

25. Ibid.; see also Lenore Skenzay, "Brand Managers Shelved? Professors Offer Alternative for Changing Market," *Advertising Age,* July 13, 1987, p 81.

26. Robert Selwitz, "Media Buying Moves In-House," *Marketing Communications,* September 1986, pp. 19–23, 79, 86.

27. M. E. Ziegenhagen, "Advertising: Which Is Best . . . In-House or Outside Agency?" *Sales & Marketing Management in Canada,* August 1986, pp. 10–11; Blois, "Do You Really Need an Agency"; Micklethwait, "Cut the Ribbon."

28. Sam Sparrow, "Design: In-House or Agency?" *Industrial Marketing Digest* (UK), 2nd Quarter 1987, pp. 35–39.

29. E. Jerome McCarthy and William D. Perreault, Jr., *Basic Marketing,* 10th ed. (Homewood, Ill.: Richard D. Irwin, 1990), p. 577.

30. "U.S. Firms with the Biggest Foreign Revenues, *Forbes,* July 23, 1990, pp. 362.

31. "Efficacy of Global Ad Prospects Is Questioned in Firm's Survey," *The Wall Street Journal,* September 13, 1984, p. 29.

32. Pradeep K. Korgaonkar and Danny N. Bellenger, "Correlates of Successful Advertising Campaigns: The Manager's Perspective," *Journal of Advertising Research,* December 1986/January 1987, pp. 29–41. See Also Pradeep K. Korgaonkar, Danny N. Bellenger, and Allen E. Smith, "Successful Industrial Advertising Campaigns," *Industrial Marketing Management,* May 1986, pp. 123–18.

33. Daniel B. Wackman, Charles T. Salmon, Caryn C. Salmon, "Developing an Advertising Agency-Client Relationship," *Journal of Advertising Research,* December 1986/January 1987, pp. 21–28.

34. "Sure You've Been a Great Agency for 16 Years, but Here's the Door," *San Diego Union,* July 7, 1991, pp. I1, 6.

35. Paul C. Katz, "Getting the Most of Your Advertising Dollars: How to Select and Evaluate an Ad Agency," *Bottomline,* March 1987, pp. 35–38.

36. Christy Marshall, "In Spite of Image, Agency-Client Links Do Often Endure," *Advertising Age,* July 1982, pp. 33–34, 41; Mat Toor, "Fear and Favour in Adland," *Marketing* (UK), November 15, 1990, pp. 30–32.

37. Paul C. N. Mitchell, "Auditing of Agency-Client Relations," *Journal of Advertising Research,* December 1986/January 1987, pp. 29–41.

38. Steven A. Meyerowitz, "Ad Agency Conflicts: The Law and Common Sense," *Business Marketing,* June 1987, p. 16.

39. Joanne Lipman, "Colgate Drops Ted Bates as Its Agency; Move Seen as Blow to Ad-Firm Mergers," *The Wall Street Journal,* June 2, 1986; see also Andy Zipser," Advertising: Mad as in Madison Avenue," *Barron's,* December 3, 1990, pp. 12–13, 32–39.

Chapter 4

1. Gary Kurzbard and Gary F. Soldow, "Towards a Parametric Definition of Marketing," *European Journal of Marketing (UK)* 21, no. 1 (1987), pp. 37–47; and O. C. Farrell and George H. Lucas, Jr., "An Evaluation of Progress in the Development of a Definition of Marketing," *Journal of the Academy of Marketing Science* 15, no. 3 (Fall 1987), pp. 12–23.

2. Adapted from American Marketing Association definition of marketing; see "AMA Board Approves New Marketing Definition," *The Marketing News,* March 1, 1985, p. 1.

3. E. Jerome McCarthy and William D. Perreault, Jr., *Basic Marketing: A Global-Managerial Approach,* 11th ed. (Homewood, Ill.: Richard D. Irwin, 1993), pp. 5–6; Louis E. Boone and David L. Kurtz, *Contemporary Marketing* (Hinsdale, Ill: Dryden Press, 1986), p. 6.

4. The classic studies on this subject were performed by Edwin A Locke, "Toward a Theory of Task Motivation and Incentives," *Organizational Behavior and Human performance,* May 1968, p. 161; and Richard M. Steers and Lyman W. Porter, "The Role of Task-Goal Attributes in Employee Performance," *Psychological Bulletin,* July 1974, p. 446; also, for a discussion of goal hierarchies, see J. Paul Peter and Jerry C. Olson, *Consumer Behavior and Marketing Strategy,* 2nd ed. (Homewood, Ill.: Richard D. Irwin, 1990), pp. 186–88.

5. William F. Allman, "Science 1, Advertisers 0: New Research is Undermining Conventional Ideas on What Sells," *U.S. News & World Report,* May 1, 1989, pp. 60–61.

6. Hank Seiden, *Advertising Pure and Simple: The New Edition* (New York: AMACOM, 1990), pp. 17–18.

7. Courtland L. Bovée and John V. Thill, *Business Communication Today* (New York: McGraw-Hill, 1989), pp. 38–40.

8. Del I. Hawkins, Roger J. Best, and Kenneth A. Coney, *Consumer Behavior: Implications for Marketing Strategy,* 4th ed. (Homewood, Ill." Richard D. Irwin, 1989), pp. 66–67.

9. The classic quote: "The medium is the message," came from Marshall McLuhan, *Understanding Media: The Extensions of Man* (New York: McGraw-Hill, 1965), pp. 45–58; see also Desmond Smith, "Tomorrow's Media Are in Place Today," *Advertising Age,* December 19, 1983, pp. M-14, M-16; Paul Levinson, "Marshall McLuhan and Computer Conferencing," *IEEE Transactions on Professional Communication,* March 1986, pp 9–11; Walter A. Kleinschrod, "The Management Message in Electronic Messaging Media," *Administrative Management,* October 1987, p. 13.

10. David Cravens, Gerald E. Hills, and Robert B. Woodruff, *Marketing Management* (Homewood, Ill.: Richard D. Irwin, 1987), p. 124.

11. Michael J. McCarthy, "Mind Probe—What Makes an Ad Memorable? Recent Brain Research Yields Surprising Answers," *The Wall Street Journal,* March 22, 1991, p. B3.

12. Robert B. Settle and Pamela L. Alreck, *Why They Buy* (New York: John Wiley, 1986), pp. 71–73.

13. Boone and Kurtz, *Contemporary Marketing,* p. 164.

14. "Maidenform Tries New Approach in Latest Lingerie Ad Campaign," *The Wall Street Journal,* April 23, 1987.

15. McCarthy and Perreault, *Basic Marketing,* p. 207.

16. McCarthy, "Mind Probe."

17. Al Ries and Jack Trout, *Positioning: The Battle for Your Mind,* rev. ed. (New York, McGraw-Hill, 1986), pp. 30–32.

18. Ibid., p. 29.

19. Adapted from Hawkins, Best, and Coney, *Consumer Behavior,* pp. 320–29.

20. John O'Toole, *The Trouble with Advertising,* 2nd ed. (New York: Random House, 1985), p. 21.

21. Larry Gaudet, "Les Annonces de Provigo," *Applied Arts Quarterly,* Spring 1990, pp. 25–28.

22. "The Yankelovich Monitor 1992," *Adweek,* November 30, 1992, pp. 20–23.

23. Peter and Olson, *Consumer Behavior and Marketing Strategy,* p.434.

24. Don E. Schultz, "Add Value to the Product and the Brand," *Marketing News,* October 23, 1989, p. 13.

25. Ken Dychtwald and Greg Gable, "Portrait of a Changing Consumer," *Business Horizons,* January-February 1990, pp. 62–74; Larry Light, "Trust Marketing: The Brand Relationship Marketing Mandate for the 90s," address to the American Association of Advertising Agencies annual meeting, Laguna Niguel, CA, April 23, 1993.

26. McCarthy and Perreault, *Basic Marketing,* p. 204.

27. B. Rice, "The Selling of Life-Styles: Are You What You Buy? Madison Avenue Wants to Know," *Psychology Today,* March 1988, pp. 46–51.

28. George P. Moschis, "The Role of Family Communication in Consumer Socialization of Children and Adolescents," *Journal of Consumer Research,* March 1985, pp. 898–913.

29. Laura Zinn, "Move Over, Boomers, The Busters are Here—And They're Angry", Business Week, December 14, 1992, pp. 74–82; "The Yankelovich Monitor 1992," *Adweek,* November 30, 1992, pp. 20–23; Jeffrey Zaslow, "Children's Search for Values Leading to Shopping Malls," *The Wall Street Journal,* March 13, 1987.

30. John Koten, "The Shattered Middle Class," *The Wall Street Journal,* March 9, 1987, p. 19.

31. Thomas G. Exter, "Blacks to 2010," *American Demographics,* December 1992, p. 63; John Wall, "Minorities Slice the Advertising Pie," *Insight,* March 9, 1987, pp. 46–47; U.S. Census Bureau, 1991.

32. Wall, "Minorities Slice the Advertising Pie."

33. Rebecca Purto, "Global Psychographics," *American Demographics,* December 1990, p. 8.

34. Laurel Wentz, "1992: A False Sense of 'Europhoria'?" *Advertising Age,* October 10, 1988, pp. 2, 74.

35. "Eastern Europe Beckons," *Advertising Age,* November 20, 1989, pp. 1, 45.

36. Boone and Kurtz, *Contemporary Marketing,* p. 174.

37. The classic studies on cognitive dissonance were initiated by Leon Festinger, *A Theory of Cognitive Dissonance* (Evanston, Ill.: Row, Peterson, 1957), p. 83; for more recent views, see also Hugh Murray, "Advertising's Effect on Sales—Proven or Just Assumed?" *International Journal of Advertising* (UK) 5, no. 1 (1986), pp. 1536; Hawkins, Best, and Coney, *Consumer Behavior,* pp. 663–65; and Ronald E. Milliman and Phillip J. Decker, "The Use of Post-Purchase Communication to Reduce Dissonance and Improve Direct Marketing Effectiveness," *Journal of Business Communication,* Spring 1990, pp. 159–70.

38. Larry Light, "Advertising's Role in Building Brand Equity," Speech before annual meeting of the American Association of Advertising Agencies, April 21, 1993.

Chapter 5

1. Adapted with permission from *Everyone Knows His First Name,* Levi Strauss & Co.

2. Hank Seiden, *Advertising Pure and Simple, The New Edition* (New York, AMACOM, 1990), p. 236.

3. *The Power of Regional Marketing* (Montreal: Association of Quebec Advertising Agencies, 1992).

4. Ken Dychtwald and Greg Gable, "Portrait of a Changing Consumer," *Business Horizons,* January/February 1990, p. 62.

5. "Forecasters Can Tell Weather to Advertise," *Advertising Age,* January 31, 1985, p. 38.

6. Values and Lifestyles Program, Descriptive materials for the VALS2 Segmentation System (Menlo Park, Calif.: SRI International, 1989).

7. William F. Altman, "Science 1, Advertisers 0: New Research is Undermining Conventional Ideas on What Sells," *U.S. News & World Report,* May 1, 1989, p. 60.

8. B. Rice, "The Selling of Lifestyles: Are You What You Buy? Madison Avenue Wants to Know," *Psychology Today,* March 1988, p. 46.

9. Rebecca Piirto, "Measuring Minds in the 1990s," *American Demographics,* December 1990, p. 33.

10. Ibid., p. 32.

11. Ibid., pp. 46–51; and B. Rice, "The Selling of Lifestyles."

12. Michael Hedges, "Radio's Lifestyles," *American Demographics,* February 1986, pp. 32–35.

13. Frank P. McDonald, "Whither the New Segmentation Systems," *Marketing & Media Decisions,* May 1985, pp. 94, 96.

14. Ed Zotti, "Thinking Psychographically," *Public Relations Journal,* May 1985, pp. 26–30.

15. John H. Mather, "No Reason to Fear Frightening Reality of VALS," *Marketing News,* September 13, 1985, p. 15.

16. E. Jerome McCarthy and William D. Perreault, Jr., *Basic Marketing,* 11th ed. (Homewood, Ill.: Richard D. Irwin, 1993), pp. 228–249.

17. David Cravens, Gerald E. Hills, and Robert B. Woodruff, *Marketing Management* (Homewood, Ill.: Richard D. Irwin, 1987), pp. 156–78.

18. Ibid.

19. McCarthy and Perreault, *Basic Marketing,* pp. 44, 83–106.

20. The now widely popularized conceptual model of the 4 Ps was originally developed by E. J. McCarthy, *Basic Marketing* (Homewood, Ill.: Richard D. Irwin, 1960); and the usage of the marketing mix derived from Neil H. Borden, "The Concept of the Marketing Mix," *Journal of Advertising Research,* June 1964, pp. 27.

21. McCarthy and Perreault, *Basic Marketing,* pp. 288–99; Harper W. Boyd, Jr., and Orville C. Walker, Jr., *Marketing Management: A Strategic Approach* (Homewood, Ill.: Richard D. Irwin, 1990), pp.250–53.

22. Meg Cos, "More Work Leaves Less Time for Arts, Harris Survey Says," *The Wall Street Journal,* March 16, 1988; also Greg Clarkin, "The Marketing Successes of 1989—Entertainment: Fast Forward," *Marketing & Media Decisions,* March 1990, pp. 57–59.

23. Boyd and Walker, *Marketing Management,* pp. 252–53.

24. Adapted from Louis E. Boone and David L. Kurtz, *Contemporary Marketing,* 5th ed. (Hinsdale, Ill.: Dryden Press, 1986), p. 228.

25. Hank Seiden, *Advertising Pure and Simple,* p. 11.

26. Allan J. McGrath, "Segmentation and Differentiation Positioning Strategies Are Timeless," *Marketing News,* October 24, 1988, p. 18; David A. Aaker and J. Gary Shansby, "Positioning Your Product," *Business Horizons,* May–June 1982, pp. 56–62; David A. Aaker and John G. Myers, *Advertising Management,* 3rd ed. (Englewood Cliffs, N.J.: Prentice Hall, 1987), p. 125.

27. Hank Seiden, *Advertising Pure and Simple,* pp. 23–30; Robert Pri-

tikin, *Pritikin's Testament* (Englewood Cliffs, N.J.: Prentice Hall, 1991), pp. 25–33.

28. Cass Bettinger, "Developing Marketing Strategy," *Banker's Magazine,* January/February 1987, pp. 64–71.

29. Tom Eisenhart, "Breaking Away from the Faceless Pack," *Business Marketing,* June 1988, pp. 74–78.

30. Ann Keely, "From Experience—Maxi-Niching the Way to a Strong Brand: Positioning According to Systemic Dynamics," *Journal of Product Innovation Management,* September 1989, pp. 20–26.

31. Larry Light, "Advertising and the Law of Dominance," *Journal of Advertising Research*, August/September 1990, pp. 49–52.

32. Kay Satow, "The Changing State of Research in the United States," *Journal of the Market Research Society* (UK), October 1989, pp. 521–25.

33. Cyndee Miller, "Jeans Maker Has No Excuses for Its Unusual Ads," *Marketing News,* November 20, 1989, p. 9.

34. See McCarthy and Perreault, *Basic Marketing,* pp. 273–74.

35. Margaret Henderson Blair, Allan R. Kuse, David H. Furse, and David W. Stewart, "Advertising in a New Competitive Environment: Persuading Customers to Buy," *Business Horizons,* November/December 1987, pp. 20–26; also, James C. Schroer, "Ad Spending: Growing Market Share," *Harvard Business Review,* January/February 1990, pp. 44–48.

36. "New products growing again," *Marketing News,* January 18, 1993, p. 1.

37. John S. Blyth, "Packaging for Competitive Advantage," *Management Review,* May 1990, p. 64.

38. Ibid.

39. Dick Berry, "Marketing Mix for the '90s Adds an S and 2 Cs to 4Ps," *Marketing News,* December 24, 1990, p. 10.

40. Shlomo Kalish, "A New Product Adoption Model with Price, Advertising, and Uncertainty," *Management Science,* December 1985, pp. 1569–85.

41. Jack Cohen, "Planning an Effective Pricing Strategy," *Supermarket Business,* January 1990, pp. 27–35, 66, 74.

42. Tom Nash, "The Price of Success," *Chief Executive* (UK), July/August 1987, pp. 14–16.

43. McCarthy and Perreault, *Basic Marketing,* p. 16.

44. U.S. Department of Commerce.

45. Janean Hube, "Franchise Forecast," *Entrepreneur,* January 1993, p. 75.

46. Terry Paul and John Wong, "The Retailing of Health Care," *Journal of Health Care Marketing,* Fall 1987, pp. 23–24.

47. Michael Etgar, "Effects of Administrative Control on Efficiency of Vertical Marketing Systems," *Journal of Marketing Research,* February 4, 1976, pp. 12–24; also Leon Richardson, "Miracles of Modern Business Method," *Asian Business (Hong Kong),* June 1990, pp. 10–45; Janean Huber, "Franchise Forecast," pp. 72–75.

48. Stephanie Barlow, "Sub-stantial Success," *Entrepreneur,* January 1993, p. 125.

49. Donald L. Baron, "A European Vocation: New Franchising Opportunities in the Old Country," *Entrepreneur,* January 1993, pp. 117–22.

50. Murray Roman, "What Telemarketing Can Do," *Banker's Magazine,* March/April 1984, pp. 55–58; see also, Stan Rap and Tom Collins, *MaxiMarketing: The New Direction in Advertising, Promotion, and Marketing Strategy* (New York: McGraw-Hill, 1987), pp. 77–82.

51. Jim Emerson, "Levi Strauss In The Early Stages of Shift to Database Marketing," *DM News,* December 7, 1992, pp. 1–2; Lisa Benenson, "Bull's-Eye Marketing," *Success,* January/February 1993, pp. 43–48.

52. Mollie Neal, "Coupon Clutter: A 'Unique' Alternative," *Direct Marketing,* November 1989, pp. 23–24, 32, 99; Associated Press, "306.8 Billion Grocery-Store Coupons Were Issued in 1990," *San Diego Union,* April 6, 1991, p. C1.

Chapter 6

1. Chuck McDonald, Robert West at Schering Canada; Daniel Rabinowicz, Nicole Lapierre, Pierre Delagrave, François Descarie at Cossette Communications-Marketing, personal interviews, August 1992 and May 1993.

2. Richard Gibson, "Marketers' Mantra: Reap More with Less," *The Wall Street Journal,* March 22, 1991, p. B1.

3. E. Jerome McCarthy and William D. Perreault, Jr., *Basic Marketing,* 11th ed. (Homewood, Ill.: Richard D. Irwin, 1993), p. 144.

4. Ibid., p. 147.

5. Jack J. Honomichl, "Marketing/Advertising Research: Top Worldwide Research Companies," *Advertising Age,* December 5, 1988, pp. S1, S11–S18; Jack Honomichl, "'The Honomichl 50': Spending for Research Shows 3.5% Real Growth," *Marketing News,* May 27, 1991, pp. H2–H34; Ken Gofton, "Market Research Maestros," *Marketing* (UK), March 19, 1992, pp. 36–42; Jack Honomichl, "Spending for Research in U.S. Shows 3.4% Real Growth," Marketing News, June 8, 1992, p. H2; Kenneth Wylie, "Dollars Grow Tight in U.S., but Foreign Research Blossoms," *Advertising Age,* June 22, 1992, pp. S1–S4; R. Craig Endicott, "Plenty of Room in Europe, 'Ripe' Asia," *Advertising Age,* June 22, 1992, p. S4.

6. McCarthy and Perreault, *Basic Marketing,* p. 144–45.

7. Jack Honomichl, "Research Cultures Are Different in Mexico, Canada," *Marketing News,* May 10, 1993.

8. "Researcher Says Test First, Then Advertise," *Bank Advertising News* 11, no. 17 (April 20, 1987), p. 7.

9. Gerald J. Eskin, "Applications of Electronic Single-Source Measurement Systems," *European Research* 15, no. 1 (1987), pp. 12–20; Don E. Schultz, Stanley I. Tannenbaum, Robert F. Lauterborn, *Integrated Marketing Communications: Putting It Together and Making It Work* (Lincolnwood, IL: NTC Business Books, 1993), pp. 149–50.

10. Dan Fost, "Business Software: Keep It Simple, Make It Fun," *American Demographics,* December 1990, p. 19.

11. Gibson, "Marketers' Mantra."

12. William F. Allman, "Science 1, Advertisers 0: New Research Is Undermining Conventional Ideas on What Sells," *U.S. News & World Report,* May 1, 1989, p. 60.

13. Robert West, Schering Canada, personal interview, May 17, 1993.

14. "Heartbeat," *Advertising Age,* January 12, 1987, pp. 3, 44.

15. Pamela L. Alreck and Robert B. Settle, The Survey Research Handbook (Homewood, Ill.: Richard D. Irwin, 1985), pp. 64–66.

16. David W. Cravens, Gerald E. Hills, and Robert B. Woodruff, *Marketing Management* (Homewood, Ill.: Richard D. Irwin, 1987), p. 639; McCarthy and Perreault, *Basic Marketing,* p. 162.

17. McCarthy and Perreault, *Basic Marketing,* p. 163.

18. Ibid.

19. Alreck and Settle, *The Survey Research Handbook,* p. 98.

20. MINITAB software for IBM-PC, for Microsoft Windows, and for academic use in an inexpensive student edition through Addison-Wesley Publishing Company, Reading, MA.

21. Michael Brizz, "How to Learn What Japanese Buyers Really Want," *Business Marketing,* January 1987, p. 72.

22. Van Wallach, "Pretesting—Necessary Evil or a Creative Tool," *Advertising Age,* February 13, 1986, pp. 18–19.

23. William R. Dillon, Teresa Domzal, and Thomas J. Madden, "Evaluating Alternative Product Positioning Strategies," *Journal of Advertising Research,* August/September 1986, pp. 18–19.

24. Michael J. McCarthy, "Mind Probe: What Makes an Ad Memorable? Recent Brain Research Yields Surprising Answers," *The Wall Street Journal*, March 22, 1991, p. B3.

25. Shona McKay, "Advertising Signs Up for Analysis," *Applied Arts Quarterly*, Spring 1987, pp. 30–32.

26. François Descarie, Director, Impact Research, personal interview, May 17, 1993.

27. Gibson, "Marketers' Mantra."

28. Robert Judson, "Marketing Mature Brands Requires Ad Analysis," *Marketing News*, January 2, 1987, pp. 20–21.

Chapter 7

1. S. C,. Gwynne, "The Right Stuff,: *Time*, October 29, 1990, pp. 74–84; Raymond Serafin, "The Saturn Story,: *Advertising Age*, November 16, 1992, pp. 1, 13, 16.

2. Alice Z. Cuneo and Raymond Serafin, "Agency of the Year: With Saturn, Riney Rings Up a Winner," *Advertising Age*, April 14, 1993, pp. 2–3.

3. William Giles, "Marketing Planning and Customer Policy," *Management Decision* (UK) 24, no. 3 (1986), pp. 19–27.

4. Margaret L. Friedman, "How to Write a Marketing Plan for Your Service Organization," *Agency Sales Magazine*, February 1987, pp. 42–46.

5. G. A. Marken, "Success Is No Accident: You Need a Plan," *Marketing News*, May 23, 1986, p. 28; Ralph S. Blois, "Do You Really Need an Agency," *Sales & Marketing Management*, October 1988, pp. 120–22.

6. David W. Nylen, "Making Your Business Plan and Action Plan," *Business*, October/November/December 1985, pp. 12–16; "Preparing a Marketing Plan," *International Journal of Bank Marketing* (UK), 1989, pp. vii–viii; Thomas McCaghren, "Putting Ill-Conceived Marketing Plans on Track," *National Underwriter*, June 5, 1989, pp. 41, 44–45.

7. S. C. Gwynne, "The Right Stuff," pp. 74–75.

8. Raymond Serafin, "The Saturn Story," p. 13.

9. David W. Cravens, Gerald E. Hills, and Robert B. Woodruff, *Marketing Management* (Homewood, Ill." Richard D. Irwin, 1987), pp. 245–46; McCaghren, "Putting Ill-Conceived Marketing Plans on Track."

10. Kenichi Ohmae, "Getting Back to Strategy," *Harvard Business Review*, November/December 1988, p. 149.

11. "Preparing a Marketing Plan," pp. vii–viii, E. Jerome McCarthy and William D. Perreault, Jr., *Basic Marketing*, 10th ed. (Homewood, Ill.: Richard D. Irwin, 1990), p. 95

12. Saturn internal figures.

13. Donald P. Robin and R. Eric Reidenbach, "Social Responsibility, Ethics, and Marketing Strategy: Closing the Gap between Concept and Application," *Journal of Marketing*, January 1987, pp. 44–58; P.Rajan Varadarajan and Anil Menon, "Cause-Related Marketing: A Coalignment of Market Strategy and Corporate Philanthropy," *Journal of Marketing*, July 1988, pp. 58–74; Mark Evens, "Education Marketing Basics: Advertising in the Classroom," *Advertising Age*, October 10, 1988, p. 18.

14. "Saturn SC1 and the Young, College-Educated Import Intenders," *1993 Case Study*, NSAC: AAF College World Series of Advertising, pp. 2, 11, 23.

15. David Woodruff, "What's This—Car Dealers with Soul?" *Business Week*, April 6, 1992, pp. 66–67; David Woodruff, "Saturn," *Business Week*, August 17, 1992, pp. 86–91.

16. David Ogilvy, *Ogilvy on Advertising* (New York: Random House, 1985), p. 12.

17. Pat Sloan, "Olay Bath Bar Takes Aim at Dove," *Advertising Age*, February 4, 1991, p.9.

18. Richard L. Erickson, "Marketing Planning: There Is No Magic," *Journal of Business & Industrial Marketing*, Fall 1986, pp. 61–67; Sharon Wolf, "Focused Strategy Can Assist the Communications Process," *Marketing News*, December 4, 1987, p. 20.

19. Robert M. Cohen, "Advertising Effectiveness; First Know Your Objectives," *Sales & Marketing Management in Canada*, October 1989, pp. 10–12.

20. John O'Toole, *The Trouble with Advertising*, 2nd ed. (New York: Random House, 1985), p. 103.

21. The classic treatise on measurable advertising objectives was written by Russell H. Colley, *Defining Advertising Goals for Measured Advertising Results* (New York: Association of National Advertisers, 1961), p. 1; see also, Russell Abratt, "Advertising Objectives of Industrial Marketers," *International Journal of Advertising* (UK) 6, no 2(1987), pp. 121–31; Steven W. Hartley and Charles H. Patti, "Evaluating Business-to-Business Advertising: A Comparison of Objectives and Results," *Journal of Advertising Research*, April/May 1988, pp. 21–27; Cohen, "Advertising Effectiveness"; Raymond R. Burke, Arvind Rangaswamy, Jerry Wind, and Jehoshua Eliasberg, "A Knowledge Based System for Advertising Design," *Marketing Science*, Summer 1990, pp. 212–29.

22. Raymond Serafin, "Riney Media Strategy Gets High Marks," *Advertising Age*, November 16, 1992, p. 15.

23. Raymond Serafin, "The Saturn Story," p. 13.

24. Adapted from Al Ries and Jack Trout, *Bottom-Up Marketing* (New York: McGraw-Hill, 1989), p. 8.

25. Robert D. Buzzell and Frederick D. Wiersema, "Successful Share-Building Strategies," *Harvard Business Review*, January/February 1981, p. 135; Siva K. Balasubramanian and V. Kumar, "Analyzing Variations in Advertising and Promotional Expenditures: Key Correlated in Consumer, Industrial, and Service Markets," *Journal of Marketing*, April 1990, pp. 57–68.

26. Lacy Glenn Thomas, "Advertising in Consumer Goods Industries: Durability, Economies of Scale, Heterogeneity," *Journal of Law & Economics*, April 1989, pp. 163–193; James C. Schroer, "Ad Spending: Growing Market Share," *Harvard Business Review*, January/February 1990, pp. 44–48.

27. William Band, "Quality Is King for Marketers," *Sales & Marketing Management in Canada*, March 1989, p. 68.

28. Bernard Ryan, Jr., *Advertising in a Recession: The Best Defense Is a Good Offense* (New York: American Association of Advertising Agencies, 1991), pp. 13–29; Priscilla C. Brown, "Surviving with a Splash," *Business Marketing*, January 1991, p. 14; Edmund O. Lawler, "A Window of Opportunity," *Business Marketing*, January 1991, p. 16; Rebecca Colwell Quarles, "Marketing Research Turns Recession into Business Opportunity," *Marketing News*, January 7, 1991, pp. 27, 29.

29. Leo Bogart, *Strategy in Advertising*, 2nd ed. (Chicago: Crain Books, 1984), pp. 45–47.

30. Schroer, "Ad Spending": John Philip Jones, "Ad Spending: Maintaining Market Share," *Harvard Business Review*, January/February 1990, pp. 38–42.

31. James M. Oliver and Paul W. Farris, "Push and Pull: A One-Two Punch for Packaged Products," *Sloan Management Review*, Fall 1989, pp. 53–61.

32. Marsha Lindsay, "Establish Brand Equity through Advertising," *Marketing News*, January 22, 1990, p. 16; Robert D. Buzzell, John A. Quelch, and Walter J. Salmon, "The Costly Bargain of Trade Promotion," *Harvard Business Review*, March/April 1990, p. 142.

33. Kent M. Lancaster and Judith A. Stern, "Computer-Based Advertising Budgeting Practices of Leading Consumer Advertisers," *Journal of Advertising* 12, no. 4 (1983), pp. 49; James E. Lynch and Graham J. Hooley, "Advertising Budgeting Practices of Industrial Advertisers," *Industrial Marketing Management*, February 1987, pp. 63–69; Pierre

Filiatrault and Jean-Charles Chebat, "How Service Firms Set Their Marketing Budgets," *Industrial Marketing Management*, February 1990, pp. 63–67.

34. Jan Calloway, "Cashing In on Your Advertising," *Cellular Business*, February 1987, pp. 20–21; Peter Barrow, "How Much Is It Going to Cost Me?" *Canadian Manager*, December 1989, pp. 14–15.

35. Gordon Willis, Sherril H. Kennedy, John Cheese, and Angela Rushton, "Maximizing Market Effectiveness: Promotion Decisions," *Management Decision* (UK) 28, no. 2 (1990), pp. 103–27.

36. Richard Vaughn, "How Advertising Works: A Planning Model Revisited," *Journal of Advertising Research*, February/March 1986, pp. 57–66.

37. Amiya K. Basu and Rajeev Barta, "ADSPLIT: A Multi-Brand Advertising Budget Allocation Model," *Journal of Advertising* 17, no. 2 (1988), pp. 44–51; Peter Doyle and John Saunders, "Multiproduct Advertising Budgeting," *Marketing Science*, Spring 1990, pp. 97–113; Glen L. Urban, John R. Hauser, And John H. Roberts, "Prelaunch Forecasting of New Automobiles," *Marketing Science*, April 1990, pp. 401–21; Bay Arinze, "Market Planning with Computer Models: A Case Study in the Software Industry," *Industrial Marketing Management*, May 1990, pp. 117–29.

38. Ahmet Aykac, Marcel Corstjens, David Gautschi, and Ira Horowitz, "Estimation Uncertainty and Optimal Advertising Decisions," *Management Science*, January 1989, pp. 42–50.

Chapter 8

1. Ellen Paris, "Welcome, Ladies," *Forbes*, September 1990, p. 96.

2. Martin Rossman, "Let's Hear It For an Agency That Hates the Ad Business," *Los Angeles Times*, February 1970.

3. Hank Seiden, *Advertising Pure and Simple* (New York: AMACOM, 1990), pp. 23–30.

4. Peter C. Yesawich, "The Final Steps in Marketing Development: Execution and Measurement of Programs," *Cornell Hotel & Restaurant Administration Quarterly*, February 1989, pp. 82, 19, 22.

5. Marvin Schoenwald, "Marketing a Political Candidate," *Journal of Consumer Marketing*, Spring 1987, pp. 57–63.

6. John O'Toole, *The Trouble with Advertising*, 2nd ed. (New York: Random House, 1985), p. 132; Fred Danzig, "The Big Idea," *Advertising Age*, November 9, 1988, pp. 16, 138–40.

7. O'Toole, *The Trouble with Advertising*, pp. 132–33.

8. John Caples, "A Dozen Ways to Develop Advertising Ideas," *Advertising Age*, November 14, 1983, pp. M4–M5; "Can Creativity Be Systemized?" *Advertising Age*, November 18, 1985, pp. 46, 48; Luther Brock and Milton Pierce, "Check Your Swipe File for Good Ideas/A Good Swipe File Is Better Than a College Education," *Direct Marketing*, December 1986, pp. 111, 116–17; Murray Raphel, "How to Get A-Head in Direct Mail," *Direct Mail Marketing*, January 1990, pp. 30–32, 52.

9. "Copy Chases: When the Client Must Take Charge," *Business Marketing*, July 1989, pp. 70–73; Julie Liesse, "Finding the Perfect Print Ad," *Advertising Age*, August 13, 1990, p. 52.

10. David Ogilvy, *Ogilvy on Advertising* (New York: Random House, 1985), pp. 17–18.

11. Milton Pierce, "How to Write a Powerful Headline," *Direct Marketing*, September 1988, pp. 90, 95.

12. Herbert L. Kahn, "Your Own Kind of Advertising for Non-Consumer Products," *Harvard Business Review*, January–February 1986.

13. E. Jerome McCarthy and William D. Perreault, Jr., *Basic Marketing*, 10th ed. (Homewood, Ill.: Richard D. Irwin, 1990), p. 175; Michael J. McCarthy, "Mind Probe—What Makes an Ad Memorable? Recent Brain Research Yields Surprising Answers," *The Wall Street Journal*, March 22, 1991, p. B3.

14. Raphel, "How to Get A-Head in Direct Mail."

15. Ogilvy, *Ogilvy on Advertising*, p. 71; Murray Raphel, "Ad Techniques—Off with the Head!" *Bank Marketing*, February 1988, pp. 54–55.

16. Ivan Levison, "Six Battle-Tested Tips for Success in Print Ads," *High-Tech Marketing*, February 1987, pp. 62–63.

17. Andrew J. Byrne, "The Most Important Part of an Advertisement," *National Underwriter*, November 7, 1986, pp. 46–49; Levison, "Six Battle-Tested Tips."

18. Robert Pritikin, *Pritikin's Testament: Miracle Ads For Big & Small Advertisers, Retailers, and Entrepreneurs* (Englewood Cliffs, N.J.: Prentice Hall, 1991), p. 25.

19. Liesse, "Finding the Perfect Print Ad."

20. Ogilvy, *Ogilvy on Advertising*, pp. 10–11.

21. Pierce, "How to Write a Powerful Headline," pp. 90, 95.

22. Harold M. Spielman, "In Copy Research, Practice Makes Almost Perfect," *Advertising Age*, November 1, 1984, pp. 16–22: "Eleven Ways to Write Copy That Gets Results," *National Public Accountant*, July 1985, pp. 31–32; "Copy Chaser Criteria," *Business Marketing*, January 1991, p. 33.

23. Ogilvy, *Ogilvy on Advertising*, p. 119.

24. Spielman, "In Copy Research."

25. O'Toole, *The Trouble With Advertising*, p. 149.

26. Ibid., p. 148.

27. Ogilvy, *Ogilvy on Advertising*, pp. 118–20.

28. Murphy A. Sewall and Can Sarel, "Characteristics of Radio Commercials and Their Recall Effectiveness," *Journal of Marketing*, January 1986, pp. 52–60.

29. Ogilvy, *Ogilvy on Advertising*, pp. 113–16; Bob Weinstein, "Radio Is a Riot," *Madison Avenue*, June 1985, pp. 70–74; Rachel Simpson, "Radio Advertisings: Creativity's Short Wave," *Marketing* (UK), December 15, 1988.

30. Ogilvy, *Ogilvy on Advertising*, pp. 103–13.

31. Steven Weed, "Expanding the Marketplace," *Direct Marketing*, November 1989, pp. 42–45.

32. Maria Katz, "No Women, No Alcohol: Learn Saudis' Taboos before Placing Ads," *International Advertiser*, February 1986, p. 11.

33. Richard N. Weltz, "How Do You Say, 'Ooops!'" *Business Marketing*, October 1990, pp. 52–53.

34. Lennie Copeland, "Foreign Markets: Not for the Amateur," *Business Marketing*, July 1984, pp. 112–18.

Chapter 9

1. Adapted from Sharon Edelson, "Elemental Considerations: Making Idyllic Images under Less than Ideal Circumstances," *American Photographer*, November 1989, pp. 18, 19, 22.

2. Murray Raphel, "Ad Techniques—Off with the Head," *Bank Marketing*, February 1988, pp. 54–55.

3. Glenn Mohrman and Jeffrey E. Scott, "Truth(s) in Advertising? Part II," *Medical Marketing & Media*, October 1, 1988, pp. 28–32.

4. J. Douglas Johnson, *Advertising Today* (Chicago: Science Research Associates, 1978).

5. John O'Toole, *The Trouble with Advertising*, 2nd ed. (New York: Random House, 1985), p. 149.

6. David Ogilvy, *Ogilvy on Advertising* (New York: Random House, 1985), pp. 88–89.

7. Ibid.

8. Ibid.

9. Richard H. Stansfield, *Advertising Manager's Handbook* (Chicago: Dartnell Corporation, 1969), pp. 640–41; Julia M. Collins, "Image and

Advertising," *Harvard Business Review*, January–February 1989, pp. 93–97.

10. Mark Spaulding, "Packaging's 100 Giants," *Packaging*, July 1990, pp. 36–54.

11. Hester Thomas, "Design Packs a Punch," *Marketing* (UK), November 20, 1986, pp. 47–50; Francis Lancaster, "Body Language in Packages," *Marketing* (UK), September 29, 1988, pp. 27, 30.

12. Walter P. Margulies, *Packaging Power* (New York: World Publishing, 1970), p. 62; Lancaster, "Body Language in Packages"; Karen Hogan, "Brand Strategy: Mint Conditions," *Marketing* (UK), February 9, 1989, pp. 27–28; Wright Ferguson, "Health & Beauty Aids," *Supermarket Business*, September 1989, pp. 194–95, 222, 230.

13. Michael Gershman, "Packaging's Role in Remarketing," *Management Review*, May 1987, pp. 41–45.

14. Sheila Clark, "Packaging—Not Just a Pretty Design," *Chief Executive* (UK), November 1986, pp. 80–81.

15. Teresa Reese, *Print Casebooks 7, 1987/1988: The Best in Packaging* (Bethesda, Md.: R.C. Publications, 1986), pp. 46–49, 88–90; Ellen Opat Inkeles, *Print Casebooks 8, 1989/1990: The Best in Packaging* (Bethesda, Md.: R.C. Publications, 1989), pp. 85, 99.

16. Karen Hogan, "Packaging/Design/Point-of-Sale: Metal Works," *Marketing* (UK), October 4, 1990, pp. 33–36.

17. Phyllis Furman, "Grocery Marketing: Redesign Puts Old Packages in New Light," *Advertising Age*, May 4, 1987, pp. S20–S21; "Marketing Guide: 14—3-D Packaging Design," *Marketing* (UK), March 29, 1990, pp. 21–24.

18. Ogilvy, *Ogilvy on Advertising*, p. 109.

19. Hank Seiden, *Advertising Pure and Simple, The New Edition* (New York: AMACOM, 1990), p. 237–38.

20. Gordon L. Patzer, "Source Credibility as a Function of Communicator Physical Attractiveness," *Journal of Business Research*, June 1983, pp. 229–41.

21. Ogilvy, *Ogilvy on Advertising*, pp. 103–13.

22. Ibid., pp. 107–8.

23. Ibid., p. 105.

24. Dylan Landis, "Sedelmaier Spots Have Alaska Airlines Roaring," *Adweek*, July 29, 1985, p. 10.

25. "Forget Jingles and Jokes in These Cinema Verité Ads," *The Wall Street Journal*, April 16, 1987.

26. Judith Reitman, "Cutting the Clutter with Computer Graphics," *Marketing & Media Decisions*, May 1985, pp. 52–58, 168.

27. Hooper White, "TV Commercial Production: Creatives Redirect a Complex Scene," *Advertising Age*, March 31, 1986, pp. S1–S2.

28. Mary McCabe English, "Test Marketing: Higher Costs Boost Test Commercials," *Advertising Age*, February 13, 1986, pp. 14–15.

29. Betsy Sharkey, "Software Lets Thrifty Clients 'CLIP' and Save," *Adweek*, November 7, 1988.

30. Terry Kattelman, "Future Shop," *Advertising Age*, January 7, 1991, p. S18.

Chapter 10

1. Gordon Graham, "Computer Wizardry: The Wild, Wild West of Desktop Color," *Applied Arts Quarterly* (Canada), Fall 1990, pp. 13, 16, 18, 20.

2. Winnie O'Kelley, "Computers Create Graphic Palette," *Advertising Age*, April 28, 1986.

3. "70 Case Studies of Computers in Business," *Technology Solutions*, supplement to *Publish*, Summer 1991, pp. 100–2.

4. Dahlin Smith White: "To the Limits of Desktop Production," *Art Direction*, August 1992, pp. 51–52.

5. "70 Case Studies of Computers in Business," pp. 61–63.

6. Kathleen Loomis, "Printing: Teach Your Boss a Lesson," *In House Graphics*, February 1990, p. 89.

7. David Ogilvy, *Ogilvy on Advertising* (New York: Random House, 1985), pp. 96–97.

8. Alex Brown, "Type Renaissance," *Macworld*, July 1991, pp. 204–5.

9. PANTONE® is a registered trademark of Pantone, Inc.

10. Stephanie Cook, "The Electronic Palette Has Retouchers on the Run," *Business Week*, Industrial/Technology edition, January 12, 1987, pp. 122H–122I; Graham, "Computer Wizardry," pp. 13, 16, 18, 20; Suzanne Weber, "Commercializing on the Power of the Mac," *Technology Solutions*, Summer 1991, pp. 61–63.

Chapter 11

1. Stewart Toy and Amy Dunkin, "Cheap Dreams: The Budget Inn Boom," *Business Week*, July 14, 1986, pp. 76–77; Beverly Narum, "Regional Profiles: Dallas," *Advertising Age*, November 9, 1988, pp. 24, 141–142; Marcia Parker, "Room at the Inn: Motel 6 Sites Finance Expansion," *Pensions & Investment Age*, December 12, 1988, pp. 27–28; Carol Hall, "Travel: Motel 6—King of the Road," *Marketing & Media Decisions*, March 1989, pp. 80–86; Skip Hollandsworth, "Ad Men at War," *Best of Business*, Summer 1991, p. 60, reprinted from *Texas Monthly*, November 1990.

2. Michael C. Keith, Radio Production, *Art and Science* (Stoneham, Mass.: Butterworth-Heinemann, 1990), p. 91.

3. Gotcha story and information adapted from Greg Hofman, "Splash Graphics That Say 'Gotcha,' " *Step-by-Step Graphics*, May/June, 1991, p. 40.

4. Miner Raymond, "How to Cut Commercial Production Costs without Anyone Knowing You've Done It," *Sales & Marketing Management in Canada* (Canada), December 1987, pp. 20–22; Janet Myers and Laurie Freeman, "Marketers Police TV Commercial Costs," *Advertising Age*, April 3, 1989, p. 51; "Marketing Guide 19: Advertising Production," *Marketing* (UK), February 7, 1991.

5. "Cost of TV Spot Production Escalates to Nearly $125,000," *Marketing News*, September 26, 1986, p. 6; Alex Ben Block, "Where the Money Goes," *Forbes*, September 21, 1987.

6. Cam Sylvester, "Mavericks: North Star," *Canadian Business* (Canada), August 1989, pp. 25–26.

7. Andrew Olds, "Creativity-Production: The Generalists," *Advertising Age*, January 1, 1990, pp. S26–S29, S31.

8. Hofman, "Splash Graphics," p. 44.

9. Joan Hamilton, "You've Come a Long Way, Gumby: Claymation Is the Hottest Thing in Commercials, and Will Vinton's Ad for California Raisins Is the Reason," *Business Week*, December 8, 1986; p. 74; Albert R. Karr, "Lively Raisins on TV are Grapes of Wrath to One Distributor," *The Wall Street Journal*, January 21, 1987.

10. Hofman, "Splash Graphics," p. 48.

11. Terry Kattleman, "Creativity: Sound Design—Roll Over Hein Hoven," *Advertising Age*, March 5, 1990, pp. SS20–SS22.

12. Ogilvy, *Ogilvy on Advertising*, pp. 113–16.

13. Miner Raymond, "How to Cut Commercial Production Costs," pp. 20–22.

14. Kenneth Roman and Jane Maas, *How to Advertise* (New York: St. Martin's Press, 1976), pp. 79–81; Miner Raymond, "How to Cut Commercial Production Costs," pp. 20–22; "Marketing Guide 19: Advertising Production," pp. 21–24.

Chapter 12

1. Joe Mandese, "Del Monte's Can-Do," *Marketing and Media Decisions*, November 1990, pp. 47–49.

2. Jon Lafayette, "Agency Media Staffs Gain Clout," *Advertising Age,* March 4, 1991, p. 12.

3. Ibid.

4. Page Thompson, "The Big Picture," *Inside Print,* 1989 Media Planner's Guide, pp. 31–33.

5. Gene Willhoft, "Is 'Added Value' Valuable?" *Advertising Age,* March 1, 1993, p. 16.

6. Joe Mullich, "The Voodoo of Value-Added," *Advertising Age,* October 26, 1992, pp. B20–B22.

7. Gary Levin, "Sports Play Integrated Marketing Game," *Advertising Age,* March 1, 1993, p. 12.

8. Joe Mandese, "Decoding the Deal," *Marketing & Media Decisions,* September 1989, pp. 33–39; Scott Donaton, "Computer-Savvy Directors Muscle Way to Forefront," *Advertising Age,* July 20, 1993, p. S6.

9. "Studying the Academic Studies," *Adweek Special Report,* December 7, 1987, p. 31.

10. David C. Lehmkuhl, "Mediology," *Marketing and Media Decisions,* May 1989, p. 79.

11. Erdener Kaynak, *The Management of International Advertising* (Westport, Conn.: Quorum Books, 1989), pp. 70, 148.

12. Jack Z. Sissors and Lincoln Bumba, *Advertising Media Planning,* 3rd ed. (Lincolnwood, Ill.: NTC Business Books, 1989), p. 126.

13. "Effective Use of Print: The Current Thinking," *Inside Print,* January 1987, p. 119.

14. Neil Kelliher, "Magazine Media Planning for 'Effectiveness': Getting the People Back into the Process," *Journal of Consumer Marketing,* Summer 1990, pp. 47–55.

15. Stephen P. Phelps, "Media Planning: The Measurement Gap," *Marketing & Media Decisions,* July 1986, p. 151.

16. Kenneth Longman, *Advertising* (New York: Harcourt Brace Jovanovich, 1971), pp. 211–12.

17. "Effective Use of Print: The Current Thinking," p. 119.

18. "The Power of Partnership," NBC Marketing Supplement, *Advertising Age,* November 16, 1992, p. 13.

19. Andrea Rothman, "Timing Techniques Can Make Small Ad Budgets Seem Bigger," *The Wall Street Journal,* February 3, 1989, p. B4.

20. Ibid.

21. Joe Mandese, "The Merge/Purge Program," *Marketing & Media Decisions,* October 1989, pp. 48–58.

22. Sissors and Bumba, *Advertising Media Planning,* p. 358.

Chapter 13

1. Mary Yeung, *The Best in Advertising/Print Casebooks 9, 1991–92 Edition* (Rockville, Md.: R. C. Publications, 1991), pp. 40–41.

2. Scott LaFee, "It's Chic, and Quite the Thing," *San Diego Union,* September 16, 1991, p. C1.

3. Pat Guy, "Circulations Drop; Shakeout Possible," *USA Today,* August 28, 1990, sec. b, p. 4.

4. Gene Willhoft, "Is 'Added Value' Valuable?" *Advertising Age,* March 1, 1993, p. 18.

5. Ibid.

6. John Potenzano, "The Added Value of Added-Value," *Marketing & Media Decisions,* June 1990, pp. 58–59.

7. Tom Goss, *The Best in Advertising/Print Casebooks 6, 1984–85 Edition* (Washington, D.C.: R. C. Publications, 1984), pp. 25–26.

8. *'90 Facts about Newspapers* (Washington, D.C.: American Newspaper Publishers Association, 1990), p. 10.

9. Ibid., p. 2.

10. Ibid.

11. Ibid., p. 3.

12. Eileen Norris, "Ad Vehicles Bombard Consumers," *Advertising Age,* November 7, 1985, p. 16.

13. Margaret Rosser, "USA Today, Yesterday, and Tomorrow," *Marketing & Media Decisions,* December 1986, p. 108.

14. *Newspaper Rate Differentials* (New York: American Association of Advertising Agencies, 1990); Christy Fisher, "NAA Readies National Ad-Buy Plan," *Advertising Age,* March 1, 1993, p. 12.

15. *'90 Facts about Newspapers,* p. 10.

16. William F. Gloede, "Newspapers Cut National Ad Rate," *Advertising Age,* June 8, 1987, p. 1; "NAA Readies National Plan."

17. "A Network of Co-op Power," *Marketing Communication,* June 1986, p. 80.

18. Fisher, "NAA Readies National Plan," p. 12.

19. Joe Mandese, Scott Donaton, "Wells Rich Tests 4A's Liability Clause," *Advertising Age,* April 22, 1991, pp. 1, 40; Willie Vogt, "Defining Payment Liability," *AgriMarketing,* May 1992, pp. 42–43.

20. Tom Eisenhart, "Opportunities Ripening for U.S. Business Publishers in Eastern Europe," *Business Marketing,* October 1990, p. 42.

21. *Guide to Consumer Magazines* (New York: American Association of Advertising Agencies, 1988), p. 10.

22. Ibid.

Chapter 14

1. Stuart Elliott, "Energizer's E. B. Parades into Ad History," *USA Today,* January 26, 1990, p. 1B.

2. Kate Fitzgerald, "Energizer Hops onto Top 10," *Advertising Age,* January 7, 1991, p. 39.

3. Julie Liesse and Ira Teinowitz, "Eveready Lashes Coors in Court," *Advertising Age,* May 13, 1991, pp. 1, 46.

4. *TV Basics 1990–91* (New York: Television Bureau of Advertising, p. 6; *Marketer's Guide to Media,* Fall/Winter 1992–93, p. 23.

5. "Tracking Ad Dollars," *The Wall Street Journal,* March 22, 1990, p. B4; *Marketer's Guide to Media,* Fall/Winter 1992–93, p. 23.

6. Joseph R. Mullie, "The United States and Canada: There Is a Difference," Address to the Canada First! Seminar, Montreal, April 19, 1993.

7. "1991 Advertisers Guide to Cable," *Advertising Age,* February 11, 1991, p. 22; *1991–1992 Television Data Book* (Don Mills, Ontario: BBM Bureau of Measurement, 1992), p. 3; Mullie, "The United States and Canada."

8. *TV Basics 1990–91,* p. 3; "Television vs. Other Media," *The Power of Spot TV,* supplement to *Advertising Age,* September 23, 1992, p. T–15.

9. *Nielsen Television Index,* Nielsen Media Research, 1990, p. 23.

10. *Marketer's Guide to Media,* Fall/Winter 1992–93, p. 50.

11. Ibid., p. 48.

12. David Samuel Barr, *Advertising on Cable: A Practical Guide for Users* (Englewood Cliffs, N.J.: Prentice Hall, 1985), p. 43.

13. "National Sales Reps Are Key to the Spot TV Mix," *The Power of Spot TV,* supplement to *Advertising Age,* September 23, 1992, pp. T–10, T–12.

14. Kathy Haley, "The Infomercial Begins a New Era as a Marketing Tool for Top Brands," *Advertising Age,* January 25, 1993, p. M–3.

15. Ibid.; Tom Burke, "Program-Length Commercials Can Bring These Six Benefits to a Major Brand Campaign," *Advertising Age,* January 25, 1993, p. M–5.

16. *Cable TV Facts 90,* p. 67.

17. Cleveland Horton, "DirecTv Offers Satellite Feed of Cable Channels," *Advertising Age,* February 1, 1993.

18. Hanna Rubin, "Home Video," *Media in the 90s,* September 11, 1989, p. 168.

19. Ibid.

20. Joanne Lipman, "Video Renters Watch the Ads, Zapping Conventional Wisdom," *The Wall Street Journal,* April 28, 1989, p. B1.

21. *Radio Facts for Advertisers 1990* (New York: Radio Advertising Bureau, 1990), pp. 34–37; *Marketer's Guide to Media,* Fall/Winter 1992–93, pp. 64, 67.

22. "Radio Ads for Athlete's Foot Medicine Outdo TV Spots," Radio Advertising Bureau.

23. *Radio Facts for Advertisers 1990.*

24. Helen Rogan, "AM Radio Fights to Win Listeners with Stereo and Format Changes," *The Wall Street Journal,* October 21, 1985, p. 25.

25. Janice Steinberg, "New Formats Gain Frequency on AM Band," *Advertising Age,* August 19, 1985, p. 18.

26. Michael Hedges, "Radio's Life Styles," *American Demographics,* February 1986, p. 3.

27. Julie Liesse Erickson, "Networks Sharing Airwaves with Syndicators," *Advertising Age,* August 29, 1985, p. 28; *Marketer's Guide to Media,* Fall/Winter 1992–93, pp. 69–70.

28. "Tracking Ad Dollars," *The Wall Street Journal,* March 22, 1990, p. B4; *Marketer's Guide to Media,* Fall/Winter 1992–93, p. 64.

Chapter 15

1. Tom Eisenhart, "Breakthrough Direct Marketing," *Business Marketing,* August 1990, pp. 20–28.

2. Carol Nelson, "If It Isn't Direct, It Doesn't Follow," *Direct Marketing,* March 1990, pp. 66–67; "Direct Marketing: A Useful Advertising Medium and a Valuable Sales Tool," *Small Business Report,* September 1985, p. 71.

3. "Tracking Ad Dollars," *The Wall Street Journal,* March 22, 1991, sec. b, p. 4; Arnold Fishman, "Mail Order Top 250+," *Direct Marketing,* July 1992, pp. 19–37; "USA Snapshots: Home Becomes the Mail," *USA Today,* December 19, 1990, sec. d, p. 1; "USA Snapshots: More Catalogs in the Mail," *USA Today,* December 19, 1990, sec. b, p. 1; Christine Adamec, "Niche Marketing by Mail," *In Business,* November/December 1986, p. 32; Jean Li Rogers, "Consumer Response to Advertising Mail," *Journal of Advertising Research,* December 1989/January 1990, pp. 18–23.

4. Albert Haas, Jr., "How to Sell Almost Anything by Direct Mail," *Across the Board,* November 1986, p. 49; Stephanie Anderson Forest and Catherine Arnst, "The Education of Michael Dell," *Business Week,* March 22, 1993, pp. 83–88.

5. Louise Tutelian, "Catalogs Turn a Page in Marketing," *USA Today,* October 17, 1986, sec. b, p. 1; Harvey D. Braun, "The Catalog Shopper of the 90s," *Direct Marketing,* March 1993, pp. 15–18.

6. John B. Hinge, "Catalog Houses That Once Boomed Find the Checks Are No Longer in the Mail," *The Wall Street Journal,* April 4, 1991, sec. b, pp. 1, 8.

7. Bob Stone, *Successful Direct Marketing Methods* (Chicago: Crain Books, 1987), p. 101.

8. William R. Morrisey, "Gain Competitive Edge with Data-Based Direct Marketing," *Marketing News,* March 15, 1985, p. 22.

9. Allen Miller, "Workshop: How to Develop a Direct-Mail Mailing List," *Public Relations Journal,* April 1988, pp. 31–32.

10. Diane C. Donovan, "Marketing," *Nation's Business,* July 1986, p. 35.

11. Peter Finch, "The Direct Marketing Data Base Revolution," *Business Marketing,* August 1985, p. 46.

12. Mary Yeung, *Print Casebooks 9: The Best in Advertising* (Rockville, Md.; R. C. Publications, Inc., 1991), pp. 19–20.

13. Riccardo A. Davis, "New Advertisers Limit Outdoor Loss," *Advertising Age,* March 15, 1993, p. 6.

14. *Billboard Basics* (Washington, D.C.: Advertising Association of America, 1991), pp. 2, 10, 14, 19.

15. Press release, Institute of Outdoor Advertising, 1991.

16. Cyndee Miller, "Outdoor Advertising Weathers Repeated Attempts to Kill It," *Marketing News,* March 16, 1992, pp. 1, 9.

17. Ruth Hamel, Tim Schreiner, and Brad Edmondson, "Billboards Want Respect: Cracking the Code," *Direct Marketing,* July 1988, pp. 45–49; Barbara Walton, "How to Reach a Very Specific Market Target Rather Efficiently," *Madison Avenue,* November 1985, p. 98.

18. Nancy L. Croft, "Spiels on Wheels," *Nation's Business,* February 1987, p. 14.

19. Speciality Advertising Association International.

20. Kevin T. Higgins, "Specialty Advertising Thrives," *Marketing News,* October 11, 1985, p. 20.

21. Richard G. Edel, "Specialties: Gifts of Motivation," *Marketing Communications,* April 1986, p. 106.

22. Avraham Shama and Jack K. Thompson, "Promotion Gifts: Help or Hindrance?" *Mortgage Banking,* February 1989, pp. 49–51.

23. Kate Bertrand, "Attention-Grabbing Trade Show Gadgetry," *Business Marketing,* November 1986, p. 106.

24. Frank Sommerfield, "The Other Show Business," *Marketing & Media Decisions,* August 1990, p. 16.

25. Doug R. Berdie and Elaine M. Hauff, "Surprises Are Found in Consumer Reactions to Ads in Yellow Pages," *Marketing News,* September 11, 1987, p. 8.

26. Edmund L. Andrews, "Changing Shopping Habits Keep Those Fingers Walking," *New York Times,* July 1, 1990, p. 4-F; "Bell South Leads in Year of Flat Growth," *Advertising Age,* August 10, 1992.

27. Ibid.

28. Carol Hall, "Branding the Yellow Pages," *Marketing & Media Decisions,* April 1989, p. 59.

29. Ibid., p. 60.

30. Ibid., p. 62.

31. Betsy Bauer, "New Quick Flicks: Ads at the Movies," *USA Today,* March 13, 1986, p. D1.

32. Joanne Lipman and Kathleen A. Hughes, "Disney Prohibits Ads in Theaters Showing Its Movies," *The Wall Street Journal,* February 9, 1990, p. B1.

33. Annetta Miller and Judy Howard, "Turning PCs into Salesmen," *Newsweek,* March 12, 1990, p. 69.

34. Lynn Coleman, " 'Smart Card,' Coupon Eater Targeted to Grocery Retailers," *Marketing News,* June 6, 1988, p. 1.

35. Cyndee Miller, "VideOcart Spruce Up for New Tests," *Marketing News,* February 19, 1990, p. 19.

36. "Electronic Promo: The Subject Was Roses," *Chain Store Age Executive,* September 1988, pp. 64–70.

Chapter 16

1. George Gendron and Bo Burlingham, "The Entrepreneur of the Decade: An Interview with Steve Jobs," *Inc.,* April 1989, pp. 114–28; Murray R. Bowes and Linda Reed Tsien, "Selling Apples by Credit Card," *Direct Marketing,* June 1987, pp. 60–65; Amanda C. Hixson, "The Reshaping of Apple," *Personal Computing,* April 1987, pp. 119–23; Paul Frieberger and Michael Swaine, "A Microcomputer Dream Ignited by a . . . Fire in the Valley," *Marketing Communications,* November 1986, pp. 113–21; Jeff Brechlin and Allison Rossett, "Orienting New Employees," *Training,* April 1991, pp. 45–51; Ikujiro

Nonaka and Martin Kenney, "Towards a New Theory of Innovation Management: A Case Study Comparing Canon, Inc., and Apple Computers, Inc.," *Journal of Engineering & Technology Management,* June 1991, pp. 67–83; Andrew Kupfer, "Apple's Plan to Survive and Grow," *Fortune,* May 4, 1992, pp. 68–72; Jerry Borrell, "An Interview with Eric Halsem," *Macworld,* September 1992, pp. 169–83.

2. Don E. Schultz, "We Simply Can't Afford to Go Back to Mass Marketing," *Marketing News,* February 15, 1993, p. 20.

3. Regis McKenna, "Marketing in an Age of Diversity," *Harvard Business Review,* September/October 1988, p. 88.

4. Regis McKenna, "Marketing Is Everything," *Harvard Business Review,* January/February 1991, p. 65.

5. Earl Lifshey, "Do Retailers Ask Too Much of Vendors?" *Scan,* March/April 1991, p. 18; "New Products Growing Again," *Marketing News,* January 18, 1993, p. 1.

6. Regis McKenna, "Marketing Is Everything."

7. William F. Arens and Jack J. Whidden, "La Pub aux États-Unis, 1992; Les symptômes et les stratégies d'une industrie surpeuplée," *L'industrie de la publicité au Québec 1991–1992* (Montreal: Le Publicité-Club de Montréal, October 1992), pp. 365–99.

8. McKenna, "Marketing in an Age of Diversity;" Don E. Schultz, Stanley I. Tannenbaum, and Robert F. Lauterborn, *Integrated Marketing Communications: Putting It Together & Making It Work* (Lincolnwood, Ill.: NTC Business Books, 1993), p. 21.

9. Karlene Lukovitz, "Get Ready for One-on-One Marketing," *Folio: The Magazine for Magazine Management,* October 1, 1991, pp. 64–70; Don E. Schultz, "Integrated Marketing Communications: Maybe Definition Is in the Point of View," *Marketing News,* January 18, 1993, p. 17.

10. Tom Duncan, "Integrated Marketing? It's Synergy," *Advertising Age,* March 8, 1993.

11. Ibid.

12. Don E. Schultz, "Integration Helps You Plan Communications from Outside-in," *Marketing News,* March 15, 1993, p. 12.

13. Regis McKenna, "Marketing Is Everything."

14. Regis McKenna, "Marketing in an Age of Diversity."

15. Paul Wang and Don E. Schultz, "Measuring the Return on Investment for Advertising and Other Forms of Marketing Communications Using an Integrated Marketing Communications Planning Approach," paper presented at the 76th Annual Convention of the Association for Education in Journalism and Mass Communication, Kansas City, August 13, 1993.

16. Don E. Schultz, Stanley I. Tannenbaum, and Robert F. Lauterborn, *Integrated Marketing Communications: Putting It Together & Making It Work* (Lincolnwood, Ill.: NTC Business Books, 1993), pp. 55–6.

17. Paul Wang and Don E. Schultz, "Measuring the Return on Investment."

18. Don E. Schultz, Stanley I. Tannenbaum, and Robert F. Lauterborn, *Integrated Marketing Communications: Putting It Together & Making It Work,* p. 58.

19. Scott Hume, "Integrated Marketing: Who's in Charge Here?" *Advertising Age,* March 23, 1993, pp. 3, 52.

20. Adapted from Mollie Neal, "Andersen Takes Great 'Panes' to Build Relationships," *Direct Marketing,* April 1993, pp. 28–30.

21. *Statistical Abstracts of the U.S.,* U.S. Bureau of Statistics, Washington, D.C., 1991; Statistics Canada, 1991.

22. MasterCard, International, 1992.

23. Elena Bowes, "Direct Response Grows in Europe," *Advertising Age,* February 15, 1993, p. I-3.

24. Junu Bryan Kim, "Databases Open Doors for Retailers," *Advertising Age,* February 15, 1993, p. 38; Francez Smith, "Long Journeys Start with Small Steps," *Direct Marketing,* September 1992, pp. 26–31.

25. Thomas E. Caruso, "Kotler: Future Marketers Will Focus on Customer Data Base to Compete Globally," *Marketing News,* June 8, 1992, pp. 21–22.

26. Ibid.

27. Don E. Schultz, "Take a Giant Step Backward? No, Thanks," *Marketing News,* December 18, 1989, p. 16.

28. "The Database Revolution," *Target Marketing,* May 1992, pp. 14–18; Junu Bryan Kim, "Databases Open Doors for Retailers."

29. Mollie Neal, "Marketers Looking Ahead in Chicago," *Direct Marketing,* March 1993, pp. 9–11.

30. Don E. Schultz, "Add Value to the Product and the Brand," *Marketing News,* October 23, 1989, p. 13.

31. Stan Rapp and Tom Collins, *Maximarketing* (New York: McGraw-Hill, 1987), pp. 56–91.

32. Ibid., p. 62.

33. Pat Sloan, "Avon Looks beyond Direct Sales," *Advertising Age,* February 22, 1993, p. 32.

34. "Losing Pitcher," *Entertainment Weekly,* May 21, 1993, p. 6.

35. Russ Bowman, "Sales Promotion," *Marketing & Media Decisions,* July 1989, p. 124.

36. Scott Hume, "Trade Promotion $ Share Dips in 92," *Advertising Age,* April 5, 1993, pp. 3, 43.

37. Larry Light, "Advertising and the Law of Dominance," *Journal of Advertising Research,* August/September 1990, pp. 49–52.

38. John Philip Jones, "The Double Jeopardy of Sales Promotions," *Harvard Business Review,* September/October 1990, p. 149.

39. Larry Light, "Trustmarketing: The Brand Relationship Marketing Mandate for the 90s," address to the American Association of Advertising Agencies annual meeting, Laguna Niguel, Calif., April 23, 1993.

40. Magid M. Abraham and Leonard M. Lodish, "Getting the Most Out of Advertising and Promotion," *Harvard Business Review,* May/June 1990, p. 51.

41. Larry Light, "Trustmarketing: The Brand Relationship Marketing Mandate for the 90s."

42. Don E. Schultz and Robert D. Dewar, "Rough Course Ahead: Retailers in Control," *Marketing Communications,* October 1985, pp. 52–68; Alvin A. Achenbaum and F. Kent Mitchel, "Pulling Away from Push Marketing," *Harvard Business Review,* May/June 1987, p. 38; Don E. Schultz, "Above or Below the Line? Growth of Sales Promotion in the United States," *International Journal of Advertising* 6, no. 1, 1987, pp. 17–27; Larry Light, "At the Center of It All Is the Brand," *Advertising Age,* March 29, 1993, p. 22.

43. David Kalish, "Creative Concepts: Space Invaders," *Marketing & Media Decisions,* November 1988, p. 31.

44. Ronald Alsop, "Retailers Buying Far in Advance to Exploit Trade Promotions," *The Wall Street Journal,* October 9, 1986, p. 35.

45. Amy E. Gross, "Promote: What Retailers Want," *Adweek's Marketing Week,* October 29, 1990, p. 42.

46. Karlene Lukovitz, "Get Ready for One-on-One Marketing," *Folio,* October 1, 1991, pp. 64–70.

47. Mollie Neal, "Coupon Clutter: A 'Unique' Alternative," *Direct Marketing,* November 1989, pp. 23–24; "Coupons Set Another Record," *Marketing News,* April 26, 1993, p. 1.

48. "Consumers' Use of Coupons Rose in 1991," Manufacturers Coupon Control Center, special release, 1991.

49. *Thirteenth Annual Survey of Promotional Practices* (Stamford, Conn.: Donnelly Marketing, 1991), p. 24.

50. "Computers Help Foil Coupon Fraud," *Marketing News*, August 15, 1986, p. 1.

51. William A. Robinson, *Best Sales Promotions*, 6th ed. (Lincolnwood, Ill.: NTC Business Books, 1987), p. 261.

52. "Study: Some Promotions Change Consumer Behavior," *Marketing News*, October 15, 1990, p. 12.

53. "Coke Disc-o," *San Diego Union*, March 6, 1991, p. E-2.

54. Regis McKenna, "Marketing in an Age of Diversity;" Kevin Doyle, "Tetley: The Shape of Things to Come," *Incentive*, April 1993, pp. 24–25.

55. Point of Purchase Advertising Institute, New York, 1987.

56. Mark Paul, "The Electronic Salesman," *Marketing Communications*, December 1986, p. 32.

Chapter 17

1. Ben Yagoda, "Cleaning Up a Dirty Image," *Business Month*, April 1990, pp. 48–52; E. Bruce Harrison with Tom Prugh, "Assessing the Damage," *Public Relations Journal*, October 1989, pp. 40–45.

2. Caleb Solomon, "Exxon Attacks Scientific Views of Valdez Spill," *The Wall Street Journal*, April 15, 1993, pp. B1, B10.

3. Amelia Lobsenz, "How to Blend PR into Your Marketing Mix," *Marketing News*, March 15, 1985, p. 37.

4. Publisher's statement, *INSIDE PR*, March 1993, p. 3.

5. "Product Survival: Lessons of the Tylenol Terrorism" (Washington, D.C.: Washington Business Information, 1982), pp.11–17.

6. Art Stevens, "How to Handle Bad News," *Industry Week*, October 14, 1985, p. 63.

7. Ibid., p. 64.

8. Doug Newsom, Alan Scott, and Judy Vanslyke Turk, *This Is PR: The Realities of Public Relations* (Belmont, Calif.: Wadsworth, 1989), p. 203.

9. "Public Relations: Creating a Company Image," *Small Business Report*, February 1987, pp. 49–54.

10. Lloyd B. Dennis, "Public Affairs; Deja Vu All Over Again," *Public Relations Journal*, April 1990, pp. 14–17.

11. "Public Relations: Creating a Company Image," p. 49.

12. Steven Morris, "Corporate Sponsorship Becomes Life of the Party," *Chicago Tribune*, March 27, 1988, sec. 7, p. 1; statistical data supplied by International Events Group, May 1991.

13. Pat McGeehan, "Signing 3M an Olympian Effort," *Advertising Age*, November 9, 1987.

14. Data supplied by International Events Group.

15. A. Craig Copetas, "Make Profits, Not War," *Inc.*, January 1986, p. 21.

16. Jane Weaver, "Perrier: Fighting Crisis with Laughter," *Adweek*, March 19, 1990, p. 12.

17. John A. Platta, "Energizing Sales with Public Relations," *Business Marketing*, June 1986, p. 133.

18. Jeanne Saddler, "Public Relations Firms Offer 'News' to TV," *The Wall Street Journal*, April 2, 1985, p. 6.

19. Corporate Advertising/Phase II, an Expanded Study of Corporate Advertising Effectiveness conducted for *Time* magazine by Yankelovich, Skelly & White, Inc. Undated.

20. Meryl Davids, "16th Annual Review of Corporate Advertising Expenditures," *Public Relations Journal*, September 1987, p. 29.

21. Ibid.

22. Newsom et al., *This Is PR*, p. 193.

23. Anne B. Fisher, "Spiffing Up the Corporate Image," *Fortune*, July 21, 1986, p. 72.

24. Tom Eisenhart, "What's in a Name? Plenty," *Business Marketing*, October 1988, pp. 88–94.

Chapter 18

1. Ralph Rubio, personal interview, January 22, 1990.

2. John E. O'Toole, "Of Dollars and Change," address to the annual meeting of the American Association of Advertising Agencies, Laguna Niguel, Calif., April 22, 1993.

3. Paul Wang and Don E. Schultz, "Measuring the Return on Investment for Advertising and Other Forms of Marketing Communications Using an Integrated Marketing Communications Planning Approach," paper presented at the 76th Annual Convention of the Association for Education in Journalism and Mass Communication, Kansas City, August 13, 1993.

4. John Freehling, "Use Drive Times to Build Trading Areas and Market Segments," *Marketing News*, May 10, 1993, p. 2.

5. Irving Burstiner, *Basic Retailing* (Homewood, Ill.: Richard D. Irwin, 1986), p. 577.

6. Eileen Norris, "Total Market Coverage: Ad Vehicles Bombard Consumers," *Advertising Age*, November 7, 1985, p. 16.

7. Thomas R. King, "In Hollywood Stars Come Out in Local Ads," *The Wall Street Journal*, July 25, 1990, p. B1.

8. Bob Hughes, "Mrs. Gooch's Makes a Fashion Statement with Its Beverly Hills Shop," *Supermarket Business*, May 1988, p. 72.

9. ADVO-System, Inc., annual report, 1990, p. 1.

10. Barry Berman and Joel R. Evans, *Retail Management: A Strategic Approach* (New York: Macmillan, 1986), p. 401.

11. James Rubenstein, "A G-R-A-N-D Opening," *Bank Marketing*, January 1989, p. 28.

12. "Younkers' Carl Zitz, Marketing VP, Tells How Store Is Changing," *Ad/Pro*, October 1986, p. 4.

13. "Creativity in Ads: How Ideas Flow," *Ad/Pro*, February 1987, p. 1.

14. "At Bullock's: Always on Sunday, in Four Color," *Ad/Pro*, March 1987, p. 1.

15. *What We've Learned about Advertising* (New York: American Association of Advertising Agencies, 1990), p. 3.

16. Data supplied by ABC, NBC, and CBS.

17. John Moes, "Military Asks What It Can Do for Recruits," *Advertising Age*, July 19, 1984, p. 36.

18. Gerry Braun, "Will High Road Lead to Victory?" *San Diego Union*, May 27, 1990, sec. a, p. 1; Patricia Sellers, "The Selling of the President in '88," *Fortune*, December 21, 1987, pp. 131, 132, 136; Walecia Konrad, "The Selling of the President, 1988" *Business Week*, September 12, 1988, p. 37.

19. "Political Ads on TV Rise," *USA Today*, September 26, 1990, sec. b, p. 1.

20. Annetta Miller, "Peddling a Social Cause," *Newsweek*, September 1, 1986, pp. 58–59.

Credits and Acknowledgments

Part I Pratt & Whitney of Canada; agency: BCP Group.

Chapter 1

Foreign Nescafé ad: courtesy Nestlé.

Exhibit 1-1 Richards Group ad: courtesy The Richards Group.

Exhibit 1-3 3M ad: courtesy Martin Williams Advertising, Inc.

Exhibit 1-4 Lee Lites jeans ad: courtesy Lee Company; agency: Fallon McElligott

Exhibit 1-5 restaurant ad: courtesy Hotel Intercontinental.

Exhibit 1-7 Boeing ad; courtesy Boeing Defense & Space Group; agency: Cole & Weber/Seattle.

Exhibit 1-8 Dutch Worldwide Fund ad: courtesy McCann-Erickson/Amsterdam; photographer: James Balog.

Exhibit 1-9 Lil Red Eden Prairie Group ad: courtesy Jean Rhode.

Exhibit 1-10 tailor's shop sign: Colonial Williamsburg Foundation.

Exhibit 1-11 health jolting chair ad: Dick Supten, *The Mad Old Ads* (New York: McGraw-Hill, 1966).

Exhibit 1-12 Palmolive ad: Reprinted from April 30, 1980, issue of *Advertising Age.* Copyright 1980 by Crain Communications, Inc.

Exhibit 1-13 Hathaway shirt ad: Courtesy Ogilvy & Mather.

Ethical Dilemma Adapted from Howard Schlossberg, "The Simple Truth: Ads Will Have to Be Truthful," *Marketing News,* December 24, 1990, p. 6; Ed Fitch, "Truth Be Told, Deception Is 'In.' " *Advertising Age,* April 20, 1987, p. 56; Robert Pitofsky, "Should Puffery Be Outlawed—Former FTC Man Says No." *Advertising Age,* April 7, 1975, p. 15; Steven Mitchell Sack, "Legal Puffery—Truth or Consequences," *Sales & Marketing Management,* October 1986, pp. 59–60; Herbert J. Rotfeld and Kim B. Torzoll, "Is Advertising Puffery Believed?" *Journal of Advertising* 3 (1980), pp. 16–20, 45; Richard Kurnit, "Truth in Advertising—The Latest Word," *Advertising Age,* July 21, 1986, p. 55; James E. Lukaszewski, "Three Grand Delusions and Five False Assumptions," *Across the Board,* November 1990, pp. 55–57; Jennifer Lawrence, "How Volvo's Ad Collided with the Truth," *Advertising Age,* November 12, 1990, p. 76; Jon Lafayette, "Scandal Puts Focus on Ad Visuals," *Advertising Age,* November 26, 1990, p. 62; Ralph Nader, "Rise of the Consumerists," *Advertising Age,* June 18, 1990, pp. 68, 72; Krystal Miller and Jacqueline Mitchell, "Car Marketers Test Gray Area of Truth in Advertising," *The Wall Street Journal,* November 19, 1990, pp. B1, B6; Paul Hawken, "Truth or Consequences," *Inc.,* August 1978, pp. 48–50, 52; Michael A. Kamins and Lawrence J. Marks, "Advertising Puffery: The Impact of Using Two-Sided Claims on Product Attitude and Purchase Intention," *Journal of Advertising* 4 (1987), pp. 6–15.

Exhibit 1-14 VW think small ad: this ad has been copyrighted by and is reproduced with the permission of Volkswagen of America, Inc.

Exhibit 1-15 California Dept. of Health nonsmoking ad: courtesy California Department of Health Services; agency: Livingston & Keye.

Exhibit 1-16 top 10 international advertisers: *Advertising Age,* November 19, 1990, p. S-4.

Exhibit 1-17 John Pemberton photo: courtesy The Coca-Cola Company.

Exhibit 1-19 old Coke coupons: courtesy The Coca-Cola Company.

Portfolio "Coke," "Coca-Cola," and the Dynamic Ribbon device are trademarks of the The Coca-Cola Company and are used with permission. Max Headroom spot, Grandpa/Art Carney storyboard, Michael Jordan spot: courtesy McCann-Erickson/New York. *Time* cover: copyright 1950 Time Inc. Reprinted by permission.

Exhibit 1-20 Coke bottles photo: courtesy The Coca-Cola Company.

Exhibit 1-21 LaLigue French cancer ad: agency: FCB, Paris; art director: Christian Vouhe; copywriter: Bruno Vasseur; photographer: Christian Thompson.

Exhibit 1-23 Bufferin photo: Michael J. Hruby.

Exhibit 1-24 Black & Decker ad: courtesy McKim Baker Lovick/BBDO.

Exhibit 1-25 oil company logos: courtesy Union Oil of California.

Exhibit 1-26 cereals: Concialdi Design.

Exhibit 1-27 Studebaker ad: Historical Pictures Service, Chicago.

Chapter 2

Jeep ad: courtesy CME-KHBB.

Exhibit 2-1 Subaru want a car ad: courtesy Wieden & Kennedy/Philadelphia.

Exhibit 2-2 Pounce ad; courtesy Harry Kerker-HCM.

Exhibit 2-3 AAAA woman shaver ad: American Association of Advertising Agencies.

Exhibit 2-4 Coppertone ad: courtesy Schering Corporation.

Exhibit 2-5 Jockey ad: courtesy Jockey® International, Inc.

Exhibit 2-6 Canon copiers ad: Canon USA, Inc.

Exhibit 2-7 Castro Oil ad: courtesy Young & Rubicam/Sydney.

Exhibit 2-9 Ray Charles for PepsiCo: ©1990 PepsiCo, Inc. All rights reserved.

Exhibit 2-10 FTC complaint flowchart: Gary Armstron and Julie Ozanne, "An Evaluation of NAD/NARB Purpose and Performance," *Journal of Advertising* 12, no. 3 (1983), p. 24. Reprinted with permission.

Exhibit 2-11 California Milk Advisory Board butter ad; courtesy Foote, Cone & Belding.

Exhibit 2-12 trademark terminology: logos courtesy of The Coca-Cola Company; GM trademark is used with permission of General Motors Corporation; Nabisco Brands, Inc.; The Prudential Insurance Company of America; The Pillsbury Company; The Du Pont Company; Federal Deposit Insurance Corporation.

Exhibit 2-13 Xerox ad: courtesy Xerox Corporation.

Exhibit 2-14 Hyatt Legal Services storyboard: courtesy Hyatt Legal Services.

Exhibit 2-15 Advertising regulations in Europe: James Maxeiner and Peter Schoffhofer, (eds) *Advertising Law in Europe and North America* (Deventer, The Netherlands: Kluwer Law and Taxation Publishers, 1992).

Exhibit 2-16 AAAA policies: ©American Association of Advertising Agencies, Inc.

Ad Lab 2-B Advertising to children: Daniel M. Gold, "The Backlash over Clutter in Kidland," *Adweek's Marketing Week,* October 8, 1990, p. 4. Storyboard courtesy The Procter & Gamble Company.

Exhibit 2-17 NAD on misleading ads: courtesy Bozell Inc./Council of Better Business Bureaus, Inc. Note: any future form of this ad will include the word *commercial* immediately prior to the last word *(advertising)* in the first paragraph.

Exhibit 2-C W. R. Grace storyboard: courtesy W. R. Grace & Co.

Exhibit 2-19 advertising principles: courtesy the American Advertising Federation.

Chapter 3

Franklin Dallas ad: courtesy Franklin Dallas Kundinger Advertising.

Exhibit 3-1 Nike ad: courtesy Muse Cordero Chen, Inc.

Ad Lab 3-A top 10 U.S. agencies: reprinted with permission from *Advertising Age,* April 13, 1992, Copyright Crain Communications, Inc.

Exhibit 3-4 LA Ads: courtesy LA Ads/Lawrence Ayliffe Advertising Inc.

Exhibit 3-5 Y&R ad: courtesy Young & Rubicam Ltd./Toronto.

Exhibit 3-6 Accord ad: courtesy Muse Cordero Chen, Inc.

Exhibit 3-7 Canon copiers ad: courtesy Canon Europa; agency: McCann-Erickson/Amsterdam/ Bugs Bunny and Elmer Fudd: trademark and copyright: Warner Bros. 1994.

Ad Lab 3-B: adapted from William F. Arens and Jack J. Whidden, "La Publicité aux États-Unis: Les symptômes et les stratégies d'une industrie surpeuplée," *L'Indusrie de la Publicité au Québec* (Montreal, Le Publicité-Club de Montreal, 1992), pp. 365–399.

Exhibit 3-8 Nike ad: courtesy Muse Cordero Chen, Inc.

Exhibit 3-9 Gigante Vaz ad; courtesy Gigante Vaz and Partners Advertising Inc.

Exhibit 3-10 Hunters & Gatherers ad: courtesy Hunters & Gatherers.

Exhibit 3-14 Minneapolis ad; courtesy Martin-Williams.

Exhibit 3-15 American Indian College Fund ad; courtesy Wieden & Kennedy/Portland.

Exhibit 3-18 Anne Klein ad: courtesy Anne Klein & Co.

Exhibit 3-19 Fallon McElligott ad; courtesy Fallon McElligott.

Ethical Dilemma Adapted from Steven A. Meyerowitz, "Ad Agency Client Conflicts: The Law and Common Sense," *Business Marketing,* June 1987, p. 16; "Saatchi and Saatchi Co. Is Brought to Court Over a Client Conflict," *The Wall Street Journal,* April 17, 1987, p. 18; Lauren Ames, "The Great Conflict Conflict," *Madison Avenue,* June 1985, pp. 66–69; Herbert Zeltner, "Conflict Issue Still a Problem," *Advertising Age,* June 16, 1986, pp. 3, 24, 28, 30–32; Marianne Paskowski, "Client Conflict Woes—As Told from the Agency Side," *Marketing & Media Decisions,* October 1984, pp. 70,, 73–74, 96; Marianne Paskowski, "Conflict Woes as Told from the Client Side," *Marketing & Media Decisions,* November 1984, pp. 61–62, 176.

Exhibit 3-21 Dentsu Xerox copier ad: client, Fuji Xerox Co. Ltd.; agency/creative, Dentsu Inc., Tokyo, production, Spoon Inc.

Exhibit 3-22 Coke storyboard: Coke and Coca-Cola are registered trademarks of The Coca-Cola Company and permission for use granted by The Company.

Exhibit 3-23 French Tang ad; courtesy GreyCom, Inc.

Exhibit 3-24 top 10 agencies: *Advertising Age*, March 26, 1991.

Checklist for Agency Review Adapted with permission from the March 30, 1981, issue of *Crain's Chicago Business.* © 1981 by Crain Communications, Inc.

Checklist of Ways to Be a Better Client Adapted from Kenneth Roman and Jane Maas, *How to Advertise* (New York: St. Martin's Press, Inc., Macmillan & Co., Ltd., 1976), pp. 151–56.

Part II The Advertising Club of Greater Boston ad; courtesy The Advertising Club of Greater Boston.

Chapter 4

Norway Post ad: courtesy Norway Post; agency: Myres/Lintas, Oslo; art director: Per Hanevik; copywriter: Kari Pedersen; photographer: Knut Bry.

Exhibit 4-1 Edsel ad: Henry Ford Museum/Edison Institute.

Exhibit 4-2 Ford Explorer ad: courtesy Ford Division Advertising Department.

Ad Lab 4-A adapted from E. Jerome McCarthy and William D. Perreault, Jr., *Basic Marketing: A Global-Managerial Approach,* 11th ed. (Homewood, IL: Richard D. Irwin, Inc., 1993), pp. 5–6.

Exhibit 4-3 Iacocca retirement ad: courtesy Chrysler Corporation.

Exhibit 4-5 Burlington Air Express ad: Courtesy Burlington Air Express.

Exhibit 4-7 Richmond Metro blood drive ad: courtesy The Martin Agency.

Exhibit 4-10 Colombian Coffee ad: courtesy The National Federation of Coffee Growers of Colombia.

Exhibit 4-11 U.S. Coast Guard ad: ©Minnesota Department of Natural Resources; agency: Carmichael Lynch Advertising.

Exhibit 4-12 Maidenform storyboard: courtesy Maidenform®

Exhibit 4-13 Lee jeans ad: courtesy Lee Company; agency: Fallon McElligott.

Exhibit 4-14 *Rolling Stone* ad: courtesy *Rolling Stone* Magazine.

Ad Lab 4-B Adapted with permission from *The Positioning Era* by Jack Trout and Al Ries, July 16, 1979, issue of *Advertising Age.* Copyright 1979 by Crain Communications, Inc.

Exhibit 4-16 Provigo billboards: courtesy Cossette Communication-Marketing.

Exhibit 4-18 Lineal Design chair ad: courtesy Lineal Group Inc.

Ad Lab 4-C adapted from Harold W. Berkman and Christopher C. Gilson, *Consumer Behavior: Concepts and Strategies,* 2nd ed. (Boston: Kent Publishing Co. 1981), p. 249. Reprinted by permission of Kent Publishing, a Division of Wadsworth Inc.: and Jack Haberstroh, "Can't Ignore Subliminal Ad Charges," *Advertising Age,* pp. 3, 42, 44, and Martha Rogers and Kirk H. Smith, "Public Perceptions of Subliminal Advertising: Why Practitioners Shouldn't Ignore This Issue," *Journal of Advertising Research,* March/April 1993, pp. 10–18.

Exhibit 4-19 social classes list: Equifax National Decision Systems.

Exhibit 4-20 Nike ad: courtesy Wieden & Kennedy/Portland.

Exhibit 4-21 Andre Agassi ad: courtesy Jim Mitchell Agency.

Exhibit 4-22 Honda ad: courtesy Muse Cordero Chen, Inc.

Exhibit 4-23 international newspapers: photo by Michael J. Hruby.

Ad Lab 4-D Jonathan's Uptown ads: art directors, Kathy Izard, Jim Mountjoy; writers, Steve Lasch, Julie Dalton; agency, Loeffler, Ketchum & Mountjoy; client, Jonathan's Uptown.

Chapter 5

Levi's ad: courtesy Levi Strauss & Co.

Exhibit 5-1 old Levi's ad: courtesy Levi Strauss & Co.

Exhibit 5-2 Levi's AIDS quilt: © 1993 Richard Morganstein.

Exhibit 5-5 Mott's Clamato storyboard: courtesy Cadbury Beverages Canada.

Exhibit 5-6 usage patterns chart: MediaMark Research, Inc.

Ethical Dilemma adapted from Michael Specter, "Reynolds Cancels Plan to Market New Cigarette," *Washington Post,* January 20, 1990, p. A3; James R. Schiffman, "After Uptown, Are Some Niches Out?" *The Wall Street Journal,* January 22, 1990, pp. B1, B6; Anthony Lewis, "Merchants of Death," *New York Times,* May 19, 1988, p. A31; Marlene Cimons, "Tobacco Firms' Sports Ties Assailed," *Los Angeles Times,* February 24, 1990, p. A23; Bryant Robey, "The 'Uptown' Fiasco Highlights U.S. Inequality," *Adweek's Marketing Week,* March 12, 1990, p. 58; Judann Dagnoli "Uptown Downfall Scares Industry," *Advertising Age,* January 29, 1990. p. 57; Editorial, "The Downing of Uptown," *Advertising Age,* January 29, 1990, p. 32; Bruce Horovitz, "Cigarette Ads: A Matter of Conscience," *Los Angeles Times,* May 2, 1989, sec. IV, pp. 1, 6; Editorial, "When Ads Leave a Bad Aftertaste," *Los Angeles Times,* January 23, 1990, p. B6; Howard Schlossberg, "Segmenting Becomes Constitutional Issue," *Marketing News,* April 16, 1990, pp. 1–2; Michael Specter, "Sullivan Denounces Reynolds Tobacco," *Washington Post,* January 19, 1990, pp. A1, A8; Alix M. Freedman and Michael J. McCarthy, "New Smoke from RJR under Fire," *The Wall Street Journal,* February 20, 1990, pp. B1, B8; Djata, "The Marketing of Vices to Black Consumers," *Business & Society Review,* Summer 1987, pp. 47–49.

Exhibit 5-7 Levi's Dockers ad: courtesy Levi Strauss & Co.

Exhibit 5-8 usage rates: adapted from Dik Warren Twedt, "How important to Marketing Strategy Is the 'Heavy User'? *Journal of Marketing,* January 1964, p. 72.

Exhibit 5-9 Vals 2 chart: Used with permission © SRI International.

Exhibit 5-10 Deloitte & Touche ad: courtesy Deloitte & Touche.

Exhibit 5-11 SIC classifications: adapted from E. Jerome McCarthy and William D. Perreault, Jr., *Essentials of Marketing,* 5th ed. (Homewood, Ill.: Richard D. Irwin, 1991), p. 156.

Exhibit 5-12 proportional map: adapted from U.S. Department of Commerce, Bureau of the Census, Census of Manufactures, Area Statistics (Washington D.C.: U.S. Government Printing Office, 1977), p. 749.

Exhibit 5-13 map: courtesy Equifax National Decision Systems, 1993.

Exhibit 5-14 Levi's loose jeans ad: courtesy Levi Strauss & Co.

Ad Lab 5-A Reebok ad: courtesy Reebok International Ltd.

Exhibit 5-15 product life cycles: adapted from Ben M. Ennis, *Marketing Principles* (Santa Monica, CA: Goodyear Publishing, 1980), p. 351.

Exhibit 5-16 Sony ad; © 1993 Sony Corporation of America.

Exhibit 5-17 Crest ad: © The Procter & Gamble Company. Used with permission.

Exhibit 5-19 Amtrak storyboard: courtesy DDB Needham Worldwide Inc.

Exhibit 5-20 Xerox ad: courtesy Young & Rubicam/New York.

Exhibit 5-21 Sunkist ad; courtesy Sunkist Growers, Inc.

Exhibit 5-22 Bass montage: client: G. H. Bass & Co., Falmouth, ME; design firm: Cipriani Kremer Design, Boston, MA; packaging team: Marcus Hewitt and Michael Peters; client liaisons: Don Sappington, President, and Mitchell Massey, Senior Vice President Marketing. Reprinted courtesy of G. H. Bass & Co.

Exhibit 5-23 Coke Classic ad: Coke Classic ad: "Coke," "Coca-Cola," and the Dynamic Ribbon device are trademarks of The Coca-Cola Company and are used with permission.

Exhibit 5-24 Quaker Oats cereals: courtesy Source Inc.

Exhibit 5-25 Certifiably Nuts ad: courtesy Thomas Binnion/Jon Reeder Design

Exhibit 5-26 supply/demand/price chart: adapted from Elwood S. Buffa and Barbara A. Pletcher, *Understanding Business Today* (Homewood, Ill.: Richard D. Irwin, 1980), p. 37.

Exhibit 5-27 Staples Office Superstore: courtesy Hill, Holiday, Connors, Cosmopulos, Inc., Advertising.

Exhibit 5-28 Mervyn's/Dockers co-op ad: courtesy Levi Strauss & Co.

Exhibit 5-29 Futurekids ad: courtesy FUTUREKIDS, Inc.; agency: Jamison/Cawdrey/Benjamin.

Exhibit 5-30 Sir Speedy photo: courtesy Sir Speedy, Inc.

Ad Lab 5-C Reebok montage: courtesy Reebok International Ltd.

Chapter 6

Optique ad: courtesy The Richard Group.

Exhibits 6-1, 6-2 Claritin ads: courtesy Cossette Communication-Marketing.

Exhibit 6-4 Equifax MicroVision ad: courtesy Equifax National Decision Systems.

Ad Lab 6-A Adapted from Natalie Goldberg, "How to Use External Data in Marketing Research," *Marketing Communication,* March 1980, pp. 76–82.

Exhibit 6-6 data collections methods: Pamela L. Alreck and Robert B. Settle, *The Survey Research Handbook* (Homewood, Ill.: Richard D. Irwin, 1985), p. 41.

Exhibit 6-7 Campbell's billboard: courtesy Ogilvy & Mather/Toronto.

Exhibit 6-8 focus group: Burgess Blevins.

Exhibit 6-9 research costs: The Professional Research Group.

Exhibit 6-10 validity/reliability matrix: Pamela L. Alreck and Robert B. Settle, *The Survey Research Handbook* (Homewood, Ill.: Richard D. Irwin, 1985), p. 65.

Ad Lab 6-B photos: adapted from *Everything You've Always Wanted to Know about TV Ratings,* A. C. Nielsen Company, 1978.

Checklist: Developing an Effective Questionnaire From Don E. Schultz and Dennis G. Martin, *Strategic Advertising Campaigns (Chicago: Crain Books, 1979).*

Exhibit 6-13 cross-tab data chart: courtesy Minitab.

Exhibit 6-14 research categories: adapted from Edmund W. J. Faison, *Advertising: A Behavioral Approach for Managers* (New York: John Wiley & Sons, 1980), p. 664.

Exhibit 6-15 Claritin print ad: courtesy Cossette Communication-Marketing.

Exhibits 6-16, 6-17 AT&T campaign from Ayer: client: AT&T-Basking Ridge, NJ; product: corp. brand; agency: Ayer New York; chief creative officer: Patrick Cunningham; director creative services: Keith Gould; creative director: Mark Ryan; art director: Nick Scordato; copywriter: Gordon Hasse; executive producer: Gaston Braun; director: David Fincher; production co:

Propaganda Films/LA; editors: Jim Haygood, Glenn Scantlebury Superior Assembly/LA; music: Elias Associates.

Exhibit 6-18 survey interview photo: courtesy Bristol-Myers Squibb Company.

Exhibit 6-19 *Parade* magazine ad: created for PARADE Magazine by Warwick Baker & Fiore Inc. Reprinted with permission.

Exhibit 6-20 TES tracking report: courtesy Impact Research.

Exhibit 6-21 Louis Kemp ad with Starch tabs: courtesy Starch INRA Hooper and Tyson Foods.

Chapter 7

UPS TotalTrack ad: courtesy United Parcel Service of America, Inc.

Exhibits 7-1, 7-2 Saturn ads: courtesy Saturn Corporation; agency: Hal Riney & Partners Inc.

Checklist Situation Analysis Adapted from Russel H. Colley, *Defining Advertising Goals for Measured Advertising Results* (New York: Association of National Advertisers, 1961), pp. 62–68.

Exhibit 7-4 U.S. Army nurse ad: Army materials provided courtesy of the U.S. Government, as represented by the Secretary of the Army.

Exhibit 7-5 Rollerblade ad: courtesy Rollerblade, Inc.; agency: Carmichael Lynch.

Ad Lab 7-A Jack Trout Al Ries, "Marketing Warfare," *Southern Advertising.* July 1978.

Exhibit 7-6 Saturn ad: © 1992 Saturn Corporation.

Exhibit 7-7 Karastan ad: courtesy Karastan Bigelow.

Exhibit 7-8 Sico Paint billboard: courtesy Sico Paint; agency: BCP Strategy Creativity.

Exhibit 7-11 Quaker Oats Plus Fiber and Life cereal ads: courtesy The Quaker Oats Company.

Exhibit 7-12 FCB grid: David Clark Scott, "Modern Advertising, 'The Subtle Persuasion,'" *The Christian Science Monitor,* January 27, 1987.

Ad Lab 7-C ADISO music ad: courtesy Parent Richards Communications; "**Naked Lunch" storyboard:** courtesy N&T/Leo Burnett, Oslo; **Missouri Humane Society ad:** courtesy Martin Williams Agency; **Chevy's Fresh Mex Storyboard:** courtesy Goodby Berlin & Silverstein; **Canadian Airlines ad:** courtesy Canadian Airlines International Ltd.

Exhibit 7-13 Saturn ad: © 1992 Saturn Corporation.

Exhibit 7-14 Domino's Pizza ad: courtesy Domino' Pizza, Inc.

Exhibit 7-15 AAAA ad: courtesy American Association of Advertising Agencies.

Ad Lab 7-D Adapted from William J. Baumol and Alan S. Blinder, *Economics: Principles and Policy,* 3d edition (New York: Harcourt Brace Jovanovich, 1985), p. 386.

Exhibit 7-16 Porsche ad: courtesy Porsche Cars North America, Inc.; agency: Fallon McElligott.

Exhibit 7-17 advertising expenditures: Reprinted with permission from *Advertising Age,* September 23, 1992. Copyright Crain Communications, Inc.

Part III Sony Walkman Poster: agency: Bartle Bogle Hegarty, London; art director: Mike Wells; copywriter: Tom Hudson.

Chapter 8

Royal Ontario Museum ad: courtesy Royal Ontario Museum; agency: Geoffrey B. Roche and Partners.

Exhibits 8-1, 8-2 4day Tire Store ads: courtesy Landsdale, Carr & Baum.

Checklist: Product Marketing Facts for Copywriters Adapted from *Advertising Today.* © 1978 by J. Douglas Johnson. Reprinted by permission of the publisher, Science Research Associates, Inc.

Exhibit 8-5 Aetna Health Plans ad: courtesy The Richards Group.

Ethical Dilemma Adapted from Darrel Muehling, Donald Stem, Jr., and Peter Raven, "Comparative Advertising: Views from Advertisers, Agencies, Media and Policy Makers," *Journal of Advertising Research,* October-November 1989, pp. 38–48; Meryl Freeman, "Comparative Cautions," *Marketing & Media Decisions,* September 1987, pp. 78, 82, 84–85; Jeffrey Trachtenberg, "New Law Adds Risk to Comparative Ads," *The Wall Street Journal,* June 1, 1989, p. B6: Liza Frenette, "Trademark Proposals Could Threaten Free Speech," *Folio: The Magazine for Magazine Management,* April 1989, p. 23; Joe Flint, "Network Handling of Comparative Ads Causing Concerns," *Broadcasting,* October 29, 1990, pp. 53, 55; Thomas King, "Comparative TV Ad Reviews Criticized,," *The Wall Street Journal,* October 23, 1990, p. B8; Steven Meyerowitz, "Brand X Strikes Back: The Developing Law of Comparative Advertising," *Business Marketing,* August 1985, pp. 81–84, 86; Slade Metcalf, "The Limits of Comparative Advertising," *Folio: The Magazine for Magazine Management,* August 1989, pp. 135–37; Cornelia Pechmann and David Stewart, "The Effect of Comparative Advertising on Attention, Memory, and Purchase Intentions," *Journal of Consumer Research,* September 1990, pp. 180–91; Caryn Beck-Dudley and Terrell G. Williams. "Legal and Public Policy Implications for the Future of Comparative Advertising: A Look at *U-Haul v. Jartran,"* *Journal of Public Policy & Marketing* 8 (1989), pp. 124–42.

Exhibit 8-6 Swiss Sunlight detergent ad: courtesy McCann-Erickson/Zurich.

Exhibit 8-8 dog trainer ad: director, James Offenhartz; writers, Marian Allen Godwin and Todd Matthew Godwin; agency, Levine, Huntley, Schmidt and Beaver; client, Luis Gomez.

Ad Lab 8-A Stanley ad: provided by Lawner Reingold Britton & Partners/Boston, MA.

Exhibit 8-9 copywriter's pyramid with ad: ad courtesy Porsche Cars North America.

Exhibit 8-10 Seiko ad: courtesy Saatchi & Saatchi Advertising/London.

Exhibit 8-11 GE lighting ad: courtesy WYZE Advertising/Cleveland; photo © D. Wilson/West Light.

Exhibit 8-12 Friki chicken German ad: agency: Springer & Jacoby/Hamburg; art director: Horst Becker; copywriter: Andre Kemper; photographer: Andrew Moran.

Exhibit 8-13 Ray-Ban Ad: courtesy Bausch & Lomb.

Checklist: Writing Effective Copy David L., Malickson and John W. Nason, excerpted from page 74 *Advertising: How to Write the Kind That Works.* © 1982 David L. Malickson and John W. Nason. Reprinted with the permission of Charles Scribner's Sons.

Exhibit 8-14 Mitsubishi ad: courtesy Chiat Day/Venice, CA.

Exhibit 8-15 Electricity Association "Frank the Tortoise" ad: courtesy GGK London Ltd.

Exhibit 8-16 NYNEX radio script: courtesy Chiat Day Mojo/New York.

Copywriter's Portfolio: Save the World ad: courtesy Cabbel Harris; **Hallmark storyboard:** courtesy Leo Burnett, U.S.A.; **Columbia Sportswear ad:** courtesy Columbia Sportswear Company; **Schwepes:** courtesy Ammirati & Puis Inc.

Exhibit 8-17 GTE/Nike Storyboard: courtesy Focus Agency.

Exhibit 8-18 radio script layout: courtesy Scali, McCabe. Sloves, Inc.

Checklist: Creating Effective Radio Commercials Peter Hochstein, "Ten Rules for Making Better Radio Commercials," *Viewpoint III* (1981).

Exhibit 8-19 AT&T storyboard script: courtesy of Ayer, Inc. Reprinted with permission of AT&T; copyright 1990, AT&T; all rights reserved.

Exhibit 8-20 Warner Lambert Lubriderm storyboard: courtesy J. Walter Thompson.

Exhibit 8-21 Canon Business Machines Dutch ad: courtesy KKBR/SMS; art director: Rob Sluys; copywriter: Tom Druppers.

Exhibit 8-22 Visa ads: courtesy Visa International.

Chapter 9

Gitano ad: courtesy Mullen Advertising/Wenham, MA.

Exhibits 9-1, 9-2 Timberland ads: courtesy Mullen Advertising Inc.

Exhibit 9-3 Hawaiian Tropic suntan oil ad: courtesy Clarity Coverdale Rueff Advertising, Inc., Minneapolis, MN.

Exhibit 9-4 Dental-Eye Camera montage: courtesy Kyocera America, Inc., Bioceram Division, and Tom Michael and Bob Hines, Market Design, Inc.

Exhibit 9-5 Holey Bagel ad: courtesy J. Walter Thompson/San Francisco.

Exhibit 9-6 French TBS shoe ad: courtesy CLM/BBDO, Paris.

Exhibit 9-7 Arian, Lowe & Travis ad: courtesy Arian, Lowe & Travis.

Exhibit 9-8 Mandarin Oriental Hong Kong restaurant ad: courtesy Backer Spielvogel Bates Ltd.

Ad Lab 9C: adapted from Walter Margulies, "What Colors Should You Use?" *Media Decisions* (New York: Decision Publications).

Art Director's Portfolio: Wamsutta sheets ad: courtesy Wamsutta/Pacific Home Products; **Metro Toronto Zoo ad:** courtesy Chiat/Day Inc. Advertising, Toronto; **Waterman Pen ad:** courtesy, Waterman Pen Company; **Egg Beaters ad:** courtesy Nabisco Brands Inc.; **Lee Euro Rider jeans ad:** courtesy The Lee Company; agency: **Fallon McElligott; SSR Travels ad:** courtesy Chistophe Guye Marketing & Kommunikations/Beratung.

Exhibit 9-9 Canadian Airlines ad: courtesy Canadian Airlines International Ltd.

Exhibit 9-10 Pasta La Bella display: courtesy American Italian Pasta Co.

Exhibit 9-11 Callahan seeds: courtesy The Majestic Group, Inc./Indianapolis, IN.

Exhibits 9-12, 9-13 Bill Demby Storyboard and sketch: courtesy BBDO/New York.

Ad Lab 9-D Adapted from Wallace A. Ross and Bob Landers, "Commercial Categories," in *Radio Plays the Plaza* (New York Radio Advertising Bureau, 1969).

Exhibit 9-14 executive spectrum: courtesy Hank Seiden;

Exhibit 9-15 Alaska Airlines sketch and storyboard: courtesy Livingston & Company/Seattle.

Ethical Dilemma Adapted from Jon Berry, "Creative Inspiration or Blatant Rip-Off," *Adweek Eastern Edition,* January 29, 1990. pp. 34–35; Bruce Horovitz, "Imitation Not Always Flattering in Advertising," *Los Angeles Times,* March 28, 1989, part IV, p. 6; David Kalish, "Copy-CAt Advertising," *Marketing & Media Decisions,* March 1987, pp. 22–23; Seymour Luft. "Imitation: The Highest Form of Blather-y," *Advertising Age,* November 15, 1982. p. M-30; Dale Arden, "Something Borrowed: When Is It Plagiarism?" *Back Stage/Shoot,* July 27, 1990, pp. 102–3.

Chapter 10

Reprozewolf ad: courtesy Trizeps/Vienna Paint, Vienna; art directors: Michael Langoth, Albert Winkler; copywriter: Fritz Grohs; photographers: Michael Langoth, Josef M. Fallnhauser; paintbox artist: Albert Winkler.

Exhibit 10-1 NYNEX ad: courtesy of NYNEX Corporation; photo by Marc Segal/PSI.

Exhibit 10-4 Dahlin Smith White agency ad: courtesy Dahlin Smith & White.

Exhibit 10-5 paste-up photos: Michael J. Hruby.

Exhibit 10-6 Celestial Seasonings ad: © 1990 Celestial Seasonings, Inc., 4600 Sleepytime Drive, Boulder, Colorado, 80301.

Exhibit 10-7 Volvo ad: courtesy Volvo North America Corporation.

Exhibit 10-9 Forest preserve shelter: John Patsch/ Journalism Services.

Exhibit 10-14 Heidelberg press: courtesy Heidelberg Eastern Inc.

Exhibit 10-15 PANTONE MATCHING SYSTEM colors: PANTONE is a registered trademark of Pantone, Inc.

Creative Department (Taster's Choice): courtesy McCann-Erickson.

Chapter 11

Polaroid ads: courtesy McKim Baker Lovick/BBDO.

Exhibit 11-1 Motel 6 radio script: courtesy The Richards Group.

Exhibit 11-2 radio commercial production: adapted with permission of Macmillan Publishing Co., Inc., from *Advertising,* by William M. Weilbacher, p. 273. Copyright 1962 by the Free Press.

Exhibit 11-3 sound decibels: Michael C. Keith, *Radio Production: Art and Science* (Stoneham, MA: Betterworth-Heinemann, 1990), p. 90.

Exhibit 11-4 Microphone: Michael C. Keith, *Radio Production: Art and Science* (Stoneham, MA: Betterworth-Heinemann, 1990), p. 90.

Exhibit 11-5 audio console: Scott Wanner/Journalism Services.

Exhibits 11-6, 11-7 Gotcha ads: courtesy Salisbury Communications.

Exhibit 11-8 Listerine Cool Mint storyboard: courtesy Warner Lambert; agency: J. Walter Thompson/New York.

Exhibits 11-9, 11-10 Gotcha ads: courtesy Salisbury Communications

Creative Department (Taster's Choice): courtesy McCann-Erickson.

Ethical Dilemma adapted from James Perry and David Shribman, "The Negative Campaign Ad Comes of Age in Eastern Races, Stealing the Limelight," *The Wall Street Journal,* November 2, 1989, p. A22; Ronald Paul Hill, "An Exploration of Voter Responses to Political Advertisements," *Journal of Advertising* 18, no. 4 (1989), pp. 14–22; Steven W. Colford, "Political Advisers Veer from Smear, *Advertising Age,* November 23, 1987, p. 53; George Will, "The Other Guy Started It," *Advertising Age,* January 18, 1988, pp. 66–67; Bob Garfield, "Let Voters Take Warning: Political Advertising in This Country Is a Travesty," *Advertising Age,* November 5, 1990, pp. 28–29; Gary Levin, "Negative Ads Win on Election Day '90," *Advertising Age,* November 12, 1990, p. 3; "One Vote for Negative Ads," *Advertising Age,* November 7, 1988, p. 16; Jack Honomichl, Rance Crain, Richard Gordon, and Steven Colford, "Negative Spots Likely to Return in Election '88," *Advertising Age,* September 14, 1987, pp. 3, 70, 72, 74, 76, 78.

Exhibit 11-13 light meters: Michael J. Hruby.

Exhibit 11-17 Panaflex camera: courtesy Panavision.

Exhibit 11-18 shooting Pepsi commercial: Diana Lyn/ Shooting Star.

Exhibit 11-19 Gotcha animation: courtesy Salisbury Communications.

Exhibit 11-20 edit bay photo: courtesy Salisbury Communications.

Part IV Manager jeans ad: courtesy Taxi.

Chapter 12

Le Redoute ad: courtesy TBWA/Brussels.

Exhibit 12-1 Del Monte super natural fruits ad: courtesy Del Monte USA.

Exhibit 12-2 Del Monte's media shift table: adapted from Joe Mandese, "Del Monte's Can-Do," *Adweek's Marketing and Media Decisions,* November 1990, pp. 47–49.

Ad Lab 12-A Shamu blimp: reprinted with the permission of Anheuser-Busch Companies, Inc. copyright 1994 Anheuser-Busch Companies, Inc. All rights reserved.

Exhibit 12-3 value-added options: reprinted with permission from *Advertising Age,* October 26, 1992. Copyright Crain Communications, Inc.

Exhibit 12-4 media planning activities: adapted from Jack Z. Sissors and E. Reynolds Petray, *Advertising Media Planning* (Chicago: Crain Books, 1976); and Jack Z. Sissors and Lincoln Bumba, *Advertising Media Planning,* 4th ed. (Lincolnwood, IL: NTC Business Books, a division of NTC Publishing Group, 1993), p. 9.

Exhibit 12-6 Del Monte trade ad: reprinted with permission of Del Monte Corp.

Exhibit 12-9 advertising expenditures: data from *The Wall Street Journal,* March 22, 1991, p. B4.

Exhibit 12-10 guide to BDI/CDI matrix: adapted from Jack C. Sissors and Lincoln Bumba, Advertising Media Planning, 4th ed. (Lincolnwood, IL: NTC Books, 1993), p. 175.

Checklist International Media Planning Courtesy Directories International, Inc.

Exhibit 12-11 Norfolk Southern storyboard: courtesy Norfolk Southern Corporation; created by J. Walter Thompson, USA.

Ad Lab 12-B Adapted from Stephen Baker, *Systematic Advertising Research Report* (New York: McGraw-Hill, 1979), p. 154.

Exhibit 12-12 readership scores: adapted from *Cabners Advertising Research*

Exhibit 12-13 evaluation of advertising media: adapted from Donald W. Jugenheimer and Peter B. Turk, *Advertising Media* (Columbus, Ohio: Grid Publishing, 1980), p. 90.

Exhibit 12-14 *Editorial America, S.A.* ad: courtesy Editorial America, S.A.

Exhibit 12-15 Cool Water ad: courtesy The Lancaster Group USA.

Exhibit 12-16 Kodacolor Amsterdam ad posters: courtesy PMSvW/Y&R.

Exhibit 12-17 GE/NBC promotion: courtesy NBC Marketing.

Exhibit 12-18 flighting/continuous/pulsing: adapted from Jim Surmanek, *Media Planning* (Lincolnwood, IL: NTC Books, 1988), p. 125.

Exhibit 12-21 Tapscan bar graph: copyright 1993 Tapscan, Inc.

Chapter 13

Forbes FYI Is Sports: courtesy Merkley Newman Harty.

Exhibit 13-1 Continental Bank ad: courtesy Fallon McElligott.

Exhibit 13-2 top U.S. magazine advertisers: reprinted with permission from ADVERTISING AGE, September 23 1992. Copyright Crain Communications, Inc.

Exhibit 13-3 ad positioning chart: adapted from "Magazine Newsletter of Research," Magazine Publishers Association, vol. 8, no. 1.

Exhibit 13-4 Sunkist grapefruit ad: courtesy Sunkist Growers; agency: Foote Cone & Belding/Los Angeles.

Portfolio of magazine ads: Singapore what's the point ad: courtesy Leo Burnett/Singapore; **Oregon ad:** courtesy Wieden & Kennedy; photo by Pat and Tom Leeson; **Liberty Scarf ad:** client: Liberty; agency: Bartle Bogle Hegarty, London; art director: Rosie Arnold; copywriter: Charles Hendley; photographer: Simon Sommerville; **Grey Poupon ad:** courtesy Lowe & Partners; illustrator: Christopher Wormell; photographer: Paul Bevitt; **Rosalp butter ad:** Werbeagentur BSW, Atelier Jaquet AG, Bern; **Lindt of Switzerland ad:** courtesy The Ball Partnership/ North Sydney.

Exhibit 13-5 Reader's Digest map: courtesy The Reader's Digest Association.

Exhibit 13-6 *Purchasing* magazine: courtesy Cahners Publishing.

Exhibit 13-7 *People* magazine advertising rates: reprinted from April 27, 1991, *Consumer Magazine* and *Agri-Media Rates & Data,* published by Standard Rate & Data Service (SRDS).

Exhibit 13-8 magazine circulation table: *Consumer Magazine and Agri-Media Rates & Data* (Standard Rate & Data Service), and *1990 Media Modules,* Grey Advertising, pp. 77–90.

Ad Lab 13-B pop-up ad: courtesy Intervisual Communications, Inc.

Exhibit 13-9 hair salon ad: courtesy Fallon McElligott.

Exhibit 13-10 top 10 U.S. newspapers: reprinted with permission from ADVERTISING AGE, September 23, 1992. Copyright Crain Communications, Inc.

Exhibit 13-11 standard advertising units grid: courtesy Standard Rate & Data Service.

Exhibit 13-12 taxidermist ad: courtesy Mad Dogs & Englishmen.

Exhibit 13-13 *Boston Globe* rate card: reprinted from May 12, 1991, *Newspaper Rates & Data,* published by Standard Rate & Data Service (SRDS).

Exhibit 13-14 Oerlikon Aerospace ad: courtesy Oerlikon Aerospace.

Exhibit 13-15 insertion order form: courtesy Donald Davis & Associates.

Checklist: What Works Best in Print Adapted from Kenneth Roman and Jane Maas, *How to Advertise* (New York: St. Martin's Press, Inc., Macmillan & Co., Ltd, 1976), pp. 32–34, 36–38.

Exhibit 13-16 *Runner's World* survey: courtesy Runner's World.

Chapter 14

Breathsavers ad: courtesy RJR Nabisco-Planters Lifesavers Co.; agency: FCB/Leber Katz Partners, New York.

Exhibit 14-1 Energizer bunny storyboard: © 1989, 1992, Eveready Battery Company, Inc.

Exhibit 14-2 top 10 TV advertisers: reprinted with permission from *Advertising Age,* September 23, 1992. Copyright Crain Communications, Inc.

Checklist (network TV rates table): reprinted with permission of *Adweek's Marketer's Guide to Media,* January-March 1991, p. 19.

Exhibit 14-4 media authority chart: reprinted with permission from *Advertising Age,* September 23, 1992. Copyright Crain Communications, Inc.

Exhibit 14-5 Weight Watchers storyboard: agency: Catchline Communications; art director: Michael van Heusden; copywriter: Han van Wel; production company: Studio Charles van Gelder; directors: Charles van Gelder, Michael van Heusden.

Exhibit 14-7 top cable advertisers: reprinted with permission from *Advertising Age,* April 6, 1992, and September 23, 1992. Copyright Crain Communications, Inc.

Exhibit 14-8 NTA ad: courtesy Network Television Association.

Exhibit 14-9 barter syndication chart: "Business Day," *The New York Times,* August 3, 1985, p. 19. Copyright © 1985 by the New York Times Company. Reprinted with permission.

Ethical Dilemma: adapted from Kim Foltz, "Kids as Consumers: Teaching Our Children Well," *Adweek,* November 30, 1987, p. 40; Noreen O'Leary, "Study Portrays Children as Complex, Savvy Media Mavens," *Adweek,* November 30, 1987, p. 42; Susan Dillingham, "Food Makers Hunger for Younger Market," *Insight,* June 18, 1990, p. 43; Patricia Sellers, The ABC'S of Marketing to Kids." *Fortune,* May 8, 1989, pp. 114–20; Ellen Graham. "Children's Hour: As Kids Gain Power of Purse, Marketing Takes Aim at Them," *The Wall Street Journal,* January 19, 1988, pp. 1, 15; "Selling to Children," *Consumer Reports,* August 1990, pp. 503,

518–21; Susan Dillingham, "The Classroom as a Marketing Tool," *Insight*, September 24, 1990, pp. 40–41; Michael J. McCarthy, "Tobacco Critics See a Subtle Sell to Kids," *The Wall Street Journal*, May 3, 1990, pp. B1, B6; John Wilke, Lois Therrien, Amy Dunkin, and Mark Varnos, "Are the Programs Your Kids Watch Simply Commercials?" *Business Week*, March 25, 1985, pp. 53–54.

Ad Lab 14-A Jack A. Sissors and Lincoln Bumba, *Advertising Media Planing* (Lincolnwood, Ill.: NTC Business Books, 1993); Scott Hume, "Nielsen vs. IRI: Battle of the Research Titans," *Advertising Age*, October 12, 1992; **people meter photo:** reprinted courtesy of Nielsen Media Research.

Exhibit 14-10 Arbitron ADI page: The Arbitron Company.

Exhibit 14-11 Blair TV spot rates: *Spot Television Rates & Data*, August 15, 1991, issue: published by Standard Rate & Data Service (SRDS).

Exhibit 14-12 Cable ad revenues: Data, Paul Kagan Associates, Inc., chart, *Cable TV Facts 1990*, p. 5.

Exhibit 14-13 daily/weekly radio reach: adapted from Radio Advertising Bureau data.

Ad Lab 14-B Reprinted with permission from *Advertising Age*, March 14, 1983. Copyright Crain Communications, Inc.

Exhibit 14-14 profile of radio listeners: used by permission of Simmons Market Research Bureau.

Exhibit 14-15 top radio advertisers: reprinted with permission from *Advertising Age*, September 23, 1992. Copyright Crain Communications, Inc.

Exhibit 14-16 network radio rates: reprinted with permission of *Marketer's Guide to Media*, January-March 1992, Network Radio Advertising.

Exhibit 14-17 KWOD-FM radio spot rates: *Spot Radio Rates & Data*, September, 1, 1991, issue; published by Standard Rate & Data Service (SRDS).

Exhibit 14-18 listening rates: courtesy The Arbitron Company.

Exhibit 14-19 courtesy Foote, Cone & Belding, 1993.

Chapter 15

Catwalk transit ad: courtesy Taxi.

Exhibit 15-1 Champion direct mail campaign: courtesy Champion International Corp.

Exhibit 15-2 Apple catalog ad: courtesy Apple Catalog Division/Apple Computer, Inc.

Exhibit 15-3 "The Ringer" infomercial: courtesy Bell Atlantic.

Exhibit 15-4 top 10 mail-order product categories: *The United States Mail Order Industry*, Maxwell Sroge Publishing, Inc., Chicago, Ill.

Exhibit 15-5 Mail Preference Service ad: courtesy Direct Marketing Association, Inc.

Exhibit 15-6 Parker Pen catalog: courtesy Parker Pen USA Ltd.

Exhibit 15-7 Doubleday Buyers list: *Direct Mail List Rates & Data (Consumer Lists)*, August 1991 issue; published by Standard Rate & Data Service (SRDS).

Exhibit 15-8 Garcia's Irish Pub billboards: courtesy Crowley Webb & Associates. This ad campaign has been copyrighted and is protected by copyright laws in the United States and Canada.

Portfolio of Outdoor Advertising: Travelodge ad: courtesy Forte Hotels; **Minneapolis Institute of Arts ad:** courtesy Minneapolis Institute of Arts; **Finisterra Hotel ad:** courtesy Forte Hotels; agency: Lord Dentsu & Partners; **McDonald's Pizza photo:** courtesy Les Restaurants McDonald du Canada Limitee; agency: Cossette Communication-Marketing; **Lexus ES 300 ad:** courtesy Lexus; agency: Team One Advertising.

Exhibit 15-9 Nike billboard: agency: Simons Palmer Denton Clemmow & Johnson, London; creative directors: Mirk Denton, Chris Palmer; art director: Andy McKay; copywriter: Tony Barry; Typographer: Barry Bond.

Exhibit 15-10 constructing billboard: courtesy Patrick Media Group, Inc.

Ad Lab 15-A Courtesy Institute of Outdoor Advertising.

Exhibit 15-11 Museum of Flight billboard: © 1991 Museum of Fliight; agency: Livingston & Co.

Exhibit 15-12 Osaka, Japan signs: Brian Lovell/ Nawrocki Stock Photo Inc.

Exhibit 15-13 map: courtesy Gannett Outdoor Advertising.

Exhibit 15-14 poster rates: Gannett's Outdoor Network, USA *1993 Ratebook & Almanac*.

Exhibit 15-15 Campbell transit ad: courtesy Campbell Soup Company; agency: Ogilvy & Mather, Toronto.

Exhibit 15-16 transit art sizes: courtesy The Transit Advertising Association, Inc.

Exhibit 15-17 Carro-Sell ad: Esprit bus stop ad: courtesy Gannett Outdoor.

Exhibit 15-18 Moscow Colgate ads: courtesy Colgate-Palmolive Company.

Exhibit 15-19 *Woman's Day* truck ad: courtesy *Woman's Day*.

Exhibit 15-20 specialty items: courtesy The Advertising Specialty Institute.

Exhibit 15-21 trade show booth: courtesy Giltspur/ Chicago.

Exhibit 15-22 Yellow Pages reach: reprinted with permission of Yellow Pages Publishers Association (YPPA).

Exhibit 15-23 top 10 Yellow Pages operators: company reports.

Exhibit 15-24 electronic couponing photo: Barth Falkenberg.

Exhibit 15-25 Carro-Sell ad: courtesy Revolving Media, Inc.

Part V McDonald's Pizza ad: © 1992 Les restaurants McDonald du Canada limitee; agency: Cossette Communication-Marketing.

Chapter 16

Canadian Saturn ad: © 1993 Saturn Corporation; agency; Cossette Communication-Marketing.

Exhibit 16-1 MacIntosh ad: courtesy Apple Computer, Inc.

Exhibit 16-2 MacIntosh storyboard: courtesy Apple Computer, Inc.; agency: BBDO/Los Angeles.

Exhibit 16-5 IMC planning process: *Integrated Marketing Communications* by Don E. Schultz, Stanley Tannenbaum, and Robert Lauterborn (Lincolnwood, IL: NTC Business Books), 1993. Used by permission.

Exhibit 16-6 factors influencing strategies: reprinted by permission from *Advertising Age*, March 23, 1993. Copyright Crain Communications, Inc.

Exhibit 16-7 Andersen Windows ad: courtesy CME/ KHBB.

Exhibit 16-8 GoodTimes magazine: courtesy Kay Bee Toy & Hobby Shops.

Exhibit 16-9 Del Monte direct mail promo: courtesy Del Monte.

Exhibit 16-10 Apple catalog ad: courtesy Apple Catalog Division/Apple Computer, Inc.

Exhibit 16-11 who watches informercials: reprinted by permission from *Advertising Age*, January 25, 1993. Copyright Crain Communications, Inc. All rights reserved.

Exhibit 16-12 promotion versus advertising spending: reprinted by permission from *Advertising Age*, April 5, 1993. Copyright Crain Communications, Inc.

Exhibit 16-13 in-store display: Ziggy Kaluzny/ Gamma-Liaison.

Exhibit 16-14 KLM sweepstakes: courtesy W. L. Harvey Communications, Inc.

Exhibit 16-15 consumer promotion scorecard: *Thir-*

teen Annual Survey of Promotional Practices, p. 27, 1991. Courtesy of Donnelley Marketing, Inc.

Exhibit 16-16 Hostess snacks ad: courtesy Continental Baking Co., Inc.

Exhibit 16-17 effect of premiums: "Study: Some Promotions Change Consumer Behavior," *Marketing News*, October 15, 1990, p. 12.

Exhibit 16-18 sweepstakes ad: courtesy Publishers Clearing House.

Exhibit 16-19 Sweepstakes participation: Reprinted with permission of *Adweek's Marketing Week*, April 9, 1990, pp. 6, 7, Sweepstakes Participation.

Ad Lab 16-B adapted from Bernard Wysocki, Jr., "Sight, Smell, Sound: They're All Arms in Retailer's Arsenal," *The Wall Street Journal*, April 17, 1979.

Exhibit 16-20 P-O-P advertising display: courtesy Lee Company.

Chapter 17

Bank of America ad: courtesy Bank of America; photo by Robert Mizono.

Exhibit 17-1 Exxon Valdez oil spill: Paul Fusco/ Magnum Photos, Inc.

Exhibit 17-2 Toshiba apology: courtesy Toshiba Americia.

Exhibit 17-3 Beatrice marathon: Eamonn Martin/ Allsport.

Exhibit 17-4 Chex Party Mix news release: courtesy Golin/Harris Communications, Inc.

Exhibit 17-5 Reebok annual report: courtesy Reebok International Ltd.

Exhibit 17-6 Claris ad: courtesy Claris Corporation.

Exhibit 17-7 Southwestern Bell ad: Courtesy Southwestern Bell Corporation; agency: DMB&B/St. Louis; photo courtesy the Missouri Historical Society.

Portfolio of Corporate Advertising: American Honda ad: courtesy of American Honda Motor Co., Inc.; **Mercedes Benz LA marathon ad:** courtesy Mercedes Benz; **Kaneka ad:** McCann-Erickson Hakuhodo, Inc.; **Hitachi ad:** McCann-Erickson Hakuhodo Inc.; **Nabisco products:** courtesy Nabisco Brands Inc.

Ad Lab 17-A David Oglivy photo: courtesy Oglivy & Mather/New York.

Exhibit 17-8 Pi Kappa Phi poster: courtesy Pi Kappa Phi Fraternity, Inc.

Exhibit 17-9 Alfa Romeo ad: © 1990, Alfa Romeo Distributors of North America. Used with permission.

Exhibit 17-10 Pratt & Whitney ad: Pratt & Whitney/ Canada; agency: BCP Strategy/Creativity.

Chapter 18

Minnesota Dept. of Health antismoking ad: courtesy Martin Williams Advertising.

Exhibit 18-1 Rubio's Fish Tacos: John Brice & Associates/Bill Pike, illustrator.

Exhibit 18-2 Richmond Symphony ad:courtesy The Martin Agency, Richmond, VA.

Exhibit 18-4 Hogan's Market logos:courtesy Hornall Anderson Design Works.

Exhibit 18-5 Yet Con restaurant ad: courtesy The Ball Partnership/Singapore; art director: Andy Clarke.

Exhibit 18-6 Arby's map: courtesy Arby's.

Exhibit 18-7 Milt Sanford ad:courtesy Kevin McCarthy.

Exhibits 18-8, 18-9 data from Newspaper Advertising Bureau, Inc.

Exhibit 18-10 *Oregonian* ad: courtesy Cole & Weber.

Exhibit 18-11 Seven Pines ad:courtesy Leland Gohlike.

Exhibit 18-12 Carlos Murphy's ad: courtesy Carlos Murphy's.

Exhibit 18-13 Atlantic Exterminating ad: courtesy Court Crandall.

Exhibit 18-14 *Les Miserables* ads: courtesy Optimum; reproduced with the permission of Cameron Mackintosh Inc. and Miruish Production.

Exhibit 18-15 Summerhill Hardware ad: courtesy Summerhill Decorative Hardware.

Checklist: Creating Local Advertising Data from Newspaper Advertising Bureau, Inc.

Exhibit 18-16 Naragansett sales ads: courtesy Leonard Monahan Lubars Kelly.

Exhibit 18-17 Portland GE storyboard: courtesy Borders Perrin & Norrander Inc./Portland.

Exhibit 18-18 London Zoo ad: courtesy Lowell Howard-Spink.

Exhibit 18-19 Pizzaiolle ad: courtesy Bos Advertising.

Exhibit 18-20 Carl Cedergren ad: courtesy Carl Cedergren.

Exhibit 18-23 Uptown District ad: courtesy Uptown District.

Exhibit 18-24 Canadian Red Cross ad: courtesy BCP Strategy/Creativity.

Exhibit 18-26 Partnership for Drug Free America ad: courtesy Partnership for a Drug Free America; agency: The Martin Agency, Richmond, VA.

Exhibit 18-27 LA July 4th fireworks ad: courtesy Larry S. Londre; agency: Fattal & Collins.

Exhibit 18-28 California Dept. of Health Services anti-smoking ad: courtesy California Department of Health Services; agency: Livingston & Keye.

Exhibit 18-29 Pharmaceutical Manufacturers ad: courtesy Pharmaceutical Manufacturers Association of Canada.

Exhibit 18-30 Alberta Canada ad: courtesy Ministry of Alberta Economic Development & Tourism.

Exhibit 18-31 Ad Council AIDS ad: courtesy Della Femina, McNamee Inc.

NAME, COMPANY, AND BRAND INDEX

Page references in **bold** print indicate exhibits. Notes show N-page number, as N-4. Glossary as G-1.

SUBJECT INDEX